COLLECTIVE VIOLENCE

LAW IN ACTION
A series edited by
Sheldon Messinger
University of California, Berkeley

COLLECTIVE

VIOLENCE

edited by

James F. Short, Jr., *Washington State University*

Marvin E. Wolfgang, *University of Pennsylvania*

Aldine · Atherton
CHICAGO AND NEW YORK

ABOUT THE EDITORS

James F. Short, Jr., is Director of the Social Research Center and Professor, Department of Sociology, Washington State University.
Marvin E. Wolfgang is Professor and Chairman, Department of Sociology, and Director, Center for Studies in Criminology and Criminal Law, University of Pennsylvania.

Copyright © 1972 by James F. Short, Jr. and Marvin Wolfgang

First published 1972 by
Aldine • Atherton, Inc.
529 South Wabash Avenue
Chicago, Illinois 60605

ISBN 0-202-23009-0, cloth; 0-202-23010-4, paper
Library of Congress Catalog Number 74-149843

Printed in the United States of America

Preface

Early in the fall of 1969, Richard Lambert, Editor of *The Annals of the American Academy of Political and Social Science,* approached us about editing an issue of *The Annals* on crowds. While this idea appealed to us, especially in view of Professor Lambert's signal contributions to understanding this mysterious aspect of human behavior, we suggested instead that some of the "unfinished business" of our service as Directors of Research for the National Commission on the Causes and Prevention of Violence was a more pressing priority. Professor Lambert agreed, and thirteen papers on the subject of collective violence were published in the September, 1970 issue of *The Annals.* Most of these papers addressed issues and controversies raised but not fully developed in Violence Commission investigations. Most of the authors of the papers were associated in some capacity with the Commission, as members of the central staff, Task Force Directors or staff members, consultants, or advisors.

We were extremely pleased with the collection of papers published in *The Annals.* Space restrictions for that issue were understandable, but quite limiting, and when Sheldon Messinger invited us on behalf of Aldine • Atherton to expand the issue for book publication we were delighted to do so. Expansion allowed us to cover new topics and to bring additional evidence and arguments to bear on topics discussed in *The Annals.* We were fortunate in being able to "recruit" most of the papers given at a special symposium on violence held at the November, 1969 meetings of the American Anthropological Association, thus bringing together one of the most comprehensive comparative examinations of the topic ever published. Additional Violence Commission contacts, and others whose work had not previously come to our attention, were persuaded to write for the expanded volume. The result, a far more comprehensive and updated compendium, stimulated us to expand greatly our "Introduction and Overview" into a more lengthy and, in some measure, synthesizing statement of the state of knowledge in this elusive area.

Papers not previously published in *The Annals* are identified by an asterisk following their listing in the Table of Contents. We are grateful to many people for their assistance, but especially to our co-authors for their contributions to this continuation of an important enterprise, to James Calonico for preparation of the indexes, and to Sheldon L. Messinger and Alexander J. Morin for their attentive aid.

Preface

Contents

* Designates new papers, published for the first time in this volume. All others appeared initially in *The Annals of The American Academy of Political and Social Science* (September 1970). Some have been expanded or altered in other ways for this volume, as footnoted individually.

COLLECTIVE VIOLENCE

Part I

Introduction and Overview

1

Perspectives on Collective Violence

By JAMES F. SHORT, JR. AND MARVIN E. WOLFGANG

James F. Short, Jr. is professor of Sociology and director of the Social Research Center at Washington State University. He served as co-director of Research for the National Commission on the Causes and Prevention of Violence. He was dean of the Graduate School at Washington State University, 1964–1968, and has taught at the University of Chicago and the University of Hawaii. He has written or edited numerous books and articles, including Suicide and Homicide *(with A. F. Henry),* Group Process and Gang Delinquency *(with F. L. Strodtbeck), and* The Social Fabric of the Metropolis. *In 1969 he was the recipient of a National Institute of Mental Health Special Fellowship and was a Fellow at the Center for Advanced Study in the Behavioral Sciences at Stanford, California.*

Marvin E. Wolfgang is professor and chairman of the Department of Sociology, University of Pennsylvania. He was co-director of Research of the National Commission on the Causes and Prevention of Violence, and is a member of the Commission on Obscenity and Pornography and of the American Bar Association Commission on Correctional Facilities and Services. He has authored and edited numerous books and articles, among which are The Subculture of Violence *(with F. Ferracuti),* Crime and Culture, *and* Delinquency: Selected Studies *(with T. Sellin). He was twice a Guggenheim Fellow, and was elected a Fellow of Churchill College in 1969 during his year as visiting professor at the Institute of Criminology, University of Cambridge.*

This is an expanded version of James F. Short, Jr. and Marvin E. Wolfgang, "On Collective Violence: Introduction and Overview," in *The Annals of the American Academy of Political and Social Science* (September 1970), pp. 1–8.

4 INTRODUCTION AND OVERVIEW

THERE seems to be no end to the many books, articles, conferences, speeches, and commissions which have analyzed, diagnosed, counselled, prescribed, or proscribed concerning violence. Violence is clearly a major social problem. Crimes of violence, riots in urban ghettos, political assassinations, and campus violence have been much responsible for the appointment of four recent national commissions: The President's Commission on Law Enforcement and Administration of Justice (1965), the National Advisory Commission on Civil Disorders (1967), the National Commission on the Causes and Prevention of Violence (1968), and —six months after the last had submitted its final report to the President (and with no public recognition of what that commission had said on the subject)— the President's Commission on Campus Disorder (1970). These commissions have engaged the efforts of many of the nation's most distinguished citizens and scholars. The volume of their reports has been prodigious and the flow of analysis, commentary, and rhetoric concerning their recommendations equally so.

Yet the problems remain. Why? Is it simply a matter of inaction, of a failure to heed the voices of reason, the recommendations of study teams? Confessing to an "increasing sense of 'commission frustration,'" Federal District Judge A. Leon Higginbotham, at the close of the Violence Commission's deliberations called for "a national moratorium on any additional temporary study commissions to probe the causes of racism, or poverty, or crime, or the urban crisis . . . (and) the prompt implementation of . . . (the) many valuable recommendations" of "the great commissions of recent years."[1] Judge Higginbotham

doubtless echoes the sentiments of many.

It is the essence of social problems, however, that people disagree about the character, causes, and cures of situations defined as problematic. It is not enough that many people find a situation distressing. Probably few would disagree about the desirability of eliminating, or at least bringing under better social control, violent crime, urban riots, and assassinations. Even those who see in such phenomena progress toward the causes they espouse hope for the control of violence once their objectives are achieved. Violence is not in this sense problematic. What is problematic is the diagnosis of violence, its causes, its justification, and its remedies. For despite (in part, because of) the efforts of study teams and commissions, journalists, commentators, and scholars of many persuasions, disagreement surrounds these issues. Even when data and theory agreeably converge on the "root causes"—for example, on the importance of racism and poverty for understanding and controlling crime and the urban crisis—there is still much disagreement about the "root causes" of racism and poverty, in turn, and about what should be done about these phenomena.

The emergence of a social problem is an important but little understood process. One important aspect of this process—the emergence at the community level of local conditions as social problems—is examined in Chapter 22, by Peter H. Rossi and Richard A. Berk. The conditions studied have to do with retail practices by ghetto merchants, and with police practices. As social problems, they become exploitation by merchants and police brutality. Rossi and Berk present an all-too-rare analysis of this kind of transformation, the

1. *To Establish Justice, to Insure Domestic Tranquility,* Final Report of the National Commission on the Causes and Prevention of Violence (Washington, D.C.: U.S. Government Printing Office, 1969), pp. 116–117.

nature of which we will discuss at a later point in this chapter.

More knowledge of these processes is very much needed. Some problems, such as war and crime, appear to have an almost universal and timeless quality, yet what is considered problematic even with respect to war and crime varies considerably from time to time and place to place. When does military action of one country against another constitute war, for example, and what types of actions are permissible? When and how does protest become revolt? What roles are played by law enforcement agents and agencies in these matters, and how do they contribute to the very behavior they are ostensibly designed to eliminate? Perhaps one of the more significant issues concerning national study commissions is whether such groups can bring themselves fully to explore and report on the role of government in perpetrating and perpetuating the violence and other social problems they wish to deter. Can or will a national advisory commission objectively examine the premises which give legitimacy to the political and economic system to which it is responsible? And to their consequences, including possible contributions to the very problems which are the subject of investigation? National commissions dealing with crime, urban disorder, and violence have faced particularly difficult problems of this sort, despite the dedication and excellence of commissioners, staff, and consultants and the generally high quality of their work.[2]

Thus, the Crime Commission virtually ignored the influence of the eco-nomically powerful in defining the nature of crime in our society, and in making and implementing laws for its control. The National Advisory Commission on Civil Disorders (the Kerner Commission) labeled as a "root cause" of ghetto riots "white racism," but failed to explore the implications for its continuance in the traditions and practices of the Congress of the United States, through seniority privileges and other means by which vested interests are protected. The Violence Commission called for a reordering of national priorities, but stopped short of full exploration of the implications for violence at home of the war in Indo-China, pleading instead for commitments to solve domestic problems "as soon as resources are available."

A complete analysis of these matters is beyond the scope of this paper and of this volume, which is devoted to the illumination of selected aspects of collective violence—with regard to which, it must be said, many conceptual problems and questions of fact remain. We neither celebrate a feast nor herald the millennium. Instead, we turn to basics in the quest for knowledge—to fundamental questions of theory, fact, and interpretation, to analysis in greater depth of data collected in the course of commission investigations, and to new investigations. These are luxuries rarely permitted in the pressure cooker atmosphere of commission studies, deliberations, and press releases.

This volume builds on—in fact, it assumes—the efforts of national commissions and other scholarly work. Many of the authors have been associated in one or more capacities with one or more of the recent national commissions most directly relevant to our concerns, and some in advisory capacities to other levels of government and to private groups, such as the National Council on Crime and Delinquency.

2. It may be argued, and has been, that the social and behavioral sciences, too, have failed in this regard. But penetrating scholarly critique of social systems is a well established tradition, operating under fewer constraints than governmental study commissions.

Several of the theoretical views discussed and the studies presented had their origins in the work of such groups.

ISSUES AND PERSPECTIVES

The volume is divided into five parts. In this beginning chapter we present an overview of the book and in some measure bring together many of the issues and perspectives and data of the chapters that follow. No attempt is made either to synthesize all the findings or to derive an overarching and complete theory. But in these chapters there are many points in common which provide a guide to better understanding and toward solving the problems which lead to collective violence. From these points, propositional statements are formed which may eventually lead to important theory.

Part II examines basic and in some instances competing theoretical issues in the explanation of collective violence. Part III begins with comparative data on modern nation states, and continues with several examples of the comparative study of violence by anthropologists. Part IV focuses on the United States, from a variety of disciplinary perspectives and on several issues, notably political violence, the Vietnam War, violence among youth (particularly campus violence), problems of the ghettos, police violence. Part V discusses nonviolent alternatives to the solution of social problems and the usefulness of commission studies in this respect.

The seven chapters of Part II begin with Allen D. Grimshaw's review of scholarly concern with collective violence, particularly psychological and sociological theories of social conflict. He concludes that superordinate/subordinate relationships *based on social categories* are inherently unstable and that social violence is very likely to occur when *accommodative structures* lose

their viability. Why they do so is the subject of several of the chapters that follow. Briefly stated, both theory and data suggest that when the assumptions underlying these relationships cease to be accepted and when their challenge by other than violent means is unsuccessful, the likelihood of collective violence is enhanced. Other factors enter in, and the form of violence (whether riots or rebellion, for example) is also problematic. It is with such matters that much of the remainder of the volume is concerned.

Chapters 3, 4, and 5 focus on "collective behavior" theories of violence. Although his title is deceptively narrow—treating of "issueless riots"—Gary Marx addresses theories of this genre at a most fundamental level, arguing that failure to make distinctions among riots based upon "their relation to ideology, social movements, and social change" is responsible for much confusion about the meaning and significance of riots.

Elliott Currie and Jerome H. Skolnick critically assess current theories of collective behavior, focusing on what they interpret to be "the anti-democratic biases in 'crowd' theory," particularly the implication that collective behavior is in some sense "irrational" behavior. A more detailed critique of one of the major representatives of collective behavior theory, Neil J. Smelser, follows, together with the suggestion that the perspective elaborated in *The Politics of Protest* offers an alternative and more valid interpretation of recent phenomena of collective violence. Smelser's rejoinder to the Currie/Skolnick paper, and his critique of the position set forth in *The Politics of Protest*, concludes this exchange.

H. L. Neiburg's discussion (chapter 6) of "rituals of conflict" leads to the suggestion that these positions may not be as far apart as they first appear.

Neiburg reviews the psychiatric, ethological, anthropological, and sociological literature concerning the importance of ritual in much behavior, and particularly that having to do with its political significance. He then analyzes the "Woodstock nation," campus demonstrations, and a variety of other forms of youthful behavior from the point of view of the symbolic significance of the behavior for its participants. The analysis is directed to non-political as well as political aspects of behavior, and of the issues to which it is related. Neiburg suggests that much political behavior has become ritualized, and that such ritualization is functional for several reasons—it is "a low-risk energy-conserving method of experimentation, learning, social choice, and consensus building." Some of the extreme forms of behavior engaged in by youth protesters, he argues, stem from the fact that the young, in contrast to the Blacks, are not a constituency. Such behavior represents "not principled testing of authority, but rather catharsis, trauma, and action for its own sake or for solidifying a remnant of a faction by high-risk commitments."

In the final analysis, Neiburg concludes, "There is a self-limiting quality in ritual rebellion and high-intensity tactics of protest. It is impossible to sustain the level of excitement." Whether or not this proves to be the case among the young, however, will depend upon the success or failure of young people in creating and sustaining the necessary ideological and structural elements which will carry beyond protest into effective social—and probably political—action. This, in turn, will depend upon a number of elements, some of which we turn to presently.

The theme for much of the book—to the extent that there is one—is set by these chapters. It is that collective violence in this country and elsewhere in

the world has political implications.[3] There is evidence that it has become *increasingly* political in focus and that it is likely to become more so. In attempting to resolve "The Paradox of American Violence" (Chapter 16), for example, historian Hugh Davis Graham concludes that "our capitalistic, federal structure has historically pitted our racial, ethnic, and economic groups against one another rather than against the state and its vital institutions." Expansion of the power of the federal government during the depression of the 1930's and following World War II appears to have altered this process fundamentally, as groups have come increasingly to look to government in search of redress of grievances from many sources. As a result, social conflicts have come to be identified with the political processes through which government, and particularly the federal government, operates.

3. The moral context within which "the climate of violence" operates has been examined by anthropologist, Anthony F. C. Wallace. Contrasting the "procedural morality" of conservatives with the "teleological morality" of revolutionaries, Wallace emphasizes that "once a moral confrontation" occurs between these groups, representing "the System and the Movement," respectively, "a climate of violence is almost certain to develop, irrespective of peaceful professions on both sides. On the Movement side, this climate is often nourished by the apocalyptic world-destruction fantasies of a prophet and his disciples, by the destructive aim of the Movement with regard to old institutions, and by the fear of retaliation by an already punitive System, which will even abandon its own procedural morality in order to destroy its enemies. On the System's side, the fear of being destroyed by self-righteous opponents who seem intent on wrecking what they do not understand, who have publicly declared their refusal to accept the traditional procedural morality, and whose professions of brother love are belied by the bellicose assaults which they launch whenever their solicitations to conversion are rejected, prompts the conservative to look to his defenses and

In a related development, there is evidence of the increased politicization of *deviant* behavior in general, as the social roots and implications of labeling as deviant, groups and behavior which are *different* from that approved by a majority (or a powerful minority) of citizens have come under scrutiny. At the same time (and in part as a result of such study?) groups labeled as deviant have come to view their problems in and with the larger society in more political terms and have sought, and in some instances achieved, a measure of political power—witness the homosexual community in San Francisco, and the efforts of many groups to change repressive laws relating to marijuana usage.[4] Similarly, other groups who have not been accorded social equality increasingly view their problems fundamentally in terms of power relations with other groups, for example, Blacks, students and youth in general, women, antiwar activists, and the poor.

These developments converge very powerfully in their impact on societies undergoing rapid social change. Tradition loses its hold on increasing numbers of citizens, institutions find their authority undermined, "rights" of property and control over the lives of employees and constituents are challenged. Conversely, many among those who feel most threatened by such changes react negatively—sometimes harshly and repressively, thus enhancing the challenge of those who protest and thereby further undermining the legitimacy of institutionalized authority. In this process, collective representations of what is considered "right" and "proper," and politically sanctioned in law and its enforcement, become changed and new conceptions are developed.

Robert E. Park, writing in 1928, caught the character of this process when he described such forms of collective violence as war, revolution, and the strike as "fundamentally . . . elementary forms of political action . . . in which issues are raised, forced upon a somewhat reluctant public, and eventually, in some fashion, settled. . . . The public has, in the long run . . . made the rules of the game, and decided the issues."[5] It is in the course of such processes that fundamental notions of property rights and the legitimacy of institutions and authority relations are forged, institutionalized, challenged, and altered. The process is continuous, as is particularly obvious in rapidly changing societies. It does not always involve violence, but violence is no stranger to such matters. We need to be reminded of this fact, and of the corollary that such violence often has led to the achievement of a more equitable and just society. While "authorities" (and many others) invariably assume that civil disorder will produce accelerating social disorganization, disrespect for law and, ultimately, anarchy . . . again and again in American history, the violence associated with decolonization has led in the direction of a new politics and a reconstructed social order."[6]

It is important to make the distinctions urged and argued by Marx, Currie and Skolnick, Smelser, and Neiburg in Part II concerning the relation of episodes and patterns of collective vio-

to wonder whether he indeed may not temporarily have to abandon the old procedural morality as it applies to violence." Anthony F. C. Wallace, "Violence, Morality, and Revitalization," in Rovert Paul Wolff, ed., *The Rule of Law*, (New York: Simon and Schuster, 1971).
4. See, e.g., Howard S. Becker and Irving Louis Horowitz, "The Culture of Civility," *Trans-action* (April 1970), pp. 12–14.

5. Robert E. Park, "Introduction" to E. T. Hiller, *The Strike* (Chicago: University of Chicago Press, 1928), pp. vii–viii.
6. Richard E. Rubenstein, *Rebels in Eden* (Boston: Little, Brown, and Co., 1970).

lence to ideology, social movements, and social change. Unless such distinctions are made, we will fail to understand the difference between "rioting mainly for fun and profit" and riots (and other forms of collective violence) which may be more politically motivated and of greater significance for both social justice and social order.[7] The fact that participants in such incidents may be variously motivated complicates the analysis but does not necessarily detract from the political significance of such behavior. For generalized beliefs and elaborated ideologies, even if largely *post hoc,* acquire a dynamic of their own. Many Blacks who have not participated in riots, for example, and who personally disapprove of them, believe that there is justification for riots and that some good results from them.[8] And, as Rubenstein reminds us, the question of whether rioters, strikers, or guerrillas "represent" their groups is extremely complex, involving analysis of "the extent to which particular episodes or campaigns of political violence correspond to the perceived interests and felt needs of particular groups."[9]

If the trends referred to above are at all accurately perceived, increasingly the most crucial question concerning collective violence will not be whether a collective belief exists but rather the stage of its development, its nature, and

the particular issues around which it develops. We may expect, furthermore, that the political challenge of social movements, of subordinate (and superordinate) groups in the social structure, and challenges to existing authority in other institutional contexts as well, will increase in scope and intensity until new accommodations are worked out.

Chapter 7, by Sandra J. Ball-Rokeach, discusses the relation of mass media to violence, focusing particularly on the complex question of its bearing on legitimacy, another complex issue with political overtones. While much research has focused on the manner and extent to which those who are exposed to various media learn violent *actions,* she argues that learning *evaluative* reactions to violence via the media is a more important consideration. Others have called attention to the role of media for both protesters and authorities, in effect making violence a weapon used by both sides because violence attracts the media. A goal for both becomes the provocation of violence by the other side so that they may be shown to disadvantage. Such provocation may be ill advised, however, for we know that a sizable majority of U.S. citizens approved of police violence at the 1968 Chicago Convention of the Democratic Party, and many felt the police had not gone far enough in this regard.[10] This makes more plausible Ball-Rokeach's notion that those whose interests are threatened, and who intensely disapprove of violent, obscene, or otherwise objectionable behavior on the part of protesters as telecast or otherwise presented by mass media, *regardless of the behavior of authorities,* may be led to support repressive measures designed to control protest behavior. The hold of the Bill of Rights

7. See Edward C. Banfield, *The Unheavenly City* (Boston: Little, Brown, and Co., 1968, 1970). See also "Banfield's *Unheavenly City*: A Symposium and Response," with reviews by Duane Lockard, Russell D. Murphy, and Arthur Naftlan, and a reply by Banfield, in *Trans-action* (March-April 1971), pp. 69–78.

8. See T. M. Tomlinson, "The Development of a Riot Ideology Among Urban Negroes," *American Behavioral Scientist* (March-April 1968), pp. 27–31; and "Report from Black America," *Newsweek* (June 30, 1969).

9. Rubenstein, op. cit., pp. 11–13.

10. For documentation of this conclusion, see Chapter 18, below.

and other constitutional guarantees on
the American people appears tenuous
indeed in the face of such evidence.

Part II closes with "some methodological notes" by Richard A. Berk on
the controversy concerning collective
violence. Berk notes that gathering data
on what happens during episodes of
collective behavior is far more difficult
than is gathering data on conditions
preceding crowd behavior and on its
results. One result of this methodological situation, he argues, is that the personal and political interests of those
who analyze collective behavior are
given relatively free reign, resulting
in a number of interpretive pitfalls.
Berk's discussion of these pitfalls is a
welcome caution against too simple
"explanations" of these complex phenomena, and his later chapter (23),
describing an "almost race riot" *in situ,*
materially contributes to the fund of
solid data in this area and to the perspective of this volume.

CORRELATES OF LEVELS AND TYPES OF
VIOLENCE: EVIDENCE FROM
COMPARATIVE STUDIES

The chapters in Part III present evidence from a variety of cultural and
social contexts related to levels and
types of violence, with particular emphasis on collective violence. Each contributes to our understanding of the
political implications of violence, though
some bear more directly than others on
the theme that violence, and particularly collective violence, is increasingly
political in nature, whether by design
or, after the fact, by interpretation.

In Chapter 9, Melvin Small and J.
David Singer, historian and political
scientist, respectively, describe "Patterns in International Warfare, 1816–
1965," based on their extensive compilation of relevant data. The picture
that emerges is not a happy one for
those who yearn for international peace.
However, as the authors note, data
now available permit "an accelerated
assault on the causes of the war problem," something past generations have
lacked woefully.

In Chapter 10, Ted Robert Gurr follows up earlier research concerning
"Why Men Rebel" with more recent
data concerning "Sources of Rebellion
in Western Societies." He concludes
that internal strife in recent years was
predictable on the basis of factors relating to the scope and intensity of collective discontent in these countries, combined with the strength of normative
and utilitarian justifications for rebellion among discontented groups and the
balance of social (political) control between contending groups. He reports
important variations in the manner in
which these factors relate to different
types of strife. Less intense forms of
strife in Western nations—such as
demonstrations and most riots, for example—"are more the result of how
people think about governments and
the desirability of protest" than they are
of the intensity of grievances. The most
serious forms of strife, however—terrorism, anti-government conspiracy,
and the more violent riots—are "a direct response to intense and persisting
frustrations, not much affected by political loyalties or traditions."

Because of its central importance in
theories of collective violence, the relationship of relative deprivation to nonviolent strife and turmoil (in contrast
with violent strife and rebellion) is
especially intriguing. Gurr defines relative deprivation as the "perception of
discrepancies between the goals of human action and the prospects of attaining those goals." When justifications
and the institutional, coercive balance
are held constant, relative deprivation
is *negatively* related to nonviolent strife
but strongly and positively related to

violent strife and rebellion. That is, nonviolent strife increases when relative deprivation is diminished, but violent strife is more likely when objective measures of relative deprivation increase. Gurr concludes that in these Western societies, "other things being equal, . . . the more discontented people are the less likely they are to resort to nonviolent protest and the more likely they are to rebel." From this, Gurr draws the implication that "in Western societies intensification of regime control seems the social policy least likely to reduce turmoil," and he advises attention to increasing the scope and activities of supporting institutions.

Returning to another line of argument, the conclusion is suggested that so long as the accommodations of subordinate and superordinate groups are regarded as legitimate, the institutions (including political institutions) which sustain them are not likely to suffer rebellion. Whether or not one grants the proposition that Superordinate/Subordinate relationships based on social categories are *inherently* unstable, it is clear that the legitimacy of such traditional bases of inequality as race, age, sex, wealth, and social position are under attack in many parts of the world. Repression of dissent and failure to redress grievances further undermine legitimacy and conduce to rebellion. Much of the literature on insurgency and counter-insurgency is based on the experience of developing societies in which the tendency has been to emphasize coercive control rather than attention to "root causes" of grievance as remedies to rebellion. [11] Gurr's analysis is especially important for the United States because it is based primarily on analyses of Modern Western societies.

The importance of cultural pattern-

ing of forms of violence is a central concern of the next several papers, based on anthropological studies in a variety of settings. For Lola Romanucci Schwartz (Chapter 11), the problem is to understand the relation between violence and social conflict in a Mexican village characterized by high levels of both but where the overlap between the two is minimal. The village, born in the Mexican Agrarian Revolution in the first quarter of the twentieth century, was without local law enforcement for several years. Most men and women were armed and violence was commonplace. More recently, there is evidence that interpersonal violence has diminished, but serious social conflicts remain. When it does occur, violence is almost exclusively male, bearing a close relationship to alcohol consumption and to the *macho* code of manliness, expressed in familar terms as *machismo*. The *macho* see themselves "as harddrinking, *enamorado,* sensitive to slights, always supposedly ready for violence and the use of a gun, given to frequenting bars and hanging out with others of their type, often involved in violence . . . and proud of all this." The subculture of the *macho* does not concern issues of social position, as such, or economic or political matters, nor does it extend to village leaders. The arena for settlement of these issues is public rather than private. Participants in long-standing conflicts avoid personal contact with one another in political and economic enterprise and contend instead in the courts.

An important principle emerges from this study and from other evidence: under conditions in which the legitimacy of the social system is solidly supported, conflicts within the system and individual violence are not generally related, and neither leads to political violence. The Mexican village studied by Schwartz is similar in this

11. Nathan Leites and Charles Wolf, Jr., *Rebellion and Authority* (Chicago: Markham Publishing Co., 1970).

respect to the United States. Individual acts of violence—homicide, aggravated assault, rape, and robbery—appear to be only incidentally associated with major social conflicts. In contrast to the experience of this country, however, the Mexican village has little or no collective violence involving social conflicts between members of subordinate and superordinate groups of an economic, racial, or religious nature. The village, Schwartz claims, is based on social mechanisms which have been developed to avoid violence—"public conflict alerts the community and its participants to the possibility of violence." Social solidarity, she suggests, "is not just the absence of pathology or of violence, but the community's capacity to contain, diminish, or limit, with a minimum of derivative violence or conflict, even the high incidence of potentially disruptive killing and violence that it has experienced."

Why has this bitter lesson not been better learned in the United States? The answer may lie in the vast heterogeneity and rapid social change which have characterized this country from its beginnings; thus, viable social mechanisms and solidarity sufficient to contain violence engendered in social conflict have not developed. We suspect the "myth of peaceful progress" and the celebration of assimilationist tendencies in American life have served to blind many to the violence of our past and perhaps to divert attention and efforts to correct the inequities and injustices in that heritage which continue to this day.[12]

The *macho* described by Schwartz is a type of *subculture of violence*—a system of values and behavior related to a larger culture, but separated from it both socially and culturally. Values supporting violent behavior, as in the settlement of disputes, the socialization of children, and the demonstration of manhood, characterize such subcultures. Aspects of social organization incorporate these values. The thesis has been most fully developed by Wolfgang and Ferracuti, and most recently documented for Sardinia, the lovely island in the Mediterranean Sea with the highest rates of homicide to be found in Italy.[13] Wolfgang notes in summary, that:

Sardinian violent offenders are reared mostly in a rural milieu that is a subculture of the Italian and even Sardinian legal values and normative culture system. Less educated, occupationally unskilled, farmers or shepherds, they generally are devoid of psychopathologies, resort to violence not within their families but within their residential environment to find targets of an economic nature connected with their honor. Their families seem supportive and understand their use of violence to resolve a problem. Without a sense of guilt, these offenders resort to a reasoned resolution of a conflict through violence rather than seek solace in a civil or criminal court. Reluctant to use the formal authority of the law, which still seems to be imposed from outside the isolationist periphery of his own culture, and supported by all the meaningful groups around him with their same value system as well as dialect, the violent Sardinian offender has significantly different attributes from the violent offenders on the mainland of Italy and from nonviolent offenders in general.

Chapters 12 and 13 present findings from extensive ethnographic studies of whole societies characterized by violent cultures. Robert B. Edgerton's discussion of "Violence in East African Societies" suggests that the "quintessential

---

12. See Rubenstein, op. cit., Skolnick, op. cit., and Graham and Gurr, op. cit.

13. Marvin E. Wolfgang and Franco Ferracuti, *The Subculture of Violence* (London; Tavistock, 1967); F. Ferracuti, R. Lazzari, and M. E. Wolfgang, eds., *Violence in Sardinia* (Rome: Mario Bulzoni, 1970).

problem" among tribal societies which lack "offices and institutions capable of ordering force in maintenance of social order" is the fact that "any act of violence between individuals is potentially, even probably, an act of collective violence" and is therefore very possibly ruinous in its consequences. Under these conditions, forms of collective violence evolve as mechanisms for the maintenance of social order, and occasionally become ritualized as means of "avoiding, attenuating, or deflecting violence." The powerful systems of supernatural beliefs which deter individual violence and feud in these tribal societies are less available to modern societies which have experienced the "disenchantment of the universe."[14] Edgerton notes that those chiefdoms in East Africa which possess offices and institutions of authority experience problems of political violence—revolt, rebellion, and conflict over succession—even as their counterparts in more modern nation-states.

In Chapter 13, L. L. Langness discusses New Guinea highland societies long noted for their violent character. Langness notes that among the Bena Bena and several neighboring societies, while warfare and other means of settling disputes "are distinguished, violence is always acceptable"; and, "for the most part, justice itself is defined by strength, as is what is moral." Violence was a daily "fact of life," and "rather than being proscribed, violent self-help was prescribed as a method of social control."

Langness notes in closing that "the materials from the New Guinea highlands illustrate lucidly that violence breeds more of the same, particularly

when there is no overriding authority and the major controls involve further violence. . . . They also illustrate the dangers of being unable to limit power when it does arise."

The development of nation-states, industrialization, and other social forces of "modernization" does not necessarily diminish violence (though the extent to which this may be the case is an important question) but they lead to changes in forms of violence and, it appears, to its politicization. Graham and Gurr refer to the "bellwether function of civil strife," reflecting "the character and social processes of the times and societies from which it arises."[15]

Melford E. Spiro's study of "Violence in Burmese History" (Chapter 14) is apposite. Spiro notes that violence has been a persistent feature of Burmese society, but its characteristic forms have changed greatly over the pre-colonial, colonial, and post-colonial periods. The pre-colonial period was characterized by culturally sanctioned warfare. Following conquest by the British, warfare was no longer permitted and other institutionalized forms of aggressive behavior (for example, intervillage races and other contests) "were abolished by the colonial government because, so it claimed, they promoted gambling and crime." Spiro attributes subsequent increases in Burma of insurgency, political violence, factionalism, and crime rates to the "restructuring of the traditional hierarchical order of the response repertoire for aggression." Burmese socialization patterns typically lead to the repression of hostility. In the absence of the traditional forms of hostile expression —external warfare and internal competition in contests—"hostile affect is expressed in disruptive political fac-

14. See Max Weber, "Science as a Vocation," in H. H. Gerth and C. Wright Mills, eds., *From Max Weber: Essays in Sociology* (New York: Oxford University Press, 1946), pp. 129–156.

15. Graham and Gurr, op. cit., p. xii.

tionalism, brutal crime, and (other forms of) violence."

In Chapter 15, John W. M. Whiting also studies violence as "a member of the more general class of social interaction usually referred to as aggression," and he also seeks a psychocultural explanation. In contrast to the broad historical level of analysis pursued by Spiro, however, Whiting focuses on social interaction among children in six cultures (communities in Okinawa, the Philippines, northern India, central Mexico, western Kenya, and New England in the United States), and on data relative to socialization and other patterns of behavior compiled from a variety of cross-cultural and cross-species investigations. Support is found for two hypotheses: (1) "that societies inducing high sex anxiety and sex inhibition are likely to permit and even to ritually require a high degree of cruelty and sadism in the treatment of prisoners of war," and (2) exclusive mother-son relationships (as, for example, in some polygynous societies in which fathers often live away from mothers and children) lead to sex identity problems for males that result in hypermasculine behavior in the form of violence.

The perspectives introduced by these anthropologists are especially valuable because they involve such a variety of cultural contexts. The enormous influence of cultural values and traditions, as well as the operation of social influences and of basic drives and energies within these cultural contexts, can thereby be better appreciated. The extent to which conclusions derived from these observations are generalizable to problems of collective violence in more modern, highly industrialized societies is, of course, problematic. Spiro specifically disclaims the applicability of his explanation of violence in post-colonial Burma to campus violence, and Whiting does not address the issue. But may

not these observations inform fundamental problems such as My Lai or ghetto violence? Regrettably, much more research is needed before such questions can be definitively answered. Surely, however, data and interpretations such as these ought to become an important part of the dialogue so important to social policy formation and implementation, and to public understanding of the complexity of issues that divide us.

In concluding our discussion of this section of the book, we return to Weber's notions concerning the "disenchantment of the universe." Weber was referring to the attitude toward natural phenomena which has accompanied the industrial revolution and the growth of science, an attitude that natural phenomena can be understood and controlled rather than merely accepted as inevitable. The related value system, discussed by psychiatrist John P. Spiegel in Chapter 19, is one of mastery over nature, as opposed to subjugation to it. Removal of the unknown and unknowable quality of natural phenomena leads also to the destruction of fatalistic beliefs which underlie many peoples' handling of disputes and aggression. The perspective of disenchantment— and of science, with its implications for understanding and control over natural phenomena—also leads to intolerance of and frustration with failure to solve problems. The response, in our society and throughout much of the world, has been to seek redress by political means.

Robert Levy presents further evidence of the extremely varied ways in which aggression is handled in societies not characterized by the disenchantment of the universe.[16] Levy describes

16. Robert I. Levy, "On Getting Angry in the Society Islands," in William Caudill and Tsung-Yi Lin, eds., *Mental Health Research in Asia and the Pacific* (Honolulu: East-West Center Press, 1969), pp. 358–380.

Tahitian society, in which angry behavior is suppressed and violence of the types referred to in this volume is unknown. "The system," Levy notes, "seems to work to prevent gross hostile action without causing strong repressed hostility, unlike the situation in other cultures where soft, gentle personality façades frequently are associated with much violent behavior.[17] The cultural system is very different from any of the others described in these chapters. Levy summarizes:

(1) Much of Tahitian socialization is directed through complex strategies, against striving. It is felt that too much striving is bad, unproductive, or may even bring punishment from nature. When one is not ambitious, he has, of course, less chance of being frustrated. (2) Emphasis is on the substitutability of goals, the objects of which are assumed to be in adequate supply. If you lose one woman, you will get another. If you do not get fish one day, you will on another. (Incidentally, there are no good luck magic and love charms. It is assumed that magic is not necessary for success and that manipulations will decrease your chances. The best way to get ahead is to take it easy.) (3) To Tahitians the actions of other people seem in some degree to represent the working out of general forces, part of the system. To the extent that actions are seen as inevitable, natural, and not arbitrary, willful, and unnecessary, they probably produce less sense of frustration and irritation.[18]

The absence of fatalistic acceptance of forces beyond understanding and control, it should be noted, need not be associated with the view that social forces (and individual actions) are arbitrary. And willfulness may come to be understood as a product of life experience. The conception of forces and actions as "natural" need not, following the "disenchantment of the universe"

17. Ibid., p. 377.
18. Loc. cit.

notion, be associated with the belief that they are "inevitable." Disenchantment may thus be the basis for a common and rational (and nonetheless humanistic) perspective on human behavior and forces which shape our lives, individually and collectively. It is this hope that motivates much of the recent scientific effort to understand the causes of violence.

DIMENSIONS OF COLLECTIVE VIOLENCE IN THE UNITED STATES

This section of the book is introduced (Chapter 16) by Hugh Davis Graham's historical examination of the paradox of an America "filled with violence," yet with vital public institutions which have enjoyed stability and continuity. Earlier, as co-directors of a Violence Commission Task Force, Graham and Gurr noted that Americans have tended to sweeten memories of the past by slighting the role of violence in our history and celebrating America and Americans as larger than life, morally superior, dedicated to and capable of achieving peaceful progress. More careful scholarship has modified this view and sobered our appraisal of the character of our society and how we have come to be what we are.

Papers in this volume by Graham and Gurr go beyond their Violence Commission assessment in analyzing forces which may contribute to future collective violence. Graham's analysis suggests that dissident groups in this country are likely to focus their discontent increasingly on political institutions, with a consequent undermining of the legitimacy of these institutions, thereby increasing the likelihood of further political violence. There are important straws in the wind—from the rhetoric of an emergent Klan to political reprisals against institutions of

higher learning.[19] The papers in Part
IV are addressed to recent events in
this country which bear upon these and
related issues.

Following Graham's historical analysis, Sheldon Levy returns to the characterological level of investigation
explored by the anthropologists in Part
III. His method is the survey interview
rather than ethnographic analysis, and
his topic, the "Psychology of (United
States) Political Activity." Levy focuses on various correlates of political
attitudes and activities. He concludes
that psychological rigidity and identification with authority as a means of reducing anxiety—both inimical to
democratic principles and effective representative government—are characteristic of persons who feel they have not
been rewarded by the political system.

*Wars, Generation Gaps, and
Collective Violence*

From historical and characterological
investigations, we turn to studies of
some of the major issues which divide
the United States, often to the point of
violence. In this section two papers by
Robert B. Smith discuss the impact of
the Vietnam War. The first, based on
national survey data, established the
proportions of "doves" (21 percent),
"hawks" (19 percent), and the silent
majority" (60 percent) among a representative sample of the U.S. adult population in the fall of 1968. Smith finds,
as have others before him, that attitudes
about the Vietnam conflict do not follow traditional lines of political cleavage in this country. "Doves" tend to be
more "liberal" concerning domestic issues such as civil rights, and they are
more tolerant of dissent and less supportive of repressive action by authorities than are "hawks." Overall, the
proportion of the American public
which supports repression appears to
be about twice that which expresses
tolerance for rebellion. Relationships
among these attitudes are complex,
however, and Smith seeks to sort them
out. In view of the shifting nature of
public opinion, and the responsiveness
of opinions concerning the war to the
course of the war, these relationships
must be viewed as suggestive rather
than definitive. But they provide important information concerning the deli-
cate balance of public attitudes and
political policies and events, a balance
far more subtle than that comprehended
in the heat of political rhetoric.

The war in Indo-China has been
much at issue in the violence which has
swept across college and university
campuses throughout the nation. A distinguished member of the President's
Commission on Campus Unrest, Erwin
D. Canham, editor-in-chief of the *Christian Science Monitor,* urges Americans
to "look beyond" the immediate issues
of campus violence and reaction to it.
"What is happening in the United
States and in much of the world," says
Mr. Canham, "goes beyond Vietnam
and social injustice and food in the
college dining halls and bombings."[20]
Mr. Canham sees in these events symptoms of "a turning point in history"
which presents opportunities for building "bridges of understanding" and for
great hope, but prospects for "great

19. Much of the rhetoric of the Klan focuses its ire against the federal government
for its role in civil rights and welfare matters. See James F. Kirkham, Sheldon Levy,
and William Crotty, *Assassination and Political Violence,* A Report to the National
Commission on the Causes and Prevention of
Violence (Washington, D.C.: U.S. Government Printing Office, 1969), especially Appendix D, pp. 319–350.

20. Erwin D. Canham, in a copyrighted
series, 1970. The quoted sentence appeared in
the *Spokane Daily Chronicle,* October 26,
1970.

anguish and turmoil" should such bridges fail or not be built.

In Chapter 19, psychiatrist John P. Spiegel conceptualizes campus unrest in terms of value conflicts. Basing his analyses on the assumption that "Students would not be protesting with such vigor were they not intensely eager for fundamental and difficult to achieve transformations, both within the university and in the society as a whole," Spiegel seeks to identify the nature of changes sought and the consequences of methods used to obtain them. His approach to this problem is based on analysis of *value orientations* of "standard (middle class) American culture," the traditional university, and the student protest movement. Spiegel sees "problems of the university in a time of value transition . . . [as] special cases of problems facing the whole society." He presents, as "informed guesses" and "based on an interpretation of changes already in process plus deductions from the logic of value conflict," proposed changes in university values which, he hopes, might bring into greater harmony conflicting values of the larger society and the students.

The changes are focused on four areas: *relational* (having to do with authority in group decision making and personal relationships within groups), *time,* (that is, the way decisions are made with respect to time), the relation of man to *nature,* and "the most valued aspects of the personality in action," or *activity.* Spiegel proposes greater emphasis in the university on individual and group decision making and less on hierarchical authority. Power in universities typically is diffused and weak, despite the apparent power of "the administration."[21] "Power," Spiegel

points out, is both stratified and divided." He continues:

Influence is commanded by informal cliques of "advisors" or "insiders" surrounding each center of power—the Board; Chancellors, Presidents and Provosts; Deans, Department Heads—down the ladder of prestige, through layers of faculty and teaching assistants to students, traditionally on a lower rung, and service employees at the bottom. As a result of the division of power, the oligarchies compete with and often neutralize each other, universities are not run very efficiently and administrators often feel frustrated. As a result of the informal nature of the decision-making clique at each center of power, the designated "head" is often a "figurehead," and it is important but difficult to know whom to cultivate in order to influence decisions. As a result of both the stratification of elites and of the obscure nature of decision-making, students have felt themselves to be without power and without knowledge of how to communicate effectively in regard to their needs and complaints, the more so since formal student governing bodies have been viewed as a part of the democratic facade governing the essentially oligarchic character of university structure.

With respect to the man/nature dimension, Spiegel proposes greater emphasis on harmony with nature, supplanting mastery over nature as the dominant value and moving subjugation to nature to the lowest priority. He points out that the proposed change is consistent with the new awareness of environmental pollution and emphasis upon the quality of life. He also suggests that changing problems of modern society require that present concerns be given equal priority with the past and the future in man's time perspective, supplanting the old emphasis on the future *over* the past which relegated

21. This diagnosis is common to many analyses of campus unrest. See e.g., Jack D. Douglas, "Youth Culture and Campus Violence," written for the President's Commis-

sion on Campus Violence, Summer 1970 (Unpublished paper).

the present to last priority. Finally, less emphasis on doing (the well-known "success" theme of American culture) and more on being-in-becoming—that is, development of a well-rounded personality without either the compulsiveness of excessive striving or the impulsiveness of activity for its own sake—is suggested.

Against this abstract consideration of value orientations, trends, and conflicts, the specifics of campus disorder often are stark and dramatic. The President's Commission on Campus Unrest highlighted two social issues which, more than any other, have been the focal point of campus disturbances: the United States' involvement in the Vietnam War and racial injustice at home. Chapter 20, by Robert B. Smith, finds Vietnam to be the primary issue in the radicalization and the violence on at least one campus, the University of California at Santa Barbara. Smith's paper is a "case study" of the Santa Barbara campus and its surrounding community.

The 1968–69 and 1969–70 academic years at Santa Barbara were marked by violent student protests over a variety of issues and, as reported by Smith, by the radicalization of a large proportion of the students. UCSB students were a good deal more "dovish" than the general adult population of the U. S. and somewhat more so than college students in general, based on estimates from other studies. The paper describes events on the Santa Barbara campus which led to confrontations involving students, faculty, administrators, and police, and which culminated in burning a local branch of the Bank of America. Issues in these confrontations were varied, from university policies relative to minority groups to the firing of a controversial faculty member and protests concerning police brutality in the "peoples' park" controversy on the

Berkeley campus of the University of California. In none, however, was the war in Vietnam an explicit issue.

Smith's task in the paper is to sift out, from many background characteristics, attitudes, and reported behaviors, the primary contributors to the violence at UCSB. He notes that at the time of his initial survey (December 1968), student militancy meant "willingness to use forceful, but nonviolent, tactics." Yet violence erupted and was widely supported among these same students.

Several points stand out in this analysis. As has been found in other studies, Vietnam "doves" are more critical of government policies unrelated to the war than are "hawks." The former are more tolerant of dissent and more "unconventional" in other ways. Some would say they are more alienated, estranged from society. Smith acknowledges that the measures of this dimension that show the biggest difference between doves and hawks may reflect "realistic cause for concern with respect to world problems." More to this point, surveys conducted in 1969 at U.C., Berkeley, and UCLA report that the views of student activists reflect beliefs about political power rather than psychological alienation. One investigator attributes campus activism primarily to participation in a counter-culture.[22] Such an explanation might be appropriate for the Santa Barbara campus, though Smith does not pursue this line of analysis. What is apparent from his data is the fact that "disaffection with the Vietam War is a primary root cause of campus violence." By the spring of 1970, nearly nine out of ten UCSB students were classified as "doves." Violent protests, threats, and physical

22. Douglas Kirby, "An Analysis of Student Demonstrators at the University of California," unpublished manuscript (Los Angeles: Survey Research Center, University of California, 1970). Mimeographed.

damage to property had increased greatly. Smith presents evidence that "disaffection from the war and demands for social justice and new domestic priorities account for about half of the variation in student militancy." He also refutes explanations which attribute student militancy and violence to the influence of "radical professors and students who 'cultivate the mystique of violence and fantasize about revolution.'"

The situation in Santa Barbara, as in every other setting in which campus violence has erupted, was—and is—extremely complex. A distinction needs to be drawn between explanation of the type provided by Smith—that is, accounting for differences in students' beliefs concerning social issues and militancy—and explanation of specific episodes involving violence (or any other type of behavior). Issues are the basis for disagreement among students and other segments of a community as well as between them. The manner in which issues are handled within and between groups has much to do with the structure and other aspects of the social systems comprised of institutions, and communities within which disagreements arise. This is a *macrosociological* level of explanation. At this level, we ask what it is about social systems that helps to explain events which occur within these systems.

Among the "macro" aspects of university life most subject to challenge in recent years, referred to by both Spiegel and Smith, is the nature of authority relations within that system. "Student Power" has become for many young people a slogan similar to "Black Power" among Black Americans, and often the two have been joined as issues in student protest. Student power typically becomes an issue in relation to university decisions relative to other issues as, for example, the relation of the university to surrounding ghetto communities, or "racist" university policies and practices, action (or inaction) relative to U.S. war policies, or the firing of a popular professor. Smith's research sorts out some of these issues in relation to the beliefs of Santa Barbara students.

It is clear from his account of events on that campus, however, that the events themselves were not solely a product of belief systems and of the nature of the university and surrounding communities as social systems. These events—the violence at Isla Vista, for example—were a product, as well, of their own unfolding. Study of this unfolding represents a *microsociological* level of explanation.[23] At this level we focus on the nature of interactive processes which produce particular episodes, on the varied roles played by participants, and on other circumstances that determine how interaction develops and outcomes result. Although various types of leadership may be important in each phase of social movements, the evidence strongly suggests that radical, and at times revolutionary, leaders have been especially crucial to campus violence in the unfolding of events rather than at the ideological or operational level of "conspiracy." Thus, for example, the President's Commission on Campus Unrest concluded. on the basis of testimony by FBI officials and other evidence, that campus unrest cannot be explained as a result of Communist subversion or conspiratorial organization. Some segments of the "New Left" have exploited the concerns of many students in creating confrontations over

23. See the distinction between microsociological and macrosociological levels of explanation, below. It is set forth and elaborated in Albert K. Cohen and James F. Short, Jr., "Crime and Juvenile Delinquency," in Robert K. Merton and Robert A. Nisbet, eds., *Contemporary Social Problems*, 3rd ed. (New York: Harcourt, Brace, and Jovanovich, Inc., 1971).

a variety of issues. Ineptness in handling such situations, over-reaction by police and national guard troops, and other factors have involved vast numbers of students in collective actions which often have included violence. In the process many of these students have become radicalized. Others no doubt have moved to more conservative political positions. The conservative Young Americans for Freedom may in fact be better organized and financed than the badly fragmented New Left. The "two cultures" of America—the old and traditional and the new "counter" culture—have emerged from the turmoil of the decade of the 1960's more polarized than ever before.

Opposition to the war in Vietnam is only one part of the disaffection, though most assuredly an important part. In an earlier analysis, Smith demonstrated that disaffection of various segments of the population and of the general public as a result of the U. S. involvement in war has varied enormously over the three most recent conflicts.[24] Disaffection in the form of negative public opinion has been far greater with respect to the Korean and Vietnam conflicts than was the case in World War II. Similarly, other measures of public disapproval and of resistance by draft-age men to service in these wars support the conclusion that the recent "limited wars" have failed to achieve the consensus which was evident during World War II, and opposition has become more widespread and intense with respect to Vietnam than was the case with Korea. Smith's analysis is confirmed by other evidence which also places today's violence-plagued era in historical perspective.

Opposition to war has been a persistent feature of U. S. history, from the American Revolution to the present. Robin Brooks concludes from his analysis of this history that the internecine strife in the American colonies and on the frontier during the war which brought the nation into being seems "to have involved less opposition to the war itself than a taking of sides in the civil war."[25] Other U. S. wars have involved vigorous antiwar sentiment and activity, often culminating in violence and official repression of dissent. On balance, violence clearly has been more frequent and intense on the part of those opposing antiwar protest than by the protestors. Brooks notes also that "in no previous American war have youth and students been significantly in opposition; previously they were a major source of patriotic sentiments . . . Nor is there any example of such widespread opposition to an American war coming from the academic and literary community."[26] Brooks' conclusion is suggestive:

We might . . . look to St. Thomas . . . [who] defined a just war as one meeting three qualifications: the ruler must be legitimate; the cause must be just; and the means employed must be proportionate to the ends in view. Apart from civil wars, there has seldom been any question about the legitimacy of American Government. Every American war has produced a few opponents who thought the cause unjust, but (perhaps duration is of significance in this equation) these have been relegated to one section or ethnic groups without greatly changing the attitudes of large

24. Robert B. Smith, "Disaffection, Delimitation, and Consequences: Aggregate Trends for World War II, Korea, and Vietnam," paper read at the annual meetings of the Pacific Sociological Association, 1969.

25. Robin Brooks, "Domestic Violence and America's Wars: An Historical Interpretation," in Hugh Davis Graham and Ted R. Gurr, *Violence in America: Historical and Comparatives,* A Staff Report to the National Commission on the Causes and Prevention of Violence (Washington, D.C.: U.S. Government Printing Office, 1969), p. 408.

26. Ibid.

patriotic majorities—again the civil wars are an important exception. Proportionality of means to ends first became a question at the beginning of the century, when Mark Twain and other intellectuals denounced the torture of prisoners in the Philippines. But atrocity stories only heightened American patriotism during World War I, World War II, and the Korean War, because Americans or neutrals were the victims of enemy barbarities. Violent opposition to the Vietnam War seems to have begun with the question of proportionality—the questions of napalm, defoliation, saturation bombing, etc.—and to have escalated to the point where a large majority of the American people question the justice of this war, and some begin to question the very legitimacy of "the system" that, in the minds of radical opponents of the war, has produced these effects.[27]

The Vietnam War has engendered both more widespread and intense opposition and more violence by protestors than any war in our history. It has done so, according to Irving Louis Horowitz, in part because it represents a broader challenge to the status quo of American society than is represented by the war itself.[28] We have moved, says Horowitz, from the politics of protest to the "politics of polarization." Just as the harassing of voter registration campaigns in the South stimulated Black militancy, the persecution of the antiwar movement made dissenters into radicals and then into revolutionaries." This has lead to escalation of the conflict by both sides. Horowitz sadly notes that "militants cheering for a Viet Cong victory emphasize a clear-cut struggle between reaction and revolu-

tion, rather than a reasoning together toward consensus."[29]

As has happened in earlier wars, antiwar protest often has been met with official, and sometimes by unofficial, violence. But this war also has resulted in official restraint and even facilitation of dissent. A quasi-experimental situation is thus created which we may study with profit. Before doing so, however, Chapter 21 further considers student dissent and its meaning for our society, and a second major issue—perhaps the most continuously divisive of all issues confronting this country over its history —is examined. The issue is race.

Youthful dissent appears to have replaced at least one of the major historical contributors to political violence in this country. A recent survey of newspaper reportage of political violence in the United States finds that "labor and racial antagonisms have dominated the picture."[30] The success of the labor movement has led to a sharp diminution of violence in this area, though it has by no means disappeared entirely. Sociologist William R. Morgan finds the labor movement instructive for understanding both contemporary student dissent and racial disorders. In Chapter 21 Morgan describes the former in terms of "formative influence relations" similar to the early labor movement. These relations are characterized by a lack of rules of fair play delimiting the range of acceptable tactics, an absence of formalized procedures for handling grievances on either side, and a high incidence of "bad faith" practices in which accommodation often breaks down and partisan conflict results. Morgan's survey of events related to anti-military recruiting demonstrations on college campuses

27. Ibid, p. 419.
28. Irving Louis Horowitz, *The Struggle is the Message: The Organization and Ideology of the Anti-War Movement* (Berkeley: The Glendessary Press, 1970).
29. Ibid., pp. 144–145.
30. Sheldon G. Levy, "A 150-Year Study of Political Violence in the United States," in Graham and Gurr, op. cit., pp. 65–77.

supports this view. Protest activity is found to be a necessary condition for administrative policy change. Predemonstration activity, Morgan reports, tended to polarize positions with respect to military recruiting on campus. The occurrence of civil disobedience as part of demonstrations against military recruiting was strongly associated with the occurrence of violence and with action by both faculty councils and student governments related to the issue. Morgan concludes that the demonstrations represented movement toward more formalized influence procedures, and suggests that the faculty is in a crucial position to mediate student-administration conflict.

This provocative formulation doubtless requires modification related to many characteristics of institutions of higher education, to the nature of problems and issues, and to the particular parties to these issues. Boards of regents, legislatures, alumni, and others in the larger society often become involved in such disputes. Faculties rather than "the administration" may be primary parties to particular conflicts. And student groups may oppose one another as primary combatants. Roles, rules, and procedures for mediating differences among such varied groups have not been formalized; indeed, it is doubtful that many have reached the stage of formative influence relations discussed by Morgan. The need to consider such matters is clear, however, as groups and institutions struggle to resolve problems of change, in the halls of academe as in the larger society.

Race and the Politics of Violence

Violence based on racial and ethnic antagonisms has been a persistent feature of the history of the United States. The newspaper survey referred to above finds that specifically racial an-

tagonisms accounted for the highest proportion of all incidents reported from 1819 through 1968. Labor violence was the only other category studied which accounted for nearly as much violence as race over this period, and during the most recent 30-year period studied, labor violence was less than half as frequently reported as was racially related violence. Labor related violence was similar in this respect to violence in "response to social conditions." Violence perpetrated "to gain political advantage" and to protest "current involvement in war" were the fourth and fifth ranking reasons for politically violent events in recent history.[31]

Racial antagonisms, and violence related to them, have been the subject of much commentary and controversy for many years. Much of the scholarly literature is touched upon in papers in this volume, particularly by Grimshaw in Chapter 2. The most notable conclusion of this literature, for present purposes, is that racial violence in this country has changed in recent years from that which "involved punitive assaults by Whites on Blacks for imag-

31. See Levy, op. cit., p. 74. The full set of "reasons" specified and their weighted averages (permitting comparison on a common standard) for the period, 1939-68, follows: *protests based on group antagonisms* (racial antagonism, 116.6; labor antagonism, 55.0; political antagonism, 15.4; differences in social viewpoints, 13.2; internal group antagonisms, 11.0; religious antagonism, 8.8), *action against authority* (respect to social conditions, 57.2; protest police action, 15.4; protest action of local officials, 13.2; to obtain a political goal, 13.2), *personal gain* (to gain political advantage, 35.2; economic gain, 13.2; personal revenge, 6.6; political disagreement, 6.6), *foreign affairs protest* (protest current involvement in war, 28.6; to protest government action in foreign affairs, 9.0), *reaction of official groups* (to maintain official authority by police, 2.2) and *to change official leadership* (to effect change in political personnel, 2.2).

ined or real violations of the status quo" to "direct assault [by Blacks] upon the accommodative structure of the society," quoting Grimshaw. Grimshaw's discussion of the general phenomenon of collective violence emphasizes factors related to the viability of accommodative structures. Among the propositions introduced to explain real or perceived changes in the distribution of power among groups in accommodative relationships, two are especially pertinent to the discussion which follows: power relationships may change when subordinate groups gain power through internal growth and organization, and when they come to realize latent power that they already possess. The legitimacy of accommodative structures may decline when those previously accorded legitimacy are perceived as having abused their power. Finally, Grimshaw notes, "If there is a belief (it need not be warranted, but not infrequently has been) that the control agencies—those institutional structures within the society which have a legal monopoly of the use of force—are weak, or partisan (or both), social violence is far more likely than if there is a belief that those agencies are strong and nonpartisan."

In "Local Political Leadership and Popular Discontent in the Ghetto" (Chapter 22), Peter H. Rossi and Richard A. Berk study personal experiences by ghetto residents, city leadership, and practices by ghetto merchants and the police. Exploitation by merchants and police brutality are the issues. When the research was begun under the auspices of the Kerner Commission, the favored model of riot causation in American cities was one stressing local conditions: on the one hand, grievances held by the Black population, and on the other, the degree of responsiveness of local city administrations. As it turned out, the research design based on such assumptions—one which would

allow comparison of riot and non-riot cities—was inadequate, as the model also proved to be. Research failed to identify systematic differences between cities which had major disorders in 1967, cities with minor disturbances in 1967 or disturbances in previous years but none in 1967, and those with no civil disorders in recent years. The disorders in April 1968, following the assassination of Martin Luther King, dealt the final blow to both the local determinism model and the research design, as three out of the five "non-riot" cities chosen for study experienced very serious disorders and one of the "medium" riot cities had its most serious disorder.

National problems may be viewed as macrosociological and appropriate to that level of analysis. They are experienced locally, however, and they become defined as national problems as a result of many individual and collective experiences. The processes by which they become manifest in local communities may also be analyzed at a macrosociological level, by viewing the local community as a social system. This is the strategy chosen by Rossi and Berk in Chapter 22.

Grievances about merchant practices and police conduct, Rossi and Berk report, have objective bases in the experience of ghetto residents. Correlations of reports by ghetto merchants and consumers and analyses of stores looted and vandalized during disorders suggest that merchant exploitation is not likely to become a source of mass dissatisfaction unless the issue is raised to the level of public controversy by local leaders. Police brutality, in contrast, emerges as a salient local issue directly out of personal experiences and is strongly related to responsiveness to Black grievances on the part of the heads of local police departments.

A good case study of this relationship, in a somewhat broader context than police brutality and in a city not included in the Rossi/Berk sample, is found in the Violence Commission's "Miami Report."[32] This report examines the disorder that occurred in Miami when the Republican National Convention was held in that city in 1968. The contrast between the county sheriff and the city police chief in their attitudes toward and relationships with ghetto residents is cited as a major factor contributing to tensions and related violence, and to their resolution. In public utterances and in attitudes and practices related to ghetto residents, the county sheriff was sympathetically responsive, but the city police chief presented a hard-line "law and order" posture that was essentially unresponsive to Black grievances. Order was finally restored by cooperation between police forces and local Black leadership. Analysis of the situation clearly reveals that the attitudes and practices of city police were a source of grievance within the ghetto, while those of the county sheriff contributed to harmonious relations within the ghetto and between sheriff's police and ghetto residents.

Rossi and Berk also report that the proportion of the population which is Black in the cities studied correlates negatively with general beliefs, personal experience, and observations of police brutality by ghetto residents, and with admitted abusive practices by police and police brutality; but the ratio of Blacks to Whites correlates positively with police knowledge of Black residents and police chief responsiveness to Black grievances.[33] These relationships

give substance to demands for "Black Power" in current controversies related to collective violence, and to a fundamental principle of Black Power— particularly in non-Southern cities, but increasingly also in the South—viz., in size there is real and legitimate political power.

A contrasting style of method (participant observation) and level of analysis (microsociological) are employed in Chapter 23. Richard A. Berk there describes and analyzes an "almost race riot," that is, a series of events which threatened but did not become a race riot. Berk's analysis of the crowds he observed suggests that participants could be characterized as "agitators" and "followers," and that persons in both roles were involved in a rational calculation of potential benefits and costs of action alternatives. In the case observed, agitators were unable to alter the payoff expectations of the followers, and so a violent confrontation was avoided. What emerged instead was ritual conflict in which minor skirmishes, gestures, verbal exchange, and symbolic paraphernalia occurred more as sport than as conflict. Following this event, inter-racial violence virtually disappeared in Baltimore, to the present writing. But ritual conflict which occurs on the basis of real antagonisms and grievances is not likely to be a long-term solution to these antagonisms and grievances. And therein lies the problem, not only of control but of justice as well.

The peculiarly sensitive role of the police in relation to group conflict is further examined in the next two chapters. In Chapter 25 Gordon E. Misner

---

32. Louis J. Hector and Paul E. Helliwell, *Miami Report* (Washington, D.C.: U.S. Government Printing Office, 1969).

33. These correlates of "general beliefs" may be particularly important to the joining of "micro" and "macro" levels of explana-

tion. See discussions of the importance of "generalized beliefs" in Chapters 3 and 5 in this volume. The concept is Smelser's. See Neil J. Smelser, *Theory of Collective Behavior* (New York: Free Press, 1962).

discusses political, organizational, ideological, tactical, and intelligence aspects
of this role. This analysis is preceded
by William A. Gamson and James Mc-
Evoy's study of police violence, which
often occurs, they note, "in a political
context with the police confronting organized groups rather than isolated
individuals."

Police may and do play very different
roles in group conflict situations. They
may adopt a neutral position with respect to issues and groups in conflict,
enforcing legal rules about permissible
conduct on the part of both sides, or
they may become partisans in the conflict, favoring one side against the
other. Cases of partisan identification
and activity often result from directives
by public officials superior to the police,
as in the case of the Democratic National Convention in Chicago in 1968.
Police violence may have been encouraged—certainly a partisan role was
encouraged—by Chicago officials in the
course of activities preceding as well
as during the convention. The "police
riot" which occurred did not involve a
majority of policemen on duty at the
time, however. Rather, it was reflected
in "the blatant misconduct and violence
by small bands of roving policemen in
the parks and streets on the city's north
side" on two nights of convention
week.[34]

The broader question examined by
Gamson and McEvoy relates to types
of constraints operating "on the use of
police as a partisan instrument against
challenging groups." More specifically,

they focus on opposition to and support
for police violence. Their discouraging
conclusion is that among adults in this
country, support for police violence
tends to be highest among privileged
groups, while opposition is highest
among groups with grievances against
the existing system of power and privilege. Given widespread public support
for police violence directed against unpopular targets, and viewing partisan
participation by police in social conflict
"as an invitation to counter-violence on
the part of challenging groups," Gamson and McEvoy find reason for serious
concern in their data. The absence of
sufficient normative constraints on police partisanship, they argue, makes
more urgent structural and organizational constraints on such partisanship.

The "other side of the coin" examined by Gamson and McEvoy is the
violence of those who protest. Evidence
relevant to the point is found in a recent survey of young (age 15–34)
Black males in the area of Newark,
New Jersey, which was wracked by
riots in the late 1960's.[35] Self-reported
participants in the rioting were found
to have greater political knowledge
(viewed as a measure of belief in the
efficacy of political action) but less
trust in existing political leadership
than non-rioters. Rioters were similar
in this respect to civil rights activists
and voters. Among the alienated—those
who scored low on both efficiency and
trust—riot participation was least frequent of all groups studied. This author
concludes that "rioting appears to be a
disorganized form of political protest
rather than an act of personal frustration or social isolation as has been
suggested in some past research."[36]

Chapter 25 examines some of the

34. Joseph R. Sahid, "Official Responses
to Mass Disorders II: The Circuit of Violence—A Tale of Two Cities," in James S.
Campbell, Joseph R. Sahid, and David P.
Stang, *Law and Order Reconsidered*, A Staff
Report to the National Commission on the
Causes and Prevention of Violence (Washington, D.C.: U.S. Government Printing Office, 1969), p. 343.

35. Jeffrey M. Paige, "Political Orientation and Riot Participation," unpublished
manuscript, 1970.

36. Ibid.

strains and the structural and organizational constraints operating on the police. Misner's focus is on police responses to collective violence, but the analysis informs as well the problem addressed by Gamson and McEvoy. The partisanship issue is complicated by several features of police work and training, and by many of the same factors which contribute to polarization of groups throughout society. Misner points out, for example, that "anger, frustration, horror, fear, and revulsion among policemen have now become a national collective phenonenon through the media of radio and television." Much of police training, a prominent police official maintains, is antithetical to democratic values, neglecting as it does "the positive values of constitutionally guaranteed rights of political dissent." Misner suggests that special care is required "to identify the ideological biases of rank-and-file policemen" and steps must be taken "to neutralize these biases" if police are to fulfill "truly impartial roles in mass demonstrations."

Police problems related to collective violence are enormously complicated, as Misner makes abundantly clear. Internal discipline and training, their relation to intelligence gathering and interpretation, civilian and political control, and tactical considerations all are problematic, often contributing to problems rather than to their solution. "The futility of placing virtually total reliance upon the police apparatus of the nation" for controlling collective violence, rather than addressing its root causes, is clear. It is also "foolish and grossly unfair," as Misner notes, "to scapegoat the police and to make them the culprits for all the social and political ills which beset the nation."

Finally, we would underscore Misner's conclusion that "unquestionably, large-scale, massive, collective violence

can be suppressed, if that is the option which is selected—either consciously or unconsciously," deliberately or by inadvertence. But it is likely that this can be done only by employing massive forces and collective violence against those who protest and seek redress of grievance. And it can be done "only at great peril to our existing political and social institutions—and at great personal risk to both citizens and civil servants!" The apparent escalation in police violence and in violent attacks on police in terrorist bombings with telephoned warnings for occupants of target buildings, may be but a prelude to violence on a much broader scale.

There is yet time, we believe, for peaceful change.[37] It may require a peaceful alteration of existing institutions if collective violence on an unprecedented scale is to be avoided. It has been suggested that the revolt of the young intelligentsia in the universities is but the first phase of "the long march through the institutions of society."[38] The problem is far deeper and more profound than a "generation gap," severe though that may be. Sociologist Richard Flacks, a founder of Students for a Democratic Society, long-time student of and sometimes spokesman for the New Left, suggests that the "trajectory" of student activism "is toward revolutionary opposition to capitalism."

37. We are inclined to believe that *Time* magazine's celebration of "The Cooling of America" (February 22, 1971 issue) is premature, though it may be accurate in a relative sense. The problems remain, as *Time* acknowledges. Whether such "cooling" as has occurred is temporary, signifying retrenchment, and whether it is likely to spread and continue, will depend very largely on social, and particularly political, responses to these problems.

38. Richard Flacks, "Young Intelligentsia in Revolt," *Trans-action* 7, no. 8 (June 1970), p. 50.

This is because capitalism cannot readily absorb the cultural aspirations of this group—aspirations that fundamentally have to do with the abolition of alienated labor and the achievement of democratic community. The incorporation of this group is made more difficult by the concrete fact of racism and imperialism—facts which turn the vocations of the intelligentsia into cogs in the machinery of repression rather than means for self-fulfillment and general enlightenment. The numerical size of this group and the concentration of much of it in universities make concerted oppositional political action extremely feasible. The liberal default has hastened the self-consciousness of students and other members of this class, exacerbated their alienation from the political system, and made autonomous oppositional politics a more immediate imperative for them. Thus, a stratum, which under certain conditions might have accepted a modernizing role within the system, has instead responded to the events of this past decade by adopting an increasingly revolutionary posture.[39]

The broadened base of "young intelligentsia in revolt" by virtue of the radicalization of students in colleges, in junior and senior high schools, among "street people" and even among members of the Armed Forces, continues to transform "the movement" and bring it closer to other movements, from the grape arbors and vegetable fields of the West to the urban ghettos. This new outlook and power base creates problems of focus and control for the movement and, we believe, enhances the prospects for its peaceful transformation. For it provides a broader base for legitimate "within-the-system" political and economic power and the achievement of change by these means, even to the transformation of the system itself. The changes required may be vast, as Flacks emphasizes. But many business and political leaders join youth in call-

ing for a reordering of priorities and for new criteria for social progress. As Flacks notes, the social and political climate "could change in a relatively short period of time as those who are now young move into full citizenship and have the opportunity directly to influence public and institutional policies. But," he warns, "what happens in the intervening years is likely to be crucial."[40] And so it is.

Mr. Canham notes that "no free society can achieve real peace with guns."[41] Many choices lie before us; many warnings have been sounded. Above all, it should be clear that repression and violence on the part of both authorities and those who protest inevitably lead to escalation of conflict and to more violence, or to such complete repression that essential freedoms are lost. Such a course would in the long run make revolution virtually inevitable. Surely this is what the small bands of embittered and naive revolutionaries in our midst want. We believe they must be denied, and they can be.

Despite the seriousness of the crises

40. Ibid., p. 54. It should be noted that preliminary analysis of a Carnegie Commission sponsored survey of a carefully selected sample of graduate students throughout the United States finds that protesters among this group are in general representative of graduate students rather than more affluent and intellectual, as previous studies have suggested. Since graduate students, as such, represent a sort of intelligentsia, this does not detract from the "intelligentsia" characterization. But it does cast doubt on contention that protesting students represent the "best" among students in institutions of higher learning. In fact, the Carnegie data suggest that approval of student radicalism tends to be negatively related to academic commitment. See Travis Hirschi and Joseph Zelan, "Student Activism: A Critical Review of the Literature and Preliminary Analysis of the Carnegie Commission Data on Graduate Students," unpublished manuscript, 1970.

41. *Spokane Daily Chronicle*, October 30, 1970.

39. Ibid., p. 50.

with which we are confronted, there is
at least some basis for optimism and
hope with which to counteract the fears
and resentment of authorities and the
general citizenry, and the despair of
those who seek change. In the past this
nation has demonstrated remarkable
resilience in the face of adversity. Today, even while fear and suspicion
divide us, we can at least agree on the
identity of common problems with
which the nation—indeed the world—
is confronted. These problems—war
and international grievance, social justice, the quality of social and physical
life—are not beyond solution. But they
will require a rearrangement of priorities, enormous expenditures of energies
and resources, and new understandings
among groups with diverse interests
and life styles. Time and need are
urgent for a new pluralism based on
mutual respect as a replacement for old
and newly arisen antagonisms.[42]

IN SEARCH OF ALTERNATIVES

That the advocacy of nonviolent
means of achieving social change has
acquired the status of a social movement speaks eloquently to the role of
violence in the regulation of human
affairs. Yet, as if in response to the
many forms violence has taken in
contemporary society, nonviolence is
"breaking out" in many forms and
many places throughout the world.
Returning to a previous reference, Wallace notes a persuasive rationale for the
development of a nonviolent perspective both on the part of those who seek
radical change and of those who are
defenders of the System:

42. Others have spoken with optimism concerning these and related matters. See, especially Charles Reich. *The Greening of
America* (New York: Random House, 1970;
and Jean-Francois Revel, *Ni Marx Ni Jesus,*
as reviewed in *Time,* (February 22, 1971),
pp. 24–25.

It is no doubt a perception of the danger
inherent in permitting the climate of violence to develop which has led some leaders of revitalization movements to insist
on nonviolence, a tactic which permits
only such violations of procedural morality which do not include physical assault
and destruction. A complimentary insistence by the System on strict adherence
to its own procedural morality by police,
courts, and the military has a similar purpose. Such devices, together with free
communication of factual information to
dispel at least gross fantasies of violence
by "the other side," may hopefully combine to establish means for effecting
change by negotiation and bargaining
rather than by internal war. Mankind
needs to find the cultural means for making violence unnecessary as a tactic for
revitalization.[43]

The social psychology of the movement in the United States is the focus
of a research team from Haverford College, headed by A. Paul Hare. What began two years ago as a study of direct
confrontation between non-violent
protestors and others (such as counter-
demonstrators or police) was broadened as a result of early research
experiences to include the study of nonviolence in life styles. Hare describes
this research in Chapter 26.

Hare's description and his presentation of preliminary findings demonstrate the increasing breadth and
sophistication of the non-violence movement in scope and in methods. They
tell us something, too, of the types of
people who are most active in the direct
confrontation aspects of the movement.
They are, Hare reports, about "equally
anxious," but less aggressive, less conforming, and more extroverted than
various samples of college students and
persons attending summer music festivals. The promise of studies such as
this—or the hope—is that processes
will be documented and mechanisms

43. Anthony F. C. Wallace, op. cit.

discovered which will be applicable on a broader scale, toward more effective grievance presentation and redress, and toward granting, even encouraging greater freedom in life styles within society at large so long as these styles do not infringe justice, domestic tranquility, and the pursuit of happiness of others.

James S. Campbell, General Counsel of the National Commission on the Causes and Prevention of Violence, concludes the book with his discussion of another type of search for these lofty goals, and specifically for alternatives to violence, viz., the national study commission. Campbell argues that such commissions are useful primarily because of the importance of their findings rather than because of their recommendations or their influence in implementing recommendations. "The real usefulness of commissions lies simply and primarily in their ability to present significant facts about national problems to those who possess political power and make political decisions." He suggests that "national advisory commissions have a distinctive fact-finding role to play that is related to—in a sense lies midway between—the respective roles of both the news media and the social sciences."

Essentially we applaud and agree with this characterization of the role of national commissions. It is important to note, however, that the social sciences have responsibilities which place them outside this implied continuum of *time* and *depth* analysis. Our responsibility is neither simply nor primarily "to present significant facts . . . to those who possess political power and make political decisions," but to present such *facts and their meaning* in terms of the accumulated body of knowledge of the science and to make this presentation to the broadest possible audience, regardless of political

power. Indeed the message of many of our younger colleagues is that we have a responsibility to broaden the base of political power and decision making rather than simply to make ourselves available to various establishments with resources to fund research.

It was the principle of freedom of communication—and Mr. Campbell was among our staunchest supporters, as was Violence Commission Chairman Milton S. Eisenhower—that led to our insistence and to Commission agreement on a publication policy for research conducted by persons employed by or for the Commission. Although all material to be published under Commission auspices was subject to Commission review, final decision about content and style belonged to the authors. The Commission had the prerogative of refusing to publish staff documents with Commission funds, in which case authors were free to publish their own material upon the expiration of the life of the Commission. As it turned out, despite sharp disagreement among Commissioners and strong reservations about some of the material submitted by Task Force directors, the Commission approved publication of all Task Force reports. Each report was twice clearly labeled on the front cover as a "Staff Report to the National Commission on the Causes and Prevention of Violence" and "A Staff Report Not a Report of the Commission."

It was this policy that made possible the publication of 13 volumes of staff reports, in addition to the well-known "Walker" (Chicago) and "Miami" reports, with the much broader circulation that is assured such publications compared to the more limited audiences of scholarly journals.[44] The Commis-

44. The reports are as follows:
Hugh Davis Graham and Ted Robert Gurr, *Violence in America: Historical and Comparative Perspectives* 1 and 2 (Washington,

sion issued a "Progress Report" to President Johnson in January, 1969, followed by a series of reports that were later incorporated into the Commission's final report to President Nixon, in December 1969.

D.C.: U.S. Government Printing Office, 1969).
Jerome Skolnick, *The Politics of Protest: Violent Aspects of Protest and Confrontation* (Washington, D.C.: U.S. Government Printing Office, 1969).
Joseph R. Salid, *Rights in Concord: The Response to the Counter-Inaugural Protest Activities in Washington, D.C., January 18–20* (Washington, D.C.: U.S. Government Printing Office, 1969).
Louis H. Masotti and Jerome R. Corsi, *Shoot-Out in Cleveland* (Washington, D.C.: U.S. Government Prinitng Office, 1969).
William H. Orrick, Jr., *Shut It Down! A College in Crisis: San Francisco State College, October, 1968-April, 1969* (Washington, D.C.: U.S. Government Printing Office, 1969).
George D. Newton and Franklin E. Zimring, *Firearms and Violence in American Life* (Washington, D.C.: U.S. Government Printing Office, 1969).
James F. Kirkham, Sheldon Levy, William J. Crotty, *Assassination and Political Violence* (Washington, D.C.: U.S. Government Printing Office, 1969).
Robert K. Baker and Sandra J. Ball, *Violence and the Media* (Washington, D.C.: U.S. Government Printing Office, 1969).
James S. Campbell, Joseph R. Sahid, and David P. Stang, *Law and Order Reconsidered* (Washington, D.C.: U.S. Government Printing Office, 1969).
Donald J. Mulvihill, and Melvin Tumin, with the assistance of Lynn Curtis, *Violent Crimes*, 3 vols. (Washington, D.C.: U.S. Government Printing Office, 1970). Several of these volumes have also been published by commercial publishers, some by more than one. Others appear likely to be commercially published soon. A volume based on the transcript of the public hearings before the Commission on the mass media and violence was not published for lack of funds.
Daniel Walker, *Rights in Conflict* (New York: Bantam Books, 1968).
Louis J. Hector and Paul E. Helliwell, *Miami Report* (Washington, D.C.: U.S. Government Printing Office, 1969).

Differences between staff and Commission Reports reflect the broader responsibilities of the scientist with respect to public issues. Staff reports contain materials that are far more critical than is the Commission report of official policy and particular groups, such as Black/White relations, the young and the poor, firearms, the media, political activities of the police and their reaction to protest activities, and, above all, about the relationship between officially legitimated violence in international relations and violence at home which is defined as illegitimate. Thus, the charge that scholarly studies "sometimes avoid the tough issues which commissions can't avoid" can be turned around. This is not to say that Mr. Campbell is incorrect. He refers primarily to the narrow and sometimes parochial focus of scholarly studies and their common failure to address significant policy issues, characteristics which surely we can neither deny nor defend entirely. We need, however, to remind ourselves and others, as Albert J. Reiss, Jr. recently did in his presidential address to the Society for the Study of Social Problems, that sociology is poorly equipped with theory that is policy oriented, and that our usefulness in other respects is further impaired by the lack of replicated studies demonstrating valid and reliable knowledge.[45]

Campbell's paper also argues co-

45. Albert J. Reiss, Jr., "Putting Sociology into Policy," *Social Problems* (Winter 1970), pp. 289–294. This same issue contains an excellent essay of a type which is directly within scholarly tradition but hardly imaginable by a national commission, because it questions the bases of power of elitist v. non-elitist groups in capitalistic systems. See Milton Mankoff, "Power in Advanced Capitalist Society: A Review Essay on Recent Elitist and Marxist Criticism of Pluralist Theory," *Social Problems* (Winter 1970) pp. 418–430.

gently for sharpening the conceptual tools of the social sciences as an aid to governmental commissions. His illustrations are well chosen, bringing us full circle to some of the basic questions of classification and interpretation with which this volume begins. Clearly much remains to be done before we can more adequately advise commissions or policy makers at any level in any cause.

From Campbell's illustrative items, however, a further point can be made concerning the use made of social science knowledge, based upon our experience with the Violence Commission. Campbell refers to the "Walker Report on the Democratic Convention disorders of 1968" as an "exhaustive, definitive account of what happened in Chicago." While the report certainly was dramatic, and it may have "made credible to millions of Americans, for the first time, the long-standing complaints of Black ghetto residents and political dissidents about 'police brutality'," it was neither exhaustive nor definitive. What it did not do—and what would have been most useful to the Commission, to the public, and to the corpus of social science knowledge —was inform us about who came to Chicago and why, who made what sorts of decisions among the demonstrators, city officials, and the media and why, and what were the processes that culminated in the violence.

The point is simply that commissions sometimes misuse and even abuse social science, even under the best of circumstances—and we believe our circumstances were unusually favorable with the Violence Commission, as we tried to make it clear in our "Preface" to the staff reports to the Commission.[46]
We commend to our readers the

reports, especially the staff reports, of national commissions on the great problems and issues related to collective violence. This volume is a continuation of the collaborative work we began with the Violence Commission. We hope and believe that these papers contribute to the illumination of collective violence. We are grateful to our co-workers in both enterprises.

IN CONCLUSION

In Hebrew the words for violence and mute have the same root. Both terms refer to the limited repertoire of response available. The mute cannot verbally articulate his intentions, frustrations, and motivations, cannot argue his case well. The person who resorts to physical violence often has limited capacity to plead his case and have his grievance resolved; responding agents often have little understanding and limited capacity to listen.

Honest analysis of problems and open discussion often are accompanied by rhetoric that does not always accurately describe our feelings and that is easily misinterpreted. We may also say hurtful things honestly about one another, about organizations, the political system, even previously sacrosanct leaders. But acceptable rules for confrontation can result in the resolution of individual and collective differences, if those in power accept the challenging voice of those not in power. Although the rhetoric of the latter often calls for the transformation of power, greater responsiveness by the possessors of power may suffice, and may in the end be the instrument of transformation.

The eruption of violence comes with self-legitimation of the use of physical force. Injurious consequences are neutralized by explicit or implied virtuous ends. These ends may be simple, individualized, and pedestrian. They are likely to become complex, universa-

46. And reprinted in *To Establish Justice, to Insure Domestic Tranquility,* op. cit., pp. 305–310.

lized, and sophisticated ideologies as intellectuals join the ranks of the violent. With polarization and the escalation of conflict, those once free may become locked into a syllogism of force.

Nations, ethnic and labor groups, neighborhoods and mates are all collectivities. We hope that sharing ideas and emotions, and the mutual anaylsis of responses and goals, will promote conciliation. In any case, change is inevitable. How well we change, how much we change, with or without overt physical violence, are matters entirely within the capacity of humanity to determine and direct.

Part II

Theoretical Issues

2

Interpreting Collective Violence: An Argument for the Importance of Social Structure

By ALLEN D. GRIMSHAW

Allen D. Grimshaw is professor of Sociology at Indiana University. He is editor of Racial Violence in the United States *(1969) and served as a consultant to the Kerner and Eisenhower Commissions. He was a fellow of the American Institute of Indian Studies in 1962–63 and director of the Institute for Comparative Sociology from 1966 to 1969. In addition to his interest in social conflict, Professor Grimshaw is currently working on the sociology of language. He is chairman of the American Sociological Association Committee on Public Policy.*

B Y way of introduction, I should like to say that eleven years ago I completed a dissertation on urban racial violence in the United States.[1] The topic was chosen not because the phenomenon was seen as a social problem of major magnitude but rather because of a general interest in social conflict as process, and because of a specific interest in replicating Richard D. Lambert's excellent study of Hindu-Muslim violence in India.[2] In 1959, few people were interested in racial violence; the perspective seemed to be that such violence was a part of our country's tawdry past—and best forgotten. A few scholars remarked on the lack of a modern sociology of conflict,[3] and Coser's excellent exegesis of Simmel[4] (following the republication of Simmel's *Conflict*[5]) stimulated some interest in social conflict processes. During the Eisenhower years, scholars seemed to be working in other areas.

1. Allen D. Grimshaw, "A Study in Social Violence: Urban Race Riots in the United States" (Ph.D. diss., University of Pennsylvania, 1959/b).

In preparing this summary article I have drawn heavily on a number of useful discussions with colleagues and students, and on my past publications. Among the former, I am most recently indebted to Jeffery M. Paige, Austin T. Turk, and Owen Thomas. Among the latter I should list particularly the preface and the introduction to *Racial Violence in the United States* (Chicago: Aldine, 1969/a); "Violence: A Sociological Perspective," *Georgetown Law Review*, vol. 37, no. 4 (May, 1969/b), 816–834, from which some sections are incorporated verbatim; and a paper on the same theme presented at the 136th meeting of the American Association for the Advancement of Science (Boston, 1969/c).

2. Richard D. Lambert, *Hindu-Muslim Riots* (Ph.D. diss., University of Pennsylvania, 1951).

3. Jessie Bernard, "Where is the Modern Sociology of Conflict?" *American Journal of Sociology* 56, no. 1 (July 1950): 11–16.

4. Lewis Coser, *The Functions of Social Conflict* (Glencoe: Free Press, 1956).

5. Georg Simmel, *Conflict and the Web of Group-Affiliations*, trans. Kurt H. Wolff and Reinhard Bendix (Glencoe: Free Press, 1955).

Even as late as 1963, only a year before the "violence of the sixties" began, I was able to write[6]:

Conflict is both a continuing theme of the world's great literature and drama and a source of grave concern for heads of states. As a social process and as an individual psychological problem it is everywhere present in human affairs. But scholarly study of violence and force (the most extreme mode of conflict resolution) has not been proportionate to the importance of violence in the affairs of men. It is not surprising that, in the nuclear years since World War II, students of society have become increasingly concerned with the nature of social conflict, particularly in international relations. Yet even today sociologists, whose disciplinary interests should lead them to a major concern with conflict, have largely neglected its systematic study. Sociologists can always defend objective research, and hence could defend study of conflict and violence as social processes. Nonetheless, they have generally shied away from this area.

Scholars in every discipline even remotely concerned with human affairs have now turned to the study of conflict; several of those disciplines are represented in this special issue. Apparently the appearance of violence in our own cities and even on our sequestered campuses has done something which more remote threats (of far off wars and impending nuclear disaster) and scholarly papers never could. One change in conflict theory in recent years has been, simply, a quantum increase in scholarly attention and attempts at interpretation. There are two other changes in perspectives on social conflict which have occurred in recent years.

The first of these is the introduction of a historical perspective into the examination of contemporary violence and

6. Allen D. Grimshaw, "Government and Social Violence: The Complexity of Guilt," *The Minnesota Review* 3, no. 2 (Winter 1963/a): 236. Reprinted in Grimshaw (1969/a).

protest. Although a few observers of the events of the sixties have seen them as following naturally from a long history, a history which included a variety of expressions of social violence in intergroup relations in the United States, most Americans—including a large proportion of those with scholarly interests —chose to view the events of the last decade as an unexpected and, in some ways, inexplicable phenomenon which somehow suddenly appeared in a full-blown and extremely threatening form.

One of the reasons for this naïvely a-historical perspective was a preoccupation with other revolutionary changes in American life in the two postwar decades; that is, there was more attention to the "affluent society" than to "the other America" and more concern with leisure than with unemployment. This preoccupation was accompanied by a pattern of wishful thinking that somehow assumed that while there are people in America who are underprivileged, even some who are systematically exploited and discriminated against, they have experienced a steadily improving situation, both through their own hard work and through legal action by the government. The continuation of highly charged conflict and violence, and its increasing tendency to spill over into new institutional areas, have forced those who would explain it to look more closely at our history. An emphasis on the continuity of violence as a characteristic of American society (and, more broadly, possibly of most societies) has informed the work of an increasing number of scholars working in a variety of disciplines.[7]

Finally, by way of introduction to my own sociological bias, I believe that we are witnessing some genuine convergences across disciplines in critical perspectives on violence. Social scientists (and humanists, for that matter) of every persuasion have attempted to isolate the causes of prejudice and discrimination (whether directed against blacks, reds, browns, yellows, poor whites, deviants, or college students), for these are social phenomena intimately related to expressions of conflict and violence. Each of the many causal explanations of prejudice has purported to isolate the major etiological factor in prejudice, and therefore in discrimination, and presumably, in social tension, social conflict, and violence. (My own work has focused primarily on racial conflict and violence, but the discussion would seem to be equally relevant to several other varieties of social conflict.) In any given instance of conflict or prejudice, however, more than one of these causal clusters has served equally well, and in practice those elements of varying theories that have best fitted immediate problems have been selected eclectically. I believe that one positive consequence of the violence and turmoil which have beset us is that scholars in different fields are now, some of them for the first time, looking seriously at the explanatory frameworks of other disciplines and systematically incorporating them into their own work. One instance of this, for example, is to be found in the suggestive work of the psychiatrist, John Spiegel. Much of his work refers more to structural factors in violence than to individual personality dynamics.[8] The fact that his work therefore becomes more meaningful to sociologists does not, I submit, make it less useful to psychiatrists.

In this article I will emphasize what I call a sociological perspective on social conflict, attending particularly to social

7. See, *inter alia,* Hugh D. Graham and Ted R. Gurr, eds., *Violence in America: Historical and Comparative Perspectives,* a report to the National Commission on the Causes and Prevention of Violence (Washington: U. S. Government Printing Office, 1969), in two volumes.

8. See citations to Spiegel in Grimshaw (1969/a).

violence. I will say something both about causation, drawing particularly on my own work on racial violence in the United States, and about similarities between that violence and violence in other institutional areas (e.g., labor or religion) as well as in other societies. Looking back over the decade since I completed my dissertation, I feel that progress has been made when I can say what I have to say in a context of general scholarly concern with social violence; a growing historical (and comparative) awareness; and the beginnings of some genuinely cross-disciplinary perspectives.

SOCIAL VIOLENCE DEFINED

Social violence is assault upon an individual or his property solely or primarily because of his membership in a social category. Some students would include the attribution of stereotypes, the accompanying use of social epithet, and a variety of discriminatory practices in their definitions (and I do not deny that words and slights can cause great pain); I include only physical assault resulting in personal injury or in damage to property. The decision to narrow the definition rests in substantial part on difficulties of measurement entailed in assessing magnitudes of, say, mental anguish or specific instances of economic deprivation.

According to this definition, a fight between two boys, one Protestant and one Roman Catholic, would not ordinarily be an instance of social violence in the United States, although there are times in our past when it would have been. If, however, the fight began because of religious insults ("Dirty mackerel snapper!") it would be, as it would become if other boys joined in on the basis of religious affiliation.[9] Similarly,

if a black robber always chose white victims because of their color rather than because of their greater likelihood of being "good" victims (two not unrelated characteristics), he would then be committing social violence. Violent events which begin as non-social violence may change during their course into social violence, as in instances where servicemen's brawls become battles between the services or when battles following high school athletic events become race riots.

During the course of American history, a very large number of social categories have been singled out for attack in patterns reflecting the complexities of intergroup contacts and conflict to be found in a pluralistic and rapidly changing society. Few types of identifiable minority social categories have been spared from attack at some time; some have been under continuous assault. Many Americans are aware, for example, that most racial minorities have been subject to social violence; somewhat fewer are familiar with the histories of nationality groups and religious bodies (there are vague memories of the reasons why Puritans and Quakers first came, somewhat vaguer recollections of Roger Williams' flight from the Bay Colony, and only minimal knowledge of pitched battles during the heyday of "Know-Nothingism," of systematic assaults on Mormons, of the history of other religious sects). There have been studies of labor violence, and Taft and Ross in their comprehensive review of this facet of our history have made available to a new generation a characterization of a set of events which has tended to be available primarily to older people.[10]

Younger Americans may also be more

9. See Lambert, op. cit., for a discussion of "insults to religion" as a factor in Hindu-Muslim conflict.

10. Philip Taft and Philip Ross, "American Labor Violence: Its Causes, Character, and Outcome," in Graham and Gurr, op. cit., pp. 221–301.

likely to view the appearance of violence toward students as a new pattern, but some people will remember that town-versus-gown disputes of the past were not always viewed as sheer sport when they occurred.[11] Shifting to a quite different set of categories, it has always been open season on homosexuals in the United States (and the mobilization of this category for protective purposes has interesting parallels to events in black groups); and there have been periods in American history when adulterers or divorcés have been subject to physical assault (by Klansmen). Finally, we have a long tradition of violence against political groups—the events in Chicago during the 1968 Democratic convention have historical continuity with patterns long ago established in "Liberty Boy" depredations against Loyalists (Tories) and in attacks on Copperheads in the North during the War Between the States, to say nothing of the inter-party and factional political violence which continued in some places in the United States well into the twentieth century.

The term *social violence* as I use it differs from the term *strife* as used by the political scientists and sociologists who have been engaged in large-scale attempts to study social conflict cross-nationally, using aggregated data.[12]

The closest parallel is with their term *turmoil,* which is considerably more inclusive than *social violence* in that it includes more general violence (viz., in which assaults are not based solely or primarily on categorical membership). Yet, I believe that the theoretical perspectives which explain social violence will also explain social protest and social turmoil, and that the same principles apply in some measure (perhaps totally) to the three phenomena which they have had under investigation.

THEORETICAL PERSPECTIVES: I. THE INDIVIDUAL

There seem to be as many explanations and interpretations of social violence as there are scholarly and applied professions interested in the phenomenon.[13] Historians speak of a tradition of lawlessness and violence; anthropologists (and some sociologists) speak of cultures or subcultures of violence; social reformers and revolutionaries speak of unjust laws; and pacifists look with horror on violence in any form and see its source in man's unfortunate but perhaps perfectible "nature." In this paper I will discuss only two of these varied explanatory perspectives: (1) those focusing on the individual and associated primarily with psychology and related disciplines, and (2) those focusing on groups and the social structure and associated primarily with sociology.

---

11. For a thought-provoking literary examination of a world in which education has come to be stigmatically defined, see Walter M. Miller, Jr., *A Canticle for Liebowitz* (New York: Lippincott, 1960).

12. For a sampling of this literature, see Rudolph J. Rummel, "Dimensions of Conflict Behavior Within and Between Nations," *General Systems: Yearbook of the Society for General Systems Research,* vol. 8 (1963) pp. 1–50; Ted R. Gurr, "Urban Disorders: Perspectives from the Comparative Study of Civil Strife," *American Behavioral Scientist,* vol. 11, no. 4 (1968) pp. 50–55, reprinted in Grimshaw (1969/a); and three articles in Graham and Gurr, op. cit.: Ted R. Gurr, "A Comparative Study of Civil Strife," pp. 443–495; Raymond Tanter, "International War and Domestic Turmoil: Some Contemporary Evidence," pp. 423–

438; and Ivo K. Feierabend, Rosalind L. Feierabend, and Betty A. Nesvold, "Social Change and Political Violence: Cross-National Patterns," pp. 497–535.

13. For examples of both sociological and non-sociological interpretation, see Grimshaw (1969/a). An excellent and more detailed account of some sociological perspectives can be found in Jeffery M. Paige, "Collective Violence and the Culture of Subordination: A Study of Participants in the July, 1967 Riots in Newark, New Jersey, and Detroit, Michigan" (Ph.D. diss., University of Michigan, 1968). Graham and Gurr, op. cit., also includes a sampling of perspectives.

The three varieties of interpretation which characterize the first perspective generally look for explanations of social violence by focusing attention on the individual. The psychoanalyst looks for violence-proneness as a characteristic of the individual personality, which is rooted perhaps in traumatic experiences of very early life but which is clearly the consequence of the interaction of uniquely personal experiences in molding an individual psyche. To the psychoanalyst, the most important traumas are usually sexual. Sexual fears and sexual competition have characterized relations between black and white people in this country since contact first occurred; it is not surprising, then, that psychoanalysts have seen sex as crucial in determining the patterns of intergroup relations—including those of violence.[14] Hersey, in his book on the Algiers Motel incident which took place during the course of the 1967 riots in Detroit,[15] criticizes the Kerner Commission for failing to acknowledge the sexual aspects of race-linked social violence in that incident.[16] The Freudian analyst, however, is likely to see social violence more generally as the acting-out of sexual traumas suffered in infancy, or as the sublimation of sexual impulses of adults rather than as direct competition over sex as a commodity. Thus, Sterba,

in his commentary on the Detroit race riot of 1943, interprets assaults by whites on black-owned automobiles and their occupants as being the acting out of white penis envy.[17] Such an interpretation lies at the fairly extreme end of the individual-versus-social explanations continuum, but continues to be subscribed to by a small but extremely hardy group of professional psychiatric and, particularly, psychoanalytic interpreters.

The psychologist, in contrast, focuses less on the characteristics of the individual personality (either as molded by experiences of infancy and childhood or as given in the adult personality) than on the dynamics of an individual's interaction with his environment. The frustration-aggression hypothesis has influenced much of the theorizing on violence by psychologists, and in their pioneering study Hovland and Sears attempted to demonstrate that the number of lynchings was directly related to economic activity, with lynchings increasing in periods of economic depression and declining in periods of prosperity.[18] Some

14. It is true, of course, that sexual fears and sexual competition have characterized relationships between imperial groups and subordinated native groups in a variety of colonial settings. It is also true that in cases where the sexual values of the more powerful groups have been more relaxed (e.g., in Portuguese-controlled as contrasted to British-controlled areas) this area of behavior has been less important in defining intergroup relationships.

15. John Hersey, *The Algiers Motel Incident* (New York: Knopf, 1968).

16. For a more extended critical commentary on shortcomings of the "Kerner Report" from a sociological perspective, see Grimshaw (1969/b), pp. 820–821, or Grimshaw (1969/a), pp. 4–6.

17. Richard Sterba, "Some Psychological Factors in Negro Race Hatred and in Anti-Negro Riots," in Geza Roheim, ed., *Psychoanalysis and the Social Sciences*, vol. 1 (New York: International Universities Press, 1947), pp. 411–426.

18. Carl I. Hovland and Robert Sears, "Minor Studies of Aggression: VI. Correlation of Lynchings with Economic Indices," *Journal of Psychology*, vol. 9 (1940), pp. 301–310. In a re-analysis of the Hovland-Sears data, Alexander Mintz, "A Re-examination of Correlations between Lynchings and Economic Indices," *Journal of Abnormal and Social Psychology*, vol. 41 (1946), pp. 154–160, concluded that the original analysis was defective: (1) because the authors had failed to distinguish between crimes against property and crimes against the person, and (2) because the high correlations were essentially statistical artifacts. The frustration-aggression hypothesis continues to be central in some influential interpretations of collective violence. See, e.g., Feierabend, Feierabend, and Nesvold, op. cit.

psychologists, of course, have focused on personality development and particular personality syndromes, e.g., the "authoritarian personality," but have extended the formative period beyond that usually emphasized by psychoanalysts and psychiatrists in the adult years. Their position would seem to be intermediate between that of the more analytically oriented student, with his view of the essential rigidity of personality, and that of the social psychologist, who has a substantially more situational interpretation of individual behavior.

Social psychologists have looked for an explanation of social violence in the acting out of prejudice (as an attitude located in the individual); they have differed from psychoanalysts and from many psychologists in their emphasis on the structural features of society which support socialization into prejudice. In the case of black rioters, they have looked for such socially generated experiences as "relative deprivation" or "a search for identity" as they may relate to individual attempts to find more congenial modes of organization of the personal field. Thus, Clark and Clark and Barker have attempted to describe the attitudinal structure of individuals who participate in social violence or who reject it, linking this attitudinal structure to the interaction of a variety of personal experiences, an interaction which is unique in the case of each individual person.[19] Ransford, a sociological social-psychologist, has attempted to isolate a number of specific attitudes, and to link these specific attitudes (e.g., isolation and powerlessness) to participation in group violence.[20] In this case, the sets of attitudes are seen as being characteristics of members of categories rather than as individual attributes. In so doing, a bridge is suggested between the social-psychological position, which emphasizes the importance of individual psychological attributes (including attitudes) in generating social tensions and violence, and the sociological perspective, which attempts to de-individualize violence phenomena by focusing on features of social structure and the location of power in the larger society. The need for some kind of bridge is obvious; few contemporary scholars of any of the three individual-oriented disciplines would argue that personality or attitudes alone can serve as an explanation for violence, and few sociologists would argue that personality factors and attitudes are irrelevant.

THEORETICAL PERSPECTIVES: II. GROUPS AND THE SOCIAL STRUCTURE

There is no space in this short paper for a systematic review of the major sociological writings on social violence, and consequently the discussion which follows will be brief and limited primarily to the perspective on social conflict associated with the name of Georg Simmel. Of the principal sociologists who have influenced my own thinking on social conflict as a process, and social violence as the extreme mode of conflict resolution—including (in addition to Simmel and his contemporary follower and interpreter, Coser) Marx, Weber, and Dahrendorf—none has ignored the individual and his personality in his writing. Indeed, Marx coined the now multifaceted term *alienation* which ap-

19. Kenneth B. Clark, "Group Violence: A Preliminary Study of the 1943 Harlem Riot," *Journal of Social Psychology*, vol. 19 (1944), pp. 319–337; Kenneth B. Clark and James Barker, "The Zoot Effect in Personality: A Race Riot Participant," *Journal of Abnormal and Social Psychology*, vol. 40 (1945), pp. 143–148.

20. H. Edward Ransford, "Isolation, Powerlessness and Violence: A Study of Attitudes and of Participation in the Watts Riots," *American Journal of Sociology*, vol. 73, no. 5 (March, 1968), pp. 581–591.

pears so frequently in psychological and social-psychological interpretations of phenomena as substantively disparate (and conceptually similar) as black ghetto violence and the "student revolution." Yet each of them in their discussions of social conflict emphasized the structural features of societies, particularly insofar as that structure is related to the distribution of power and its exercise.

In brief outline, the perspective from which Simmel viewed social conflict was simple indeed.[21] He asserted that it is possible to make an analytical distinction between the forms which interaction takes and the content of any given interaction. The forms can be discussed and understood in the abstract, without regard to the personalities or other characteristics of the particular incumbents in the particular roles involved. He identified four such *forms,* all of which ultimately refer to the inevitability of conflict.[22]

(1) People (or groups, or collectivities, or, more generally, parties) are continuously attempting to maximize their share of scarce resources; when they do not know one another or are not aware of another party (e.g., a national scholarship competition, or small producers in a vast, anonymous market) the form (or process) is labeled by Simmel as *competition.*

(2) When the person or group with whom one is competing is identified (as in the instance of electing a president), or when members of only one group can have the power of making allocative decisions (e.g., students *or* administra-

tors, blacks *or* whites, management *or* workers), this competition becomes personalized and the form becomes *conflict.* This does not, of course, exclude the possibilities of sacrifice, abnegation, coöperation, or collusion. It should also be noted that others have defined the difference between competition and conflict along other dimensions.[23] (I have found Simmel's distinction to be the most useful for my own work.)

(3) When conflict is resolved, either by the defeat of one party or through stalemate, the form which results is *accommodation.* Accommodation is always unstable, since at least one party is forced to settle for less than he (it) wants.

(4) Only when *assimilation* occurs, a form of interaction in which the differences between those interacting have disappeared (the goal, variously, of Americanization programs for immigrants, "integrationist" policies in race relations, and attempts to socialize young people into acceptance of "adult" values)—or when one party has been totally destroyed—is there an ultimate resolution of conflict. Even in the case of assimilation, new differences are likely to emerge as different persons or groups begin to accumulate power and invest that power in attempts to maximize their share of scarce commodities ("commodities," as used here, includes prestige and status as well as Cadillacs and caviar).

Accommodation, which is the characteristic form of interaction between potentially conflicting parties (groups or individuals) in all societies in periods when there is no open conflict, can be discussed and analyzed without reference to the characteristics of the parties involved. Thus, in the classic accom-

21. In addition to Simmel, op. cit., see especially *The Sociology of Georg Simmel,* Kurt Wolff, trans. (Glencoe: Free Press, 1950).

22. There is no space in this paper for a discussion of the interesting questions of whether or not conflict is inevitable and, if it is inevitable, whether it is to be viewed as being primarily functional or primarily dysfunctional. See Grimshaw (1969/c).

23. See especially the excellent review article by Clinton F. Fink, "Some Conceptual Difficulties in the Theory of Social Conflict," *Journal of Conflict Resolution,* vol. 12, no. 4 (December, 1968), pp. 412–460.

modative relationship of superordina-
tion/subordination—which can be exemplified on the group level by such
relationships as nobility and vassals or
(in Northern Ireland) Protestants and
Roman Catholics, and on the individual
level by relationships of master/slave,
officer/enlisted man, and so on—it is
expected that demands and directives
flow in one direction and deference and
compliance in the other.[24]

Two points should be made. The first
is that there are classes of both individual and group relations of super-
ordination/subordination which persist
for long periods of time without substantial attempts by the subordinated
party to change the relationship (e.g.,
patria potestas in Rome, or classic caste
relations in India). The second is that
there are instances of personal interaction where incumbents of institutionally
subordinated roles may nonetheless
dominate—because of joint participation
in another accommodative relationship
in which they are superordinate, or because of personality, or because they
possess resources external to the particular relationship, and so on. In the case
of group relationships, however, sharp
disparities in power are likely to be
translated into attempts to reverse the
relationship or, at the very least, to establish parity. This may possibly be a
cross-cultural universal, although the
anthropological literature provides us
with some questionable cases; and there
are substantial definitional difficulties in
attempting to determine exactly how
superordination and subordination can
be measured in different societies. At
the very least, exceptions to behavioral

expectations in superordinate/subordi-
nate relations, whether on the group or
on the individual level, are interesting,
reportable and non-random.

Seen from the perspective described
above, a number of substantively quite
different cases of large-scale conflict and
social violence (as well as instances of
interpersonal conflict) turn out to be,
analytically, quite similar. Historically,
relations between blacks and whites
in American society have represented
almost a type-case of the superordi-
nate/subordinate variety of accommodative relationship.[25] There have been,
in American society, other groups than
blacks which have been subordinated to
the majority community and to the
holders of power in the establishment.
Some of the ethnic and other socially
distinguishable groups in the United
States which have been categorically
subjected to attack, ranging from economic and legal discrimination through
occasional violence to full-scale violence
and even to military assault, have been
mentioned above.[26]

Similarly patterned superordinate/sub-
ordinate relationships between social
categories have obtained elsewhere, in
every country and in every period of
man's history. Wherever there has been
a peasantry, there have been landlords;
wherever there have been urban rich,
there have been urban poor. In many
instances these group relations have had
superimposed upon them a rich variety
of ethnic, linguistic, and religious strati-
fications—sometimes with the further

24. In accommodative relationships between
groups, most but not all individual members
of the groups are involved in individual accommodations with members of the other
group; most individual accommodative relationships, but not all, belong to classes of relationships which when aggregated become accommodative relationships between groups.

25. Jeffery M. Paige has suggested that a
more precise description of these relations
would be that of "unstable accommodation al-
ternating with periods of open conflict" (Personal communication, 1969).

26. For a brief review of some of these cases,
see Allen D. Grimshaw, "Lawlessness and Violence in America and Their Special Manifestations in Changing Negro-White Relationships,"
Journal of Negro History, vol. 44, no. 1
(1959/a), pp. 52–72.

addition of colonial or imperial subjugation. It is not surprising, then, that
social conflict generally, and social violence more specifically, have been endemic accompaniments of man's social
condition. I have discussed the specific
instance of racial violence in a number
of publications over the last several
years; other instances are mentioned in
this special issue and in citations to
many of the other articles.[27]

TWO GENERALIZATIONS ON
SOCIAL VIOLENCE

In a series of publications extending
over the last decade, I have emphasized
two conclusions on the phenomenon of
racial (black and white) violence in the
United States. They are not original
but derive historically from a long sociological tradition, including writers such
as Simmel and, more recently, from related conclusions reached by Lambert in
his study of Hindu-Muslim violence in
India. Their lack of novelty makes
them no less useful, and I think events
of recent years have underlined their
theoretical validity. They also seem almost simple-minded, once stated (I am
a firm believer in simplicity and parsi-
mony as centrally important criteria for
good theory). But, simple or not, they
appear to hold equally well when we
examine careful comparative studies of
social violence in different institutional
areas (as in labor/management) and in
different societies (as in religious conflict involving Hindus and Muslims in
India).

The first conclusion is that superordi-
nate/subordinate relationships in which
the parties are classified by social categories are fundamentally unstable, and

that social violence is likely to occur
when such an accommodative structure
loses its viability. Initially, and drawing solely on urban racial violence in
the United States before 1960, I had observed, somewhat more narrowly, that:
(1) social violence occurs as a result
of real or perceived assaults upon the
accommodative structure; (2) violence
can occur in the absence of conscious
decisions by the leadership of either
party to use it—indeed, it may actually
occur in spite of leadership decisions
against violence; and (3) the violence
need not be reciprocal, and may take
forms in which there are no direct cross-
category confrontations and violence.
American racial violence prior to the
mid-twentieth century most frequently
involved punitive assault by whites on
blacks for imagined or real violations of
the status quo (attempts to vote, or to
increase the black share of economic
goods on the one hand; assaults upon
white women or white dignity on the
other). Disturbances of recent years
have differed from those of the past in
that violence, rather than being largely
a response of the dominant group against
an "uppity" minority, seems increasingly
to have been part of a direct assault
upon the accommodative structure of
the society.[28]

This change does not invalidate the
overall interpretation suggested, that social violence occurs when the accommodative structure loses its viability. But
simply to assert this would be tauto-
logical. It is my claim, however, that
the conflict/accommodation perspective
subsumes a great variety of other ex-

27. See, *inter alia*, the bibliography in Grim-
shaw (1969/a); references in Graham and
Gurr, op. cit.; and the twelve-year index of the
Journal of Conflict Resolution, vol. 12, no. 4
(December, 1968), pp. 533–550.

28. Allen D. Grimshaw, "Changing Patterns
of Racial Violence in the United States,"
Notre Dame Lawyer, vol. 60, no. 5 (1965), pp.
534–548; Symposium: Allen D. Grimshaw,
"Three Views of Urban Violence: Civil Disturbance, Racial Revolt, Class Assault," *American Behavioral Scientist*, vol. 11, no. 4 (1968),
pp. 2–7. Both of these papers are reprinted in
Grimshaw (1969/a).

planatory perspectives, including many but not all of those which are built on individual-oriented (psychological) bases. Accommodative structures can lose their viability in a number of analytically separable but theoretically "inter-implicated" ways. There may be real or perceived changes in the distribution of power: (1) when superordinate groups lose their vitality (as in Pareto's circulation of elites); (2) when subordinated groups gain in power, either through internal growth and organization (e.g., some indigenous revolutionary movements, or the American labor movement) or through outside assistance (possibly some of the contemporary revolutionary movements of Southeast Asia); (3) when subordinated groups come to realize latent power they already possess (perhaps various militant groups in the contemporary United States). There may be a decline in the legitimacy accorded the superordinate category, or even the regime itself.[29] This can occur: (1) when those previously accorded legitimacy are perceived as having abused their power (e.g., university support of an "immoral war"; exposés of governmental "corruption"); (2) when new perspectives on legitimacy are introduced to a social system, partly from outside (e.g., anti-colonialism and some national independence movements since World War II). There may be real or perceived changes in the amounts of commodities available (as broadly defined above) or in patterns of allocation, producing perceived deprivation,[30] systemic frustration,[31] or sudden declines in satisfaction following periods of improvement and rising hopes.[32] All of

these types of social events, and the listing here is not exhaustive, occur within different environing social contexts which influence the probability of social violence. Moreover, the outbreak of violence is also conditioned by such variables as the size and strength of contending parties and the intensity of concern over the issues at stake. Nonetheless, it seems to me that a persuasive argument can be made that the conflict/accommodation perspective serves most usefully as an organizing theoretical frame within which to include a wide variety of empirical conclusions and "middle-range" theoretical interpretations.

The second major conclusion, again quite simple (if seldom seen as a factor in making policy), emphasizes the central importance of the posture and strength of control agencies in the determination of the occurrence or nonoccurrence of social violence. Lambert, in his study of Hindu-Muslim violence in India, concluded that there were four possible relationships between government and subordinated groups: (1) the government itself may directly assault a subordinated group or groups; (2) the government may take a passive posture while tacitly approving assaults by one group upon another; (3) the government may take a "hands off" position while favoring neither of two groups involved in social violence (this can happen either because the government is too weak to enforce peace or because the government hopes to gain from the mutual weakening of the groups engaged in conflict); and (4) a subordinated group may itself assault the government.[33] If there is a belief (it need not

29. See especially William A. Gamson, *Power and Dissent* (Homewood, Illinois: Dorsey, 1968).

30. Gurr, op. cit.

31. Feierabend, Feierabend, and Nesvold, op. cit.

32. James C. Davies, "The J-Curve of Rising and Declining Satisfactions as a Cause of Some Great Revolutions and a Contained Rebellion," in Graham and Gurr, op. cit., pp. 547–576.

33. Lambert, op. cit. I have reviewed some of Lambert's discussion of control strategies elsewhere, especially in Grimshaw, "Actions of

be warranted, but not infrequently has been) that the control agencies—those institutional structures within the society which have a legal monopoly of the use of force—are weak or partisan, or both, social violence is far more likely than if there is a belief that those agencies are strong and nonpartisan. Lambert has spelled this out in a series of propositions on the control of social violence, based on his aforementioned study.[34]   Events in Chicago in the summer of 1968 and in Berkeley in the spring of 1969 seem to substantiate this conclusion.[35]

SUMMARY

Scholarly attention to the phenomena of social violence has increased markedly in recent years in the United States, in part as a result of new or resurgent manifestations of turmoil and public strife wracking American society—the accompaniment to reassessments of the social and political legitimacy of long-

standing accommodative relationships. In recent years this increased attention has, to a greater extent than was true in past research, included the incorporation of a sounder historical and comparative perspective and more self-conscious attempts at genuine interdisciplinary perspectives (this volume itself is an example of both developments).

Scholars have directed their attention to social violence—defined as assaults upon individuals or their property solely or primarily because of their membership in a social category—from a number of perspectives, most noticeably those which emphasize either individually oriented or social-structurally oriented interpretations.   This paper has emphasized the social-structural perspective, searching for the source of social violence in differential access to power and the rewards of that power which result from location in the social structure.   Such a perspective implies a conflict/accommodation theory of social conflict and violence, asserting that social violence occurs when accommodative structures lose their viability.   The claim is made that a number of other interpretations belong structurally under this rubric.   A brief concluding comment emphasizes the importance—in determination of occurrence or nonoccurrence of social violence—of the strength and partiality of control agencies exercising a legal monopoly of force.

Police and the Military in American Race Riots," *Phylon*, vol. 24, no. 3 (1963/b), pp. 271–289; reprinted in Grimshaw (1969/a). Some moral implications of the several government postures are discussed in Grimshaw (1963/a).

34. See the original dissertation, Lambert, op. cit., or Grimshaw (1963/b).

35. See, e.g., Jerome H. Skolnick, dir., *The Politics of Protest: A Task Force Report Submitted to the National Commission on the Causes and Prevention of Violence* (New York: Simon and Schuster, 1969).

3

Issueless Riots

By Gary T. Marx

Gary T. Marx is lecturer in the Department of Sociology, Harvard University, and research associate at the MIT–Harvard Joint Center for Urban Studies. He is the author of Protest and Prejudice *(1967) and editor of* Racial Conflict: Tension and Change in American Society *(1970). His articles have appeared in the* American Sociological Review, Trans-Action, Encyclopaedia Britannica, Journal of Social Issues, *and other journals. He was on the staff of the Kerner Commission and is currently an associate editor of* Social Problems. *He is spending the year in France and England as a Guggenheim Fellow studying the police and social movements.*

WE have come a long way in our
view of collective violence since
early pioneering theorists such as G.
LeBon, E. D. Martin, and E. A. Ross
emphasized the emotional character of
crowd behavior. For them, the crowd
evoked lurid images of opportunism and
destruction where the basest of human
impulses were expressed. They wrote of
"herd instincts" and "the group mind,"
the "atavistic vulnerability of civilized
men," "dirty people without name," and
the "dangerous classes." The crowd
was thought to be like-minded, destructive, irrational, fickle, and suggestible,
and made up of social misfits, criminals,
and riffraff.

Fortunately, the basic theoretical assumptions of collective behavior theorists (as expressed most clearly in the
work of Neil Smelser), empirical research, and the ideological predispositions of contemporary social analysts
have shattered this one-sided image of
riotous crowds.

The excessively negative and psychological image of the crowd has been
undermined by certain theoretical developments in sociology. Neil Smelser, in
reacting against earlier characterizations
of crowd action as "irrational," "unpredictable," "purposeless," and "unrestrained," has performed a valuable
service in arguing that "collective behavior is analyzable by the same categories as conventional behavior." [1]
Much of man's action, whether collective or in a more institutionalized setting, can be seen as goal-directed and
purposive, involving a response to the
exigencies of social life, affirmation of

I am grateful to Greg Johnson, Leon Mann,
and Art Liebmann for their helpful comments.

1. Neil Smelser, *Theory of Collective Behavior* (Englewood Cliffs, N.J.: Prentice-Hall,
1963). See also the useful discussion by C.
Couch, "Collective Behavior: An Examination
of Some Stereotypes," *Social Problems* 15, 3
(1968), 310–322.

that response by the assignment of positive values to it, and a definition of the
situation in which it occurs. Ideas and
beliefs about the world play an important role here. Furthermore, collective
outbursts show something of the patterning and structure of ordinary social
life. The threatening and sometimes ex-
otic nature of collective behavior led
earlier conservative theorists to ignore
its similarities to more conventional behavior.

RUDÉ'S STUDIES CITED

In the case of empirical research,
Rudé's studies of the crowd in France
and England between 1730 and 1848,
and recent research on black rioters,
offer slight support for the image of the
crowd participant held by earlier observers. Rudé, in using police and judicial
records, finds that criminal and lumpen-
proletariat participation was slight.
Eighteenth century British and French
rioters were not those at the margins of
society; rather, they tended to be well
integrated into local settings and had
specific grievances. The mob consisted
of the ordinary urban poor, known as
the *menu peuple*—small workshop masters, shopkeepers, apprentices, crafts-
men, and laborers: employed people with
settled abode and without criminal conviction.[2] Similarly, research on black-
riot participants in the 1960's suggests
that in many ways rioters were broadly
representative of Negro youth.[3] They
were not disproportionately unemployed,
criminal, or recent migrants, and had a

2. Rudé, *The Crowd in History* (New York:
Wiley, 1964).
3. R. Fogelson and R. Hill, "Who Riots?
A Study of Participation in the 1967 Riots,"
in *Supplemental Studies for the National Advisory Commission on Civil Disorders* (Washington, D.C.: U. S. Government Printing Office, 1968) and the studies summarized in N.
Caplan, "The New Ghetto Man: A Review of
Recent Empirical Studies," *Journal of Social
Issues* (Winter, 1970).

strong sense of indignation over the place of Negroes in American society.

An additional factor in the debunking of classical riot views has been the sympathy shown by many American social scientists for current rioters. In direct contrast to certain early conservative theorists such as LeBon, most American sociologists studying collective behavior hold liberal-to-left political perspectives. They rather naturally and correctly reject the Gustave LeBon–Ronald Reagan "mad dog" image of rioters, though in so doing there is a tendency to ignore variation and see all violent outbursts as "rational," "intrinsically political," and "instrumental and purposive." Their analysis and ideology lead them to see black, student, and "third world" collective violence as intricately tied to injustice and strain, and often to imbue all crowd participants with ideological ends and a disinterested morality.[4]

For quite different reasons, some very conservative observers such as Senator McClellan's internal security sub-com-

mittee members are also stressing the political nature of recent civil disorders. It is interesting that a somewhat similar interpretation of events can be made to serve very different ends. On the one hand, radicals justify recent riots by seeing them as a natural response to oppression (one even guaranteed in the U.S. Constitution). They are seen to involve a higher, protest morality, and the appropriate response is to end oppression which generates protest. On the other hand, for conservatives a political, conspirational interpretation of riots makes it easier to justify the need for massive repression than would less threatening interpretations stressing expressiveness, opportunism, and personal pathology.

A HEALTHY CORRECTIVE

The factors mentioned have produced a healthy corrective to the image of the crowd held by earlier theorists and still held by a large proportion of the American public. Yet I think they have caused a pendulum to swing too far away from LeBon; or, at least, we have ceased paying attention to those instances of rioting crowds where protest, ideology, and grievance are relatively absent. When, out of interest or by definition, attention is focused on crowds that have an ideological purpose, are involved in the process of social change, and are related to social movements, rioting crowds are then taken, by default, to have the above characteristics. I think such characterizations of recent American collective violence tend generally to be correct, though there is much variation between riots. Such characterizations are also politically pleasing to most social analysts, so long as the view is not applied to the collective violence of groups they disagree with (as the KKK or the Minute Men).

Yet there are numerous occasions where, outwardly at least, men collec-

4. For example, for a sampling of numerous articles where this theme is explicit or implicit: R. Fogelson, "Violence as Protest," in R. Connery, ed., *Urban Riots: Violence and Social Change* (New York Academy of Political Science, 1968); T. M. Tomlinson, "The Development of a Riot Ideology among Urban Negroes," *American Behavioral Scientist* 11 (March–April, 1968), 27–31; J. Geschwender, "Civil Rights Protest and Riots: A Disappearing Distinction," *Social Science Quarterly* 49, no. 3 (December, 1968); R. Rubenstein, *Mass Political Violence in the United States* (Boston: Little, Brown, 1970); I. L. Horowitz and M. Liebowitz, "Social Deviance and Political Marginality," *Social Problems* (Winter, 1968); some of the essays (particularly chs. 1 and 9) gathered together in J. Skolnick, *The Politics of Protest* (New York: Ballantine Books, 1969).

The less negative view of riots currently held by social scientists may also be because contemporary riots are more restrained than earlier ones and, given effective, worldwide coverage by the mass media, have become almost daily, routinized events that no longer seem so out of the ordinary.

tively seem to be doing many of the same things—battling authorities and each other, attacking symbols, looting, stealing, and destroying property—but where the elements of protest, ideology, grievance, strain, lack of access to channels for redressing complaints, social change and social movements, are relatively insignificant factors, if not absent altogether.

Such situations can be called "issueless riots." In such riots, I do not mean to imply that behavior is necessarily, on the average, any more or less rational, emotional, or destructive than in non-crowd circumstances, nor that it may not be individually instrumental. Such riots are issueless in the sense that a critique of the social order and the belief that violence will help bring about needed social change are relatively unimportant as motivating factors.

In discussing deviant behavior, Robert Merton has made a distinction between deviance which is *nonconforming* and that which is *aberrant*. This distinction would seem to have application to types of riot and riot participants. Nonconformity is seen not as ". . . . a private dereliction but a thrust toward a new morality."[5] The nonconformist legitimates his disinterested deviance in terms of higher values, he publicly challenges norms and practices that he sees as morally suspect, and he aims to replace them with new norms. In contrast, the individual engaged in aberrant behavior deviates out of expediency and for the momentary gratification of personal ends, without seeking social change.

What Neil Smelser has called a generalized belief, and has taken to be a crucial, defining characteristic of collective behavior, does not seem applicable to all situations of non-institutionalized, hostile, collective action. For Smelser,

collective behavior represents "the action of the impatient," and involves a response to strain which attempts to modify some component of social action. A generalized belief is seen as one of the necessary conditions for the occurrence of an episode of collective behavior. The generalized belief identifies sources of strain and calls forth an appropriate response. In the case of a riot or hostile outburst, this belief assigns responsibility for an undesirable state of affairs to a particular individual, institution, or symbol, and argues that things will be improved if only the latter is attacked or destroyed. In offering a coherent and systematic framework, rich with examples, Smelser has made a significant contribution to the study of collective behavior, yet I think his definition unduly restricts the field, at least as far as collective violence is concerned.

The exclusive contemporary focus on one type of riot (however interesting and accessible), where, in Merton's sense, behavior can often be seen as nonconforming and where elements of a generalized belief are clearly present, may obscure certain general predisposing factors, psychological states, social processes, and consequences found in the most diverse types of riot. Such a focus may also inhibit the comparative analysis of different types of violent outburst.

DEFINING A RIOT

I would prefer to define a riot as "relatively spontaneous group violence contrary to traditional norms."[6]

Within this general definition, riots may be seen to vary from one another along numerous dimensions. The number of attributes to be used in characterizing riots is large, and we lack a generally-agreed-upon set of concepts or measures for classifying them. Most

5. R. Merton and R. Nisbet, *Contemporary Social Problems* (New York: Harcourt, Brace and World, 1966), p. 810.

6. Whether all riots are illegal is not an issue raised in this definition.

earlier theorists, while classifying types of crowd, did not single out riots or deal with types of riot. Crowds were characterized in terms of whether or not an objective was present, the type of objective present, the psychological states of the participants, the nature of their interaction, and criteria of group membership. Park and Burgess differentiated between passive and active crowds.[7] Herbert Blumer makes a distinction between the casual, conventionalized, expressive crowd and the "acting, aggressive crowd."[8] Turner and Killian differentiate between individualistic/solidaristic, focused/volatile, and active/expressive dimensions of crowds.[9] Roger Brown divides crowds into mobs and audiences, and sees four types of the former: aggressive, escape, acquisitive, and expressive.[10]

Many scholars have differentiated riots from revolutions, rebellions, and the like, depending on whether an intent to overthrow the government is present; but there have been relatively few efforts to deal systematically with types of riot.[11] Racial violence in different time periods has been contrasted by considering the group dominating the rioting (whites or blacks) and the primary object of attack (people or property).[12] The few quantitative studies that have been done on riot occurrences (as against studies of riot participants) generally fail to deal much with variation in types of riot. This failure may partly explain why they usually come up with fairly weak correlations in relating background variables to the occurrence of a riot.[13]

The one effort that has dealt most with variation between riots, focusing on severity rather than occurrence, although using items that are not theoretically very significant (such as whether or not the National Guard is called out), reports more and stronger correlations when various background measures are considered than do several of the above studies that treat riots as

7. R. Park and Burgess, *The Science of Society* (Chicago: University of Chicago, 1924).
8. H. Blumer, "Collective Behavior," in H. Lee, *New Outline of the Principles of Sociology* (New York: Barnes & Noble, 1961).
9. R. Turner and L. Killian, *Collective Behavior* (Englewood Cliffs, New Jersey: Prentice-Hall, 1957), pp. 84–89.
10. R. Brown, *Social Psychology* (New York: Free Press, 1965).
11. An important exception is Tilly's use of historical data to trace a development from "primitive" to "reactionary" to "modern" violence, depending on shifts in the organizational base (communal to associational) and the relation to the structure of power (acquiring, maintaining, or losing position): C. Tilly, "Collective Violence in European Perspective" in H. D. Graham and T. R. Gurr, *Violence in America* (New York: New American Library, 1969). "Primitive violence" would seem to fall often in cell IV of the typology which follows, with the other two types falling in cell I and, to a lesser extent, II.

12. Morris Janowitz, *The Social Control of Escalated Riots* (Chicago: University of Chicago, Center for Policy Studies, 1968). Distinguishes between "communal" and "commodity" riots. The latter refers to recent ghetto riots, although they are also characterized by the increased use of arms. The move from white-dominated attacks on blacks to biracial rioting, to black-dominated, property-oriented rioting, is observed by L. Masotti, J. Hadden, K. Seminatore, J. Corsi, in *A Time to Burn?* (Chicago: Rand McNally, 1969), ch. 5.
13. S. Lieberson and Silverman, "The Precipitants and Underlying Conditions of Race Riots," *American Sociological Review* (December, 1965), 887–898; M. Bloombaum, "The Conditions Underlying Race Riots as Portrayed by Multidimensional Scalogram Analysis: A Reanalysis of Lieberson and Silverman's Data," *American Sociological Review* 33 (February, 1968), 77; B. Downes, "Social and Political Characteristics of Riot Cities: A Comparative Study," *Social Science Quarterly* 49, no. 3 (December, 1968); S. Spilerman, "The Causes of Racial Disturbances: A Comparison of Alternative Explanations," *American Sociological Review* (August, 1970). In excluding racial disorders that developed out of focused institutional contexts, Spilerman finds that riot proneness is largely a function of one factor—the size of the Negro community.

if they were internally homogeneous phenomena.[14]

Recent research efforts like that of the Kerner Commission have given most attention to rather easily quantifiable or descriptive factors, such as how long the riot lasts, the number of people involved, injured, and arrested, the amount of damage done, the type of hostile activities present, the extent of social control mobilization, and the nature of the precipitating event.

NEGLECTED FACTORS

Relatively less attention has been focused on the nature of the legitimating belief (or whether it is even present), consequences of various types of riot, the type of prior context out of which the riot emerges, different patterns of development, the kinds of psychological states characterizing rioters, selectivity in attack, and questions of a sociological nature which can be asked about any group activity (such as its degree of cohesion, planning, the importance of leadership, and the type of roles present).

The variables one emphasizes in building a typology depend on the questions one is concerned with. I think a major focus of the study of riots should be their relation to ideology, social movements, and social change. Thus, two of the most important dimensions would seem to be: To what degree is a generalized belief present? and, To what degree are riot actions themselves instrumental in collectively solving a group's problem?[15] When these dimensions

14. J. Wanderer, "An Index of Riot Severity and Some Correlates," *American Journal of Sociology*, 64, no. 5 (March, 1969).

15. In riots characterized by a generalized belief, there is no assumption that *all* riot participants share the belief nor that other motives are not present. As in any complex event, motivation for participation is diverse and may change over time, though this is not to suggest that the same kinds of motives in the same frequencies are found in all instances

are combined, we have the following typology:

GENERALIZED BELIEF PRESENT

		YES	No
COLLECTIVELY INSTRUMENTAL	YES	I Bread riots Luddites Prison riots	III Riots misinterpreted by authorities
	No	II Pogroms Communal riots	IV Riots during police strikes Riots in victory

This framework could be elaborated by considering the nature of the generalized belief. Following Smelser, does it envision fundamental changes in values, or changes only in norms; or simply see an attack on particular individuals as sufficient to alleviate the source of tension? Does the change aim at creating entirely new social arrangements, or is it an effort at restoring a prior state of affairs?[16] What kind of substantive elements does the belief involve—class, racial, religious, national? To what extent does the belief have a magical quality to it, which distorts reality and "short-circuits" the paths to change?

If the riot is seen as instrumental, we may further ask if the violent action

of disorder. The personally disorganized, those with pronounced antisocial tendencies, criminals, and individualistic looters may take advantage of the general confusion in a riot to further their own ends. There are many recent and historical examples of such people being drawn into a riot, unconcerned, and perhaps even unaware of the broader issues. Riots clearly offer a cover for normally prohibited behavior. Yet such people are always present, while riots of type I and II occur infrequently and are very much related to broader social, political, economic, religious, and racial issues. An explanation that seeks the source of these riots only in the nature of man, or of certain men (such as those in the lower social classes), cannot account for their variation in place and time.

16. For example, Rudé's distinction between "backward-looking" and "forward-looking" riots. Op. cit., pp. 214–234.

itself directly solves the problem—such as in storming a jail to release prisoners, destroying or driving away all one's enemies, or gaining retribution and avenging a perceived wrong—or if it is instrumental in the sense of being a resource and a threat, which compel's one's adversary to negotiate and offer concessions? Regardless of the generalized belief, what kind of changes actually occur—the removal of particular agents seen as troublesome, the redistribution of resources, the appearance of new roles and organizations, alternations in values and/or norms? Attention could also be focused on those outbursts which, beyond not helping to solve a group's problem, positively hinder it by misplaced attack or by stimulating repression and retrenchment.

The above typology could be expanded and refined (and perhaps made more difficult to comprehend) by considering the above distinctions, or any of a large number of others. However, its present simple form may suggest certain questions and various hypotheses.

PROTEST OR CRIME?

In a useful article, Ralph Turner has called attention to some factors involved in subjective definitions of disorders as either protest or crime on the part of various publics. In contrast to many observers who see "protest" and "political" meaning in any collective disorders or deviant activity, merely because an oppressed group is involved, without considering the ways in which such actions vary or what types of evidence would prove or disprove such interpretations, Turner "scrupulously avoid[s] assuming that there are objectifiable phenomena that might be classified as deviance, as protest, or as rebellion."[17]

17. R. Turner, "The Public Perception of Protest," *American Sociological Review* (December, 1969).

Clearly, there is an arbitrary element here, and definitions adopted bear some correspondence to ideology and whatever public-policy axe the definer is wielding; yet I think there are "objective" factors which might lead a no-less-scrupulous investigator to differentiate disorders which are protest from those which are merely deviance. One of the most important of these is the presence of a generalized belief. Additional factors that make a protest definition more applicable are: the development of the disorders out of a prolonged community conflict and out of a focused context, an overlap in roles between conventional political activists and riot participants, the presence of riot spokesmen, the presentation of demands, selectivity in attack, and a link between the source of the trouble as identified in the generalized belief and those targets actually attacked. To be sure, rarely will these all vary perfectly with one another, or approach either end of the continuum.

Riots of a protest nature fall in cells I and II. The "principled" rioting of these cells can be differentiated from the "unprincipled" or issueless rioting of cell IV.

Among some hypotheses which hopefully are not unduly circular, and which in most cases are based on nothing more than hunches, are the following:

Riots of type I (generalized belief, instrumental) may be more controlled and patterned and do less damage than types II (generalized belief, not instrumental) or IV (no generalized belief, not instrumental).

To the extent that they are present, the supposed psychological characteristics of crowd members (reduction in self-control and self-consciousness) and traditional crowd processes (milling, collective excitement, contagion) may characterize cells IV and II to a greater extent than cell I.

There will be a tendency for a dissatisfied group to move from type II to type I riot, and from there to less spontaneous, carefully planned guerrilla warfare and sabotage activities. But as a given type I or II riot develops, the proportion of ideological rioters will decline when more opportunistic types move in to take advantage of the situation.

If true, this may operate to underestimate the degree of selectivity of attack in such riots. If studies on the patterning of looting and burning of ghetto stores in the 1960's riots had been able to separate early from late attacks, I think an appreciably greater amount of selectivity might have been found. As it was, in some cities, but certainly not all, considerable selectivity by race, reputation, and type of store was present—although in one city, the eventual spread of fires by strong winds led one researcher to conclude nothing more than that those stores that had combustible material in them burned.

The generalized belief present in type II riots is more likely to have a magical, short-circuiting-of-reality quality than that in type I.

Riots of types II and IV will inspire less serious and punitive efforts at social control than will I; although the nature of the social-control response plays an important part in any collective outburst, variations in it will be felt to a greater extent in types II and IV than I.

Participants in type IV riots, on the average, will be lower in social position and less well integrated into the society than those in I and II, and this will be true of type II relative to I; riots of types IV and II are more likely to involve groups receiving their solidarity on the basis of ascriptive type criteria than type I. Targets in type IV riots are likely to be more diffuse than in I and II; targets in type I are more likely to be a powerful group than in II, where targets are likely to involve an ethnic

minority or other powerless group; riots of type IV are likely to have a less hostile, more playful and expressive character than I or II, with attacks on authorities motivated to a greater extent by self-defense than in types I and II.

Examples of riots where a generalized belief is present and where riotous action is instrumental in helping solve a group's problems (type I) may be seen in the eighteenth and nineteenth century European food and industrial riots studied by Rudé and Hobsbawn. They represented a means, understood by the people as well as their rulers, by which those with few political or economic rights might gain concessions.[18]

The main thrust of food riots was a demand to buy food at a "just price." Demonstrations would be mounted against those presumed to be profiteering through the shipment or hoarding of grain. If the authorities failed to act and impose a just price on merchants, millers, farmers, or bakers, grain and its products would be seized and sold at a lower price with the proceeds going to the owner.

In what Hobsbawn has called "collective bargaining by riot," workers, lacking other means, pressed their demands through attacks on industrial property, workshops, mines, mills, and machinery, and by pulling down the employer's house. Violence was used as a means of dealing with wage cuts and price increases, or so as to protect the workers' livelihood against the threat of new machinery. Nineteenth-century Luddism moved from a seemingly spontaneous demonstration of stocking workers "clamoring for work and a more liberal price" to a well-organized movement whose small, disciplined bands moved swiftly at night. Machines rather than people were attacked, until the authorities began attacking the

18. G. Rudé, op. cit.; E. Hobsbawn, *Primitive Rebels* (New York: W. W. Norton, 1959).

Luddites. Attacks were selective and restrained, and frequently preceded by a letter warning the employer to change his ways or face the consequences.

GHETTO RIOTS

Black ghetto riots of the 1960's have been complex and quite diverse, varying from the multi-faceted disorders of Watts, Newark, and Detroit, to those that emerged in self-defense against overly eager control forces caught up in a riot self-fulfilling prophecy as in Jersey City, to those that were characterized primarily by looting or were largely expressive (as in many of the 1964 riots or in the 1966 Dayton riot), or were not much more than traditional Saturday night brawls but which happened to occur during the height of the riot season and were labeled "riots" by the mass media (as was the case in Tucson, Arizona), to those that were most clearly political, as in Plainfield, where demands were presented and negotiations between ghetto youth leaders and city officials alternated with violence.[19]

Most ghetto riots—coming after a decade of civil rights activity and promises, in a context of severely restricted channels for the effective redress of grievances, sometimes growing out of focused community conflicts with a degree of selectivity in attack, and with the presence of slogans and *ex-post facto* legitimations discovered by social science research and journalists—clearly fit in cells I and II. From the riots in 1964 to those occurring later, there appears to be a tendency for the generalized belief to develop more fully and to reach an even larger number of people, and perhaps for the violence to become more instrumental or to be responded to by authorities as if it involved grievances as well as rule-breaking.

Riots of type I are likely to involve a dissident group against the government and civil authorities, or a particular, focused, institutional context such as a factory or school; whereas riots of type II are likely to have a more diffuse character, often involving violence between groups divided on the basis of religion, ethnicity, ideology, race, or region, with the government as a bystander. Most pogroms and communal riots fall here. In these cases, a generalized belief is present defining a group as aliens, outsiders, troublemakers, inferiors, degenerates, subversives, or racially or culturally impure, and holding them responsible for various social ills and historical sins. Elements of wish fulfillment, and what Smelser calls "short-circuiting" (a jump from very general levels of blame to an attack on specific concrete agents) seem more characteristic of this type of outburst. Although there may be elements of realistic competition present, and the clash of divergent life styles and values, such riots tend not to deal directly with the source of strains experienced by the group or lead to changes in public policy. Instead, they can represent a displacement of anger onto an accessible target. Such riots may inhibit social change and, as in the case of earlier American race riots or Russian pogroms, may occur with the explicit or implicit encouragement of elite groups.[20]

As noted earlier, much has been writ-

19. In addition, two generally neglected factors in some of the destruction in certain cities were (a) merchants who paid black youth to firebomb their stores in order to collect insurance, and (b) efforts of organized crime to sanction or destroy noncoöperating businesses.

20. For a consideration of the scapegoat and displacement of aggression functions of such riots, see H. Otto Dahlke, "Race and Minority Riots—A Study in the Typology of Violence," *Social Forces* 30 (1951–52); and M. Simpson and G. Yinger, *Racial and Cultural Minorities* (New York: Harper & Row, 1965), ch. 4.

ten about the type I and II riots. Their importance in causing (and reflecting) social change and their dramatic nature help explain why. Appreciably less attention has been given to violent outbursts where a generalized belief is lacking and which are not instrumental in solving a group's problem (type IV). Considering such neglected riots offers an indication of the range of material that a comprehensive sociological analysis of riots should deal with.

I wish briefly to describe issueless riots which develop out of two kinds of circumstances: (a) in the face of a pronounced weakening of the agents of social control, and (b) expressive outbursts which occasionally accompany victory celebrations or ritualized festivals.

RIOTING WHEN POLICE GO ON STRIKE

Under some conditions, the weakening or absence of external controls may greatly increase violations of traditional rules. The disorders that have emerged when police go on strike or in the disorganization of war periods indicate this. Following a strike in 1919 by the Liverpool police, riotous behavior occurred over a two-day period, necessitating the calling out of soldiers and the use of 850 special constables. As helmeted soldiers with fixed bayonets patrolled the streets, a *London Times* correspondent reported "Central Liverpool tonight represents a war zone. . . . Anarchy broke out, and even in Liverpool's unfortunate history of strike troubles, the position was apparently never more serious." [21] In what was described as an "orgy of destruction," predominantly youthful rioters held the upper hand in the densely crowded streets for two nights. The dominant activities seemed to be looting, destroying property, drinking, generally rebellious behavior, and attacks on police

21. *London Times*, August 4, 1919.

and soldiers trying to maintain order. Streets were littered with merchandise, from watches to costumers' dummies.

The riot, at least initially, seemed to have a less hostile tone than those where a well-developed generalized belief is present. Thus, in one instance, from Crane's shop of musical instruments "looters dragged pianos out into the open and thumped them in a frenzied endeavor to demonstrate their defiance of law and order. Here, between 1 and 2 this morning, a baton charge was made by the police and the *al fresco* concert was suddenly ended and the crowd dispersed." However, less expressive activities were also present, such as stoning and mobbing of soldiers—which resulted in (or stemmed from) soldiers offering volleys of rifle fire and bayonet charges.

A similar situation prevailed at nearby Birkenhead, where almost half the police force went on strike. The Riot Act was read, forty shops were wrecked and looted, fifty people were arrested, street fighting occurred, and police and soldiers were attacked as rioters made sorties from their strongholds in narrow back streets.

A similar phenomenon occurred in Boston a month later, when two-thirds of the police went on strike and then-Governor Calvin Coolidge and his police commissioner refused to call out the 3,000 available state troopers. Boston was without police protection for two days and, according to a recent article, "the mob ruled the streets." [22]

The rioting and lawbreaking that accompanied the 1969 strike of the Montreal police also seemed to have

22. F. Russell, "The Strike that Made a President," *American Heritage* 14 (October, 1963), 44–47, 90–94; and R. Bartlett, "Anarchy in Boston," *American Mercury* 35 (1935), in part reprinted in R. Turner and L. Killian, *Collective Behavior*, op. cit., pp. 22–23. Also, W. Heaps, *Riots, U.S.A.* (New York: Seabury Press, 1966), pp. 118–130.

several elements of issueless rioting; though given the issue of French separatism, student and labor dissatisfactions, and economic rivalries, this is less clearly the case than in Liverpool or Boston. Looting, vandalism, and arson were reportedly widespread, a policeman was killed by sniper fire, and scores were injured. One shop owner reported, "You've never seen the city like this. It's like the war." [23] Disorders also were reported in Stockholm, Malno, Goteburg, and other Swedish cities following the equivalent of a police strike on June 7, 1970.

Roughly comparable situations could be seen in some European cities at the end of World War II, when rioting and a general breakdown in order occurred as the Axis Powers retreated.

RIOTS IN VICTORY AND CELEBRATION

The category of riots in victory, or the somewhat traditional violent outbursts that follow particular holidays and social events (or that accompanied the fairs and feasts of pre-industrial Europe and the brawls between rival craft guilds or volunteer fire departments in nineteenth-century America), do not so clearly fit into the category of collective behavior as the events considered above. They may have a ritualized aspect and be "institutionalized," in the sense that participants and controllers expect them to happen. The element of spontaneity, which is a crucial component of collective behavior, is less clearly present.

Yet no one knows exactly when the violence will begin, who will play what roles, and/or how far what begins as merry-making activity will go. It thus clearly has an element of spontaneity to it, even if not so clearly pronounced as is the case with other kinds of riot.

The element of fun, kicks, the quest for excitement, and a general expressiveness characterizes such disorders, though if social control agents are highly repressive this can quickly change. The riot in victory or as recreation is particularly interesting in light of theories that see rioting always tied to strains and the absence of appropriate means for redressing grievances.

Among well-known examples of such riots are many of the youth disturbances which occur with some regularity at resorts during vacation periods,[24] and the antics of an earlier generation of college boys, whose victory celebrations sometimes moved from tearing down goal posts and overturning streetcars to brawling, looting, and battling authorities.

Less well known but having something of the same character was an August 1945 riot in San Francisco, which followed the Japanese surrender. As San Francisco "opened all vents in celebration of the war's end," thousands of dollars of damage was done.

According to a report in the *Los Angeles Times*, "police stood by powerless as the crowds broke windows on Market and adjoining streets." [25] The crowd attacked streetcars, overturned scores of automobiles, looted stores, and tore down posters that reminded them of the war.

While clearly marginal to the category of issueless riots, the series of violent outbursts that occurred around the career of John Wilkes are interesting. They suggest the fluid link between celebration and destruction, and how past

23. *New York Times*, October 9, 1969.

24. Though as American youth has become more politicized in the 1960's, such outbursts less clearly fit in this category.

25. *Los Angeles Times*, August 14, 1945. Of a more mixed variety is the riot in an army rehabilitation center which also broke out on the night of victory over the Japanese, reported in J. Abrahams and L. McCorkle, "Analysis of a Prison Disturbance," *Journal of Abnormal and Social Psychology* 42 (1947).

memories of oppression, as well as current dissatisfactions, may lead to violent action even on the occasion of partial victories. More than half of the Wilkite riots reported by Rudé developed out of seeming victories and celebrations. For example, Wilkes' supporters greeted his election (not his defeat) to Parliament in 1768 "by tumultuous riots in the cities of London and Westminster which, for two days on end, the forces of law and order were quite inadequate and unable to contain." [26] The windows of the rich were smashed with little distinction made between government and opposition members. With "gay abandon," less serious but similar activities also occurred on his birthday, twice on his release from prison, his later election to Parliament, and on his election as Lord Mayor of London. In each of these instances it is difficult to see how the precipitating incident confirms or sharpens strain, or the generalized belief in any of five ways listed by Smelser, such as introducing a sharp new deprivation, symbolizing a failure which demands explanation, or being a response to the sudden closing of channels for peaceful protest. [27]

STRAIN A NECESSARY FACTOR?

To be sure, if one looks long enough and carefully enough into the nooks and crannies of any complex body of riot data, he can probably find some evidence of strain and at least a proto-ideology. For example, in the police strike riots, some people no doubt were angry at the city government for what they saw as a government attack on trade unionism, yet this factor does not characterize issueless riots, particularly when they are contrasted with riots at the other end of the continuum. In neither

26. Rudé, op. cit., p. 55.
27. N. Smelser, op. cit., pp. 249–251.

Liverpool nor Boston was it possible to identify ". . . a belief in the existence of extra-ordinary forces—threats, conspiracies, etc.—which are at work in the universe" nor an ". . . assessment of the extra-ordinary consequences which will follow if the collective attempt to reconstitute social action is successful." [28]

In some of the riots in victory, it has similarly been difficult to identify sources of strain, such as racial discrimination or competition, low salaries and job insecurity, colonial domination and the like—though, as the riot develops, people experiencing an array of strains may become involved. [29]

The occurrence of such "issueless" riots in the face of weakened social control, together with those that emerge out of victories, suggests that pronounced strain and the presence of a generalized belief are not necessary conditions for the occurrence of a riot, though mixed with other factors they are certainly sufficient conditions.

This does not mean one must adopt a Hobbesian beast-in-the-breast-kept-in-check-only-by-external-force image of riots. [30] Nor is it to deny that riots often have a protest character and are inspired by indignation and ideology, and that a

28. N. Smelser, op. cit., p. 8.
29. An important and rather neglected issue is the systematic study of the process whereby the focus and/or types of participants in a crowd change.
30. A pronounced weakening of social control is neither a necessary nor sufficient condition for the occurrence of a riot. For example, in 1919, although riots occurred in Boston and Liverpool, they did *not* occur in London or Birmingham, where police also were on strike; nor did they occur in all Italian and German cities when social control agents withdrew as Allied forces came near.

Indeed, in some cases the reverse may occur. In Detroit in 1967, during the "blue flu" (when large numbers of police failed to report for duty, claiming to be sick during a dispute with the city), crime reportedly went down. In some ghetto areas, riots essentially ended crucial factor in accounting for major shifts in the rate of hostile outbursts is the political system itself. It is to call attention to variation in types of riot.

To be sure, hostile outbursts involving well-developed generalized beliefs are more interesting and likely to be more significant for social change, and perhaps occur with far greater frequency than the relatively issueless riots described here. Yet this should not lead us to ignore—or worse, deny—the presence of the latter.

To note the distinctions made in this paper is certainly not to argue that current black and student disorders are unaffected by a generalized belief, or occur in a context where serious grievances and issues are lacking. Unlike a recent paper by a political scientist, in which the political implications are

rather more clear than the scientific, I am not suggesting that current riots occur "mainly for fun and profit." [31] However, I am suggesting that our understanding of riots, social movements, and change would be broadened by some consideration of other kinds of riots that are less tied to protest and ideology.

If this were done, we might become more aware of:

A) How different types of riot (and riot participants) relate to each other (e.g., the process whereby issueless riots become articulate and instrumental, or how ideologically motivated rioters affect opportunistic rioters);

B) Sources of motivation beyond a generalized belief and disinterested protest;

C) The expressive consequences of riots beyond their instrumental group conflict aspects;

D) The need to restrict theories about the importance of strains, lack of political access, and the role of ideology to one of several types of violent outbursts.

We might also be better able to document and understand the protest nature of much recent American collective violence, by contrasting it with other types of riot where this is clearly absent.

---

when police were withdrawn, though in others disorders greatly escalated when this occurred. In a number of recent "rock" festivals, the absence of a visible police presence and self-policing by youth marshals appear to have minimized disorder. However, in one unfortunate incident the announcement that, after strenuous negotiations, there were no police present at the festival, led to wild cheering, but also led to an immediate outbreak of purse-snatching, robbery, and gate-crashing. An important variable in the withdrawal of regular police is the strength and legitimacy granted indigenous controllers.

31. E. Banfield, *The Unheavenly City* (Boston: Little Brown, 1970), ch. 9.

4

A Critical Note on Conceptions of Collective Behavior

By Elliott Currie and Jerome H. Skolnick

Elliott Currie is assistant professor of Sociology, Yale University; Ph.D. candidate in Sociology, University of California, Berkeley; formerly research assistant, Center for the Study of Law and Society, Berkeley; formerly assistant director, Task Force on Violent Aspects of Protest and Confrontation, National Commission on the Causes and Prevention of Violence; co-editor Crisis in American Institutions *(1970).*

Jerome H. Skolnick is a professor at the School of Criminology and research sociologist, Center for the Study of Law and Society, University of California, Berkeley; senior social scientist, American Bar Foundation; formerly director, Task Force on Violent Aspects of Protest and Confrontation, National Commission on the Causes and Prevention of Violence; editor or author of the following: Crisis in American Institutions, *with Elliott Currie (1970);* Society and the Legal Order, *with Richard D. Schwartz (1970);* The Politics of Protest *(1969);* Justice Without Trial *(1966);* Problems of the Family, *with Fowler V. Harper (1962). Author of numerous articles, consultant to various commissions, and formerly professor of Sociology, University of California, San Diego; associate professor of Sociology, University of Chicago; and assistant professor of Law and Sociology, Yale.*

THE study of "collective behavior" has always had a curious place in sociology. No one has ever been happy with the state of the field; much effort is spent periodically in trying to define its boundaries and to pin down its elusive subject matter. This sort of effort is, of course, not confined to the analysis of "collective behavior," but it can be reasonably argued that it assumes a more conspicuous place in that field than in most others. The fault has usually been attributed to a lack of serious effort at systematization of the field, or of carefully constructed empirical research, or both.[1] No one seems to have seriously asked the logically prior question: Is there something about the way we conceive of "collective behavior," in the first place, that militates against our making successful use of the idea? In short, does the concept of "collective behavior," as it is usually applied, have much heuristic value?

Increasingly, empirical work is beginning to chip away at some of the staple notions of early "collective behavior" theories.[2] In an earlier discussion, we explored some of the assumptions of these ideas and their relevance for understanding contemporary group violence. Our analysis centered on the following points:[3]

FOUR CONSIDERATIONS

1. Collective behavior theory has its roots in the antidemocratic theorists of nineteenth-century Europe, best represented by LeBon.[4] In being transferred to American social science, the antidemocratic biases in "crowd" theory were modified but not abolished.

2. Perhaps the most fundamental of these biases is the implication that collective behavior is in some sense "irrational" behavior. This bias may be traced in LeBon's distaste for the mystical loss of individuality and civilized behavior in the "crowd," and reaffirmed in modern "riot control" manuals, as well as most contemporary social-scientific approaches. In line with the emphasis on irrationality, collective behavior has usually been seen as destructive and, in most treatments, inappropriate and distasteful. Unlike conventional behavior, it is conceived by collective-behavior theorists as "likely to be foolish, disgusting, or evil."[5]

3. This conception is neither empirically valid nor theoretically justified. Studies of riots, in particular, show them

1. For general treatments of the "state of the field," see Herbert Blumer, "Collective Behavior," in *Review of Sociology; Analysis of a Decade,* J. B. Gittler, ed. (New York: Wiley, 1957); R. H. Turner and L. M. Killian, *Collective Behavior* (Englewood Cliffs, N.J.: Prentice-Hall, 1957); Neil J. Smelser, *Theory of Collective Behavior* (New York: Free Press, 1962); Kurt Lang and Gladys Engel Lang, "Collective Behavior," in *International Encyclopedia of the Social Sciences,* 1968, pp. 556–564.

2. For example, Carl J. Couch, "Collective Behavior; an Examination of Some Stereotypes," *Social Problems,* vol. 15, no. 3 (1968), pp. 310–322; Robert M. Fogelson and Robert B. Hill, "Who Riots? A Study of Participation in the 1967 Riots," *Supplemental Studies for the National Advisory Commission on Civil Disorders* (Washington, D.C.: U.S. Government Printing Office, July 1968); Jules J. Wanderer, "1967 Riots; A Test of the Congruity of Events," *Social Problems,* vol. 16, no. 2 (1968), pp. 193–198; and, for historical materials, see George Rudé, *The Crowd in His-*

tory, 1730–1848 (New York: Wiley, 1949), and Eric Hobsbawm, *Primitive Rebels* (New York: Norton, 1959).

3. Jerome H. Skolnick, dir., *The Politics of Protest* (New York: Simon and Schuster, 1969), especially pp. 329–346, and 3–8. This discussion was a collective effort; particular mention should be made of the contributions of Charles Carey, Anthony M. Platt, and Richard Speiglman.

4. Gustave LeBon, *The Crowd* (New York: Viking, 1960). For a discussion of the background of theories of collective behavior, see Leon Bramson, *The Political Context of Sociology* (Princeton, N.J.: Princeton University Press, 1961).

5. Roger Brown, *Social Psychology* (New York: Free Press, 1965), p. 709.

to be far more structured than collective-behavior theory would suggest, far more attuned to the redress of specific grievances and to the selection of limited and understandable targets. This is true both historically and currently.[6] On the other hand, the implication that the behavior of authorities is more moderate or rational seems countered by the most cursory examination of social life, particularly if we observe such carefully considered policies as weapons development, policies of mass extermination, incarceration of minorities, or religious persecution. On a more immediate level, such conceptions obscure the interactive nature of episodes of collective action: not only in that the "response" of agencies of social control may affect the *outcome* of the episode, but also that they may *constitute* much of the episode itself, especially in terms of its destructiveness and human cost. Police or other officials may initiate a riot, may carry out most of the destructive behavior, and may be responsible for the escalation of the merely disorderly into the tragic.[7]

These considerations suggest that conventional approaches to collective behavior obscure more than they illuminate, and are therefore of little help in understanding collective violence or in providing a framework for careful consideration of the issues of public policy

and political action surrounding such violence. Moreover, many conventional treatments display an inherent bias toward an "official" perspective on collective action, one that tends to discredit the claims and perspectives of the participants while uncritically accepting those of constituted authorities and agents of social control.

We are not opposed to the study of the phenomena that fall conventionally under the rubric "collective behavior." *The Politics of Protest* (a discussion directed by Skolnick and later published) is an analysis of such phenomena, and the reader may refer to it both as an illustration of our approach and for further reference to the sorts of studies and approaches we regard as more or less helpful. In *The Politics of Protest* we argued, as an alternative procedure for comprehending the nature and significance of collective violence, a more critical and concrete approach that would take seriously the historical and political context of the collective events and the point of view of the people involved, as well as the specific "natural history" of episodes of collective violence.[8]

A reasonable criticism of that earlier discussion is that it condensed its analysis of collective-behavior theory to such an extent that it blurred some important differences among various theorists and tended to lump together perspectives that differ from one another in important ways. With this in mind, we have decided to focus in this note on the work of one recent theorist: Neil J. Smelser.[9]

6. In addition to the studies cited in note 2, see Robert Blauner, "Whitewash Over Watts," *Trans-Action* 3 (March–April 1966), pp. 3–9, 54; Anthony Oberschall, "The Los Angeles Riot," *Social Problems*, vol. 15, no. 4 (1968), pp. 322–342; Robert M. Fogelson, "Violence as Protest," in Robert H. Connery, ed., *Urban Riots; Violence and Social Change* (Proceedings of the Academy of Political Science, Columbia University, New York, 1968), pp. 25–41.

7. See *The Politics of Protest*, op. cit., ch. 7; National Commission on the Causes and Prevention of Violence, Chicago Study Team, *Rights in Conflict* (New York: Bantam, 1968).

8. *The Politics of Protest*, op. cit., especially pp. 3–8.

9. Our analysis is confined to Smelser's *Theory of Collective Behavior*, op. cit. (hereafter *TCB*) and *Essays in Sociological Explanation* (hereafter *Essays*), (Englewood Cliffs, N.J.: Prentice-Hall, 1968), especially ch. 5, "Social and Psychological Dimensions of Collective Behavior," pp. 92–124.

SMELSER'S THEORY

Our singling-out of Smelser is neither accidental nor malicious. Smelser is an important writer in this field, and his contributions are relatively recent and systematic; they constitute, in fact, the most significant recent effort to organize systematically the idea of collective behavior and to surmount some of the perennial problems associated with the field. Moreover, Smelser views his work as an important step beyond earlier approaches—indeed, as a radical departure from at least some of the perceptions of those earlier approaches.[10] We disagree. We will argue in this paper that Smelser's theory suffers from an excessive emphasis on systematization; that, although superficially plausible, it does not move our understanding much beyond earlier approaches to collective behavior; that it is held together largely through undemonstrated assertions about the "exaggerated" character of "uninstitutionalized" beliefs and behavior; and that it seems to adopt an administrative or managerial perspective on collective behavior, in which unacknowledged evaluations take the place of forthright assertions of the social values underlying the study of collective action.

Like many earlier theorists, Smelser approaches collective behavior as a formidable problem of definition and classification. He suggests that "in all civilizations men have thrown themselves into episodes of dramatic behavior, such as the craze, the riot, and the revolution."[11] But the field of collective behavior has often viewed these things as the result of the operation of mysterious forces; there is much indeterminacy and imprecision in the typical approach to these dramatic episodes. Therefore, the first problem is one of definition; what do we include in the concept of collective behavior and what do we leave out?

For Smelser, collective behavior has three defining characteristics. First, it is behavior based on a *belief* which "redefines social action," i.e., is aimed at some level of social change. Second, the beliefs guiding collective behavior *differ* from those guiding ordinary behavior: they are exaggerated; they involve the idea of the "existence of extraordinary forces—threats, conspiracies, etc.—which are at work in the universe."[12]

These beliefs, both in the existence of "extraordinary forces" and in the assessment of "extraordinary consequences," lead to behavior that "short-circuits" normal channels. Thus, according to Smelser, collective behavior is "the action of the impatient."[13]

Third, collective behavior is "not institutionalized behavior."[14] It is not altogether clear what "institutionalization" refers to in this scheme. Sometimes Smelser contrasts "collective" behavior with "conventional" behavior,[15] sometimes with "established" behavior,[16] and sometimes with behavior that is *not* aimed at social change.[17] The inability to pin down the meaning of "institutional" behavior makes for a serious ambiguity, and we will return to this point later on. An immediate question is whether or not these attributes— (1) "uninstitutionalized," (2) directed toward social change, and (3) exaggerated—necessarily "hang together"? Is there something about behavior that challenges existing social conditions, on whatever level, in "unconventional"

10. *TCB*, p. 20.
11. Ibid, p. 1.

12. Ibid., p. 8.
13. Ibid., p. 72.
14. Ibid., p. 8.
15 Ibid., p. 67.
16. Ibid., p. 71.
17. "The 'uninstitutionalized' character of collective behavior is also implied by the fact that the high level component (of social action) is redefined or reconstituted"; *TCB*, p. 71 fn.

ways, that makes it more likely to be rooted in exaggerated or distorted beliefs than other kinds of behavior? If not, the linkage of these three attributes seems strained and artificial. And if this connection is in fact strained and artificial, the parallel linking of Smelser's various "forms" of collective behavior— "panics," "crazes," "hostile outbursts," and "norm-oriented" and "value-oriented" social movements [18]—would appear to be equally strained and artificial.

Smelser recognizes that these three components of "collective behavior" are not *necessarily* connected. For example, "generalized beliefs" may be institutionalized: the "hysterical belief" that underlies panic may also be found in "institutionalized beliefs, such as superstitions, fears of witchcraft, demons, spirits, and the like." [19] "Reconstitution" of social action—that is, social change— may clearly be "institutionalized," and Smelser illustrates this with the example of the post-Sputnik effort to boost American technological capacity.[20] (Clearly, too, some institutions have as a main purpose the reconstitution of some component of social life; we think, particularly, of established agencies of social reform and amelioration or, in another sense, appellate courts.)

Furthermore, dramatic episodes of collective action, even highly destructive action, may take place in "conventional" or "institutionalized" settings. Smelser notes that this is true of some kinds of ceremonials or patriotic outbursts: but

Even though these celebrations may provide the setting for genuine collective outbursts—e.g., the patriotic demonstration that turns into a riot—they are not in themselves examples of collective behavior. True, they are based often on generalized values such as the divine, the nation, the

monarchy, or the alma mater. True, they are collective. True, they may release tensions generated by conditions of structural strain. The basic differences between such ceremonials and collective behavior—and the reasons for excluding them—is that the former are institutionalized in form and content. The index of their institutionalization is that such events are often scheduled for definite times, places, and occasions, and are shrouded in formal rituals such as chants, or semi-formal "ways of celebrating" such as drinking, whooping, marching, and so on.[21]

Moreover, Smelser is aware that certain kinds of behavior, such as lynching, for example, may be a "genuine hostile outburst" *or* a "quasi-institutionalized form of justice." This

should remind us that in many cases history does not always produce instances that fit neatly into our analytic definition of collective behavior. We must examine carefully the context of the event in question before we decide upon its relevance for study.[22]

A FUNDAMENTAL DIFFICULTY

Granted that classificatory schemes always have elements of arbitrariness, and that he recognizes that events in the real world may be more complex than his categories, there remains a more fundamental difficulty with Smelser's variant of the "structural-functional" approach to social theory. Like some others in this tradition, Smelser typically fails to clarify the relationship between his conceptual scheme and the real world, and does not provide adequate criteria for testing this relationship.[23] For example, was the Free Speech Movement at Berkeley a "norm-oriented" or "value-oriented" movement? Which be-

18. *TCB*, pp. 79–130.
19. Ibid., p. 85.
20. Ibid., pp. 67–70.

21. Ibid., p. 74.
22. Ibid., p. 75.
23. For a discussion that touches on this problem in the work of Talcott Parsons, see Tom Bottomore, "Out of This World," *New York Review of Books*, Nov. 6, 1969, pp. 34–39.

liefs of which participants are we to accept as the "generalized beliefs" of the movement? Whose beliefs were exaggerated? Those of all the participants, some, the leaders? Were the beliefs of the authorities (about the movement) distorted? Which of the contradictory accounts of distinguished social scientists, concerning the validity of student beliefs, are we to accept?

Smelser's lack of criteria must lead to considerable confusion for anyone attempting to employ his analysis of collective behavior. Smelser sometimes seems to suggest that protest movements are, by definition, instances of collective behavior, because they inherently or typically possess the three relevant conceptual attributes. At other times, he seems to suggest that whether actual protest movements qualify as "collective behavior" is a matter for empirical investigation. But an empirical investigation obviously would assess the beliefs and goals of (say) a protest movement, the social and political context in which it takes place, and so on. It would also include criteria for determining whether the underlying beliefs were exaggerated. Having thus studied the movement (and not otherwise), we would presumably be in a position to decide whether the movement qualified as "collective behavior." Why bother? Why—given that we must study the movement in order to ascertain its "relevance for study"—need we utilize Smelser's conception of "collective behavior" at all, with its potentially misleading implication that social movements are necessarily based on distorted beliefs?

We may put this in another way. The notion of the "generalized belief" —an idea that links Smelser's work with the earlier stress on the "irrational" nature of collective behavior [24]—is central

to Smelser's explanatory scheme. Presumably, those who do not hold distorted beliefs seek social change through established institutions. Thus, without the idea of belief distortion, Smelser's model becomes capable of explaining most group behavior directed toward changing a "component of social action." Smelser himself notes that "relaxed in appropriate ways," his model could be used for other kinds of behavior.[25] Yet, as already noted, the assessment that the beliefs underlying any actual instance of collective behavior necessarily involve "exaggerated" conceptions of the role of hostile forces and agents, fantasies of the exaggerated effectiveness of the movement, and so on, must be either (a) a matter for careful empirical analysis or (b) a doubtful theoretical premise. But (1) if it is either of these, it clearly has no place in an acceptable explanatory model; and (2) if it is *removed*, Smelser's model lacks explanatory power. Thus, says Smelser,

The master proposition is . . . people under strain mobilize to reconstitute the social order in the name of a generalized belief. Stated so generally, this proposition is not very helpful in interpreting the actual data of collective outbursts.[26]

But, according to Smelser, by specifying further conditions we can arrive at statements such as this one regarding panic:

Panic will occur if the appropriate conditions of conduciveness are present, *and* if the appropriate conditions of strain are present, *and* if a hysterical belief develops, *and* if mobilization occurs, *and* if social controls fail to cooperate.[27]

notion of irrationality is a defining characteristic of collective behavior. How else, though, are we to take the idea that collective behavior involves distorted beliefs, feelings of "anxiety, fantasy, hostility, etc." (*TCB*, p. 11) and so on?

25. *TCB*, p. 387.
26. Ibid., p. 385.
27. Ibid., p. 385.

24. We are aware that Smelser does not identify his work in this way—that, indeed, he often rejects the idea that some simplistic

To arrive at this proposition, of course, requires many pages of exegesis of the meaning and significance of these terms within the "action" scheme derived from the work of Talcott Parsons.[28] Yet on examination, the statement seems still to tell us very little that we did not know before—or could not have assumed by ourselves, with one important exception. If we take out the exception—the idea that panic is based on a "hysterical belief"—Smelser's statement seems to tell us little more than that panic will occur if the conditions under which it could occur are present, and if counter-conditions are not present. To give concrete meaning to all this would require that we engage in actual study of some instance of panic, which is precisely what we would have done had we not had the explanatory scheme.

Moreover, and this seems crucial, if we remove the *a priori* characterization of the belief as "hysterical" (or some other variant of the "generalized belief"), the model no longer differentiates "collective" from other forms of behavior. But it is not clear that we can properly use the idea of "generalized belief" in this way, even in the case of panic. As Smelser himself notes, panic may be based—as in the "classic" panic situations of fire in a theater or a sinking ship—on a realistic threat and hence not on a "generalized belief" at all.[29] Thus, as part of the conceptual scheme, in the case of panic as well as other forms of collective behavior, the idea of the "generalized belief" is problematic. As an assertion of predictable empirical regularities underlying actual instances of the various forms of collective behavior, the notion of "generalized belief" is *defensible* only if it can be empirically demonstrated; and it is *useful*

only if it can be shown that such beliefs do not regularly underlie "institutional" behavior as well.

SMELSER'S INTERPRETATION OF DATA

How does Smelser go about demonstrating the role of distorted, exaggerated beliefs in collective behavior? What kinds of evidence does he provide for this fundamental idea of a contrast between collective and conventional behavior on the basis of types of belief? In practice, Smelser's approach to this problem often blends an indiscriminate use of the empirical literature with a certain tendency toward *a priori* discrediting of behavior that challenges existing social conditions in ways that bypass or reject "normal channels." Used in this fashion, the notion of "collective behavior" becomes a means of making evaluative judgments about social behavior without coming to grips with the problem of specifying and defending the values underlying those judgments.

This process may be seen in several of Smelser's illustrations of the nature of collective behavior. Thus, the factory agitation in Britain in 1831–33 was "accompanied by many extravagant claims concerning the effects of machinery and the factory on the health of the children, the morals of the factory population, and so on."[30] Early industrial protests in England were compounded of "anxiety, hostility, and fantasy."[31] Speaking of the failure of impartiality of the police in the 1919 Chicago race riot, Smelser tells us that "the individual conduct of policemen was probably not so unfair as Negroes claimed."[32] None of these assertions is accompanied by empirical support. Consider this illustration from the literature on prison riots:

28. See, especially, the discussion in *TCB*, ch. 2.
29. *Essays*, p. 113.

30. Ibid., p. 85.
31. Ibid., p. 79.
32. *TCB*, p. 268.

In the prisons, the inmates' grievances centered around conditions such as "poor, insufficient, or contaminated food; inadequate, unsanitary, or dirty housing; sadistic brutality by prison officials," or some combination of these. These reality conditions, combined with the exaggeratedly suspicious attitudes toward authority on the part of the selected prison population, made for a high level of hostility.

On what grounds are the prisoners' attitudes termed "exaggeratedly suspicious"? Again, we are offered neither empirical evidence for this assumption nor criteria for assessing it. What we are in fact offered seems little more than a diffuse tendency to discredit the attitudes and beliefs of those who challenge "conventional" conceptions of political propriety or "institutionalized" definitions of social reality, and a tendency to accept the definitions offered by authorities.

We are not suggesting that *all* of Smelser's illustrative material is devoid of empirical support. What we are suggesting is that the *a priori* attitude that Smelser's model brings to the analysis of collective behavior makes for an absence of consistent concern for the empirical evidence. This lack of concern, in turn, allows Smelser to keep the conceptual scheme, with the central importance of the "generalized belief," intact. This, in its turn, allows Smelser to discredit the beliefs of the participants in collective action on *a priori grounds*. The process is circular and self-justifying.

Moreover, such a perspective means that certain kinds of people standing in a particular relationship to authority—prison inmates, lower-class people, students, children, women—will be *most likely* to have their behavior characterized as odd or threatening, and most likely to have their beliefs and attitudes discredited on *a priori* grounds.

Thus, Smelser suggests that collective behavior is clustered most often among

such groups as "adolescents, recent migrants, and unemployed people."[34] This raises several issues. A main problem with this conception is that—as we noted above—empirical research does not consistently support it; ghetto rebellions, for example, are characterized by the participation of a far broader spectrum of people than the conventional picture suggests. But the basic problem is deeper; it is the failure to specify the criteria on which attitudes are judged "exaggeratedly suspicious," or what have you. Lacking such criteria, we simply have no way of adequately assessing Smelser's contentions. Whether the behavior involved is that of rioters or feminists, stockbrokers or segregationists, the assessment of their attitudes in Smelser's work seems quite arbitrary. Clearly *some* criterion is being used; but we are not told what it is, and it is of course quite possible that Smelser is also unaware of its nature.

From an official or managerial point of view, it is subordinates who are likely to be most threatening insofar as they behave "collectively" in challenging and unconventional ways, and it is generally to the interest of officials to discredit such behavior and to attempt to "channel the energy of collective outbursts into more modest kinds of behavior."[35] But to recognize this fact is one thing: to present sympathy with official perspective as social science analysis is another thing altogether.

Smelser's tendency to discredit arbitrarily the beliefs of *some* of the participants in collective action is coupled with a complementary tendency to accept uncritically the testimony of "official" commentators or of clearly hostile observers such as LeBon. The early theories of the crowd were "top-down" theories, reflecting the fears and resent-

33. *Essays*, p. 112.
34. Ibid., p. 97.
35. *TCB*, p. 73.

ments of antidemocratic thinkers facing the aspirations of formerly excluded and exploited groups. This is especially true of LeBon, and it is therefore remarkable that Smelser places such credence in LeBon's "insights" into the "mysteries" of the peculiar thought processes of crowds.[36] It is even more remarkable that Smelser frequently relies on official "riot control" manuals for empirical descriptions of the "hostile outburst," without so much as suggesting the need for exercising caution in the use of such sources.[37]

MANAGERIAL PERSPECTIVE

Again, this suggests a diffuse but pervasive tendency toward what might be called a managerial or administrative perspective on collective action. Such a perspective carries the implication that collective behavior is something requiring "control" or "containing" or "handling and channeling," an emphasis not nearly so apparent in the work of such writers as Blumer, Turner and Killian, and Lang and Lang.[38] For Smelser, the issue becomes whether or not control is applied in effective fashion in order to ensure the strict "maintenance of law and order."[39] Such imagery underestimates the role of agencies of social control in the origins and the content of the "outburst" itself, rather than merely affecting its outcome. It is surely such an overly sanguine interpretation of the meaning of "social control" that enables Smelser to criticise the "weak governor who shilly-shallies in deciding to call in the National Guard to put down a dangerous riot."[40] And it is surely the same uncritical attitude that permits Smelser to present as an "objective" assessment the statement of E. S. Bo-

gardus that a "mob in full fury will not listen to reason; it can be stopped only by force, by tear bombs, by bayonets."[41] Smelser's discussion of hostile outbursts recognizes the impact of government, as in the Red Scare following World War I, and in the McCarthyism of the 1950's, in fomenting hostile outbursts. Indeed, he claims not to venture judgment even on the desirability of violence; which, says Smelser, is "sometimes . . . necessary to smash a brittle social order; sometimes it merely adds to social chaos."[42] Yet this recognition of the possible complicity of the government and its agents fails to inform Smelser's entire discussion of the "Control of Hostile Outbursts," which moves little beyond the level of the "riot control" literature on which it is heavily based. This section offers little more than the conventional view of the nature of riots, mystified by the attachment of a complicated, cumbersome, and confusing classificatory scheme. Thus mystified, these essentially commonsense attitudes about riots and their control may have a formidable effect on the unwary reader, who will doubtless feel confronted by "social science" at its most impenetrable and forbidding. But they do not suffice as an empirical examination of riot behavior, or as a convincing illustration of the utility of Smelser's analytical scheme.

In a more recent paper, Smelser has attempted to come to grips with the issue of the relation between social and psychological aspects of collective behavior. Here, too, unfortunately, the approach seems conditioned by an empirically unfounded and theoretically questionable tendency to discredit the beliefs underlying collective action. This seems evident in the way in which Smelser conceives of the "psychological" aspect of the behavior: collective behavior is held

36. Ibid., p. 80.
37. Ibid., pp. 222–268.
38. Cf. fn 1 and *Essays,* 79–80.
39. *TCB*, p. 266.
40. Ibid., p. 262.

41. Quoted in *TCB*, p. 267.
42. Ibid., p. 227.

to have a psychological as well as a social dimension, since the "deepest and most powerful human emotions—idealistic fervor, love, and violent rage, for example—are bared in episodes of collective behavior, and since persons differ psychologically in their propensity to become involved in such episodes." [43] This seems to imply that collective behavior is "psychological" because it is "emotional"—indeed, that "psychological" behavior is "emotional" behavior. Surely there is more to the "psychological" dimension of social behavior than this. This perspective seems to suggest that "psychology" is something we use to uncover the peculiar aspects of unconventional behavior, and not, for example, to expose what may be the deeper pathologies of "normal" social life.

Consider the discussion, in this more recent paper, of the psychological aspects of protest movements. Smelser notes:

Harshness and rigidity (in the response of authorities to protest) provide the participants with "evidence" of the vicious character of the authority, and thus justify extreme and militant tactics; weakness or collapse in the face of threats provides "evidence" that these extreme tactics are in fact effective, and encourages participants in protest movements to give credence to their own fantasies of omnipotence.[44]

The question arises: when is evidence not really evidence? Why put "evidence" in quotes? Why characterize the participants in protest movements as motivated by fantasies of omnipotence? If this is intended as an empirical assessment, Smelser provides no evidence for it. If it is intended as a theoretical premise, it must be said to prejudge the issues rather heavily.

More generally, Smelser's analysis of

the "psychological level of explanation" of protest movements concludes that their psychological aspect lies in the fact that they allow repressed Oedipal conflicts to "emerge and be gratified." This is held to explain the ambivalence toward the "leader" that Smelser tells us characterizes protest movements. On the one hand, such movements are characterized by "unqualified love, worship, and submission to the leader." [45] On the other hand, such movements display "unqualified suspicion, denigration, and desire to destroy the agent felt responsible for the moral decay of social life and standing in the way of reform." [46] Does this apply to the NAACP? the SPCA? the UMW? Again, no evidence—not even, in this case, that of hostile accounts—is provided for those assertions.

All of this should not be taken to imply that we reject the attempt to investigate the psychological aspects of social movements. We do insist, however, that, as Allan Silver has remarked, "men who engage in dangerous and desperate behavior—indeed, any behavior—have a certain claim to have taken seriously the meanings which they see in their own acts, and wish others to see in them." [47] Moreover, the interactive aspect of social behavior applies to its psychological dimensions as well as its social ones: it is misleading to focus on the hidden psychological motives of one set of participants in a protest situation while leaving the other side unexamined, as John P. Spiegel has recently suggested regarding student protest:

It simply isn't reasonable to raise questions about the irrational, unconscious motivations of students without also probing the behavior of faculties and administration in a similar vein. Such a procedure not only reveals (embarrassingly, one would have

43. *Essays*, p. 92.
44. Ibid., p. 114.

45. Ibid., p. 119.
46. Ibid., pp. 119–120.
47. Allan Silver, "Official Interpretations of Racial Riots," in Connery, op. cit., at p. 154.

thought) the blind spots of the observers; it also prejudges the question of where the pathology lies.[48]

There is also the question of the appropriateness of the analysis, the extent to which it fairly engages the major issues in the situation. Thus, we could have concentrated in this discussion on the psychological motivations for Smelser's "exaggerated" concern for systematization, his distaste for a "lax eclecticism," [49] and the general tendency to discredit behavior that is in some sense out of control.

Such an analysis would be "psychological"; it might even be useful, under different circumstances. But we do not think it is a fair or especially helpful way to engage the issues involved in the study of collective behavior. Likewise, Smelser's invocation of the Oedipal conflict to explain some of the characteristics of protest movements would be useful *if* it were a response to the issues raised by careful empirical analysis of protest movements; if, that is, there were well-observed phenomena surrounding such movements that seemed difficult to explain without some such approach. As it is, however, Smelser's treatment, since it is *not* grounded in such careful assessment of the issues, appears forced and out of place. It is hardly reassuring, therefore, to be told that this exercise represents an effort to transcend one-sided interpretations of collective behavior in the interests of a "synthetic" approach.[50]

CONCLUSION

Lacking consistent empirical foundation, Smelser's characterization of collective behavior as mobilized on the basis of some form of "generalized be-

48. John P. Spiegel, "Campus Conflict and Professional Egos," *Trans-Action*, October 1969, at p. 42.

49. *Essays*, p. 91.

50. Ibid., p. 121.

lief" seems little more than a prejudgment. If so, the somewhat tenuous relation between the several "forms" of collective behavior would appear to be most questionable, as would the utility of the conceptual edifice invoked to explain it. Furthermore, Smelser's tendency toward an administrative perspective is related intrinsically to the idea of isolating a class of kinds of behavior related solely by virtue of their (a) orientation to change, (b) "unestablished" character, and (c) purportedly distorted or exaggerated perspective. Such a conception virtually builds in the idea of "control," the attempt to "channel" such behavior into paths more acceptable from the viewpoint of the maintenance of some set of (usually unspecified) social and political conditions. When applied to the real world of social conflict and political struggle, "collective behavior" theories based on such a conception often acquire the appearance of a literature of counter-insurgency. Worse, associated with a claim of neutrality, they tend to drift into this attitude, without consciously and explicitly defending it.

In addition, the arbitrary linkage of social movements of all kinds with so-called "panics" and "crazes," the traditional approach to the study of "collective behavior," seems to us to be misleading on its face. To link these phenomena means that those richer in social and political meaning tend to be reduced to a common and basically trivial level. One *can*, of course, compare the hula-hoop "craze" of a few years ago with the Cuban revolution of roughly the same time, and doubtless discover some similarities and points of comparability. But these are likely to be unilluminating and quickly exhausted; if taken as definitive, they are likely to blind us to what is most compelling, both analytically and politically, about the latter event.

We are not suggesting that it is pointless to study such things as "panics" or "crazes" or behavior in disasters or social movements or revolutions: far from it. We *are* suggesting, however, that the boundaries holding together the traditional field of collective behavior are conceptually weak and empirically misleading. Creative work in the several areas it has covered can be done, and done better, without them. What Professor Smelser has to say about actual instances of collective behavior, for example, could still be said without his model, and said more simply, more persuasively, and more readably. Certainly, the study of protest and movements for social change is better off if it is less tendentious, less evaluative in hidden ways, and yet more attuned to the moral and political issues that surround these phenomena.[51]

CONCEPT OF INSTITUTIONS

One step in this direction might involve the use of a richer and more explicit conception of what we mean by

51. We recommend, as illustrations of theoretical work that is empirically grounded, the major investigations of such men as Eric Hobsbawn, George Rudé, Arthur Waskow, and Barrington Moore, Jr.

"institutions." We suggest above that the idea of "institutional" behavior is unclear in Smelser's perspective, and that this leads to some ambiguity about whether "institutional" behavior means behavior that is structured, or behavior that is conventional or accepted, or some combination of these. We may suggest another idea of the meaning of institutions, which conceives of institutions as having a potential for the development and maintenance of human values—values such as democracy, participation, and the reduction of the repressive aspects of social life. From this perspective, we would want to look at various forms of collective action—whether within or beyond the "normal" or conventional social and political arrangements—in the light of their capacity to promote (or retard) the creation and maintenance of these values. Such a conception would thus place the values that guide our research at the threshold of the inquiry, rather than at the back door, and would avoid the equation of the "institutional" with the merely routine, the reflexive affirmation of the usual, and the implication that the nonconventional is a "problem" to be investigated with an eye to control and containment.

5

Two Critics in Search of a Bias:
A Response to Currie and Skolnick

By Neil J. Smelser

Neil J. Smelser, Ph.D., is professor of Sociology at the University of California at Berkeley. He is author of Economy & Society, *with Talcott Parsons (1956);* Social Change in the Industrial Revolution *(1959);* Theory of Collective Behavior *(1963);* Essays in Sociological Explanation *(1968). Professor Smelser is a member of the Council of the American Sociological Association, and between 1962 and 1965 he served as editor of the* American Sociological Review. *He served in an advisory capacity for two commissions: the National Advisory Commission on Civil Disorder and the Commission on the Causes and Prevention of Violence.*

WHEN the editors approached me to contribute to this issue, I understood that it would be my assignment to respond to a statement by Jerome Skolnick, in which he was to make explicit the theoretical underpinnings of his book, *The Politics of Protest*,[1] and perhaps to contrast it with other perspectives on protest and collective behavior. I was mildly surprised to discover, upon receiving the essay by Elliott Currie and Skolnick, that they had, instead, prepared a somewhat elaborated version of Skolnick's assertion, ventured first in *The Politics of Protest*, that despite appearances, I am an ideologue in social scientist's clothing, and that I fall into the antidemocratic, irrationalist tradition identified mainly with Gustave LeBon.[2]

I am pleased to respond to their statement—it is always fun to mix it up with one's critics—even though my assignment must now be a bit different from the one I originally agreed to undertake. Nevertheless, I do plan to raise a few questions about the guiding assumptions of *The Politics of Protest* that also arise in reading Currie and Skolnick's essay.

Currie and Skolnick's statement is a good example of a very ancient sport in sociology, which might be termed "bias-hunting." [3] This sport seems to have become more popular than ever in the past few years. Also in keeping with a modern trend, Currie and Skolnick find my work to smack of establishmentarianism, even counter-insurgency, and to treat protesters and underdogs as generally peculiar, irrational people to be contained or managed. I want to dispute this diagnosis, and to examine some of the implications of what I gather to be Skolnick's positive theoretical alternative to what he thinks I am doing, even though he has seldom spoken of that alternative, and then only in very general terms.

SOME ERRORS AND MISINTERPRETATIONS

One of my main complaints about Currie and Skolnick's essay is that they do not appear to have read my work very carefully. Time after time they say that my statements on collective behavior "seem to suggest" some kind of "diffuse but pervasive tendency" on my part to adhere to some position, when in fact I have been perfectly explicit on that position. Consider a few examples:

(1) They assert that my conception of collective behavior has a "potentially misleading implication that social movements are *necessarily* based on distorted beliefs." Not only did I make the opposite statement explicitly—when I stated that "many movements . . . achieve their ends without ever developing generalized beliefs" [4]—but I inquired into the conditions under which demands for normative change are likely to develop generalized beliefs.[5]

(2) They argue that I maintain that "the beliefs guiding collective behavior *differ* from those guiding ordinary behavior." Yet—as they also note—I explicitly indicate that generalized beliefs are sometimes institutionalized, and

1. *The Politics of Protest*, under the direction of Jerome H. Skolnick (New York: Simon and Schuster, 1969).

2. Ibid., pp. 330–339.

3. My own view is that bias-hunting has both potentially positive and potentially negative aspects. On the one hand, if it can be demonstrated that a bias systematically leads the investigator to ignore important problems and sources of data, or to distort his empirical information, it is a valuable exercise. On the other hand, if it does little more than try to demonstrate that another investigator is "conservative," "radical," "moderate," and so forth, without reference to the consequences of that bias for scientific inquiry, the exercise can degenerate into a kind of invidious labeling.

4. Neil J. Smelser, *Theory of Collective Behavior* (New York: Free Press, 1962), p. 271.

5. For example, ibid., pp. 292–296.

therefore are among the factors that influence behavior other than that which I define as collective behavior. In addition, Chapter V of *Theory of Collective Behavior*, which is devoted to describing generalized beliefs, contains numerous examples of such beliefs drawn from institutionalized religion, magic, folklore, and so on. My position is that generalized beliefs are indeed one defining feature of what I characterize as collective behavior, but the same kinds of beliefs operate as general determinants of behavior in combinations of determinants other than the combinations I studied. I do not, as they assert, rest my analysis on the "fundamental idea of a contrast between collective and conventional behavior on the basis of types of belief."

(3) In the introduction to my essay on the social and psychological dimensions of collective behavior, I illustrated my general assertion that this behavior has a psychological dimension by indicating that powerful human emotions are bared in such behavior and that people differ psychologically in their propensity to become involved in episodes of collective behavior. Currie and Skolnick seized this illustration and converted it into an unrecognizable series of assertions. First, they took my illustrations to imply that "collective behavior is 'psychological' because it is 'emotional'—indeed, that 'psychological' behavior is 'emotional' behavior." In turn this "seemed to suggest" to them that I hold to the view that " 'psychology' is something we use to uncover the peculiar aspects of unconventional behavior. . . ." There is something quite remarkable about the way they used logical gymnastics to turn my rather casual illustration into a fixed set of definitions and propositions, and then into a fixed ideological position. They could have saved themselves all this trouble if they had read one page further and discov-

ered my explicit working definition of a psychological system, which is constituted by the "drives, affects, skills, defenses, and so on" of the individual, as well as that which is emotional and peculiar about him.[6]

My citation of these errors and misinterpretations is, I grant, a bit tedious, and I promise the reader to turn to more substantial matters presently. But since Currie and Skolnick did build their case on them, I felt compelled to mention a few of the more obvious howlers.

STRATEGIES IN "UNCOVERING" THE "BIAS"

My main objectives in writing *Theory of Collective Behavior* were (1) to select a range of empirical variability—in this case, those phenomena falling loosely under the conventional heading "collective behavior"; (2) to attempt to define and classify these phenomena as consistently and rigorously as possible; and (3) to identify typical combinations of determinants that would help explain when, where, and in what form episodes of collective behavior occur. In connection with this last objective, I developed a "value-added" explanatory scheme, consisting of several determinants— structural conduciveness, strain, growth and spread of a generalized belief, mobilization of participants for action, and the operation of social controls—which were ordered in a hierarchy of diminishing generality. Far from arguing that collective behavior is something that has to be explained by factors that are special and unusual, I based the book on the premise that "collective behavior is analyzable by the same categories as conventional behavior."[7] In another

6. Neil J. Smelser, *Essays in Sociological Explanation* (Englewood Cliffs, N.J.: 1968), p. 93.

7. *Theory of Collective Behavior*, p. 23.

article in this issue of The Annals, Gary Marx correctly perceives that my theoretical position—and its implementation—is one of several challenges to the "one-sided" theories of the riotous crowd of LeBon, Martin, and Ross in recent times.[8]

Given my explicit theoretical position, how do Currie and Skolnick haul me back to the position of LeBon? In examining their essay I have located three main lines of argument, each one of which involves a serious distortion of my own position:

(1) Choosing one determinant and making it into an explanation. Most of Currie and Skolnick's case is based on one ingredient of the value-added scheme—the generalized belief. As I indicated before, they erred in converting this kind of belief into something that is connected *exclusively* with collective behavior and not other kinds of behavior. Having done that, they then picked up my observation that generalized beliefs are likely to be exaggerated in terms of the forces at work in the world, the efficacy of the movement to transform the world, and so forth, and argued that "the notion of 'generalized belief' . . . links [my] work with the earlier stress on the 'irrational' nature of collective behavior." What astounded me about this reasoning was the fact that they ignored the remainder of the value-added scheme, particularly the variables of structural conduciveness and strain, which provide the basis for analyzing the "historical and political context" of the growth of generalized beliefs and the occurrence of collective events—a context that Currie and Skolnick and I feel must be taken into account. My basic theory of generalized beliefs is that they are purposive collective efforts to redefine and restructure the social environment, that crystallize

when individuals and groups are subjected to certain stresses (strain) and certain types of constraints on their opportunities to resolve these stresses (conduciveness). This is a far cry from LeBon's "image of man as irrational and selfish, as heavily subject to impulse and caprice or to wicked rationality, as agent and victim of unthinking violence and pious fraud,"[9] and that these features of man are the basic causes of crowd behavior. Yet Skolnick and Currie have taken my observation that generalized beliefs are likely to be exaggerated in their diagnosis of the social situation and in their envisioned solutions and have tried to argue that I share LeBon's causal assumptions.

(2) Collapsing attributes that are analytically separate. Currie and Skolnick assert simply that in my view generalized beliefs are exaggerated, and, by extension, "irrational" in the sense that LeBon would hold them to be. A reading of Chapter V of my book indicates that my only assertion is that generalized beliefs are *likely* to be exaggerated because they involve a cognitive structure that short-circuits many logical and empirical contingencies. Never do I equate "generalized" with "exaggerated." In fact, I explicitly dissociate the two qualities by noting that generalized beliefs may give a true account of a social situation,[10] and that even when the belief is accurately based on objective circumstances—as in the case of the "classic" panic situations of the fire in the theater or a sinking ship—the belief is still a generalized one.[11] Yet

9. Robert K. Merton, "Introduction," to Gustave LeBon, *The Crowd* (New York: Viking Press, 1960), p. xv.

10. *Theory of Collective Behavior*, p. 94.

11. For this reason, Currie and Skolnick are inaccurate in their statement: "As Smelser himself notes, panic may be based—as in the 'classic' panic situations of fire in the theater or a sinking ship—on a *realistic* threat and hence not on a 'generalized belief' at all." My

8. "Issueless Riots," pp. 21–33 of this issue.

Skolnick and Currie freely substitute words like "exaggerated" and "distorted" for "generalized."

The fact that they have collapsed these attributes—which are analytically separated in my own work—raises serious doubts as to their claims about my interpretation of data. I did gather a great deal of empirical data throughout the volume to demonstrate that ideas associated with collective episodes do possess the attributes of generalized beliefs. That seems to me to be important empirical data to assemble. Because Currie and Skolnick collapse "generalized belief" and "exaggerated belief" and treat them as one, they insist that I took upon myself the task to prove that every generalized belief is exaggerated. That, I did not undertake to do. Their criticisms therefore seem misplaced, because they read my theory differently from what it actually is.

(3) Turning the choice of a determinant into a simple value-preference. Currie and Skolnick are correct that I regard social controls as major variables in determining the direction, timing, and content of episodes of collective behavior. I divided controls into two broad types: (a) those that affect conduciveness (an example would be the actions of a government that close off or open up avenues for exerting political influence) and strain (an example would be the actions of a government that relieve the unemployed in a distressed sector of the economy); (b) those controls that come into play after a collective episode has begun to materialize; examples would be actions of the police, the courts, the press, and so on. I tried to illustrate the importance of these types of controls in connection with the development of various types of collective behavior, all the way from the panic and craze to the value-oriented movement.

Currie and Skolnick take up this point, and claim that I share the ideological viewpoint of the agents of social control, label the views of underdogs as odd or threatening, and thereby discredit them. Arguing from my discussion of the role of the police and military in controlling hostile outbursts, they maintain that I "underestimate . . . the role of agencies of social control in the origins and the content of the 'outburst' itself." Generally, they claim, my work tends to "acquire the appearance of a literature of counter-insurgency."

Once again, it would have been nice if they had read a bit more carefully With respect to concentrating only on "underdog" movements, I would think my inclusion of the Red Scare, the scapegoating of the business community by the Roosevelt administration, as well as officially encouraged mob violence, would dispel the notion that I limit my accounts of the hostile outburst to society's down-and-outers. (There is good reason to suspect, however, that these outbursts will in fact occur more often among society's disinherited, both because they are disinherited and because they have less access to alternative avenues of political expression.)[12] And had Currie and Skolnick made reference to my discussion of the determinants of value-oriented movements, they would have discovered that I noted and documented extensively the following situations in which value-oriented beliefs typically congeal:

(1) among politically disinherited peoples, especially recent migrants;
(2) among colonially dominated peoples;
(3) among persecuted minorities;
(4) in inflexible political structures;
(5) in post-revolutionary situations;

explicit position is that such beliefs are *both* realistically based *and* generalized.

12. *Theory of Collective Behavior*, pp. 227–247.

(6) in situations marked by the failure of government by political parties.[13]

Each of these situations is clearly one in which the political powers, through repression and unresponsiveness, are directly involved in "the origins and the content of the 'outburst' itself." As for the charge that my discussion of "control" of hostile outbursts was "heavily based" on the riot-control literature, a perusal of the footnotes would indicate that my theory of control does refer to that literature, but is also built substantially on the scholarship of such ideologically diverse figures as Georges Sorel, Crane Brinton, and Leon Trotsky, as well as dozens of historical monographs.[14]

In sum, Currie and Skolnick have extracted one of many perspectives that I used in my work—the perspective of the generalized belief—have isolated it from the rest of the analysis, have misinterpreted it in several ways, and then have blown it up again, claiming that it informs my whole work.

The Issue of Discrediting

One of Currie and Skolnick's main claims is that I try to "discredit" people that protest their situations by becoming involved in social outbursts and social movements. I have tried to demonstrate that they have not made their case. Nevertheless, they have raised a very old and pervasive issue in social analysis: how seriously or how literally to take what people say they are doing as explanatory theories of their own behavior.

People—whether acting as individuals or in groups—typically carry at least an implicit "explanation" of what they are doing. If we ask a man why he holds

a job, he will probably reply that he has to earn a livelihood and to support his wife and children. If we ask a member of a protest movement why he is protesting, he will reply that he is dissatisfied with some kind of injustice or inequity, and that he is working to remove it and thereby improve the political situation. These explanations typically contain an empirical diagnosis of some features of the world, implied reasons or motives for the actors' behavior, and some notion of the consequences of their behavior.

Furthermore, to confront an actor with *any* statement that he is not doing what he thinks he is doing, that he has different motives than he thinks he has, or that the state of the world is not as he views it, is to discredit, in some way, his own account of what he is doing. But much of social science involves making just that kind of statement. Consider the Marxian statement that religious leaders are not saving souls as they think they are, but are, in fact, helping to oppress the exploited. Consider the Freudian explanation of why artists smear paint, a far cry from artists' explanations of their esthetic mission. Consider Bendix's analysis of managerial ideologies as, in part, instruments of worker domination, an analysis that does not always accord with managers' own ideological notions. Consider my own exploration of determinants of behavior of those committed to social movements of various types, which does not always square with the diagnosis and explanation of the world contained in their ideologies. All such explanations can be read as "discrediting," because they imply that the people being studied are in some way limited or mistaken in their own explanation of what they are doing.

Currie and Skolnick are very sensitive about discrediting. They insist, with Allan Silver, that "men who engage in

13. Ibid., p. 325. For documentation, see pp. 325–334.

14. Ibid., pp. 262–268; 364–379.

dangerous and desperate behavior—indeed, any behavior—have a certain claim to have taken seriously the meanings which they see in their own acts, and wish others to see in them." Silver's statement contains some rather vague words—words such as "certain claim" and "taken seriously"—so it cannot be taken as a statement of a definite methodological position. Nevertheless, it does suggest a kind of appreciative, phenomenological, naturalistic methodology, by virtue of which the investigator takes as an explanation of behavior that which he finds in the ideology of those who are participating.

Skolnick has never outlined that methodological position clearly, but many of his statements in *The Politics of Protest* indicate that he does in fact subscribe to something of the sort. This is how I read his assertion that "mass protest is an essentially political phenomenon engaged in by normal people" [15]—people, that is, who are not peculiar, abnormal, or otherwise "acting out" something unrelated to the protest. Further, he argues, protesting students' outlook and behavior "cannot be explained away by referring to personality problems or to youthful intransigence or delinquency." [16] Instead, Skolnick argues, we understand why students protest by referring to the following kinds of factors:

Stridency has increased with political frustration related to civil rights and the Vietnam War. Campuses have become the headquarters of anti-war protest. Not only have students challenged the war on its merits; they have also questioned whether a free society should force young men to fight a war they do not support, and whether school attendance and grades should be criteria for exemption from military service. They have been especially critical of the university's coöperation with the Selective Service System and of that system's policy of "channeling" students into careers and occupations deemed to be in the national interest by the director of Selective Service.

They have come to see the university as implicated in the industrial, military, and racial status quo. Disaffection has been intensified by the response of certain university administrations, which have been perceived as more susceptible to conservative pressures than to underlying issues.

In short, Skolnick is saying that we explain student militancy mainly in the same terms as student militants would use to explain their behavior—in terms of perceiving injustices and setting them right. These are the "claims" of militant students that have to be "taken seriously" and Skolnick surely does so, since he builds much of his explanation out of theirs.[17]

SKOLNICK'S POSITION

Skolnick's methodological position, then, seems to be that the analysis of protest "cannot focus solely on the character or culture of those who protest the current state of the American political and social order." Rather, he suggests, "mass protest is an outgrowth of social, economic, and political conditions." [18] And taking his observations on student unrest into account, we must add that at least some mass protest is an outgrowth of those conditions *as they are diagnosed by those who protest*.

Skolnick applies this appreciative methodology more or less consistently in analyzing student protest, anti-war pro-

15. *The Politics of Protest*, p. xxi .
16. Ibid.

17. Gary Marx perceives this characteristic of Skolnick's work when he observes that "Their analysis and ideology [of Skolnick, among others] lead them to see black, student, and 'third world' collective violence as intricately tied to injustice and strain, and often to imbue all crowd participants with ideological ends and a distinterested morality." Op. cit., this issue, p. 23.
18. *The Politics of Protest*, p. 4.

test, and black militant protest. He treats the social facts on which these groups base their ideology and their actions as objective and real and hence as important determinants of their protest behavior. Yet he does not apply the methodology consistently. In considering the racial attitudes of white Americans, for example, he freely addresses the subject of "personality and politics," and approvingly applies neo-Freudian statements such as "for many individuals, their own unacceptable and unconscious impulses and desires may be an important cause of prejudice," and that, in projecting such impulses and desires, these people distort the character of the social world.[19] Oversimplified stereotypes also function to "save [the bigoted individual] the mental effort of considering the complex historical, political, and economic factors. . . ."[20] And in discussing the outlook of the police, Skolnick assesses various police "theories," such as the "rotten apple" theory of man, as distorted, in so far as it excludes social factors such as poverty, discrimination, inadequate housing, and the like, and therefore runs "contrary to the teachings of all the behavioral sciences."[21] Holding these kinds of views, the police are "ill-equipped to understand or deal with dissident groups."[22] In reading *The Politics of Protest*, one gains the impression that Skolnick wears bifocals. He seems to have in mind two kinds of protesters—those who diagnose objective circumstances correctly and those who do not—and, as a consequence, two types of methodologies and two overlapping but partly differing sets of determinants to account for the behavior of each.

To change the metaphor, such strategies of analysis may make sweet music

19. Ibid., p. 192.
20. Ibid., p. 193.
21. Ibid., p. 259.
22. Ibid., p. xxiv.

for the ears of readers who share Skolnick's preferences, and may register as sour notes on those who don't. But as far as advancing our consistent understanding of social movements in general is concerned, I find strategy of one-methodology-for-one-kind-of-movement, another-for-the-other, to be unhelpful and probably mischievous. As for my own personal preferences, I also support movements I think are instrumental in reducing injustice and inequity, and oppose those that aim to perpetuate those conditions. But as a social scientist I feel compelled to try to bring consistent methods of analysis to bear on the explanation of both kinds of movements.

My position on participants' explanations of their own behavior attempts to avoid both the extreme of "appreciation" and the extreme of "debunking." On the one hand, it is essential to describe faithfully and accurately the beliefs of the participants in movements, because these beliefs constitute the network of meanings that define the movements' goals and guide the behavior of their participants. For this reason I felt it necessary to take the "generalized belief" as the starting point in identifying the major types of collective behavior. For the same reason, I felt it necessary, in my book *Social Change in the Industrial Revolution*, to give an extensively documented account of the ideology of the movement agitating for factory reform in nineteenth-century Britain—an ideology portraying the worsening physical, medical, and moral condition of the working classes.

In addition, however, I found the implicit "explanations" contained in this ideology inadequate to account for the course of the movement itself. According to the ideology, the reformers were moved to agitate because of their worsening conditions. Yet an exhaustive examination of the historical sources indicated that periods of agitation did not correlate very well with the conditions specified in the ideology, and in some cases the agitation swelled during periods in which these conditions were improving. I therefore went beyond the ideology's implied explanation of the participants' behavior, inquiring into conditions *other* than those specified in the ideology. In this inquiry I found that fluctuations in the content, timing, and intensity of the factory reform movement could be related closely to structural changes in the family system that were being generated by the changing technological and industrial structure. I concluded that line of analysis as follows:

We must take care . . . not to fall into the biases of the 1830's and assume one of two stands on the charges against the factory: (1) that these charges were true and the humanitarians were right [the appreciative extreme], or (2) that the claims were untrue and hence dismissible as a sort of sham or rationalization on the part of the agitators [the debunking extreme]. It seems to me that a third explanation accounts for the apparent exaggerations and paradoxes connected with the factory agitation. Because the family economy was passing through the early stages of differentiation, the social context for responsible attention to physical evils was in a precarious state. Therefore, oversensitive reformers were quick to generalize and attack the factory system for the *worsening physical condition of the children.*[23]

My methodological position, then, is to attempt to find causal links between social variables and the ideologies and behavior of participants in a movement. This position seems to me to avoid the problems that arise in *either* converting the ideology of the participants into a theory for the investigator, *or* "explaining away" that ideology, *or* doing the

------

23. Neil J. Smelser, *Social Change in the Industrial Revolution* (Chicago: University of Chicago Press, 1959), p. 279.

------

former for some ideologies and the latter for others.

THEIR CONCEPT OF INSTITUTIONS

As I have indicated, neither *The Politics of Protest* nor Currie and Skolnick's essay makes any substantial effort to lay out an explicit theoretical framework for the analysis of protest or collective behavior. Nevertheless, toward the end of their essay, they did give a hint as to how they would want to study collective action. They suggest a conception for the sociological concept, "institutions." They see institutions as having "a potential for the development and maintenance of human values— values such as democracy, participation, and the reduction of the repressive aspects of social life." Given this definition, the purpose of analysis becomes to assess all collective action in terms of its "capacity to promote (or retard) the creation and maintenance of these values." The justification of this general program for research is that it would "place the values that guide our research at the threshold of inquiry. . . ."

It is difficult to pin down the exact meaning of these statements, since Currie and Skolnick do not develop them beyond the sketchy phrases I have quoted. What they seem to have in mind is a kind of "evaluation research," taking certain traditional Western values or goals and then judging how well social arrangements realize these goals. This is certainly one defensible approach to research. In fact, it is much in evidence in contemporary sociology. Much of the research in areas like social mobility and race relations, for example, is directed to discovering how close—or how far—contemporary American institutions are to the. ideal of equality of opportunity.

Nevertheless, Currie and Skolnick's

formulation has some limitations as a *general* strategy for social research on collective action. First, it does not necessarily bring the investigator's own values closer to "the threshold of inquiry." It is perfectly possible to evaluate the extent to which institutions realize democratic ideals without necessarily positively valuing those ideals, just as it is possible to evaluate the extent to which European social arrangements in the eleventh and twelfth centuries realized the ideals of medieval religious philosophy, without necessarily positively valuing those ideals. Second, Currie and Skolnick's suggested program narrows the research enterprise unduly. To focus on the consequences of collective action for one certain set of human values, however important these may be, seems to downplay an interest in the determinants of this action on the one hand, and to downplay an interest in other types of consequences, both of which are essential to our scientific understanding of the collective action in question. And third, their suggested program seems especially limited as a perspective for a comparative analysis. While it has a valuable place in the comparative study of societies in which the particular human values they mention have been important historically, it does not seem to generate the most relevant kinds of questions about those societies in which those values have not been salient. A somewhat more inclusive conception of values would seem to be indicated. In sum, it appears to me that Currie and Skolnick, in the context of a negative polemic, have casually tossed in an alternative, and have not bothered to inquire into its theoretical and methodological implications.

6

Agonistics—Rituals of Conflict

By H. L. NIEBURG

H. L. Nieburg, Ph.D., is professor of Political Science at the State University of New York, Binghamton. Professor Nieburg is author of Nuclear Secrecy and Foreign Policy *(1964),* In the Name of Science *(1966), and* Political Violence: The Behavioral Process *(1969).*

ACTS of violence, even suicide, may be the enactment of a ritual which for a person in an extreme situation appears inescapable, reasonable, and legitimate. Wahl analyzes suicide as a "magical act," pointing out that the purposes of this symbolic solution are such that the actual death of the individual may be looked upon merely as a bonus effect, the necessary price of his action.[1] All behavior is problem-solving in some sense even though, in terms of value premises of the observer, this is not always obvious. The ritualization of behavior must be interpreted as a functional and problem-solving process, however disagreeable or even self-destructive its form.

Psychiatrist Ronald R. Laing argues for the validity of fantasy as "a mode of experience," equal in its effect on personal development and behavior to objective experience. Fantasy colors and embroiders sensory inputs with all the permutations and combinations of memory and prophecy engendered by the anxiety of existence. Laing writes: "Unfortunately, fantasy has not received the consideration it demands from an existential and phenomenological perspective. . . . No adequate existential account of the relation of self and other can afford to ignore fantasy."[2] Like ritual, of which it is an intrinsic part, fantasy is the real thought process that links action and response, that intervenes between all sequences of action and reaction, modifying behavior through a learning curve.

Even if unconscious, inarticulate, unsophisticated, the fantasy process mobilizes and weighs the options and potentials of response in every human interaction. Every possibility is reviewed for pertinency and efficacy. Thus, in some mysterious way, fantasy colors and determines behavior. All the materials of one's experience, conscious or unconscious—including the secondary inputs of observation, example, and symbolic communication, and the tertiary inputs of artful forecasting dramatized by theater, by plot and story conveyed through the media, as an art form, or through rumor, hearsay, ideology, or peer group instruction—are mobilized through fantasy by a process which is not necessarily improved by education. This process garners, activates, and selects the appropriate coils of the human memory bank, shapes the perception, and determines the circuit of the body's complex systems of electro-motor responses.

It is through fantasy that ritual behavior is projected and assimilated. That is why symbols can have powerful psychic and bodily effects, acting from a distance without physically touching the individual. What passes for "external reality" for the individual is a compendium of life experiences and organic conditions—those tested by trials-and-errors of the past, as well as those observed or communicated—all of which condition the response to new sensory inputs. *Reality*, therefore, is a modified fantasy which in its group manifestations becomes ritual and culture.

Secularization and science have imposed self-righteous blinkers upon modern man. We see the ritual dimension of primitive societies and of the unwashed and uneducated as a form of magic and superstition. We disguise the pervasive and inescapable ritual dimension which continues unabated even in a highly industrialized and sophisticated society, obscured by our myths of objectivity and science, yet expressed in the ritual of "news," the conventions of entertainment and art, the rubric of our

1. Charles William Wahl, "Suicide as a Magical Act," in Edward S. Schneidman and Norman L. Farberow, eds., *Clues to Suicide* (New York: McGraw-Hill, 1957), p. 24.

2. R. D. Laing, *The Self & Others: Further Studies in Sanity & Madness* (London: Tavistock Publications Ltd., 1961), p. 3.

political lives and ideologies, the omni-present network of electronic communications, and so forth. The rapidity of change, the search for novelty, as well as the highly specialized skill groups that innovate our culture, obscure the mystical quality of subjective culture forms. We live in a sea of mental images and ritual practices, including the magical prescriptions of science written on a bottle of pills and the transitory fads of language, dress, and manners.

THE ETHOLOGICAL CONTRIBUTION

"Agonistic" is a term used by ethologists to denote animal conflict behavior that is playful, symbolic, or ritualistic. The Greek word "agon" refers to the traditional ceremonial games played by young men and women from which came the international Olympics. Interest in ritual behavior has honorable roots in the social sciences (especially in anthropology and sociology), but the political functions of symbolic presentation, aggressive display, playful attack and defense, conventionalized interaction, have not been accorded much attention by political scientists. In the light of recent civil disturbances, the study of human agonistics (Woodstock, ritual-like confrontations) may have relevance as a proper area of theory and analysis.[3]

The ethological literature shows a remarkable consensus about the social function of agonistic animal behavior—it is political. Out of it come dominance/subordination patterns which constitute the complex authority and status structures of the group or pack. Through an intense agonistic phase, the young members discover, learn, and communicate their place in an ordered

set of relationships. Such structures endure as the animals mature, accommodating themselves to the existing relationships of older members and maintaining a set of behavior norms and culture patterns which perpetuate the group, which enable all members to coördinate behavior for the common good, which maximize the stability and success of the group in relation to the physical environment as well as to other groups of the same or of different species.[4]

Hinde discusses "the ritualization of behavior" among animals. Over several generations, behavior tends to evolve "to improve its adaptive value and the functional context in which it appears." Rituals of display and presentation have the principal function of "communication with other individuals." Such behavior, whatever its origins, tends to become modified to serve this purpose (although in some cases there is a "need for crypticity," that is, disguise of the behavior and/or the communication in order to protect against predators or for other purposes).[5] "Ritualization" includes changes in the display movement itself and the development of conspicuous physical structures by which the movement is enhanced. Actual physical changes in the species may respond to a behavior pressure of this type.[6]

3. The term itself is interesting. "Agony" is an "acted out display" of one in the throes of an agon, or a symbolic ritual of conflict. "Antagonistic" refers to real hostility; reduced to its roots, it means "pre-ritual conflict."

4. See John Paul Scott and John L. Fuller, *Genetics and the Social Behavior of the Dog* (Chicago: University of Chicago Press, 1965); Robert A. Hinde, *Animal Behavior: A Synthesis of Ethology and Comparative Psychology* (New York: McGraw-Hill, 1966); Margaret Bastock, *Courtship: An Ethological Study* (Chicago: Aldine, 1967); Desmond Morris, ed., *Primate Ethology* (Chicago: Aldine, 1967); Lorus and Margery Milne, *Patterns of Survival* (Englewood Cliffs, N.J.: Prentice-Hall, 1967); S. A. Barnett, *The Rat: A Study in Behaviour* (Chicago: Aldine, 1963).

5. Hinde, op. cit., p. 432.

6. See N. Tinbergen, "Derived Activities: Their Causation, Biological Significance, Origin and Emancipation During Evalution," *Quar-*

During ritualization, some behavior takes on a "typical intensity" which makes it distinctive from otherwise similar behavior. The key definition of "ritualization" arises from the "motivational changes" controlling the movement, governed by causal factors quite different from those which motivated the behavior in its original, simple reflex or trial-and-error forms. For example, the purpose of a specific act of feeding may be not to gain nourishment but to display a nonchalance in another animal's presence, as part of an encounter or confrontation.[7]

In the definitive Scott/Fuller study of dogs, agonistic behavior tends to stabilize to reflect rank relationships among a group of individuals, but it continues after ranking is well-recognized and stable. In effect, it comes to be ritualized in terms of a wide variety of motives other than those creating authority relationships: e.g., confirming and demonstrating relationships, ceremonial repetition as a symbol of group unity, low-risk testing of the structure by subordinate individuals (who, if they detect indifference or inattention, will persevere in seeking other indulgences above their rank, if not an escalated reopening of the original agonistic relationship with a possible reversal of roles as the outcome),[8] appeals for indulgences by subordinate individuals, repetition as a form of operant conditioning by individuals seeking to repeat an associated anticipation or reaction, repetition as a form of search behavior

in reacting to an unfamiliar stimulus, repetition as an inappropriate response to an ambiguous stimulus, and so forth.[9]

Among dogs about seven weeks of age (the time when final weaning begins and mothers begin to threaten their offspring), puppies leave their mothers and begin to attack each other in groups. In most breeds, this "ganging up" is temporary and playful. A definite dominance/subordination pattern emerges by fifteen weeks of age, after which the incidence of actual fighting is much reduced—although symbolic or ritualistic conflict behavior continues and may even increase in frequency.[10] This is the most critical period in the life of the animal. In addition to the determination of social relationships, the emotional sensitivity and sitll undeveloped motor and intellectual capacities of the puppy suggest that this may also be a critical period for possible psychological damage. "Emotional sensitivity is apparently a necessary part of the social process, and this automatically makes the animal susceptible to psychological damage as well."[11]

RITUAL IN ANTHROPOLOGY/SOCIOLOGY

Mumford and others suggest that the task of elaborating the social order is the primary task of human groups the most elemental human drive toward creativity, ritual, and play gives rise to

terly *Review of Biology*, 27 (1957), pp. 1–32; and A. D. Blest, "The Concept of Ritualisation," in W. H. Thorpe and O. L. Zangwill, eds., *Current Problems in Animal Behavior* (Cambridge: Cambridge University Press, 1961).

7. See F. McKinney, "An Analysis of the Displays of the European Eider and the Pacific Eider," in *Behaviour, Supplement No. 7;* and Hinde, op. cit., p. 433.

8. Scott and Fuller, op. cit., p. 77.

9. Scott and Fuller, ibid., also illustrate this point: "Some dogs simply growi at each other and move apart. More typically, the dominant dog places his feet on the back of the other, growling as he does so, while the subordinate one keeps his head and tail lowered. Still more subordinant animal may roll over on his back while the dominant one stands over him, head to head; the subordinate animal rapidly snaps his teeth and yelps. Sometimes, the dominant animal makes a few threatening snaps at the subordinate one" (p. 77).

10. Ibid., p. 109.

11. Ibid., pp. 107, 110–111.

manners, ceremony, social systems, inventions, and technologies.[12]

Since the last quarter of the nineteenth century, analysis of ritual has ranged from Durkheim's theories (1925) to Gough's work (1959) on the Nayar cults of the dead. One extremist usage has been to define ritual as "any expression of cultural form." Another would limit it to the performance of religious acts. Psychoanalytic theory uses the term for repetitive, involuntary sequences of behavior stemming from compulsion. Most anthropologists think of ritual as any proscribed form of behavior that is not essential to technical and practical affairs. Malinowski, Redfield, and others have demonstrated the interpenetration of ritual and non-ritual experience.

Ritual and one of its forms—political ideology—are parts or dimensions of culture, and may be thought of as the link in the network by which the social meaning of actions and relationships is exchanged and communicated. Thus, ritual is an expression or articulation, often non-verbal, of the values, attitudes, theories, interpretations, potential actions, and expectations of individuals in a community. Fairkind provides the classic formulation of ritual as "the collective representation" of the group, which he divides between "sacred" and "profane," a dichotomy which we are tempted to abandon.[13]

The ritual dimension of behavior is described by anthropologist Max Gluckman as "the mystical form of the political system" which reflects the common interests of all members of the society as well as the interconnected rights, duties, and sentiments which make it a single community. Ritual embodies the general interest in fertility and prosperity, the need to respond to changes in the physical environment and technology, and the adjustment of internal and external conflict. In addition to food planting, production and exchange, marriage, procreation, and so on, every action has, in Gluckman's terms, a "moral aspect" expressing sentiments, mobilizing social relationships, expressing claims and anticipated responses, confirming or altering social relationships, maintaining a reciprocal and mutually balancing system.[14]

In these terms, ritual is perhaps the unique and essential aspect that makes all behavior "social" rather than individual and isolated. Pseudo-events, such as elaborate ceremonials, are thus significant events which affirm and perpetuate the social group. Gluckman: "The distribution of ritual power helps achieve a balance against competing secular interests." This can be applied not only to organized religions, the role of the chaplain and the sanctuary of the church, but also to spontaneous secular rituals of all kinds and of all degrees of permanence and substance. Gluckman concludes that ritual develops most strongly in those situations where moral judgments on actions affect many social relationships.[15]

Ritual action is the redressive, reconciling means of reaffirming loyalties, testing and changing them at times or offering new ones to replace the old, but expressed in a kind of muted symbolic display with a symbolic response which changes attitudes and values without major and unlimited conflict, and without the necessity for total and simul-

12. Lewis Mumford, *The Myth and the Machine: Technics and Human Development* (New York: Harcourt, Brace & World, 1967), p. 3.
13. Paul Friedrich, "Revolutionary Politics and Communal Ritual," in Marc J. Swartz, Victor W. Turner and Arthur Tuden, eds., *Political Anthropology* (Chicago: Aldine, 1966), pp. 191–193.

14. Max Gluckman, *Politics, Law and Ritual in Tribal Society* (New York: New American Library, 1965), p. 280.
15. Ibid., pp. 281–300.

taneous involvement in the new value systems by all members of the society. The potential for disruptive revolutionary change by escalated violence and internal warfare is always present, unpredictable in its outcome, costly in its logistics, dangerous in the secondary conflicts which may be engendered; ritual controls and moderates these undesirable tendencies.

Ritual is distinguished from *ceremony*. The former we use to designate the general tendency for actions to acquire a symbolic meaning which tends to have a function different from the raw act. Ceremony is used to describe a specific, highly conventionalized performance.

Anthropologists report a common feature of every culture: the ceremonial occasion in which all the proscriptions on behavior, the constraints and requirements of self-discipline, are set aside for a prescribed period. Puritanical societies may approve harvest rituals in which lewd songs and sexual displays are permitted, even by staid matrons. Many cultures provide occasions on which ceremonial participants go into a mystic trance, during which they are expected to do unmentionable and forbidden things. Western culture has long smiled with tolerance and a knowing wink at Saturday night and special holidays that unleash a wild set of provocative conventions: New Year's Eve, the Tuesday preceding Lent, the Christmas office party, New York City following the Mets' victory in the World Series, V-E Day. Alcohol, cocaine, costumes, dances, mummery, mimicry, love-making and outrageous flirtations, intimate encounters with strangers in dark alleys or side streets—such Saturnalias of sexuality and exhibitionism can be found in every culture as part of a ceremonial occasion or as a spontaneous reaction to a happy or terrible event.

The ancient Greeks had a holiday in which the slave/master relationship was reversed and the slaves were served by their masters for a day. This is not unlike a ritual practiced in the United States one day a year, when school children reverse roles with teachers and principals, sometimes with mayors and governors. This is a form of ritual which has not been given much attention by social scientists. In a recent study of drunken comportment, two sociologists conclude that most behavior supposed to result from alcohol is rather conventionalized ritual for whose performance little alcohol is necessary, which cannot be performed at all if too much alcohol is imbibed. Drunkenness is seen as ritualized behavior which is "time out" from the normal discipline of life. Under the role of drunkenness, all kinds of behavior are excusable, even charming, which would not be tolerated under the conventions of sobriety.[16]

In primitive societies, ritual aims at dramatizing the critical turning points in the life histories of individuals, the turning of the seasons, major historical events of the group, as well as current crises. Ritual functions "to release beneficent power," and is effective because "it exhibits all the tensions and strife inherent in social life itself," according to Gluckman. All the disturbances of the natural world, including the transformation of role from child to youth to man or woman, transferring land, moving a village, reorganizing activities, all threatening disturbances are amended and assimilated through a process of ritualistic pseudo-events.

All behavior is a social communication as well as a goal-directed activity. That is why men conduct themselves differently depending upon the audience for the performance. Even when alone, fantasy conjures up various audiences for every act, even those acts deliber-

16. Craig MacAndrew and Robert B. Edgerton, *Drunken Comportment: A Social Explanation* (Chicago: Aldine, 1969).

ately shrouded in secrecy and darkness. This is an aspect of the socializing function of interaction.[17] Man is a social creature, even or especially when he masturbates alone in the coalbin.

Every act has multiple levels of meaning, whether confirming, influencing, or challenging the expectations of others to respond to or repeat the act. Any act which does not conform to the appropriate social code which governs it makes news because, in Goffman's words, it "disconfirms the selves of the participants."[18] Man is a social being, living in manmade culture; therefore, all actions, inactions, and reactions express social values and communicate a highly significant symbolism. Every movement for accomplishing a given act, even one of simple physical manipulation, has social meaning. The fact that the act is done, the way in which it is done, its timing in relation to sequences of acts by oneself and others, are pertinent dimensions which communicate something. The act may become pure ritual in that the dominant intention of the actor is the communication and not the physical outcome. Whether alone, in a small group, or in front of a television camera, the social dimension can become dominant, either confirming or challenging values and social groupings. In all their actions, persons "must sense that they are close enough to be perceived in whatever they are doing, including their experiencing of others, and close enough to be perceived in this sensing of being perceived."[19] All behavior changes its social meaning,

17. See Robert C. Carson, *Interaction Concepts of Personality* (Chicago: Aldine, 1969); also Eric Berne, *Transactional Analysis in Psychotherapy* (New York: Grove Press, 1961).
18. Erving Goffman, *Interaction Ritual* (Garden City, N.Y.: Doubleday, 1967), p. 51.
19. Goffman, *Behavior in Public Places: Notes on the Social Organization of Gatherings* (New York: Free Press, 1963), p. 17.

though its physical form be the same, depending upon its setting, its intended audience, and its intended effect. The level and scope of "mutual monitoring" is what defines a "gathering," in which loosely organized group behavior occurs, having a social meaning distinct and distinguishable from that which the same sequence of actions might have in a different gathering.

A ceremonial rule is defined by Goffman as a conventionalized means of communication whose primary significance lies in the communication rather than the direct outcome of the action. By means of this communication, the individual "expresses his character or conveys his appreciation of the other participants in the situation."[20] Behavior may be seen as part of a symbolic bargaining relationship: by presentation and display, individuals, much like the lower animals, seek to trade-off values or otherwise influence each other's behavior.

A study in political anthropology (the annual fiesta round at Naranja, in Mexico) concludes that "the ritual cycle vouched for and in a sense periodically regenerated the legitimacy of the political system." In the same way, the profanation of ritual or the development of counter-ritual (Black Mass, witches' rites, and the like) are designed to challenge the legitimacy of the political system. Ceremonial behavior creates a "power of the weak" expressing what might be called the emerging influence of new groups in the informal political systems, thus offsetting and countervailing the power of the strong. Power which rests on the formal institutional structure (property, law, and the monopoly of legality and police power of the state) may be offset and limited by informal ritual practices, including claims of special knowledge and power

20. Goffman, *Interaction Ritual*, p. 54.

deriving from the practices. A study of African micropolitics [21] finds a society in which the father has almost absolute power, while the mother has control of religious ritual in the family and is able to check, if not overcome, the formal system.

In brief, the functions of agonistic behavior are (1) to provide a means of low-risk testing in the continuing conflict for precedence among rising and declining social groups and values; (2) to transmute events into a form of knowledge, learning, and consensus which modifies the behavior of those involved and others who are affected; (3) to provide a continuous source of experimentation and culture inputs; (4) to provide a means of confirming and maintaining social groups and culture forms; and (5) to offer a means of buffering the group against crises and threatening disturbances by assimilating the unfamiliar into a familiar process. Mass ceremonials and demonstrations, in addition, are in part a display of force, a threat to others, and a source of reassurance and manifest power for those directly involved. Parades, marches, mass meetings and the like, whatever their avowed purpose, demonstrate commitment, solidarity, and strength, and thereby have great political potency, influence, and deterrent power arising from the mere fact that they occur, quite apart from the rhetoric or declaratory threats of the leaders. Military displays, fly-bys, troop maneuvers, draft-eligibles by the thousands singing *Alice's Restaurant,* all are mass ceremonials whose main effect is a show of force.[22]

21. See Friedrich, op. cit., pp. 187–219; and Victor W. Turner, "Ritual Aspects of Conflict Control in African Micropolitics," in Swartz, Turner, and Tuden, ibid., pp. 239–246.

22. See Glenn H. Snyder, *Deterrence and Defense: Toward a Theory of National Security* (Princeton, N.J.: Princeton University Press, 1961), pp. 254–255.

"THE WOODSTOCK NATION"

To begin to understand the tactics of certain groups of the young, one needs to look at the ritual behavior provided by certain public settings and occasions. The street party, the carnival, the Mardi Gras, and ritual vandalism, all have much in common with political demonstrations of recent years. The "be-in," the 1969 Woodstock Festival and its countless imitations, are recognized street occasions in which roofless and open space, usually in mild weather, becomes by definition a stage for socially-defined behavior unlike that which is appropriate in a private setting. The very fact of group encounter, strangeness, anonymity, the reinforcement of numbers, inverts the normal sense of danger and the reflexes of self-protection, liberating people from their usual private roles. Street theatre is a kind of "open region" where instant social accessibility is recognized and facilitated, where extravagant and fleeting claims upon life may be projected by every repressed ego. Even Wall Street bankers had a famous "be-in" during the summer of 1969, celebrating a young girl with an abnormally large bust in much the same way as the young rebels on the campus seize as excuse the obvious sins and faults of society.

People who are forced together or come together voluntarily on such ceremonial occasions radiate the assumption of mutual trust and good will. This value system is built into such open regions. It is the only way a crowd protects itself from the implicit dangers of sudden social fusion. The same system of values manifests itself during a natural disaster, when individuals suddenly find themselves locked together in a predicament. Tragedy has struck and may strike again, and all are suddenly aware of their mutual dependence for information and help. All the ordinary constraints upon communication among strangers are put aside. The anxiety and tension which exist in all relationships are liberated as a kind of free-floating energy.

Many have remarked upon the curious paradox that natural disaster creates a sense of gaiety and excitement whose contagion overrides even the tragedies of the moment. Like lemmings trampling each other in their haste to commit suicide, a disaster creates a ceremonial occasion with many of the same dynamics as those seen in convivial carnivals and costumed street demonstrations. The Woodstock Festival is cited as evidence that half a million people can create a new culture, one which enables them to live for three days under disastrous conditions with bountiful toleration, mutual help, and an intense sense of the moment. In this instance, the aftertaste was good, the disappointments, inconvenience, and disorientation of the event were temporary. For many of the participants, it was the first great ceremonial occasion of their lives, a mass post-puberty rite in a world that offers the young few meaningful ceremonies. Thus, it provided the impetus for a mystique and a cult which Abbie Hoffman has called "the Woodstock nation." It was an ordeal and a ritual such as earlier generations achieved at summer camp in the mountains or during a Boy Scout Jamboree.

Most private encounters are motivated by the various needs, designs, and incentives of the participants. The usual forms of polite social intercourse provide methods of gradual exchange of values or non-provocative withdrawal. Social distance and manners tend to protect, buffer, and test the development of mutuality of interest. On the other hand, the ceremonial occasion of a carnival or a disaster guarantees that encounters are not and should not be the basis for lasting relationships and ex-

changes of values. Consequently, many of the safeguards for negotiating long-term relationships are relaxed. It becomes possible to grab a value here or there with the hope of not paying for it. Individuals may fornicate amid the shrubs and cows in much the same way as black teenagers loot liquor and department stores during a ghetto riot.

In such a situation, values are born every minute as persons ratify each other's acts by imitation, signs of approval, and mutual participation. It is this process that makes it possible for crowds to become mobs, capable of the most unlikely and despicable actions. A desperate youth stands on the ledge of a high building while, amid laughter and obscenities, the crowd yells, "Jump, man, jump!" Even short of mob action, a ceremonial crowd encourages behavior that is improvised rapidly from materials at hand, whose imitation by others becomes a test of loyalty to the occasion's code.

The ritual of spontaneous ratification of innovative acts leads to crowd actions that may have political consequences and characterizations. It may also lead to uncontrollable situations, violent attacks, counter-attacks, and/or preëmptive attacks. Mass hysteria may arise from this process, as a form of inappropriate and harmful ritual.[23]

MASS HYSTERIA

Instances of mass hysteria are frequently noted. In 1955, London's Royal Free Hospital reported an upsurge of 300 cases with identical symptoms and no verifiable disease. Like witchhunting in New Salem or the dancing manias of Germany in the Middle Ages, contagious hysteria has been well documented in many kinds of situations.

23. The definition of *hysteria* contains a value assumption: "inappropriate" and "harmful" is ascribed to the outcome of such behavior, thereby implying a post hoc evaluation.

Events of recent years give us insight into the process. Possibly the study of such historical incidents would indicate that they were not isolated outbreaks but were related to conflict groups and social change in much the same way as the mass behavior of militant students in 1970, burning and ravaging Isla Vista and Harvard Square.

The waves of student rebellion in the past two years bear an unmistakeable resemblance to the mania for the early Beatles on their first American tour, the hoola-hoop craze, fraternity raids, the spring madness of beach riots—rituals which college students in their campus ghettos invent as a way of demonstrating their insulation and insularity.

However, such ritual occasions by their very nature cannot be sustained indefinitely. Behavior which seems so appropriate, original, exciting, amusing, and intelligent in the ceremonial setting is soon found to be quite otherwise when the occasion ends, as it must. The memory of the emotional binge creates a great incentive to look for socially legitimate occasions, at least from the point of view of the intended audience, for calling the tribes together again for a reënactment. It is never the same. Disillusionment and reservation must set in.

This syndrome may help to explain some of the imitative behavior of the so-called political encounters that have come to characterize certain elements of the young. The most liberal and free universities were the first targets. In their guilt and uncertainty, the authorities sought to renew their legitimacy by capitulations to demands, however shallow. They were startled and dismayed that such capitulation seemed to precipitate an escalation of demands and a renewal of the ceremonial forms of mass protests. Studies of campus rebellions show that such actions tend to run a natural course, ending after about two weeks—as fatigue, boredom, and the call

of private values and life situations reassert themselves, soaking up the vast reservoir of free-floating fantasy which had been directed into the street performance. The natural demise of the ceremonial has often had the effect of isolating the activists and forcing them into attempts to re-energize and radicalize their comrades by more extreme and provocative actions. Such tactics are designed to draw the authorities into mistakes and over-reactions which may renew the unity of the participants. Tear gas, tanks, and machine guns resurrect the image of the demonstrators as put-upon and manipulated innocents, who must stand together to face the official terror of the authorities.

As police and administrators have learned to avoid the use of terror tactics as a response to low levels of provocation, the provocation level of the activists has risen—as if to force an hysterical reënactment of the old situation. After hit-and-run guerrilla tactics at the University of Wisconsin, combined with window smashing, overturning cars, and throwing fire-bombs, the young people walked hand-in-hand down State Street singing "We Shall Overcome." A sense of injured righteousness pervaded them. Perhaps, ritualistically, they were the tormented blacks of Alabama led by Martin Luther King, walking with truth and God at their side, heads held high, right in the face of Chief Bull Connor and his red-neck storm troopers.

Erving Goffman's observations are perceptive and germane. Confrontation politics uses the system he calls "a focused gathering" or "a situated activity system." By emphasizing the social communication that surrounds behavior, Goffman grapples with the ritual, symbolic, and ceremonial dimensions of behavior. Culture is manmade and makes man, and it is constantly in a state of becoming. If persons come together into a focused gathering and stay for a time, certain "systems problems" will have to be solved: "the participants will have to submit to rules of recruitment, to limits on overt hostility, and to some division of labor." In addition, they will have to discover and create some kind of hierarchy of influence, so that even a transitory group may coördinate the activities of its participants.

GROUP CHARACTERISTICS

A focused gathering may be preliminary to the creation of a social group, or it may take on some of the characteristics of a social group for a limited purpose and occasion and then dissolve. All social groups possess common organizational characteristics, including rules of entering and leaving, rules for collective action, specialization of function within the group (i.e., leadership), routines of socialization, and some means of satisfying certain individual values, of adjusting internal conflict, of relating the group to its physical setting and the rest of society. Whether formal or informal, these characteristics are found in all social relationships and are most perfectly developed and formalized in groups whose activity is of longer duration, frequency, and importance to the participants—whether it is a relationship between two persons, a network interlocking a set of friends, a complex organization, a set of business men, or a group of players in a game.

Shared spontaneous involvement in a mutual activity brings the sharers into some kind of exclusive solidarity and permits them to express relatedness, psychic closeness, and mutual respect; failure to participate with good heart can therefore express rejection of those present or of the setting. Involvement and acceptance of the focus of attention and the improvised rules of behavior of a gathering in an open region, like participation in any social group, confirms the reality of the world prescribed by group unity and by the ratification of each participant's actions in the approval and reaction of his peers. In the same way, this reality tends to deny the reality of other potential worlds inhabited by outsiders. Participants enjoy a secret standing which they communicate by little signs and fragments of speech which are unintelligible to others. The bafflement of the outsiders adds a delicious quality of amusement and pleasure for the insiders who share a secret truth.

The constraints and behavior norms of a ceremonial gathering, while they generate an enhanced sense of freedom and novelty, are in fact in every way as compulsory upon the participants as those of everyday private life. A gathering of strangers, held together in the magic bond of a special occasion, is capable of punishing infractions of the rules, doubts, or skepticism, flagging energy, attempts to withdraw, challenges of the norm, even more viciously and directly than the brutal reprisals built into polite society. However, the elements of coercion are muted by the unanimity and high spirits of the occasion, even as the group turns on a doubter or punishes the waverer.

The gathering, the most informal and loosely constructed precursor to the social group, will, depending upon the outcome of its activity, be strengthened or weakened accordingly, moving toward more lasting forms of behavior or, in the face of ill success, falling apart and rendering the participants available for reformation in other activity groups.[24] If the outcomes are favorable, forms of organization and activity emerge which are likely to be continued or repeated and the gathering will be marked by the participants as a "memorable event," out of which some kind of group forma-

24. Goffman, *Encounters: Two Studies in the Sociology of Interaction* (Indianapolis: Bobbs-Merrill, 1961), p. 14.

tion will retain a call upon the future loyalty of the individuals involved, limiting their availability for regrouping, or dividing their loyalties in other groups. It is a common phenomenon for the survivors of a disaster to feel such a strong sense of identity as to want to keep alive the cause of their group formation, celebrating it in story and song, and organizing annual reunions. One of the survivors may fall into the pathology of striving to reënact the disaster, actually or fraudulently, in an effort to recapture the sense of meaning, community, and dignity which his subsequent life did not match. This pathology may lead the survivor of a spectacular fire to become an arsonist.

Individual behavior can be understood only in relation to group values, interests, and norms. Even the anomic individual acts in reference to groups. Such an individual seeks reinforcement and legitimacy for his actions. "Reference group theory" has proved useful in accounting for criminal behavior. The "reference group" is "that group whose perspective constitutes the frame of reference of the actor" without necessarily being the group in which he is accepted or aspires to be accepted.[25] Ralph H. Turner calls such behavior "role-playing"; the individual, even though disoriented and socially isolated, takes the role of a member and adopts the group's viewpoint as his own.

INDIVIDUAL AND GROUP

But reference group behavior on the part of an individual (whether in or out of such groups) may be viewed as rationalization. A great deal of extreme individual behavior occurs as impulsive reflex to provocative stimuli not fully comprehended by an excited actor. His attempts to legitimize his reflex will

25. Tamotsu Shibutani, "Reference Groups as Perspective," *American Journal of Sociology* 60, 3 (May 1955), pp. 562–563.

exploit any material he believes to be plausible to an auditor, and will therefore be of little diagnostic or analytical value. The dismissal of such rationalization, however, ignores a fundamental principle of all behavior: that its causes are always imperfectly understood by the actor and he always seeks legitimacy by aligning himself with such individuals and groups as may reinforce and accept him.

Reference behavior of this kind is a projection of fantasy and a ritual, because it may be otherwise unrelated to organizational or purposeful behavior of group members. The hijackers of the ship *Columbia Eagle* declared that they were acting as part of an SDS-sponsored campaign to sabotage arms shipments to Southeast Asia. In fact, it turned out that neither of them had any direct contact with SDS and had been spending most of their time at sea prior to the hijacking. Their fantasy of reference group behavior seeks to rationalize and justify their action by the standards of legitimacy achieved by the slogans of SDS. All the crew members reported that the two hijackers were unpopular from the beginning, unwilling to do tasks that were assigned to them, and spent most of their time smoking marijuana out of sight.

Many of the tactics of present-day extremists are in the nature of ceremonial profanations, as in the use of four-letter words, public fornication, incivility, the disruption of dialogue, and so forth. Ceremonial profanation is an accessible means of action, of attack against another group's unity and self-confidence. The breaking up of public meetings and religious services has proven efficacious as an attention-getting device for small groups. Such tactics are designed to shock and to disorient. In the search for new ceremonies to profane, anti-war protestors break up speeches by Senator William Fulbright, and the November Action Coalition, a so-called Left faction of SDS, launches attacks against Moratorium marches and the New Mobilization.

Behavior of the so-called "Smashers" of the Left has been ritualized into a highly conventionalized performance. It is comparable in motive and effect to that of "food throwers," inmates in prisons or mental hospitals who bring a predictable disorder to the meal hour. This role endows them with a certain amount of influence and special attention. Like the common variety of kickers, spillers, or stealers found in nursery schools and families, the behavior has distinctly social-psychological components. Being a form of direct action, it can hardly be ignored, and by threat of escalation it neutralizes control action based upon superior or even overwhelming force. However, violation of situational proprieties has piquancy only so long as there is an element of surprise. If such behavior is generalized as a new norm, it quickly loses its charm.

A school fire drill is a form of ritual whose function as training for emergencies is obvious. However, the ritual has other effects. It manifests the unified whole of the school, it confirms the power of the principal, and it provides the students an opportunity of mass assembly. Most important, of course, it teaches behavior which can be invoked in the event of a real fire. The inability of most of the students to distinguish between the real and the ritual is one of the most important results which the drill achieves, making evacuation of the building possible without panic and even with considerable gaiety.

The requirements of group life impose many difficult actions upon individuals. Individuals suffer and die in order that group purposes may be achieved. Rituals like a fire drill teach group unity and facilitate leadership control over certain kinds of behavior from the group members. Most primitive societies have warfare rituals celebrated as great occasions, even in peace time. These rituals make it easier to mobilize the group's war-making resources and manpower when policy requires.

In the same way, ritual can lead individuals into inappropriate and self-destructive behavior, in which ritual and real action are confused until it is too late. For example, young radicals use a rhetoric of provocation and violence of the most extreme kind. When the acts that implement rhetoric lead to real confrontation with the police, tear gas, split heads, and arrests, the youngsters experience a sense of having been betrayed. People were not supposed to take much of the rhetoric seriously; they were not supposed to respond with violence. The ritual was supposed to be performed as a kind of metaphor and symbolic warning. There is, they charge, something grossly unfair in the tendency of the police to take them at their word and respond accordingly. The uses of ritual are thus ambiguous, performing a number of needful social functions but also being subject to abuse, dysfunction, and excess.

FORMS OF SYMBOLIC THREAT

There are many forms of symbolic threat intended to influence behavior at minimum risk, like the dead kitten at the door of an unpopular neighbor, the telephone call in which no threat is uttered, only heavy breathing, the package of dung delivered in the mail. The celebrated Mafia symbolism, the system of graded warnings, from the cutting down of a vine and the maiming of a mule to the deposit at a man's door of a beheaded dog or a sheep with its throat cut—are all found in widely spaced areas of the world. Similar contrivances, ceremonies of sacrifice, initiation, blood-drinking, artifacts of death connected with mystical rites, frequently are in-

corporated into group symbols and ceremonials as a kind of implicit threat
against member disloyalty or as a means
of intimidating outsiders.

Dark glasses and black leather jackets
are rich in symbolism. The jacket goes
back to the Gestapo. Picked up by the
British Rockers, the American Hell's
Angels and Outlaws motorcycle gangs,
it expressed a threat of merciless violence. The dark glasses of the Black
Panthers derive from jazz musicians.
The style has threat value also. The
wearer can stare at another person sur-
reptitiously. The object is unable to
read the intention of the person whose
eyes are shielded. The role of the Black
Panthers as the "muscle" of the latter
stages of the civil rights movement
brings to the black community a stage
of development for which sociologists
have been searching in vain—that is, a
form of "police enforcement," which
can provide a base not only for organized criminal activities, but also for
organized political influence. Earlier
waves of immigrants who took up residence at the bottom of the pecking order
in American cities eventually formed
criminal syndicates and gangs, which
aided the fight of the group into the
social, economic, and political systems,
into the suburbs, and into a loss of
group identity and an end to the need
for a kind of "military muscle."

It is charged that great numbers of
modern youth are occultists and tribal-
ists and that this is the result of the
sterility of ritual in modern life. I propose the opposite thesis, not as proven,
but for examination: namely, that the
contemporary fads, forms, and life styles
are rather an expression of pluralism—
too many images, too much variegated
and conflicting fantasy, a surplus of
riches—culture spawned, generated, used
up and discarded at an incredible rate,
in such an even-handed way as to permit
every contribution to have provisional

legitimacy for some group in society,
providing it is fresh and imaginative.

A phrase arises from a new television
program and goes the rounds to become
common coin, a ritual incantation by
which all the individuals who adopt it
prove thereby to be "with it," that is,
tuned in to the source of culture input.
Yet within a few months the phrase is
stale; it has been replaced by so many
new candidates that only a complete
"square" or a child will be found guilty
of the *faux pas* of using it. Later, the
phrase might evolve into a new stage
of freshness in which it become "camp"
or a deliberate malapropism, deriving a
new but brief freshness because of
the inversion of its meaning, expressing
not the original sentiment but rather
recognition of its vulgarity.

In much the same way, the movement
of "flower children" evolved in the brief
span of five years through all the
changes of political tactics, going from
throwing flowers to throwing dung and
bombs. The gentle Mods and the tough
Rockers in Britain, or the Hippies and
the motocycle gangs in the United
States, evolved apart, together, and
apart again, an aspect of the relent-
less process of culture change and
innovation.

The overload of inputs and the rapid
exhaustion of culture forms is an aspect of ritual in a society undergoing
vast and important changes. Such a
swift current of culture consumption,
uncomfortable to some, exciting to
others, may be necessary as a means of
experimentation, of the emergence of
new groups and constituencies, new
value systems of behavior. Some of
these may be assimilated into enduring
forms and institutions while others are
discarded as a transitional phase of
growth for some individuals.

An industrial society based on high-
level production and consumption makes
novelty itself a positive value and an ob-

ject of much social behavior. The parameters of our lives are changing rapidly, due not only to social and political
factors but also to the unrelenting pace
of technological change. This pace requires a constant replenishment of new
values and behavior forms. Through a
process of testing and competitive group
formation, some of these forms may survive in cloistered confines of this or
that special activity or interest group,
while others may be generalized for a
longer or shorter time as an approved
value with prescribed behavior patterns
for the whole society. That this process
should be transformed into symbols and
ritual is not surprising. Symbolic and
ritual behavior is a low-risk, energy-
conserving method of experimentation,
learning, social choice, and consensus-
building. Artificial constraints or the
use of state authority to stanch, limit,
or channel the flow are part of the win-
nowing process, but hardly determining.
Attempts to use state power in a controlling fashion are bound to lead to a
variety of protective responses, resistance, concealment, challenge of the legitimacy of state power, and other such
forms, in order to safeguard the need
for a continuous and pluralistic input of
new values, patterns of behavior, and
group loyalties.

RITUAL POLITICAL BEHAVIOR

An understanding of the dimensions
of ritual in political behavior may lead
one to greater sanguinity about the jar-
ring affronts of the cultural revolution.
If you don't like the forms this year,
to quote Casey Stengel, "wait until next
year!" Understanding the process of
ritual and its essential functions may
serve to quiet our apprehension. The
chief factor that can arrest the tide of
culture experimentation would be the
overreaction of those vested with formal
authority seeking to obliterate the challenge of change and collect all the strings

of power from above. To do so would
invalidate the sense of community and
of united purpose which some of the
most extreme groups are hawking in
the streets. Such a reaction would tend
to delay the inevitable fragmentation of
the ritual "Woodstock nation" and its
variants.

Uncivil and disruptive behavior, stylized as ritual, must be looked upon as
adaptive and practical in some sense,
rather than as merely pathological or
erratic. The self-justifying rhetoric of
the youth cult includes: everyone else's
guilt and hypocrisy, claims that the
values of Western civilization are daily
corrupted and contradicted by war,
atomic weapons, police brutality, ethical
ambiguity, reliance on force and raw
power, and the dalliance and relativism
of the middle-aged liberals. Somehow
the fathers have cheated the children,
creating an impossible world overshad-
owed by nuclear missiles, ugliness, and
unspeakable stupidity, invoking in the
young a sense of anxiety, helplessness,
and rebellion. All nations, but especially the rich and powerful, are rotten,
their leaders have lost the way and are
unable to cope either with injustice,
racism, and environmental despoliation
or the challenge of the poor, the Blacks,
and the young.[26]

The ritualization of politics during
this troubled period may be serving the
same function that apolitical culture
forms served in other generations, as
rites of passage, courtship ritual, or
rites of spring. There is the example of
the Black civil rights movement and the
emergence of the Black constituency, its
success, and the success of virtually all
its imitators, including the anti-war
movement, Indians, homosexuals, and
the new feminists. There is the unique
historical sequence of the last few years,
when the pressure of international crises

26. For example, see Jeff Nuttall, *Bomb
Culture* (New York: Delacorte Press, 1969).

suddenly disappeared. Communism and the dangers of war receded even as the morass of Vietnam deepened, wrenching loose all the priorities which had so rigidly commanded our values and institutions for thirty years. There were the accumulated deficits of domestic problems, and the unrecognized new groups demanding their places in the sun. There is the breakup of old coalitions: nationality groups that finally took their place as "real Americans" parting company with the labor movement which, together with crime and politics, became their instrument of upward mobility. The coalitions of the power establishment which conducted World War II and the Cold War collapsed when success and power eliminated their reason for vigor and unity. This establishment, the tired and aging revolutionaries of the New Deal, reached a turning point. The end of the Cold War, the breakdown of communism, the disruption of the regional ghettos (e.g., of Jews, Italians, Poles) as a base of political power in American cities, the loss of credibility and self-confidence in the face of Vietnam and Black uprisings—all such factors made the time ripe for new groups, more dissatisfied, more unified by geography and inequality, to march, to manifest their unity, and to force the established groups to admit them as full partners in all institutions, from television networks to political offices.

These trends explain the timing and success of the Black Revolution. They also account for the period of intensified domestic conflict, the violence of Right and Left, which have characterized the politics of adjustment.

The Blacks are a real constituency. The question is no longer Black power or White power, but how to orient, relate, and use the tremendous power which Blacks have already acquired and to which Whites now defer in many areas

where previously White supremacy ruled with impunity. The Black success has spawned a host of imitators and claimants within and without the Black community. As for middle-class white youth, the question arises as to whether they are in fact a *constituency?* Certainly, in numbers they have a potential far more awesome and overwhelming than that of the Blacks. But are they a constituency? Do they share a deep sense of common grievance? Do they really crave the responsibility of power? the drudgery of administering the complex and thankless tasks of public policy and government—sewage treatment? mail delivery? educational planning and scholarship? Are they united by overriding interests? or divided by the same pluralism that divides their elders?

If an observer puts the slogans and clichés aside, it soon becomes clear that among the young people themselves are deeper cleavages and gaps than those between the generations. Recent events and numerous studies reveal that young people are fractured, fractious, and various.[27] They are not a constituency. In fact, many of the troublesome rituals of political violence arise from this. Irrational forms of extremism, counterproductive, unpolitical, and self-destructive tactics currently in use, demonstrate this point. Even with help from state legislators and police departments, who through intimidation and repression tend to foster a degree of political unity among the young, the young people may be too divided and disparate to provide the kind of constituency that can lead to positive and constructive reintegration and sharing of power in reformed civil institutions.

After two years of enormous success,

27. See study by Urban Research Corporation, "Student Protests, 1969" (Chicago, January 1970). A summary of the findings is in *The New York Times*, January 14, 1970, p. 51.

SDS dissolved into a mélange of factionalism and futility. Having aroused the sleeping giant of American college youth as it has never been aroused before in American history, the promoters and organizers fell into disarray. Some of them began experimenting with tactics which alienated vast uncommitted groups. The rituals of guerrilla tactics, the bombing, vandalism, anonymous hit-and-run tactics, the anonymity of the leaders of each day's tactics, the demand in advance for amnesty, the refusal to negotiate demands—all these stylized rituals represented not principled testing of authority but rather catharsis, trauma, and action for its own sake or for solidifying a remnant of a faction by high-risk commitments.

THE POLITICS OF YOUTH

The youth cult has been co-opted. Many corporation executives wear long hair and sideburns, some sporting bell-bottom multicolored trousers and brilliant waist sashes. The leading fashion designers have adopted hippie styles, while the wives of suburbia are furnishing their homes with psychedelia.

The culture forms and rituals of the "flower children," including leading performers of "acid rock," sexual freedom in the media, the language of "uptight" and "turn-on," provide the season's most popular television series. The so-called "underground" is now so far above ground that middle-aged investors are signing up rock groups and building strangely incongruous lines of latrines across the countryside where the youth tribes may reassemble. AM and FM radio stations across the country don the "underground" style; the *Village Voice* becomes as respectable as *The New York Times,* and is purchased as an investment by a conglomerate holding company. Abbie Hoffman franchises a shirt manufacturer to produce his American flag shirt, and Jerry Rubin grants a sweatshirt manufacturer the right to use the title of his book (*Do It!*).

Student radicals appear thus far to have failed to create a youth culture or a youth constituency, as well as failed in their efforts to align themselves with the Black militants and with the "working class." The disaffected groups in our country seem to be going back to "working through the system" and looking for ways to bring influence to bear through the political process.

There is a self-limiting quality in ritual rebellion and high-intensity tactics of protest. It is impossible to sustain the level of excitement. Most people respond to persistent disorder by raising the threshold of sensitivity. A higher degree of disorder becomes bearable, thereby denying the instigators of disorder the fruits of their efforts.

Readers of Daniel Bell's *The End of Ideology* are astonished to find youth going back to Marx and Lenin, Trotsky, Mao, Che, Regis Debray, and Frantz Fanon. To some, it is something of a pity to see the exuberant early slogans of the youth movement suddenly revert to the leaden hues of rigid ideology. This is perhaps an attempt to hold together by the ritual of ideology the remnants of a movement for which the rituals of political action are collapsing.

Much of this can be explained, not as politics (although having political effects) but as ritual and culture. In a recent documentary film, French movie producer Frederick Rossif comes to the same conclusion about violence in America. "Everything in America is a spectacle, everything answers to a profound and original rhythm—strikes, music, a presidential election, baptism of Blacks in the Mississippi, crazy speculation in Wall Street." Everything in America is transformed into art, entertainment, and music. "The Charleston, jazz, assembly-line work, hunger

marches, billionaires and public enemies—everything is animated by a vital
sense of growth that left Europe a long
time ago. In American brutality there
is less underhanded egotism than in the
apparent gentleness of European life." [28]

Not only are purely entertainment
shows aspects of culture symbolism and
forms, but even *news* plays a similar
ritual role. The focus of attention and
perspective on events tends to reflect the
underlying symbolic consensus of a
culture and a time. The media in a
sense transmit a wide variety of acts
which are designed to get attention, to
dramatize and display value patterns of
conflict groups. The media merely extend the range, scope, and speed by
which the symbolic and ritual dimension
of behavior is communicated. Real
events and pseudo-events blend in an
omelet that cannot be unscrambled.
The moon landing, the funeral of JFK
or of Martin Luther King, Jr., an eclipse
of the sun, a campus riot, all of these
blend and merge into a uniform ritual
indistinguishable from wholly pseudo-
events like a sports match or a St.
Patrick's Day parade. Although many

28. Quoted in *The New York Times*, April
13, 1970, p. 13.

events are not artificially contrived,
every event contains a strong element of
contrivance on the part of the actor.

All state systems and societies must
integrate into the power structure at
least those groups that are self-conscious, organized, interested, and capable
of exercising private power in some
manner, especially if excluded from the
formal vantage points of institutional
and economic power. This is true of the
Blacks, as it is of many new groups who
are demanding recognition. Should the
young emerge as a genuine constituency,
then they must be assimilated into the
vantage points of power. This is already a trend—with the lowering of the
voting age, reform of the draft system,
and the election of under-thirty candidates to university and corporation
boards and other public bodies. The
prospect before us is continued change
and clamorous demands from many
quarters for attention. Conflict is an
essential aspect of growth, one that we
can neither fully control nor prevent,
nor should we wish to do so. Yet, social
life exhibits a strong strain toward
humanizing power and dampening extreme oscillations of change. Ritual is
one of the important social processes
that aids these ends.

7

The Legitimation of Violence

by SANDRA J. BALL-ROKEACH

Sandra J. Ball-Rokeach is presently a visiting assistant professor in the Department of Sociology, University of Western Ontario, while on a leave of absence from Michigan State University. She was co-director, Task Force on Mass Media and Violence for the National Commission on the Causes and Prevention of Violence. She is co-author of Media and Violence *(With Robert K. Baker).*

THE main purpose of this chapter is to explore some neglected aspects of the legitimation of violence. Conditions which affect the legitimacy of violent behavior, different types of involvement in violent behavior, and the ways in which violence is commonly justified are examined. In the latter portion of the chapter, questions are posed concerning the possible role of television programming and practices relative to the legitimation of violence.

In everyday language, "violence" typically refers to illegitimate or undesirable forms of activity. Gang fights, for example, are called acts of violence, while the behavior of soldiers killing one another on a battlefield is likely to be referred to in terms of heroism, courage, or patriotism. An elaborate system of official and unofficial sanctions reinforces these definitions.

The social force of labelling actions as "violent" or "nonviolent" goes deep into the structure of our society. In the political realm, coercive power in the form of legitimated violence rests largely with representatives of political institutions. These representatives may legitimately employ physical force to protect and maintain political institutions, while those who seek power or who seek to attack political institutions may not legitimately use physical force. Although the kind of physical force used in both instances may be identical, the actions of those attacking existing political institutions are far more likely to be identified as acts of violence.

This labelling process is an interesting research problem for social scientists, and it has been much commented on in recent years.[1] However, research on violence, much like previous research on prejudice, deviant behavior, or conflict, often suffers by witting or unwitting adoption of pre-judgments. Most particularly, certain types of questions are unlikely to occur to investigators who assume that violence is illegitimate:

1. How does violence become legitimated or how does it lose its legitimacy?

2. What are the manifest and latent functions of violence for individuals, groups, collectivities, or societies? For example, under what conditions is violence an effective way of bringing attention to a cause, clarifying issues, or promoting inter-group communication?

3. Why does symbolic violence, such as the use of obscene language, call forth intense reactions?

4. Is the threat of violence or violence itself an important facet of maintaining a democratic form of government? To what extent, for example, does the threat of violence provide organized minorities with bargaining power that they would not otherwise possess?

For purposes of this discussion, violence is defined as the threat or exertion of physical force which could cause bodily injury. This definition permits neutrality with respect to legitimacy. It also allows the investigator to avoid the whole issue of the intent of the person employing physical force.

LEGITIMACY AND VIOLENT BEHAVIOR

Legitimacy is defined here as a collective judgment that attributes the qualities of "goodness" or "morality" or "righteousness" to behavior. The ascription of legitimacy is a powerful social force having important consequences for the manner in which persons regard themselves as well as how they will be regarded and treated by others. Persons engaged in legitimated violent behavior are rewarded by others

1. See, for example, Howard S. Becker, *Outsiders* (New York: Free Press, 1963); and Howard S. Becker, ed., *The Other Side* (New York: Free Press, 1964).

with praise, acceptance, status, etc. They can also see themselves as moral, responsible, and good people because their behavior is so regarded by themselves and others.

When a person or group participates in legitimated violent behavior, no social forces are precipitated which would lead them to question why they behaved violently, or even to label the behavior as "violent." Thus, justifications of legitimated violence are neither so necessary nor as likely to occur.

However, there are probably only a very few situations in which an act of violence is clearly legitimate in the eyes of all concerned. Legitimacy is a complex social product which reflects peoples' subjective states—attitudes, values, needs—as well as their objective states—structural position, rank, etc. Variations in the evaluations of the legitimacy of violent acts can be expected whenever people vary greatly in terms of such subjective and objective variables.

Subjective and objective characteristics of assailants and victims also affect legitimacy judgments. For example, evaluations of the legitimacy of killing may depend upon such things as the known or imputed motives and values of the assailant and victim, and the occupation, life style, race, age, or sex of the assailant and victim.

Thus, evaluations of the legitimacy of any specific act of violence will be the product of salient subjective and objective characteristics of the evaluators and the perceived subjective and objective characteristics of the assailant and victim.

Although there may be sharp disagreement about how an act of violence should be evaluated, legitimacy judgments which are enforced via formal social controls in any society are those of the dominant or powerful groups in that society. Indeed, the relative freedom to define which acts of violence are legitimate and illegitimate, and to enforce these judgments, is an important source of power in a society.

A common correlate of political conflict is intense disagreement about the right of dominant groups to employ violence as a means of maintaining power and of preventing minority groups from achieving power. The deep political conflicts between Blacks and Whites, for example, are reflected in their different evaluations of the legitimacy of police violence.*

Data collected in a national survey of a representative sample of adults shows a high degree of consensus between Blacks and Whites in their evaluations of legitimacy of violent acts except when the person employing violence is a policeman.[2] Policemen are regarded by many Blacks as the direct implementors of both the position of power and codes of moral/legal conduct of White society. Many Blacks also see themselves as the most likely victims of police violence. Thus, it is not surprising to find that Blacks attributed legitimacy to acts of violence committed by policemen much less frequently than did Whites.

CONDITIONS WHICH LEAD TO JUSTIFICATIONS OF VIOLENCE

Justification refers to an explanation or rationalization of behavior. Justifications for violent actions are not inherently properties of events, but develop as part of events in process. When legitimacy of a violent act is clear and unquestioned, evaluation in the form of justification is "built in" to the event.

*Editor's note: see also Chapter 23, below.

2. R. K. Baker and S. J. Ball, *Violence and the Media*, A Report to the National Commission on the Causes and Prevention of Violence (Washington, D.C.: U.S. Government Printing Office, 1969), pp. 341–358.

When this is not the case, justification becomes problematic.

Lack of Consensus Concerning Legitimacy

1. Effects on violent actors.

Violence in war, in campus demonstrations, abortion, capital punishment, euthanasia, attacks on civilian populations during war, and corporal punishment of children are all acts of violence about which there is disagreement or low consensus with respect to their legitimacy. When these acts occur, some people may respond with approval, others with disapproval, and still others may make no overt response. The effect of low consensus regarding legitimacy judgments upon persons or groups who commit acts of violence depends, in part, upon the social psychological distance between the actor and the persons who regard his acts as illegitimate. It depends also on legal status of the act.

When the person committing an act of violence is in a close social psychological relationship with persons who regard his behavior as illegitimate, such as a friendship or family relationship, he is likely to feel a need to justify his actions to these persons. The intent of justification, in this case, is to persuade others that the violent behavior should be regarded as legitimate so that informal punishments, such as disapproval or rejection, will not occur. The need to justify will be directly related to the level of punishment which the violent actor anticipates and the degree to which he values his relationship with these persons.

These are cases where an act of violence is committed which is evaluated as legitimate by all persons in a close relationship to the violent actor, but which is legally defined as illegitimate. Klu Klux Klan bombers of Black churches in the South, for example,

may have encountered little informal or interpersonal negative evaluations of the legitimacy of their acts, but still had to anticipate severe formal punishments if they were apprehended by law enforcement authorities. In such cases, if the violent actors are apprehended, they will either attempt to evade or deny the charges or, failing this, offer extenuating circumstances as justifications for their behavior in the hope of reducing or removing threatening legal punishments.

Low consensus does not in and of itself lead violent actors to offer justifications for their behavior. For there are instances of violence about which there is intense disagreement with respect to legitimacy, but which don't require justification. For example, there are different evaluations of the legitimacy of parental use of corporal punishments as a method of discipline and punishment; yet many parents spank, whip, or strap their children without ever feeling the need to justify their behavior. The need to justify such violent behavior is likely to be low because legal legitimacy is not involved (except in case of clear excess), and there is much support for exercising a strong hand in the discipline of children.

Low consensus creates a situation of potential threat to violent actors insofar as there are differences of opinion about the legitimacy of actions. The violent actor's need to justify will hinge on how seriously he regards the views of those who view his behavior as illegitimate and the extent to which his self-esteem and welfare are threatened by others' negative evaluations of his behavior.

2. Issues regarding violent acts.

Low consensus regarding the legitimacy of violent acts may directly precipitate justification processes involving persons who have never committed these acts. When disagreement becomes visible, the legitimacy status of an act of violence, such as capital punishment or abortion, may become an issue.

When legitimated violent acts become issues for public debate, they generally take the form of a challenge to the validity of justifications which are the rationale for legitimacy. However, advocates favoring the legitimacy of a violent act customarily resort to reiteration of established justifications.

Thus, when the legitimacy status of a violent act becomes an issue, the main focus and content of the ensuing debate is the validity of justifications offered as a rationale for the attribution of legitimacy.

Ambiguity Regarding Legitimacy

When legitimacy is ambiguous, it is difficult for people to know how to react to violent acts, and for violent actors to evaluate themselves or predict how others will evaluate them. Violent actors are likely to seek to resolve ambiguity by offering justifications for their behavior which are intended to convince themselves and others that their actions are legitimate. Persons who feel the need to react in a meaningful manner will also seek to resolve ambiguity. Resolution may entail rejection or acceptance of justifications offered by the actors, or the reactor formulating his own justification for deciding that the violent act should be regarded as legitimate or illegitimate.

Two primary sources of ambiguity with respect to the legitimacy of violent acts are (1) lack of knowledge and (2) value conflict.

1. Lack of knowledge.

When novel acts of violence are introduced, such as the atom bombing of Hiroshima, people have so little knowledge about the effects of the act and the motivations of the actors that legitimacy judgments may be withheld until such knowledge becomes available. In the case of Hiroshima, use of the bomb by the victorious Americans justified, for many, the violent act. When some people began to doubt that the bomb had been decisive in ending the war, however, the legitimacy of its use came under severe attack.

Hearings held to assess the legitimacy of police or citizen acts of violence often take place when there is ambiguity about the necessity of such acts. In such cases, specific information about the situation in which violence occurred is often required before evaluations of legitimacy can be made. The killings of students at Kent State and Jackson State have been examined by a number of groups seeking to resolve exactly this sort of ambiguity. Most investigating groups seemed to be trying to determine if the violent acts of the guardsmen were a legitimate application of their rights of self-defense.

2. Value conflict.

Many acts of violence on the contemporary scene elicit contradictory legitimacy judgments arising out of value conflicts. Some revolutionaries, for example, have little trouble legitimating their collective acts of violence against property, but appear to experience ambiguity about the legitimacy of acts which result in injury or death to persons. The common practice of giving prior warning when a building is to be bombed may be regarded as an attempt to resolve the ambiguity arising from the possibility that violence against property will also lead to violence against persons. In the case where an "innocent" person is killed in a bombing, the political values of the revolutionary may lead him to regard this act as legitimate, while his humanitarian values may lead to quite an opposite evaluation. He may seek to resolve this ambiguity either by changing his values with regard to violence against persons, thereby removing his value conflict, or by formulating a justification which will permit him to evaluate his behavior as legitimate (for example, loss of life was accidental and everything possible was done to avoid it, but when you're a revolutionary, you must accept such unfortunate events as inevitable).

Illegitimacy.

When an act of violence occurs which is consensually regarded as illegitimate, persons or groups committing the act often attempt to justify their behavior. Violent actors who have been caught "red-handed" in such behavior may offer justifications aimed at gaining sympathy or understanding. A man who murders his wife, for example, might point to the incorrigibility and disloyalty of his wife as the cause of this "immoral" act.[3]

Similar modes of justification which may be offered by persons who admit having committed illegitimate acts of violence consists of shifting or denying responsibility. For example, a gang rape may be presented as an entirely victim-precipitated event, thereby shifting some of the onus and blame for this illegitimate act to the victim.

While most persons who commit illegitimate acts of violence would probably seek to evade informal and formal punishments and to obviate the need for justification to others, they still may have to find a way to justify their behavior to themselves. In this case, the major motivation for justification would be protection of self-esteem. They may, for example, tell themselves that the world is a jungle in which everyone resorts to violence when they need to, so they are no dif-

ferent, or that they have been so mistreated, deprived, and unlucky when behaving non-violently that they have finally seen that violence and taking what you want is the only way for them to succeed.

LEGITIMATION AND DE-LEGITIMATION

Change in the boundaries of legitimate violent activities may be either a consequent or determinant of changes in both subjective and objective conditions of groups. An example of the former is found in the worldwide development of revolutionary groups. As Palestinian refugees, American Blacks, students, and French Canadian separatists developed increasingly negative attitudes towards established governments and became increasingly convinced that nonviolent means of bringing about social change were ineffective, they began to extend their definitions (boundaries) of the legitimacy of violence to include destruction of property and, later, political kidnapping and assassination.

Such changes in the legitimation of violence by militants, in turn, has been a major determinant of changes in non-militants' attitudes toward dissenters, including the legitimation of increasingly violent means of controlling dissent and revolutionary activities. Perhaps the most visible indicator of imminent change in the legitimacy status of violent acts is found in the polarization of justifications offered for those acts. Such polarization may be viewed as a prelude to the collective re-examination of the legitimacy of violence.

The process of legitimation, whereby an act of violence which was at one time judged illegitimate becomes legitimated, does not usually occur without the intervening process of articulation of justifications and successful persuasion of groups to accept the validity of

3. Cf. David Matza, *Delinquency and Drift* (New York: Prentice-Hall, 1964); David Matza, *Becoming Deviant* (New York: Prentice-Hall, 1969).

those justifications as sufficient for a change in legitimacy status.[4]

Likewise, the process of de-legitimation usually entails effective attacks upon justifications which persuade people that an act of violence should no longer be considered legitimate. Corporal punishment in the public schools, third degree methods of interrogation, and flogging of prison inmates are all acts of violence which have undergone the process of de-legitimation in recent American history.

Consensus with regard to the legitimacy status of a violent act declines with polarization, but is restored once new definitions have been agreed upon. The process is never complete, though periods of ferment—sometimes including violence—and stability follow one another. Because change in legitimacy status often has direct and different implications for the political or economic welfare of groups, inter-group conflict is likely, wherein one group attempts to maintain while another seeks to change legitimacy status. Groups in power have considerable advantage in this process, in part because of their greater access to the mass media.

Successful completion of the process of legitimation is evident when people no longer refer to an act as violent. Conversely, successful de-legitimation is evidenced when the label of violence becomes incorporated into common language references to those acts.

4. As Robert E. Park indicated many years ago. See his discussion of role played by war, revolutions, and the strike in changing collective representations concerning a variety of issues. See Park's "Introduction" to E. T. Hiller, *The Strike: A Study in Collective Action* (Chicago: University of Chicago Press, 1928). See also Short's application of these notions to contemporary violence in James F. Short, Jr., *The Social Fabric of the Metropolis* (Chicago: University of Chicago Press, 1971), pp. xliii–xliv.

DEHUMANIZATION: A METHOD OF OBVIATING THE NEED FOR JUSTIFICATION

In most societies, violence of certain kinds is accepted without any question as to its legitimacy, and therefore is never labeled "violence." Perhaps the most common kind of living object against whom people are given free license to use violence are certain animals and insects. Killing a "bug" is not considered an act of violence or in any way illegitimate because bugs are devalued. No social or psychological forces are therefore activated which would require justifications.

Throughout the history of mankind there have been numerous instances in which human beings have been similarly devalued or bestialized; violence against them is regarded in much the same way as violence against non-human objects. Slaves, women, heathens, members of ethnic, religious, and racial outgroups have been dehumanized to the point where they are regarded as chattel or beasts to be trained or controlled by physical force.

Dehumanization may sometimes be deliberately planned in order to facilitate participation in violence with minimum qualms about morality legitimacy. Soldiers in wartime, for example, may be taught to regard the "enemy" as something less than human.

Once dehumanization of the victims of violence has been successful, the idea that such actions are violent is no longer necessary. Devaluation of human beings against whom violence is perpetrated obviates the need for justifications of violence.

COMMON MODES OF JUSTIFICATION OF VIOLENCE

Three common types of justifications of violence are evident from an informal examination of historical and current events. They are probably not mutually exclusive, nor are they likely to be exhaustive.

1. Violence as a means to desired ends.

Values play a primary role in justifications of violence. Terminal values, or preferred states of existence, are frequently the ends for which violence is employed. Several sub-types of this mode can be identified:

A. Security and survival (e.g., Israeli bombings of Egypt, or an individual who kills to defend himself).

B. Social control and law and order (e.g., parent spanking a disobedient child, police clubbing unruly demonstrators, or capital punishment).

C. Social change (e.g., French, American, and Russian Revolutions).

D. Progress and growth (e.g., treatment of the Indians and Mexicans in the westward expansion).

E. Winning or success (e.g., football games or boxing).

F. Entertainment (e.g., gladiator matches, or television watching).

G. Education (e.g., instilling and enforcing societal values via violent means, such as corporal punishment).

2. Duty and obedience.

Throughout man's history, obedience to the commands of a supernatural being has been employed as a justification for violence. Responsibility for making certain ends mandatory or desirable is attributed to forces beyond man's control. The Crusades and the Salem witch burnings are examples of violence justified in the context of obedience to a supernatural being.

Similar justifications are offered by persons who disclaim responsibility for their violent actions on the ground that they were simply obeying orders. Subordinates in a hierarchical command structure, such as the military, have referred to their values of duty and obedience to justify their participation in violence. This mode of justification was typical at the Nuremberg War Crimes trials, and may be heard once again in the trials of soldiers allegedly involved in the My Lai massacre.

3. Extenuating circumstances.

A third mode of justification emphasizes the loss of personal control over one's behavior. In such cases, participants in violence may justify their behavior by reference to "extenuating circumstances" such as fear, exhaustion, temporary insanity, demon possession, or the influence of drugs or alcohol.

TYPES OF PARTICIPATION IN VIOLENCE

Attention may be drawn to three types of participation in violence: advocacy, action, and reaction. For the most part, the roles of advocacy and reaction have been neglected, while the action role has received considerable attention by the public and by social scientists. It is probably necessary to consider all three in order to understand and explain the many ramifications of violence, particularly legitimization and de-legitimization of violence.

Advocacy

Advocates of violence, whether they be national leaders, political theorists, revolutionaries, or counter-revolutionaries, have played significant roles in the genesis, maintenance, and ideological justification of violent behavior. The Weathermen, Nazi officials, or the founding fathers of America, for example, have provided ideological justifications for violence. In the case of the Nazis and the founding fathers of

America, these justifications were accepted and became the basis of legitimated violence.

Advocacy can play an essential role in maintaining or altering conceptions of legitimate violence. For example, debates on the repeal of abortion laws usually involve advocates who attempt to alter the conception of abortion as an illegitimate act of violence against the unborn, and other advocates who seek to maintain that conception.

A more subtle form of advocacy and way of maintaining the legitimacy status of violent behavior is evident in public ceremonies rewarding or honoring persons who have taken violent actions. When the President awards the Medal of Honor to a soldier for killing the "enemy," the President is playing the role of advocating a certain form of legitimated violence.

Advocacy can also be essential in the de-legitimization of violence. Abolitionists successfully attacked the brutal treatment of slaves and, indeed, the whole institution of slavery as inhuman. Advocates against violence have also played significant roles in the de-legitimization of violent treatment of prison inmates, suspects in criminal investigations, bacteriological warfare, disarmament of police on some campuses, etc.

Action

Acts of violence, particularly illegitimated acts, are the primary reason for public concern about violence. In regard to the topic of legitimization of violence, violent actions which elicit justifications are perhaps the most salient. Specifically, interest lies with those violent actions which, by their relationship to advocacy and reaction, precipitate change in the boundaries of legitimated violence.

Reaction

There are at least two types of reactions to violence: evaluations and overt behavior responses. The former is central to the problem of legitimization, while the latter is an essential consideration for analysis of the dynamics of violence.

Overt evaluative reactions, such as approval or disapproval, are not only the most direct indicators of the legitimacy status of violent actions, but also act as social control mechanisms. As social control mechanisms, evaluative reactions reward legitimated violence and punish illegitimated violence, which has the effect of maintaining established legitimacy boundaries. Change in the legitimacy status of a violent act requires change in the nature of evaluative reactions.

People are not always in a position to express openly or act upon their evaluative reactions to violence. For example, the immediate problem of a college president faced with student violence is to devise a strategy of overt behavioral reaction which will put an end to the violence. He may personally think that the students who took violent actions are "bums" or self-righteous hypocrites. Public expression of such evaluations would probably seriously aggravate the situation. Thus, he may feel forced to keep his evaluative reactions private, at least until the threat of violence has subsided. Likewise, the college president's overt behavioral response may not necessarily be dictated by his private evaluations, but by the strategic requirements of the situation.

During this brief analysis of the conditions which gives rise to justification and legitimization of violence, little has been said about *how* people learn or alter conceptions of the legitimacy of violence. This issue is examined in terms of one major source of exposure to violence: television. Specifically, we ask, what role does television play, via its programming and practices, in the legitimization of violence.

TELEVISION AND THE LEGITIMIZATION OF VIOLENCE: QUESTIONS FOR FUTURE RESEARCH

Of all mass media, television is the most accessible, utilized, and credible.[5] Violence, whether it be in news or entertainment programs, is a pervasive element in television presentations.

Television viewing is the primary vehicle through which the majority of persons come into contact with violence. Via television, millions of people have the daily opportunity to observe and, thus, indirectly participate in real and fictional violent events. Both legitimated violence, such as occurs in war and football games, and violence which is defined as illegitimate, such as assault or murder, are frequently presented and observed.

Television Programming

Since the advent of television, citizens and social scientists have been concerned about the effects of mass exposure to television programs, particularly violent programs. This concern has most commonly focused on the effects of violent entertainment programs upon children. The "effects question" which has been given the most public and scientific consideration is most often phrased as: "Does exposure to television portrayals of violence increase the probability that audience members will engage in illegitimated violent actions?".

Reviews of the social science research on this "effects" issues are available in the literature.[6] The research which is most relevant to the question of the legitimization of violence is that of Bandura and others regarding observational learning of violent actions from audio-visual portrayals of violence.[7] Bandura has shown that children can learn violent actions by observing models in audio-visual portrayals, and, under certain conditions, will overtly engage in learned violent acts.

An observational learning approach to the study of the television effects can be extended to include effects which are directly related to the legitimation of violence. The following questions are examples of the kinds of effects and research questions which would be important to consider.

If people learn violent actions from observation of television portrayals of violence, do they also learn:

1. Overt behavioral reactions to violence?

2. Conceptions of legitimated and illegitimated violence?

3. Modes of justification for violence?

4. Evaluative reactions to violence?

These questions would be equally ap-

5. Jack Lyle, "Contemporary Functions of the Mass Media," in R. K. Baker and S. J. Ball, op. cit., pp. 187–216.

6. For example, see Richard Goranson, "A Review of Recent Literature on Psychological Effects of Media Portrayals of Violence," in R. K. Baker and S. J. Ball, ibid., pp. 395–413.

7. For example, see Albert Bandura, "Influence of Models, Reinforcement Contingencies on the Acquisition of Imitative Responses," Journal of Personality and Social Psychology 1 (1965), pp. 589–595; A. Bandura, D. Ross and S. A. Ross, "Transmission of Aggression Through Imitation of Aggressive Models," Journal of Abnormal and Social Psychology 63 (1961), pp. 575–582; A. Bandura, J. Grusec, and F. Menlove, "Observational Learning as a Function of Symbolization and Incentive," Child Development 37 (1966), pp. 499–506; D. Hicks, "Imitation and Retention of Film-Mediated Aggressive Peer and Adult Models," Journal of Personality and Social Psychology 2 (1965), pp. 97–100.

plicable to news as well as entertainment programming, and legitimated as well as illegitimated violent actions and reactions.

Perhaps the most important effect to consider in this regard is learned *evaluative reactions* to violent actions. For to the extent that people learn evaluative reactions, they are also learning justifications for violence and conceptions of legitimated and illegitimated violence.

In many respects, the social implications of people learning evaluative reactions to violence from television programs are more significant than those of learning violent actions. One reason is that many persons may learn violent actions, but they are rarely in a situation in which they can act upon this learning. This is not the case with respect to learned evaluative reactions. It is difficult to go through a day without hearing about or observing acts of violence via exposure to the mass media. Thus, most persons have daily encounters with situations in which they may employ evaluative reactions to violence learned from television.

The social and political impact of violent actions is mediated, and sometimes determined, by the manner in which people react. For example, intensely disapproving reactions to the violent actions of a few political protesters have led to public support of new "riot" control laws, increased appropriations for police personnel and equipment, and an extension of legitimated techniques of crowd control, to name a few consequences. In this case, violent actions had little significance in terms of property damage or injury to persons, but precipitated evaluative reactions which have had far-reaching social and political consequences.

In order to examine the long-run effects of television programming on the legitimization of violence, questions which go beyond strictly observational learning effects would have to be considered. For example:

1. What effect does television programming have on broadening or narrowing established boundaries of legitimated violence?

2. To what extent are the conceptions of legitimated and illegitimated violence, modes of justification, and reactions to violence presented in television programming similar to those present in society?

3. To what extent does prolonged exposure to television portrayals of violence produce a generally affectless reaction to violent events?

4. What effect does the role of TV "good guys" who employ violence as a means to their own personal ends have upon children's conceptions of legitimated violence?

5. Is violence which is *labelled* "violence" treated differently in news broadcasts than violence which is not so labelled? For example, are justifications given by the persons advocating or engaging in violent actions presented in both instances?

Each of these questions has direct implications for the role of television programming in the legitimization of violence.

Television News Practices

It may also be worthwhile to explore briefly the question of how television news practices affect the legitimation of violence. News practices with respect to coverage of violent actions can, in themselves, be considered evaluative or overt behavioral reactions to violence. Violence is regarded by most newsmen as newsworthy, an evaluative reaction to violence *per se*. Spectacular violent events elicit almost immediate on-the-scene coverage, an overt behavioral reaction.

A number of questions can be asked about the effects of television newsmen's reactions to violence upon the legitimization of violence. It is widely believed, for example, that violent actions are engaged in by protesters in order to provoke even greater violence by police so as to draw the attention of news media. Do leaders of social movements who advocate or engage in violence gain in status or power as a result of news coverage?

Television provides a key communication link between people who advocate or engage in violent actions and people who react to such behavior. Television, therefore, has the potential to enter the legitimation and de-ligitimation process in a most significant manner. Doubtless it is doing so, but systematic knowledge of its effects is lacking.

Concluding Remarks

Violence, regardless of whether it is labelled as such, is a common form of individual and collective activity. Some forms of violence, particularly those involving collectivities, can operate as effective mechanisms of maintenance and change of society. Violence plays an indispensable role in power acquisition and maintenance. Those who have the freedom which derives from the right to use legitimated violence are in a much better position to acquire or maintain power than are persons lacking this freedom to challenge it successfully. Any change which extends or restricts the boundaries of legitimated violence is likely to affect directly the distribution of power, thereby affecting the nature of social relations within and between groups.

This relationship between power and violence is only one major reason why it is important to understand the processes of legitimation and de-legitimation of violence. Legitimation and de-legitimation of violence having significant political and social consequences does not occur without advocates, justifications, and alteration of public reactions and conceptions. Often violent actions precipitate consideration of the issues. This discussion only scratches the surface of the range of questions and issues that will have to be considered before we will be able to explain and predict changes in the legitimation and de-legitimation of violent behavior.

8

The Controversy Surrounding Analyses of Collective Violence: Some Methodological Notes

By Richard A. Berk

Richard A. Berk, Ph.D., is an assistant professor in the Sociology Department and Center for Urban Affairs, Northwestern University; formerly a research associate in the Department of Social Relations, Johns Hopkins University, and lecturer in Sociology, Goucher College. He is co-author with Peter H. Rossi of a book on class and racial conflict in American cities, to appear late in 1971; and has authored articles in the areas of political sociology, social change, and methodology.

I wish to thank Lee Bradford for her help, and especially acknowledge the useful suggestions of Howard Becker and Peter Rossi.

ANALYSES of crowd behavior have continually generated vast amounts of controversy, and the sources of these debates can be traced in part to the consequences of many actions taken in this collective context.[1] Frequently there is violence and destruction of property. But probably more important in understanding the intensity of the dialogue is the fact that many kinds of crowds have significant political impact on important sectors of the larger society. The gathering of a crowd often suggests the presence of grievances and/or unmet needs, and actions taken by mobs can sometimes challenge the legitimacy of the social order. It should come as no surprise, then, that many analysts of collective behavior are acting on more than a casual academic interest in the subject.

This is not to say that research substantially motivated by personal and political concerns is bad. It is probably true that much of the best social science research is produced by effectively channeling such concerns. The problem with the controversy surrounding crowd behavior is that coupled with the intense motivation is a lack of good data on many crucial aspects of the phenomenon—a situation which too frequently finds researchers taking long speculative leaps from their data, causing all parties to talk past each other. Scarcity of data which should encourage prudence, seems to encourage uncommon confidence. This chapter will examine the apparent paradox with the hope that an honest recognition of the absence of certain kinds of factual material and resulting potential distortions in analysis could temper the debate, and many of the more aggressively presented assertions might be then properly labeled as empirical questions.

1. For a good example of such a debate, see chapters 4 and 5 in this volume.

It is relatively easy to gather information about conditions *preceding* crowd behavior because most of the measurement techniques commonly employed by social scientists are applicable. One can look at demographic characteristics of the population in question, survey potential actors, and seek a variety of unobtrusive measures. Further, there is plenty of time to access the facts. Similarly, the *results* of crowd behavior are easily measured. Crowds usually leave plenty of data in their wake which can be analyzed in a relatively leisurely manner. In contrast, for many reasons mob process is extremely difficult to study. Some of the more common problems complicating the collection of such data are:

1. Events during crowd behavior usually occur rather quickly.
2. Many events occur at once.
3. Actions are often taking place over a relatively wide geographical area.
4. The occurrence of collective behavior is difficult to anticipate, so that investigators interested in the phenomenon usually miss the activities.
5. Mob processes (as compared to the results of mob processes) leave few traces, and frequently the best one can do is gather retrospective accounts.
6. Crowd participants are unlikely to take time out from what they are doing to cooperate with an investigator. And even if they would, the suspicion that a researcher might be a police officer or informant would mitigate against a sincere inter-action.
7. Crowd participants or persons who happen to be present during collective violence frequently have very salient vested interests in the interpretation of the phenomenon. Their accounts are thus especially

vulnerable to conscious and un-conscious distortions.[2]

8. The high risk of personal injury persuades many researchers to study crowds from a distance.

The relative ease in gathering data on conditions preceding crowd behavior, and on the results of the crowd behavior when combined with the extreme difficulties in gathering data on group processes, results in analyses of crowds that can best examine input and output, but little in between. One consequence is that many researchers wisely concentrate their analyses on the precursors of mob actions and on the results of mob actions. A perusal of most of the recent edited volumes on civil disorders, for example, will indicate that examinations of crowds *per se* get very limited attention.[3] A second consequence, and the one in which we shall be most interested here, is that some researchers choose to focus on the collective violence group process in spite of a lack of data on what crowds actually do, which makes their interpretations vulnerable to a number of potential distortions, especially when the investigator acts impulsively on his political and personal concerns.

We now turn to some of these interpretive pitfalls, noting in advance that although they are presented separately, in actual manuscripts they tend to occur together and inter-act.

Crowd behavior is sometimes characterized as implicitly irrational and/or other-worldly, and as a result crowds are seen as somehow demonic, or at least lacking in many of the more pedestrian human qualities found in other groups of people. Mob participants are viewed as transformed from their natural state into creatures of passion who cease to possess rational and moral thought. And even when such terms are not employed, too often crowds are viewed as mysterious phenomena in which individuals are caught up and lost.

The crowd, suddenly there where there was nothing before, is a mysterious and universal phenomenon. A few people may have been standing together—five, ten, or twelve, not more; nothing has been announced, nothing expected. Suddenly everywhere is black with people and more come streaming from all sides as though streets had only one direction.[4]

It seems reasonable to attribute parts of such interpretations to the fact that through scarcity of empirical data, individuals and small groups are indeed usually lost. What happens to people in crowds is an empirical question on which we have little information, and into this factual vacuum are drawn a variety of speculations—speculations that place crowd behavior above (or below) other group phenomena. With a lack of good information about mob process, concerned social commentators who feel compelled to make pronouncements about crowd behavior sometimes tell us more about themselves than the events. Analyses of mobs may then more closely approximate a projective test than an examination of collective behavior. In short, descriptions of crowds often take on an other-worldly flavor because we have little data with which to anchor crowds to this world.

A second interpretive pitfall is closely related to the first. In place of either good description or sound theory, one frequently finds extensive use of metaphor. Impulses surge through crowds,

2. For example, see John Hersey, *The Algiers Motel Incident* (New York: Bantam Books, 1968).

3. For example, see Louis H. Masotti and Don R. Bowen, *Riots and Rebellion* (Beverly Hills, Calif.: Sage Publications, Inc., 1968).

4. Elias Canetti, *Crowds and Power* (New York: Viking Press, 1966), p. 16.

mobs act without conscience, and riots are irrational. Part of the blame for the use of metaphors rests on sloppy thinking, but sloppy thinking is encouraged by the lack of data on mob process. In the absence of facts, one is tempted to slip into metaphors.

Slowly—in a pattern whose origins remained mysterious—a small number of *provocateurs* infiltrated the mob. They would go farther than the mass in confronting the police; when the chips were down, they were the ones who shouted orders. But as the ranks grew, the agitators became indistinguishable from others in the crowd. It was all one big frantic family.[5]

The frequent use of metaphor in a wide variety of social science analyses in spite of counter-methodological counselling suggests that the presence of metaphors cannot be cavalierly dismissed. Obviously, in some situations competent researchers find them useful. Probably the crucial notion underlying criticisms of metaphor is the degree to which they are employed to introduce into the analysis ideas that are not explicitly examined. Frequently a reader is left to sift through a number of carelessly implied connotations, and in some more insidious situations the author purposely uses metaphor to bring in ideas that would not stand up under scrutiny. In contrast, using metaphors to summarize ideas that have been analyzed or to introduce ideas that will later be thoroughly examined can be a handy, honest tool which frequently adds much needed color to otherwise bland manuscripts. Unfortunately, collective violence research, plagued by the absence of mob process data, too often resorts to metaphor in ways that obfuscate the issues.

5. Allan Priaulx and Sanford J. Ungar, *The Almost Revolution* (New York: Dell Publishing Company, 1969), p. 37.

A third interpretive pitfall stems from the several levels of analysis from which mob process may be viewed and the availability of data at the different levels. Generally, the larger the unit of analysis of crowds, the easier it is to gather information. For example, it may be fairly easy to chart the path of a riot through a shopping district of a city, but much harder to trace the actions of individuals. Similarly, it is easier to note the overall size of a crowd than to document who is talking to whom. One result of the relative ease of getting data on the larger levels is that researchers are influenced to build their analyses on theoretical constructs best employed on large aggregates. This in itself is not a problem, but too often one finds these collective concepts used to analyze the actions of individuals. Then, descriptions of mob behavior slide between several levels without the alteration of theoretical concepts to fit the unit under study. A statistical example of this kind of error can be found in the "ecological fallacy" when correlation coefficients are employed to explain behavior at the wrong level of analysis.

A similar danger emerges if concepts developed for smaller units are applied to larger units. Even when the investigator is explicit about his use at one level of analysis of concepts generated at another level, it is an open question whether explanation by what at best is analogy is especially useful.

The basic postulate here is that the standard practice by which any society or group defends itself against demoralizing tendencies are in some sense analogous to the characterological defenses of individuals. They mobilize sentiment and affect to support and maintain social solidarity. This mobilization of sentiments to uphold a threatened norm is evident in loyalty parades or propaganda rallies to counter-act "heresies."[6]

Probably many researchers should be more careful in noting the level of analysis from which the data is gathered and then apply concepts appropriate to that level. If analogies are to be employed, they should be seen as first approximations from which more useful concepts will be developed. One should keep in mind that the notion of structural strain tells us little about individuals in crowds, and the concept of rationality tells us little about the behavior of a group.

A fourth kind of interpretive pitfall involves the assumption that people in crowds tend to be motivated by the same interests or that they are nearly identical in other ways. Even when such notions as "group mind" are not used as metaphors, they can still obfuscate the issues by transforming empirical questions of individual similarities into assertions.

Within a crowd there is equality. This is absolute and indisputable and never questioned by the crowd itself. It is of fundamental importance and one might even define a crowd as a state of absolute equality. A head is a head, an arm is an arm, and differences between individual heads and arms are irrelevant. It is for the sake of this equality that people become a crowd and they tend to overlook anything that might detract from it.[7]

Part of an attempt to impose what may be artificial homogeneity on a crowd can be traced to a desire to build order from a variety of events, or to summarize—obviously useful enterprises. However, too often the homogeneity emerges because of an absence of data. People in crowds are viewed as similar because the crude methods of gathering facts fail to measure individual differences. In this light, such concepts as Smelser's "generalized belief" must be applied with extreme care and not be automatically attached to any active gathering of people. The researcher may be led to infer that there is a generalized belief simply because his data is not rich enough to show important individual variation. Similarly, Gary Marx's concept of "issueless riots" should be applied only when the data are of sufficient quality to make a "null" finding a reasonable conclusion.[8]

A fifth potential distortion comes from the tendency to speculate about mob process primarily from events preceding the collective behavior and from the results of the collective behavior. With little information about mob process, researchers are tempted to describe the intervening activities by some sort of extrapolation (forward or backward). This point is best illustrated by telling a story.

Picture a small group of scientists travelling across a desert. For two days they have been without water and finally they come upon a water hole. In spite of their extreme thirst, they are aware that the water could be poisonous and as a result do not immediately begin to drink. They hurriedly talk over the situation and try to ascertain if the drinking water would be dangerous. They consider such problems as alkaline content and bacteria that may be present in stagnant water. After several minutes of deliberation, one of the group volunteers to taste the water, and he judges that the water is fit to drink. At that point, everyone jumps into the water hole. All drink as much and as quickly as they can. Then they splash, bathe, and dance about. Most engage

6. Kurt Lang and Gladys Engel Lang, "Racial Disturbances as Collective Protest," in Louis H. Masotti and Don R. Bowen, op. cit., p. 122.

7. Canetti, op. cit., p. 29.

8. See Chapter 3 in this volume.

in horseplay, yelling and cheering. Eventually they fill up their canteens and move on.

If someone wanted to analyze the events above, think how the interpretation would be affected by the availability of data for different actions in the sequence. If only the facts about the thirst and the behavior in the water hole were known, one might characterize all of the behavior as impulsive, irrational, or childish—an example of man driven by the most rudimentary needs. In contrast, extrapolating forward from actions preceding those in the water hole would suggest that the men were probably operating in a sensible way and not swept up in the passions of the moment.

The point of the story is that collective violence involves a series of complex events and researchers who extrapolate forward from data preceding crowd behavior, and backward from the results of crowd behavior (or from only the most visible aspects of the mob processes), are speculating from data that may give a distorted picture of crowds. For example, the fact that a riot may not have accomplished a set of goals that one might attribute to the rioters (and it is not usually clear how one decides what the goals of the rioters were without good data on what occurred during the riot) may allow a commentator to say that the "tactics" were incorrect, but it does not permit a characterization of the processes operating in the crowd.[9] Yet too often this is just the kind of analysis that is presented.

This discussion should not be construed as attacking the technique of postulating intervening processes between measured independent and dependent variables (elaboration). The point is not to simply criticize the typical elaborative speculations about mob process, but rather to encourage researchers to gather data relevant to their speculations. One would hope that notions about mob process would compel investigators to seek data on what mobs actually do, and that in the relative absence of such data researchers would be more prudent in their assertions.

A good example of extrapolation and a series of resulting distortions can be seen in the interpretations of the 1964 Watts riot presented by the McCone Commission. Using as a primary data base the most visible consequences of the civil disorder and a variety of retrospective accounts, the riot participants were characterized as "riffraff"—a small proportion of the ghetto population who were principally from the lowest socioeconomic elements of the ghetto. Rioters were described as generally the unemployed, the least educated, the most recent migrants, and possessing the worst criminal records. As a result, the *crowd processes* were blamed on agitators and criminals whose sole purpose was to stir up trouble and/or loot local retail establishments. [10] More thorough data gathered in later civil disorders not only contradicted the "riffraff" theory but suggested that there was much more to riot behavior in Watts than the actions of agitators and criminals.[11] Clearly, political considerations had much to do with the "findings" of the McCone Commission, but

9. Turner and Killian have also made this point. See Ralph H. Turner and Lewis M. Killian, *Collective Behavior* (Englewood Cliffs, N.J.: Prentice-Hall, 1957), chap. 1.

10. *Violence in the City—An End or a Beginning, A Report by the Governor's Commission on the Los Angeles Riot,* December 2, 1965.

11. For example, see Robert M. Fogelson, "Who Riots? A Study of Participation in the 1967 Riots," in *Supplemental Studies for the National Advisory Commission on Civil Disorders* (Washington, D.C.: U. S. Government Printing Office, July 1968).

it would have been more difficult to impose such a convenient interpretation had there been better data on rioters and riot process.

A more recent example of similar analytical style can be seen in Banfield's *The Unheavenly City*.[12] After defining the lower class as those people who are incapable of planning for the future and stating that ghetto conditions are objectively not bad (and are improving), Banfield characterizes urban civil disorders of the late 1960's as "mainly for fun and profit." By describing preceding conditions in terms of psychological handicaps among ghetto dwellers and minimal objective poverty, he then extrapolates that the resulting mob processes *initiating* most civil disorders are due to the "animal spirits" of lower class male participants.[13] Banfield's preconditions of civil disorders are certainly debatable, but even given these preconditions, his extrapolations to the motivations of riot participants and mob processes are speculations at best, and are based on little data on what happens to crowds during urban riots. Unfortunately, the speculations are presented to the reader as if there were a wealth of empirical evidence in support of his analysis.

CONCLUSIONS

The social scientist speculating from limited data is not a new phenomenon, nor one that is limited to the study of crowd behavior. However, people who study crowds are often highly motivated by personal and political concerns and are plagued by a number of unique problems created by the differential accessibility of data. The relative absence

12. Edward C. Banfield, *The Unheavenly City* (Boston: Little Brown & Co., 1968), chap. 9.
13. Ibid, pp. 190, 197–198.

of information about mob process coupled with intense motivation means that some investigators feel compelled to "analyze" crowds and take a position on the issues when good judgment would suggest more caution. This situation is frequently aggravated by pressure on investigators from political groups (such as the Kerner Commission) to come up with "the answer."

The discussion above suggests that the shape of the controversy surrounding crowd behavior is a function of the motivation of the investigator and the kinds of data that are available in the study of crowds. It is probably undesirable (and impossible) to alter the motivation of students of collective violence. However, one might hope that social scientists who are interested in crowds might take more care to examine the bases of their assertions, and come to realize that if they are going to try to characterize mob process they will have to collect far more data on what happens in crowds. Preceding conditions and resulting consequences leave too much in the middle unmeasured.

It should also be clear that the five kinds of interpretive pitfalls, though discussed as analytically separate, rarely occur by themselves. Rather, they tend to interact, building on one another and reinforcing a picture of crowd behavior that may be fraught with inaccuracies. For example, metaphors based on preceding conditions in individuals are employed to characterize mobs as homogeneous and acting on "instinct." And if one looks for the empirical base of such explanations, one often finds poor data and sloppy interpretations. Thus, students of crowd behavior should be constantly vigilant about the sources of their material and wherever possible seek the original data, and not interpretations of that data.

Part III

Comparative Perspectives

9

Patterns in International Warfare, 1816-1965

By MELVIN SMALL AND J. DAVID SINGER

Melvin Small, Ph.D., is an associate professor in the History Department of Wayne State University. A specialist in American diplomatic history, he is editor of Public Opinion and Historians *(1970) and co-author of* The Wages of War 1816–1965: A Statistical Handbook *(1970). Professor Small was a recipient of an American Council of Learned Societies Study Fellowship and was a Fellow at the Center for Advanced Study in the Behavioral Sciences at Stanford, California.*

J. David Singer, Ph.D., is professor of Political Science at the University of Michigan and is also a research political scientist at the university's Mental Health Research Institute. Professor Singer is author of Financing International Organization *(1961),* Deterrence, Arms Control, and Disarmament *(1962), and co-author of* The Wages of War *(1970), and editor of* Human Behavior and International Politics *(1965) and* Quantitative International Politics *(1968). He was a Fulbright Fellow in Oslo in 1963–1964 and a visiting scholar at the Carnegie Endowment for International Peace in Geneva in 1967–1968.*

SINCE Thucydides, scholars and statesmen have speculated about the causes and consequences of conflict between nation states. Despite the earnest efforts of countless generations of investigators, it is only within the past several decades that any promising attack on the problem of the causes of war has been mounted. In our judgment, the important turning point in man's long quest to understand this recurrent phenomenon occurred in the 1930's, when Quincy Wright and Lewis Richardson began to employ operational, quantitative techniques in the description and analysis of the most pernicious product of international relations.[1]

Inspired by the work of these pioneers, and borrowing many of their methodological and theoretical innovations, we have initiated a project whose major objective is to identify the variables that are most frequently associated with the onset of war, from the Congress of Vienna to 1965.[2] Our first requirement was to describe and measure the dependent variable, and ascertain the trends and fluctuations in the frequency, magnitude, severity, and intensity of war during that period. This task has now been completed and the data base we have developed allows us to generalize with some degree of confidence about patterns in international violence over the last century and a

half.[3] Before we turn to such generalizations, however, we should explain briefly the data acquisition and coding procedures employed in our study.

IDENTIFYING THE WARS

Most major studies of war suffered from an absence of methodological precision and an invisibility of coding rules.[4] These practices often resulted in the impressionistic analysis by anecdote of a few famous and large wars by political theorists, or the hyper-empirical analysis of every conceivable sort of violence by scholars with a mathematical orientation. Aware of the pitfalls inherent in both approaches, we have adopted criteria and rules which we feel allow maximum practicality and efficiency but which do not violate intellectual standards of reliability and validity.

Thus, we began by delimiting the system in which we were interested. Although it would be useful to know something about violence in all polities for all recorded time periods, such an approach would find us laboring far into the foreseeable future in the often overgrown and uncultivated vineyards of the historians. The period since 1815, which is manageable in terms of the availability of historical sources, satisfies our need both for systemic conti-

---

1. Quincy Wright, *A Study of War*, 2 vols. (Chicago: University of Chicago Press, 1942); Lewis F. Richardson, *Statistics of Deadly Quarrels* (Chicago: Quadrangle, 1960). In the third volume of his *Social and Cultural Dynamics* (New York: American Book, 1937), Pitirim A. Sorokin also applied empirical techniques to a longitudinal study of warfare.

2. For a complete description of the project, see J. David Singer, "Modern International War: from Conjecture to Causality," in Albert Lepawsky et al., *Essays in Honor of Quincy Wright* (in press).

3. Most of the material in this article is reported in other forms in J. David Singer and Melvin Small, *The Wages of War, 1816–1965: A Statistical Handbook* (New York: John Wiley, 1970).

4. Even Wright and Richardson's pathbreaking works suffer from these shortcomings to some degree. Except for the most recent period, Wright did not order his study of wars in terms of magnitude or severity, nor did he present operational criteria for defining his universe. For his part, Richardson did not distinguish between the status of political entities engaged in conflict, nor was he interested in the casualties suffered by the separate participants in the wars he studied.

nuity and for a time span long enough to allow for any permutations in the level of violence to evidence themselves. Within these temporal bounds, we were concerned with wars fought by members of the international system against fellow members (interstate wars) and against independent or colonial entities which did not qualify for membership in the system (extrasystemic wars). To qualify for membership in the international system, a state needed to have a population of at least 500,000 and diplomatic recognition from legitimizers within the international community.[5] In the period after 1920, membership in the League of Nations or the United Nations was used as an alternate criterion in some cases. The adoption of such a scheme results in a system with 23 members in 1816, 34 in 1870, 61 in 1920, and 124 in 1965.

As for the wars themselves, we gathered data on those conflicts in which the battle-connected deaths for all systemic combatants taken together surpassed 1,000. A slightly more complicated procedure was used to determine the inclusion or exclusion of some extra-systemic wars.[6] (Civil wars, even those with foreign intervention, were not considered in this stage of the project.) All the qualifying wars were codified in terms of severity (or battle deaths of system-member participants) and magnitude (or total number of nation months that system-member partici-

pants spent in combat). The 93 wars which met our criteria are listed in chronological order in Table 1, with the 50 interstate wars shown in italics. Alongside each war is its rank position in terms of battle deaths, nation months, and a simple intensity measure—number of battle deaths divided by number of nation months.[7]

TRENDS AND CYCLES

After the basic data were reordered according to the amount of war begun, under way, and terminated each year, we were able to search for secular trends and periodicity over the past century and a half. Looking first at secular trends, contrary to what might have been expected, no trend, either upward or downward, is evident. That is, whether we concentrate upon frequencies, magnitudes, severities, or intensities, we do not find appreciably more or less war in any of the sub-epochs covered. Of course, there were more battle deaths in the twentieth century than in the nineteenth (thanks to the impact of the two World Wars and the Korean conflict), but when the figures are normalized for the number of nations in the system, this trend disappears. International war, therefore, appears to be neither on the rise nor the decline. It is true, however, that extra-systemic wars have been decreasing in frequency; but this is entirely a product of the liquidation of formal colonial empires and the expansion of the international system to include all independent entities.

While such findings might cheer those who intuitively feared that we have been experiencing an ever-increas-

5. A complete explanation of membership criteria is found in J. David Singer and Melvin Small, "The Composition and Status Ordering of the International System, 1815–1940," *World Politics* 18, no. 2 (January 1966), 236–282.

6. Because many nineteenth century imperial conflicts achieved a casualty level of 1,000 battle deaths only after five or ten years, we decided that such a conflict had to average 1,000 battle deaths a year for the system member in order to qualify for inclusion in our list.

7. Battle death and nation month scores for extra-systemic wars reflect only the war experiences of system members. Many of these wars would have ranked considerably higher on all indices had we included non-member battle deaths and nation months.

TABLE 1—BASIC LIST OF INTERNATIONAL WARS, 1816-1965
(N = 93)

NAME OF WAR	RANK POSITION		
	BATTLE DEATHS	NATION MONTHS	BATTLE DEATHS PER NATION MONTH
British-Maharattan, 1817–1818	73.5	70	68.5
Greek Independence, 1821–1828	37.5	12	70
Franco-Spanish, 1823	89	52.5	90.5
First Anglo-Burmese, 1823–1826	37.5	29	52
Dutch-Javanese, 1825–1830	37.5	17	70
Russo-Persian, 1826–1828	58	45	67
Navarino Bay, 1827	69	86.5	24.5
Russo-Turkish, 1828–1829	9	26.5	11
First Polish Insurrection, 1831	37.5	66	22
First Syrian, 1831–1832	46.5	52.5	46
Texan-Mexican, 1835–1836	89	70	83
First British–Afghan, 1838–1842	30	18	59
Second Syrian, 1839–1840	46.5	78.5	20
Peruvian-Bolivian, 1841	89	91	35
First British-Sikh, 1845–1846	78.5	83	54.5
Mexican-American, 1846–1848	34	19	60.5
Austro-Sardinian, 1848–1849	50.5	62.5	40
First Schleswig–Holstein, 1848–1849	55	47	62.5
Hungarian Revolution, 1848–1849	17.5	58	9
Second British–Sikh, 1848–1849	78.5	78.5	66
Roman Republic, 1849	73.5	70	68.5
La Plata, 1851–1852	82	56.5	85
First Turco-Montenegran, 1852–1853	58	81	26.5
Crimean, 1853–1856	6	6	17
Anglo-Persian, 1856–1857	73.5	65	72.5
Sepoy Mutiny, 1857–1859	66	35.5	82
Second Turco-Montenegran, 1858–1859	69	56.5	71
Italian Unification, 1859	26	70	14
Spanish-Moroccan, 1859–1860	46.5	62.5	35
Italo-Roman, 1860	89	91	35
Italo-Sicilian, 1860–1861	89	75	79.5
Franco-Mexican, 1862–1867	30	7	75.5
Second Polish Insurrection, 1863–1864	58	50	64.5
Ecuadorian-Columbian, 1863	89	91	35
Second Schleswig–Holstein, 1864	61	59.5	62.5
La Plata, 1864–1870	11	5	41.5
Spanish-Chilean, 1865–1866	89	47	92.5
Seven Weeks, 1866	23	49	16
Ten Years, 1868–1878	12	8	41.5
Franco-Prussian, 1870–1871	7	30	8
Dutch-Achinese, 1873–1878	55	16	87
Balkan, 1875–1877	46.5	38	57
Russo-Turkish, 1877–1878	5	43	3
Bosnian Insurrection, 1878	66	83	31
Second British Afghan, 1878–1880	63.5	43	72.5
British-Zulu, 1879	66	75	50
Pacific, 1879–1883	41	4	88.5
Franco-Indochinese, 1882–1884	61	31	75.5

TABLE 1—(Continued)

NAME OF WAR	RANK POSITION		
	BATTLE DEATHS	NATION MONTHS	BATTLE DEATHS PER NATION MONTH
Mahdist Insurrection, 1882–1885	30	21	54.5
Sino-French, 1884–1885	42	33	54.5
Central American, 1885	89	91	35
Serbo-Bulgarian, 1885	73.5	91	18
Sino-Japanese, 1894–1895	37.5	47	38.5
Franco-Madagascan, 1894–1895	55	64	48
Cuban Revolution, 1895–1898	20	24.5	28
Italo-Ethiopian, 1895–1896	50.5	61	43
First Philippine Insurrection, 1896–1898	73.5	35.5	88.5
Greco-Turkish, 1897	73.5	75	64.5
Spanish-American, 1898	46.5	67	30
Second Philippine Insurrection, 1899–1902	61	20	85
Boer, 1899–1902	27	28	47
Russo-Japanese, 1904–1905	9	22.5	13
Central American, 1906	89	75	79.5
Central American, 1907	89	75	79.5
Spanish-Moroccan, 1909–1910	46.5	43	51
Italo-Turkish, 1911–1912	30	32	45
First Balkan, 1912–1913	15	39.5	10
Second Balkan, 1913	16	80	4
World War One, 1914–1918	2	2	5
Russian Nationalities, 1917–1921	20	22.5	29
Hungarian-Allies, 1919	43	55	44
Greco-Turkish, 1919–1922	20	13	49
Riffian Revolt, 1921–1926	.25	15	60.5
Druze Rebellion, 1925–1926	63.5	35.5	75.5
Manchurian, 1931–1933	17.5	26.5	20
Chaco, 1932–1935	9	14	20
Italo-Ethiopian, 1935–1936	30	52.5	26.5
Sino-Japanese, 1937–1941	4	9	7
Russo-Japanese, 1939	33	59.5	23
World War Two, 1939–1945	1	1	1
Russo-Finnish, 1939–1940	14	70	6
Indonesian Rebellion, 1945–1946	81	35.5	92.5
Indochinese Rebellion, 1945–1954	13	10	38.5
Madagascan Rebellion, 1947–1948	78.5	39.5	90.5
First Kashmir, 1947–1949	78.5	52.5	85
Palestine, 1948–1949	52	41	58
Korean, 1950–1953	3	3	12
Algerian Revolution, 1954–1962	37.5	11	79.5
Tibetan Revolt, 1956–1959	22	24.5	32
Russo-Hungarian, 1956	24	86.5	2
Sinai, 1956	69	86.5	24.5
Sino-Indian, 1962	89	86.5	54.5
Second Kashmir, 1965	53	83	15

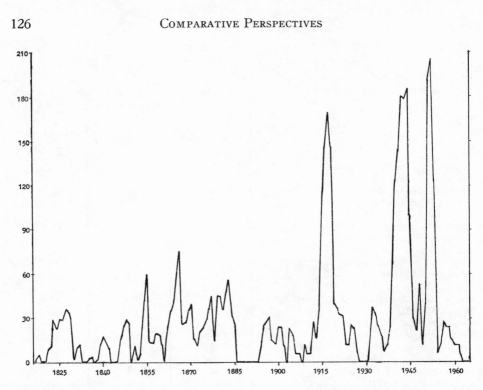

FIGURE 1. ANNUAL AMOUNT (IN NATION MONTHS) OF INTERNATIONAL WAR UNDER WAY
1816–1965

ing amount of war as we approach the apocalypse, they must be balanced with the more dismal finding that there appears to be a strong tendency toward periodicity in the system's war experiences. Although cycles are not apparent when we examine the amount of war beginning in each year or time period, a discernible periodicity emerges when we focus on measures of the amount of war under way. That is, discrete wars do not necessarily come and go with regularity; but with some level of interstate violence almost always present, there are distinct and periodic fluctuations in the amount of that violence. The 20-year cycle in the amount of nation-months of war is partially visible in the graph in Figure 1, and becomes more apparent when these data are subjected to a spectral analysis.

Others have discerned similar cycles

which could be related, among other things, to the time needed for a generation to "forget" the last bloody conflict.[8] It must be remembered that such analyses assume an interdependence between the martial activities of all system members, and that, for example, the incidence of war in the Balkans presumably affects the incidence of war on the Iberian Peninsula or even in

8. See, for example, Frank H. Denton, "Some Regularities in International Conflict, 1820–1949," *Background* 9, no. 4 (February 1966), 283–296; Frank H. Denton and Warren Phillips, "Some Patterns in the History of Violence," *Journal of Conflict Resolution* 12, no. 2 (June 1968), 182–195; Edward R. Dewey, *The 177 Year Cycle in War, 600 B.C.–A.D. 1957* (Pittsburgh: Foundation for the Study of Cycles, 1964); J. S. Lee, "The Periodic Recurrence of Internecine Wars in China," *The China Journal* 14, no 3 (March 1931), 111–115, 159–162.

Southeast Asia. Interestingly, no cyclical patterns are apparent when we examine the military experiences of the individual nations which participated in several wars. Thus, we must be rather tentative in affirming the existence of periodicity in the incidence of war, for our one strong pattern shows up only when we isolate one set of variables among many. Much more work needs to be done before we can accept completely the notion of a 20-year cycle, although these preliminary findings suggest the direction in which this work should go.

SEASONS AND WARS

Another way to approach the temporal variable is to examine the relationship between season and month and the incidence of war. According to the folklore, the onset and termination of war should be determined, in part, by climatological conditions which might affect military mobility and efficiency, and the growing and harvesting seasons which might, in turn, affect provisioning and recruiting an army. Some contemporary analysts would expect most wars to begin between March 22 and April 20 under the sign of bellicose Aries, and the fewest to begin between September 24 and October 23 when the gentle Libra is dominant.

To some degree, our data support the common folklore although the verdict is mixed for the astrologists. Of the 93 wars, 64 began in either spring or autumn and only 29 in summer and winter. Moreover, this pattern does not change much over time; for example, 11 of the 21 wars fought since 1920 began in autumn. As for specific months, April and October saw the initiation of 28 of the 93 conflicts. No one season or month stands out when it comes to the termination of war. This latter finding, when compared to the

onset patterns, lends credence to the thesis that policy makers are influenced by the season when they consider a war/no-war decision, but that once the war is under way, more nonrational factors militate against weather or supplies playing such a crucial role. Of course, much of this is conjecture. Before we can attest with certainty to the proposition that weather and climate weigh heavily with the decision-maker, we must compare similar sets of crises, which did and did not terminate in war, with specific seasonal variables.

THE WAR PRONENESS OF NATIONS

Whereas systematic patterns of international violence are most interesting to the political theorist, the record of individual nations' martial activities has long fascinated historians. Many have argued that some nations (perhaps during certain periods) are more aggressive than others, or that some ethnic groups are naturally warlike whereas others are naturally pacific. At the same time, repeated involvement in war may not necessarily relate to any innate characteristic but merely to the misfortune of being geographically proximate to predator powers or valuable territory. By computing the number and severity of wars experienced by each nation during its tenure in the system, we can obtain a more accurate indication of the distribution of wars among the nations, and whether, indeed, certain nations, or certain classes thereof, are more prone to war involvement than others.

In terms of the sheer number of international wars, France and England lead the field with 19 each, Turkey participated in 17, Russia 15, and Italy (including its predecessor, Sardinia) 11. All of these nations were members of the system for the full 150 years. Spain, which fought in 9 wars, and the United States, which fought in 6, are two other

TABLE 2—NATIONAL PERFORMANCES IN INTERNATIONAL WAR, 1816–1965

NATION NAME	ALL WARS	INTERSTATE WARS	NATION NAME	ALL WARS	INTERSTATE WARS
England	16–2	6–0	China	3–4	2–4
Russia	13–2	8–2	Bulgaria	1–3	1–3
France	14–4	9–2	India	1–2	0–2
Italy (Sardinia)	8–3	8–2	Mexico	1–2	1–1
United States	5–0	4–0	Peru	1–2	1–1
Brazil	3–0	2–0	Salvador	1–2	1–2
Japan	5–2	5–2	Ecuador	0–1	0–1
Yugoslavia (Serbia)	4–1	4–0	Hanover	0–1	0–1
Rumania	4–1	4–1	Hesse Electoral	0–1	0–1
Austria-Hungary	5–3	3–3	Hesse Grand Ducal	0–1	0–1
Belgium	2–0	2–0	Iraq	0–1	0–1
Chile	2–0	2–0	Jordan	0–1	0–1
Germany (Prussia)	4–2	4–2	Lebanon	0–1	0–1
Greece	4–2	4–2	Mecklenburg-Schwerin	0–1	0–1
Holland	3–1	1–0	Persia	0–1	0–1
Israel	2–0	2–0	Saxony	0–1	0–1
Mongolia	2–0	2–0	Syria	0–1	0–1
Spain	5–4	2–3	Bolivia	0–2	0–2
Australia	1–0	1–0	Denmark	0–2	0–2
Canada	1–0	1–0	Finland	0–2	0–2
Colombia	1–0	1–0	Honduras	0–2	0–2
Czechoslovakia	1–0	1–0	Morocco	0–2	0–2
New Zealand	1–0	1–0	Papal States	0–2	0–2
Nicaragua	1–0	1–0	U.A.R. (Egypt)	0–2	0–2
Norway	1–0	1–0	Hungary	0–3	0–3
Pakistan	1–0	1–0	Turkey	5–11	4–6
Paraguay	1–0	1–0			
Portugal	1–0	1–0			
Poland	1–0	1–0			
South Africa	1–0	1–0			
Baden	1–1	1–1			
Bavaria	1–1	1–1			
Ethiopia	1–1	1–1			
Guatemala	1–1	1–1			
Two Sicilies	1–1	1–1			
Württemberg	1–1	1–1			
Argentina	1–1	0–1			

charter members of the system with significant war experience. Those with a shorter tenure are led by Austria-Hungary and China with participation in 8 wars, Greece and Japan with 7, and Germany (including its predecessor, Prussia), with 6. As might be expected, these nations also sustained the most battle deaths, with Russia, Germany, China, France, Japan, England, Austria-Hungary, Italy, and Turkey, in that order, all suffering 750,000 or more. Moreover, 39 percent of all the

system's nation months of war were accounted for by 5 nations—France, England, Turkey, Spain, and Russia—and 39 of the 43 extra-systemic wars were fought by 7 states—England 12, France 7, Turkey 6, Russia 5, Spain 4, Holland 3, and Austria-Hungary 2.

Obviously, major powers were the most war-prone, with Turkey, Spain, and Greece the only non-majors to appear in this firmament.[9] No major

9. Our major powers (reflecting the historians' consensus) were England 1815–1965,

powers were able to escape this scourge, which may, in fact, turn out to be a prerequisite for achievement of that exalted status. On the other hand, most of the smaller states, and especially those in extra-European regions, enjoyed a fairly pacific record in terms of international war. Many of these, of course, experienced long and bloody civil conflicts. Still, the fact that more than half the nations (77 out of 144) which were at one time or another members of the system were able to escape international war entirely, suggests that military conflict between nations is not so common a systemic activity as some have posited.

NATIONAL MILITARY ACHIEVEMENT

Although some nations have fought in more wars than others, they have done so with varying degrees of success. Indeed, success in warfare might predict to frequency of involvement. A nation which loses several wars might behave with great circumspection in order to avoid the necessity of having to go to war again. Alternately, a military loss might foster a revanchist spirit, or worse yet, it could tempt a third power which felt it could easily defeat the nation whose military record was less than impressive. The data upon which one might base such generalizations are offered in Table 2, which shows each nation's record of victories and defeats in all international wars, followed by its record for interstate wars only.[10] Experiences in the one

stalemate (the Korean war) have been excluded from this tabulation.

Thanks to their choice of enemies and allies, as well as their military capabilities and skills, most of the major powers have done rather well. The 9 nations which were at one time or another major powers hold 6 of the first 7 positions and 8 of the first 13 in terms of won-lost records. The one major power absent from this galaxy, China, achieved its poor record while it was a minor power—since 1950 China has won two wars and tied in another. Turkey, as was expected, has a dismal history in this realm, but the Italians, often maligned for their legendary military ineptitude, nevertheless emerged victorious in 8 of their 11 engagements.

THE INITIATION OF INTERSTATE WAR

A history of involvement in international war is a necessary but not sufficient indication of a nation's bellicosity. The determination of the initiator of military conflict, however, may tell us a bit more about a nation's aggressive proclivities. When we speak of initiation here, we are merely identifying the nation(s) which made the first attack on an opponent's armies or territories. Clearly, initiator and aggressor are not always identical, as a participant might provoke its adversary into military action by mobilization or other aggressive diplomatic or economic actions. But the designation of the initiator of military aggression should nevertheless provide some tentative clues as to the relative belligerency of system members.

In examining the 49 interstate wars

France 1815–1940, 1945–1965, Germany 1815–1918, 1925–1945, Russia 1815–1917, 1921–1965, Austria-Hungry 1815–1918, Italy 1860–1943, United States 1899–1965, Japan 1895–1945, and China 1950–1965.

10. In some cases, the distinction between victor and vanquished was difficult to make, but in the end we "declared" a victor in all but one of the wars. For our purposes, nations like Poland and Belgium in World War

II, while defeated in the initial stages of the war, were considered victors since they emerged at war's end on the side of the winning coalition. Italy, Rumania, and Bulgaria, who joined the Allies after being defeated as members of the Axis, were considered as having been both winners and losers.

in which we were able to make this designation, we find that Italy was the
actual initiator (or on the side of the
initiator) on 8 occasions, France played
that role on 6 occasions, Germany and
Japan on 5, and Austria-Hungary,
Russia, and Bulgaria on 4.[11] But when
we turn from sheer number of initiations to the frequency of initiation compared to the total number of war experiences, some of the nations on this in-
famous list look a little less bellicose.
Whereas Italy initiated or fought on the
side of the initiator in 8 of her 10 interstate wars, Germany in 5 of her 6,
Japan in 5 of her 7, Austria-Hungary
in 4 of her 6, and Bulgaria in all of her
4, France initiated only 6 of her 12
interstate wars and Russia only 4 of
her 10. Among those nations with significant war experience which are absent from this list and therefore, perhaps, more pacific, are: the two "sick
men" of Asia, Turkey and China; three
Balkan states, Greece, Rumania, and
Yugoslavia; and the two Anglo-Saxon
major powers, England and the United
States.

The decision to initiate hostilities is
related, in part, to the expectation of
victory. Few governments would move
first militarily unless they expected that
such preëmption had a high probability
of victory or, at least, of national survival. Not surprisingly, then, we find
that initiators emerged victorious in 34
of the 49 interstate wars although they
lost 14 times and experienced one stalemate. As for battle fatalities, in 36 of
those 49, the initiators lost fewer men
than their opponents, and they were victorious in 6 of those 13 wars in which
their losses were greater than their opponents'. This is an impressive record

when one considers that an attacking
force is generally assumed to lose more
men than a defending force in a given
engagement.

Of course, in almost 40 percent of the
cases, the initiator turned out to be a
major power attacking a minor power.
Of the 19 wars which saw such a one-
sided confrontation, the major power
initiated hostilities on 18 occasions and
won 17 of those 18 contests.[12] When
minors fought minors, the initiator won
14 times and lost 7, but when majors
fought majors, the intiators won 3 times
and lost 5. Thus, initiation of hostilities
appears to have been a major advantage
to the combatants, but an advantage
which decreased in importance when
the two sides were more nearly equal in
power.

TRADITIONAL ENMITIES AND
FRIENDSHIPS

A nation's record of participation, as
well as of success and of failure, in war
has something to do with its historic
long-term relationship to other nations.
Historians and political scientists have
written about the importance of traditional enmities and friendships between
nations, and speculated as to whether
similar governments, religions, ethnicity, or stages of economic development
affect the propensity of nations to war
against, or ally with, one another. Moreover, the experience of conflict against
or alliance with a state in one war
should affect future relations with that
state in other wars and crises. In *Statistics of Deadly Quarrels*, Richardson
reported that 48 percent of the pairs
who fought on opposite sides in all wars
from 1820 to 1949, fought against each
other on more than one occasion. But
he also found that 29 percent of those
pairs who had been allies in one war

11. The one case which we did not include
in this part of the study was the Navarino
Bay incident of 1827. In several other wars,
the labeling of one side as initiator came only
after long and troubled consideration.

12. In 17 of these wars, the major power
shared a border with the minor power.

had already fought against each other in an earlier experience.[13] Looking at our more restricted set of wars, we find somewhat less evidence for the prevalence of historical enmities and alliances.

Of the 209 pairs who fought opposite each other in our 50 interstate wars, only 19 percent had fought against each other before, while 21 percent had actually been allies in an earlier war. As for those pairs with more than one experience in war (136), of the 95 pairs with some experience as opponents, 77 of them also fought at least once on the same side.

Thus, in terms of war experience, few friendships or enmities have held up throughout our 150–year period. When we look only at those nations with 3 or more experiences as allies and none as opponents in that period, we find that France and England have been partners on 6 occasions, Greece and Yugoslavia on 4, and Belgium, England and France, Greece and England, Holland and England, and the United States, England, and France on 3. As for historical enmities, those with 3 or more experiences as opponents and none as allies are Russia and Turkey with 5 conflicts, Austria-Hungary and Italy, and China and Japan with 4, and Germany and France with 3. While these listings conform to the historians' generalizations, the large

13. Richardson, op. cit., 196–199.

number of possible dyadic relationships requires us to conclude that the notion of enduring and traditional relationships in war applies only to a limited number of famous pairs.

CONCLUSION

The above figures provide a brief, and necessarily superficial, overview of the incidence of war in the modern international system. While they are of some intrinsic interest, their major value is more instrumental in nature. That is, with such data as summarized here (and reported more fully in our *Wages of War*) an accelerated assault on the problem of the causes of war becomes feasible. A variety of researchers, reflecting diverse disciplines and numerous theoretical orientations, can now undertake a systematic search for the factors which account for this organized tribal slaughter. Whether the focus be on economic or strategic, psychological or technological phenomena, the dependent variable data are now at hand. Our major purpose was to make such research possible, and as we explore the problem from our particular point of view, we hope others will do likewise. Although the odds do not seem particularly favorable, we might just unravel the mystery of war's regularity before we stumble into its final occurrence.

10

Sources of Rebellion in Western Societies:
Some Quantitative Evidence

By TED ROBERT GURR

Ted Robert Gurr, Ph.D., is associate professor of Political Science at Northwestern University and research associate of the Center of International Studies, Princeton University. He is author of Why Men Rebel *and* The Conditions of Civil Violence *as well as a number of monographs and articles; co-author of* American Welfare; *and co-editor of* Violence in America: Historical and Comparative Perspectives. *In 1968–69 he was co-director of a task force of the National Commission on the Causes and Prevention of Violence, and in 1970 held a Ford Foundation Faculty Research Fellowship while doing research in England.*

The research reported here was supported partly by the Advanced Research Projects Agency of the Department of Defense. This support implies neither sponsor approval of the article nor the author's approval of policies of the U.S. government toward civil strife. A preliminary version of this paper was presented at a seminar at the Richardson Institute for Peace and Conflict Research, London.

Norman Jacknis and Erika Gurr assisted in the preparation, revision, and analysis of the data.

THIS is one in a series of reports on the development and assessment of a general theory of the causes of civil disorder.[1, 2, 3, 4, 5] The theory is neither time-bound nor culture-specific, hence it has no special relevance to the social ills of Western societies. But since the theory and the measures devised to test it are by intention universally applicable, they should be no less relevant to Western societies than to others. Thus, they afford a partial test of assertions that the contemporary resurgence of strife in the West is either epiphenomenal or, on the contrary, attributable to flaws unique to complex modern societies. By old-fashioned statistical and substantive criteria, the results of this aggregate statistical analysis of conflict and its asserted causes suggest quite strongly that the general causes and patterns of strife in Western nations are not unique but common. Much the same sorts of conditions distinguish peaceful from turbulent Western societies as have made the difference between civil peace and civil disorder in other societies and other eras.

1. Gurr, T. R., and C. Ruttenberg, *The Conditions of Civil Violence: First Tests of a Causal Model*, Research Monograph 28, Center of International Studies (Princeton: Princeton University Press, 1967).

2. Gurr, T. R., "Urban Disorder: Perspectives from the Comparative Study of Civil Strife," *American Behavioral Scientist*, 11 (March 1968), 50–55.

3. Gurr, T. R., "A Causal Model of Civil Strife: A Comparative Analysis Using New Indices," *American Political Science Review*, 62 (December 1968), 1104–1124.

4. Gurr, T. R., "A Comparative Survey of Civil Strife," in H. D. Graham and T. R. Gurr, eds., *Violence in America: Historical and Comparative Perspectives* (Washington, D.C.: National Commission on the Causes and Prevention of Violence, 1969), chap. 17.

5. Gurr, T. R., *Why Men Rebel* (Princeton: Princeton University Press, 1970).

THE THEORETICAL ARGUMENT

Collective discontent is the necessary precondition for civil strife; the statement is all but truistic. What is not truistic is the hypothesis which proceeds from it: that the greater the intensity and scope of discontent in a population, the greater the magnitude of strife. By strife we mean all collective, overt, nongovernmental attacks on people or property that occur within a political system, including both violent and nonviolent, symbolic attacks. The concrete phenomena included range from demonstrations and interracial clashes to coups d'état and guerrilla wars. The violence used by regimes to maintain social control is not included in strife. It may be closely related to strife, as cause or consequence, but it typically has different origins and effects, which dictate its separate theoretical and empirical treatment.

Discontent is a psychological variable which is difficult to assess except by reference to its collective outcomes. There are social conditions from which it can be inferred and predicted, however. We conceptualize its social origins in terms of relative deprivation, that is, widespread perception of discrepancies between the goals of human action and the prospects of attaining those goals. Several objective patterns of social conditions are theoretically associated with perceived deprivation. Among them are a group's relative or absolute decline from a previously enjoyed condition; a prolonged improvement in a group's condition followed by abatement of progress; and social inflexibilities that differentially restrict a group from attaining conditions enjoyed by other groups. (For a systematic analysis of perceived deprivation and its social causes, see *Why Men Rebel.*[6])

Discontent and strife are causally connected both rationally and nonrationally. Rationally, angry men may resort to public protest and violence on the basis of their estimation that it will help improve their circumstances. Nonrationally, there is extensive psychological and ethological evidence that aggression against someone who frustrates or threatens is self-satisfying.[7] Often these two motivations reinforce each other; at other times the nonrational impulse to aggression may be inhibited by the perception or belief that it is undesirable. This suggests the second basic proposition of the theoretical argument: the greater the normative and utilitarian justifications for strife in a discontented group, the greater the magnitude of strife. Normative justifications are the basic attitudes men have about the desirability of violence, ranging from culturally implanted dispositions about how to deal with anger, to traditions and ideologies that variously praise order or celebrate violence. Utilitarian justifications are beliefs about the success of strife, beliefs which are as likely to be derived from others' successes as from concurrent calculation.

Justifications like discontent are psychological variables, difficult to observe collectively except from their overt consequences of order or violence—which in any case have other causes as well. One condition that can be included in an evaluation of strife over a period of time is the historical extent of the condition. We would expect groups and societies with high levels of past strife to hold attitudes and beliefs that offer greater justification for future strife than societies with more peaceful histories. The success of strife in the past

ought also to leave attitudinal residues that help justify future strife. A psychological correlate of attitudes about political violence is the legitimacy of political systems: the more legitimate they are, the less likely their citizens are to be willing to attack them. Two objective conditions of political legitimacy, which can be used to index it, are the durability of a political system and the extent to which it is an indigenous rather than an imposed system.

The outcome of motivational and attitudinal dispositions to strife is finally and most immediately determined by two aspects of social organization: the balance of social control and the balance of institutional support between contending groups. In contemporary societies, the contending groups most often involved in strife are the regime and those who support it, on the one side, and those who oppose or ask concessions of it on the other. In support of this assertion, we reported elsewhere findings that the initiators in 93 percent of some 1,100 occurrences of strife in 114 nations, 1961–65, had significant political motives, as inferred either from their demands or actions.[8]

The institutional balance between regimes and dissidents refers to their relative capacity to organize and command; if regimes are supported by a dense and pervasive network of organizations, dissidents have little space in which to organize, much less to take concerted action. The coercive balance refers to the capacities of the contenders to use force; if dissidents can arm substantial cadres or win over some of the military, they can carry on a protracted internal war. The hypothesis is that the greater the institutional and coercive capacities of the dissidents relative to regime capacities, the greater the magnitudes of strife. The relation should hold only

6. Ibid., chs. 2–5.
7. Ibid., ch. 2.

8. *Violence in America,* op. cit., pp. 458–460.

up to the point of equality; beyond the point at which dissidents gain the upper hand, regimes will collapse more quickly and the violence contingent on their collapse is likely to be less. In the contemporary Western societies that are the subject of this study we would expect to find few if any cases of dissident predominance.

MAGNITUDE OF STRIFE

Data have been collected on each reported occurrence of strife in twenty-one nations of the Western community for the years 1961 through 1965, using procedures described elsewhere.[9] In the previous studies [10] we assessed the magnitude of strife in these and other countries by taking into account its relative duration, pervasiveness, and intensity (the latter indexed by casualties), and distinguished among three forms of strife: turmoil, conspiracy, and internal war. Revised measures and different distinctions are used in this study. Magnitude of strife is indexed here using man-days of strife per 100,000 population, which combines duration and pervasiveness, and deaths from strife per 100 million population, which excludes injuries—reports of which are usually less precise and often missing. The distinctions made are between *violent* and *nonviolent* strife, and between *turmoil* and *rebellion*. Turmoil is relatively spontaneous, unorganized strife with substantial popular participation. Rebellion includes events previously characterized as conspiracy (highly organized strife with limited participation) and internal war (highly organized strife with widespread popular participation). Rebellion is a misnomer for a few events thus included—for example, the racial terrorism practiced by the Ku Klux Klan in the American South—but is

9. Ibid.
10. See notes 2, 3, 4.

otherwise appropriate: the central objective in most of these events is fundamental political change. For all practical purposes, nonviolent strife is a subset of turmoil: it consists almost entirely of peaceful demonstrations and general strikes.

There are no strong relationships among the relative levels or types of strife, as is apparent from the data shown graphically in Figures 1 and 2. For example, we might expect that peaceful protest would be more common in less violent societies, and rebellion most common in the most violent ones. Contrary to these expectations, man-days of peaceful protest are greater in violent than nonviolent countries; rebellion is equally common among low-strife and high-strife countries, but has somewhat greater magnitudes in the latter. The man-days and deaths measures, logged, have only a weak correlation of .44. It is evident, though, that countries having one type of strife are quite likely to experience others as well. Seven of the sixteen countries with any strife at all had all three types—violent and peaceful turmoil plus rebellion—while six others have two of the three. Figure 2 shows that deaths were proportionally greatest in South Africa, Rhodesia, and France. Comparison of the relative rankings of man-days and deaths shows that South Africa has a very high incidence of deaths relative to man-days of strife, and Rhodesia and the U.S.A. had substantially higher-than-average incidences. These figures reflect the relative intensity of protest and rebellion, and of severity of coercive response to it, in these countries. By contrast, strife was rather extensive but largely or wholly peaceful in Italy, West Germany, Austria, and Australia.

Two kinds of summary measures of strife are used. For purposes of statistical comparison, the "man-days" and "deaths" figures for each type of strife for 114 countries were logged, converted to standard scores, and added. These summary scores for total magnitude of strife for the Western community nations are shown in Table 1. For the graphic comparisons shown subsequently, the summed standard scores were converted to 100–point scales in which countries with no strife of a particular kind are scored 0 and those with the maximum are scored 100. These more-readily-compared measures are shown in Table 1 for total strife, nonviolent strife, turmoil, and rebellion. The averages show that the Western nations have lesser magnitudes of all four types of strife than the entire universe of 114 contemporary nations; the discrepancy is greatest for rebellion, least for non-violent strife. Most of the strife measures are closely associated with one another. Total strife correlates .81 and .92 respectively with its nonviolent and violent facets, and .96 and .61 with the turmoil and rebellion components. The extent of rebellion is largely independent of the magnitude of the less intense forms of protest, though; it correlates only .40 with peaceful protest and .43 with all turmoil.

THE EXPLANATION OF STRIFE: RELATIVE DEPRIVATION

To what extent do variations in discontent among Western peoples determine national differences in strife? Our evidence suggests they do so only in part. Three summary measures of different kinds of deprivation were con-

FIGURE 1: Man-days of Participation in Civil Strife per 100,000 Population 1961–65, by Type of Strife

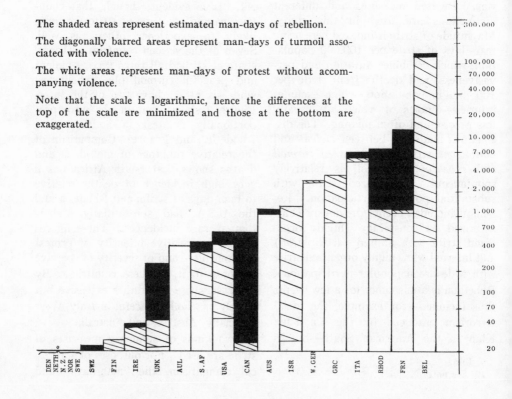

The shaded areas represent estimated man-days of rebellion.

The diagonally barred areas represent man-days of turmoil associated with violence.

The white areas represent man-days of protest without accompanying violence.

Note that the scale is logarithmic, hence the differences at the top of the scale are minimized and those at the bottom are exaggerated.

FIGURE 2: Deaths from Civil Strife per 100 Million Population, 1961–65, by Type of Strife

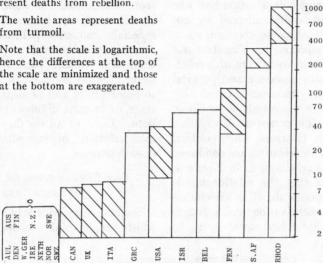

The diagonally barred areas represent deaths from rebellion.

The white areas represent deaths from turmoil.

Note that the scale is logarithmic, hence the differences at the top of the scale are minimized and those at the bottom are exaggerated.

structed, based on information on short-term economic declines, on burdensome new political restrictions and governmental regulations, and on persisting structural conditions that cause enduring discontent (such as discrimination, lack of educational opportunities, religious cleavages, and separatism).[11] Short-term political deprivation and persisting deprivation both are correlated moderately with total strife, .50 and .39, respectively.[12] When the two measures are combined and plotted against total strife, in Figure 3, it is apparent that most of the correlation depends on a handful of cases. The seven countries

11. See note 3.
12. For 21 cases, correlations above .43 are significant at the .05 level; those above .55 are significant at .01. For this analysis of what is nominally the whole universe of contemporary nations in the Western community (aside from very small ones), we regard correlations of .30 or more as supporting the causal arguments. Lesser correlations, though they may reflect true relations, are too weak to be of substantive significance.

with deprivation scores of 16 or more all have relatively high levels of strife, but for the 14 countries with less indicated deprivation there is no consistent pattern—except that as a group they have a considerably lower average level of strife than the seven.

What of economic discontent? Among 114 nations we found a significant correlation of .34 between short-term economic deprivation and total strife; among the 21 Western nations the correlation is an inconsequential .06. In other words, setbacks of economic progress in the short run seem to have little to do with public protest and violence in Western countries. But persisting grievances about its distribution, as reflected in economic discrimination and lack of educational opportunities to increase wellbeing, are evidently among the consequential causes of strife.

When the different components of strife are examined, we find evidence of important variations in apparent causation. Levels of peaceful protest are not significantly affected by *any* of the deprivation measures. Total turmoil, violent as well as nonviolent, is not associated with economic deprivation but, like total strife, somewhat affected by political and persisting deprivation, r's = .40 and .37, respectively. The strongest causal connections by far are with rebellion. Here both economic and political deprivation are important, correlating .44 and .73 with magnitude of rebellion, respectively, while persisting deprivation correlates .55. However, when political and persisting deprivation are combined and related to rebellion, as in Figure 4, we find again that the relationship is largely a function of the close association between high deprivation and substantial rebellion for a few cases.

Briefly, the substantive implications of these results seem to be these: intense and persisting discontents in Western societies are most likely to lead to the more intense and violent kinds of strife we call rebellion. The same discontents, especially immediate political grievances, may episodically lead to peaceful protests and violent turmoil, but these latter events vary principally according to more subtle and unmeasured discontents, or to quite different conditions, or both. Least of all do they seem to be manifestations of immediate economic dissatisfactions.

THE EXPLANATION OF STRIFE: JUSTIFICATIONS

Societies vary widely in the extent to which people think violent protest and

TABLE 1—RELATIVE MAGNITUDES OF STRIFE 1961–65

COUNTRY	ALL STRIFE (standard scores)	ALL STRIFE (scaled)	NONVIOLENT STRIFE (scaled)	ALL TURMOIL (scaled)	REBELLION (scaled)
Rhodesia	0.82	33	57	48	40
Belgium	0.78	33	56	55	1
France	0.30	28	65	33	34
Italy	−0.17	23	80	37	23
Greece	−0.24	23	62	38	0
South Africa	−0.27	22	44	37	21
Israel	−0.41	21	30	36	0
West Germany	−0.43	21	73	34	0
Austria	−0.63	19	66	30	13
U. S. A.	−0.70	18	36	30	16
Canada	−0.79	17	0	9	22
Australia	−0.93	16	55	26	0
United Kingdom	−1.03	15	5	17	18
Ireland	−1.54	10	0	16	1
Finland	−1.67	9	0	14	0
Switzerland	−2.52	1	0	0	1
Denmark	−2.54	0	0	0	0
Netherlands	−2.54	0	0	0	0
New Zealand	−2.54	0	0	0	0
Norway	−2.54	0	0	0	0
Sweden	−2.54	0	0	0	0
Averages:					
W. Community	*−1.05*	*16*	*30*	*22*	*9*
114 nations	*0.00*	*25*	*33*	*30*	*24*

Type of scores, for scaled scores, minimum = 0, maximum = 100.
Scores are not additive. See text for their derivation.

FIGURE 3—TOTAL MAGNITUDE OF STRIFE, 1961–65, AND
POLITICAL + PERSISTING DEPRIVATION

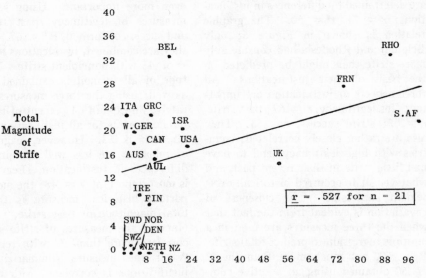

Political + Persisting Deprivation

Note: Scores on both variables are converted to scales in which the lowest observed score in 114 nations = 0, the highest = 100. The best-fit lines in this and subsequent figures were fitted by inspection.

rebellion are justified. Our measures of the justification of protest and rebellion among the Western nations proved more important causes of total strife and turmoil than actual deprivation, but they were less important causes of rebellion. Three measures suggested by the theoretical discussion, above, were used: governmental legitimacy; the relative extent of past strife, 1946–59, distinguishing among levels of turmoil, conspiracy, and internal war; and the historical success of strife. The construction of the first two measures is described in an earlier article.[13] To estimate the third, success of strife, each country was judgmentally coded on three variables: the relative scope and success of internal wars, if any, fought between 1850 and 1960; the relative frequency and success of coups and other con-

13. See note 3.

spiracies between 1900 and 1960; and the extent to which riots, demonstrations, or general strikes contributed to favorable policy or regime changes between 1940–60. A six-point scale was used for internal war success, five-point scales for the others. When all three scores were combined, the "strife success" scores for Western countries ranged from 0 (for the three Scandinavian countries and Switzerland) to 11 (Greece). For specific analyses we used measures of justification appropriate to the type of strife being explained, e.g., past levels of turmoil and success of popular strife to explain differences in turmoil. For the general analysis we used a single measure combining all justifications: the sum of standard scores on legitimacy (high scores = low legitimacy), total past strife, and strife success.

Fully half the differences in magnitudes of strife among Western nations are determined by differences in justifications: $r = .71$, $r^2 = .50$. The graphic relation is shown in Figure 5; only Belgium and Rhodesia had considerably more strife than might be predicted on the basis of their justifications. All three aspects of justification are important: for legitimacy, $r = .67$; past strife, $r = .62$; strife success, $r = .53$. They also are rather closely correlated: countries with high legitimacy tend to have had little strife in their recent past, and whatever strife occurred historically was seldom successful. The closeness of covariation is evident from the fact that when the three measures are used in a multiple regression to predict total strife, $R^2 = .60$, not much more than the r^2 of .50 obtained using an additive combination of the three.

Do these results also hold for the various forms of strife in Western nations? For nonviolent strife, justifications are even more important. Using separate measures of legitimacy, past turmoil, and success of turmoil, $R^2 = .67$. When they are combined, justifications have an r^2 of .45 with nonviolent strife. Magnitude of all turmoil is explained about as well: using the three measures separately, we explain 64 percent of the differences, while for all justifications combined, r^2 is .53. However, magnitudes of rebellion are less well explained by differences in justification. Legitimacy is most important, $r = .48$; the most important historical measure is that of total magnitude of past strife, $r = .44$. None of the measures of strife success correlate more than .34 with rebellion. When the measure summarizing all justifications is correlated with magnitude of rebellion, $r^2 = .20$.

The substantive implications of these

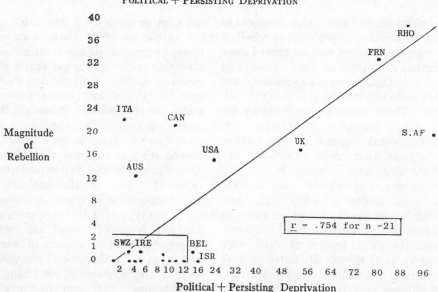

FIGURE 4—MAGNITUDE OF REBELLION, 1961–65, AND
POLITICAL + PERSISTING DEPRIVATION

Note: The lower left corner of the graph is expanded to show better the distribution of cases there. The countries on the 0 magnitude of revolution axis, left to right, are Sweden, Norway, West Germany, Denmark, Finland, Netherlands, Greece, Australia, New Zealand, Israel. Also see note on Figure 3.

FIGURE 5—TOTAL MAGNITUDE OF STRIFE, 1961–65, AND
ALL JUSTIFICATIONS FOR STRIFE

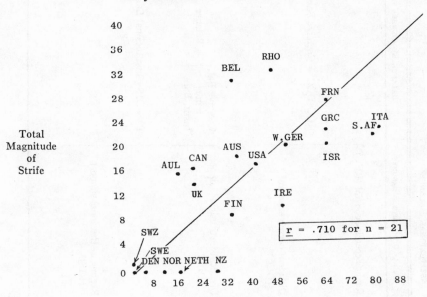

All Justifications for Strife

results, when compared with the analysis of discontent, are quite clear. The less intense forms of strife in Western nations—demonstrations and most riots—are more the result of how people think about governments and the desirability of protest than of intense grievances. In countries with unpopular governments and traditions that sanction protest, even minor grievances will precipitate public protest. The pattern has long characterized France and has been evident in Greece and Italy since World War II; it began to appear in the United States during the early 1960's and by 1970 seemed firmly established. In the late 1960's, similar developments seemed to be occurring in the United Kingdom and West Germany. But the most serious forms of strife—terrorism, antigovernment conspiracy, and the more violent riots—are in Western nations a direct response to intense and persisting frustrations, not much affected by political loyalties or traditions.

THE EXPLANATION OF STRIFE: THE COERCIVE AND INSTITUTIONAL BALANCES

The most immediate and therefore statistically strongest of causes of strife is the pattern of institutional support and coercive control which channels the expression and repression of collective motivations to violence. We constructed and combined a large number of measures of the relative capacities of regimes and dissidents; these indices and their progressive combinations are shown in Figure 6. Five are discussed here: the four group measures—dissident and regime coercive control and institutional support—and the summary index of balance. The correlation coefficients for these measures with some of the strife measures are shown in Table 2.

The most important structural determinants of strife are those directly affecting dissidents, that is, the scope and strength of their organizations and

FIGURE 6—MEASURES OF COERCIVE AND INSTITUTIONAL BALANCE

PRIMARY MEASURES	FIRST COMPOSITE MEASURES	GROUP COMPOSITE MEASURES	BALANCE MEASURES
Military personnel[a,d] Internal security force personnel[a,d] Historical loyalty of coercive forces to the regime[b]	Population in cities of 20,000+[a] Coercive force status[c]	Regime coercive control (RCC)[c]	
	Frequency of military participation in anti-regime strife 1961-65[a]		
Foreign support for dissidents, 1961-65 —Level[b] —No. of countries providing[a]	Foreign support for dissidents[b]	Dissident coercive control (DCC)[c]	RCC−DCC = Coercive Balance
Dissident groups —Size[a,d] —Organization[b] —Isolation[b]	Remote-area concentration of dissidents[c]		
Communist parties —Size[a,d] —Oppositional status[b]	Organized Communist dissidence[c]	Dissident institutional support (DIS)[c]	Coercive Bal. minus Instit. Bal. = Balance
Labor movement status —Union membership[a,d] —No. of political strikes 1956-66[a] —Political autonomy of labor movement[b]	Labor union dissidence[c] Labor union support for regimes[c]		
Gross Domestic Product[a] Central government budget[a]	Regime economic influence[a]	Regime institutional support (RIS)[c]	RIS−DIS = Institutional Balance
Voting participation[a] Government party seats[a] National political integration[b] Political centralization[b]	Regime political support[c]		

[a] Interval-measured data, usually from published studies, normalized by rescaling.
[b] Judgmentally-coded scales, some from published studies.
[c] Summary measures combined by addition or multiplication of component measures, in some cases rescaled.
[d] Measures weighted by population.

TABLE 2—CORRELATIONS OF COERCIVE CONTROL AND INSTITUTIONAL SUPPORT
WITH STRIFE IN THE WESTERN COMMUNITY

BALANCE MEASURE	CORRELATIONS WITH STRIFE MEASURES (n = 21)			
	ALL STRIFE	NONVIOLENT STRIFE	TURMOIL	REBELLION
Regime coercion	−23	−17	−12	−47*
Dissident coercion	67**	37	53*	84**
Regime support	−57**	−52*	−54*	−57**
Dissident support	72**	74**	71**	39
Balance	*−74** *	*−64** *	*−67** *	*−72** *

Product-moment correlation coefficients × 100.
 * Significant at the .05 level.
 ** Significant at the .01 level.

the degree of coercive capacity. Their importance vis-à-vis one another varies with the type of strife: increases in dissident institutional support are likely to lead to greater nonviolent protest, whereas increases in their coercive capacities enhance the prospects for rebellion. Regime institutional support, as measured here, is moderately and consistently important in minimizing all forms of violence. The coercive capacity of regimes, however, has very little effect on the extent of any type of strife except rebellion, which it tends slightly to minimize.

The summary measure of balance is

FIGURE 7—TOTAL MAGNITUDE OF STRIFE, 1961–65, AND
COERCIVE/INSTITUTIONAL BALANCE

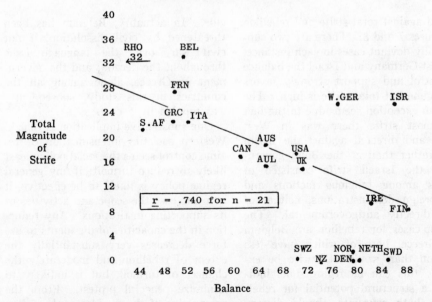

Note: High balance scores indicate relatively high institutional and coercive support for the regime vis-à-vis dissidents. Also see note on Figure 3.

FIGURE 8—MAGNITUDE OF REBELLION, 1961–65, AND
COERCIVE/INSTITUTIONAL BALANCE

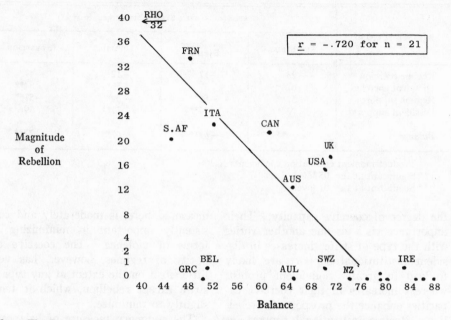

Note: The lower portion of the graph is expanded to show better the distribution of cases there. The countries on the 0 magnitude of rebellion axis, right to left, are Finland, Israel, Sweden, Netherlands, Denmark, Norway, West Germany, New Zealand. Also see note on Figure 3.

plotted against total strife and rebellion in Figures 7 and 8. There are two substantially deviant cases in each instance. In West Germany and Israel the balance of control and support strongly favors the regime but total strife is high. The German exception seems due to the fact that most strife there was in West Berlin and directed against the Berlin Wall rather than at the Bonn government; the Israeli strife consisted of clashes among religious factions and anti-foreign demonstrations, neither of them directly antigovernmental. The deviant cases for rebellion are Belgium and Greece, both of which have less rebellion than would otherwise be expected; this can be regarded as indicating a structural potential for rebellion in both countries, should discontents and attitudes supporting it coin-

cide. In actuality, Belgium has been threatened by civil dissolution, if not civil war, over the language issue throughout the decade; and the government of Greece, alone among all the countries in this study, subsequently was toppled by a coup.

One substantive implication is that in Western societies intensification of regime control seems the social policy least likely to reduce turmoil; if any general regime policy is likely to be effective, it is to increase the scope and activities of its supporting institutions. Any reduction in the capacities of dissidents to use force decreases very substantially the extent of rebellion and moderately the chances of turmoil, but is unlikely to minimize peaceful protest. From the perspective of the dissidents, the policy to be preferred depends upon their ob-

TABLE 3—MULTIPLE REGRESSIONS: TYPE OF STRIFE BY RELATIVE
DEPRIVATION, JUSTIFICATIONS AND BALANCE

| TYPE OF STRIFE | CONSTANT | INDEPENDENT VARIABLES AND STANDARD WTS. | | | VARIATION EXPLAINED $(R^2 \times 100)$ |
		RELATIVE DEPRIVATION	JUSTIFICATIONS	BALANCE	
All	= 0.538 −	0.009* (.53, −.01)	+ 0.466 (.71, .60)	− 0.525 (−.74, −.58)	71.5%
Nonviolent	= 2.275 −	0.367 (.26, −.43)	+ 0.523 (.67, .61)	− 0.632 (−.64, −.62)	65.8%
Turmoil	= 1.221 −	0.088* (.44, −.11)	+ 0.546 (.73, .64)	− 0.468 (−.67, −.51)	67.2%
Violent	= 0.017 +	0.176* (.62, .23)	+ 0.414 (.68, .55)	− 0.418 (−.73, −.48)	69.6%
Rebellion	= −0.647 +	0.482 (.75, .53)	+ 0.066* (.45, .10)	− 0.377 (−.72, −.43)	66.4%

The initial correlation coefficients and partial coefficients are shown in parentheses below each equation. The partial represents the proportion of variation explained by a variable when the effects of other variables are removed or held constant.

* These weights are significant at less than .10 using the one-tailed t-test.

jective. If it is rebellion or revolution, coercive capacities should be increased; if they hope to organize political pressure by means of demonstrations and riots, organizational efforts seem in order. Of course the evidence is cross-sectional, not based on the experience of particular groups and governments across time; it says nothing about the effects of various kinds of intensities of strife, nor about the effects of specific kinds of tactics. The analysis of these questions requires more detailed studies and measures.

THE EXTENT OF EXPLANATION

Taking all three levels of explanation into account, we can specify which are most important and how much of the differences in strife among Western nations they account for. Three summary measures—political plus persisting deprivation, all justifications combined, and balance—were used in multiple regressions, with the results summarized in Table 3. Looking first at the proportions of variation explained, they are all

high and almost identical: the three measures account for two thirds or more of the differences among Western nations in all five aspects of strife, total strife being slightly better explained than any of its components. In other words, if the same independent variables were measured for the decade of 1960's, we would expect to be able to predict with an accuracy of 65–70 percent the extent of different kinds of strife in Western countries in the first five years of the 1970's.[14]

14. The component measures of the independent variables in fact represent various time periods, but the only consequential qualification to the over-time predictive capability of the model is that a few of these measures are synchronous with those for strife. Short-term political deprivation and four of the 21 measures used in constructing the social balance measure make significant use of information from the early 1960's, some of which was influenced by the occurrence of strife that we purport to explain. We would expect that if we replaced synchronous measurement for these variables with time-lagged measurement, the levels of prediction would decrease slightly but not substantially.

FIGURE 9—STRIFE POTENTIALS AMONG WESTERN NATIONS

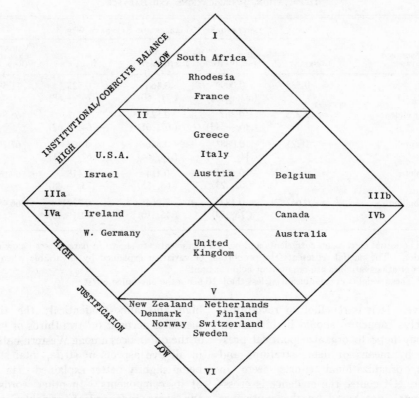

Nations in the top half of each diamond had high levels of discontent in the early 1960's vis-à-vis those in the bottom half. Overall potential for strife decreases from top to bottom of the larger diamond. See text.

The variables are not consistently important in the explanation of all forms of strife, as we noted previously. Their importance can be compared by examining their standard weights in the five equations, and their partial correlations; the comparisons are approximately equivalent. Balance is a consistently important and a negative determinant of variations in strife of all forms, although the more violent the form of strife, the less relative importance social balance has. Justifications for violence are positive causes of strife and approximately equal in importance to balance, except for rebellion. Relative deprivation has the most anomalous results.

Variations in deprivation are not an important direct determinant of total strife, turmoil, or violent strife; in all three instances their effects are largely determined by the justifications and balance. In real-world terms this does not mean that deprivation is unimportant as a cause of these forms of strife, but that the magnitude of its effect depends on how it is channeled by peoples' attitudes and social situations. The most striking direct effects of relative deprivation are on variations in nonviolent strife and rebellion. When other determinants are held constant, deprivation is a significantly *negative* cause of nonviolent protest and the strongest *positive* cause of rebellion. Other things being equal (literally so, in a statistical sense), the more discontented people are, the less likely they are to resort to nonviolent protest and the more likely they are to rebel. The statistical results may seem anomalous; their substantive interpretation is quite in accord with our intuitive and theoretical expectations about actual behavior.

The results are consistent with those examined above. Discontent is evidently a first cause of strife, but if it is relatively mild its popular manifestation is determined not by its extent or intensity but by popular attitudes about the desirability of governments and of violence. The more intense discontent is, the less likely is it to be either moderated or intensified by such attitudes and the more likely it will lead to severe violence. Mild or intense, the final and most immediate determinants of how discontent is expressed are the social circumstances of the discontented. If the social balance is substantially against them, expressions of discontent will be partially but not entirely muted; the greater their freedom of action and capacity to strike, the greater the strife—if they are already motivated to it. But if the psychological conditions of rebellion are not present, there will be little or no strife, whatever the social balance may be.

CONCLUSION

The statistical results of this study provide strong support for the hypotheses sketched at the outset. The occurrence of strife in the twenty-one Western nations included in this study is not inexplicable or unexpected in any general sense; in fact, its occurrence, with recent variations among countries, is largely explicable even by rather crude techniques of quantitative analysis. Some of our findings and their implica-

tions are summarized in the graphic categorization of Western countries in Figure 9.

The institutional/coercive balance between regimes and their opponents, and justifications for protest and violence, are equally strong determinants of magnitudes of strife in these nations; they also tend to persist over time with relatively little change, so categorization ought to begin with them. In the early 1960's, according to our measures [15] the countries in the top diamond of Figure 9, categories I and II, all had a high level of justification for strife and a social balance relatively favorable to dissidents. Those in the bottom diamond, V and VI, had the combination most likely to minimize strife: few kinds of justification and a social balance strongly favoring the regime. The remaining two diamonds contain countries having disparate combinations of predisposing conditions, one facilitating and the other mitigating against strife. Within each diamond, the countries are listed according to decreasing levels of discontent in the early 1960's. This follows from our finding that variations in discontent affect magnitudes of strife largely through the mediation of justification and balance. The close correspondence of the ranking from top to bottom with the rank-order of magnitudes of strife in 1961–65 (Table 1) reflects the power of statistical explanation of the variables used in the study.

For each of the categories we can specify what kinds and levels of strife countries in them were likely to experience in the first half of the 1960's, and indicate their potentials for subsequent strife. The judgments in these predic-

15. The independent variables were dichotomized at the point which seemed most plausible on inspection of the data plots in Figures 3, 5, and 7: the cutting points were 15 for deprivation, 36 for justifications, and 66 for balance.

tions are relative to other countries in the Western community, not to all nations, which on the average have somewhat more turmoil and much greater magnitudes of rebellion.

I. High-magnitude turmoil and rebellion so long as discontent remains high. Should discontent decline, prospects are for moderate turmoil but little rebellion.

II. Moderate turmoil but little rebellion so long as discontent remains low. Intensification of discontent would probably lead to high-magnitude turmoil and rebellion.

IIIa. High turmoil so long as discontent is high, moderate turmoil when it declines. Attempts at rebellion occur where the discontented have relative freedom of action, but this they are unlikely to have in large measure.

IIIb. High turmoil and rebellion so long as discontent remains high; low turmoil and rebellion if it declines.

IVa. Low turmoil and rebellion so long as discontent remains. Intensification of discontent is likely to lead to high turmoil and attempted but unsuccessful rebellion.

IVb. Low turmoil and rebellion so long as discontent remains low.

Intensification of discontent is likely to lead to high turmoil and rebellion.

V. Moderate turmoil when discontent is high, otherwise little or none. Rebellion unlikely unless the intensely discontented get relative freedom of action, which is unlikely.

VI. Little or no turmoil or rebellion. Intensification of discontent is likely to lead at most to moderate turmoil but not to rebellion.

The predictions for the first half of the 1960's are mostly accurate, despite the fact that the categorization of countries glosses over many differences within them. Considerations of those differences account for several of the few exceptions. Several countries experienced higher magnitudes of rebellion in the 1960's than their categorization suggests, including the U.S.A., Italy, and the United Kingdom (in Ulster). In each case, rebellion was perpetrated by relatively small, intensely discontented groups, for whom there were some justifications for violence and some freedom of action, groups whose differences from their countrymen were washed out in statistical aggregation. The reader may judge whether the contingencies suggested account for events of the last half of the 1960's, and their applicability to the future.

11

Conflict Without Violence and Violence Without Conflict in a Mexican Mestizo Village

By Lola Romanucci Schwartz

Lola Romanucci Schwartz is director of Contemporary Issues and Cultural Traditions, John Muir College at the University of California, San Diego; and lecturer in the Department of Community Medicine at the UCSD School of Medicine. She has taught anthropology at the University of Hawaii and San Fernando Valley State College. Her anthropological fieldwork in Mexico was done in collaboration with Erich Fromm and Ted Schwartz, and in Melanesia with Margaret Mead and Ted Schwartz as the American Museum of Natural History Expedition to New Guinea and the Admiralty Islands.

This paper was prepared for the Symposium on Violence at the meetings of the American Anthropological Association, New Orleans, Louisiana, 1969.

IT may be expected, perhaps, that in a community manifesting both much conflict and much violence, the two would be closely related. Conflict should lead to the violence which in turn should lead to more violence and conflict. It might also be expected that the high incidence of both would lead to disruption and instability in the community. Rather surprisingly, these expectations were not met in the study here reported. Conflict and violence tended to remain in separate spheres of social disruption, limited and eventually reduced. Major conflicts showed continuity over the years as the issues changed, but the reverberation of violence into further conflict and violence was effectively damped, each event kept isolated by a number of implicit social devices and by the ambiguities of the moral code itself.

This chapter is based on a study of a progressive Mexican mestizo village in central Mexico. The village, a product of the Mexican Agrarian Revolution, was an *ejido* community built around the shell of a burned-out *hacienda* by former *peones* who had come from several states to claim land parcels that were distributed. The period under consideration runs from 1924 to 1960. During this period, especially in the late 1920's and the early 1930's, the community grew from a few families that had lived around the *hacienda* before the Revolution, to about 800 persons in 1961. A fairly stable pattern of social relations, a community image, and traditions, were formed during this period. A process of rapid social stratification took place within the village, leaving a dozen *patroncitos* in place of the pre-revolutionary single great *patron*. A succession of related deep and bitter conflicts developed over status, land, and other economic interests, and over political power within the village and the region. The village and those

villages from which many of its new inhabitants came had been at the heart of the Revolution. It was abandoned much of the time while people hid in the hills from the raids of both sides. For years there was no local law enforcement, a state of statelessness. Most men and many women were armed, often with guns, or at least with weapon-implements such as *machetes* and knives. Violence was commonplace after the formation of the *ejido* and of new forms of local government in 1927, when municipality and village records were started. Thirty-two murders took place between 1927 and 1960 within the village or its environs, involving residents of the village. In addition there were 77 incidents of violence that stopped short of killing, but in which there were serious injuries or wounds. The range was from 0 to 5 killings a year, with an average of .94 killings per year. My compilation is based on all killings and incidents of serious violence mentioned to me during my three years of study of this village, as well as an examination of village and municipality records. I went from court records to further inquiries in the village which revealed further cases and added to the specification of those encountered in the records. At least in the case of the killings it was possible to conduct systematic inquiry.

In my relation with the women of the village I had access to the abundant circulation of a kind of malicious gossip, which I have described elsewhere as constituting a moral accounting system. Such gossip is known as *chismes,* and in effect I was able to do a *chismografiá* of the village, "chismography." My studies of the court records, in cross-checking *chismes,* indicated that this information has a high degree of reliability.

The murder rate per 100,000 over this period depends on what one takes as the average population figure. According to my estimate it grew from about 250 to 800 during the period, the average was most likely about 400, which would yield a murder rate of 235 per 100,000. Taking 525 as a midpoint of this population expansion, we would get 178 per 100,000. The true figure probably lies somewhere between these. This agrees fairly well with figures for the state, as well as with other studies of violence in Mexican villages, particularly those by June Nash and Paul Friedrich.[1] Generally, they report rising murder rates, with a high incidence of motivated and also political killings, while in this report I will offer evidence that, for the village in question, which is mestizo in contrast to the two Indian villages (Mayan and Tarascan) referred to in the Nash and Friedrich studies, the murder rate is declining and that the great majority of all murders can be described as motiveless, that is, mostly unconnected with stable or persistent conflicts.

Because of the history which I have reconstructed of hostile major conflicts in the village as well as a prevalence of minor conflicts involving fewer persons and lesser interests, I was surprised to find that very few of the cases of violence were connected to these conflicts, and that the effect of violence in generating conflict leading to further violence was minimal. I will suggest explanations for this disjunction between conflict and violence.

The extremely numerous, relatively minor conflicts so overtly contested among the women of the village were connected with only occasional and

very minor violence and almost never reached the level of weapon use. Killing is exclusively a male activity—none of the killings were carried out by women, although one influential and "wealthy" woman was suspected of having hired assassins in two killings. Allegations about hired assassins are not uncommon, but in no case could any of these be verified. It is a suspicion that must be taken as more general than its realizations, and it is often alleged in conflict between important persons, even when no assassination takes place. In 77 instances of violence involving 176 persons, there were 79 men and 9 women among the so-called aggressors, and 80 males and 8 females among the victims. The difference between aggressor and victim is sometimes clearcut, sometimes narrow, depending, in part, on the fortunes of combat. Among those killed, only 2 of 32 were women.

This brings us to perhaps the single most important factor in the occurrence of murder and violence. There appears to be an overwhelming correlation between these violent acts and the state of intoxication. This cannot be established definitely, but the evidence is highly suggestive of it. The much lower involvement of women in violence appears to be correlated with their non-drinking. Women drink only at *fiestas,* and then in moderation. They do not participate in drinking in non-ceremonial contexts such as bars.

Intoxication is mentioned in the court records in 8 of 32 killings. It is also mentioned in 17 cases of violence, and though less explicit, it seems highly probable in 35 of the others, either from the location in bars or from the behavior described. We made lists of village alcoholics and heavy drinkers quite independently of the compilation of the lists of murderers and of the violent, and for other purposes, primarily to study the problem of alco-

1. Paul Friedrich, "Assumptions Underlying Tarascan Political Homicide," *Psychiatry* 25 (1962), 4:315–327; June Nash, "Death as a Way of Life: The Increasing Resort to Homicide in a Maya Indian Community," *American Anthropologist* 69 (1967), 5:455–470.

holism and for a characterological sub-typing of the village. The alcoholic was classified as the person who became as intoxicated as possible as often as possible, and whose drinking very greatly interfered with his maintaining a regular work schedule. It is also associated with (this is not a criterion) a very sharp drop in productivity, in that these men, when they were *ejidatarios*—that is, had a land parcel—tended to be farming less than the full extent of their available land, and whether *ejidatario* or not, they very often worked less than a full work-week. The heavy drinker was the man who was very often intoxicated, but usually on weekends and holidays, and who generally carried on his work activities without either a reduction in productivity or cutting into his work-week.

There is a very high co-incidence between the lists of the violent and the lists of alcoholics and heavy drinkers. The problem of habitual intoxication is indicated by the following figures: of 165 males in the village over twenty years of age, 17.6% are on the alcoholic list, and 16.3% are on the heavy drinker list. Combining the two lists, 34% of all males over twenty years of age are found on these lists. For reasons that will be discussed below, only three of those who have murdered in the village remain in the village. One of these is a non-drinker; he is also the clearest case of having committed an act of deliberate and premeditated murder with definite motives. (He ambushed and shot his father-in-law after his wife had left him, complaining of too frequent beatings.) The other two are on the alcoholic or heavy drinker lists. Forty-two of the people on the list of aggressors were no longer in the village at the time of our study. Of the 22 males from this list who remained in the village, two were non-drinkers and the rest were all on the alcoholic or heavy

drinker lists—in other words, almost all of them came from among the 34% of the village males to be found on these lists.

The village is obviously not homogeneous, either characterologically or in social status, or in participation in the main lines of village conflict. If 34% of the village males were alcoholic or heavy drinkers, the rest were not. The leaders of the village and the more successful in the process of rapid social stratification tended to be men who emphasized sobriety, did not socialize in bars, and did not "hang around" the streets. They maintained large and stable families, and their concerns were the struggles in the economic and political arena. These men were also the leaders and at the center of the main conflicts around which so much of village life revolved. Their general non-involvement with intoxication is one of the most important factors in the disjunction between violence and conflict. The violent tended to come from a social and characterological sub-group that are identified with *machismo,* that is with the *macho* code of manliness. (*Machismo* is well known in the literature on Mexico and can only be mentioned very briefly here.) *Macho* they were in every motion, thought, and self-image—derived, as it were, from a kind of free-floating social image of manliness based in part on the *vaquero,* or the cowboy, and in part on a remnant of chivalry. The *macho* saw himself as hard-drinking, *enamorado,* sensitive to slights, always supposedly ready for violence and the use of a gun, given to frequenting bars and hanging out with others of his type, often involved in violence of the variety we have called motiveless, and proud of all this.

Violence often occurs, unanticipated, among friends who drink together. A joke that is told in the village expresses the pattern very well. A group of men drink together in a bar. After a few drinks they call each other friend; a few more and they call each other *compadres;* another round or two and they have all become brothers. They embrace each other with protestations of affection, and after still more drinking one says to another *"Yo soy tu mero papá"* (I am your very father), and there is a killing. This kind of insult to one's mother is known as a *mentada de madre* and is actually mentioned in a number of court records. We have seen at least one instance of violence that lived up literally almost to the dialogue of the joke: a *mentada* either invites one to have access to one's mother with all sorts of elaborations on this, or uses a term which implies that one's mother has been violated or that she is promiscuous. Such expressions are often used jokingly among these men when they are *en su juicio* (possessing judgment—in their "right minds") without leading to violence, but in an intoxicated state they might start a fight. Under these circumstances a *macho* will not brook a *mentada* and other forms of insult, although these come readily to his lips when he is offended. Other incidents included a drink refused, an attempt to leave a drunken all-night gambling session, a bit of joking or teasing which is suddenly taken seriously. Jealousy entered into one of the killings which took place under intoxication, but generally the motives are momentary and transient. The aggressor would not have behaved as he did had he been sober. The aggressor later is often bewildered by the effects of his action. One man who had hacked up his friend with a *machete* in such a quarrel went around for years protesting his hurt that this friend, now crippled, would no longer associate with him. In their readiness to fight, the *machos* are referred to as *justanciosos*

(from *justa,* the joust, i.e., jousters). It is beyond the scope of this paper to take up the complex question of why people in this village fall into various socio-characterological sub-groups. But the disjunction between this group which has been the source of so much violence and another group which is the source of so much of the conflict is basic to the distribution we are discussing.

Generally for men the show of aggression is suppressed; men are cautious in their interactions with one another. Gossip, which is so common an activity of women, is greatly inhibited among men, even when in safe company. Intoxication seems to be required in almost all cases to release aggression to expression in violence. It seems to be true that in many cultures and situations, some kind of distantiation may be necessary for people to be able to kill each other—that is, the other has to be seen impersonally or seen as a member of an enemy group, or a person removed from normal society in some way. For the situation which we are analyzing, however, distance seems clearly to be protective. The killings are often among those who are in intimate contact with one another —even more so, given the effect of intoxication. The killings are most often horizontal in terms of social status, although only in the lower portion of the hierarchy. They are greatly inhibited horizontally among those at the top. Most of the mechanisms we shall discuss which are called into play to inhibit violence and the reverberations of its effect, and which prevent a conversion of conflict into violence, depend upon distance. Vertical relationships seem almost totally immune to violence. Such relations, given the social structure of this community, are mainly those of patronage/clientage, but there is the possibility of one patron's client killing another patron, at his behest. This is used at times as a threat or voiced as a suspicion. The greatest status envy or disdain was usually for those most immediately above or below one's own position. There was extraordinarily little resentment by the poorest members of the village of those who were the wealthiest in the village. Instead, there was either dependence or the hope that the patron would act in the social image of the benevolent patron. The upper status people were strongly antagonistic to one another and usually involved in bitter conflicts of interest of long duration. Cool and cautious about friendships and less apt to depend on them, they spent little time in socializing outside of their families. They cultivated patronage with those clearly above and below them rather than horizontal relationships. They tended not to be sensitive to slight or rejection, but rather suspicious or wary in advance. They were able to accept considerable social disapprobation in matters of their own interests.

Such men live in public conflict, and public knowledge of conflict is protective—it leads to avoidance, wariness, and the expectation of possible violence, including the possibility of hired killers as well as fear of direct violence from their antagonists. First we find separateness of the distinct segments of the population from which the violent and the main parties to conflict are drawn. Secondly, conflict alerts participants in the community to the possibility of violence. These are the major causes for the disjunction between the violent and those in conflict.

Those involved in major conflicts often take recourse to a protective preestablishment of blame in litigation, that is, it is a common practice for the municipal court to deliver a warning of mutual responsibility for harm to litigants. The major conflicts have long

histories, and such mutual grievances are neither transient nor private. A rapid upwelling of grievance or sense of insult seems to be a prerequisite for the conversion of grievance to violence. Intoxication is probably also necessary. Conflictants do not drink together and do not attend the same *fiestas* in their avoidance of each other. Insult is not usually exchanged among the participants in major conflicts. Further, the participants in major conflict are skilled conflictants. Their conflicts are expressed in political terms. Legitimate means are pursued in competitive patronage and clientship, in the building of separate networks of influence and protection, in the use of litigation and petition in courts and to higher authorities, the building of factions, the use of mechanisms of political control (i.e., contesting in local elections and for village and regional offices), the use of threats and of legal protection. The threats may go so far as to involve frequent talk about violence—this is especially likely from the retainers of each of the conflictants. But in spite of all of this, direct violence is avoided.

Violence itself leads to remarkably little conflict, especially to violence-producing conflict. The social mechanisms that operate seem sufficient to prevent the reverberation of violence, so that the high level of violence and high frequency of murder is not being generated by the kind of chain of feuding and vengeance that is so often reported elsewhere.

One reason for the failure of violence to beget violence is that with a high degree of regularity, either murderers or people involved in serious violence leave the village temporarily. Forty-two of the 77 involved in violence are no longer in the village at all. Those who leave for this reason are being drawn from a limited pool, tending over a time to diminish violence. They are not being replaced at the same rate due to countervailing processes of culture change. Most of the court records end with the note that the suspect is *en fuga* (in flight). In some cases, village officials and others intervene to prevent immediate reprisal, and it seems that if violence does not come immediately then it usually does not come at all. The necessity of flight, sometimes temporary, sometimes only a short distance, is symbolic, since the whereabouts of the person is often known. The necessity to leave the village seems to be one of the sanctions operating against the occurrence of major violence.

Does stability deter violence? The village is composed mainly of immigrants but it has become increasingly stabilized and most of its present residents have either an *ejido* and a house site, or a house site and a set of patronage relationships with those who have *ejidos*. Most have some stake in the village and have no wish to leave. (Of 418 people over 16 years of age, 118 or 27% were born in the village, and, of these, less than half have at least one parent born in the village.)

Five of those who were killed were *ejidatarios,* and there are *ejidatarios* among the violent. Fear of punishment does not seem to act as much of a deterrent. Only 3 of 32 murderers were jailed for very short periods. One died in prison after his second murder, having been declared insane. One killed a former village mayor. He is the only one to be pursued beyond the village and to receive a five-year prison term. On his return he was treated without stigma and was given another *ejido* parcel for the one taken away from him. He was offered every post in village government and occupied several. Another man spent two years in the penitentiary and did not lose his *ejido* parcel. He later served as justice of the

peace. Where people do not flee and are apprehended for violence, fines are commonly assessed and paid—in many cases charges are not pressed. Some cases are heard only in the village, where they are treated mildly.

We have said there is evidence of a sharp diminution of violence, in spite of its high average rate over the period —in the 34 years that this survey covers, there were 21 killings in the first 17 years, and only 11 killings in the second 17 years. Of the 11 killings in the second 17 years, all occurred in the first 12 of those 17 years. There are no killings at all on record from 1956 through 1960. Comparison of the first and second halves of this 34-year period in which the number of killings drops to about half represents even more of a diminution when one considers that over this whole period the population tripled. Considering a rough estimate of the probable population averaged over the first half of this period, compared wtih the second half, then the rate drops from about 300 deaths per 100,000 in the first half, to 95 in the second half. The data indicate a less marked decline of non-lethal violence which cannot as reliably be estimated due to the greater probable incompleteness of the collection of violence cases. The violence rate appears to be relatively constant comparing the first half and the second half of the period. The number of incidents of violence appearing in court records and village gossip increases considerably, but when allowance is made for increase in population it appears as a constant. If further allowance could be made for the greater likelihood of appearance of cases of non-lethal violence in court records in more recent years, then one would note a decline, though much less marked.

What might be the reasons for this diminution of violence? One is the draining off of the violent by flight, and incomplete replacement of their numbers either through immigration of other violents who have fled from other villages, or of the *macho* type that is their main source. Self-elimination takes place also by the tendency of the violent to eliminate each other. The diminution must also be traced importantly to social and cultural changes militating against the relatively free and ready violence of the early period of the formation of the village following the Revolution. After a long period of virtual statelessness during the Revolution and immediately following it, the formation of the village, the organization of the municipality with the gradual assertion of its law enforcing institutions, and the effect of the local state government[2] on the suppression of violence contributed to its decrease.

In the early period after the Revolution each village maintained its own militia and all were armed. The militia itself and its members were often involved in violence. Since these militia were disbanded, periodic campaigns of "depistolization," as it is called, are sponsored by the state government to reduce arms ownership and use. There are laws against the carrying of arms now, but enforcement is sporadic. The presence of law enforcement officers in the countryside is rare, and pursuit of fugitives is uncommon. Nevertheless, the increased presence of a state following the period of statelessness must be held to account for part of the diminution. The increased stabilization of the population, the formation of new villages, and the gradual reduction of the rate of immigration must also be in part responsible.

A process of acculturation also militated against violence and replenishment of the *macho* sub-group from which so much of the violence came.

The *macho* code had old Hispanic roots. Perhaps from the first, there was some ambivalence about its place in an overall moral code. It was in competitive conflict with other levels of that code. I have elsewhere described the complexity of the moral codes of the village under study.[3] I found a hierarchically layered system of co-operant moral codes. There is a general moral code that people will often cite, greatly affected by Catholic religious principles, that deplores violence, exalts familial stability and obedience, and is opposed to the principles of *machismo*. Prudence and caution are among its primary values which, as we have seen, have effect on the behavior of persons in public conflict. *Machismo* appears as another layer in the overall set of moral codes. It also serves as a kind of free-floating social identity, available to those who most require it. But its principles are co-occurrent with their opposite—such notions as prudence, sobriety, and progress. Even in the general moral code, there is widespread social approval of the basic principles of manliness and yet, even on its own level, this approval co-exists with its contrary. There are many sayings to the effect that the *macho* is a coward: *"el macho vive mientras el cobarde quiere"* (the *macho* lives as long as the coward wills it). There is a folk perception of the shallowness of *machismo* and its association characterologically with the opposite of what it seems to be.

The complexity and ambivalence of the moral code can be clearly seen in the notions of vengeance and honor. Everyone speaks about violence as if there is a certainty of vengeance—they

2. "State government" refers to the federal states of Mexico, whereas "state" refers to the political concept of a government exercising control over the use of force.

3. Lola Romanucci Schwartz, *Morality, Conflict and Violence in a Mestizo Village,* doctoral dissertation (University Microfilms, Ann Arbor, Michigan, 1963).

will speak of themselves as being vengeful, and there is pronounced obligation of members of a family or kindred, even of friends, to avenge the death of a person. In numerous conversations I found that it came as a shock to villagers to have it demonstrated to them that, in fact, not one single murder since the village had been formed had ever been avenged. Leaving the village temporarily releases both the fugitive and those obliged to pursue him from vengeance. Despite the code, there is no appetite for deliberate violence.

Lack of awareness of departure from the general moral code is also instanced by the *macho* code which would enjoin murder or violence over jealousy. Supposedly, a man who is betrayed will kill. There is the saying, very often reiterated: *"mujer mala matarla o dejarla"* (kill or leave the immoral, betraying woman), but it is in fact rare in the frequent enough instances in which a man believes himself betrayed for him either to kill the woman or to leave her. Women, even with children, do leave men from time to time, for their philandering, physical abuse or drinking. The moral code then is stratified, allows for choice, involves alternatives and ways out of the value traps that would otherwise lead to violent behavior.

Similarly, there is a kind of ambivalence about violence at times: pride in their violent nature, pride in their peacefulness contrasted to neighboring Indian villages. There is an ambivalent identification of violence with the Indian component of the mestizo heritage, often considered to be a direct consequence of Indian blood. At times this will be spoken of with pride and at other times with disparagement, in the same opposed senses as one might say *"soy hombre malo."*

The people regard their village as peaceful and progressive. They do not have a cumulative sense of the amount of violence that has occurred. In casual discussion they begin to recall cases and "add them up," surprised by their frequency. One other thing also leads to the perception of the village as essentially peaceful, and that is that in many of the cases involving violence, they will say that the people involved *"no son de aqui"* (are not of this village). This, however, is applied to anyone who was not born in the village or whose parents were not born there, and this includes most of the village, as we noted above. A person's "place" is where he was born, where his parents were born. Even the immigrants to a village perceive many of the violent who have left the village as not having been from the village, in that their stay was temporary.

Violence is also attributed to a *falta de cultura* (i.e. cultivation, education, literacy, civility, respect for the law), a lack of civilization, of culture. They see themselves as being more advanced than surrounding places (which are seen as more violent)—as having more *cultura,* though unevenly distributed within the village, a situation similar to that described by Charles Leslie for Mitla.[4]

To summarize: We have examined the high but diminishing rates of murder and violence in a single Mexican mestizo community, and have noted and tried to account for a disjunction between the occurrence of conflict and the occurrence of violence, and have pointed out several bases for this disjunction. These include a social and characterological difference of provenience between the participants in public conflict and the violent; the mechanism whereby public conflict alerts the com-

4. Charles M. Leslie, *Now We Are Civilized: A Study of the World View of the Zapotec Indians of Mitla, Oaxaca* (Detroit: Wayne State University Press, 1960).

munity and its participants to the possibilities of violence leading to avoidance which greatly reduces the possibility of violence; and the mechanisms whereby violence, when it does occur, is limited in its possible reverberation in conflict and in further violence. Thus, in examining conflict and violence we learn something about social solidarity and social mechanisms for reducing and limiting violence. Solidarity, like health, is not just the absence of pathology or of violence, but the community's capacity to contain, diminish, or limit, with a minimum of derivative violence or conflict, even the high incidence of potentially disruptive killing and violence that it has experienced.

12

Violence in East African Tribal Societies

By ROBERT B. EDGERTON

Robert B. Edgerton is associate professor of anthropology (in residence) in the Departments of Anthropology and Psychiatry, University of California at Los Angeles. He is also the co-ordinator of the Socio-Behavioral Research program, Mental Retardation Center, UCLA. He has written and edited various articles and books, among which are The Cloak of Competence, The Individual in Cultural Adaptation, Drunken Comportment *(with C. MacAndrew), and* Changing Perspectives in Mental Illness *(with S. Plog).*

This paper was prepared for the Symposium on Violence at the meetings of the American Anthropological Association, New Orleans, Louisiana, 1969.

I wish to acknowledge the assistance of the Social Science Research Institute (NIMH Grant MH-02243) and the East-West Center at the University of Hawaii in preparation of this paper.

IN writing about violence the social scientist faces certain hazards. For one thing, any subject as fashionable and important as violence is likely to lure the unwary social scientist into premature expression of his beliefs or findings. There are several recent and well-publicized volumes dealing with violence to demonstrate (should there have been any lingering doubt) that the social sciences have yet to exhaust their extraordinary capacity for producing pretentious and vacuous accounts of complex and vital human concerns. Another hazard is encountered when one attempts to decide just where on earth he is to begin, for where on earth, almost literally, is there not—or has there not at one time been—human violence in the most appalling abundance? And how is it possible to add anything of significance to all that has been said of this violence by history's chorus of voices? But there is also an advantage here, for so plentiful are these examples, today and in the past, and so horrendous are they to contemplate that it is almost literally impossible to be guilty of hyperbole in discussing violence.

And yet it is possible that there *has* been exaggeration in some of our common-sense and scientific views of today's violence. Even a cursory examination of the dismal record of violence throughout history reveals that a recurrent theme in human thought in many of the places where records have been kept is the belief that violence had reached unprecedented and intolerable levels.[1] Surely there are few among us today who seem eager to suggest that the violence or threat of violence in our daily lives is either ordinary or tolerable. Without for a moment suggesting that I find the current dimensions of violence in the world either morally pleasing or lacking the most serious apocalyptic potential, I would ask how much we really know about man's ability to live with violence, to control it, and to endure it. Since I believe that our received answer to this question is at best inadequate and may well be highly misleading, it may be possible for us to improve our understanding of violence by reviewing what is known of violence in a part of the world unlike our own—tribal East Africa.

EAST AFRICA IN HISTORY

Although most of East African history is still known only in sketchy outline, certain facts are now reasonably well attested. If there is still too little evidence for us to say just how fanciful is Ardrey's vision of an East Africa populated by territorially violent primates and men, the record of history is quite ample to convince anyone that even if early man were a paragon of peace (as some would have it), recent men in East Africa have made up for lost time.[2]

While the interior of East Africa has remained very poorly documented until quite recent times, the east coast of Africa has been known to history since the *Periplus* of about A.D. 100, and it may have been known to Phoenecians several centuries earlier.[3] Romans,

1. Gustav Bychowski, *Evil in Man: The Anatomy of Hate and Violence* (New York: Grune and Stratton, 1968); H. D. Graham and T. R. Gurr, eds, *The History of Violence in America: Historical and Comparative Perspectives* (New York: Frederick A. Praeger, 1969); Fredric Wertham, *A Sign for Cain: An Exploration of Human Violence* (New York: MacMillan, 1966).

2. For a collection of largely polemical responses to Ardrey, see Ashley Montagu, M.P., ed., *Man and Aggression* (New York: Oxford University Press, 1968).

3. Gervase Mathew, "The East African Coast Until the Coming of the Portuguese," in R. Oliver and G. Mathew, eds., *History of East Africa* 1 (Oxford: Clarendon Press, 1963).

Greeks, Chinese, Arabs, Indians, and others later left evidence of their trade wares and entrepôts along various parts of the coast from Somalia to Tanzania. Since slaves were being exported from East Africa as early as the *Periplus,* it is likely that from the very beginning this trade sent waves of violence well into the interior.[4] Certainly, early documents of East African trade leave no doubt that violence was common on the coast, but little of this coastal mayhem seems to have involved African tribal peoples until the late sixteenth century, when a tribe known to history as the Zimba swept up the coast, annihilating Arab and Portugese colonies here and there and killing over 3,000 of the inhabitants of Kilwa. As one European observer put it, these tribesmen killed and ate ". . . every living thing, Men, Women, Children, Dogs, Cats, Rats, Snakes, Lizards, sparing nothing. . . ."[5] But when it came to unrestrained violence, although the Portuguese did not deign to eat their victims, they did mutilate them horribly in the zeal of their mission as well as in the collection of valuables on fingers, in teeth, or thought to be hidden away in more intimate orifices.[6]

As the Arab slave trade intensified in the eighteenth or nineteenth centuries, the violence of the coast was extended to the interior. In many areas along the slave caravan routes, combat was virtually continuous as large armed bands of Arab slavers and African tribesmen alternately co-operated and clashed. In addition, tribal warfare

also occurred in the interior quite apart from any involvement with the slave caravans.

When the European powers began to take an active interest in East Africa —whether to explore, to suppress slavery, to spread enlightenment, or to open new markets—it was probably inevitable that East African tribesmen, long accustomed to the depredations of slavers and to hostilities between tribes, would resist the efforts of the British and Europeans to impose European ideas of law and order upon them. European efforts to pacify the tribes were often tragic, with senseless killing on both sides. Colonel Meinertzhagen, then a young British officer, gives the flavor of these military forays when he recounts, as in the conflict with the Kikuyu and Nandi, how certain of his African soldiers and a few European officers keenly enjoyed both shooting Africans and referring to them as apes.[7] In return, Africans from many tribes produced a good many dead bodies as evidence of their military competence and their outrage. In some instances, the reciprocal killing became particularly ugly (as, for example, in one case when a European settler was killed by having large numbers of men and women urinate into his mouth until he drowned).[8]

Eventual establishment of peace did reduce inter-tribal war greatly and, with rare exceptions, it eliminated the slave trade altogether. In return, however, Britain and Germany brought to East African men the horrors of military service in two World Wars. And while European law brought with it many undeniable advantages, it also brought flogging, imprisonment, and hanging, often for reasons that Africans found unfair or inexplicable. Eventually, colonial law probably served to

4. Kenneth Ingham, *A History of East Africa* (New York: Frederick A. Praeger, 1962) ; R. Oliver and G. Mathew, eds., *History of East Africa,* 2 vols (Oxford: Clarendon Press, 1963).

5. Mathew, op. cit., p. 138.

6. Justus Strandes, translated by J. F. Wallwork, *The Portuguese Period in East Africa* (Nairobi: East African Literature Bureau, 1961).

7. R. A. Meinertzhagen, *Kenya Diary, 1902–06* (Edinborgh: Oliver and Boyd, 1957).

8. Ibid.

reduce capital crime and it brought juridical stability to areas which had formerly been in political turmoil, but it could hardly have been expected to eliminate all forms of violence, and it did not do so.[9]

On some occasions, various economic and social problems that were occasioned by German and British administration led directly to long and bloody rebellion. In 1905 many tribes of Tanzania rose against the German administration in what was known as the Maji Maji rebellion, and it was not until 1907 that German machine guns put an end to the uprising. There was heavy loss of life on both sides. The Mau Mau rebellion of the Kikuyu brought several years of terror or warfare to Kenya in the 1950's. Although European deaths, both military and civilian, did not exceed a few hundred, more than 10,000 Kikuyu died. Since the three East African nations have achieved independence, some intertribal warfare has occurred, there has been renewed rebellion (for example, the Konzo-Amba revolt in Uganda), certain military units have rebelled (in one instance British troops had to be called upon to restore order) and important political leaders have been assassinated.[10]

9. For a useful review of colonial impact upon tribal societies, see P. H. Gulliver, *Social Control in an African Society. A Study of the Arusha: Agricultural Masai of Northern Tanganyika* (Boston: Boston University Press, 1963).

10. See, for example, Ingham, *op. cit.* (1962); P. H. Gulliver, ed., *Tradition and Transition in East Africa: Studies of the Tribal Element in the Modern Era* (Berkeley: University of California Press, 1969); A. A. Mazrui, *Violence and Thought: Essays on Social Tensions in Africa* (London: Longmans, Green, 1969); Eugene V. Walter, *Terror and Resistance: A Study of Political Violence; With Case Studies of Some Primitive African Communities* (New York: Oxford University Press, 1969).

This background to East African violence has been provided for those who lack acquaintance with the area, as well as to give some indication of the varieties of violence that have been experienced in East Africa's past. This is not to suggest, even for a moment, that East Africa is, or was, the most spectacularly violent place on earth. In my view, the record of violence established on our own frontier, in Europe, in Indonesia, in China, and elsewhere, can hardly be matched by East Africa.

VIOLENCE IN EAST AFRICAN TRIBAL SOCIETIES

The following remarks are based upon field research conducted in 1961-62.[11] The four societies in question are the Hehe of the southern highlands in Tanzania, the Kamba of central Kenya, the Pokot of northwest Kenya, and the Sebei of the northern slopes of Mt. Elgon in Uganda. These four societies reflect much of the variety that is typical of tribal East Africa. The Hehe are a large, formerly dominant tribe of southern Tanzania; they represent some thirty or more chieftaincies which were amalgamated under the leadership of two famous chiefs in the nineteenth century. At their apex, the Hehe not only controlled a vast area of Tanzania, they confronted and defeated the Germans before yielding to superior force of arms. The Kamba are a still larger tribe, but one a good deal less complex in political organization; related to the Kikuyu, they number close to 1,000,000 people. The Pokot are a far smaller society, one whose history lies not with the Bantu speaking tribes (such as the Hehe and Kamba) but with the Kalenjin speakers (such as the Nandi).

11. This research was supported by a research grant from the National Science Foundation, and NIMH Grant M-4097. My special thanks are due Walter Goldschmidt, the director of this project.

Their remote location has left them beyond the reach of most modernizing influences and they remain relatively little acculturated. The Sebei, like the Pokot, are a small, Kalenjin speaking people, but one with a lesser devotion to pastoralism and a greater involvement with agricultural life on the densely populated slopes of Mt. Elgon. Thus, while four societies do not represent the full range of social and political complexity in tribal East Africa, they do provide a varied introduction to violence and its control in that region. The descriptions that follow refer to the period 1961–62, which was in all cases prior to independence.[12]

Throughout East Africa, especially in the low-lying savannah areas that are farther from the highlands and the European settlements, the environment itself is suffused with violence. Novelists have used the ever-present sharp thorns of the trees and brush to symbolize the harshness of this world, but this harshness is more visible and dangerous in animal form—crocodiles, poisonous snakes, lions, leopards, hyenas, rhino, elephant, buffalo, and many others bring violent death to animals and men alike. And over much of the same area there is the constant threat and the occasional actuality of warfare involving the universal prize, cattle. Such armed conflicts are most common in the lowlands of northern Kenya and

12. For an introduction to these tribes, see G. G. Brown and A. McD. Hutt, *Anthropology in Action* (London: Oxford University Press, 1935); Walter Goldschmidt, *Sebei Law* (Berkeley, University of California Press, 1967); Gerhard Lindblom, *The Akamba in British East Africa* 17, 2nd ed. (Uppsala Archives d'etudes Orientales, 1920); J. G. Peristiany, "The Age-Set System of the Pastoral Pokot," *Africa* 21 (1959), pp. 188–206, 279–302; H. K. Schneider, "The Subsistance Role of Cattle Among the Pokot in East Africa," *American Anthropologist* 59 (1957), pp. 278–300.

Uganda, but armed conflict took place in all four societies during 1961–62. The Hehe fought several skirmishes with raiding Gogo and Baraguyu, the Sebei engaged in lethal hostilities with Karamojong cattle raiders, the Pokot and Turkana were never fully at peace, and the Kamba and Masai joined in a battle so large it required the intervention of British police and troops. Typically, such battles were encounters undertaken to steal cattle, but should men or boys defend their cattle, then spears and arrows (still poisoned in many areas) were used with all the vigor of old. The administration sometimes countered an increase in warfare by mounting punitive or preventive forays of troops into an area in need of pacification. These measures, earlier known as "showing the flag," were occasionally draconian, for these troops were sometimes disposed to employ their automatic weapons for purposes other than display.

But the ambiance of violence does not derive wholly from such dramatic occurrences and symbolic presences. The texture of everyday life is a product of many routine acts of violence. For example, it is not uncommon in East Africa to find a kind of casual cruelty to animals that Europeans find appalling, a cruelty in which children torture small animals with a seemingly supreme indifference to their pain. And while East African adults sometimes treat their livestock with great compassion, they sometimes inflict what to Western eyes is outright cruelty, as when some tribesmen castrate their cattle or when goats are smothered for ceremonial use. What is more, these are societies in which eveyone knows that animals sometimes take human life and humans often take the lives of animals. Whether it is a leopard stealing a child or a man downing an antelope, everyone knows that violent death of this kind has occurred and will occur again. Perhaps this knowledge makes the casual evisceration of a small animal, or the laughter that follows the fall of a blind man, comprehensible. Perhaps it does not. All we can know with certainty is that such acts do take place.

Although it is my impression that East African parents are remarkably gentle with their children (at least by European standards), there is no absence of violence in the family. Husbands often assault their wives, sometimes with a slap, sometimes with a fist, a foot, or a stick. Especially when the marriage is new or the husband is drunk, these blows can be harsh enough to leave the bruised faces of wives as anything but an uncommon sight. Sexual relations, too, can be violent, and not in the sense of mutually esteemed passion. Few East African societies share with the Gusii their extremes of sexual violence in which the infliction of pain is a sovereign goal,[13] but all four of these societies sometimes express manifest violence in their sexuality. The Kamba, for example, approve a form of sexual intercourse in which the man is expected to take the wife with a maximum of force and a minimum of concern for her feelings, and the Pokot have institutionalized a form of rape in which married men may forcibly and, if necessary, painfully rape unmarried girls.

Brawling is another regular feature of life in these societies. While fighting with fists, sticks, or clubs may be no more frequent than comparable fights are in the West, verbal abuse is a seemingly ubiquitous aspect of life. Sometimes these raucous insults or subtle inuendos lead to physical attack, with women punching each other and pulling hair and men exchanging blows. These conflicts appear to be most frequent among young men of warrior age who are expressing the animal spirits expected of them or fighting over girls, and among older persons over beer. Quarrels that begin over the beer pot may lead to comic violence, as among the Kamba where otherwise dignified elders will, once they are in their cups, undertake to flail feebly at one another or to wrestle ignominiously in the dust. Or the violence may be serious, as among the Sebei, where the aggrieved party has been known to lie in ambush in order to murder his adversary, or among the Hehe, where a drinker's argument has been known to erupt into sudden violence with one man butting another with his head with murderous intent and fatal outcome.

Murder may also take place by less direct means, as for example, when an entire family is burned to death in their sleep by an unknown enemy. Arson of this sort was practiced and feared in all four societies. And yet there can be no doubt that more murder was intended and accomplished by witchcraft than by any other means. It might be argued that witchcraft (be that understood as an immanent power for evil or the intentional practice of sorcery) is hardly violence in the same sense as a clout on the head. But in my view, and in the view of many anthropologists who have done research in East Africa, nothing creates more terror nor gives rise to more overt acts of violence than the covert menace of witchcraft.[14] Surely, no account of violence in these four societies would be complete without an emphasis upon witchcraft. In these societies it is no exaggeration to say that everyone believes in the terrible power of witchcraft to sicken or kill, and that everyone at one time or

13. Robert LeVine, "Gusii Sex Offenses: A Study in Social Control," *American Anthropologist* 61 (1959), pp. 965–990.

14. John Middleton and E. H. Winter, eds., *Witchcraft and Sorcery in East Africa* (New York: Frederick A. Praeger, 1963).

another in his life—if not at all times—lives in dread that he has become a victim of this malevolence. An ethnographer has little difficulty locating men and women who admit that they are practicing witchcraft against someone, and threats and accusations of witchcraft are commonplace. What is more, people express their fear of witchcraft almost continually and they forever search for protective counter-magic. The use of poisons to assure injury to persons who are also being bewitched is likewise common, and terrifying, especially among the Kamba. As a result, serious illness and misfortune—common enough matters anywhere—are usually taken to be evidence of human malevolence as it is communicated in witchcraft.

The result of this system of supernatural malevolence is fear and hostility, and even in 1961–62, despite administrative prohibition against killing suspected witches, some persons whose witch power was greatly feared were killed. Others were forced to flee for their lives. Even if no blow is struck in the name of witchcraft, and the killer is unknown, the intent is murderous nonetheless and the body is no less dead. People in these societies treat witchcraft as something not merely akin to violence, but as violence of the most horrifying and lethal kind.

This brief account of some of the kinds of violence that take place in these four East African societies is intended to suggest the range, kind, and frequency of violence that routinely occurs in everyday life. As you will already have discerned, however, the examples of violence mentioned thus far are primarily individual in nature. The reason for discussing individual violence in an essay concerned with collective violence will be discussed in a moment, but before doing so I want to indicate something of the range of collective violence that also occurs in these societies.

In the following examples of collective violence, I exclude the Hehe because they are a chiefdom rather than a segmentary tribal society lacking central political authority. My reasons for this exclusion will be discussed later.

SOME EXAMPLES OF COLLECTIVE VIOLENCE

The brawls that occur between individuals may also occur among larger numbers of persons who represent regions, clans, or age-sets. For example, young men of an age-set may band together to beat or whip one of their number who has committed an offense, and it is not uncommon for members of a clan or lineage to take action—violent action if need be—against a fellow clansman whose behavior is incorrigible. The action may take the form of physical restraint, beating, or even execution.

But it is not only in such commonplace ways that collective violence is expressed. The Pokot practice of marriage-by-capture (kïcitït) is a ceremonial epic of violence in which kin and age groups vie with one another in ritualized displays of violence, while unmarried women stand in immediate danger of forcible abduction by groups of men. When such a girl is captured, she may be tied and raped over a period of several days (in one instance reported by Conant, a girl's pelvis was dislocated by the violence of the assault). Throughout this dramatic occurrence, men threaten armed violence—and sometimes their posturing does develop into a general affray—while women are subject to imminent capture, rape and, sometimes, marriage by force.[15]

15. Francis Conant, "The External Coherence of Pokot Ritual Behavior," *Philo-*

In these tribal societies, a woman's choice of her spouse is a good deal less than free. Typically, young women form romantic relationships with young men only to find that their romantic inclinations do not often correspond to those of her family who wish a happy and secure marriage but who also wish one in which a sizeable brideprice is paid. When young women refuse to marry the man their family finds most suitable, or best able to pay the brideprice, they may (and often do) attempt to run away, but since this maneuver has been anticipated, it is seldom successful. Instead, the girl is likely to be apprehended and subjected to varying degrees of force until she accepts the designated husband. This force may consist in nothing more than confinement and haranguing, but it may also involve a prolonged beating at the hands of her brothers and father. Similarly, a women who deserts her husband, either to run away with another man or merely to escape from an unpleasant marital relationship, may be captured and beaten by her family or by interested clansmen until she agrees to return to her husband. Many women flee their husbands several times, only to be apprehended and coerced back into the marriage. However, it is also the case that a husband who regularly or flagrantly abuses or mistreats his wife may be seized by his clansmen and beaten. In both cases, the family and the clan are concerned that the marriage—and their reputation as people from whom good marriages may be expected—be maintained and that neither husband nor wife do anything to destroy the marriage. The use of violence against runaway women is a good deal more common than it is against mis-

behaving husbands, but collective violence may be directed against either.

In at least one of these societies, a wife has the right to take violent action against a husband who fails in his marital obligations. Among the Pokot, a man who is excessively abusive toward his wife, or beats her too often or too vigorously, or fails to take her satisfaction into account in their sexual relations, may fall victim to what is known as *kilapat*, something done or organized secretly. When a wife is legitimately aggrieved, she may collect half a dozen or a dozen other wives and together they may seize the unfortunate husband in his sleep, tying him securely and roughly to a nearby thorn tree. These women may then proceed to revile him, referring to inadequacies of his character and sexual anatomy alike, all the while laughing and mocking him as a man. Next they may beat him with sticks and whips, concentrating upon his testicles. They may also urinate and defecate upon him, and they may place their naked vulvas directly before his face so that he is compelled to see this otherwise always hidden and avoided organ. Finally, they may slaughter his favorite and most valuable ox and eat it before his now disbelieving eyes. The severity of the beating a man may receive varies greatly, as does the value of the ox or goat that is demanded by the angry women. To evaluate this behavior it must be understood that for women to so organize themselves against men—and no man may interfere in this ordeal—to insult and beat them and destroy their property, is extreme, even by Pokot standards of violence.[16] Similar expressions of collective power by women have been reported in other tribal societies of East

sophical *Transactions of the Royal Society of London*, Series B, no. 772 (1966), pp. 505–519.

16. R. B. Edgerton and Francis Conant, "Kilapat: The 'Shaming Party' Among the Pokot of East Africa," *Southwestern Journal of Anthropology* 20 (1964), pp. 404–418.

Africa. For example, Lindblom, writing of the period 1911–12, reported a highly similar practice among the Kamba—again, women had the right to band together to insult, assault, and threaten the property of any husband whose behavior had gone too far (I do not believe that this form of collective violence was still being expressed among the Kamba in 1961–62).[17]

Turning to a different context, it should be noted that collective violence is a recurrent feature of initiation ceremonies in these societies. Over much of tribal East Africa, both males and females undergo initiation. These ceremonies often involve circumcision, which for the girls may range from the minor excision of a portion of the hymen and the clitoris to the removal of the clitoris as well as large portions of the major and minor labia. These operations are violent enough in themselves, with pain and gore in abundance, but in addition the intiation ceremonies may include a period of violent behavior that is both directed toward the initiates and performed by them.

The Kamba provide one example of what is a more general East African pattern. The Kamba send males through a series of initiations, in some areas including a third and most secret ceremony. The initiates participate in a period of license during which time they roam about together, begging, marauding, and threatening. They may demand or destroy certain kinds of property and they may also assault or rape any uninitiated persons who are unfortunate enough to cross their path. Although these assaults are sub-lethal today, it is reported that in the past deaths might sometimes result.[18] At other times during the ceremonies, however, fully initiated men may haze the initiates and subject them to painful and humiliating experiences in which the initiate must eat excrement, commit sexual improprieties of a most flagrant sort, and submit to degrading ordeals and beatings.

The solidarity of men who experience these initiations together is directly seen in their assumption of the role of warriors within an age-graded system. However, these men also possess the potential for collective violence within the society. For example, if a Kamba council of elders, supported by divination, agrees that a person is an incorrigible thief, or a menace to life, they may order his execution. The execution is carried out by all the young men in the district who together form what is known as the *kingole*. In the manner of vigilantes, these men rush upon the victim and riddle him with poisoned arrows.

Similarly, the Sebei extend coercive power to the community by the ceremony of *ntarastit*. This ceremony invokes strong supernatural support for the right of the community to employ force in its maintenance of order. *Ntarastit* punishment is inflicted upon both murderers and thieves, and, like the Kamba, Sebei men descend upon the culprit en masse, but unlike the Kamba, the Sebei confine their punishment to the destruction of property.[19]

In addition, these societies have the potential for a collective response not unlike vigilantism in its spontaneity, but possessing organization along kinship lines. Thus, while an unsuccessful prophet may be killed by a more or less *ad hoc* assemblage of men who may or may not belong to the same age-set, most parties of men who undertake violence within these societies are carefully composed to include close relatives of the person who is about to be killed.

17. Lindblom, op. cit., p. 181.
18. Ibid., p. 66.

19. Goldschmidt, op. cit., pp. 255–259.

DISCUSSION

Mark Twain said, "Every man is a moon and has a dark side which he never shows to anybody." I have no doubt that most men have a dark side, but I think it could be argued that all too many show their dark side all too readily. In tribal East Africa, as in so many parts of the world, violence is never far from the center of human affairs. But beyond noting this grisly fact of human existence, what can we learn by examining violence in these tribal societies?

I should note once again that while it is doubtful that people in these East African tribal societies have achieved a more violent way of life than that of many other societies, they have certainly made violence a conspicuous part of their lives. By any criterion, these *are* violent societies. Yet it should also be noted that this violence is patterned. It occurs in more or less predictable ways and at more or less predictable times. What is more, it is responsive to ecological molding, for in each tribe the farmers (who must live amicably together on land that is in short supply) eschew direct or overt violence in favor of indirect means of aggression, while pastoralates (who can quite literally move away from trouble without harm to social or economic life) can and do express aggression more directly.[20] But none of this is startling, for human violence is probably always shaped by cultural considerations of what is or is not appropriate, just as it is often—perhaps always—influenced by ecology.[21]

But there is something about violence in these tribal societies that is less obvious and that warrants further comment. What these societies share—in addition to certain similarities in culture—is a tribal form of sociopolitical organization. Opposed to chiefdoms with their offices and institutions capable of ordering force in maintenance of social order, tribal societies lack offices and institutions of authority. Not only are they acephalous in their lack of political centralization, ideally they extend to no man the right to command the behavior of any other man. It was due to this fundamental difference that I omitted the Hehe from the earlier discussion of collective violence. The Hehe possessed a paramount chief supported by many sub-chiefs, as well as an extensive political apparatus which could order and compel forced labor, conscription into military service, division of land, and the like. Tribal societies such as the Kamba, Pokot, and Sebei are without such institutions for enforcement. Instead, as is well known to students of African societies, tribally organized societies (sometimes known as segmentary societies) must maintain social order by achieving a balance of power between contending and potentially hostile age, sex, territorial, and, principally, kinship groupings.[22]

20. R. B. Edgerton, *The Individual in Cultural Adaptation: A Study of Four East African Societies* (Berkeley: University of California Press, 1971).

21. See Gulliver, op. cit. (1963), and Paul Spencer, *The Samburu: A Study of Gerontocracy in a Nomadic Tribe* (Berkeley: University of California Press, 1965) for two excellent accounts of violence and its control

in East African tribal societies. For additional examples, see Paul Bohannan, ed., *African Homicide and Suicide* (Princeton, N.J.: Princeton University Press, 1960).

22. Well-known accounts are available in E. P. Evans-Pritchard and Meyer Fortes, eds., African Political Systems (London: Oxford University Press, 1940); Lloyd Fallers, *Bantu Bureaucracy: A Study of Integration and Conflict in the Political Institutions of an East African People* (Cambridge: East African Institute of Social Research, 1959); Meyer Fortes, *The Web of Kinship Among the Tallensi: The Second Part of an Analysis of the Social Structure of a Trans-Volta Tribe* (London: Oxford University Press, 1949).

This, then, is the central dilemma of these societies: how to resolve disputes and avoid violence in the absence of institutions capable of the enforcement of social order. What may be less well understood is the fact that the failure to control violence would be ruinous. It is no exaggeration to say that the control of violence in tribal societies is the quintessential problem, for in these societies any act of violence between individuals is potentially, even probably, an act of collective violence. That is so because the units of these segmentary societies (clans, lineages, etc.) are corporate groups that respond to aggression against one of their members with collective retaliation, not only against the individual aggressor but often against any or all members of his clan. Clan feuds of this sort can be bloody and prolonged because tribal societies typically lack any infallible means of arbitration or peacemaking. Some tribal societies, such as the Kaingáng of South America, have seen their feuds proliferate so wildly that their survival as a people is in doubt.[23] East Africa has often witnessed the destructive consequences of such feuding, as in the case of the Kamba, many of whose districts were long at war with the district of Kilungu, or the debilitating feuds of the Kikuyu, or the massive conflicts that splintered the Masai. Feuds not only bring death and terror to the involved segments of the society, they weaken all segments of the society against military attack by neighboring societies. If feuds are not prevented, everyone loses.

Therefore, individual violence must be aborted or attenuated before it becomes collective violence. As we have seen, however, these East African societies are not without forms of collective violence. Yet, as the examples illustrate, this collective violence is characteristically either an obvious mechanism for the maintenance of social order, or it is a ritualized means of avoiding, attentuating, or deflecting violence. Socially divisive forms of collective violence—for example, revolt, rebellion, conflict over succession—are primarily seen in chiefdoms, not tribal societies.[24]

While it is true that these East African tribal societies lack legal means of enforcing order, it is not true that they lack all means of coercion in mitigating violence and preventing feud, for they do possess a powerful deterrent in their system of supernatural beliefs. For example, while witchcraft can—and does—precipitate violence and lead to feud, the fear of witchcraft also causes many persons to avoid conflict, and if conflict begins, these persons often seek protection in counter-magic (or witchcraft of their own), not merely in retaliatory violence. And all of this exchange of witchcraft and sorcery can be managed so covertly that open clan confrontation need not be risked. Furthermore, misdeeds of all sorts can also be deterred by belief in a variety of forms of "moral" magic which are used to guard a man's property and his rights.[25] Hence, rather than face the danger of running afoul of a man's protective magic, persons may avoid theft, adulterous liaison, harsh words, or thoughtless blows. Similar deterrence resides in the curse which may be employed by fathers against their children, or the old against the young. This power—which may disable or kill only when it is used in proper support of what is just and moral—is greatly feared. Used by the old in defense of the social order, it is

23. Jules Henry, *Jungle People: A Kaingáng Tribe of the Highlands of Brazil* (Richmond, Va.: J. J. Augustin, 1942).

24. Max Gluckman, *Order and Rebellion in Tribal Africa* (London: Cohen and West, 1963).

25. E. V. Winans and R. B. Edgerton, "Hehe Magical Justice," *American Anthropologists* 66 (1964), pp. 745–764.

a potent means of preventing or punishing misconduct and mitigating violence. Finally, there is the oath which, like the curse, is widespread. The oath invokes supernatural sanction for many ceremonies, for the detection of wrongdoers, and for the punishment of such persons. Both the Kamba *kingole* and the Sebei *ntarastit* rely upon such oaths, and without these means of collective enforcement both societies would run a greater risk of feud. And without the constraint of supernatural powers such as these, the control of violence in tribal societies would be a far more difficult matter.

I think it is fair to conclude that tribal societies in East Africa have brought a number of forces to bear in their efforts to avoid feud and other forms of divisive collective violence. These forces have included a sense of common interest, various forms of collective prevention, and supernatural constraints, among others. That these societies have succeeded in their efforts may be thought obvious, for they have survived as societies and have increased their populations. Yet, of course, we cannot be absolutely certain that without the presence of colonial government with police, courts, and soldiers, these societies would have enjoyed the same degree of success. What is more certain is this: while the best efforts of tribal and colonial wisdom have sufficed to control collective violence, these efforts have *not* controlled individual violence which continues to occur frequently and in a variety of forms.

This fact suggests more general inferences. We might, for example, conclude that despite all that tribesmen and European officials can do, man's violent nature will continue to express itself where it can—in this case in noncollective violence. Or we could conclude that, given the nature of tribal society, and the constraints of colonial

law, individual violence is an inevitable outcome. For example, the pre-colonial system of intra- and inter-tribal conflict was never truly eradicated, and such colonial interventions as the prohibition on the killing of flagrant witches must have led, among other things, to more withcraft, more hostility, and more violence. Alas, the current state of our knowledge is insufficient to permit us to decide which of these or several other alternatives best accounts for the facts of East African tribal violence. Perhaps we shall never know enough to be able to answer this question. However, it seems to me that the question with which I began this inquiry can be answered. How great is man's ability to live with violence? Very great. Whether in a military campaign, a besieged city, a concentration camp, a plains Indian society, a modern urban ghetto, or an East African tribal society, man can and does live with a continuous threat and frequent realization of violent death. He may hate his life under such conditions or he may exult in it. In either case, he displays immense capacity for living with violence.

To extend the speculation stimulated by this East African example, I would say that while men must control certain sorts of collective violence, they can achieve this control while tolerating a high level of violence that offers no collective threat. We might be in error if we attribute the occurrence of such violence to man's nature; the origin of violence is not likely to be understood so simply. However, neither can we rely upon man's nature to put an end to violence simply because it has reached a high level.[26]

26. Also see R. B. Edgerton, "On the 'Recognition' of Mental Illness," in S. Plog and R. Edgerton, eds., *Changing Perspectives in Mental Illness* (New York: Holt, Rinehardt and Winston, 1969).

13

Violence in the New Guinea Highlands

by L. L. Langness

*L. L. Langness,Ph.D.,is an Associate Professor of Anthropology in the Depart-
ment of Business, Government and Society and the Department of Anthropology
at the University of Washington. In addition to articles on New Guinea, he is the
author of* The Life History in Anthropological Science *(1965) and co-editor of*
Melanesia: Readings on a Culture Area *(1971). His field work in the New
Guinea Highlands in 1961–62 was financed by the National Institute of Mental
Health. In 1969–70 he was Research Associate at the Social Science Research
Institute and East-West Center, University of Hawaii. In 1970–71 he did further
field work in the New Guinea Highlands financed by the Australian-American
Educational Foundation (Fulbright) and the New Guinea Research Unit of the
Australian National University.*

The observations which make up part of this acocunt were carried out in 1961–62, at which
time I held a Predoctoral Fellowship of Mental Health, United States Public Health Service.
I wish also to acknowledge the assistance of the Social Science Research Institute (NIMH
Grant MH-09243) and the East-West Center at the University of Hawaii.

VIOLENCE, like pig raising and horticulture, is characteristic of all highlands New Guinea societies, from Kapauku[1] in the west of West Irian, to Tairora[2] in the east of the Territory of New Guinea. Although most ethnographers in this area have commented on its presence, no detailed account of violence, as such, exists. The purpose of this paper is to give such an account, concentrating on the Bena Bena peoples of the Eastern Highlands district of the Territory of New Guinea.[3] Comparative illustrations will be taken from the literature.[4]

1. Leopold Pospisil, *Kapauku Papuans and Their Law* (New Haven: Yale University Publications in Anthropology, no. 54, 1958); *The Kapauku Papuans of West New Guinea* (New York: Holt, Rinehart and Winston, 1963).

2. James B. Watson, "Tairora: The Politics of Despotism in a Small Society," *Anthropological Forum* II (1967), pp. 53–104.

3. L. L. Langness, "Notes on the Bena Council, Eastern Highlands, New Guinea," *Oceania* 33 (1963), pp. 151–170; "Some Problems in the Conceptualization of Highlands Social Structures," *American Anthropologist* Part 2, 66 (1964), pp. 162–182; "Hysterical Psychosis in the New Guinea Highlands: A Bena Bena Example," *Psychiatry* 28 (1965), pp. 259–277; "Sexual Antagonism in the New Guinea Highlands: A Bena Bena Example," *Oceania* 37 (1967), pp. 161–177; "Bena Bena Political Organization," *Anthropological Forum* II (1968), pp. 180–198; "Courtship, Marriage and Divorce: Bena Bena," in R. M. Glasse and M. J. Meggitt, eds., *Pigs, Pearshells and Women* (Englewood Cliffs, N.J.: Prentice-Hall, 1969), pp. 38–55; "Political Organization," in *Encyclopedia of Papua-New Guinea* (Melbourne, 1970, in press).

4. Strictly speaking, my materials apply only to a portion of what are nowadays referred to as the Bena Bena. Specifically, Korofeigu in the Southeast of the language area and similar groups adjacent to them. Korofeigu is not necessarily typical. They were larger and more successful than most groups in the traditional environment. Also, they are grassland rather than bush dwellers, a fact which may be of some significance

Violence here is defined as the use of forcible means to attain goals. Used in this way, the term contrasts with "gentleness," "passivity," "persuasion," and "reason." For example, a man arguing with his wife would be apt to shout at and beat her rather than reason with her or sit sulking in silence. If someone is wronged, he will attempt to use physical means to redress the grievance rather than merely engage in public debate or take the issue to a court of law. I *do not* mean to imply that people *always* use force, or that the alternatives specified are *never* used, nor that the people are necessarily incapable of using them. I mean to say that forcible means are more *characteristic* of the Bena Bena than, say, middle class Americans. In this sense forcible means are more likely to be expected by the members of these cultures and are less likely to be considered deviant, unusual, or morally offensive. This implies a quantitative judgment as well—there is much violence. But as there are no precise measurements for amounts of violence available, at least cross-culturally, the reader will have to judge for himself from these pages and from other published accounts.

In the Bena Bena and environs children are encouraged to be violent and aggressive.[5] Tantrums are frequent and are usually ignored. Boys are especially encouraged in aggressive behavior. Play is rough and unsupervised, and

when it comes to warfare and raiding. Nonetheless, I believe what I describe will be similar throughout the area and to a somewhat lesser extent throughout the Eastern Highlands. Patterns of violence in some other areas of the highlands, except in a more general sense, may not be similar.

5. Ronald M. Berndt, *Excess and Restraint* (Chicago: University of Chicago Press, 1962); R. M. Glasse and Shirley Lindenbaum, "South Fore Politics," *Anthropological Forum* II (1969), pp. 308–326.

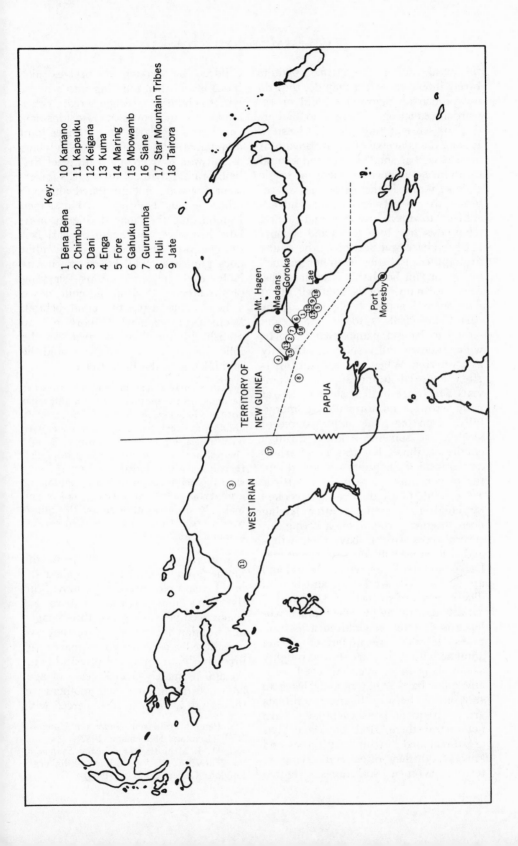

Key:

1 Bena Bena
2 Chimbu
3 Dani
4 Enga
5 Fore
6 Gahuku
7 Gururumba
8 Huli
9 Jate

10 Kamano
11 Kapauku
12 Keigana
13 Kuma
14 Maring
15 Mbowamb
16 Siane
17 Star Mountain Tribes
18 Tairora

Mt. Hagen
Madans
Goroka
Lae
Port Moresby

TERRITORY OF NEW GUINEA

PAPUA

WEST IRIAN

the weak suffer the strong. Adults rarely intervene and if they do, they do not punish an aggressive child or reward a weaker one. There is no "underdog" or sense of "fair play," as western Europeans conceive of them. Boys beat girls as well as smaller boys and several children sometimes torment a single child. Likewise, the deformed or retarded are targets of derision and are subject to much teasing and abuse. Tiny boys are given sticks and encouraged to chase and beat girls, the adults urging them to "stick it up her vagina" or "go on, hit her hard." Children also hear the many stories men tell about fighting and about strong men of the past. The ideal is to be brave and strong to have a name—that is, to be widely known and respected, primarily as a warrior. When one is small this is often achieved at the expense of animals which are beaten, stoned, shot at with arrows, and tormented unmercifully. Even pigs, the major source of wealth, are sometimes killed through children's abuse, but this is a serious matter, and if the guilty are found out, the owner must be reimbursed. Birds are caught, plucked alive, and cooked by children, sometimes after having been dragged around on a string for several days. Insects have their wings and legs torn off or are sometimes hacked to bits. Dogs, which abound and are seldom fed, are kicked and beaten. The concept of a "pet" is absent.

Although rarely punished, much violence is directed at children at certain times. If they are underfoot during adult activities, they are shoved roughly aside, slapped, or even switched, usually quite hard. They quickly learn to stay out of the way. Castration threats are so frequent boys eventually learn not to fear them. Both boys and girls are threatened "in fun" with axes and knives and they often run crying in terror. Women sometimes frighten

children by making themselves look hideous and then bursting into a house where children are gathered. When adults are mourning a close kinsman, small girls regularly have a finger joint amputated. I know of one case in which a man was so overcome with grief that he bit rather than cut off a girl's finger. Bena boys are not mutilated although other highland boys may be, but as men in mourning they may decide to mutilate themselves by slicing an earlobe.[6] On the rare occasions when an adult does punish a child, he or she invariably uses physical means—slapping or threatening to drop the child down a hole or to leave the child behind. Women are somewhat more apt to punish children than are men, but the following, from the Enga, would be unthinkable in the Bena Bena:

A father early warns his children that the gardens are the mother's domain and must not be visited without her permission. A child who steals is lucky to escape with only a beating from the mother. Should she tell her husband, he is likely to punish the offender with great severity. He may slice the child's palm with a knife, lop off a fingertip, cut off an earlobe, cook it and make the child eat it, or smoke the culprit over a fire. At the least he will administer a sound thrashing.[7]

Both boys and girls sleep in the mother's house until they are about 10 or 11 years old, when boys move into the men's house, leaving mothers and sisters behind. There are three stages of initiation for males before they are considered adult enough to marry, all involving both force and physical pain. At approximately 5 to 7 years of age, boys are taken from their mothers for the day to have their ears pierced with

6. Peter Matthiesson, *Under the Mountain Wall* (London: Heinemann, 1962).

7. M. J. Meggitt, *The Lineage System of the Mae-Enga of New Guinea* (Edinburgh, London: Oliver and Boyd, 1965).

a sharp bone. Subsequently they are feasted with pork. Because this event occurs only every three or four years, boys who experience it together are "age mates" and will continue a close relationship as such for life. When they are from 9 to 11 years, they are again seized, to have their septums pierced in the same manner. At this time they also have sandpaper-like leaves thrust repeatedly up their nostrils, causing them to bleed. When 12 or older, the major initiation ceremony occurs, and this time, youths are secluded from women entirely for a month or more. Again the leaves are thrust up their nostrils, and in another ceremony a miniature arrow with a sharp stone point is shot into both the tongue and the uretha until bleeding occurs. Finally the initiates are forced to swallow bent lengths of supple cane which are worked down their throats, causing them to vomit.

The purpose of these rites is to free the youths from female pollution, make them strong, healthy, and virile, and to emphasize the solidarity and significance of the male community. They are also, at this time, reminded who they are, who their enemies are, what they must do to them and how, and other things tradition demands. Initiations appear to have used less violent means to attain similar goals in other parts of the highlands, but training for war was always an integral part of growing up and being initiated.

Females do not escape this ethos of violence, especially in the Bena Bena. Although they do not have the violent initiation of males, they are seized to have their nostrils bled with leaves, and all girls have their noses pierced, either by their mother or by a female friend. They are married against their wills, attempts to resist result only in their being beaten and sometimes even

dragged to their weddings.[8] Interestingly, the ceremony involves the symbolic forcible removal of the bride from her own people.[9] If they then attempt to run away from their husbands they are beaten and returned. Married women brutally fight with their co-wives or potential co-wives and in some cases, albeit rare, fight to the death. Even so, once a woman has settled down with a man for some time she will cut off her own fingers in mourning for him should he die or be killed. Widows are frequent suicides, usually by hanging themselves in a public manner.[10]

The amount of violence towards women varies across the highlands.[11] Precision is extremely difficult in determining the status of women or measuring male-female hostility, as Strathern has recently reminded us.[12] However, violence could be and was used by husbands everywhere. Although among Kapauku, "An ideal husband . . . should not punish his wife physically—a reprimand should be his harshest treat-

8. R. M. Glasse, "Marriage in South Fore," in R. M. Glasse and M. J. Meggitt, eds., op. cit., pp. 16–37; Langness (1969), op. cit., pp. 38–55; K. E. Read, *The High Valley* (New York: Scribners and Sons, 1965).

9. Langness (1969), op. cit.

10. It is sometimes the case that women do not want to cut off their own fingers and have to be bullied into doing so by men; but this is not always the case. One might also say that a widow committed suicide only because her future prospects could be so undesirable. But husbands and wives do develop very strong emotional bonds over time. Whatever, the violence involved is the same.

11. Langness (1967), op. cit.; M. J. Meggitt, "Male-Female Relationships in the Highlands of Australian New Guinea," *American Anthropologist* Part 2 (1964), pp. 204–224; K. E. Read, "Nama Cult of the Central Highlands, New Guinea," *Oceania* 23 (1952), pp. 1–25.

12. Andrew Strathern, "Descent and Alliance in the New Guinea Highlands: Some Problems of Comparison," *Proceedings of the Royal Anthropological Institute for 1968, 1969* (1969), pp. 37–52.

ment," nonetheless a man may punish his wife, "even by wounding her or, for a serious offense such as adultery, by killing her. . . . [13] Violence toward wives appears to have been more common among the Maring, but some men were believed to be exceptions.[14] Among the Bena Bena, some men have a reputation for wife beating and some do not;[15] but the violent punishment of women described by Read for the nearby Gahuku would be most unusual.[16] The following, from Mendi, would not have happened at all:

This kind of economic pressure obviously leads to a form of blackmail, with the wife threatening to go home unless the husband makes repeated payments to her kin. This is, however, a risky game—a form of "brinkmanship" which balances the respective political influences of the wife's and the husband's kin groups. If the wife loses, her husband may kill her publicly with a red-hot stone in her vagina; I know of two cases in which this did in fact happen.[17]

This is not to say that Bena Bena men did not at times kill their wives, but it was uncommon and did not employ such a premeditated technique. Also, although rape occured in the Bena Bena and all lone women were usually "fair game," rape was not formally regulated in war as seems to have occurred in Kapauku:

. . . married women escape any molestation, an unmarried girl is invariably raped if caught by the advancing enemy. Since it

is taboo for the enemy to rape girls of the opposite camp, it is the friends and "in-law" relatives of the enemy who violate the girls.[18]

The amount of violence associated with warfare and raiding, although known to vary, has not been the subject of intensive study. Berndt points out in his brief survey article that highlands warfare is often described as "chronic," "incessant," or "endemic,"[19] but the meaning of these terms remains far from clear. Barnes summarized the New Guinea literature and suggested "a great(er) emphasis is placed upon killing for its own sake."[20] At the same time, warfare has been described as merely an "antagonistic game,"[21] a "serious game resembling European tournaments,"[22] or an "athletic match."[23] Indeed, Gardner and Heider have said the Dani engage in war to promote their general well-being and happiness:

In the first place, the Dani engage in "war" to promote the success and well-being of their social order. In large measure, their health, welfare, and happiness depend on the pursuit of aggression against their traditional enemies. Since their enemies share a common culture, the same considerations motivate them.[24]

13. Pospisil (1958), op. cit., p. 57.
14. Cherry Lowman-Vayda, "Maring Big Men," *Anthropological Forum* II (1968), pp. 199–243.
15. Langness (1969), op. cit., p. 49.
16. K. E. Read, "Morality and the Concept of the Person Among the Gahuku-Gama," *Oceania* 25 (155), pp. 234–282.
17. D'Arcy Ryan, "Marriage in Mendi," in R. M. Glasse and M. J. Meggitt, eds., op. cit., pp. 159–175.

18. Pospisil (1958), op. cit., p. 91.
19. Ronald M. Berndt, "Warfare in the New Guinea Highlands," *American Anthropologist* Part 2 (1964), pp. 183–203.
20. J. Barnes, "African Models in the New Guinea Highlands," *Man* 62 (1962), pp. 5–9.
21. Berndt (1964), op. cit., p. 444.
22. Jan Pouwer, "A Social System in the Star Mountains: Toward a Reorientation of the Study of Social Systems," *American Anthropologist* Part 2, 66 (1964), pp. 133–161.
23. G. F. Vicedom and H. Tischner, *Die Mbowamb: die Kultur der Hagenberg Stamme in Ostlichen Zentral-Neuguinea*, 3 vols. (Hamburg: de Gruyter, 1943/48).
24. Robert Gardner and Karl G. Heider, *Gardens of War* (New York: Random House, 1968).

In any case, the causes of war were fairly uniform—women, deaths from sorcery that had to be avenged, theft of pigs, failure to live up to obligations, insults, and disputes over various kinds of property. Land was a cause of war in some areas[25] whereas in others it is reported not to have been.[26] In some cases people were driven from their land but later invited to return, the possession of territory not being, in itself, an issue:

Warfare here is not a consequence of hunger for food or, as a general rule, for land. The capture of women, pigs or even children is incidental. The struggle, basically, is for power and for the prestige that goes with it. Just as rivalry within the district is a feature of relations between adult male peers, particularly in terms of their relative strength, so the relations between districts are marked by the same desire to show the superior strength of one against another. This can be achieved, in a small way, by destroying gardens, burning houses, stealing pigs, and other provocative acts, or, on a larger scale, by driving away whole villages or districts. But the real test is to show that one has the power of life or death over members of another district—to kill without being killed in return, and to taunt the bereaved district with its defeat.[27]

The weapon of greatest importance in the east of the highlands was the bow and arrow. Bows were made of black palm and employed unnotched, reed shafted arrows with heads of carved hardwood or bamboo, the hardwood points made wickedly barbed and difficult to remove. The many arrow types had individual names and were highly decorated. Spears were present everywhere but were used more widely by some people than by others. The Kapauku in West Irian had them but, interestingly, did not use them in battle.[28] The Dani used both bows and arrows and spears.[29] Axes and clubs were used also but seem not to have been of primary importance as weapons of war in most areas. Wooden war shields were present in many places but varied in size, design, and frequency of use. Matato, the great Tairora leader described by Watson, was recognized in battle because of his "great black shield."[30] The Dani apparently did not use shields at all,[31] and in Kapauku shields were used, but not by the brave.[32] Fire was widely employed in fighting, entire villages sometimes being burned out in the Bena Bena area and in Kapauku.[33] Prior to administrative control in the Bena Bena, villages were located on ridge tops and fortified with high fences of timber, bamboo, and cane. There was usually only one entrance through which men and women left in the morning for the gardens—the men to watch and guard from the ridge tops, the women to work. But the Enga and others in that area did not live in villages, being dispersed over the landscape in women's houses around a centrally located men's house.[34] In the West Irian highlands, the pattern varies from small dispersed hamlets or compounds among the Dani,[35] to the villages of the Kapauku.[36]

25. Meggitt (1965), op. cit.

26. Langness (1964), op. cit.; Marie Reay, "Structural Co-Variants of Land Shortage Among Patrilineal Peoples," *Anthropological Forum* II (1967), pp. 4–19.

27. Berndt (1962), op. cit., p. 414.
28. Pospisil (1958), op. cit., p. 91.
29. Gardner and Heider (1968), op. cit.
30. Watson (1967), op. cit., p. 64.
31. Gardner and Heider (1968), op. cit.
32. Pospisil (1958), op. cit., p. 64.
33. Langness (1968), op. cit.; Pospisil, ibid.
34. Meggitt (1965), op. cit.
35. Gardner and Heider (1968), op. cit.; Denise O'Brien, "Marriage Among the Konda Valley Dani," in R. M. Glasse and M. J. Meggitt, eds., op. cit., pp. 228–234.
36. Pospisil (1963), op. cit.

Tactics varied from place to place although small hit-and-run raiding occurred with varying frequency everywhere. Major campaigns in the Bena Bena usually took place in the very early morning. Men crept up to an enemy village to work their way through or over the fortifications. They first approached the men's house to tie the doorway shut. If successful, they set fire to the men's house and shot anyone who attempted to break out. After this had been accomplished, they turned their attention to the women's houses. On large raids everyone encountered was killed—young, old, male, female, healthy or infirm. Afterward, with the help of their women and children, the victors would loot the gardens, ringbark the trees, take whatever they could find, and depart. Raids of this magnitude are of unknown frequency, but judging from the earliest accounts (diaries, patrol reports) and from the statements of informants, they were by no means uncommon.[37] Most common were the small raids in which a number of men would ambush or creep up and slay one or two unsuspecting or careless people. Again, no regard for age and sex was involved, and children were killed as readily as adults. It appears that a roughly similar pattern existed among the Kapauku:

It happens, sometimes, that one side starts winning, having succeeded in killing a few enemies and pushing the rest of them toward their village. The war leaders shout in order to stop the retreat. They scold and insult the panicky individuals but in vain. The retreat may be temporarily halted near the houses where barricades are made of short plants driven vertically into the earth. Soon the invading forces penetrate the village, looting and burning the houses, raping the unmarried girls, shooting pigs, cutting down banana trees and fences, and destroying the crop

in the fields. After this is accomplished, the victors withdraw with their loot and leave the remnants of the village and crop to the beaten enemy. Land is never taken away from the defeated party.[38]

Descriptions of warfare from other areas, by contrast, have emphasized its orderliness and relative lack of violence. Here it appears that large-scale battles were fought on prepared battlegrounds. The opposing sides, forewarned and dressed for the occasion, lined up to taunt one another. The lines would move forward and backward, dodging, mocking, catcalling, with few casualties, until evening, when they would quit. Inclement weather, a single death, or even an injury could call off the day's "festivities."[39]

Although Gardner and Heider point out that "war" may not be the proper term for the behavior they describe for the Dani, they do not suggest there might be, in addition, other forms of behavior more properly called war.[40] Nor do they discuss raiding in detail. Similarly, Ploeg reports that the Mbogoga Dani "like fighting for its own sake,"[41] but at the same time, he reports people fleeing from war and moving to new territories, a fact at variance with the picture of Dani warfare as ritualistic and bringing about happiness and well-being.[42] At this point it is clear only that there is much variation across the highlands. Whether some or any are merely "fought for fun" is open to question. There do seem to have been more highly developed rules and regulations regarding warfare, and it may have been more serious, more violent,

37. Langness (1969, 1970), op. cit.

38. Pospisil (1958), op. cit., p. 93.
39. Gardner and Heider (1968), op. cit.; A. Ploeg, *Government in Wanggulam* (The Hague: Martinus Nijhoff, 1969).
40. Gardner and Heider (1968), ibid., p. 135.
41. Ploeg (1969), op. cit., p. 116.
42. Ibid., p. 2.

more "unregulated" and more common in the Bena Bena and contiguous groups than in most other areas.[43] But the Huli,[44] further to the south and the west, also seem to have played a "serious game" indeed:

Until the 1950's warfare was the dominant orientation of Huli society. Every boy was taught to fight and every man was expected actively to defend his own interests. People fought to avenge killings, sexual offenses and property infractions. A major war mobilized up to a thousand warriors, lasted for four or five months and resulted in fifty deaths. The victors plundered the losers' gardens, destroyed their homes and slaughtered their pigs. Great fighters were highly esteemed and prowess in war qualified a man for leadership in other fields.[45]

But violence is characteristic of the New Guinea highlands and Bena Bena quite apart from war. The settlement of disputes is a good example. It is significant that although the Bena, like several of their neighbors to the west, distinguish between warfare and other means of settling disputes, violence is always acceptable. Within the Siane

phratry, according to Salisbury, "warfare is forbidden, although fighting with non-lethal weapons such as clubs is common when disputes need settling."[46] The same is true for the Gahuku, as well as the Gururumba:[47]

The authority structure itself is not so much a source of cohesion as is the fact that the phratry is considered a field of action for reaching a settlement of matters under dispute. This is exemplified in the notion of two kinds of warfare. One is called *roBo*, warring with deadly weapons such as spears, axes, and arrows. The other is called *nande*, fighting with sticks, stones, and hands. In addition, *roBo* connotes fighting with the intent to decimate the enemy, while *nande* connotes fighting that can be halted short of extensive killing or property destruction and, further, that a settlement of the dispute giving rise to the fight can be reached by nonviolent means. It is said that people of different phratries war (*roBo*) with one another, while people of the same phratry only fight (*nande*).[48]

Newman's use of the word "nonviolent" is not clear. The distinction does not seem to be on the basis of the presence or absence of *violence in general*, but on whether *killing* (or "extensive killing") is allowable in particular. Traditionally, few disputes would have been settled by nonviolent means in the Bena, although they make a similar distinction. Arguments between husbands and wives, for example, were rarely settled by any form of arbitration, but far more frequently by an argument or a beating or both. They might have been settled by one partner refusing to perform some vital domestic task until the other capitulated. The

43. Langness (1968, 1970), op. cit.

44. R. M. Glasse, "The Huli of the Southern Highlands," in P. Lawrence and M. J. Meggitt, eds., *Gods, Ghosts and Men in Melanesia* (Melbourne: Oxford University Press, 1965), pp. 27–49.

45. As an example of the difficulty involved in assessing the extent and importance of warfare, it is interesting to note that while Glasse says 50 deaths in a four- or five-month period constitutes a major war (and by implication is undesirable), Gardner and Heider believe that from 20 to 40 deaths a year from warfare is not "excessive": In a year, the toll on each side of deaths resulting from wounds received in formal battle, ambush or raids will number between ten and twenty. An equal or even greater number of Dani perish prematurely from complications arising from the common cold; hence, as Dani war is an institution involving virtually all male members of the society, the death rate is not excessive (see Gardner and Heider, 1968: p. 144).

46. Richard F. Salisbury, *From Stone to Steel* (Melbourne and Cambridge: The University Presses, 1962).

47. Read (1952, 1955, 1965), op. cit.

48. Philip Newman, *Knowing the Gururumba* (New York: Holt, Rinehardt and Winston, 1965).

ubiquitous disputes over pigs, in which one person's pig violates another's garden, were frequently settled by killing the pig and paying compensation, but only after considerable argumentation and sometimes by fighting. Arguments themselves are often violent displays of intemperance, with men threatening —and even at times attempting—to burn down or pull down their houses, throwing their axes dramatically on the ground, and engaging in histrionics of all kinds. Newman cites a Gururumba case in which a man publicly strangled his dog in an argument with a woman over a chicken.[49] The male partner in an adulterous affair is shot in the thigh with a special arrow by the offended husband, the woman most usually receiving a beating. Punishment for adultery can be far more violent, however, in other parts of the highlands. Stealing is punished by a beating if the offended party is strong enough to administer it. And one must forcibly retrieve his possessions if he wants them back. Thus if a man is wronged, he typically either threatens or uses violence in redress. If he does not, he merely suffers because of his impotence. He must demonstrate his personal strength, or strength of support, or both, if he is to obtain what he desires. Matthiesson stated it succinctly, "A man suffers offenses according to his inability to defend himself . . . "[50] Thus, these are not only systems of self-help, they are systems of self-help which typically employ violent means—the strong get away with what they can and the weak fall. For the most part, justice itself is defined by strength, as is what is moral. It is good to be strong—physically strong and strong in numbers. It is only when two disputing groups are so large and/or

evenly matched they cannot come to a settlement without threatening the survival of the larger group itself that nonviolent settlement becomes desirable and the community steps in on their behalf:

Internal strife is always possible. Interpersonal conflicts might at any time flare up into intergroup fights, but the protagonists need to gather their supporters. While the tribe is working toward a major enterprise, internal conflicts may not be supported. The universal desire for the enhancement of tribal reputation may override private interests.[51]

The machinery for settling disputes in this way was not highly developed, however, so that whether disputes were settled amicably or not probably depended upon the effectiveness of the leadership available at the time.[52] The question of leadership itself clearly brings out the place of violence in the lives of these people.

Leaders were expected to, and often did, settle their disputes with violent means. Consider the following Maring example:

Mbamp yu are said to be physically strong and vigorous men. . . . They are quick to bursts of temper and quick to action, and they may commit acts of physical violence against those who antagonize them. Men who are mbamp yu may therefore depend on physical coercion to sanction and maintain their own vested interests. . . . Angry mbamp yu have been known to beat persons offending them with the back side of a steel axe or to shoot an arrow or throw a spear. Such assaults within the clan are not considered serious unless blood is drawn. Maring informants say that people do not die of arrow or spear wounds unless the "liver" is penetrated. . . . Despite the

49. Ibid., p. 103.
50. Matthiesson (1962), op. cit., p. 32.

51. Paula Brown, "From Anarchy to Satrapy," *American Anthropologist* 65 (1963), pp. 1–15.
52. Langness (1968, 1970), op. cit.; Watson (1967), op. cit.

fact that relatively few intraclan assaults result in death, they do result in injury.[53]

To what extent a violent nature was required for positions of leadership in different parts of the highlands is not well known. Some accounts have emphasized that leaders, to be truly successful, must be capable of patience, restraint, good judgment, and "equivalence," rather than—or in addition to—being strong men or forceful warriors.[54] Others have emphasized the reverse, the necessity for primarily violent action.[55] Still others have emphasized organizational ability and entrepreneurship, or have distinguished between different kinds of leaders:

I should point out that, in the present paper, I am not writing about those men to whom the Mae occasionally refer as *kamunggo* merely because they are active warriors, killers of enemies of the clan and clever at setting ambushes. Such men are rarely the true *kamunggo* who plan military strategy and direct tactics from behind the lines. Indeed, many Mae believe that the very quality of unreflecting violence that distinguishes a man in battle may make him a great nuisance at other times; they echo Clemenceau in arguing that the fruits of war are too important to be left in the hands of warriors.[56]

Not all highlanders were as clear on this point, however, nor do they all distinguish between different kinds of leaders. The Bena Bena did not make such a distinction nor are they explicit on what qualities were necessary for leadership other than strength and success in war. But the Bena Bena would not express it as tersely as the Wanggulam Dani apparently do: "Wanggulam say that the big man, *ap ngwok*, are those who kill. . . . The more people a man kills, the bigger he grows."[57] They also recognize the "criminality" of wanton killers, as in this example from the Dani:

. . . in the Hisaro clans to the southward there is a kain who is said to have taken more than one hundred lives. . . . In the course of an ordinary lifetime of tribal wars and raids it would not be possible to kill one hundred people, but this kain is not an ordinary man. A fanatic warrior in battle, he prowls as well on solitary raids into the country of his enemies, killing quietly where chance offers. On one occasion he accosted a woman on a lonely path: the woman, assuming the stranger was bent on rape, lay down philosophically to receive him. His spear lay beside them, and, instead of raping her, he drove the spear inside her. . . . Despite the number of enemies to his credit, this man's need to take life is unfamiliar to the Dani and makes even his own people uneasy. The criminality of his acts is recognized; unlike Wereklowe, he is despised as well as feared.[58]

It is important to recognize here that although this man was feared, even despised, and in spite of his recognized criminality, he remained, apparently for a long time, a well-known Dani leader. Killing is usually a prerequisite for leadership in the highlands, but it becomes difficult to draw the line between criminal acts of killing and glorious achievements in battle or raids. It would appear that a man remained a leader, no matter how despotic he was, until some other men supplanted him either through treachery or bravery. The limits of power, like justice and

53. Lowman-Vayda (1968), op. cit., p. 215.
54. Paula Brown, (1963), loc. cit.
55. Langness (1968, 1970), op. cit.; Richard F. Salisbury, "Despotism and Australian Administration in the New Guinea Highlands," *American Anthropologist* Part 2, 66 (1964), pp. 225–239; Watson (1967), op. cit.
56. M. J. Meggitt, "The Pattern of Leadership Among the Mae-Enga of New Guinea," *Anthropological Forum* II (1967), pp. 20–35.

57. Ploeg (1969), op. cit., p. 75.
58. Matthiesson (1962), op. cit., p. 76.

morality, were confirmed only by action—violent action. This is one of the great paradoxes of highlands political systems, especially in the Bena Bena.[59] Watson has cogently summarized the dilemma for Tairora:

Intimidation, fear, and awe are, in Matato's case, inherently unilateral responses proper to a complementary relationship, not a reciprocal one. Arguing that it is these relationships *per se* that violate Tairora morality, because it is an egalitarian and reciprocal morality, practically implies that the Tairora political order is an inherently leaderless ("acephalous") one, or one in which leaders can only seem to lead while really being but custodians of the *vox populi*. It is my impression, on the contrary, that the pre-contact Tairora are quite accustomed to strong men and that in essence their strength is necessarily expressed in some differentiation, through behavior, from men of lesser strength. Surely, I do not say that Tairora politics is therefore inherently the politics of despotism. Indeed, I have argued above that despotism is rather a condition to which the political order is susceptible and occasionally succumbs, but for various reasons is not its constant state. I do, however, tend to reject the image of intrinsically headless political groups in the Tairora area except where headlessness occurs—as it often does occur—by default of adequate leader recruitment.

The issue may come down to whether a better case can be made that (1) Tairora have a leaderless political morality, though intermittently experiencing strong, even arbitrary leaders, or that (2) the political ideal rather calls for the leadership of men of strength but, when they arise, the Tairora often experience with them the moral conflict expressed in characterizing them as bad.

In either case there would be an incongruity between morality and real experience.[60]

It should be apparent that violence in the Bena Bena was a daily fact of life as well as a part of the continuing cycle of war. Rather than being proscribed, violent self-help was prescribed as a method of social control. But as Pospisil observed for Kapauku, violence was not highly elaborated. The concept and practice of torture, for example, did not exist.[61] Also, as Watson mentions for Tairora, there were no trophies of war.[62] Bena warfare was consistent with this overall emphasis on practicality. It had much less ritual significance and elaboration than the behavior described as war for the Dani.[63] Its consequences also appear to have been more serious.

But this is not to suggest there was no ritual elaboration of violence in the Bena Bena. Indeed, most of their rituals include or express violence in some form. For example, when men return with a bride price, a group of women waylay and attack them with sticks and stones. This is more than mere play, as people are injured and pigs get killed.[64] A similar ritual battle occurs during male initiations. The largest ceremonies held are to pay back for help given in war, and the rituals at this time express strength and success in war. Violence is thus acted out when it does not actually occur. Also, for every ritual purpose, pigs are slaughtered in a noisy, violent display expressing the wealth and achievement of the group. At a death, in addition to the previously mentioned violence of mourning, male relatives of the deceased come armed in order to shoot the pigs they are entitled to receive.

I have not mentioned sorcery or cannibalism. Sorcery is not practiced often

59. Langness (1968, 1970), op. cit.
60. Watson (1967), op. cit., pp. 102–103.

61. Pospisil (1958), op. cit., p. 77.
62. Watson (1967), op. cit., p. 65.
63. Gardner and Heider (1968), op. cit.
64. For accounts of very similar rituals, see Read (1965), op. cit.

in the Bena Bena (at least nowhere near as often as it is discussed), but is greatly feared. It is part of the overall atmosphere of violence although basically it employs nonviolent means to achieve its violent ends. Cannibalism was associated with violence only in that some people who died or were killed were sometimes eaten. They were never killed for this purpose and were consumed only by specific kinsmen. Infanticide and senilicide, both practiced occasionally, were not associated with any ritual, being regarded as practical necessities.

Violence, then, was an important element of life all across the highlands, but the specific content of violent acts and their precise direction varied from place to place. It is difficult, however, to determine to what extent, if any, violence was considered by the highlanders themselves to be a "problem" or just another fact of life. It could have been considered both—a possibility which has sometimes been overlooked. There has also been confusion at times over whether the point of view expressed by a particular author is his own or that of his subjects. Dani warfare, it would appear from Gardner and Heider's account, was not considered a problem by anyone:

In the first place it [war] is as positively sanctioned as any major institution in the culture. The Dani fight because they want to and because it is necessary. They do not enter into battle in order to put an end to fighting. They do not envisage the end of fighting any more than the end of gardening or of ghosts.[65]

These authors, having already claimed war promotes general well-being and happiness, go on to suggest the culture might not survive without war "except parasitically as the novelty of mission-

aries or policemen.[66] At the same time, according to Matthiesson's account, the Dani do experience the moral dilemma over the limits of power as outlined by Watson.[67]

The Bena Bena universally condemn war. It is true that men do recount deeds of bravery and boast of their prowess in battle, but soldiers in many societies do this also, without positively sanctioning warfare. It would seem to have been a classic situation of violence begetting violence. The theft of a pig or a woman resulted in fighting, which in turn resulted in injury or death, which in its turn would have to be paid back. But in the course of doing this, others would become involved, or some innocent bystander would get hurt, and a new series of raids and counter-raids would begin. Further, since it was believed that deaths (except for old age and those in battle) were caused by sorcery, and sorcery only emanated from other groups, whenever a person died, from whatever cause, a raid usually ensued. Because no system of control existed other than what physical coercion could be exercised by individuals and groups, there was no way of stopping the cycle; and although the ultimate possibility of amicable settlement was held out ideologically, the possibility was recognized only by a small group and was seldom utilized unless some larger threat also existed. Even within groups, violence was the most typical means for settling disputes. The following statement makes this point very well:

Wanggulam have a strong feeling of being their own masters. The ultimate means of force in their society rests with the individual adult members. There are no functionaries or groups of functionaries with a monopoly of the means of force. People

65. Gardner and Heider (1968), op. cit., p. 135.

66. Ibid., p. 144.
67. Watson (1967), op. cit.

do not refrain from using force, and the number of fights, whether with fists, or with clubs, or with bows and arrows, is large. They often occur between close relatives, for example, between full brothers, and people do not object to such fights. Intervention in fights rarely occurs.[68]

This would be quite a fair statement for the Bena Bena as well, although Bena leaders, if strong enough and if so inclined, might intervene. But because the system existed, for whatever evolutionary, historical, or psycho-biological reasons, children were trained for it because such training was necessary for survival. The natural aggressive acts of children, instead of being suppressed, were encouraged and shaped by the culture for its own ends. There was no place for the weak and cowardly in such a world. The religious system, which excluded females entirely, stressed male solidarity, strength, and bravery. In this respect, it did not tolerate much deviation from the norm, nor was there much.

Although violence was widespread in daily life and in war, it was obviously not the case that rules governing it did not exist at all. The difficulty with the rules is that they applied to such a narrow range of persons and could not be enforced by further violence.[69] All of these societies had extensive and quite specific rules known to all. Among the Kupauku, for example, violence directed against a grey-haired man would be unthinkable[70] and a man should not beat his wife.[71] Among Gahuku, and elsewhere, "big men" are supposed to exercise restraint as well as power.[72] For the Kamano, and others, there are rules prohibiting the

killing of in-laws in battle.[73] Among the Bena, a man should not fight within the group, most importantly, not with brothers or age mates, but strictly speaking, not with anyone. However, "big men" did not always exercise restraint, people did fight with their brothers, in-laws were sometimes killed, and whatever public opinion might have been, by itself it was seldom enough. It must not be overlooked, however, that within the group, people were quite capable of acts of considerable tenderness and affection and there were strong emotional ties. The people were not devoid of motive and emotions apart from violence in spite of their centrality in this particular paper and in much of the literature.

The violence of Bena Bena was primarily situational; it cannot be said that fundamentally the Bena Bena enjoyed fighting or killing. Certainly they did not enjoy dying, whether in battle or otherwise. Their own explanation for infanticide and senilicide tends to condemn them both as a result of war. Even the most successful groups have unpleasant memories of fleeing into the grass or the bush or taking refuge with other people. The idea of fighting for "causes" rather than practical necessity (if they could be said to have even a concept of that sort) did not appeal to them. (Practical necessity would include, of course, revenge for sorcery, theft of women and pigs, etc.) They report that they fought incessantly and did not have enough time to build substantial houses or put in large gardens. They also emphasize that they were almost constantly afraid. Thus, although the Bena Bena may have viewed warfare as "an integral part of living," they do not seem to have regarded it

68. Ploeg (1969), op. cit., p. 69.
69. Read (1955), op. cit.
70. Pospisil (1958), op. cit., p. 59.
71. Ibid., p. 57.
72. Read (1959), op. cit.

73. Reo Fortune, "The Rules of Relationship Behaviour in One Variety of Primitive Warfare," *Man* XLVII (1947), p. 1-15.

as "something good in itself."[74] And it is of great significance that warfare in the Bena was abandoned fairly quickly after contact with Europeans and at a time when there were few patrols to adequately enforce the laws that accompanied contact.[75] There are very few Bena, if any, who want to return to the traditional wars. With the passing of war a number of other institutionalized behaviors are disappearing—the

men's house, traditional religion, and the basic relations of hostility between the sexes. But in spite of this, there is no evidence the people are falling into "parasitism" or that they have not benefitted from the suppression of hostilities.

The materials from the New Guinea highlands illustrate lucidly that violence breeds more of the same, particularly when there is no overriding authority and the major controls involve further violence. But they also illustrate the dangers of being unable to limit power when it does arise. Finally, they put to the test our somewhat exaggerated notions about the harmony and solidarity of small-scale pre-contact societies.

74. Berndt (1962), op. cit., p. 164.

75. I recognize it is possible that warfare in this area was not as total or as practical as I have claimed, and that an alternative explanation for its early disappearance is that it was more ritualistic and/or unimportant. Obviously, I do not believe this to be the case.

14

Violence in Burmese History:
A Psychocultural Explanation

By MELFORD E. SPIRO

Melford E. Spiro is professor and chairman of the Department of Anthropology, University of California, San Diego. He has authored and edited numerous books and articles, among which are Kibbutz: Venture in Utopia, Children of the Kibbutz, Context and Meaning in Cultural Anthropology, Burmese Supernaturalism, Buddhism and Society. *He has conducted field work in Micronesia, Israel, and Burma, and has been a Fellow at the Center for Advanced Study in the Behavioral Sciences, and at the Social Science Research Institute, University of Hawaii.*

This paper was prepared for the Symposium on Violence at the meetings of the American Anthropological Association, New Orleans, Louisiana, 1969.

THIS chapter is a precis of a more comprehensive comparative study of social control in three distinct periods in Burmese history: the pre-colonial, colonial, and post-colonial, or independence, periods (but excluding the period, beginning with the 1962 coup, of the present military dictatorship). The post-colonial or independence period is marked by at least four threats to social order, most of them violent in nature: insurgency (both political and ethnic), political disruption, factionalism, and a high crime rate. All of these threats, so I argue in the larger study, not only represent aggression on the behavioral level, but they reflect hostility on the characterological level. (As I use these terms, "aggression" refers to overt behavior, while "hostility" refers to a motivational disposition.)

Compared to the pre-colonial period, aggression—and by aggression here I mean intra-group aggression—in the colonial and post-colonial periods differs from aggression in the pre-colonial period in three important dimensions: in quantity—it became much more frequent; in motive—it changed from a sportslike phenomenon to a deadly serious enterprise; and in quality—it came, increasingly, to exhibit violence and cruelty.

Given, then, that intra-group violence became (and has remained) an acute problem in Burma primarily after the British conquest, are we to assume—following some currently fashionable political interpretations—that this sociological change was brought about by colonial oppression, resulting either in an increase in hostility or in a lowering of the Burmese threshold for frustration tolerance? Or, rather, are we to assume—following other theories of social change—that this sociological change is an index of characterological change? Or, finally, can we assume, as

I shall suggest, that neither is the case, but that, instead, this sociological change is a result of colonially-induced cultural deprivation which has produced a psychological change at the action system level only?

Before proceeding, the terms of the last alternative (which contains the argument of this paper) must be defined. By "cultural deprivation" I refer to that condition which, with respect to any need, results from the extinction of traditional social and cultural institutions for the satisfaction of that need. By "action system" I refer, with respect to any need, to the hierarchical order of an actor's response repertoire for its satisfaction. That is, given that for any need there is available within the behavioral repertoire of any actor a *range* of potential behavioral responses by which it might be satisfied, it follows that any *actual* response represents a choice from within that range. For every need, then, the actor has (what might be termed) a response repertoire. Typically, the responses which comprise such a repertoire have different psychological valences for the actor; they form a hierarchy ranging from those which, for him, are prepotent to those which are barely conceivable. It is this hierarchical order of a response repertoire which I am calling an "action system." Hence, although action is instigated by needs (or, more properly, by the wish to satisfy them), the behavioral form in which action at any choice point is expressed, and by means of which a need is channeled and (it is hoped) satisfied, is not determined by the instigating need but by the action system associated with it. On the societal level, an action system represents the modal hierarchical order of a group's response repertoire.

It is my thesis, then, that the increase in violence in the last two periods of Burmese history represents a restructuring of the modal Burmese action system for aggression.

AGGRESSION NEED PRESS IN CONTEMPORARY BURMA

As I interpret the data, the violence found in contemporary Burma is an expression, on the behavioral level, of a hostile affect or drive, found on the psychological level, which, moreover, has been a persistent (and modal) attribute of Burmese personality. To support this thesis it is necessary, of course, to adduce some measures of hostility independent of the violence itself; otherwise the argument is circular. Again, in this short paper I can merely mention, rather than document, the grounds of this thesis.[1] Before doing so, however, I wish to emphasize that in referring to Burmese hostility I am not implying that its level or intensity either absolutely or relatively is uniquely Burmese. Indeed, I am confident that the level of hostility is much lower in Burma than in a variety of other societies, in some of which there is greater, and in others of which there is less, overt aggression. Some of the possible reasons for these different behavioral vicissitudes of characterological dispositions to aggression are discussed be-

low. Nor am I implying that hostility is the most salient of the Burmese characterological dispositions. The Burmese are famous for their hospitality, warmth, sense of humor, and so on, which—because this paper focuses on the problem of violence—are not discussed here.

To return, then, to the indices of hostility: in the first place, the careful observer of Burmese interpersonal and social behavior is struck by what appears to be a phobic attitude on the part of the Burmese to the expression of their own hostile impulses. Although this observation can be validly interpreted in a number of ways, I am here concerned with only one of its interpretations: clinically, a phobic attitude toward one's own hostile impulses is an index of rather strong hostility.

Another index of Burmese hostility is their ubiquitous and persistent criticism of others. Over and over again, one is told by the Burmese that all other—or most other—Burmans are liars, thieves, stupid, ignorant, dishonest, impious, etc., and that he (the speaker) alone is honest, or intelligent, or pious, and so on.

Still another index of Burmese hostility is their distrust and suspiciousness of the aggressive intentions of their fellows. This distrust, of course, may be interpreted either as a realistic assessment of the intentions of others, or as a projection of their own hostility. Although this difference in interpretation is an important difference, for our present purpose it need not detain us, for either interpretation supports the thesis that the Burmese are characterized by strong hostile impulses.

The Burmese fear of the aggressivity of others (whether realistic or projective) extends beyond the "human" world. Ghosts and demons, witches, and malevolent spirits abound in the Burmese behavioral world—the belief in evil supernaturals, no doubt, repre-

1. Documentation for this thesis may be found in Geoffrey Gorer, *Burmese Personality* (New York: Institute for Intercultural Relations, 1943), mimeo; Everett Hagen, *On the Theory of Social Change* (Homewood, Ill.: Dorsey Press, 1962); L. M. Hanks, "Individual Autonomy in Burmese Personality," *Psychiatry* 12 (1949), pp. 285–300; Hazel M. Hitson, *Family Patterns and Paranoidal Personality Structure in Boston and Burma*, Ph.D. thesis (Cambridge: Radcliffe, 1959); Lucian W. Pye, *Politics, Personality and Nation Building* (New Haven: Yale University Press, 1962); U. Tu Sein, "The Psychodynamics of Burmese Personality," *Journal of the Burma Research Society* 47 (1964), pp. 262–286; James Steele, *A Preliminary Analysis of the Burmese Rorschachs* (unpublished manuscript).

sents a projection of hostile impulses—and numerous types of magic are employed for protection against their maleficient intentions.[2] The projection of hostility is strongly indicated, as well, in the Burmese projective test protocols.

Let me mention only one more—but a most important—index of Burmese hostility, *viz.*, their authoritarian character structure, which, according to certain psychological formulations, is a clear sign of hostility.

Despite these indications of Burmese hostility—and there are others—only rarely is their hostile affect focused to form hostile drives, and even when it is, the drives are typically suppressed (and, perhaps, repressed), so that the affect is not discharged in behavior. The result is that hostile affect builds up until it can no longer be contained, and then it is expressed explosively in acts of cruelty, violence, and rage.[3]

AGGRESSION NEED PRESS IN TRADITIONAL BURMA

Since the above picture, even if valid, portrays hostility in *contemporary* Burma alone, perhaps it might be argued that Burmese hostility, like their violence, is a post-colonial phenomenon, produced—as one theory has it—by the frustrations of British colonialism. Seductive (and fashionable) though it is, the historical data do not support this argument. All of the indicators of contemporary hostility were present as well in pre-colonial Burma, as a careful survey of the historical literature reveals.

If, then, so far as hostile affect is concerned, there is little difference be-

tween the contemporary and the pre-colonial periods of Burmese history, and if, nevertheless, these periods differ markedly in violence (on the peasant level, at least, pre-colonial Burma seems to have been characterized by very little intra-group violence), how are we to explain the dramatic increase in violence in the modern period?

There are, I believe, two answers to this question: first, hostility in the pre-colonial period was expressed (displaced) socially in the culturally sanctioned violence of warfare, and, second, it was sublimated through a variety of institutions which, psychologically viewed, may be interpreted as culturally constituted defenses against violence. With the coming of the British the first expression was rendered inoperative, and the second was suppressed. I can only state, without examining them, each of these arguments in turn.

Culturally Constituted and Socially Sanctioned Aggression

Early observers of Burmese behavior were often struck by—and happily for us, they often remarked upon—the difference between the kindly, often gentle, Burman at home, and the brutal, even ferocious, Burman at war. The following quotation is typical.

The conduct of the Burmans, in their predatory excursions, is cruel and ferocious to the last degree, and scarcely any people of Asia have more greatly abused the right of conquest. They are not themselves unaware of the barbarous spirit in which their wars are conducted. "You see us here," said some of the chiefs to Mr. Judson, "a mild people, living under regular laws. Such is not the case when we invade foreign countries. We are then under no restraints—we give way to all our passions—we plunder and murder without compunction or control. Foreigners should

2. Melford E. Spiro, *Burmese Supernaturalism* (Englewood Cliffs, N.J.: Prentice Hall, 1967).

3. Melford E. Spiro, "Politics and Factionalism in Upper Burma," in Marc Swartz, ed., *Symposium on Local Level Politics* (Chicago: Aldine, 1968).

beware how they provoke us when they know these things."[4]

If it be remembered that the Burmese army was a conscript, not a professional, army, I think it is reasonable to conclude that Burmese brutality in war (and the Burmese were constantly at war with their neighbors) is not only an index of traditional Burmese hostility, but that this very brutality was a crucial means by which their hostile affect was socially expressed. Since their hostility was periodically abreacted in violence directed against foreign enemies, the Burmese were able in part to remain kindly and nonaggressive at home. This, at least, is my argument.

All this changed, however, with the British conquest: first, because as a British colony, the Burmese were no longer permitted to wage war, and, second, because the British government deliberately refrained from conscripting ethnic Burmese into its colonial army. Hence, deprived of a foreign enemy against whom they could express violence, the Burmese (as Crawfurd—and others—implied that they would do) turned their violence onto domestic targets. Inter-group became intra-group aggression.

But warfare was not the only means in traditional Burma for the expression of hostility—though it was certainly the most violent. Traditional Burmese culture was rich in a variety of internal institutions marvelously used—if not always intended—as a means by which hostile impulses could be sublimated. Descriptions of traditional boat races, pony races, buffalo fighting, and cockfighting (among others)—most of which took the form of inter-village contests—vividly portray the sublima-

tory character of these "old-fashioned amusements," as the colonial administration quaintly called them. Their importance, for our present thesis, consists not so much in the opportunity afforded the participants for the expression of hostile (and other kinds of) energy, but, more importantly, as an opportunity for the expression of an incredible amount of affect by the spectators. "Incredible" is used advisedly, as the following account of an inter-village boat race reveals.

But when the contest is decided, no words can fully picture the scene presented by the wild, yelling, roaring, dancing, laughing, crying crowd. The losers all seem to have disappeared, and the winners all to have gone mad. Here you see a grave, respectable, wealthy, corpulent elder who in ordinary times would consider anything beyond a smile unsuited to his dignity, with his "putsoe," or kilt, tucked up round his thighs, his headkerchief torn off and waved wildly in his hand, his few long grey hairs streaming in the wind, dancing and giving vent to his feelings in the most frightful whoops. Sometime the farce is heightened by the imperturbably and exaggerated gravity of his countenance during this absurd performance. Here is a woman, the wife of an official, an old respectable lady, who in natural manner and good breeding might pass muster anywhere, with her handkerchief tied around her waist, dancing wildly to the music that adds its din to the uproar. To a stranger it would seem at first to be a vast crowd of furious drunkards; but I will be bound there is not one really drunken man among the thousands, though they do seem to be mad for the time. I have often laid my hand quietly on some old man, whom I did not like to see thus making himself absurd; he has sat down with a look as if thanking me for recalling his senses, and remained looking on quietly for some minutes, then suddenly jumped up again, as if unable to control himself, and joined in the wild "sabbat." This is not owing solely or chiefly to the sordid pleasure of gaining the money staked, though thousands of

4. J. Crawfurd, *Journal of an Embassy from the Governor General of India to the Court of Ava in the Year 1827*, 2 vols. (London: Henry Colburn, 1834).

rupees change hands on a great race, but to the excitable and irrepressible disposition of the Burman.[5]

Other contests, sports, and customs enabled the Burmese to discharge hostile affect which might otherwise have been expressed in other—antisocial and violent—forms. Indeed, this is precisely my argument: pre-colonial Burma was characterized by a limited degree of intra-group violence and brutal crime because, in addition to war, hostility was provided various other institutionalized and culturally sanctioned forms of expression. These institutionalized expressions were not only non-disruptive of the social fabric, but they were sufficiently satisfying that non-institutionalized, socially disruptive expressions were not sought to any marked degree.

With the coming of the British, however, all of this, too, was changed. Some of these customs and institutions disappeared, for reasons I have been unable to discover; still others—the inter-village races and contests—were abolished by the colonial government because, so it claimed, they promoted gambling and crime.[6]

To summarize, then, an important (though not exclusive) cause of the violence found in post-colonial Burma, and extending to the present, has been the scarcity of social institutions—the functionally equivalent institutional alternatives to those extinguished by British rule—for socially acceptable expressions of hostility. Given that the Burmese tend to suppress their hostile drives, so that hostile affect (when it is expressed) is discharged explosively, the near-absence of such institutions is *in this context* especially dysfunctional.

Deprived of their traditional culturally sanctioned and socially functional means for the expression of hostility, hostile affect is expressed in disruptive political factionalism, brutal crime, and violence.

If so, the increase in intra-group violence found in modern Burma does not reflect an increase in hostility produced by British colonialism; it reflects, rather, a decrease in the traditional, institutionalized means for its expression —which, in turn, has led to a restructuring of the traditional hierarchical order of the response repertoire for aggression. Intra-group violence, a former low-valence means for the expression of hostility, has become (for many Burmese) a prepotent one.[7]

I would conclude this truncated case study with two general observations. First, if the analysis of this case is valid, it follows that dimensions of social character may persist over long periods of historical time, despite changes in macro-social and macro-cultural structures, so long as one microsocial structure (family and socialization systems) remains fairly constant. In the Burmese case, the latter structure has remained fairly constant and it is this structure which, in my opinion, produces the motivational disposition to violence found in that country. Second, I do not believe—though here I am merely speculating—that this analysis explains the contemporary, worldwide phenomenon of student violence. The latter, I believe, is a function of the breakdown of authority patterns and conceptions of legitimacy which, in turn, reflect important macro- and micro-structural changes, alike. But that is a topic for another paper.

5. C. J. Forbes, *British Burma and Its People* (London: John Murray, 1878).
6. John S. Furnivall, *An Introduction to the Political Economy of Burma* (Rangoon: People's Literature Committee and House, 1931).

7. For detailed historical documentation of the argument, and a full explication of its theoretical foundations, see Melford E. Spiro, "Colonialism, Culture Change, and Some Psychological Aspects of Social Control," in George DeVos, ed., *Cultural Change and Psychological Adjustment* (in press, 1971).

15

The Place of Aggression in Social Interaction

By JOHN W. M. WHITING

John W. M. Whiting is professor of social anthropology, Department of Anthropology and the Department of Social Relations, Harvard University. He is director of a Child Development Research Unit at the University of Nairobi in Kenya, where such studies as the effect of stress and nutrition on growth, the effect of urbanization on child behavior, etc. are carried out. He is the author of Becoming a Kwoma, Child Training and Personality *(with I. Child),* "Sorcery, Sin and Superego," "Effects of Climate on Certain Cultural Practices," "Infantile Stimulation and Adult Stature in Males" (with T. K. Landauer) and "The Learning of Values" (with E. H. Chasdi and H. Antonovsky).*

This paper was prepared for the Symposium on Violence at the meetings of the American Anthropological Association, New Orleans, Louisiana, 1969.

VIOLENCE or violent behavior is, to my mind, a type of the more general class of social inter-action usually referred to as aggression. This chapter is concerned with this more general domain.

As part of a study of socialization in six communities carried out by Thomas and Hatsumi Maretzki in Okinawa, William and Corinne Nydegger in the Philippines, Leigh Triandis and John Hitchcock in northern India, Kimball and Romaine Romney in central Mexico, Robert and Barbara LeVine in western Kenya, and John and Ann Fischer in New England, standardized observations were made of the social inter-actions of children between the ages of 3 and 11. In all, 134 children were observed, matched by sex and age and roughly by culture. When finally coded, the observations provided by the field teams yielded a data bank of nearly 8,000 inter-acts. This permitted us to construct a transcultural paradigm of social acts and a tentative set of rules for the syntax of sequences of social inter-action.

We found that the type of social inter-action observed could be defined as an exchange of goods between two persons. The paradigm for defining social acts thus consists of a classification of the goods to be exchanged in the transaction, cross-cut by the prime beneficiary of the exchange. Although our initial code listed some 75 categories of goods, we found that they could be reduced into the following four major categories: (1) help, (2) dominance, (3) perception of injury, and (4) sociality. Perception of injury, the primary concern in this chapter, may not seem to be a "good," but from our observations it is evident that when a child successfully insults another, the "put-down" is clearly perceived as enjoyable. The beneficiaries of social inter-action are easier to define. They are (1) the self, (2) the other, and (3) the group. Social behavior in which the self is the primary beneficiary may be referred to as *egoistic,* the other as *altruistic,* and the group as *responsible.*

This paradigm, if all distinctions could be made and all combinations occurred, would yield 12 behavior types. Such was, however, not the case. It was impossible to judge reliably whether the beneficiary of offered help was the *other* or the *group,* or whether the beneficiary of sociable inter-action was *self* or the *other.* Furthermore there were no coded instances of altruistic

FIGURE 1. A PARADIGM OF SOCIAL BEHAVIOR BASED ON THE OBSERVATION OF CHILDREN IN THE SIX CULTURES

	BENEFICIARIES		
	SELF (EGOISTIC)	OTHER (ALTRUISTIC)	GROUP (RESPONSIBLE)
help	seeks help	offers help	
dominance	seeks dominance		suggests responsibly
injury	acts aggressively		punishes
sociability	acts sociably		

(Goods)

Some examples of behavioral sequences illustrating syntactic rules.

MAND	STYLE AND RESPONSE
1. A seeks help	simply; B complies.
2. A seeks help	simply; B non-complies;
3. A seeks help	threateningly; B complies.

dominance or altruistic injury. The final paradigm then defines seven behavior types: (1) seeks help, (2) offers help, (3) seeks dominance, (4) suggests responsibly, (5) acts aggressively, (6) punishes, and (1) acts sociably.

Social inter-action as we observed it does not, of course, consist of a single isolated act but occurs in a sequence which has formal properties similar to that of a sentence. We have, therefore, borrowed the notion of syntactic forms from linguistics. Three forms emerged in our syntactic analysis of behavior. (1) a *mand,* (2) a *style,* and (3) a *response.* A mand is form found in the initial position of a social inter-action. It is an attempt by the initiator to influence or change the behavior of another —to force or persuade him to give up or accept some good. Mands can be made in a wide variety of styles. They may be simple, polite, obsequious, or threatening. In other words, the *style* form bears an adverbial relationship to the *mand* form. Finally the response of the person, the target of the mand, consists either of compliance which ordinarily marks the end of the inter-action, or non-compliance which ordinarily leads to a continuation.

Most of the seven behavior types described above can occur as any of these three syntactic form classes. Thus a child can assault his younger sibling with the intent to injure him—*an aggressive mand.* He can assault his younger sibling after the latter has refused to comply to a mand—an aggressive mand style. Finally he can use aggression as *an act of non-compliance.* Although our analysis is as yet incomplete, it is our strong impression that aggression occurs by far the most commonly as a mand style or technique of persuasion, usually following non-compliance to some other mand. Next most common is its occurrence as the re-sponse to a mand to symbolize the refusal to comply. This type of aggression is commonly referred to as defensive aggression. Aggression of the first form—the seeking of injury for its own sake where the good is to see someone else suffer—occurred rarely in our sample of children. This type would be commonly referred to as sadistic.

Having placed aggression in semantic space, we are able to turn to the main concern of this chapter: to develop some hypotheses and present some evidence concerning those factors that would predispose a person or the members of a society to be aggressive. In other words, having provided a cognitive map we can turn to the guts of the problem.

In the first place it is assumed that the same factors will not apply with equal force to the six types of aggression that have been specified above. A theory that would account for them all would be too complex to present in this brief chapter. The discussion will therefore be limited to two of these categories: (1) egoistic aggressive mands —the seeking of injury for its own sake for selfish reasons, and (2) aggression as a style used in conjunction with an egoistically dominant mand. A child who uses an aggressive style to persuade another to accept his dominance would be a case in point.

We have already suggested that egoistic mands which seek injury for its own sake can be thought of as sadistic. Without going into details let us accept the Freudian hypothesis that sadistic pleasure has a sexual component and one who enjoys seeing others suffer is anxious and inhibited at the genital sexual level. There is enough clinical evidence in support of this hypothesis to take it seriously as an explanation of sadistic behavior in individuals. As far as I know, no one has asked whether this hypothesis is applicable at the level of culture. If it is so applicable, it should follow that those societies in which the rules governing sex are rigid, and where sexual behavior is punished during childhood, should at least permit—if not positively value—sadistic behavior.

Fortunately we were able to test this hypothesis by turning to Textor's *Cross Cultural Summary,* in which indices of both sadism and sex inhibition are available and correlated. The index of sadism is particularly appropriate for this symposium. It is the rather elegant scale that Philip E. Slater and his wife developed for their cross-cultural study of narcissism. The scale is labelled "Killing, Torturing, or Mutilating the Enemy." The high point on the scale is defined as follows: "When members of the tribe habitually take prisoners in warfare or raids for the explicit purpose of torturing them; or when prolonged or elaborate torture of captives is mentioned as a common phenomemon; or when prisoners are regularly sacrificed under conditions that approximate torture (slow, painful death, dismemberment while still alive, eaten alive, etc.); or when particularly large numbers of prisoners are slaughtered in ways that produce a rapid but especially painful or terrifying death." The medium position on the scale was defined as follows: "When none of the above are present but, Warriors are said never to take prisoners in battles or raids but have a policy of killing all the enemies on the spot; or headhunting or scalp hunting is said to be practiced on a wide scale, and provides a major source of prestige or status; or killing is a prerequisite of manhood." A society was coded low on this scale if "none of the above are present and the tribe is described as peaceful, gentle, kindly, etc.; or "Prisoners are taken and kept as slaves or otherwise incorporated into the society; or there is no consistent policy regarding

prisoners; or prisoners are not taken but battles or raids are typically concluded before everyone is killed, i.e. when some objective is obtained or when ritual expression of defeat is rendered by the enemy, or wars and raiding are rare."

Ninety societies well distributed over the culture areas of the world were rated on this scale. Fourteen scored high, 23 medium, 47 low, and 6 could not be rated. For the results to be reported below, the high and medium cases were combined and contrasted with the cases that scored low.

This scale seems to be a reasonable measure of an over-determined positive evaluation of egoistic mands in which the good is the perception of injury. The typical members of a society scoring high on this scale should get more pleasure from performing sadistic acts than a typical member of a society scoring at the low point of the scale.

Scores of sex inhibition are provided by Ford and Beach, who rated 42 societies overlapping with the Slater sample on whether extramarital sex was permitted or punished. Of the 23 societies that prohibited premarital sex, 18 scored high or medium and only 5 low on the sadism scale. Of the 19 tribes that were judged to permit extramarital sex, only 5 scored high and 14 low on the sadism scale. This contigency yields Phi value of .47 and a significance level of .002.

It is interesting to note that the *Ethnographic Atlas* scales on *premarital sex* did not show up in Textor's tables to be significantly related to the Slater scale.

An orthodox Freudian would, I am sure, object to cultural rules governing the sexual behavior of adults as a "cause" of over-determined sadistic impulses. They would require some events that could be said to customarily occur during the process of socialization when "personality" is being formed.

The treatment of children's sexual behavior during childhood was scored by Whiting and Child. Although the 39 cases that overlap with the Slater sadism scale are associated in the predicted direction, the relationship does not attain statistical significance.

William Stephens' composite predictor of castration anxiety, however, is significantly related to the Slater sadism score (Phi value = .32 p < .05). The Stephens score includes both the punishment for masturbation and sex during childhood, and the importance and strictness of the father as a disciplinarian.

In sum, there seems to be some support for the hypothesis that societies inducing high sex anxiety and sex inhibition are likely to permit and even to ritually require a high degree of cruelty and sadism in the treatment of prisoners of war.

The second aggressive factor to be considered is the use of aggression as a style in seeking egoistic dominance. The behavior of non-human primates provides the clue to an understanding of this behavior. In these animals, this type of behavior occurs primarily as a manifestation of masculine prowess. If we assume that this is also true of human primates, and the fact that in the six-culture study, boys showed significantly more egoistic dominance than girls, supports this view. The problem is to specify the conditions under which men should have an overdetermined need to prove their masculinity. Beatrice Whiting, in a recent paper on "Sex Identity Conflict and Physical Violence," has suggested an answer to this question. She cites evidence that an exclusive relationship between a mother and son during infancy should lead to a feminine identity which conflicts with his need to be a

man. This conflict results in hypermasculine behavior in the form of violence. I have used this hypothesis to interpret the functions of male initiation rites.

Confirming evidence for this thesis can also be found in Textor. Slater again provides the appropriate scale for the dependent variable—in this case the pursuit of military glory. The scale is defined as follows:

"High: When the ethnographer says that members of the tribe seek death in battle, or regard it as preferable to defeat and behave accordingly, or see it as the principal road to earthly or other-worldly glory. Or, when war is said to be considered by the tribe as glorious, the primary source of status and prestige, or to be waged principally for the purpose of obtaining rank, honor, or fame. Or, when military virtues, such as valor, recklessness, fighting skill, etc., are said to be the most important ones in the society. Or, when military trophies are said to be the principal source of rank or prestige in the society.

"Moderate: When none of the above are present but: Defensive virtues are said to be valued—military resistance, endurance, fortitude, etc. Or, values other than military ones predominate, though the latter are important; or, contests of bravery, skill or endurance (e.g., ability to withstand pain) are an important feature of masculine relationships; or, raids, etc., are frequent, but conducted primarily for economic reasons.

"Low: When none of the above are present and: Ethnographer says military virtues are not valued. Or, some indication is given that saving one's own life in battle is considered normal and appropriate behavior. Or, war is regarded as abhorrent."

If glory in war is taken to be a reasonable index of hypermasculinity or the exaggerated need for men to defend themselves against femininity, then it should be found more commonly in societies with an exclusive relationship between a boy and his mother during his infancy, combined with a low salience of the father during this period. Such turns out to be true. Polygynous societies in which the child remains with his mother but whose father often sleeps and eats elsewhere are more likely to value glory in war than do monogamous societies. The Phi value of this relationship is .28 (P < .009). Exclusive mother-son sleeping arrangements—a more explicit measure of a condition likely to produce cross-sex identity—is also significantly associated with the glory in warfare score (Phi = .40P < .01).

In sum, certain values and practices associated with warfare—specifically, the treatment of prisoners and the evaluation of military glory—can be interpreted to be explained in part by a model which sets aggression within a coherent structure of social behavior and which borrows from Freud principles of defense against conflict.

It is hoped that this analysis will contribute to some small degree to an understanding of violence at the cultural level.

BIBLIOGRAPHY

Six Cultures; Studies of Child Rearing—Beatrice B. Whiting, John Wiley and Sons, Inc., New York, 1963.

Mothers of Six Cultures—Leigh Minturn and William W. Lambert, John Wiley and Sons, Inc., New York, 1964.

Child Training and Personality—Irvin L. Child and John W. M. Whiting, Yale University Press, New Haven, 1953.

A Cross Cultural Summary—Robert B. Textor, HRAF Press, New Haven, 1967.

The Oedipus Complex: Cross Cultural Evidence—William N. Stephens, The Free Press of Glencoe (A Division of the MacMillan Co.), New York, 1962.

"Sex Identity Conflict and Physical Violence: A Comparative Study" in *The Ethnography of Law* and *The American Anthropologist* (1967) Part II, pp. 123–140. First published in 1965 (*The Ethnography of Law*).

Part IV

Dimensions of Collective Violence in the United States

16

The Paradox of American Violence:
A Historical Appraisal

By Hugh Davis Graham

Hugh Davis Graham, Ph.D., is associate professor of History at the Johns Hopkins University and assistant director of the Institute of Southern History. He is author of Crisis in Print *(1967), co-editor of* Violence in America *(1969), and editor of* Huey Long *(1970). In 1968–69 he was co-director of the History and Comparative Task Force of the National Commission on the Causes and Prevention of Violence. He has been awarded a Guggenheim Fellowship for 1970–71.*

IT IS today a commonplace observation that American historiography has long been flawed by a self-congratulatory parochialism. The consensus historians who dominated their craft during the "complacent 1950's" celebrated American uniqueness, and the corollary myths of individual assimilation and peaceful progress, in tones reminiscent of Bancroft, and their generally conservative ideology implicitly sustained the Cold War as a kind of latter-day projection of Manifest Destiny. Then came the contagion of violence that swept the nation during the 1960's, and with it the resurgence of radicalism and the challenge of the new left. Historians were impelled to reassess their history in light of the tumultuous new era, and since the question of the antecedents of nonmilitary violence—or at least its popularity—was relatively new, most of the old books had little to tell us.

While this dramatic new concern for the history of American violence tended inherently to compensate for the self-congratulatory or myopic tendencies of the past, the danger remained that American historians would reassess the meaning of their past in light of the new question but within the confines of the old parochialism. If the essence of social science is comparison, the new question invited not only a historical or vertical comparison—i.e., to what degree our past has been more or less violent than our present—but also a cross-national or horizontal comparison—i.e., how have our patterns of violence contrasted with those of other societies?

TASK FORCE ON VIOLENCE

This conviction that maximum insight would flow from a focus on the intersection between the vertical dimension of historical analysis and the horizontal dimension of cross-national comparison guided the research design of the Historical and Comparative Task Force of the National Commission on the Causes and Prevention of Violence, of which I was co-director with Ted Robert Gurr, a political scientist. Hence our report, *Violence in America*,[1] not only delved into the various historical categories of American violence—frontier and vigilante, labor, racial and ethnic, violent crime, antiwar protest; it also contained cross-national comparisons that, while lacking in historical depth, were particularly revealing of the paradoxical relationship between the high incidence of American violence in comparison with other nations and, at the same time, the relative stability of institutions that has mitigated the severity of our violence.

One study of cross-national data on political violence in the last twenty years concludes that when greatest weight is given to the frequency of violent events, the United States ranks 14th among 84 nations.[2] Yet when the major criterion is the severity of all manifestations of political instability, violent or not, the United States stands below the midpoint, 46th among the 84. A more detailed comparison of the characteristics of civil strife in 114 nations and colonies in the 1960's concludes that in total magnitude of strife the United States ranks first among 17 Western democracies and 24th in the overall sample.[3] Yet, again reflecting the relative stability of the American social structure, most demonstrators and rioters in the United States were protesting rather than rebelling or engaging in organized violence. As a consequence, even though

1. Hugh Davis Graham and Ted Robert Gurr, eds., *Violence in America: Historical and Comparative Perspectives* 2 (Washington, D.C.: U.S. Government Printing Office, 1969).

2. Ivo K. Feierabend, Rosalind L. Feierabend, and Betty Nesvold, "Social Change and Political Violence: Cross-National Patterns," in *Violence in America* 2, pp. 497–542.

3. Ted Robert Gurr, "A Comprehensive Study of Civil Strife," in *Violence in America* 2, pp. 443–96.

about 220 Americans died in violent civil strife in the five years before mid–1968, the rate of 1.1 deaths per million population was exceedingly low compared with the average for all nations and colonies of 238 deaths per million, and it was also less by half than the European average of 2.4 deaths per million.

If our report documented this paradoxical relationship and catalogued a tumultuous history that our selective recollection had previously obscured, yet it failed adequately to explain why our consistently high levels and lethal thrusts of collective violence have largely been deflected from our vital institutions. We historians dearly love paradox, but by its nature it explains nothing.

THE PARADOX CONSIDERED

Any paradox must contain two ostensibly contradictory assertions—in this case, that the American past has been filled with violence, and that the stability and continuity of America's vital public institutions have been extraordinary. How can we account for this? Let me consider these assertions in reverse order. One plausible, albeit only partial, reason why violence has not been directed against public institutions in the United States to the degree that it has in so many other nations may be (at least until the recent period) that, given America's federal, capitalistic structure, state institutions have historically been less important than private institutions or than public institutions in other societies. Capitalism pitted labor against industry, farmers against the railroad or an impersonal market system. Consider our long and turbulent history of frontier and agrarian discontent: the Paxton Boys; the New Jersey land rioters; the New York anti-rent movement; the North Carolina Regulators; the New Mexico White Caps; the Shays, Whiskey, and Fries

rebellions; the Western Claims Clubs; the Kentucky tobacco coöperatives; the Grangers, Greenbackers, Alliancemen, Populists; the Green Corn Rebellion; Oklahoma socialists; the Farmers' Holiday Association—the list stretches from Nathaniel Bacon (excluding the American Indians) to Cesar Chavez.[4] Yet most frontier and agrarian violence was not directed against the state, and when it infrequently was, it was quickly and usually easily put down. Our labor history is of more recent vintage, but also more bloody. It is true that the state frequently lent its National Guard and occasionally federal troops to the support of the industrialists, and that police and sheriffs as agents of the state were also rarely neutral. But the carnage associated with the Molly Maguires, Homestead, Coeur D'Alene, the Black Hole of Ludlow, and Gastonia was not primarily directed at, or even by, the state. It was Judge Gary, not President Cleveland or Justice Field, whom the embattled and enraged steelworkers alleged had never seen a blast furnace until the day he died.

There are, of course, notable exceptions. To the Indians, the state was devastatingly important, much as it was to slaves and, to a much lesser extent, the Mormons. But the Indian wars were remote from public institutions, slave rebellions were few and abortive, and the Mormons perforce modified one of *their* peculiar institutions to fit the preconditions of the monogamous state. The crowning exceptions were, of course, the Revolution and the Civil War. But their circumstances were so unusual that, crucially important as they were, they skew the picture of workaday violence

4. See Richard Maxwell Brown, "Historical Patterns of Violence in America," in *Violence in America* 1, pp. 35–64. Brown's 156 references constitute a comprehensive bibliography of the historical literature on American violence.

in America—and, in any event, the state and its dominant institutions, with the crucial exception of chattel slavery, emerged greatly fortified from both conflagrations.

A second reason why the thrust of American violence has been largely directed away from the nation's vital institutions is our unparalleled racial and ethnic pluralism. Consider how much of our collective violence has been intergroup, how frequently group frustrations have generated displaced aggression against racial and ethnic scapegoats: the Know-Nothings and the American Protective Association; the anti-abolitionist mobs; the Irish rampage against Negroes in New York in 1863; the chastisements of the first and third Ku Klux Klans, and at least the rhetoric of the second Klan; the predominantly southern lynching of Negroes; the Western attacks upon Orientals; the massive white urban rioting against blacks in the pre-Harlem pattern of race riots, and the destruction of symbolic private property in the post-Harlem pattern. Perhaps those New York Irishmen in 1863 should logically have protested an inequitable conscription by attacking the government, but to do so would have been suicidal. Until very recently, no single racial or ethnic group has been numerous or strategically located enough to venture serious frontal aggression against the state. This, of course, does not apply to the dominant Anglo-Americans, but the behavior of the state far less often militated against their interests.

Yet a third reason has been American affluence. Too much could be made of this, for we know that the abundance has been unequally distributed and that such economic inequities may generate violent protest. And we also know that societies characterized by abject poverty and minimal expectations are unlikely to spawn revolutions. But students of

the American franchise have concluded that the increase in national wealth has been paralleled by a general decline of voter participation, to such an extent that only two-thirds of qualified twentieth century Americans bother to vote even in presidential contests. Contrast this to the extremely high percentage of voting that characterizes the impoverished Latin American nations, where the relationship to those in power is so crucial to livelihood and where violence and political instability are endemic. Apparently, prosperity as well as poverty can generate apathy. By implication, those tens of millions of Americans who have been insufficiently concerned with public policy to bother casting their votes (this, of course, excludes those disfranchised) are unlikely candidates for attacks on the government; and, of course, those who do vote are more unlikely still.

A fourth reason is closely linked to the economic performance discussed above. The rewarding payoff of American material progress reinforced faith in the legitimacy of the system and sanctified the dominant institutions of the state. It has been a faith of astonishing tenacity, deeply rooted in the wisdom of the Founders; the American Dream of a New Jerusalem, of a City on a Hill; the fetish of Constitution-worship; the rags-to-riches, log cabin-to-White House mythos; the iron, conservative grip of the liberal consensus—what Daniel Boorstin has called the sense of "givenness" of American institutions.[5]

5. Daniel J. Boorstin, *The Genius of American Politics* (Chicago: University of Chicago Press, 1953). Boorstin has been preëminently cited as representative of the consensus school of American historians. See also David M. Potter, *People of Plenty* (Chicago: University of Chicago Press, 1954); and Louis Hartz, *The Liberal Tradition in America* (New York: Harcourt, Brace & World, 1955). Unlike Boorstin and, to a lesser extent, Potter, Hartz has been more critic than celebrant of the consensus.

To appreciate the ubiquity of this nationalistic faith, to acknowledge its awesome power, is not necessarily to celebrate it after the fashion of Boorstin and the consensus historians. From the perspective of our more cynical era, how astonishing it is to contemplate its historic grip upon millions of black Americans, whose everyday lives for centuries cruelly mocked and belied it.

THE EUROPEAN STATE COMPARED

The European state, lacking the broad sanction of such a secular faith, encumbered by a feudal past, generally endowed with greater and more centralized power, its population less divided by ethnic and racial heterogeneity, perforce was more vulnerable to collective violence—more given to destruction or to totalitarian self-defense. In Europe, Charles Tilly has traced the evolution of three basic forms of collective violence.[6] The first, "primitive" violence, was characterized by diffuse and unpolitical objectives and was based upon communal forms of organization that produced apolitical village brawls and guild clashes, the mutual attacks of hostile religious groups, and the peasant *Jacquerie*. In America, the rioting in colonial seaports, the slave rebellions, the celebrated family feuds, town and gown clashes, the frontier lynching mobs, and wars between sheepmen and cattlemen partook of this primitive, communal character. But lacking a feudal past— to the exclusion of the South's abortive "Reactionary Enlightenment"—America's primitive violence has a more truncated history and has been far less pervasive than that of Europe.

Tilly's second category is "reactionary" violence.

Reactionary disturbances are also usually small in scale, but they pit either communal groups or loosely organized members of the general population against representatives of those who hold power, and tend to include a critique of the way power is being wielded. The forcible occupations of fields and forests by the landless, the revolt against the tax collector, the anticonscription rebellion, the food riot, and the attack on machines were Western Europe's most frequent forms of reactionary collective violence. The somewhat risky term "reactionary" applies to these forms of collective violence because their participants were commonly reacting to some change that they regarded as depriving them of rights they had once enjoyed; they were backward-looking.[7]

It is at this level that differences between American and European violence are most striking, for the "representatives of those who hold power" in Europe were far more often representatives of the state and its public institutions than has been the case in America. We have had our Whiskey Rebellions, to be sure, but far more predominant in America has been the racial, ethnic, and economic violence of the extrapolitical and intergroup nature that has been discussed above.

And why has there been so much violence in America? Theoretically, in a democratic republic, violence would be neither necessary nor tolerated. Accordingly, our civics textbooks have combined with historical amnesia to foster the familiar myth of melting-pot assimilation and pacific progress. Now that we are becoming increasingly aware of our violent past, how do we account for it?

6. "Collective Violence in European Perspective," in *Violence in America* 1, pp. 5–34.

7. *Ibid.*, p. 14. Tilly's third category, "modern" violence, is based upon a broad associational base that is conducive to large-scale activities which are not intrinsically violent, such as the strike or demonstration, and that provides leaders with a greater measure of control in striking for rights considered due them, but not yet enjoyed. The modern American labor and civil rights movements are obvious examples.

THE FOUR FACTORS RECONSIDERED

One might begin to account for it by reconsidering the influence of the four factors previously adduced as to why American violence has been deflected from our vital public institutions: the federal, capitalistic structure; racial and ethnic heterogeneity; affluence; and the American Creed as reflective of our national character. In a society as thoroughly capitalistic as ours has been, private hands have been endowed with great power to bestow rewards or mete out punishment; in the absence of a powerful state equipped with physical controls sufficient to quickly and effectively punish aggression, private sources of economic power became lightning rods to attract protest. And what generated the lightning? In large part, class, ethnic, and racial competition for the promised abundance. As a pluralistic society, probably the most pluralistic major society in the world, America has been especially vulnerable to the frustration of disappointed expectations, because historically we have employed the political process of generating demands through pressure groups as a means of leverage to bring about change and progress. But the very success of this process has generated new demands on the part of newly emergent groups, and renewed resistance on the part of groups defending earlier achievements.[8]

Given these self-reinforcing engines of aggression, and given the ready access

8. I have argued elsewhere that the seeds of our discontent were to a large extent embedded in those same ostensibly benevolent forces—pluralistic immigration, the frontier, the Revolution, the liberal consensus, urbanization and industrialization, and abundance—that consensus historians have cited as productive of our benign uniqueness. See "Violence in American History," in *To Establish Justice, To Insure Domestic Tranquility:* Final Report of the National Commission on the Causes and Prevention of Violence (Washington, D.C.: U.S. G.P.O., 1969), pp. 1–16.

to such instruments of aggression as firearms, American society has been poorly equipped historically to cope with the violence it has generated. At the root of our national character has been an obdurate commitment to the notion of equality—more specifically, as De Tocqueville perceived it, to equality of opportunity. David M. Potter, the preëminent student of the American national character, has seen as "the most pronounced of all the concrete expressions of American beliefs in equality" the rejection of authority, a pervasive taboo that has led to an extraordinarily strong emphasis on permissiveness.[9] This taboo on authority has, in turn, been shaped and reinforced by a frontier individualism and a sympathy for the underdog that has endowed with the mystique of Robin Hood such spectacular agents of violence as the James brothers, Billy the Kid, Pretty Boy Floyd, John Dillinger, and Bonnie and Clyde. Add to this the Higher Law doctrine that was embodied in the Revolution, the abolitionist crusade, and the trials at Nürnberg, and it is not difficult to fathom why America—despite official rhetoric to the contrary—has never been a very law-abiding nation.

SYMPATHY WITH LAW BREAKERS

Within the last quarter century there have been four large-scale situations wherein major public sympathy in America was with the lawbreakers: (1) with Germans who rejected Nazi law, and particularly with those who attempted to assassinate Hitler; (2) with Americans who refused to obey racial segregation laws in the South; (3) with protesters who violate law in their demonstrations against the Vietnam War; and

9. David M. Potter, "The Quest for the National Character," in John Higham, ed., *The Reconstruction of American History* (New York: Harper & Brothers, 1962), p. 216.

—more recently in our hardening times —(4) with whites who refuse to obey decrees to integrate their schools. There has even been some sympathy for looters who are trapped in poverty, and for law-breaking students who regard school authorities as contemptuous of their consent. The sword of the Higher Law is, of course, two-edged: one strikes for equality, the other for liberty—a basic contradiction that has been generally unappreciated by generations of Americans, who have thoughtlessly equated liberty and equality, and who have consequently misread the powerful ambiguities in American life and have remained oblivious to the violence in our past and puzzled by the violence in our midst.

In the conclusion to our report, we noted this abiding conflict that is inherent in a dual commitment to liberty and equality, although we did not expand upon it. But it may be that American violence is rooted in American values. De Tocqueville observed long ago that the materialistic Americans exploited their political liberty in an insatiable quest for equality of opportunity.[10] Their democratic individualism led them to reject the sanctions of tradition, family, church, and state; and this unique freedom from external, institutional restraints required a self-restraint that imposed an enormous psychic burden upon the individual, in the unending quest for material equality. Persistently faced with a social reality that denied such equality, the frustrated American democrat became peculiarly vulnerable to seizures of violent aggression. Given a remarkably fluid society, a boom-and-bust economy, relatively minimal state

sanctions, and an unparalleled racial and ethnic heterogeneity, private targets for violent aggression—whether displaced or direct—have been plentiful and inviting.

In recent years, two theories have been advanced that attempt to explain violence in terms that are quite contradictory—the one appealing to the ideological right, the other to the left. At the root of the first is the ancient notion, recently resurrected and refurbished in scientific garb, that man is instinctively aggressive. According to this thesis, which has been most prominently advanced in the scientific writings of the Austrian ethologist Konrad Lorenz and the popular expositions of Robert Ardrey,[11] the cynical Roman epigram, *homo homini lupus*—man is a wolf to man—represents a libel on the gentle wolf. Equipped by evolution with such puny physical weapons, man perforce developed a minimal instinctive restraint to bridle his intra-specific aggression. Consequently, when his ingenious technology produced weapons capable of massive destruction, he became the planet's most truly immoral creature, singularly given to self-destruction. The origin of the Freudian death wish, *Thanatos*, had been located immutably in Darwinian terms.

In an age of missile silos, rampant overpopulation, and environmental pollution, it is understandable that liberal and radical social scientists should be appalled by the profoundly conservative implications of the assertion that man is instinctively aggressive, and that they should deplore an inherent fatalism which bases man's hope for survival on such frail reeds as the promotion of a kind of symbolic, safety-valve competi-

10. I am indebted to John William Ward for his perceptive comments on the paper by Michael Wallace, "The Uses of Violence in American History," read at the meeting of the American Historical Association in Washington, D.C., 28 December 1969.

11. Konrad Lorenz, *On Aggression* (New York: Bantam Books, 1967); and Robert Ardrey, *The Territorial Imperative* (New York: Dell Publishing Co., 1966). For a liberal critique, see M. F. Ashley Montagu, ed., *Man and Aggression* (New York: Oxford University Press, 1968).

tion in international sports and in space. I confess that I have been disappointed, if not really surprised, at the degree to which the mere mention of Lorenz or Ardrey in liberal academic circles is likely to elicit a dogmatic and emotional outburst that ill consorts with the social scientists' ostensible commitment to entertain any reasonable hypothesis concerning human behavior. But the social scientist is surely on sound ground in insisting that culture is a powerful, if not omnipotent, determinant of man's propensity for violence—witness the melancholy fact that Manhattan Island, with a population of 1.7 million, has in recent years produced more murders per year than all of England and Wales, with a combined population of 49 million. One need not become entangled in the interminable hen-and-egg debate over the nature-versus-nurture controversy to perceive that man has the cultural capacity to minimize as well as maximize his recourse to violence.

TO MARX AND BEARD

But the thesis that man is innately aggressive, when advanced as a blanket explanation for human violence, founders not only on the shoals of comparative evidence. It also runs afoul of a fundamental moral objection. For if all are guilty, none is guilty. Keenly sensitive to this moral dimension, and appalled by the Hobbesian view of human nature that is implicit in the thesis that human aggression is innate, contemporary historians of a "new" leftish persuasion have turned not to Darwin or Freud but to Marx—or at least to Beard: American violence has been primarily a consequence of repressive men wielding the power of the state in defense of privilege and the status quo. According to this formula, American violence has not been paradoxical, because "violence and stable institutions, in-

stead of being opposites, become co-partners." [12]

Such a denial of the paradox, however, misconstrues the argument here, which is not that violence and stable institutions are *necessarily* opposites. Obviously, violence and stable institutions *may* become co-partners, as in totalitarian societies in which the reign of terror sustains the state in the absence of perceived legitimacy. Clearly, such assertions reflect a present-minded and burgeoning animosity on the left toward the behavior of the American government since World War II—for reasons that are painfully apparent and need not be adumbrated here. But these ominous postwar events seem to reflect a fundamental discontinuity with our past, for even if the historical commonality of American violence is demonstrable, the power and activity of the American state have grown enormously during the postwar years. Despite the recent popularity of hyperbolic allusions to the Third Reich, the United States has not been a totalitarian society, and historians angered at the contemporary state's behavior should beware of projecting these assumptions backward onto our past.

This is not to deny that much of our historic violence has "served the dominant establishment"—has generally been "generated from the top of society, not the bottom, and has aimed at repression, not innovation." [13] The repressive nature of American nativism is an old and familiar story. The leading authority on American vigilantism, Richard Maxwell Brown, has described vigilante groups as predominantly local

12. Comment by Douglas T. Miller on an earlier version of this paper, read at the meeting of the Organization of American Historians in Los Angeles, 16 April 1970.

13. *Ibid.* Michael Wallace similarly argued that the preponderance of American violence has been repressive, whereas that of Europe has been expressive and generated from below.

elites, organized to uphold community values and property—eminent men for whom it would be easy to compile a " 'Who's Who' of American vigilantism." [14] And in a recent study, Leonard L. Richards has described the leaders of the anti-abolitionist mobs in Jacksonian America as "gentlemen of property and standing." [15] To survey the history of American violence from "the bottom up" is not to imply that the preponderance of the violence emanated from the lower social orders. The point of this analysis is rather to emphasize that our capitalistic, federal structure has historically pitted our racial, ethnic, and economic groups against one another rather than against the state and its vital institutions, which until the very recent past have been, in comparison with other societies, unusually sanctified, insulated, even indifferent—occasionally an aggressor, to be sure, but rarely a target. To assert that a society's vital public institutions have been remarkably immune from the tumult that has surrounded them is not to deny the moral indictment that they presided over internecine pain and anguish. It is only to attempt to explain an important historical phenomenon that historical and comparative evidence have brought to light—one that appears to be ostensibly paradoxical, but that has nevertheless been very real.

14. See "The American Vigilante Tradition," in *Violence in America* 1, pp. 121–70.

15. *Gentlemen of Property and Standing: Anti-Abolitionist Mobs in Jacksonian America* (Oxford University Press, 1970).

17

The Psychology of Political Activity

By Sheldon G. Levy

Sheldon G. Levy, Ann Arbor, Michigan is associate professor of Psychology and research associate in the Center for Urban Studies at Wayne State University. He was an assistant professor at the University of Michigan after receiving his Ph.D. there, and has spent visiting years as an associate professor at Brandeis University (1968–69) and Rice University (1970). He also served as a co-director of the task force studying assassination and political violence with the National Commission on the Causes and Prevention of Violence. His publications include Inferential Statistics in the Behavioral Sciences *(1968) and co-editorship of* Assassination and Political Violence *(1969).*

THIS paper examines attitudes toward political violence that were obtained from a national sample of almost 1,200 adults, 18 years of age or older. The major purpose of this presentation is to develop theoretical ideas that will organize and explain the findings, portions of which have been presented in a series of earlier papers by the author (which will be cited as they become relevant).

Because part of the data has already been examined, the theory represents an effort to explain the results rather than to make a *priori* predictions. Consequently, the full test of the theory as well as the attempt to broaden it to a wider range of data must wait upon further research. Hopefully, these ideas will lay a foundation for those efforts.

THE THEORY OF REDUCED ALTERNATIVES

The major objective of this analysis is to predict the political behavior of individuals. This behavior is considered the outcome of an interaction between the contemporary social environment and the psychological characteristics of the individual. The theory focuses on the effect of a cognitive and behavioral reduction in the number of alternatives for political action upon attitudes toward authority.

The starting point of the discussion is the past social experience of the individual, which is considered to be a major determinant of his psychological

orientation. The concepts of systemic reward and punishment are used to define the major relevant components of this experience. (For discussions of concepts relevant to this presentation, such as relative deprivation, systemic frustration, and rising satisfaction, see Gurr, Feierabend et al., and Davies.[1]) Systemic reward is said to have occurred when an individual receives benefits, real or psychological, that are consistent with his desires within the society. Systemic punishment occurs when such benefits fall short of those wishes. There is, of course, good reason to expect that the concept of systemic reward/punishment is multidimensional.

The next problem is to examine the consequences of reward and punishment on political behavior and political attitudes. The first assumption is that the greater the punishment, the lower will be the level of political responsiveness and the greater will be the rigidity in the response repertoire.

Systemic punishment has a corresponding psychological consequence, namely, frustration, which leads to a cognitive reduction in the number of potential response alternatives. It is, of course, recognized that a narrow range of behavioral-cognitive alternatives may also arise from limited individual or cultural learning experiences.

The rigidity of response induced by punishment leads to anxiety over those situations that require or even allow a

The interviewing was conducted October 1-8, 1968, by Louis Harris and Associates for the National Commission on the Causes and Prevention of Violence. The portions of the survey reported here were under the direction of the author, who was co-director of the Task Force on Assassination and Political Violence. Richard Link was particularly helpful in the statistical analyses.

It should be noted that the source of the data restricts present applicability of the theory to a large, modern, democratic society.

1. Ted Robert Gurr, "A Comparative Study of Civil Strife," I. Feierabend, R. L. Feierabend, and B. A. Nesvold, "Social Change and Political Violence: Cross-National Patterns," and James C. Davies, "The J-Curve of Rising and Declining Satisfactions as a Cause of Some Great Revolutions and a Contained Rebellion," in Hugh Davis Graham and Ted Robert Gurr, eds., *The History of Violence in America*, Report to the National Commission on the Causes and Prevention of Violence (Washington, D.C.: U.S. Government Printing Office, 1969), 572–730.

variety of responses. Consequently, the individual develops a more general psychological rigidity, which manifests itself in a preference for less complex situations and a positive evaluation of those circumstances that more precisely define role expectations. Another way to express this is to say that the punishment-induced sequence leads to an intolerance of social ambiguity.

Although the reduction in anxiety is partially accomplished through psychological rigidity, additional defense mechanisms may be necessary. One way in which security can further be achieved is through identification with authority. In the political sphere, this may be one of the most important mechanisms for anxiety reduction. The greater the trust or faith in, or reliance upon, authority, the less is the need for individual decision-making. This defense should manifest itself in the support of authority even when its action is questionable, and an unwillingness to attack authority even when the freedom of the individual is infringed upon. Very likely, the politically insecure individual is unwilling to admit that the attacks of authority are directed at him; that is, the individual rationalizes the action of authority to maintain his favorable attitude.

Identification is not the only defense mechanism. Behavioral withdrawal (with the corresponding psychological state of alienation) is also an important outcome. The reasons for alienation rather than identification are not clear. One possibility is that alienation is more likely to occur when authority provides insufficient symbols upon which identification can be based. Another possibility is that a threat that leads to great anxiety is more likely to result in withdrawal to insure the anxiety will be sufficiently reduced. These two possibilities combine in the case of value

conflict. That is, if the value system of the individual and that represented by authority are greatly discrepant, withdrawal rather than identification is the likely consequence of prior systemic punishment. Within this formulation, neither identification nor withdrawal leads to interest in the operation of government. The identified are disinterested because governmental decision-making introduces a complexity into the environment that is anxiety-arousing, whereas the alienated have already removed themselves behaviorally and psychologically from such concerns. There is, however, an observable difference between the two groups. Those who have identified with authority will be more supportive of authoritarian actions and more antagonistic toward attacks upon authority than will the alienated.

It will be noted that the above discussion indicates that systemic punishment leads to eventual political passivity on the part of the individual. If this were the only outcome, there would never be protest or revolution. It seems apparent that protest represents an attempt to remove an interference to goal achievement and, therefore, is indicative of frustration in the individual.

The theory of *reduced alternatives* proposes that one major distinction between the politically active and the politically passive is that the former have available a wide range of response and cognitive alternatives. This allows a flexible rather than a rigid outlook and approach to problems. Consequently, the need for identification with authority in order to reduce anxiety is absent. Thus, authority can be veridically perceived, and opposition to threats from such authority can be initiated.

To recapitulate: a response to a threat, such as governmental oppression, requires the perception of the threat. The more dependent the individual is on the government, the less likely a threat will be perceived. Individuals who have a limited repertoire of political responses will be more dependent upon the government than those with a wide range of responses. Consequently, the latter are more likely to perceive a threat and more likely to oppose it. Of course, the greater the dependence upon the authority, the greater will be the opposition to attacks upon it.

In addition to having less ability to perceive a threat, those who have few available political responses will prefer simple situations. They will be less interested, therefore, in the operation of government and will be more likely to prefer authoritarian government; whereas those who have a range of responses will prefer more complex situations and more democratic government. The latter will express greater interest in the operation of government and will be more likely to oppose attacks upon democratic institutions.

The major determinant of the range of available political responses is the amount of past systemic punishment the individual has experienced, although individual and cultural learning is also important.

If anxiety cannot be adequately reduced through dependence on the government, withdrawal (alienation) may occur. If withdrawal is prevented under such circumstances, attack upon authority is likely as the only remaining alternative.

Relevant individual factors, such as intelligence and tolerance for anxiety, have not been included in this presentation.

OPERATIONALIZATION OF THE THEORETICAL CONCEPTS

The purpose of this section is to examine the questionnaire variables that represent operationalization of the concepts.

The theory is outlined in Figure 1.

Indices of Systemic Punishment

Operationalizing systemic punishment is extremely difficult in general, and especially so when it is applied to a survey that has already been conducted. The concept involves a discrepancy between the individual's desired level of achievement and his actual level. Thus, eventually, its measurement might greatly benefit from panel studies.

In this study, several demographic variables that had high predictive power were obtained from a multiple regression. The use of systemic punishment represents an attempt to understand one reason why the variables were predictive.

Education will be used as one index of systemic reward and punishment. The assumption is that in the United States a low level of education is generally indicative of punishment to the individual, because it represents achievement below his desired level. It thus results in psychological frustration. It may also be an indirect index of other punishing experiences, such as lowered income and reduced status. Although income was a fairly good predictor by itself, it did not give sufficient additional information beyond that which was available from the educational level.

Similarly, being nonwhite may also be considered evidence of systemic punishment, such as that which occurs through racial discrimination; and it may also be an indirect index of other punishing experiences, such as lowered education, lowered income, and reduced status. However, in this country, being white does not appear to be an index of systemic reward—although in other countries, such as South Africa and Rhodesia, it might well be.

Finally, residence in the South was taken as indicative of systemic punishment. (Empirically, the region of the country in which one resided was a good

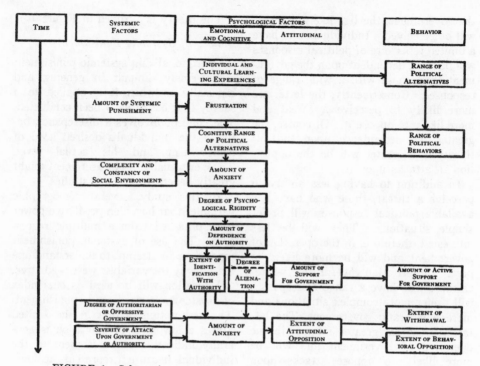

FIGURE 1. Schematic representation of the theory of reduced ALTERNATIVES.

predictor.) The other regions were not considered indices of either reward or punishment. This interpretation for the South is, of course, debatable. Income, however, is lowest in the South. Further, the South has been punished historically through losing the Civil War and the subsequent Northern occupation. In addition, the norms of the white South with respect to the races have continued to conflict directly with the federal government in all its branches. Finally, the migration patterns of Southern residents, at least during the past thirty years, may be evidence that the South represents a "punishing" environment relative to other sections of the country. All these arguments are tenuous. But at this stage of theoretical development, residence in the South may be reasonably treated as indicative of systemic punishment, al-

though other reasons for the results may, of course, be applicable.

Behavioral Alternatives

To examine the number of political activities the individual engaged in, respondents were asked the following question:

People take many kinds of action to express their views about political or social issues. Please tell me which of these actions you have ever taken to express your opinion on a social or political issue: discuss with friends, write a letter to a newspaper or to an elected official, contribute money to an organization concerned about the issue, sign a petition, express your opinion in person to a government official, organize a group, participate in a legally permitted demonstration, participate in an illegal but non-violent demonstration, participate in a riot.

Rigidity and Support of Authority

In order to examine these psychological traits, responses to 25 items were studied.[2] The first 10 factors of a principal axis solution were rotated to a varimax criterion. Five rotated factors appeared important enough for detailed analysis. These factors accounted for 11 percent, 9 percent, 7 percent, 7 percent and 6 percent of the total variance.[3] The 1st, 3rd and 5th factors were taken to represent psychological rigidity and support for authority, and will be briefly presented.

RIGIDITY

The 6 items that comprised the most important factor seemed to indicate an intolerance for social ambiguity. The percentage of either agreement or strong agreement is given in parentheses, based on a weighting of the sample so that it would conform more closely to national demographic characteristics.

1. A few strong leaders could make this country better than all the laws and talk. (53 percent)

2. People were better off in the old

2. The 25 items included some from standard psychological tests as well as others which were designed by William Gamson and James McEvoy. McEvoy suggested the factor analysis.
For additional analyses of this material, see Sheldon G. Levy, "The Psychology of the Politically Violent," paper presented before the Pacific Sociology Association, Seattle, Wash., April 24, 1969; and Levy, "Assassination—Levels, Motivation, and Attitudes," Peace Research Society (International) Papers (in press).
3. The factor analysis is discussed in Levy, "Attitudes Toward Political Violence," J. F. Kirkham, S. G. Levy, and W. J. Crotty, eds., Assassination and Political Violence, Report to the National Commission on the Causes and Prevention of Violence (Washington, D.C.: U.S.G.P.O., 1969), 383–417.

days when everyone knew just how he was expected to act. (47 percent)

3. Justice may have been a little rough and ready in the days of the Old West, but things worked better than they do today with all the legal red tape. (56 percent)

4. What is lacking in the world today is the old kind of friendship that lasted for a lifetime. (72 percent)

5. Everything changes so quickly these days that I often have trouble deciding which are the right rules to follow. (50 percent)

6. What young people need most of all is strong discipline by their parents. (86 percent)

SUPPORT FOR AUTHORITY

Two factors emerged that appeared related to this concept. One indicated support for the police and the other dealt with the government's use of force in international relations.

Support for the police (Domestic Force)

1. The police are wrong to beat up unarmed protestors, even when these people are rude and call them names. (49 percent) (45 percent disagree or strongly disagree)

2. The police frequently use more force than they need to when carrying out their duties. (28 percent) (65 percent disagree or strongly disagree)

3. Any man who insults a policeman has no complaint if he gets roughed up in return. (56 percent)

4. Sex criminals deserve more than prison, they should be publicly whipped or worse. (40 percent)

International use of force

1. In dealing with other countries of the world we are frequently justified in using military force. (62 percent)

2. Our government is too ready to use military force in dealing with other

countries. (39 percent) (53 percent disagree or strongly disagree)

3. It is unfortunate that many civilians are killed in bombing in a war but this cannot be avoided. (73 percent)

RESPONSE TO GOVERNMENTAL REPRESSION

The problem of studying the responsiveness of both those that identify with and those that oppose authoritarian political action is a difficult one. The procedure that was designed for this study was to develop hypothetical situations of governmental repression or injustice. For each situation, an attitude was first obtained that extended from strong approval to strong disapproval. Then a set of responses was presented that varied from mild activities (discussion with one's friends, signing a petition, and organizing a group) to more severe activities (illegal sit-ins and armed action or physical assault). The interview instrument was designed to examine both the endorsement of the responses and the likelihood of personal behavioral responses to governmental activities involving repression or injustice.

The hypothetical situations of governmental repression were:

1. Imagine that Congress has passed a law that makes you pay just as many dollars in taxes as people who make a lot more money than you do.

2. Imagine that Congress has just passed a law prohibiting anyone from saying anything against the government.

3. Imagine that the government has just arrested and imprisoned many of the Negroes in your community, even though there has been no trouble.

4. Imagine that, in order to keep control of the country, the government starts arresting and shooting large numbers of innocent people, including members of your family.

After the degree of approval or dis-approval was ascertained, the respondent was asked to indicate each action that he felt it would be all right to take. These were:

A. Express an opinion to friends on what is happening.

B. Sign a petition about what is happening.

C. Organize a group that is interested in what is happening.

D. If nothing else works, participate in an illegal sit-in, to express one's feelings about what is happening.

E. If nothing else works, participate in a physical assault or armed action, because of feelings about what is happening.

The responses were designed so that a person could not say no to one of the illegal responses because he felt a legal response would do the job. Thus, those actions that would ordinarily be considered illegal (D and E responses) were introduced with the phrase, "If nothing else worked. . . ."

After the "all rights" were recorded, the respondent was asked, "How about you, personally? Are you likely, or unlikely, to do this as a reaction to (the particular situation) we talked about?"

Schematically, the design of these items can be represented in three dimensions: (1) the degree of provocation offered by the situations, (2) the degree of reaction offered by the response alternatives, and (3) the personal endorsement alternatives. Figure 2 presents this conceptualization for the four hypothetical situations.

RESULTS

The first prediction is twofold. It is that greater systemic punishment (as represented by amount of education) will result in both:

a) reduced political activity on the part of the individual, and

INCREASING DEGREE OF GOVERNMENTAL INJUSTICE

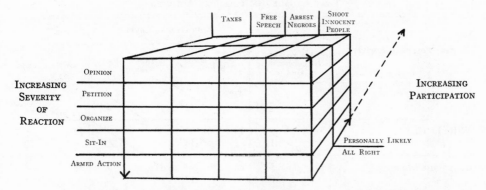

FIGURE 2. CONCEPTUALIZATION OF GOVERNMENTAL INJUSTICE ITEMS

b) greater rigidity in political responsiveness in the individual.

Education and Amount of Past Political Activity

Respondents were divided into four educational levels. These were: up to and including 8th grade, some high school, high school graduate, some college. The results for each of the past political activities as reported by the respondents are given in Table 1.

Except for the first response, which almost everyone participated in, and the last response, which practically no one participated in, there is a consistent increase in reported participation with increasing educational level.

Measuring the rigidity of the responsiveness is more difficult. The concept of rigidity means an inability or unwillingness to deviate from a particular mode of behavior. One measure of rigidity that seems reasonable is the variance. If several different responses are equally or almost equally preferred, then the behavior would not be considered rigid and the variance would be small. The more variable the responses are from each other, the greater the rigidity. In order to make the distributions comparable for level of activity, the proportions of the group that have

engaged in a particular activity have been divided by the sum of the proportions of the group across all the responses. Thus, each activity is evaluated in terms of the proportion of the total activity of the group that it represents. These figures are included in the triangle in each cell. The variances are included at the bottom of each column.

It is apparent that rigidity in political behavior, as measured by the variance, decreases steadily as the educational level increases. Thus, systemic punishment, as measured by educational level, appears to lead to both a reduction in political behavior and greater rigidity in the behavior that does occur.

Polarized Subgroup Analysis

It should be evident that any single demographic variable, even education, only roughly indexes the amount of systemic punishment. It would be far better if several variables could be used simultaneously. Polarized Subgroup Analysis (PSA) accomplishes this by determining homogeneous subgroups in the population that differ maximally from each other. First, a set of predictor variables is used in a stepwise multiple regression to predict to a number of indices and variables in the particular questionnaire. The most impor-

TABLE 1—EDUCATIONAL LEVEL AND PROPORTION OF RESPONDENTS
THAT ENGAGED IN POLITICAL ACTIVITIES

PAST POLITICAL ACTIVITY	EDUCATIONAL LEVEL			
	UP TO AND INCLUDING 8TH GRADE	SOME HIGH SCHOOL	HIGH SCHOOL GRADUATE	SOME COLLEGE
Discuss with Friends	97* .54**	97* .44**	96* .38**	97* .27**
Write Letter	31 .17	40 .18	58 .23	72 .20
Contribute Money	17 .09	26 .12	31 .12	53 .15
Sign Petition	15 .08	22 .10	25 .10	52 .15
Express Opinion in Person	15 .08	19 .09	24 .10	45 .13
Organize a Group	4 .02	7 .03	7 .03	16 .04
Participate in Legal Demonstration	1 .01	6 .03	6 .02	15 .04
Participate in Illegal Demonstration	0 .00	2 .01	3 .01	6 .02
Participate in Riot	0 .00	0 .00	0 .00	1 .00
Variances among Proportions in Triangles	.0259	.0166	.0142	.0073

* Proportion based on weighted sample.
** Proportion of total activity of the group represented by this response.

tant and consistent predictors are then used to develop subgroups defined by simultaneously used levels of the variables. The method is more fully described in Levy[4] and Conant, Levy and Lewis.[5]

In this study, the following variables were selected: race (white, nonwhite), education (for nonwhites, up to and including 8th grade, some high school, high school graduate, college; for whites, some high school, and high school graduate or above), past political activity (low, medium, and high),[6] sex, and region of the country, (East, West, Midwest, and South).

4. S. G. Levy, "How Population Subgroups Differed in Knowledge of Six Assassinations," *Journalism Quarterly* 46, No. 4 (1969); 685–698.

5. R. Conant, S. G. Levy, and R. Lewis, "Mass Polarization," *American Behavioral Scientist* 13, no. 2 (1969), 247–263.

6. The measure of previous political activity has just been discussed. The respondent was placed in the low category if he responded to 0 or 1 action, in the medium category if he responded to 2, 3, or 4, and in the high category if he responded to 5 or more.

TABLE 2—CODES AND SUBGROUPS USED IN POLARIZED SUBGROUP ANALYSES (PSA)

8 = NONWHITE

8-1 = Low Activity n=103	8-2 = Medium Activity n=87	8-3 = High Activity n=28	8-4 = 8th Grade or Less n=70	8-5 = Some High School n=61	8-6 = High School Grad n=52	8-7 = College n=33	8-8 = Male n=115	8-9 = Female n=102	8-0 = East n=68	8-X = Midwest n=30	8-Y = South n=97	8-T = West n=23
+P	O	I	+P	O	O	I	-P	-P	-P	-P	+P	-P

9 = WHITE

NOT HIGH SCHOOL GRAD

9-1 = Male, Low Activity n=99	9-2 = Male, Medium Activity n=74	9-3 = Male, High Activity n=10	9-4 = Female, Low Activity n=96	9-5 = Female, Medium Activity n=72	9-6 = Female, High Activity n=6
+P	O	I	+P	O	I

HIGH SCHOOL GRADS AND COLLEGE

9-7 = Male, Low Activity n=57	9-8 = Male, Medium Activity n=157	9-9 = Male, High Activity n=74	9-0 = Female, Low Activity n=80	9-X = Female, Medium Activity n=178	9-Y = Female, High Activity n=28
I	O	+R	I	O	+R

10 = WHITE

NOT HIGH SCHOOL GRAD

10-1 = East n=94	10-2 = Midwest n=109	10-3 = South n=109	10-4 = West n=47
-P	-P	+P	-P

HIGH SCHOOL GRAD

10-5 = East n=158	10-6 = Midwest n=184	10-7 = South n=120	10-8 = West n=115
-R	-R	I	-R

MALE

10-9 = East n=126	10-0 = Midwest n=145	10-X = South n=118	10-Y = West n=84
O	O	-P	O

FEMALE

10-T = East n=126	10-U = Midwest n=148	10-V = South n=108	10-W = West n=78
O	O	-P	O

11 = WHITE

LOW ACTIVITY

11-1 = East n=94	11-2 = Midwest n=104	11-3 = South n=104	11-4 = West n=34
-P	-P	+P	-P

MEDIUM ACTIVITY

11-5 = East n=130	11-6 = Midwest n=158	11-7 = South n=107	11-8 = West n=91
O	O	O	O

HIGH ACTIVITY

11-9 = East n=32	11-0 = Midwest n=31	11-X = South n=18	11-Y = West n=37
-R	-R	I	-R

Because a national sample of 1,200 adults yields a small number of non-white cases, this group was treated with only one additional attribute at a time.

Repeated use of the same individual was also the case in the analysis of whites. However, because the number of cases was larger, it was possible to use a larger number of traits simultaneously in this category. The combinations used were: education—sex—previous political activity; political activity—region; education—region; and sex—region. A list of the subgroups, the identifying code, and the number of cases in each is given in Table 2.

It can thus be seen that the subgroups are defined by variables that index previous systemic punishment as well as the level of political behavior (i.e., behavioral alternatives).

Predictions to Rigidity, Support for Authority, and Responsiveness to Governmental Oppression

The theoretical argument that has been presented states that the behavioral rigidity that results from systemic punishment should lead to a corresponding psychological rigidity and support for authority. Both of these traits will be measured by factors that emerged from the factor analysis of the psychological items. In addition, the high systemic punishment groups should be relatively unresponsive to the hypothetical situations of governmental injustice when compared with the high systemic reward groups.

The procedure for examining the results will be as follows: For each of the measures, the highest six and the lowest six subgroups will be specified. Although the PSA subgroups in this analysis resulted in the same individuals being used more than once, the subgroups can be examined for the consistency of their traits with the theory.

For the factors, the basis for determining whether a subgroup placed at an extreme is simply the factor score it received. For the responsiveness to governmental injustice, three measures were developed; one was the number of times a subgroup appeared among either the highest six or lowest six in strong disapproval of the hypothetical situations. Another was the number of times the subgroup appeared at an extreme on each of the legal responses for each of the four situations. The maximum number of appearances, therefore, was 12.

The third measure was the number of times a subgroup appeared at either the highest or lowest extreme for the two responses that would ordinarily be considered illegal, with the maximum, of course, being 8. Note that only the "all right" results and not the "personally likely" ones were examined. The results are presented in Table 3.

In order to evaluate the results more efficiently, each of the PSA subgroups had been labeled with an additional code in Table 2, representing the degree of systemic punishment or reward, as well as the range of behavior alternatives. The codes are based on the following decisions:

1. Low education or residence in the South is taken as indicative of systemic punishment. High education is taken as evidence of systemic reward. Low past political activity is taken as indicative of a narrow range of political behavioral alternatives, and high political activity, a wide range.

2. Subgroups are classified as follows:
   A. *Subgroups defined by consistent traits.*

   +P: Subgroups that have at least two supporting punishment/behavior attributes, e.g., Southern non-whites or less than high

TABLE 3 —SUBGROUP (S), SUBGROUP CLASSIFICATION (C), AND NUMBER OF OCCURRENCES (N) FOR SELECTED VARIABLES

SUBGROUPS	RIGIDITY S	RIGIDITY C	POLICE FORCE S	POLICE FORCE C	INTERNATIONAL USE OF FORCE S	INTERNATIONAL USE OF FORCE C	SUBGROUPS	DISAPPROVAL S	DISAPPROVAL n	DISAPPROVAL C	LEGAL RESPONSES S	LEGAL RESPONSES n	LEGAL RESPONSES C	ILLEGAL RESPONSES S	ILLEGAL RESPONSES n	ILLEGAL RESPONSES C
Highest	10-4	-P	10-4	-P	11-X	I	Lowest	11-2	4	-P	9-1	8	+P	10-4	6	-P
	8-4	+P	9-1	+P	9-7	I		8-X	3	-P	9-3	8	I	9-6	5	I
	9-4	+P	11-3	+P	8-X	-P		8-4	2	+P	10-4	5	-P	9-1	4	+P
	9-1	+P	10-2	-P	10-X	-P		9-3	2	I	11-3	5	+P	9-4	4	+P
	11-3	+P	11-1	-P	10-7	-P		10-2	2	-P	9-7	5	I	11-1	3	-P
	9-5	0	9-3	I	8-1	+P		9-4	2	+P	10-X	5	-P			
	11-9	-R Revol.	8-7	I Revol.	11-9	-R		10-9	2	0	9-6	7	I	8-3	8	I Revol.
	9-Y	+R	8-3	I Revol.	9-Y	+R		9-9	2	+R	8-2	8	0	8-0	5	-P
	11-Y	-R	8-2	0	8-7	I Revol.		11-9	2	-R	11-0	7	-R	8-X	5	-P
Lowest	8-7	I Revol.	8-X	-P	8-3	I Revol.	Highest				8-9	5	-P	9-9	3	+R
	9-9	+R	8-0	-P	8-2	0					8-4	4	+P	11-9	3	-R
	8-3	I Revol.	8-T	-P	8-0	-P					8-3	4	I Revol.	11-0	3	-R
											9-9	4	+R			
											8-Y	4	+P			
											8-0	4	-P			

For identification of Subgroups(S) and Classifications(C), see Table 2.

school graduates (< HSG), male, low activity, whites.

+R: Subgroups that have at least two supporting reward/behavior attributes.

−P: Subgroups that have one punishment/behavior attribute, e.g., low activity, Midwest, white.

−R: Subgroups that have one reward/behavior attribute.

B. *Subgroups defined by inconsistent traits within the theory.*

I: Groups that are defined by inconsistent punishment/behavior attributes, e.g., HSG and more, male, low activity, white; less than HSG, female, high activity, white; and college, nonwhite.

C. *Other groups.*

O. Those that are defined either by neutral traits, e.g., medium activity, West, white, or by potentially mildly conflicting traits, e.g., some high school, nonwhite (which might also have been classified −P) or HSG+, male, medium activity, white (which might also have been classified −R).

DISCUSSION OF RESULTS

The results in Table 3 give very strong support for the theoretical propositions that have been presented. If the theory were totally supported, one would expect the upper half of the table to contain only +P or −P subgroups. Of the 35 subgroups listed, 26 (or 74 percent) received these codes, as opposed to only 20/53 or 38 percent of the original groups which were so coded. There

are no directly inconsistent groups, that is, there are no groups coded either +R or −R in the upper half of the table. The only group coded O tends toward a −P evaluation. All the remaining groups are coded I, and demonstrate the importance of the PSA in allowing interaction effects among a set of traits to provide different results from those expected in a simple additive model. (It should also be noted that 4 of the 8 I notations are provided by groups with extremely small n's, namely 9–3 (n = 10) and 9–6 (n = 6).

The bottom half of the table also provides strong support for the hypotheses of the theory. If there had been perfect prediction, all the subgroups should have been +R, −R, or I (revolutionary). The actual results show that 37 percent were coded +R or −R, as opposed to 8/53 or 15 percent of the original groups. Further, 8 of the 9 I codes consisted of either highly active nonwhites (8–3) or nonwhites with at least some college (8–7). These groups qualify under the concept of revolutionary, or protesting, as presented in the theory. That is, they consist of individuals who have undergone (and continue to undergo) large amounts of systemic punishment, but whose behavioral alternatives have been widened—as evidenced by either reward in the area of education (high level of education), which broadens cognitive alternatives, or actual high levels of political activity. Of the remaining groups (7 were coded O; 8 were −P; and 3 were +P), all but one are nonwhite. Thus, of the 23 subgroups that are not coded either +R or −R, 21 are nonwhite.

Part of the explanation for the above results could be the fact that nonwhites have not even had symbols within the dominant authority structure which would allow them to identify with it. In addition, the open and widespread communications system, great mobility, and high literacy levels lead to an increase in the number of alternatives compared to what otherwise would be expected. In any event, a combination of the above factors appears to have limited the amount of identification among non-whites with authority. This is especially noticeable on the support of the police factor and on the legal responses to the hypothetical situations of governmental injustice.

Conclusions

Although the data presented here are limited, they give strong support to the notion that systemic punishment leads to behavior-cognitive restriction in political action and this restriction leads to psy-chological rigidity and identification with authority to reduce anxiety. Even strongly oppressive governments may capitalize upon the identification mechanism to reduce opposition to the government, especially if it provides appropriate symbols with which to identify. Central to opposition to authority appears to be a broadened outlook, a flexibility of perceived and practiced action. Nazi Germany and Stalinist Russia give evidence that severe oppression in itself does not insure active opposition.

Democratic societies may best safeguard their form of government by providing rewards to all their citizens and by both maintaining open channels of political communication and encouraging their use.

18

Rebellion and Repression and the Vietnam War

By ROBERT B. SMITH

Robert B. Smith teaches research methods and political sociology at the University of California, Santa Barbara. He is preparing several books for publication. He is editor of Social Science Methods, *(1971), a new introductory methods text, and author of* Why Soldiers Fight *(1971), an empirical corroboration of the group cohesion theory of combat motivation. His papers in this volume are part of a larger study of the social costs of the Vietnam war.*

The author is indebted to Richard Flacks, Daniel Willick, and Thomas Wilson for helpful comments, and to Anthony Shih for technical assistance. Thanks are due to Dr. John P. Robinson of the National Institutes of Health for releasing the restrictions on his survey data about the Chicago Police Department. Grants of computer time were provided by the National Institute of Mental Health and the Computer Center of the University of California, Santa Barbara.

THIS paper seeks to consolidate and extend research concerning the domestic social consequences of the Vietnam war, by focusing on public attitudes about the war and about rebellion and repressions and the independent effect of Vietnam war attitudes on the latter.[1]

The analysis is based on data from the 1968 national presidential election survey, carried out by the Survey Research Center of the University of Michigan. In this survey a total of 1,557 citizens of voting ages were interviewed, most of them before and after Election Day.[2]

THE VARIABLES

*Disaffected doves, the
silent majority, harassed
hawks—the pivotal
independent variable*

Attitudes about the Vietnam war are gauged by the two items presented in

Table 1. The first item gauges whether or not our involvement in Vietnam is felt to be a mistake. The second item inquires as to what should be done now, with options of pulling out, maintaining the status quo, or taking a stronger stand.

The responses to these items suggest that most Americans believe that our involvement in the fighting in Vietnam was a mistake, but only 20 percent are in favor of immediate withdrawal, compared to slightly more than a third who want to maintain the status quo, and another third who want to take a stronger stand.[3]

These two items can be combined to form an index that distinguishes between what we shall call *disaffected doves*, the *silent majority*, and *harassed hawks*. The disaffected doves believe that our involvement in Vietnam was a mistake, and that we now should pull out entirely. The harassed hawks believe the opposite—we were right in getting involved, and we now should take a stronger stand. The silent majority, comprised of people with divided opinions on the war, is intermediate between these two extremes. Some think our involvement was a mistake, but we now should maintain the status quo or take a stronger stand. Others think our involvement was not a mistake, but we now should pull out as soon as possible. Among the 1,194 respondents who have definite opinions on both items, 21 percent are disaffected doves, 19 percent

1. For documentation of the relation of the war in Vietnam to domestic turmoil in this country, to public disaffection, and polarization of the citizenry, cf. Robert B. Smith, "Disaffection from War, Delegitimization, and Consequences," paper presented at the annual meeting, Pacific Sociological Association, Seattle, Washington, April, 1969; Tom Hayden, *Rebellion and Repression* (Cleveland: World Publishing, 1969), 21–35; Philip E. Converse et al., "Continuity and Change in American Politics: Parties and Issues in the 1968 Campaign," *American Political Science Review* 63 (December, 1969), 1083–1105; Raymond Tanter, "International War and Domestic Turmoil: Some Contemporary Evidence," ch. 16 in Hugh Davis Graham and Ted Robert Gurr, eds., *Violence in America* (Washington, D.C.: U.S. Government Printing Office, 1969); Jerome H. Skolnick, *The Politics of Protest* (Washington, D.C.: U.S. G.P.O., 1969); Daniel Walker, *Rights In Conflict* (New York: Bantam Books, 1968); John P. Robinson, "Public Reaction to Political Protest: Chicago, 1968," *Public Opinion Quarterly* 34 (Spring, 1970); Sidney Verba et al., "Public Opinion and the War in Vietnam," *American Political Science Review* 61 (June, 1967), 317–333.

2. The data cards were obtained from the Inter-University Consortium for Political Research.

3. The distribution of responses is very similar to that obtained by Gallup in the fall of 1968. The public was asked this question:

"In view of the developments since we entered the fighting in Vietnam, do you think the U.S. made a mistake sending troops to fight in Vietnam?"

YES	No	No Opinion	Total
53%	35	12	100%

For the trend, see the *Gallup Opinion Index* for September, 1968.

TABLE 1—Two Items About Vietnam

"Do you think we did the right thing in getting into the fighting in Vietnam, or should we have stayed out?"

Yes, Right Thing	Other; Depends	No, Should Have Stayed Out	Don't Know	Total
30%	1%	52%	17%	100%

"Which of the following do you think we should do *now* in Vietnam?"
1. Pull out entirely.
2. Keep our soldiers in Vietnam but try to end fighting.
3. Take a stronger stand even if it means invading North Vietnam.

Pull Out	Status Quo	Stronger Stand	Don't Know; Other	Total
20%	37%	34%	9%	100%

are harassed hawks, and 60 percent belong to the silent majority.

Because discerning the consequences of attitudes about the Vietnam war is our major concern, it is necessary to insure that the index actually measures what it is intended to measure. This index does meet the three standard criteria for validity usually followed in survey research: [4]

First of all, the two questions about the war and the three categories of the index have face validity. They seem to measure what they are supposed to measure. Each item directly gauges sentiment about the war. The two dimensions defining dove/hawk sentiment —whether or not the war is a mistake, and whether or not we should de-escalate—are commonly used to distinguish between doves and hawks. Also, our definition of the silent majority as those who are neither dove nor hawk conforms to President Nixon's usage of the term.[5] The index classifies a majority of the respondents (60 percent) as belonging to the silent majority.

Secondly, the index is internally consistent. Its internal consistency is indicated by the high intercorrelation be-

tween the two items (Gamma is .533), and by the fact that each item singly has similar consequences for a range of related items.

Finally, the index is externally valid, in that it predicts responses to items that are not a part of the index, but which are related to, or alternative measures of, the concepts the index purports to measure. Table 2 compares responses of doves, hawks, and the silent majority on a seven-point rating scale ranging from advocacy of immediate withdrawal (point 1) to advocacy of complete military victory (point 7). For purposes of comparison, points 1 and 2 on the scale were combined to gauge strong support for immediate withdrawal, points 6 and 7 to represent support for military victory, and points 3, 4, and 5 a middle-of-the-road position. The findings demonstrate that respondents classified as disaffected doves are more likely to give strong support to immediate withdrawal, while harassed hawks tend strongly to support complete military victory, and those classified as silent majority are more likely to take a middle-of-the-road position in this respect.

*Tolerance for rebellion
and support for repression;
the pivotal dependent variable*

Tolerance for rebellion and support for repression of protest can be gauged

4. For an excellent discussion of these criteria, see Gary T. Marx, *Protest and Prejudice* (New York: Harper & Row, 1967), 45–68.
5. See *The New York Times*, Wednesday, November 5, 1969.

TABLE 2—EXTERNAL VALIDATION OF THE DOVE/SILENT MAJORITY/HAWK INDEX

		DISAFFECTED DOVES	SILENT MAJORITY	HARASSED HAWKS	DIFFERENCE
Strong Support for Immediate Withdrawal (points 1 & 2)		55%	17%	7%	48%
	Number	(209)	(575)	(196)	
Strong Support for Complete Military Victory (points 6 & 7)		15%	26%	55%	− 40%
	Number	(209)	(575)	(196)	
Middle-of-the-Road Position (points 3, 4, or 5)		31%	57%	38%	
	Number	(209)	(575)	(196)	

by the two questions presented in Table 3. Responses which indicate tolerance for rebellion are coded 1; those indicating support for repression are coded 0. While some ambiguity is introduced in the first item by the phrasing "sit-ins, mass meetings, demonstrations *and things like that*," the intent of the item clearly implies nonviolent means of protest.[6] While protests may be quite disruptive, they are nonviolent in that the demonstrators do not intentionally use force to injure or kill people, or to destroy property. The second item ascertains respondents' feelings about the use of. force by the police to break up mass demonstrations such as occurred during the week of the 1968 Democratic National Convention.[7]

The responses to these questions do not present an optimistic picture to the civil libertarian. More than half the public clearly disapproves of such protest, compared to only 6 percent who clearly approve, and an additional 14 percent who are at least somewhat approving.

By way of contrast, answers to the second question indicate little public disapproval of the use of force by the police in handling demonstrations and protest. Only 16 percent say that the Chicago police used too much force against the demonstrators at the Democratic National Convention. About half of those questioned said either that the Chicago police acted properly or did not use enough force with the demonstrators. Police tactics on this occasion subsequently were labelled a "police riot" by a governmental investigating task force.[8] Of those who were aware and expressed an opinion, fully 75 percent approved these police tactics. Support for repression of mass demonstration and protest thus appears widespread and strong.

An index of tolerance for rebellion and support for repression can be derived from these items by simply summing the pro-rebellion responses coded 1, and the pro-repression responses coded 0. Interviewees with an index score of 0 strongly support repression of protest, by disapproving mass demonstration and protest and approval of police force against demonstrators. Of the 956 respondents with opinions on both of these items, a clear majority (63 percent) support repression of protest in this sense. In subsequent analyses, the remaining 37 percent who do not support repression are grouped together. Of these, about 11 percent have *high*

6. This item was the last in a series of three concerning protest. The first question in the series gauged attitudes about orderly demonstrations that were permitted by the local authorities. The second question asked about individual civil disobedience. Responses to these items were not related to attitudes about Vietnam. (Italics were added.)

7. See John P. Robinson, op. cit., for an intensive analysis of the correlates of this item.

8. See Daniel Walker, op. cit., 10–11.

TABLE 3—TWO ITEMS ABOUT REBELLION AND REPRESSION

"Suppose all other methods have failed and the person decides to try to stop the government from going about its usual activities with sit-ins, mass meetings, demonstrations, and things like that. Would you approve of that, disapprove, or would it depend on the circumstances?"

APPROVES (1)*	DEPENDS (1)	DISAPPROVES (0)	OTHER (DK, NA)	TOTAL
6%	14%	58%	22%	100%

"Thinking back to the 1968 Democratic National Convention in Chicago, do you think the police used too much force, the right amount of force, or not enough force with the demonstrators?"

TOO MUCH FORCE (1)	RIGHT AMOUNT (0)	NOT ENOUGH (0)	UNAWARE	NO OPINION	TOTAL
16%	28%	21%	11%	24%	100%

* Responses coded 1 indicate tolerance for rebellion, those coded 0 indicate support for repression.

tolerance for rebellion, an index score of 2. These respondents approve of confrontation protest and disapprove of police violence against demonstrators. The other 26 percent have *some* tolerance for rebellion, an index score of 1. These citizens either approve of confrontation protest and also the use of police violence to control them, or they disapprove of both police violence and confrontations.

Validity of the dichotomized index is established on the basis of the three criteria for validity discussed earlier: (1) the two questions about protest and the two categories of the index have face validity; (2) the index is internally consistent as indicated by the high intercorrelation between its component items (Gamma is .630) and by their similar effects on other items; and (3) the index is externally valid as demonstrated by the data of Table 4. Here respondents classified as having at least some tolerance for rebellion, relative to those supporting repression, are much more likely to approve of meetings, marches, and civil disobedience as forms of protest, but are much less likely to recommend the use of all available force to maintain law and order as a solution to the problem of urban unrest and rioting.

TEST FACTORS

In the subsequent analyses of the affect of Vietnam disaffection on tolerance for rebellion, the effects of four other explanatory variables (test factors) will be quantified and controlled. One of

TABLE 4—EXTERNAL VALIDITY OF THE REBELLION AND REPRESSION INDEX

	TOLERANCE FOR REBELLION	SUPPORT FOR REPRESSION	DIFFERENCE
Approves of Protest Meetings or Marches Permitted by Local Authorities	68%	34%	34%
Number	(352)	(488)	
Approves of a Person Refusing to Obey a Law Thought to be Unjust	54	27	27
Number	(347)	(583)	
Says That the Best Way to Deal with the Problem of Urban Unrest and Rioting Is to Use All Available Force to Maintain Law and Order	16	41	−25
Number	(348)	(585)	

TABLE 5—AN ITEM ABOUT CIVIL RIGHTS

"Some say the civil rights people have been trying to push too fast. Others feel they haven't pushed fast enough. How about you: Do you think that civil rights leaders are trying to push too fast, are going too slowly, or are they moving at about the right speed?"

	TOO FAST (0)*	ABOUT RIGHT (1)	TOO SLOWLY (1)	DON'T KNOW, NO ANSWER	TOTAL
1968	62%	27	7	5	101%
1964	62%	25	6	8	101%

* Responses coded 0 indicate unfavorable civil rights attitudes; those coded 1, favorable attitudes.

these, attitudes about civil rights, is a social psychological variable. The other three variables are sociological. These are: (1) ethnicity, (2) socio-economic status, and (3) age.

Attitudes about civil rights

Attitudes about the civil rights movement are gauged responses to a question about the pace of social change presented in Table 5. This question ascertains whether the civil rights leaders are perceived to be pushing too fast, going too slowly, or moving at the right speed. The latter two responses are combined to measure favorable attitudes; the "too fast" response category is used to measure unfavorable attitudes. This dichotomized item validly gauges civil rights attitudes because it has both face validity and external validity; it has the expected effects on other items related to civil rights. For example, respondents classified as favorable to civil rights support the integration of schools, neighborhoods, and public places. They also want Blacks to get fair treatment in jobs. Moreover, they perceive that recent Black protest has been peaceful and beneficial.

Table 5 reports that in 1968, 62 percent of the public was unfavorable to the civil rights movement, compared to 34 percent (27 percent and 7 percent) which was favorable. This represents a ratio of about 2 to 1 against civil rights. This finding cannot be attributed to "white backlash" against Black protest.

This question was also included in the 1964 Michigan election survey, which was taken prior to the recent wave of ghetto riots. The responses to this earlier survey are almost identical: 62 percent was unfavorable, compared to 31 percent which was favorable.[9]

Ethnicity

Two items about race and religion were combined to classify the respondents according to ethnicity. The ethnic *minority* category is comprised of those who are not White Protestants: Blacks, Catholics, Jews, and people without a religious affiliation. The ethnic *majority* category is comprised of White Protestants. The survey data suggest a relationship between ethnicity and residence. The minorities tend to live in large cities, the majority in rural areas and in small towns (Gamma is .470).

Socio-economic status

Two items about occupation and education were combined to gauge socio-economic status. Respondents classified

9. This finding of no backlash also holds when the responses of whites only are tabulated:

WHITES ONLY

	TOO FAST	ABOUT RIGHT	TOO SLOWLY	DON'T KNOW/ NO ANSWER	TOTAL
1968	68%	23	4	5	100%
1964	68%	21	3	8	100%

This data corroborates J. Michael Ross' analysis which was described in Skolnick, op. cit., p. 144.

as *high* socio-economic status have a white collar occupation (or are housewives) and more than a high school education.[10] Those who do not have these attributes have *low* socio-economic status. This simple index meets the usual criteria for validity: (1) the two items and the two categories have face validity; (2) the index is internally consistent (Gamma for the two items is .344); and (3) the index is externally valid—it correlates very highly with the respondents' subjective rating of their social class (Gamma is .653), and with their perceptions of how others rate them (Gamma is .726).

Age

The respondents were grouped into two age categories by inspection of the relationship between age and rebellion. Those classified as *younger* are no more than 39 years old. Those classified as *older* are 40 or more years old.

PROCEDURE

To measure the independent effects of Vietnam war attitudes and other determinants of rebellion and repression, we employ the method of multivariate analysis developed by Coleman.[11]

Causal ordering of the variables and analysis of the two pivotal variables, Vietnam war attitudes and rebellion and repression, are established by means of the elaboration procedures for survey analysis developed by Lazarsfeld and Hyman.[12] We will find that the relationship between these pivotal variables is specified by the test factors. That is, whenever a category of a test factor is supportive of rebellion, then the relationship between Vietnam disaffection and rebellion is increased. In the higher order tables these specifications will be quantified by applying Coleman's multivariate procedure separately to the sets of conditional tables defined by the categories of the test factors. Inasmuch as all the test factors are dichotomous, this will result in two "conditional" effect parameters per test factor for the pivotal independent variable: the first based on the conditional tables of the positive category of the test factor; the second, on the conditional tables of the negative category. For example, the effect of Vietnam disaffection on rebellion will be quantified for those who favor civil rights, controlling for the effects of the other variables, and for those who are against civil rights. The Coleman effect parameter for this independent variable is simply the weighted (by number of

10. Housewives were classified as white collar occupation in order to preserve the sample size. This expediency has almost no effect on the zero order relationship between socioeconomic status and tolerance for rebellion. But it does reduce the intercorrelation of the two items comprising the index. When housewives are excluded, Gamma is .538.

11. See James S. Coleman, *Introduction to Mathematical Sociology* (New York: Free Press, 1964). This technique is very closely analogous to the regression analysis of dummy variables. See Richard Boyle, "Causal Theory and Statistical Measures of Effect: A Convergence," *American Sociological Review* 31 (December, 1966), 843–851. The "effect parameters" of Coleman's model quantify the independent effects of the explanatory variables and are closely analogous to unstandardized regression coefficients. In a higher order table,

the effect parameter for a particular explanatory variable quantifies the amount of variation in the dependent attribute explained by that explanatory variable, controlling for the effects of the other explanatory variables (test factors). The "total random shocks" of Coleman's model provide a measure of unexplained variation in the dependent attribute which is somewhat analogous to "unexplained variance" in traditional regression analysis. The total random shocks quantify how much variation in the dependent attribute there remains to be explained.

12. For a concise statement of these procedures, see Paul F. Lazarsfeld, "Evidence and Inference in Social Research," in Daniel Lerner, ed., *Evidence and Inference* (Glencoe, Ill.: Free Press, 1959).

cases) average of these two conditional effects.[13]

FINDINGS

Public opinion and the Vietnam war

In their survey of public opinion and the war in Vietnam, which was conducted in late February, 1966, Verba and his colleagues found that attitudes about Vietnam did not follow the usual lines of political cleavage. They concluded:

Variables of social status—occupation, income, or education—do not relate to policy preferences on the Vietnamese war; nor do such variables as religion or region. . . . In addition, party affiliation does not relate to policy preferences; a fact that illustrates why it is difficult to make foreign policy the subject of political campaigns. . . . Two differences among social groups do stand out, however. One is the difference between men and women, with women more in favor of de-escalation; and the other between whites and Negroes with the Negroes more in favor of de-escalation.[14]

For the most part, Verba's findings of no effects are corroborated by the data in Table 6 from the 1968 Michigan election survey. No social statuses have large zero order effects on attitudes

13. The equations below describe the relationship between the total effect and the two conditional effects.

(1) Total effect $= \dfrac{\text{effect when test}}{\text{factor is } (+)}$

$$\times W_1 + \dfrac{\text{effect when test}}{\text{factor is } (-)} \times W_2$$

(2) $W_1 = \dfrac{\begin{array}{c}\text{Number of cases in}\\ (+) \text{ conditional tables}\end{array}}{\text{Total cases}}$

(3) $W_2 = \dfrac{\begin{array}{c}\text{Number of cases in}\\ (-) \text{ conditional tables}\end{array}}{\text{Total cases}}$

(4) Total Cases = sum of cases in both (+) and (−) conditional tables

14. Verba et al., op. cit., p. 331.

TABLE 6—ANTIWAR SENTIMENT AND SOCIAL STATUSES

SOCIAL STATUSES	COLEMAN EFFECT PARAMETERS	SOMERS' dyx's
Farmers	.080	.141
Income Less than $6,000 Per Year	.089	.151
Less Than a High School Education	.099	.170
Jews and No Religious Affiliation	.128	.202
Democrats	.024	.035
Women	.085	.143
Blacks	.095	.156

Zero order effects on dove/silent majority/hawk index.

about the Vietnam war, but several attributes do have small effects. Farmers are more likely to be doves than respondents with either white-collar or blue-collar occupations. Those with very low income or education are more antiwar than those with higher socioeconomic status. Jews and religiously unaffiliated are more likely to be doves than Protestants and Catholics. Party affiliation has almost no effect. But women and Blacks are more antiwar. It seems that in both 1966 and in 1968, disaffection from the Vietnam war was not congruent with the traditional lines of political cleavage in American society.

Space limitations preclude detailed consideration of relationships between attitudes about Vietnam, toleration of rebellion and repression, social statuses, and attitudes concerning domestic issues and foreign policy.[15] Suffice to say that, although few individual effects are large, doves are more likely to be of lower socio-economic status, and to belong to racial and religious minorities. On this basis one would expect doves to take a liberal position on domestic issues re-

15. These matters will be considered at greater length in a later paper.

TABLE 7— REBELLION AND DISAFFECTION

	DIS-AFFECTED DOVES	SILENT MA-JORITY	HARASSED HAWKS
Tolerance For Rebellion	49%	41%	23%
Number	(148)	(457)	(168)

$a \cdot 1$ = effect of dove relative to
$\qquad$ silent majority = .077
a_1 = effect of silent majority
$\qquad$ relative to hawk = .183
$a_1(OV)$ = overall effect of dove relative
$\qquad$ to hawk = .260
r = random shock toward
$\qquad$ rebellion = .226
s = random shock toward
$\qquad$ repression = .514

lated to social welfare and civil rights, and they do. Doves tend to be less concerned about foreign policy than about domestic issues, and to be against foreign aid. My interpretation of these findings is that the doves place a heavier emphasis on solving the domestic problems of American society, rather than involvement in a costly foreign war. Since the doves disagree with the basic tenor of the United States' Vietnam policy, one would expect the doves to support dissent. Empirically, the index of tolerance for rebellion and support for repression has correlates similar to the dove/silent majority/hawk index. Similarly, minority ethnicity and attitudes favorable to civil rights are positively related to norms supportive of protest and to anti-authoritarianism, and through these, to tolerance of rebellion. High socio-economic status and being younger are related to feelings of political efficacy and, in turn, also to tolerance of rebellion.

Causes of tolerance for rebellion and support for repression

Our major hypothesis is that disaffected doves are more likely to have tol-erance for rebellion. Because of the bi-polarity of the two pivotal variables, this implies that harassed hawks are more likely to support repression. Our underlying model is quite simple. The events of the Vietnam war and our middle-of-the-road policy produces severe strains for both doves and hawks. For the doves, disaffection from the war acts as a stimulus which engenders tolerance for rebellion and subsequent protest behavior. For the hawks, the harassment from the war acts as a stimulus which produces support for repression of protest.

These mechanisms also can be conceptualized sociologically as anomic in character, in the Mertonian sense.[16] Doves strongly hold a goal, namely, to end the war in Vietnam. But their access to this goal is limited; we are not terminating the war; we will not pull out. The doves adapt to this situation by developing a tolerance for rebellion, and by subsequent protest behavior.[17]

A similar process operates for the hawks, who also strongly hold a goal, viz., to win the war in Vietnam. But access to this goal also is limited; we will not (or cannot) escalate the war enough to win; we do not strive for complete military victory. Hawks adapt to this anomic social structure by supporting the repression of protest. This is a form of ritualism, since the original political goal of the war has been de-emphasized, but there is a heavy emphasis on the means—excessive use of force not only against the enemy in Vietnam, but also against antiwar and other protestors who might well be perceived as aiding the enemy, or as disloyal Americans.[18]

16. For Merton's theory of anomie see Robert K. Merton, "Social Structure and Anomie," ch. 4 in *Social Theory and Social Structure* (Glencoe, Ill.: Free Press, 1957).
17. Ibid., p. 140.
18. Ibid., p. 140.

Independent effects

Table 7 substantiates the relationship between disaffected doves and tolerance for rebellion for the individuals in the Michigan survey. As expected, disaffected doves have more tolerance for rebellion than harassed hawks; the overall effect is .260. Perhaps surprisingly, the silent majority is rather similar to the doves. A difference in effect of only .077 separates them from the doves, less than half the .183 separating them from the hawks. In this table the random shock toward rebellion, r, is .226. This parameter can be interpreted as the underlying probability that a person will have some tolerance for rebellion even without feeling any disaffection from the war.[19] The random shock toward repression, that is, the underlying probability that a person will support repression of protest even without feeling any harassment from the war, is .514. The ratio between these two parameters is slightly more than 2 to 1 in favor of repression of protest. Thus, given no external stimulus, such as the Vietnam war, the public appears twice as likely to support the repression of protest as to have tolerance for rebellion, as we have defined these terms.

The same patterns of effect can also be discerned in Table 8, in which the four test factors—favorable civil rights attitudes, minority group membership, high socio-economic status, and age—have been simultaneously controlled. The overall effect of being a dove on tolerance for rebellion is .204. This is the largest independent effect. It is comprised of a small difference in effect, .039, between the doves and the silent

majority, and a large difference in effect, .165, between the silent majority and the hawks. Once more, the silent majority is much less willing than the hawks to support repression of protest, and just slightly more willing than the doves.

Tolerance for rebellion also is strongly affected by the four test factors: the effect of favorable civil rights attitudes is .181; the effect of minority ethnicity is .177; the effect of high socio-economic status is .146; and that of being younger (less than 40 years old) is .126. These variables combine to account for all of the unexplained random shock toward tolerance for rebellion. Unexplained random shock toward support for repression remains, however (s = .166). This lack of equality between the two random shocks corroborates our earlier conjecture that the public is more disposed to support repression than to have tolerance for rebellion.

Specifications

Whenever a zero order relationship between an independent and a dependent variable is analyzed in light of a third variable which is antecedent in time to the independent variable, the original relationship is said to be specified when one of the two partials is larger than the original relationship.[20] Each of the four test variables—civil rights attitudes, minority ethnicity, socio-economic status, and age—is antecedent to the pivotal independent variable, attitudes about Vietnam, and specifies its effect on tolerance for rebellion.

Table 9 reports the effects. The sizes of the effect parameters for the various categories of the test variables indicate that the overall effect of disaffection (dove relative to hawk) is enhanced whenever the category of the test variable has a positive effect on tolerance,

19. This interpretation for the random shocks was first suggested by J. Michael Polich, "The Coleman-Boyle Techniques and Multiple Regression Analysis" (Senior honors thesis, Dartmouth College, 1967).

20. See Lazarsfeld, op. cit., p. 128.

and it is reduced whenever a category has a negative effect.

This pattern is a consequence of an interesting social process. Whenever individuals are predisposed by the test factors to have tolerance for rebellion,

TABLE 8—CAUSES OF TOLERANCE FOR REBELLION AND SUPPORT FOR REPRESSION

	DISAFFECTED DOVES	SILENT MAJORITY	HARASSED HAWKS
	(proportion with some tolerance for rebellion)		
Younger/High SES/Minority			
For Civil Rights	.923	.789	.286
Number	(13)	(19)	(7)
Against Civil Rights	.500	.667	.429
Number	(2)	(15)	(7)
Younger/High SES/Majority			
For Civil Rights	.900	.733	.143
Number	(10)	(15)	(7)
Against Civil Rights	1.000	.417	.250
Number	(1)	(36)	(12)
Younger/Low SES/Minority			
For Civil Rights	1.000	.765	1.000
Number	(4)	(17)	(3)
Against Civil Rights	.667	.375	.222
Number	(3)	(16)	(9)
Younger/Low SES/Majority			
For Civil Rights	.600	.462	.400
Number	(5)	(13)	(5)
Against Civil Rights	.400	.167	.192
Number	(5)	(30)	(26)
Older/High SES/Minority			
For Civil Rights	.667	.478	1.000
Number	(6)	(23)	(3)
Against Civil Rights	1.000	.588	.286
Number	(3)	(17)	(7)
Older/High SES/Majority			
For Civil Rights	.625	.455	.000
Number	(8)	(22)	(4)
Against Civil Rights	.278	.391	.125
Number	(18)	(46)	(16)
Older/Low SES/Minority			
For Civil Rights	.727	.556	.250
Number	(11)	(18)	(4)
Against Civil Rights	.333	.280	.167
Number	(12)	(25)	(12)
Older/Low SES/Majority			
For Civil Rights	.000	.429	.182
Number	(5)	(28)	(11)
Against Civil Rights	.067	.189	.100
Number	(30)	(90)	(30)

$$a \cdot 1 = \text{effect of dove relative to silent majority} = .039$$
$$a_1 = \text{effect of silent majority relative to hawk} = .165$$
$$a_1(OV) = \text{overall effect of dove} = .204$$
$$a_2 = \text{effect of being for civil rights} = .181$$
$$a_3 = \text{effect of minority affiliation} = .177$$
$$a_4 = \text{effect of high socio-economic status} = .146$$
$$a_5 = \text{effect of being younger} = .126$$
$$r = \text{random shocks toward rebellion} = .000 \ (-.014)$$
$$s = \text{random shocks toward repression} = .166$$

TABLE 9—SPECIFIED EFFECTS
OF DISAFFECTION

CATEGORY OF TEST FACTOR	EFFECT OF DOVE RELATIVE TO SILENT MAJORITY	EFFECT OF SILENT MAJORITY RELATIVE TO HAWK	OVER-ALL EFFECT OF DOVE RELATIVE TO HAWK
	(effects on tolerance for rebellion)		
For Civil Rights	+ .108	+ .244	+ .352
Against Civil Rights	− .013	+ .133	+ .120
Minority Ethnicity	+ .154	+ .162	+ .316
Majority Ethnicity	− .033	+ .167	+ .130
High SES	+ .089	+ .276	+ .365
Low SES	+ .001	+ .089	+ .090
Younger (less than 40)	+ .176	+ .165	+ .341
Older	− .022	+ .165	+ .143
Total Effect Parameter	+ .039	+ .165	+ .204

the disaffected doves differentiate themselves from the silent majority by having more tolerance. The average of the four dove relative to silent majority effects is +.132 (.108 + .154 + .089 + .176 ÷ 4). Whenever they are predisposed to support repression, the average of the four partial effects is only −.017 (−.013 − .033 + .001 − .022 ÷ 4). This small negative effect suggests that among people predisposed to support repression, the silent majority is slightly more tolerant of rebellion than the doves. But in all circumstances the doves and the silent majority have more tolerance for rebellion than the hawks.

SUMMARY

Attitudes about the war in Vietnam define three social types: the disaffected doves strongly oppose the war; the

harassed hawks are strongly committed to it; and the silent majority is in the middle. Attitudes about the war do not follow the traditional lines of political cleavage in American society, but there are important differences between these three social types. Doves are more concerned about domestic problems, take a more liberal position on civil rights and social welfare, and have greater tolerance for rebellion. This latter variable is also associated with liberal positions on civil rights and social welfare.

The proportion of the American public which is supportive of repression appears to be about twice that which expresses at least some tolerance for rebellion. Surprisingly, the silent majority has almost as much tolerance for rebellion as the doves. Both are significantly more tolerant than the hawks. Four test factors also affect tolerance for rebellion. Attitudes favorable to civil rights, minority ethnicity, high socioeconomic status, and being younger (less than 40 years) have positive effects on tolerance. The first two variables are related to general norms supportive of protest and to anti-authoritarian values, the latter two, to feelings of political efficacy.[21]

These factors also affect the relationship between the two pivotal variables. The overall effect on tolerance of being a dove is increased whenever a category of a test factor predisposes toward tolerance. Whenever a category predisposes toward repression, the doves are less tolerant and are similar to the silent majority. But these two social types are always more tolerant than the hawks.

21. For a review of the literature related to this point, see Seymour Martin Lipset, *Political Man* (Garden City: Doubleday, 1960), ch. 6.

19

Cultural Value Orientations and Student Protest

By John P. Spiegel

John P. Spiegel, M.D., is director of Lemberg Center for the Study of Violence, Brandeis University. Formerly he was an associate clinical professor of psychology and a lecturer in the Department of Psychiatry, Harvard Medical School. He has served as associate attending physician, Cook County Psychopathic Hospital; chief of the psychiatric clinic, and associate director, Institute for Psychiatric and Psychosomatic Research and Training, Michael Reese Hospital; and a research associate in the Laboratory of Social Relations, Harvard Medical School. Dr. Spiegel has written extensively on neuroses and psychoanalysis, including "Psychological Factors in Riots—Old and New," Mental Health Digest *(March 1969); and* "The Social and Psychological Dynamics of Militant Negro Activism: A Preliminary Report," in Psychiatric Spectator *(1968).*

This paper was prepared for the annual meetings of the American Political Science Association, Los Angeles, 1970.

A BASIC assumption in any discussion of student protest involves the question of social change. Students would not protest with such vigor were they not intensely eager for fundamental and difficult-to-achieve transformations, both within the university and in the society as a whole. These changes are presumed to be difficult to achieve because they run counter to some of the basic values which are accepted by most Americans and which are firmly embedded in university practice. Accordingly, the protests and demands of the students encounter considerable resistance. The resistance, so it is held, vastly increases the militance and force with which students push their protest, giving rise to techniques of generating change which tend to feature violence.

If these assumptions are correct, then any discussion of the consequences of student protest for the university must be divided into three parts: (1) What changes are the students attempting to bring about and what effects would flow from these changes? (2) What are the consequences of the methods students use to bring about change? (3) What are the consequences of the methods used by faculty and administration to deal with both the techniques of protest and with the demands for change?

Despite the accumulating body of writings on the subject, it is obviously difficult to discuss the topic of desired social changes because of the tremendous amount of variation in goals of student groups, both between universities and on any one campus. Nevertheless, there is a potential solution to the problem. The variability exists principally at the level of concrete issues. There appears to be much more consensus about the changes in general value orientations which students would like to have instituted. In current studies of this sphere of belief and behavior, the staff of the Lemberg Center has been using the theory of variations in cultural value orientations proposed by Florence Kluckhohn.[1] I would like, therefore, to begin our discussion of the effects of student protest in the context of this theory of change in cultural values.

The theory proposes five categories of value dimensions based upon common human problems with which every society must deal. Three solutions are proposed for each of these common human problems, and differences between cultures (or subcultural groups) is assumed to rest upon differences in the order of preference for the solutions. I shall briefly discuss four of these categories, omitting the fifth for the sake of brevity. For the same reason, I shall not discuss the theoretical assumption nor the empirical data on which the generalizations which follow are based.

The first of these value dimensions is concerned with the *time* orientation— that is, the way decisions are made with reference to time. The prevailing pattern of preference for standard American culture is Future in the first position, Present second, and Past in the weak, third-order position. The degree to which Americans ordinarily plan for a far-flung future conceived in terms of something bigger and better needs no spelling out here. This emphasis is, of course, especially pressing in the educational area because of the need for parents and children to plan ahead for school, college, and career in the usual lock-step progression. Present time concerns are saved mainly for recreational situations—for entertainment, eating

1. F. R. Kluckhohn and F. L. Strodtbeck, *Variations in Value Orientations* (Evanston, Ill.: Row, Peterson & Company, 1961). Also, J. P. Spiegel, *Toward a Theory of Collective Violence* (in press).

and sex. The Past, in accordance with our anti-traditional bias, receives rather short shrift. Americans generally are too busy looking ahead to care about the past, tending to deal with both national and personal history in terms of superficial stereotypes.

Universities and colleges are somewhat variant with respect to this pattern of preference. So far as the usual curriculum is concerned, the Past receives a heavy emphasis in departments of history, classics, archeology, language, and other humane studies. The Past is also represented in a variety of quaint academic rituals and labels reaching back to the medieval origins of the university, as well as in the traditional songs, Latin mottoes, heraldic symbols, and other decorative mementos which distinguish one university from another. The Future is represented by the sciences with their stressing of research, change, and problem-solving. Quite aside from specific teaching programs, students are continually reminded that undergraduate or graduate studies are preparations for something that lies ahead, future examinations, other goals to be reached, jobs to be obtained, failures to be avoided. Thus, the pattern of preference for the *time* dimension in the university is Future/Past/Present.

To this pattern of value choices students have responded with demands for more attention to Present time. The "tune in, turn on, drop out" slogan proposed by Tim Leary in the early 1960's for drug users represented a cry for the re-arrangement of time values which has now been institutionalized in the drug and hippie culture. It is not within the scope of this paper to inquire deeply into the underlying motives for the switch to the Present. That it is connected with fear of the draft, horror of the war in Vietnam, anxieties about the Bomb, and general

doubts about survival in a polluted world have all been commented on. For our purposes, we are confronted with the more difficult question: how is the university to deal with the re-ordered *time* dimension—Present/Future/Past—incorporated in the student protest movement? What are the political and academic consequences of accepting or rejecting this revision of values? How is one to cope with the problem that dominant American middle-class culture, the university, and the student protest movement, each stress a different and seemingly incompatible value pattern in this area?

The second value category is concerned with the relation between man and nature (or super-nature). The order of preference for solutions to the *man/nature* category in main-stream America is first, Mastery over Nature; second, Subjugated to Nature; and third, Harmony with Nature. The first and most popular choice, Mastery over Nature, is consonant with our desired (and demonstrated) technological mastery of problems. Technical competence has fulfilled most of the dreams of antiquity as well as the fantasies of science fiction. For the few problems that remain unsolved, such as chronic illness and death (overlooking war, weather, and overpopulation, which remain on the agenda for technical mastery), the second choice, Subjugated to (super-)Nature plugs the gap. In this case, man can recognize his weakness and, in accordance with the Judeo-Christian or other religious belief, pray for deliverance from pain and misery. The third order solution, Harmony with Nature, avoids the concept of a struggle between man and nature. Rather, it emphasizes, somewhat on the pattern of the pre-Christian, polytheistic cults, that nature is herself full of contending forces loosely orchestrated on a grand but rather mysterious plan with which mankind must try to stay on good terms in order to avoid misfortune.

The Harmony with Nature position has, until recently, seemed at best charming and anachronistic, at worst magical and threatening, at any rate unrealistic to a science oriented culture. The student protest movement, however, is attempting to elevate Harmony with Nature into the first-order position. Students involved in protest have become disillusioned with the first two value choices. Mastery over Nature has been used for evil purposes, as exemplified in the war, the Bomb, and the computerized invasion of privacy. In addition, our vaunted technology has filled the firmament and our one only planet, earth, with waste products which it is incapable of disposing of in a safe and sane way. So much for technology. Finally, Mastery over Nature leaves no room for tragedy. A tragic event occurs when somebody goofs, pulls the wrong switch, prescribes the wrong medicine, fails to fasten his seat belt, takes an overdose of drugs, or foolishly falls into some other avoidable mishap. Aside from blaming the experts, there is no psychological relief available, since religion and the whole Subjugated to Nature orientation fails to carry conviction.

To many students born and raised in the Age of Aquarius, the rationalism of science and technology appears pretentious and somewhat menacing. Its failures loom as large as—if not larger than—its triumphs. On the other hand, the peculiar irrationalism of organized religion, with its singularly remote and unhelpful deity and its self-serving puritanical morality, seems even more objectionable. That a confused adult world should continue to honor a religion it does not and cannot use effectively tends to undermine the credibility of non-protesting adults who offer

themselves as models for the young. Thus, a Harmony with Nature position, however expressed—through astrology, magic, ecology, "humanistic" psychology, hostility to research, or to reason itself—tends to capture the imagination of those involved in protest. Given the traditional values of the university, this switch in values presents a problem of staggering dimensions.

The third value category is concerned with the most valued aspects of the personality in action, and is therefore called the *activity* dimension. The order of solutions for Americans in this category is first, Doing; second, Being; and third; Being-in-Becoming. Doing represents the success theme in American life—the externally made judgment that a person has "made it," has achieved in the eyes of others. Being, on the other hand, places chief value on spontaneity, on the expression of feeling, and on revealing the inner man in a straightforward way. Being-in-Becoming places its emphasis on the rounded development of the personality over time. The aim is to bring all aspects of the person together and into fruition, overlooking both the nose-to-the-grindstone pressures of Doing and the impulsiveness of Being.

The student protest movement has rejected this typical rank-order of *activity* values in favor of the sequence: Being-in-Becoming/Being/Doing. The emphasis on achievement for its own sake, on hard work for success, is regulated to the third place, probably because it has been so over-emphasized to date and because it is not seen as leading to personal satisfaction or happiness. On the contrary, it is perceived as forcing people ruthlessly into career lines and personal conduct which falsify the individuality and inner meaning of a person to himself, somewhat along the lines of the "Death of a Salesman" theme. For this undesirable outcome,

Being-in-Becoming is proposed as a corrective. For young people especially, it offers opportunity to explore themselves and their world(s), to avoid being pushed into premature career choices, to take time out from the "rat race," in the interests of finding for themselves a satisfactory niche and a happy combination of roles in the domestic, occupational, and recreational areas of life.

To the university, this re-ordering of values is not as troublesome as it may seem at first glance. Being is retained in the second position, where it has always been. To be sure, its range is now broadened. When Being follows Doing, as in the typical American sequence, its range is restricted because of the need to suppress inner feeling for the sake of success in whatever terms are laid down by "the establishment." If Being follows Being-in-Becoming, there is more room for spontaneity and the honest expression of inner feelings, often brought out with sufficient vehemence to unsettle the "traditional" calm and reserve of the academic mind. Nevertheless, academia has always honored, though it has not sufficiently emphasized, the Being-in-Becoming value orientation. With the exception of occasional publish-or-perish overkill, universities have always made room for teachers and scholars not particularly interested in the external success market. Though a heavier investment in the Being-in-Becoming value choice would require some readjustments in university programs, the strains would not be overwhelming.

The fourth value category is concerned with group decision-making and with personal relationships within groups. Called the *relational* value orientation, it is the most sensitive and problematic of all the value dimensions for the structure of universities, and is most highly involved in issues of dissent and protest. The preferred American pattern is Individualism first, Collateral second, and Lineal third. In most American groups, the individual is expected to behave in an independent fashion, to make up his own mind about what he wants, and to feel that he is as good as the next person. Tough group decisions are settled by majority vote. Collaterality, the second choice, emphasizes the horizontal, team-like structure of the group. Everyone is considered to be on the same plane but group harmony is more important than the individual wishes and opinions of a group member. Decisions are therefore made by concensus, a process that requires a good deal of prolonged discussion in order to overcome disagreements. The Lineal choice refers to group arrangements based on a vertical hierarchy. Decisions are made by a boss and are handed down the ladder of authority. Attention is paid to status within the group, to power issues, and to ranking in terms of superiority and inferiority.

There is much empirical evidence at our disposal that the Individual/Collateral/Lineal sequence is heavily endorsed by most Americans. It represents the national egalitarian ethos. The fact that most middle-class families are run on the basis of the Individual/Collateral/Lineal pattern often gives rise to the criticism that today's parents are too permissive. The fact that the criticism is made at all suggests that some parents (particularly among working-class, ethnic groups) still give considerable weight to a Lineal, authoritarian value system which is in conflict with middle-class culture. The Collateral aspects of groups are emphasized in all sorts of recreational and informal activities where the maintenance of group harmony and loyalty to the group is more important than recognition of individual rights. The lowly position of Lineality is expressed in resentment toward overweening authority and in our traditional sympathy for the underdog.

Nevertheless, despite the evidence that the Individual/Collateral/Lineal rank-order is representative of American ideals and that it is institutionalized within the middle-class family structure, most large-scale bureaucracies in the areas of business, government, education, and health are based on a variant pattern. Such organizations emphasize the Lineal, vertical structuring of relational values to a degree that is inconsistent with the ideal rank-order. They are characterized by stratification, superior/inferior status relations, one-way communications (from the top down) which impose excessive impersonality on human relations, and massive control over decision-making in the hands of those at the top of the bureacracy. This is not to say that the elitism of such organizations thoroughly invalidates the principle of individualism, but merely that individualism is much weakened by the heavy emphasis on Lineality. Thus, the operating sequence of relational values in many large-scale business organizations is Individual/Lineal/Collateral. And in some organizations, such as the military, the police, city governments, federal agencies, hospitals, and universities, the Lineal choice emerges in the first-order position, so that the resulting rank-order is Lineal/Individual/Collateral.

The discrepancy between the ideal and the operative relational values is nowhere more apparent than in the areas of race relations and foreign policy. The elitist principle that holds down Blacks, Spanish-Americans, Indians, and other minority groups, and the "world power" principle that governs our international relations are both

similarly evolved from a Lineal perspective on human relations. The word "perspective" is used advisedly in this connection since values pertain not to the nature of reality but to the way reality is viewed. Clearly, there are many persons who would see no justification in reality for racial oppression but who would still view the war in Vietnam as justified by the world power struggle between democracy and communism. But there are a growing number of persons who would regard this justification as unreal—as a disguise for a policy of economic domination of foreign markets.

To students involved in the protest movement, the connection between racism and war is quite real, and the implication of the universities in both issues is equally real. Universities are viewed as having actively endorsed our military policies by participating in generously financed war-related research and as having implicitly subscribed to racism by the exclusion of Blacks, their history, and their culture from any significant role in campus life. Reinforcing these conjoined issues is the students' view of the structure of the university itself as excessively Lineal. To university administrators impressed with the very real limitations on their authority and power, this view of the university often comes as a shock. It is true that power in the university is decentralized and that college presidents, deans, and department heads cannot have their way simply by issuing commands. But the fact that universities are not dictatorships does not mean that they are democracies. Possibly the most appropriate label for the political structure of the average university would be "decentralized oligarchy." Power is both stratified and divided. Influence is commanded by informal cliques of "advisors" or "insiders" surrounding each center of power—the Board;

chancellors, presidents and provosts; deans; department heads—down the ladder of prestige, through layers of faculty and teaching assistants, to students, traditionally on a lower rung, and service employees at the bottom. As a result of the division of power, the oligarchies compete with and often neutralize each other, universities are not run very efficiently, and administrators often feel frustrated. As a result of the informal nature of the decision-making clique at each center of power, the designated "head" is often a "figurehead," and it is important but difficult to know whom to cultivate in order to influence decisions. As a result of both the stratification of elites and of the obscure nature of decision-making, students have felt themselves to be without power and without knowledge of how to communicate effectively in regard to their needs and complaints, the more so since formal student governing bodies have been viewed as a part of the democratic facade covering the essentially oligarchic character of university structure.

Since many of the students who become involved in protest have entered the university already strongly opposed to the Lineal values manifested in the racist and military policies of the nation, it is not surprising that this opposition should be strengthened when they discover that the university is itself organized on Lineal lines. When a student learns that he is expected to know his place in the hierarchy of elites, comply with a complicated network of rules and regulations about which students have generally not been consulted, and suffer without complaint the punishment of probation or expulsion for breaking the rules, he is confronted with a system of human relations greatly at variance from those he learned within his family. The response to this value conflict, around which protest is organized, consists of promoting the Collateral value choice into the first-order position. The protesting students would like to see the university function as a community, on the order of a vastly extended family. Members of such a community would not be overly concerned with prestige or status. Decisions would be made by taking into account the wishes and feelings of all community groups in order to arrive at a reasonable consensus. Given the implications of such a horizontal, egalitarian triumph over the traditional, hierarchical decision-making, one could assume that such ill-fitting anomalies as racism and wars in defense of puppet governments or client states could no longer be tolerated within the university. For the image of the university as a consensually responsive, intercommunicating, and conflict-resolving community is meant to be a model for the nation as a whole—or even for the whole world. The relational profile incorporated into this model is Collateral/Individual/Lineal.

If we are correct in assuming that the concrete needs and complaints articulated in the various student protests and "demands" are responsive to value strains within and without the university, then we should try to inventory the discrepancies cited above in order to pinpoint the dilemma in which the universities find themselves as a result of the protest movement. Table I is designed for this purpose. It compares the ideal value patterns which are actualized in the American middle-class family with the value patterns represented in the structure of the university and in the forms of student protest. The *relational* patterns within the parentheses are reminders that the *operative* patterns associated with large-scale organizations tend to be at variance with both ideal and middle-class family values. This contrast is also a reminder

TABLE I—COMPARISON OF VALUE ORIENTATION PROFILES

	MIDDLE-CLASS FAMILY	UNIVERSITY	STUDENT PROTEST
Time	Fut > Pres > Past	Fut > Past > Pres	Pres > Fut > Past
Man/Nature	Over > Subj > Harmon	Over > Subj > Harmon	Harmon > Over > Subj
Activity	Doing > Be > BIB	Doing > BIB > Be	BIB > Be > Doing
Relational	Ind > Col > Lin (Ind > Lin > Col) (Lin > Ind > Col)	Lin > Ind > Col	Col > Ind > Lin

that the problems of the university in a time of value transition are merely special cases of problems facing the whole society.

Still, despite this across-the-boards sharing of value conflicts, the fact remains that universities have been singled out for attack. Protesting students have, in effect, declared that it is within the university that these problems of social change must be identified, confronted, fought out, resolved. Many persons within the university complain that this strategy is unfair, that colleges and universities cannot be expected to solve all the problems of the nation or of the world. Such complaints are probably based on a false premise. The student protest movement, in all likelihood, does not expect the university to come up with instant solutions. Rather, it hopes that the university will function as a model for the way social problems are to be approached. The expectation assumes that since universities prepare the young for the future, and since that future is already heavily implicated in the current value conflicts, it is the special obligation of the university to face up to the associated political problems both on and off the campus, and to make a determined attempt to deal with them.

A glance at Table I shows immediately that this expectation presents the university with an immensely complicated task. At the simplest level, no large, traditional organization can undergo structural change without tremendous strain and discomfort being imposed upon its incumbents. For those that have been in office for any length of time, the change in habits and role expectations generates much personal stress, reduces efficiency, and often leads to psychosomatic illness, death, or premature termination of employment. But this universally disabling effect of organizational change could be more easily accepted and overcome were the direction of change to be clear-cut and the scheduling of change accomplishable on an easily understood plan. Employees and other members of the academic community could respond more easily to a "like it or not, this is what's going to happen" policy than to the current situation of ambiguity and uncertainty.

Ambiguity, unfortunately, is built into the current value snarls illustrated in Table I. The values representative of the university fit neither with the idealized values of the middle-class family nor with the patterns being promoted by the student protest movement. To be sure, with the exception of the *relational* orientation, university values are closer to middle-class family values than to those of the student movement. In this respect, the student movement is radical in more than the political connotations of this word. It is radical in substance—that is, in the degree to which it alters traditional views of human relations and the meaning of life.

If its aims were to be realized, the *norms* for behavior within the university and, subsequently, within the social system as a whole would have to undergo extensive transformation.

It is obvious that the university, caught in the middle between two extremely different value patterns, is in trouble. No matter which way it moves it will be in trouble, and if it stands still without change, it will remain in trouble. Nevertheless, the university is a self-directed organization. No matter how battered it may be for some time to come, it will have no choice but to cope with its problems in its own time and in its own way, unwilling and unable to respond passively or mechanically to pulls from either (or any) direction. In the intervening time, however, during which it is undergoing intense internal turmoil and confusion sometimes bordering on paralysis, it cannot respond rapidly enough nor appropriately to pressure for change. The stress is too great and the insight into the appropriate response too dim.

Despite these difficulties, many universities have been attempting to experiment with new structural and functional arrangements. Such efforts, however, are difficult to analyze and to assess because they are so intricately interwoven with the implications of the second question we asked at the beginning of this chapter: What are the political consequences of the methods students use to bring about change? And the question itself is not a simple one. The methods of student protest have ranged from non-violent techniques, such as polls and boycotts, through disruptions of classes and takeovers of buildings, to violent attacks on personnel and property. To complicate matters further, the methods used by protesting students are usually responsive to previous administrative reactions to a set of prior demands for change put forth by some of the more radicalized students. In a previous publication, this escalation of conflict leading toward disorder was described as a process of action and reaction occurring in five stages of progression.[2] In that paper it was postulated that despite the presence of small groups of students (such as the various SDS factions) fixated on violence and disruption as the only effective technique for reaching their revolutionary goals, large-scale, persistent disorder within the university was usually the product of a series of errors on the part of the administration. Most of these mistakes consisted of failures of communication: the invisibility and inaccessibility of top administrative figures for both students and faculty; failure to take early requests for change with sufficient seriousness; neglect or mismanagement of the negotiating process; and carelessness and misjudgment in the use of police, national guard, and other law enforcement agencies.

It is not within the scope of this paper to discuss the process of escalation of disorder. For the university, the political consequences of student protest and disorder are fairly well known. They have tended to divide the American public into sharply polarized groups: (1) a very small group who sympathize both with the aims and the methods of radical protest, (2) a somewhat larger but still minority group which sympathizes with some or all of their aims but disapprove of their methods, and (3) a much larger group, probably a majority, which disapproves of both their aims and their methods. This external public response has produced an acute problem for university administrators. How are they to deal with the negative attitudes toward stu-

2. J. P. Spiegel, "Campus Conflict and Professional Egos," *Trans-action* (October 1969), pp. 41–50.

dent protest outside the university while still maintaining a reasonable stance toward the considerable pressure for change within the student body and within much of the faculty?

There are three possible ways of coping with this situation: (1) the Conflict-resolving Response, (2) the Conflict-deterring Response, and (3) the Mixed Response. The Conflict-resolving Response is a strategy based on anticipating student demands wherever possible so that they can be made the subject of university-wide discussion. Such early discovery of potential sore-spots, so the strategy goes, leads to a "defusion" of tension and toward a potential concensus on the basis of which the administration can take action without too much backlash from whatever quarter. Thus, although it is resented as co-opting the movement by some of the more radical students, it tends to avoid disorder and the need to call in external law enforcement agencies. To be successful, it requires an inordinate amount of communication, meetings, trial-and-error, feed-back, correction of mistakes, and just plain hard work on the part of all concerned. The time consumed in all the necessary work may prevent ordinary tasks from being completed and may easily wear out those who have responsibility. Since it does not provide an iron-clad guarantee that there will be no disruptions at all, it may be seen as too "soft," leading to loss of support from large donors, alumni, and state legislators, who disapprove of any departure from the traditional Lineal structure of the university.

The Conflict-deterring Response is less inclined to anticipate the *content* of student protest, more inclined to plan for dealing with the method of protest on a tough, law-and-order, "no-nonsense" basis. It relies on the infiltration of dissident student groups so as to have maximum information on plans for disruptions. Students are warned of exactly what will happen to them if they should break university rules in carrying out protest, and the warnings are backed up by prompt action by the police and disciplinary committees within the university and by court action off campus. Various divide-and-conquer techniques are applied for the sake of breaking up refractory student organizations. Disorder is deterred by intimidation. The firm thrust of this response may earn the university the praise of Lineally-minded segments of the public, but the conflict management technique severely limits student freedom while anger seethes, however well concealed. Aside from repressive vigilance, no change in the structure of the university is likely to take place under these circumstances. Oddly enough, despite the approval of "hard line" segments of the public, universities using this approach seem not to reap any particular financial benefits as a reward, either from state legislators or from wealthy, private donors.

Although this represents a much-needed area of research and the facts are not certain, it would appear that only a handful of universities employ either a pure Conflict-resolving or Conflict-deterring strategy. Most prefer to try some conflict-resolving methods for as long as possible, using conflict-deterrence when the situation threatens to or actually gets out of hand. This Mixed Response seems less rigid and arbitrary. Perhaps it is more adaptive than the other two precedures, but without more experience and comparative research no final conclusions are available. It has the possible disadvantage of appearing, under certain circumstances, as vacillating, contradictory, or weak, thus stimulating distrust among students and disgust in the ranks of the disaffected public. At the present time, the actual proportions and sequencing of conflict-resolving and conflict-deterring procedures in the "mix" varies considerably from campus to campus. The "mix" seems to be a product of many factors: the personal "style" of the president of the university, the previous history of the university within its community, the region or state in which the university is located, private versus public and rural versus urban contrasts, and probably other considerations difficult to discern at present.

Because of our ignorance and the absence of a body of comparative research, to make any generalizations about the consequences of the various techniques of conflict-management seems risky. It has been suggested that ill-conceived conflict deterrence employing badly trained personnel, such as the use of the national guard at Kent State and of the police at Orangeburg, South Carolina and Jackson, Mississippi, leads to the unnecessary and tragic killing and injury of students. This is probably true, but it is necessary to await the outcome of various official investigations before coming to firm conclusions. At the present time, the only generalization in which one can have confidence is that, whatever the technique of conflict-management, its purpose (as opposed to its effects) is to keep the university relatively stable and free of inordinate turbulence so that the needed changes can be worked out with care.

This situation, interestingly enough, cuts both ways. Many universities administrators complain that they are so busy coping with protest, and its consequences, that they do not have the time to concern themselves with educational reform. On the other hand, many persons, particularly students and reform-minded faculty, believe that it is only because of the protest activity that universities have become interested in making changes in the first place. Both views are probably correct, in part, though the facts would seem to indicate that no matter how busy the administration, most universities are currently undergoing change of some sort. The chief obstacles to change would appear to lie not in the areas of time and technique but in the realm of values and value conflicts. This consideration suggests that we should not conclude this chapter without giving some thought to the options open to the university for solving the value problems illustrated in Table I.

The statements which follow are based on an interpretation of changes already in process plus deductions from the logic of value conflict. However, they represent at best informed guesses. For the sake of avoiding repeated qualification, they are expressed in positive terms but they are not meant to be considered as guidelines or recommendations. They are merely ideas proposed for the sake of stimulating discussion.

The key position of the *relational* values as the point of attack of student protest suggests that this area receive top priority in any consideration of structural change. In addition, relational values are more highly implicated in contradiction and confusion than are the other value dimensions. They are the source of that "hypocrisy" to which the student protest movement is so sensitized. How can the university escape from the contradiction between the ideal Individual/Collateral/Lineal sequence, which it is presumably promoting at the level of belief, and the operative Lineal/Individual/Collateral pattern which it so vigorously practices?

The solution proposed by protesting students is to promote the Collateral choice into first-order position and to demote the Lineal to the third-order position. At first blush this may seem a good solution. It is true that in most large universities, fragmentation and isolation of individuals and groups is severe. Except in the course of a crisis, there is little overall community feeling. But the effort to highlight and maintain Collaterality in the first position suffers from several inherent weaknesses. As the experience of student militant organizations demonstrates, collaterally organized groups easily undergo fission, particularly in the context of crisis situations when consensus about difficult decisions is hard to reach. Furthermore, in such emergencies, after collateral fission takes place, the split groups usually adopt a fiercely competitive, rivalrous stance toward each other. Under these circumstances, with the survival of the groups at stake, the submerged Lineality tends to reassert itself in an intense and anomalous form. Group leaders begin to behave in an authoritarian manner quite in contradiction to the official ideology of the group. The fact is that emergencies featuring dangerous, inter-group rivalry require a Lineal organization of decision-making. In threatening, fast-moving circumstances, there simply is not time for Collateral or Individual decision-making to take place. This is why military and quasi-military organizations are structured on a Lineal basis. A strong authority must make the decision quickly and see that it is executed lest he be outmaneuvered and his cause lost.

Radical student organizations are frequently accused of being "fascist" because of the unexpected prominence of Lineality. It would seem, however, that the term is in error as the authoritarianism of such groups is not a matter of ideology but of group dynamics. The attempt to cope with the problem by the constant rotation of leaders is of some help. But there is always the danger that, having been driven into authori-

tarian practices, the group members will, unconsciously at least, begin to place some value on Lineality for its own sake as the means by which they are able to be successful. Examples of this outcome in history are not hard to find.

If the first-order Lineality of the university system is inappropriately elitist and not particularly efficient and the first-order Collaterality of the student protest movement is unstable, then perhaps a better arrangement would be represented by the ideal, American pattern of Individual/Collateral/Lineal. If this pattern could be instituted, the gap between ideal and operative relational values would disappear and the problem of "hypocrisy" would be eliminated. Current structural changes directed at dealing with this problem, however, would not be sufficient. The placing of a few students on various university committees and boards, whether as voting or non-voting members, does not materially alter the Lineal structure of the bureaucracy; though it may result in better feed-back from below to the top. In order to preserve Individualism in the first-order position, an arrangement featuring both representation of constituencies and participation in university governance must be found. The format recently installed at the Free University of Berlin constitutes one such arrangement. Governance is in the hands of a tripartite elected University Council composed equally of students, faculty, and administration, with Council decisions being taken by vote. Since this format constitutes a real rather than a *pro forma* distribution of power, students and faculty tend to vote in larger numbers than previously in order to elect members who will represent their views. However, this is only one model and it may not be suitable for American universities. In this case, some other

TABLE II–Comparison of Actual and Proposed Values for the University

	ACTUAL	PROPOSED
Time	Fut>Past>Present	Fut=Past=Present
Man/Nature	Over>Subj>Harmony	Harmony>Over>Subj
Activity	Doing>BIB>Being	BIB>Doing>Being
Relational	Lineal>Ind>Col	Ind>Col>Lineal

format capable of reaching the same goals will have to be invented and tried. What is important is change in the profile of values rather than the particular structures in which the change is embodied.

Once the relational problem is resolved, the other value dimensions should be easier to handle. In my opinion, it would be best to leave the *time* dimension open. Instead of attempting to create a new rank-ordering of time values, why not let each choice have equal weight? Clearly, present time considerations have received insufficient attention in the university, and they now require heavier accenting. But the future and the past are also of great importance. If each choice were to be equal to the other two, then students and other members of the university community could create their own patterns rather than being forced into a fixed time mold.

In the *man/nature* dimension, the Harmony with Nature/Mastery over Nature/Subjugated to Nature profile being sponsored by the student movement seems a wise choice. Mastery over nature has been stretched out of all relationship to the ability of man to attain this position. If it is retained in the second position, the Harmony with Nature choice, divested of its magical overtones, would represent a more rounded, humanistic approach to the relation between man and nature. The demotion of the Subjugated to Nature choice is in line with changes already taking place—even within divinity

schools where theology tends more and more to be taught within a comparative, historical frame of reference.

In the *activity* dimension, the university profile places too much emphasis on Doing while the student protest sequence gives it too little stress. At the present time, Doing—that is, hard work for the sake of achievement—is so little honored among dissident students that they often cannot maintain protest over sustained periods of time. After a crisis, their attention is apt to be diverted to some other activity that captures their interest as they follow their Being-in-Becoming explorations, or become involved in the spontaneity of Being, perhaps with the aid of drugs. On the other hand, the university's emphasis on Doing stimulates an excessive amount of competitiveness, anxiety about grades, and about performance in general. For both student and junior faculty, the worry about whether one will be able to "make it" are pervasive. This is one of the reasons that junior faculty are apt to associate themselves with student causes.

A possible solution to this value conflict would be the sequence, Being-in-Becoming/Doing/Being. With Doing in the second position, the exploratory and relaxed character of Being-in-Becoming would reduce the harsh, compulsiveness of the "success theme" while the demotion of Being would screen expressiveness for its own sake, holding it to those areas of emotional behavior in which a safety valve function is important.

Table II summarizes these suggested changes by comparing the actual value profiles characteristic of the university at present with those proposed in the preceding discussion. Whether the suggested value changes are appropriate and helpful cannot be determined at this stage of the on-going value transitions. It is hoped, however, that they will contribute to an objective discussion of a topic often loaded with emotion and controversy.

20

Campus Protests and the Vietnam War

By Robert B. Smith

I am indebted to many colleagues for their comments on an earlier draft. Generous grants of computer time were provided by the National Institute of Mental Health and the Computer Center of the University of California, Santa Barbara.

THIS chapter seeks to clarify how disaffection from the Vietnam war affects aggressive student protests against university administrators. On the basis of their recent analysis of chronologies of student protests, the Urban Research Corporation concluded that the Vietnam war is not a major cause of campus unrest because the war was an issue in only 2 percent of the student protests occurring between January and June 1969.[1] Contrary to this interpretation, the survey analysis reported in this chapter finds that disaffection from the war is a major determinant of student militancy even in protests that are manifestly not about the war.[2]

This analysis is based primarily on a survey of undergraduates at the University of California at Santa Barbara (UCSB) during the 1968–1969 academic year. This branch of the university is a relatively new institution which draws students mostly from affluent white upper middle-class California families. At the time of the survey there were 12,619 students enrolled; 86 percent were undergraduates.[3] About 95 percent of the undergraduates were residents of California prior to their admission, at least 93 percent are white, about 80 percent come from white collar and professional families, and 70 percent have fathers with at least some college education.

The attitudes and behaviors of these students are of interest because these students have been noted for surfboarding, sun bathing, and conservative political apathy, rather than activism. Only a year after this survey was taken, however, many of these same students were actively confronting police both on campus and in Isla Vista, the privately owned student community adjacent to the campus, during several months of intensive protest behavior. In the course of these protests the Isla Vista branch of the Bank of America was destroyed by fire, a student was killed by the police, and about 900 students, faculty, and residents of Isla Vista were arrested.

This survey was carried out as part of an introductory research methods course. The students in the course designed the questionnaire under the capable direction of the teaching assistant, Byron Eckerson. A systematic sample was drawn from the *Hustler's Handbook*, an alphabetical listing of the names and addresses of the students. The questionnaires were given out in December 1968, during "dead week," the week before final exams. By January 1969, 287 questionnaires were returned to ballot boxes located in various places both on and off campus. The anonymity of the respondents was protected by having them detach from the questionnaire an extra sheet which carried their name. This sheet was collected separately and destroyed immediately after checking off that the respondent had returned his questionnaire. During the spring quarter, just after the Berkeley "People's Park" protests in which a bystander was killed

1. John Naisbitt, *Student Protests, 1969 Summary* (Chicago: Urban Research Corporation, 1970).

2. The impact of the war on student antiwar protests has been described in other studies. See Allen H. Barton, "The Columbia Crisis," *Public Opinion Quarterly* 49 (Fall 1968), pp. 333–351; Richard Flacks, "Who Protests: The Social Basis of the Student Movement," in Julian Foster and Durward Long, eds., *Protest* (New York: Morrow, 1970), pp. 134–157; Edward E. Sampson, "Student Activism and the Decade of Protest," *Journal of Social Issues* 23 (July 1967), pp. 1–33; and Jerome Skolnick, *The Politics of Protest* (New York: Simon and Schuster, 1969), pp. 27–124.

3. These statistics were reported by the Office of Analytical Studies, University of California, Santa Barbara, in their Fall 1968 report.

TABLE 1—AN ITEM ABOUT DISAFFECTION FROM THE VIETNAM WAR

"People are called 'hawks' if they want to step up our military effort in Vietnam. They are called 'doves' if they want to reduce our military effort in Vietnam. How would you describe yourself—as a 'hawk' or a 'dove'?"

	HAWK	DOVE	NO OPINION	TOTAL
UCSB Students (Dec. 1968)	12%	74%	14%	100%
Public (AIPO) (Oct. 1968)	44	42	14	100

by the police, there was a follow-up contact for 61 randomly selected non-respondents. These people were given a second questionnaire which contained additional questions about the Berkeley protests. The resulting sample of 348 students represents a satisfactory response rate of 53 percent.[4] Comparison of early and late returns does not show any large differences or important trends. In general, there are no important differences between the marginal distributions of sex, grade in school, academic major, and attitude about the war for the returned sample and the undergraduate population.[5] Estimates of population characteristics may be off by 5 or 10 percent due to bias, but relationships between variables and the magnitudes of their effects which are our main concerns, should be correct.

4. This is about the same response rate as that reported by Barton in his studies of the Columbia protests. See Barton, "The Columbia Crisis," op. cit., p. 335.
5. In this sample about 74 percent say they are doves on Vietnam. In a student referendum in November 1968, *El Gaucho*, the UCSB student newspaper, reported that 76 percent of the students who voted desired an immediate and total withdrawal of all troops from Vietnam. In this same referendum, 86 percent of the voters stated that politics is playing too large a role in the governing of the University. On a very similar item, 85 percent of the survey respondents felt that the autonomy of the University is threatened by politics. These small differences between the survey respondents and the student voters indicate that the survey sample is representative of the UCSB undergraduates.

THE VARIABLES

Disaffection from the Vietnam War: The Pivotal Independent Variable

Disaffection is defined as the absence or withdrawal of affection or loyalty, as disagreement, or discontent. It also connotes alienation, estrangement, and dislike.[6] Student disaffection from the Vietnam war is gauged by the Gallup poll (AIPO) item used to assess whether a person is a "dove" or a "hawk"—that is, whether he wants the war in Vietnam de-escalated or escalated. Table 1 presents the exact wording of the question, and response distributions for the UCSB students and for the American public. The marginals indicate that at the time of this survey the UCSB students were considerably more "dovish" than the public. The difference is 32 percent.[7]

Because disaffection from the war is the pivotal independent variable, we must insure that the above item validly gauges this concept. This single indica-

6. *The American College Dictionary* (New York: Random House, 1948), p. 343.
7. UCSB students are considerably more dovish than most college students. In the spring of 1970, a *Playboy* survey found that 65 percent of all college students were doves on Vietnam. Of these, 36 percent wanted an immediate withdrawal from Vietnam and 29 percent wanted a speeded-up withdrawal. In the spring of 1970, about 87 percent of the UCSB students were doves, a difference of +22 percent from the student public. For data about the student public, see *Playboy* 17 (September 1970), p. 182.

TABLE 2—EXTERNAL VALIDATION OF THE DOVE/HAWK INDEX OF DISAFFECTION AMONG UCSB STUDENTS

DIMENSIONS OF DISAFFECTION	DOVES	HAWKS	DIFFERENCE
Disagreement with Government Policies			
Vietnam war a mistake	89%	30%	59%
Radical or Liberal	60	18	42
No restrictions on marijuana	75	48	27
Free availability of drugs	30	15	15
Disrespect for Laws and Institutions (delegitimation of authority)			
Protestors need not always use existing channels of communication and authority	20	3	17
Leniency for protestors who use nonviolent civil disobedience	51	33	18
Smoked marijuana at least once, thereby breaking a law	57	24	33
Less conventional career plans	67	46	21
Alienation and Estrangement			
Feels lonely	60	47	13
Worries about personal and world problems	69	35	34
Tried pep pills	32	18	14
Tried LSD and other psychedelic drugs	25	9	16

tor does fulfill the two usual criteria for an index comprised of a single item in terms of face validity and external validity. Table 2 presents strong evidence for the latter.

Students who are doves tend strongly to disagree with government policies on important issues, and to do so to a far greater extent than those who declare themselves to be hawks. Doves also express disrespect for laws and institutions, indicating a delegitimation of authority. Finally, doves also are more alienated than hawks, though differences here are somewhat smaller than on the other two dimensions, particularly if one grants realistic cause for concern with respect to world problems. This item might then be considered an indicator of identification—even compassion—for humanity and its problems.

Student Militancy: The Pivotal Dependent Variable

Student militancy against university administrators is defined as readiness to press aggressively for changes in the structure of the university. The face

TABLE 3—AN ITEM ABOUT STUDENT MILITANCY

"When existing channels of communication prove inadequate or unsatisfactory, students should then directly confront administrators with their grievances, even if this entails civil disobedience in some form or other." Do you:

AGREE	DISAGREE	NO OPINION	TOTAL
68%	29%	3%	100%

TABLE 4—Student Militancy and Support for Forceful, Nonviolent Protests Against University Administrators

UCSB Student Protests	Militant	Conservative	Difference
Black Student Union Protest (October 2–17, 1968)			
BSU sit-in justifiable	80%	40%	40%
Favored take-over of computer center	85	50	35
Favored chancellor's handling of the matter	74	53	21
Berkeley Solidarity Protest (May 22–27, 1969)			
Favored protesting excessive use of force by police	93	50	43
Favored student strike	64	15	49
Participated in 2 or more activities	69	23	46
Bill Allen Controversy* (January 20–February 12, 1970)			
Administration was unresponsive to petition signed by 7,776 students	84	33	51
Allen was right in trying to change anthropology department's decision to fire him	88	40	48
Allen was right to encourage rallies and demonstrations to protest his being fired	69	7	62
Student representatives should vote in department faculty meetings	86	39	47
Student representatives should vote in the academic senate	88	43	45

* Data from a survey about the burning of the Isla Vista Bank of America (March 1970).

validity of the item in Table 3 is obvious. Militants are defined as the 68 percent who agree with this statement.[8]

At the time of this survey, militancy connoted a willingness to use forceful, but nonviolent, tactics. Several facts

8. For an excellent survey analysis of student militancy at the University of California, Berkeley, see Robert H. Somers, "The Mainsprings of the Rebellion: A Survey of Berkeley Students in November 1964," in Seymour Martin Lipset and Sheldon S. Wolin, eds., *The Berkeley Student Revolt* (Garden City, N.J.: Anchor Books, 1965), pp. 530–557. Somers classified about 30 percent of the Berkeley students as militant during the Free Speech Movement. These students supported both the goals and the tactics of the demonstrators.

suggest this, and at the same time are strong evidence for the external validity of the item. First, there is a high association (Gamma = .635) between the militancy item and an item about leniency for participants in nonviolent protests, i.e., protests in which there is no damage to property, and no people are hurt. Second, only 8 percent of the militant students *say* they are radical, and it would be the radical students who would be most likely to support violence as a tactic.[9] Third, until a year

9. Data from a later survey about the burning of the Bank of America corroborate this assertion. Students who support the Radical Union are more likely to agree that when grievances pile high, violence may be the

after this survey was taken, violent protests were very infrequent at UCSB. Finally, there are strong relationships between militancy and support for non-violent, but forceful, protests.

Table 4 describes the reactions of militant and conservative UCSB students to three protests against University administrators. The war in Vietnam was not an explicit issue in any of these protests. The first two, the Black Student Union and Berkeley Solidarity protests, took place during the 1968–69 academic year and are described by data from this survey. The Bill Allen controversy took place the next year, just prior to the burning of the Isla Vista branch of the Bank of America, and is the subject of a later survey.

Black Student Union protest

The Black Student Union protest began October 1, 1968, when twelve Black athletes met with the chancellor to object to the athletic department's attitudes and policies toward Black athletes. Eventually, a list of 13 grievances was formulated. These included demands for the hiring of more minority group teachers and the admission of more minority students, a Black studies department, the establishment of a commission designed to investigate the causes and consequences of institutional and personal racism at UCSB, and the firing of several coaches perceived to be prejudiced. These demands were enforced when 16 Black students took over the campus computer center

for most of the day of October 14, 1968. The administration met many of their demands, and the Blacks withdrew from the computer center. There was no damage to any equipment and no one was hurt during the sit-in. Since the protest was nonviolent and the grievances were real, the protestors received only minimal punishment—suspended suspensions.[10]

Although a few White students and faculty were vocal in their opposition to the Black's tactics, the vast majority of the students supported the BSU. About 75 percent of the students thought the sit-in was justifiable, 60 percent favored the take-over, and 68 percent approved the chancellor's handling of the matter: he kept the police off campus, negotiated with the students, and was lenient with the demonstrators.

Berkeley Solidarity protest

The Berkeley Solidarity demonstrations took place toward the end of the academic year in order to protest police brutality against the Berkeley community and the presence of the national guard on the Berkeley campus. Street people and students had converted an empty lot south of the campus into a "people's park." The university decided to use this land for other purposes. On Thursday, May 15, 1969, about 1,500 people held a rally at the university's Sproul Plaza and called for a march on the lot. Demonstrators were met by

only effective response (49 percent difference), are less likely to totally reject violence as a means of political dissent (41 percent difference), are more likely to agree that violent tactics do not subtract from the just goals of protests (42 percent difference), and to agree that legitimate channels of protest are not effective (43 percent difference).

10. This description of the BSU sit-in is based on my own observations of the events, and on newspaper reports in *El Gaucho*, the UCSB student newspaper, and in the *Santa Barbara News-Press*.

The BSU takeover was the first forceful sit-in at UCSB. Prior protests had been characterized by non-forceful, nonviolent tactics. Typically, they were staged by antiwar White students who gathered petitions, deployed ineffectual picket lines, and marched for peace in the city of Santa Barbara.

the police, and a violent confrontation ensued. Students and street people threw rocks and bottles at the police, who in turn used rocks, guns, and teargas to disperse the crowd. Several bystanders were hit by police gunfire. One person was seriously wounded. His death the following Monday touched off a series of protests at other campuses of the university.

At UCSB, the Berkeley Solidarity protest began on Thursday, May 22, with a rally in the Free Speech area behind the University Center. On Friday the chancellor cancelled classes at 3:00 P.M. for a university convocation at the athletic field. After the speeches there was a call for a two-day strike on Monday and Tuesday. On these days most classes were either cancelled, poorly attended, or devoted to discussing the events at Berkeley and means for achieving constructive social change. On Tuesday there also was a peaceful march on Santa Barbara to explain student views on the Berkeley situation, as well as to increase rapport between the students and the community.[11]

As might be expected, militant students, to a greater extent than conservatives, supported these demonstrations. Responses are shown in Table 4.

The Allen controversy

The Bill Allen controversy became very visible during the winter quarter of the next academic year. On January 20, 1970, the student newspaper announced that 6,000 students, faculty, and staff had signed a petition asking for an open hearing for William Allen, as assistant professor in the UCSB anthropology department. The preceding

11. The description of the events at Berkeley was gleaned from a careful reading of reports in the *New York Times*, the *Santa Barbara News-Press*, and *El Gaucho*. The description of the events at UCSB is based on my own observations.

spring Allen had been notified that his contract would not be renewed. Consequently, he had a terminal appointment for 1969–70. The petition called for an open hearing which would require the anthropology department to state the exact reasons for firing Allen, and allow Allen to present a defense to these reasons. Many students felt that Allen had complied with the major requirements for advancement (viz., he was a good teacher and a productive scholar) and that he was being fired unjustly for his radical political beliefs and for his permissive life style.

By the end of the week the number of signatures had reached 7,776, and the petitions were presented to the anthropology department. The vice chancellor for Academic Affairs, who was acting chancellor while the chancellor was out of the country, chose to respond to the students because the chancellor had previously ratified Allen's dismissal. In his reply (which by happenstance was released on Monday, the first day of a very salient ecology week commemorating the first anniversary of the Santa Barbara oil spill), the acting chancellor refused the petition. He stressed that Allen was not fired capriciously, that Allen's political beliefs were not a factor, and that even though students were being asked to participate at all levels of campus activities, academic personnel decisions should be made by professional peers and the administration.

Two days later, on January 28, 1970, to protest the Santa Barbara oil spill disaster, the more militant, ecologically oriented students, along with Bill Allen, staged a "wharf-in" at Stearn's Wharf in the Santa Barbara harbor. This wharf includes restaurants and facilities for servicing small ships, the latter being used by oil companies to load and unload small transport vessels which service the offshore oil rigs.

About 75 demonstrators slept on the pier that evening, preventing would-be diners from eating at the restaurants. The owner of the restaurants has a concession from the city which enables him to control the pier. The demonstrators restricted access to the restaurants in order to protest the oil companies' use of the pier's maritime facilities. Thursday morning, under the threat of arrest, the demonstrators left the pier and returned to campus to attend a massive noon rally in support of Allen. This rally, and subsequent rallies during the controversey, were held in a restricted non-free-speech area directly in front of the administration building. The rally was sponsored by the Radical Union and the 7,776 signers of the petition, by the Black Student Union, and by the Santa Barbara chapter of the New University Conference, an organization of radical professors. All three parties in the coalition demanded an open hearing for Allen and greater student participation in the governance of the university.

On Thursday and Friday, crowds of demonstrators sealed off the entrance of the administration building, and the building was evacuated except for security personnel. For the most part, both the police and the demonstrators were nonviolent. In public statements student leaders often stressed the importance of nonviolence, and compared to the police in Berkeley during the People's Park protest, the police at Santa Barbara did not use excessive force. On Thursday, however, a short scuffle between the dean of men and a few students apparently stimulated a spontaneous charge by a group of club-swinging campus policemen who temporarily dispersed the crowd. Campus police broke a few windows when they charged out of the administration building, and a few students were injured.

Soon after, several more windows were broken by the demonstrators.

Friday morning an attempt to reach a negotiated settlement failed. The students wanted a tripartite committee to review the Allen case and to make a recommendation to the chancellor. After making their recommendation the committee would also study the long-range possibilities of student participation in the hiring and firing of academic personnel. The acting chancellor rejected this proposal but stated that the administration would urge all department chairmen to set up meetings with students to discuss "student input" on matters of hiring and firing. The students did not accept this counter-proposal, and continued to seal off the administration building.

That afternoon about 300 state police and sheriff's deputies arrived on campus in response to the acting chancellor's request for assistance. This was the first time in the history of UCSB that outside police were called to campus to quell a student protest. The police formed a skirmish line and moved in unison, pushing the crowd back with shields and billy clubs. The students' strategy was to move back, regroup, and march back to the administration building, where the whole process was repeated. In their attempts to disperse the students the police used a minimum of force—only a few demonstrators were hurt—and the students remained nonviolent.

In contrast to the sit-in at the computer center the year before, the administration and the police took a "hard line" during the Allen controversy. On Monday, February 2, the police arrested 19 students and student leaders for participating in the demonstrations. Many of these students had publicly advocated nonviolence during the protests. The administration also punished these students by suspending them from school and barring them from campus. "Double jeopardy," the perceived political nature of the arrests, and demands for amnesty soon became major issues in the controversy.

On the same day as the arrests, and on the following Tuesday, the police established control over the grounds near the administration building. However, demonstrators ringed police lines and talked with individual policemen, there were marches around the campus, protest meetings were held in other restricted areas, and the faculty club was taken over by students. The demonstrators threatened a direct confrontation, by marching in unison toward the police, but they stopped just short of the police line and there was no violence. On Wednesday the police left the campus, and support for the demonstrations dropped off. A strike called for Thursday and Friday was only moderately successful.

In negotiations with the students, the administration and the academic senate would not compromise on the various issues. On Tuesday, February 3, the academic senate voted against open hearings in personnel matters and also against a tripartite committee to study and make recommendations to the chancellor concerning the Bill Allen case. The next day, the Committee on Privilege and Tenure of the academic senate voted not to review the Allen case in a formal hearing, stating as their reason that there was no evidence that Allen's termination was based on other than professional or academic considerations. On Thursday, the acting chancellor released his final statement on the controversy, stating that he had initiated disciplinary action against Allen for unprofessional conduct. He also threatened university discipline for students who would disrupt the orderly functioning of the university or violate university-wide or campus regula-

tions. However, he also reaffirmed his desire to devise ways for students to aid in the evaluation of academic personnel.

In response to the chancellor's return to campus on Sunday, February 8, the students declared a moratorium on demonstrations, hoping that he would offer a compromise on the Allen decision and that charges might be dropped against the 19 arrested students. But the chancellor's statement released on Wednesday, February 11, reaffirmed the decisions made in his absence. The statement also promised more student participation in the future and encouraged the formation of undergraduate organizations in each department in order to provide input to departmental decision-making processes, especially concerning the teaching abilities of professors.

Except for a brief encounter between a few students and campus police when Allen went to the administration building to talk with the chancellor, on February 12, the demonstrations ended with the chancellor's statement. The next week the students' attention shifted to the conclusion of the conspiracy trial in Chicago. To some students and faculty, the prosecution of the "Santa Barbara Nineteen" for participation in the Bill Allen protests was directly analogous to the prosecution of the "Chicago Seven" for their participation in the demonstrations in Chicago during the week of the Democratic National Convention.[12]

Two weeks after the Bill Allen controversy, on February 25, UCSB students burned down the nearby Isla

12. This description of the Allen controversy is based on my own observations and notes, on a careful analysis of the events reported in *El Gaucho*, and on newspaper reports in the *New York Times* and in the *Santa Barbara News-Press*.

Vista branch of the Bank of America.[13] Soon after this violent protest took place, an extensive survey of students' political attitudes and behavior was instituted. This survey included several questions about the Bill Allen controversy.[14]

The survey indicated solid student support of the Bill Allen protests. About 63 percent of the students thought the administration was unresponsive to the petition for an open hearing, 67 percent supported Allen's attempt to change the decision to fire him, and 54 percent of those with an opinion thought Allen was right to encourage rallies and demonstrations in his behalf. With respect to student participation in the governance of the uni-

13. The bank-burning culminated two evenings of sporadic violence against property and police in Isla Vista. On Tuesday, February 24, 1970, Isla Vista street people and UCSB students confronted police who were attempting to arrest two residents of Isla Vista. That evening demonstrators started fires in trash cans, broke the windows of several realty companies and the Bank of America branch. The next day, after a speech by William Kunstler and a forcible arrest of a former student, enraged students and street people drove the police out of the business district, vandalized the realty companies, destroyed a police car, and burned the bank. For more details see the text below and Winthrop Griffith, "The Isla Vista War—Campus Violence in a Class by Itself," *New York Times Magazine*, August 30, 1970.

14. The survey was administered to a random sample of 36 small classes and discussion sections of large classes during "dead week" of the winter quarter, about two weeks after the bank burning. The teachers usually permitted the questionnaires to be passed out in class, but seldom permitted the students to use class time to fill out the questionnaire. The classes were contacted at subsequent meetings and the filled-out questionnaires collected. About two-thirds of the questionnaires were returned. A detailed comparison of sample and population characteristics is not yet available, but a preliminary analysis suggests that this sample is at least as accurate as the 1968–69 survey.

versity, 69 percent wanted student representatives to be able to vote in the academic senate and 66 percent wanted representatives to vote in department meetings. Table 4 reports the views of militant and conservative students on these items. By wide margins, the militants were more favorable to Allen and supported more student participation. The data in Table 4 thus clearly validates the militancy item. It is important to emphasize that the war in Vietnam was not an issue in any of these protests.

THE TEST VARIABLES

In the analysis of the relation of Vietnam disaffection to student militancy, the effects of six other explanatory variables will be quantified and controlled. These test variables are attitudes favorable to Black Power, complaints about the university, three social statuses (religion, father's occupation, and student's sex) and an index of predisposition toward militancy based on these attributes.

Attitudes toward Black Power

Attitudes about Black Power are gauged by responses to a direct question (see Table 5) about how the student reacts to Black Power. The direct nature of this question and its correlates insure both internal and external validity.[15]

15. For documentation of the importance of support for civil rights and demands for social justice as an explanation for student militancy, see the following sources: Robert H. Somers, "Mainsprings of the Rebellion," op. cit., p. 532; Seymour Martin Lipset and Philip G. Altbach, "Student Politics and Higher Education in the United States," in Seymour Martin Lipset, ed., *Student Politics* (New York: Basic Books, 1967), pp. 201–202; Edward E. Sampson, "Student Activism and the Decade of Protest," op. cit., pp. 25–26; Allen Barton, "The Columbia Crisis," op. cit., pp. 349–350; Jeanne H. Block, Nor-

TABLE 5—THE BLACK POWER ITEM AND ITS EXTERNAL VALIDATION

BLACK POWER AND CORRELATES	FAVORS BLACK POWER	DOESN'T	DIFFERENCE
The item:			
"Black Power" strikes different chords in different people. What is your reaction?			
Percent of total	55%	45%	—
External validation:			
Reads books by Blacks	42	25	17%
Activated by King's death	79	54	25
BSU sit-in justifiable	88	60	28
Favored take-over of computer center	79	35	44

Complaints about the University

The 1968–69 student survey included questions about several complaints that were then focuses of discontent—complaints about courses and professors, noise in Isla Vista, "slum" housing, restrictive rules and regulations, etc. Only two of these complaints are consistently linked to student militancy: (1) complaints about restrictive housing regulations (no pets allowed, no visitors after certain hours, no musical instruments, etc.), and (2) complaints about irrelevant courses (see Table 6). These two items have been combined to form a complaints index by simply counting the number of complaints. The resulting index was dichotomized by grouping together the 79 percent with one or two complaints versus the remaining 21 percent with none.

Again, this simple index fulfills the usual criteria for validity. The two items have face validity; the index is internally consistent since both items are similarly related to militancy and

ma Haan, and M. Brewster Smith, "Activism and Apathy in Contemporary Adolescents," in James F. Adams, ed., Understanding Adolescence (Boston: Allyn and Bacon, Inc., 1968), pp. 198–231; and Daniel Bell, "Quo Warranto," The Public Interest 19 (Spring 1970), pp. 53–68.

are intercorrelated; and it is externally valid. Students high on the index also complain about other matters. They are more likely to report that their living accommodations hinder studying (13 percent difference), that regulations hinder their social life (14 percent difference), that they don't enjoy most of their courses (25 percent difference), and that only a few of their professors are good teachers (16 percent difference).

Social statuses predisposing toward militancy

Religion

The students were asked to report their religious preference as Protestant, Catholic, Jewish, agnostic, or other. Inspection of the relationships between these categories and student militancy suggests that those who are not Protestant are more militant. Consequently, religion has been dichotomized into non-Protestant (Catholic, Jewish, agnostic, atheist, and other) which comprises 60 percent of the students, and Protestant, which comprises the remaining 40 percent. Of the 60 percent who are non-Protestant, about 40 percent say they are atheists, agnostics, or other. Most probably, many of these

TABLE 6—COMPLAINTS ABOUT THE UNIVERSITY

"If there are any regulations governing students where you live, what do you think of them?"*

(1) TOO RESTRICTIVE	(0) NOT TOO RESTRICTIVE	(0) NOT APPLICABLE	TOTAL
16%	43%	41%	100%

"On the whole, how relevant to your future would you say your courses so far have been?"

(1) NOT RELEVANT	(0) RELEVANT	TOTAL
76%	24%	100%

* Responses coded 1 indicate complaints about the University; those coded zero are not complaints.

students come from Protestant families, but are not now religious.[16]

Father's occupation

Student responses concerning their father's primary occupation were coded into four categories: (1) professional (and businessman), (2) white collar, (3) blue collar, and (4) other. Inspection of the relationships between these categories and student militancy suggests that children from the more affluent professional (and business) families are more militant. Consequently, father's occupation was dichotomized into *professional* (including businessman) and *non-professional* (white collar, blue collar, and other). About 37 percent have professional fathers; the remaining 63 percent, nonprofessional.[17]

16. For documentation about the role of religion in student militancy, see Richard Flacks, "The Liberated Generation," *The Journal of Social Issues* 23 (July 1967), pp. 52–75; Robert H. Somers, "Mainsprings of the Rebellion, op. cit., pp. 547–548; and Seymour Martin Lipset and Philip G. Altbach, "Student Politics and Higher Education in the United States," ibid., pp. 220–221.

17. For documentation of the effect of father's occupation on militancy, see Richard Flacks, "The Liberated Generation," p. 65; Lipset and Altbach, "Student Politics and Higher Education in the United States," op. cit., pp. 217–222; and Richard Flacks, "The

Student's sex

Since male students are more militant than the females, sex is included as a test variable.[18]

Predisposition toward militancy

Simultaneous control for the effects of attitudes about Black Power, complaints about the university, and the three social statuses, necessitates combining the latter into an index which we have called predisposition toward militancy. This has been done by simply counting the number of statuses

Revolt of the Young Intelligentsia," in Norman Miller and Rod Aya, *Revolution Reconsidered* (New York: The Free Press, 1970). Data at UCSB from the survey about the bank burning indicate that there is little difference in militancy between students from professional or managerial families. About 86 percent of the students from professional families are militant compared to 81 percent from managerial families. Blue collar, engineering, and white collar (clerical) fathers' occupations are associated with low militancy.

18. The finding that the male students are more militant than the females is consistent with past research on voting which has found men to be more politicized than women. I have not found any studies of student activists in which male-female differences in militancy have been noted. For the voting studies, see Bernard Berelson, Paul F. Lazarsfeld, and William N. McPhee, *Voting* (Chicago: University of Chicago Press, 1954), Appendix A.

predisposing a student toward militancy. The resulting index ranges from a score of zero (Protestant, non-professional father, female) to three (nonprotestant, professional father, male). The index has been dichotomized by inspecting the relationships between the index scores and student militancy and by considering natural inflections in the data. As a result, students with either zero or one predisposing status have been grouped together as *low predisposition* toward militancy; and those with two or three, as *high predisposition*. About 58 percent have a low predisposition in these terms; the remaining 42 percent, a high predisposition.[19]

PROCEDURE

Multivariate Analysis of Survey Data

To measure the independent effects of Vietnam disaffection and other determinants of student militancy, we employed the method of multivariate analysis developed by Coleman.[20] His continuous time, discrete space, stochastic model for multivariate analysis defines three types of parameters: the substantive effect parameters (a_i's), the random shock toward the positive category of the dependent attribute (r), and the random shock toward the negative category of the dependent attribute(s). The sum of these latter two parameters is called the total random shocks.[21] The total random shocks provide a measure of unexplained variation in the dependent attribute somewhat analogous to "unexplained variance" in traditional regression analysis.[22]

Elaboration Procedures

The causal effect of the explanatory variables is measured only if the causal ordering of the variables is correct.[23] In order to establish a correct causal ordering and to interpret the findings, the elaboration principles and procedures developed by Lazarsfeld and Hyman have been applied.[24] Quite simply, the pivotal independent variable, Vietnam disaffection, and the test variables are either antecedent in time or in structure, or they are more general concepts than the specific pivotal dependent variable, student militancy.[25] Consequently, it is more plausible to assume

19. For a similar index of political predisposition, see Paul F. Lazarsfeld, Bernard Berelson, and Hazel Gaudet, *The People's Choice*, 2nd ed. (New York: Columbia University Press, 1948).

20. James S. Coleman, *Introduction to Mathematical Sociology* (New York: The Free Press, 1964), chap. 6.

21. In this application of Coleman's method the effect parameters are identical to those that would be obtained from a dummy-variable regression analysis of this data. This is so because all of the variables have been dichotomized, and Boyle's weighting procedure has been used. See Richard Boyle, "Casual Theory and Statistical Measures of Effect: A Convergence," *American Sociological Review* XXI (December 1966), pp. 843–851. For the same reasons, the parameters are very similar to those that would be obtained by calculating partial dyx's using Somers' procedure. See Robert H. Somers, "Simple Measures of Association for the Triple Dichotomy," *Journal of the Royal Statistical Society*, Series A, 127, pp. 409–415.

22. The total random shocks quantify how much variation in the dependent attribute remains to be explained. For an insightful analysis of the meaning of random shocks, see J. Michael Polich, "The Coleman-Boyle Techniques and Multiple Regression Analysis," Senior Honors Thesis (Hanover, N.H.: Dartmouth College, June 5, 1967).

23. Coleman, op. cit., chap. 3.

24. See Herbert Hyman, *Survey Design and Analysis* (Glencoe: The Free Press, 1955), and Paul F. Lazarsfeld, "Evidence and Inference in Social Research," in Daniel Lerner, ed., *Evidence and Inference* (Glencoe: The Free Press, 1959).

25. These principles are explicated by Paul F. Lazarsfeld in his introduction to Hyman, ibid.

that these variables affect militancy than to assume the opposite. Whenever possible, the effects of the explanatory variables will be interpreted—that is, the reasons underlying these effects will be studied.[26]

ANALYSIS

Before the pivotal analysis of Vietnam disaffection and student militancy is presented, the social bases of disaffection from the war will be examined, along with some important correlates of student militancy.

Social Bases of Vietnam Disaffection

Recent research of the social bases of disaffection from the Vietnam war has been based on national cross-sections of the adult population.[27] Typically, these studies report that attitudes about the war do not decisively follow the usual lines of political cleavage in America.[28]

Social background is also indistinctly related to Vietnam attitude among students at UCSB. Table 7 reports these effects. Only two social statuses—non-Protestant religion and minority ethnic-

ity—have statistically significant zero-order effects.[29] Father's occupation, father's education, and student's sex are unrelated to disaffection. Differences in academic major have large effects, with more Letters and Science majors evidencing disaffection than students majoring in the performing arts, engineering, or physical education. There are no statistically significant relationships between being a "good student" (B or higher grade point average), or being an upperclassman, and attitude about the Vietnam war.

The latter finding, coupled with the earlier lack of relationship between student's sex and disaffection, suggests that differences in eligibility for the draft are not a major determinant of disaffection.[30] Clearly, men are more eligible for the draft than women, and upperclassmen are more threatened by the draft than freshmen or sophomores. But the zero-order effects of these variables are negligible and so are the effects when the two variables are simultaneously controlled. When this is done, the independent effects of these variables are both .017. For most students, disaffection from the war is linked to the perception that American intervention in Vietnam is a catastrophic mistake, and to demands for social justice and new domestic priorities.[31]

26. Lazarsfeld and Hyman point out that a relationship between an independent and a dependent variable is interpreted when an intervening test factor reduces the original relationship. For examples of interpretations, see ibid., chap. 7.

27. For examples of research on this topic, see Sidney Verba, et al., "Public Opinion and the War on Vietnam," *American Political Science Review* LXI (June 1967), pp. 317–333; Philip E. Converse, et al., "Continuity and Change in American Politics: Parties and Issues in the 1968 Campaign," *American Political Science Review* LXIII (December 1969), pp. 1083–1105; and Philip E. Converse and Howard Schuman, "Silent Majorities and the Vietnam War," *Scientific American* 222 (June 1970), pp. 17–25.

28. See the citations and my analysis of these relationships in "Rebellion and Repression and the Vietnam War," my other chapter in this volume.

29. The *Playboy* poll corroborates the zero-order relationship between non-Protestant religion and disaffection, as measured by wanting an immediate withdrawal from Vietnam. The September 1970 issue reports the following data (p. 184):

PULL OUT NOW—BY RELIGION

Protestant	27%
Catholic	30%
Jewish	51%
Other	40%
None	63%

30. For corroborating evidence, see Barton, "The Columbia Crisis," op. cit., pp. 348–349.

31. *Ibid.*, pp. 349–350.

TABLE 7—Effects of Social Background on Disaffection
(Coleman Effect Parameters)

	Zero-order Effect on Disaffection	Effect, Control War Mistake	Effect, Control Black Power	Effect, Control Both Variables
Social Statuses				
Non-Protestant religion or no affiliation	+.121	+.049	+.085	+.022
Minority ethnicity	+.123	+.106	+.068	+.061
Professional father	+.022	—	—	—
Father with some college	+.044	—	—	—
Males	+.020	—	—	—
Academic Statuses				
Letters and Sciences	+.242	+.157	+.238	+.178
"Good Student" (B or higher grade point average)	—.060	—	—	—
Upperclassman	+.017	—	—	—

Table 7 also clarifies the manner in which religion, ethnicity, and academic major affect disaffection. These variables are interpreted by the intervening variables (1) evaluating our involvement in Vietnam as a mistake, and (2) supporting Black Power. The first interpretive variable is related to perceptions of the government's ineffectiveness and to subsequent delegitimation of authority. It is measured by the standard Gallup poll (AIPO) Vietnam mistake item which is presented in Table 8 along with the marginal distributions for the UCSB students and the American public. These data indicate that more students evaluate our involvement as a mistake. The second interpretive variable is linked to demands for social justice and for a

greater emphasis on domestic priorities, as measured by the Black Power question described earlier. When the mistake item is controlled, the effect of non-Protestant religion is reduced by almost two-thirds, and the effect of academic major by about two-fifths. But when the Black Power item is controlled, these effects are reduced to a lesser degree, suggesting that for the majority of White students perceptions of governmental ineffectiveness and delegitimation more directly interpret the effects of social background than do demands for social justice and new domestic priorities.

The opposite pattern characterizes minority students. For these students, when attitudes about Black Power are controlled, the zero-order minority eth-

TABLE 8—An Item about the Vietnam War

"In view of the developments since we entered the fighting in Vietnam, do you think the U.S. made a mistake sending troops to fight in Vietnam?"

	Yes, Mistake	No	No Opinion	Total
UCSB Students (Dec. 1968)	70%	20%	10%	100%
Public (AIPO) (Oct. 1968)	54	37	9	100

FIGURE 1. Causes of disaffection

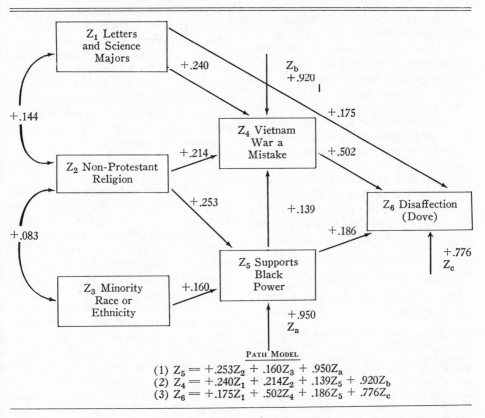

PATH MODEL

$$(1) \quad Z_5 = +.253Z_2 + .160Z_3 + .950Z_a$$
$$(2) \quad Z_4 = +.240Z_1 + .214Z_2 + .139Z_5 + .920Z_b$$
$$(3) \quad Z_6 = +.175Z_1 + .502Z_4 + .186Z_5 + .776Z_c$$

nicity effect on disaffection is reduced by one-half. But when attitudes about the war are controlled, this effect is virtually unaffected. This suggests that for minority students, demands for social justice and new domestic priorities more directly interpret their disaffection than do perceptions of governmental ineffectiveness and delegitimation. For neither minority nor majority students do social background variables (except academic major) directly influence disaffection.

The indirect linkages between social background and disaffection are made more explicit by the causal diagram presented in Figure 1. This diagram synthesizes three separate multivariate analyses of the causes of: (1) support for Black Power, (2) evaluating the war as a mistake, and (3) disaffection from the war.

The diagram clearly shows that for the UCSB students, religion and ethnicity do not directly affect disaffection, but operate via the two intervening variables. Academic major affects disaffection indirectly via its effect on the "Vietnam is a mistake" variable, but it also has a direct effect on disaffection. Through disaffection it eventually affects student militancy.[32]

32. In these applications the Coleman effect parameters are identical to path coefficients since each coefficient has been standardized by multiplying it by the ratio of the standard deviations of the independent and dependent variables. This enables the zero-

The Militancy Syndrome

Militancy is a pivotal characteristic that distinguishes one student from another. Early studies of militant students found them to be idealistic, intellectual young people committed to social change via nonviolent tactics.[33] Now they are sometimes characterized as unstable personality types ready to use deceit and violence to gain their ends.[34] In order to help clarify what the militant students are like today, some behavioral and attitudinal correlates of militancy will be described. This militancy syndrome has three aspects: (1) political and social attitudes, (2) life style, and (3) support for violent dissent.

Political and social attitudes

Table 9 reports the political and social attitudes of militant and conser-

---

order relationship (measured by Phi) between any two variables to be decomposed into direct and indirect effects. For more information about the path analysis of attributes, see Raymond Boudon, "A New Look at Correlation Analysis," in Hubert M. Blalock and Ann B. Blalock, *Methodology in Social Research* (New York: McGraw-Hill Book Company, 1968), pp. 216–220. The sizes of the direct and indirect effects of the three status variables on disaffection are below:

	PHI	DIRECT EFFECTS	INDIRECT EFFECTS
Letters and Science Majors	.321	.176	.145
Non-Protestant Religion	.226	.000	.226
Minority Ethnicity	.068	.000	.068

33. See Somers, "Mainsprings of the Rebellion," op. cit.; Lipset and Altbach, "Student Politics and Higher Education in the United States," op. cit.; Block, Haan, and Smith, "Activism and Apathy in Contemporary Adolescents," op. cit.; and Kenneth Keniston, "Notes on Young Radicals," *Change in Higher Education* 1 (Nov.-Dec. 1969), pp. 25–33.

34. Bell, "Quo Warranto," op. cit., pp. 65–66.

vative UCSB students. Like militant students in earlier studies, those at UCSB tend to support the New Left. The major surprise in these data, however, is the extent to which these beliefs are also held by conservative students. Similarly, idealism, as indicated by concern for underprivileged minorities and social problems, is much stronger among militants, but not uncommon among conservatives.

Life style

The life style of today's UCSB militants appears to differ from those described in earlier studies. The militants at UCSB are not more intellectual than the conservative students, as evidenced by data presented in Table 10.[35] When disaffection is controlled, the negative effect of militancy on good grades completely disappears.[36] Similarly, when disaffection is controlled, the negative effect of militancy on being a conscientious student is specified.[37] A further analysis (not shown in the table) demonstrates that when students are disaffected, there is a negative relationship between militancy and being a conscientious student (the difference is −14 percent). But when students are not disaffected, there is a positive relationship between militancy and being a conscientious student (the difference is +38). The weighted average of these effects (−.08) reported in

35. The earlier studies that found the activists to be more intellectual are Somers, "The Mainspring of the Rebellion," op. cit., p. 544, and Flacks. "The Liberated Generation," op. cit., pp. 69–70.

36. This means that the zero-order effect is explained by disaffection. See Lazarsfeld, "Evidence and Inference in Social Research," op. cit., pp. 129–131.

37. A relationship is specified when an antecedent test factor modifies an original relationship such that in one comparison there is a larger effect, and in the other, a smaller effect. See *ibid.*, pp. 128–129.

TABLE 9—POLITICAL AND SOCIAL ATTITUDES
OF MILITANT AND CONSERVATIVE STUDENTS*

POLITICAL AND SOCIAL ATTITUDES	MILITANT	CONSERVATIVE	DIFFERENCE	PERCENT OF TOTAL
New Left Politics				
Radical or Liberal	81%	33%	48%	60%
Supports Radical Union	41	0	41	19
America is an imperialist nation	84	44	40	58
Capitalism is largely responsible for the ills of American society	67	24	43	52
Vietnam war a mistake	95	76	19	84
Social Problems Orientation				
Supports civil rights	74	26	48	51
Supports Black Power	68	17	51	41
Supports Chicano Power	72	20	52	34
Supports ecological action	98	76	22	87

* Data from a survey about the burning of the Isla Vista branch of the Bank of America (March 1970).

Table 10 is not statistically significant. In sum, these data indicate that in terms of academic criteria, UCSB militant students are neither more nor less intellectual than the conservative students.

A second difference between the earlier student activists and today's UCSB militants is the involvement of the latter in the new sensibility of American society.[38] The new sensibility is a form of cultural radicalism which dictates that all realms of experience must be opened and explored.[39]

The militant students are definitely involved in the new sensibility, as evidenced by use of hallucinogens, approval of premarital sex, and interest in The New Consciousness, a program of confrontation and sensitivity training groups.

Earlier in this paper (Table 2) similar correlates between disaffection and drug usage were reported. But disaffection from the Vietnam war does not explain the relationship between militancy and the new sensibility. When disaffection is controlled (last column, Table 10), these effects of militancy are unchanged. This suggests that the new

38. For an earlier study of the new sensibility at UCSB, see Edward A. Suchman, "The 'Hang Loose' Ethic and the Spirit of Drug Use," *Journal of Health and Social Behavior* 9 (June 1968), pp. 146–155. Some of the data used from this study in later tables were reported in the pre-publication draft of Suchman's paper and not in the published version.

39. Daniel Bell describes the new sensibility in these terms: "What is celebrated is expression rather than idea, improvisation rather than text, sincerity rather than judgment. The psychedelic experience and the drug culture,

the search for the "high," and for extended awareness are the mass manifestations of this phenomenon. In this fierce anti-intellectualism, feeling and sentiment, not cognition, are considered more important. Education becomes not the transmission of learning but a search for 'meaningful identity' to be gained by 'dialogue,' 'encounter,' and 'confrontation.'" See Bell, "Quo Warranto," op. cit., p. 60.

TABLE 10—Life Style and Militancy

Life Style	Militant	Conservative	Difference	Effect, Control Disaffection
Intellectual Level				
Good grades (B or more)	35%	41%	— 6%	—.01
Conscientious student	71	75	— 5	—.08
Plans for graduate school	70	69	+ 1	+.03
Involvement in the New Sensibility				
Has smoked marijuana	61	21	+40	+.40
Has tried pep pills	38	8	+26	+.26
Has tried LSD	26	3	+23	+.26
Approves of premarital sex	78	50	+28	+.26
Interested in the New Consciousness*	62	38	+24	+.18
Personal Problems				
Unsatisfactory social life	12	25	—13	—.13
Feels lonely	58	57	+ 1	0
Often worries	69	65	+ 4	—.02
Worries about gossip	33	38	— 5	—.06
Worries about personal and world problems	56	52	+ 4	—.04

* Data from a survey about the burning of the Isla Vista branch of the Bank of America (March 1970).

sensibility is an intrinsic part of the new militancy.[40]

The militants' search for experience and subsequent drug usage does not imply that they are unstable personality types. Indeed, militants report fewer personal problems than do conservatives. When disaffection is controlled, militants are *less* likely to report an unsatisfactory social life or that they worry about gossip or personal and world problems.

Violence

After the Bill Allen controversy, many militant students at UCSB began to support and to participate in violent protests in Isla Vista. These demonstrations were directed against the police, the local real estate companies, and the Bank of America branch. On Tuesday afternoon, February 24, 1970, sheriff's deputies arrested two residents of Isla Vista, a student and a community organizer, who were standing on a street corner. A crowd began to gather. They tried to free the prisoners by pulling them away from the police and by immobilizing the patrol car (the keys were taken from the ignition, the

40. Marijuana smoking is a key aspect of the new sensibility. This is a serious problem because it implies a violation of a law, not because of the psychological consequences for the user. The data indicate that there is no association between using marijuana and the indicators of personal problems used in Table 10. The effects are below:

Unsatisfactory social life	—.051
Feels lonely	+.041
Often worries	—.030
Worries about gossip	—.114
Worries about personal and world problems	+.073
Average of effects	—.016

tires deflated, and gasoline poured on the tires and set afire). Police reinforcements put the fire out, and after a scuffle with the crowd they left with the prisoners. That evening several hundred students and street people protested this arrest by starting fires in trash cans and by breaking windows at real estate companies and at the Bank of America.

The next evening, after a speech by William Kunstler about the Chicago conspiracy trial and after a forcible arrest of a former student who was carrying a bottle of wine, about a thousand students went on a rampage. Police were stoned and driven from the business area, a patrol car was destroyed, real estate companies were vandalized, and the Isla Vista branch of the Bank of America was burned.[41] The precise causes of support for the burning of the bank cannot be analyzed here, but it is possible to describe the new relationship between student militancy and support for violent tactics, and the causes of the shift from nonviolence to violence.

41. This description of the bank burning is based on my own observations, discussions with students and colleagues, news reports from the UCSB radio station, a chronology of events prepared by *El Gaucho*, and newspaper reports in the *New York Times* and the *Santa Barbara News-Press*. For an interesting discussion of these events, see Richard Flacks and Milton Mankoff, "Revolt in Santa Barbara: Why They Burned the Bank," *The Nation*, March 23, 1970. The *Playboy* poll indicates that a minority of the student public would support such a protest, but the exact precentage is difficult to determine, given the response distributions below, reported in the September 1970 issue (p. 184):

VIOLENT DEMONSTRATIONS

Violence is unjustifiable under any circumstances	53%
Violence is justified only when provoked by authorities	33%
Violence is the only way to make the establishment respond	14%

Table 11 reports relevant data. Support for violence is divided into three dimensions: (1) perceptions of the ineffectiveness of nonviolence, (2) tolerance for violent dissent, and (3) support for the burning of the Isla Vista branch of the Bank of America. Each of these dimensions is gauged by two items. The table reports the percent of the students who agree with each item, the zero-order effect of militancy on each item, and the reduction in the zero-order militancy effect when various antecedent test variables are individually controlled. A large reduction in the zero-order effect means that the test variable explains a large part of the original relationship between militancy and violence.[42] That is, a test variable causes a shift from nonviolence to violence if the relationship between militancy and support for violence is reduced when the test variable is controlled. This principle of elaboration enables us to discern which of the numerous hypothetical explanatory variables in fact cause militant students to become violent.

The data indicate that many of the students think nonviolence is ineffective, and support violent dissent when grievances pile high and most leaders represent established authority. Active support for the bank burning is small, but nearly one-third say the burning of the bank was emotionally satisfying, and more than one-half say they would not help put out the fire, even if there was no personal danger.

The data also suggest that the previously nonviolent militant students now support violent tactics. They believe nonviolence is ineffective (the average of the two effects is .418), they have tolerance for violent dissent (the average of the two effects is .492), and they

42. Lazarsfeld, "Evidence and Inference in Social Research," op. cit., pp. 129–131.

TABLE 11—Violence and Militancy*

		Reduction in Zero-order Militancy Effect Caused by:						
Aspects of Violent Dissent	Zero-order Militancy Effect	Military Violence in Vietnam	Unresponsiveness of UCSB Administration and Academic Senate	Police Too Eager to Arrest for Marijuana	Demands for Social Justice (Pro Black Power)	Hearing Kunstler's Speech	America is an Imperialist Nation	Capitalism Causes Ills of American Society
Ineffectiveness of Nonviolence								
Aggressive students cannot bring about changes in the University by working through legitimate channels (46% agree)	.453	−.124	−.177	−.119	−.101	−.035	.000	−.043
Legitimate channels of protest—petitions and the like—are not effective means for bringing about change (50% agree)	.382	−.093	−.112	−.074	−.044	−.053	−.010	−.067
Tolerance for Violent Dissent								
When grievances pile high and most leaders represent established authority, then violence may be only effective response (47% agree)	.500	−.174	−.120	−.153	−.128	−.050	−.090	−.065
Americans should not completely and totally reject violence as a means of political dissent (42% agree)	.484	−.188	−.130	−.117	−.132	−.055	−.058	−.034
Support for the Burning of the Bank of America								
Forgetting about rational considerations, the burning of the bank was emotionally satisfying (30% agree)	.376	−.155	−.140	−.130	−.144	−.061	−.076	−.074
Would not help put fire out, even if there was no danger from the police, the demonstrators, or the fire (53% agree)	.451	−.162	−.170	−.123	−.130	−.065	−.095	−.064
Average Reduction in Militancy Effect	—	−.149	−.141	−.119	−.113	−.053	−.055	−.058

* Data from a survey about the burning of the Isla Vista branch of the Bank of America (March 1970)

also support the bank burning (the average of the two effects is .414).

Finally, these zero-order effects are substantially reduced by four of the seven test factors. The test variables that explain the shift from nonviolence to violence are (in order of their explanatory power): (1) agreeing that the military violence in Vietnam is worse than the violence of protesters in America (−.149 average reduction in the militancy effect), (2) the unresponsiveness of the administration and academic senate to student requests for participation in the governance of the University (−.141 average reduction), (3) the perception that the police are too eager to arrest students for smoking marijuana (−.119 average reduction), and (4) demands for social justice and new domestic priorities as indicated by support for Black Power (−.113 average reduction).

The three test variables that do not explain the shift to violence are "outside agitators" and the two indicators of New Left beliefs. Hearing Kunstler's speech reduces the militancy/violence linkage the least (it has the smallest explanatory power of the seven variables, −.051 average reduction). Moreover, the explanatory power of each of the two New Left beliefs is only slightly larger (−.055 average reduction for "America is imperialist" and −.058 for "capitalism causes the ills of American society").

These data strongly suggest that campus violence will not be reduced by barring controversial speakers from campuses or by demanding ideological conformity from teachers. Indeed, restrictions on free speech and academic freedom in the name of law and order seem likely to cause rather than prevent campus disorders.[43] The data also sug-

gest that if violent campus protests are to be prevented, the root causes of the shift to violence must be mitigated.

Campus Protests and the Vietnam War

Disaffection with the Vietnam war is a primary root cause of campus violence. When disaffection is high, campus protests are frequent, whether or not the protests are manifestly about the war or war-related issues. In the past, protests at UCSB were virtually devoid of violence. During the academic year 1969–70, however, both demonstrators and the police were ready to use violence.

Aggregate trends

Table 12 documents these trends in disaffection from the war, campus protests, and repression of protest at UCSB during the last three academic years. Disaffection from the Vietnam war, gauged by the number of students who are doves, has increased from 56 percent in 1967–68 to 87 percent in 1969–70. The trends of two important correlates of disaffection show similar increases. The number of students who evaluate the war as a mistake has increased by 33 percent, and the number who smoke marijuana (thereby breaking a law) has increased by 45 percent.[44]

This disaffection expresses itself in campus protests that are increasingly issueless and violent, and only tangen-

43. Restrictions on free speech and academic freedom were largely responsible for the Free Speech Movement at Berkeley. See almost any chapter in Lipset and Wolin, *The Berkeley Student Revolt.*

44. The UCSB students are considerably more likely to have smoked marijuana than the student public. The *Playboy* poll reports that 47 percent of all college students have smoked marijuana at least once, compared to 66 percent for the UCSB students, a 19 percent difference. The higher rate of marijuana usage at UCSB is probably a consequence of the higher rate of disaffection from the war. Like most usage of drugs, marijuana smoking is a form of retreatism, in this case in response to the anomie engendered by the war. See the discussion below and Robert K. Merton, "Social Theory and Anomie," in *Social Theory and Social Structure* (Glencoe: The Free Press, 1957), chap. 4.

TABLE 12—DISAFFECTION, CAMPUS PROTESTS, AND PUNITIVE ACTIONS
(UNIVERSITY OF CALIFORNIA, SANTA BARBARA, 1967–70)*

	1967–68	1968–69	1969–70	TREND
Disaffection and Correlates				
Dove	56%	74%	87%	+31%
Vietnam war a mistake	51	70	84	+33
Smoked marijuana at least once, thereby breaking a law	21	47	66	+45
Campus Protests Reported in EL GAUCHO				
Antiwar or war-related	50	6	7	—43
nonviolent, non-forceful	100	90	75	—25
Nonviolent, forceful	0	6	13	+13
Violent	0	4	12	+12
Total number of reported protests	(22)	(48)	(114)	(+92)
Indicators of Turmoil from University Records				
Fire bomb threats	(1)	(6)	(128)	(+127)
Broken windows	(0)	(2)	(50)	(+50)
Punitive Actions Reported in EL GAUCHO				
By the University administration	(0)	(0)	(6)	(+6)
By the police	(0)	(14)	(43)	(+43)

* The disaffection of the students in 1967–68 was gauged by data from Edward Suchman's survey of UCSB undergraduates. See Edward Suchman, "The 'Hang-Loose' Ethic and the Spirit of Drug Use," *Journal of Health and Social Behavior* 9 (June 1968), pp. 146–155. The 1969–70 disaffection data is from the survey about the burning of the Bank of America branch in Isla Vista (March 1970). The number of fire bomb threats was gleaned from UCSB fire department records. The number of broken windows was estimated by the UCSB chief of police. The events coded from *El Gaucho* in 1969–70 do not include Isla Vista III and therefore are very conservative estimates of police repressions.

tially about the war in Vietnam, the major cause of the discontent. During the 1967–68 academic year *El Gaucho,* the student newspaper, reported 22 student protests at UCSB.[45] Of these, 11 (50 percent) were explicitly about the war in Vietnam or other war-related issues. Confrontation and violent tactics were not used in any of these protests, which consisted of non-disruptive sit-ins, teach-ins, picket lines, rallies, marches, and petitions.

In contrast, during 1969–70, *El Gaucho* reported 114 protests, eight (7 percent) of which were explicitly about

45. The coding of the *El Gaucho* reports was done by Mr. Sandy Rhone, an undergraduate student in the UCSB sociology department. In 1967–68, there were reports of 6 non-forceful sit-ins, 5 teach-ins, 2 picket lines, 7 rallies, one march, and one petition.

the war or war-related issues. Seventy-five percent of the reported protests were nonviolent and non-forceful, a decrease of –25 percent. This decrease is compensated for by increases in forceful but nonviolent (confrontation) protests and by violent protests. During the academic year 1969–70, confrontation tactics—strikes and disruptions—were used in 13 percent of the reported protests. The remaining 12 percent were violent protests, as described above.[46]

46. During 1969–70, the detailed breakdown of reported protest events is as follows: *Nonforceful, nonviolent*—three sit-ins, one trash-in, 5 boycotts, 4 picket lines, 36 rallies, 20 marches, and 17 petitions; *forceful, nonviolent*—eight strikes, 7 disruptions; *violent events*—four severe violence to property events, 2 fire bombings, 3 vandalisms, and 4 window-breaking events.

Data from university records coroborate these trends toward violence. Fire bomb threats have increased from one during 1967–68 to 128 during 1969–70. Similarly, the number of windows broken in campus buildings has increased from none to about 50.

As might be expected, there has been a parallel increase in administration and police punitiveness. During 1967–68 *El Gaucho* reported no punitive actions by either the administration or the police. During 1969–70 there were reports of six punitive actions by the administration and 43 by police, sheriff's deputies, and the national guard.[47] Demonstrators and others were subjected to curfews, beatings, arrests, threats of violence, tear gas, thrown rocks, and gunshot; one student was killed.

Individual correlations

The relationship between disaffection and campus protests documented by these aggregate trends also holds true for individual students. Table 13 reports the relationship between the two pivotal variables, disaffection from the Vietnam war and student militancy. Students who are doves are considerably more militant; the zero-order effect is .383.

TABLE 13—DISAFFECTION AFFECTS
MILITANCY (1968–69)

	DOVES	HAWKS
Percent militant	76%	38%
	(252)	(32)

a_1 = zero-order effect of disaffection = .383
r = random shock toward militancy = .375
s = random shock toward
          conservatism = .242

47. During 1969–70, the reported academic and police punishments were as follows: six academic suspension events, one killing by the police, 7 threat of guns events, 8 beating events, 24 arrest events, one harassment event, 2 curfew events. These data exclude Isla Vista III and are conservative statements of police repressions.

The underlying model is quite simple. The events of the Vietnam war and our Indo-China policy produce severe strains for students who are doves. This engenders disaffection from the war which is expressed in militancy and in campus protests that often are not explicitly about the war.

This mechanism also can be conceptualized sociologically as anomic in character, in the Mertonian meaning.[48] Doves strongly hold a goal, namely, to *end* the war in Vietnam. But access to this goal is restricted; the war drags on. Many disaffected doves adapt to this situation by rebellion. They reject societal goals and means, and live in a youth counter-culture that is antiwar, anti-establishment, and involved in the new sensibility.

Before accepting this explanation of the linkage between the Vietnam war and campus protests, it is necessary to demonstrate that the pivotal relationship between disaffection and militancy is causal rather than spurious, and to show that contradictory explanations of student militancy are incorrect.[49]

Table 14 reports the effect parameters for four multivariate analyses that corroborate the causal relationship between disaffection and militancy. In each of these analyses, three antecedent test variables are simultaneously controlled: (1) demands for social justice and new domestic priorities, indicated by support for Black Power, (2) complaints about the university, and (3) a variable of social status. In the first analysis, the social status is religion; in the second, father's occupation; third, student's sex; and finally, an index comprised of all three statuses.

48. Merton, op. cit., chap. 4
49. A relationship between an independent and a dependent variable is casual if it does not disappear when a range of antecedent test variables is controlled. If it disappears, then the relationship is spurious. See Lazarsfeld, "Evidence and Inference in Social Research," op. cit., pp. 129–132.

TABLE 14—DISAFFECTION AFFECTS MILITANCY, CONTROL BLACK POWER, COMPLAINTS, AND SOCIAL BACKGROUND (1968–69)

VARIABLES	EFFECTS WHEN STATUS IS NON-PROTESTANT RELIGION	EFFECTS WHEN STATUS IS PROFESSIONAL FATHER	EFFECTS WHEN STATUS IS MALE	EFFECTS WHEN STATUS IS Ad Hoc INDEX	AVERAGE OF EFFECTS
Doves	.187	.211	.222	.162	.195
Black Power	.283	.280	.263	.284	.277
Complaints	.088	.096	.118	.102	.101
Status Variable	.083	.118	.150	.142	.123
Random Shock toward Militancy	.155	.237	.182	.182	.189
Random Shock toward Conservatism	.132	.058	.065	.128	.096

The last column in Table 14 presents averages of the effects across the four analyses from the 1968–69 survey. Disaffection from the war consistently has the second largest direct effect on student militancy ($\overline{X} = .195$). Only the effect of the closely related variable, support for Black Power, is larger ($\overline{X} = .277$).[50] Taken together, disaffection from the war and demands for social justice and new domestic priorities account for about half of the variation in student militancy. The random shocks are further reduced by the effects of the other test variables. The

50. During the 1968–69 academic year, Black Power was a very salient issue on campus because it was the first year of the E.O.P. program which brought 200 new Black students to campus. This probably accounts for the larger effect of this variable. During 1969–70, disaffection is clearly the major determinant of militancy. When disaffection from the war, support for Black Power, and complaints about the unresponsiveness of the University are simultaneously controlled, the effects on militancy are as follows:

a_1 = disaffection from the war = .465
a_2 = support for Black Power = .187
a_3 = unresponsiveness of University = .223
r = random shock toward militancy = .168
s = random shock toward conservatism = .000 (—.043)

average of the effects of complaints about the University is .101, and for the predisposing status variables, .123.

Contradictory explanations

In response to the recent turmoil at UCSB, moderate and conservative members of the academic senate have created a new organization called Faculty for Academic Responsibility (FAR). This organization was formed to counter "certain groups of faculty and students who seek to impose their ideologies on the academic community by undemocratic, indeed by uncivilized, means."[51] Some of the specific areas of concern are the political involvement of faculty, student/faculty polarization, and the role of the student newspaper in contributing to the latter. The leadership in FAR appears to believe that the recent disorder and violence at UCSB was caused by radical professors and students who "cultivate the mystique of violence and fantasize about revolution."[52]

51. This statement of principles about FAR was reported in the *Isla Vista Viewpoint*, Friday, July 31, 1970, p. 2.
52. This phrase was part of the testimony to the Santa Barbara Citizen's Commission on Civil Disorder by a leader of FAR. It was reported in *ibid*. In his testimony the speaker also stressed that the students as a group were distressed about the war.

The empirical adequacy of the FAR explanation is questionable, on the basis of data presented in Table 11 concerning the unimportance of New Left beliefs as an explanation of the shift to violence. Further, the FAR explanation logically implies a *shift* in the social and political composition of faculty and students, since disorder and violence have become commonplace at UCSB only during 1969–70, and since according to FAR, "irresponsible" (i.e., radical and liberal-left) professors and students cause these events. However, the data do not support such a shift. Table 15 reports the three-year trends in the political and social composition of faculty and students. Faculty politics are gauged by mail ballots on proposed antiwar legislation sponsored by either radical or liberal-left faculty in the academic senate. During 1967–68 the issue voted on was war-related research and support for students who staged a non-forceful sit-in against Dow recruiters; the next year, legislation to withdraw academic credit from ROTC; and in 1969–70, a strong resolution against the invasion of Cambodia and support for student antiwar demonstrators. Each year about 30 percent of the academic senate votes in favor of these resolutions.[53]

Table 15 also conclusively documents no gross change in student recruitment, but a strong shift to the left politically. But the latter is more likely a consequence of antiwar disaffection and police repression than an independent determinant of campus protests.

Since there has been no change in the number of radical or liberal-left professors, and no overall change in the social and political character of the students except for the very large (+31 percent) increase in the students' disaffection from the war, this pivotal variable provides a more general and empirically adequate explanation for the increase in campus turmoil than does the FAR hypothesis.[54]

Summary and Implications

This survey analysis has shown that disaffection from the Vietnam war is a pivotal determinant of student dissent even in campus protests that do not explicitly concern the war. At present, about 87 percent of the UCSB undergraduates are disaffected from the war and from other important aspects of American society.

53. The percent voting favorable is even less on purely radical resolutions. For example, a resolution in support of William Allen sponsored by a radical professor and opposed by the majority leader of the UCSB senate gathered only a 14 percent favorable vote in a mail ballot (Resolution E, April 23, 1970). When the resolution is jointly liberal-left and radical, it will draw about one-third of the senate votes. For example, see resolution A, April 23, 1970, which supported Jerry Rubin's right to speak at UCSB and criticized the chancellor. The vote was 34 percent in favor. Consequently, in 1969–70, the radical and liberal-left block is comprised of about 14 percent radical and about 20 percent liberal-left professors. This estimate of the number of radical professors is a little lower

than the estimate for the preceding year. In 1968–69, about 18 percent of the senate voted in favor of setting up courses in guerrilla warfare for Blacks, the NLF, etc. For details, see addendum #5 to the call (5/8/69) for reconsideration when reconvened (5/27/69), minutes, UCSB academic senate.

54. Marijuana smoking, which is in part determined by disaffection from the war, probably exacerbates the disaffection and protest because it is illegal. Smoking marijuana makes a person a law-breaker and engenders a fear of the police, which increases the delegitimation of authority. Edward Suchman concluded his report on the spirit of drug use at UCSB by the following insightful observation, with which I totally agree: "Surely, it should be possible to express one's disapproval of marijuana and to seek its control without making its use a crime against society." See Suchman, "The 'Hangloose' Ethic and the Spirit of Drug Use," op. cit., p. 155.

TABLE 15—THE POLITICAL AND SOCIAL COMPOSITION OF FACULTY AND UNDERGRADUATES
(UNIVERSITY OF CALIFORNIA, SANTA BARBARA, 1967–70)*

	1967–68	1968–69	1969–70	DIFFERENCE
Faculty				
Votes for strong antiwar resolutions in academic senate	30%	27%	33%	+3%
Students				
Militancy-related Statuses				
Letters and Science majors	95	95	95	0
Father's occupation (income more than $20,000)	30	—	30	0
Non-Protestant (of those with affiliation)	30	33	31	+1
Males	48	50	51	+3
From militant counties (L.A., Alameda, Monterey)	42	41	39	−3
From conservative counties (Tri-counties and Orange)	23	23	23	0
Out-of-state residents	5	5	5	0
Political Attitudes				
Militant (of total)	—	67	64	−3
For Black Power	—	58	57	−1
Radical or liberal	—	50	66	+16

* The faculty votes were reported in the minutes of the UCSB Academic Senate; the characteristics of the students were reported by the UCSB Office of Analytical Studies; and the students' attitudes in 1969–70 were gauged by the survey about the burning of the Isla Vista branch of the Bank of America (March 1970).

The students express their disaffection in militancy and in subsequent campus protests that are increasingly only tangentially about the war, the primary source of their disaffection. At UCSB about two-thirds of the students are now militant. About half of the students now think nonviolence is ineffective, and will support violent protests under certain circumstances. These percentages are considerably higher for the militant students.

Four variables largely explain the militants' shift from nonviolence to violence. These are: (1) the military violence in Vietnam, (2) perceived unresponsiveness of the university, (3) police harassment for smoking marijuana, and (4) the militants' desire for social justice and new domestic priorities. New Left beliefs and "outside agitators" do not explain this shift to violence.

At UCSB disaffection from the war provides the most powerful explanation for the change in student militancy and campus protests. The level of disaffection has increased tremendously over the three academic years studied, while the levels of the test variables and the political and social characteristics of the faculty and students have remained constant. These are the parameters of the system. It is the change in the level of disaffection that has caused the change in the frequency of campus protests and a decline in the quality of intellectual life.

An end to the war in Vietnam will undoubtedly decrease campus turmoil, but it is not likely to end the rebellion of the younger generation. For many, the war has highlighted the unresponsiveness and ineffectiveness of American political and social institutions, and this has led to delegitimation of authority.[55] Until the political system and the universities are more responsive to the goals of the students and more

effective in their attempts to bring about social justice and peace, there will be campus protests.[56]

---

55. For a clear statement of the effectiveness/legitimacy hypothesis, see Seymour Martin Lipset, *Political Man* (Garden City, N.Y.: Doubleday and Co., 1960), pp. 77–96. This hypothesis can explain why students rebel in other countries where the war in Vietnam is not an issue. In these other rebellions, the sources of the ineffectiveness and delegitimation are different) viz. in South America the military elites might be a problem; in France, the opportunity structure might have been the issue, etc.); but the consequences are the same—student protests.

56. For an insightful discussion of the transformation of unresponsive societies, see Amitai Etzioni, *The Active Society* (New York: The Free Press, 1968), chap. 18.

21

Campus Conflict as Formative Influence

By WILLIAM R. MORGAN

William R. Morgan, Ph.D., is an assistant professor of sociology, Indiana University. His published writings include experimental studies of bargaining behavior and empirical work on student and Black protest. He is currently preparing a monograph detailing the argument sketched in this chapter.

This chapter is based on research conducted for the author's doctoral dissertation, "Student Protests and Racial Disorders: Formative Influence Relations" (Department of Sociology, The University of Chicago, 1970). Valuable advice during this research came from Richard Flacks, Jack Sawyer, and Fred L. Strodtbeck. Research expenses were paid from grant MH-14305 and a predoctoral fellowship, both from the National Institute of Mental Health. Whitney Pope and Austin T. Turk made helpful comments on the draft of this paper.

We seek the establishment of a democracy of individual participation, governed by two central aims: that the individual share in those social decisions determining the quality and direction of his life; that society be organized to encourage independence in men and provide the media for their common participation.

—Tom Hayden, Students for a Democratic Society, 1962[1]

IN the early days of the current American student movement, its principal goals were encompassed in the SDS call for participatory democracy. This condition was sought as an end in itself, as suggested in the above quotation. In addition, however, participatory democracy was seen as the essential precondition for resolving the various American injustices in internal and external relations. The campuses, in turn, were seen as the starting place for the development of participatory democracy.

In retrospect, we know that the student movement has proceeded in diverse directions since the drafting of the Port Huron Statement, excerpted from above. Its political ideology has become more revolutionary. The initial sociopolitical emphasis has been supplemented by important sociocultural dimensions. For various reasons, radical students increasingly have given up participation in protest demonstrations for a more self-encompassing state of protest—membership in campus "counter-cultures,"[2] where students and non-

students live and assert the virtues of a life style in extreme opposition to conventional American values. Highly-publicized acts of property violence, engaged in by a very few, and at best incompletely approved by the majority of the radical population, have colored the political impact of the radical movement. The fate of the movement, as it is known to members—including its probable duration, its course, and the extent to which it will reshape various American institutions—is highly uncertain.

Of principal interest in this chapter is an examination, not of where the movement is going, but what it has left behind. In particular, we are concerned with the ways in which campus protests may have transformed the internal political organization of the institutions where they occurred. The main thesis is that the student protests of the 1960's, and the campus response to them, represent the precursors of more formalized influence relations of students to administrators and faculty.

Because of these protests, administrators and faculty are paying a great deal more attention than they did five years ago to students' own statements of their interests. Instructional and curricular reforms, often largely student-defined, have hastened. There has been increased receptivity to direct student participation in university-wide policy formation, at all levels, as well as in the more conventionally-defined student affairs policies. This increased university recognition of student opinion and sharing of decision-making is a turn of events quite consistent with the early activist goals of participatory democracy. Paradoxically, however, the current, more revolutionary-minded radicals often see this reform either as unwelcome or irrelevant. For the most part it is the mainstream, formerly inactive students who are now benefiting

1. Tom Hayden, "The Port Huron Statement," in Paul Jacobs and Saul Landau, eds. *The New Radicals: A Report with Documents* (New York: Vintage, 1966), p. 152.

2. Theodore Roszak, *The Making of a Counter Culture* (Garden City, N.Y.: Anchor, 1969). For an assessment of the utility of this construct, see J. Milton Yinger, "Contraculture and Subculture," *American Sociological Review* 25 (October 1960), pp. 625–635.

from the trend toward greater student participation.

FORMATIVE INFLUENCE

What is it about campus disorders that has brought about this change? They represent a type of formative influence, or non-institutionalized bargaining, whereby a previously inactive, unpoliticized group (in this instance students) act upon their discontent in an effort to win concessions from authorities (in this instance administrators). To the extent such a newly active set of partisans is successful, their influence relationship with the authority becomes more symmetric. A mutual recognition develops that influence can also flow from partisans to authorities, not just vice versa as in the past.[3] The attainment of such mutuality is an essential requisite for the development of cooperative bargaining, defined elsewhere as the attainment of joint agreements through mutual adjustment of conflicting expectations.[4]

During this formative period the activities of the contending parties may not appear fully rational when contrasted with the formal procedures and "rules of the game" followed in more institutionalized bargaining settings, yet as a recurrent form of social behavior non-institutionalized bargaining possesses a pattern of its own. Exactly what this pattern is has remained elusive, as was pointed out in a recent review of conflict resolution research. As stated there, ". . . the institutionalization of social decisions and of social conflict resolution is only a crust over the great ambiguities of non-institutionalized bargaining—bargaining that starts from scratch and knows no overarching principles or third parties."[5]

Probably the most basic characterization is that there are few rules of fair play delimiting the range of acceptable tactics, as in formalized bargaining. If the authorities' aim is to preserve the status quo and thus to avoid making concessions, their primary strategy will be to ignore partisan influence attempts as much as possible, to prevent the latter from gaining a semblance of recognition as bargaining equals. Partisans, in order to gain this recognition and have their demands acted upon, will create a situation sufficiently uncomfortable to the authorities that they cannot be ignored.

If eventually some form of negotiations do get underway, there are no guidelines to prevent all kinds of what experienced bargainers would refer to as "bad faith" practices. Without a fixed contract period and agenda or some analogous arrangements, neither side is able to make a rational assessment of what are just demands and concessions. For example, partisans, perhaps feeling that by their pressuring they have worked the authorities into an appeasement posture, may respond to each small concession begrudgingly granted by authorities with a new demand instead of agreeing to one set of concessions to extend over a definite period of time. Authorities, however, may renege on terms of agreement, using the justification that the concessions had been made under illegitimate duress. Additional antagonisms are liable to develop during these serial

3. A partisan-authority influence model is developed more fully in William A. Gamson, *Power and Discontent* (Homewood, Ill.: Dorsey Press, 1968).

4. William R. Morgan and Jack Sawyer, "Bargaining, Expectations, and the Preference for Equality over Equity," *Journal of Personality and Social Psychology* 6 (June 1967), pp. 139–149.

5. Elizabeth Converse, "The War of All Against All: A Review of the Journal of Conflict Resolution, 1957–1968," *Journal of Conflict Resolution* 12 (December 1968), p. 523.

negotiations. They arise partly because the negotiations tend never to reach a natural ending point at which to climax and cool off and partly because there are no accommodative provisions to "leave room for bargaining," each successive demand and concession generally being cast as a "take-it-or-leave-it" offer.

The absence of any restrictions on who can participate in the negotiations complicates formative influence relations. Deadlocks occur quite frequently because the parties may refuse to consider seriously each other's offers when they anticipate that they will win support of a critical third party. By contrast, the voluntary agreement to limit negotiations to two parties, avoiding all third-party arbitration, helps to prevent deadlocks.

The force impelling these pseudo-negotiations onward is usually some form of ongoing protest activity. A fuller discussion of these activities, to be called negative inducements, will be presented later. The point now is to contrast the atmosphere of tension and uncertainty prevalent during these ongoing activities, such as a series of student sit-ins, with the situation of calm urgency created by the more distant and impersonal strike deadline of formalized labor/management negotiations. In the formal rules of contemporary collective bargaining, the strike deadline is the critical parameter that negotiators keep in mind in moving toward an agreement.[6] This deadline is not a threat in the sense that a strike is contingent on some particular course of action by the other, but rather it is contingent on not having reached agreement by a particular time. It is well to keep in mind, however, how industrial strikes began as relatively spontaneous

workers' protests and only slowly became institutionalized and legalized as the prime influence mechanism of labor unions, and a basic right of workers.[7]

The likelihood of institutionalized bargaining continuing between parties over an extended period of time is low. For most parties the energy expended in working out these complexities is drawn too heavily from other essential activities so that a yearning for a return to "normalcy" often eventuates in the voluntary acceptance of a more workable, formalized influence relationship. But in addition to this tendency toward voluntary acceptance, there is a built-in dynamic in these negotiations toward more formalized influence relations. Each act of gaining a concession is also a gain in prestige, reducing this difference between partisans and authority, and as a result each subsequent concession is gained a little more easily. As the prestige differential continues to decrease, a form of mutuality develops that allows for the working of joint problem-solving approaches at least within a limited set of decision areas. Of course, with the antagonisms and uncertainties inherent to these formative influence relations there is likely to be a great deal of "slippage," and the interventions by strong third parties may change the outcome entirely.

There are two basic considerations in applying this formative influence model to campus disorders. The first is to examine the extent to which the activity surrounding protests does in fact resemble a form of negotiations. The second is to assess any indications of a movement toward more formalized influence relations. In the survey results that follow, an effort has been made to offer evidence on both these concerns.

6. Robert M. Stevens, *Strategy and Collective Bargaining Negotiations* (New York: McGraw Hill, 1961).

7. Arthur M. Ross, "The Natural History of the Strike," in Arthur Kornhauser, Robert Dubin, and Arthur M. Ross, eds., *Industrial Conflict* (New York: McGraw Hill, 1954).

THE ANTI-RECRUITING
PROTEST SURVEY

During the 1967–68 academic year there occurred a large number of student protests against allowing war-related recruiting on campus. So numerous were these protests, along with other antiwar demonstrations, that one university administrator was led to assert that the Vietnam war was being fought on two fronts: one in Southeast Asia and the other on American university campuses.[8] Approximately one of every four accredited four-year colleges and universities in the United States had an organized student protest against armed services recruiting. One of every five had a protest against recruiting by either Dow Chemical Company, as the manufacturers of napalm, the CIA, or some other war-related agency.[9] At a majority of these schools the protests were restricted to mild demonstrations of moral witness, while at the others militant students purposely disrupted recruiting efforts in hopes of bringing about a policy of banning recruiters from campus. These students justified their use of direct action as a means of compelling non-cooperation with an alleged illegal war effort, in view of the additional belief that allowing these recruiters, along with other activities, made their schools guilty of complicity in American imperialism.

Administrators based their unwillingness to ban war-related recruiters on three points. First, they stated that

8. Cox Commission Report, *Crisis at Columbia* (New York: Random House, 1968), p. 10.

9. Richard E. Peterson, *The Scope of Organized Protest in 1967–1968* (Princeton, N.J.: Educational Testing Service, 1968), p. 14.

such a ban on a particular set of recruiters would be a violation of the free speech policy of keeping the campus open to all outsiders. Second, they said that it would infringe on the rights of those students wishing to see the recruiters. Finally, they expressed the norm that the use of coercion by students was an unacceptable means of influence on campus.

In terms of social research objectives, the widespread occurrence of these demonstrations provided the opportunity for a controlled study of the dynamics of student protests. Their occurrence at a large and varied set of schools enabled the use of statistical controls for institutional variables known previously to affect the nature of protest activity. The overall uniformity of the protest issue across schools enabled an assessment of the impact of varying qualities of protest and aftermath activity on a specific institutional policy consideration, on-campus recruiting. Finally, the occurrence of most of these protests at one period in time, the fall months of October through December, enabled an examination in late May of post-demonstration changes that took place within a roughly equal time interval, and under similar historical circumstances.

Preliminary information on the anti-recruiting protests was obtained from a large number of newspaper accounts, compiled by a professional newsclipping agency and a national student press organization. Questionnaires were mailed in late May to persons at the protest institutions identified from the articles. Schools with demonstrations in the fall, but which were known also to have had anti-recruiting demonstrations during the previous year, were excluded, as were any schools where demonstrations did not occur until after December. This made it possible to assess the impact of demonstrations and the development of conflict over a constant time period, roughly that of one academic year.

At the same time, a general questionnaire on demonstrations and student affairs was mailed to a set of schools where no anti-recruiting demonstrations had taken place. These schools had been selected to match with a representative sub-set of the protest schools on institutional characteristics —academic quality, total enrollment, type of control, and regional location— previously shown to predict administration liberalism.[10] This matching enabled an assessment of protest activity relatively independent of variations in response predisposition due to administrative liberalism.

The questionnaires called mostly for factual information, but because judgment and selective recall were involved in the responses, an effort was made to get a variety of viewpoints on the demonstrations. At least one administrator, one faculty member, and two students from each school were mailed a questionnaire, each being told that others at their school were receiving the same form. Whenever possible, persons identified in the newspaper articles as prominent participants in the demonstrations or their aftermath were selected. If no specific names were available, questionnaires were sent to the dean of students or similar officer, to a social science faculty member identified in his school catalogue or professional directory interest listing as someone likely to be concerned with student affairs, and to students affiliated with the campus newspaper or student government.

10. Paul F. Lazarsfeld and Wagner Thielens, Jr. *The Academic Mind* (New York: Free Press, 1958); E. G. Williamson and John L. Cowan, *The American Student's Freedom of Expression* (Minneapolis: University of Minnesota Press, 1966).

The overall institutional response was high—96 percent of the colleges and universities surveyed returned at least one questionnaire, giving a total of 106 protest schools and 26 matched nonprotest schools for analysis. The individual response rates varied from 59 percent for administrators, to 42 percent for faculty, and 38 percent for students, yielding totals over the 132 schools of 118 administrators, 73 faculty, and 136 students. Response agreement within schools was generally high, with disagreements for the most part occurring randomly among the respondents. The major exception was that administrators consistently gave lower estimates of protest size than either faculty or students. An analysis of response bias (which cannot be reported here) suggested that information could reliably be pooled into composite school scores. The procedure wherever possible was to average responses on each item or, in the case of disagreement on certain open-ended questions, to select the response giving the maximum amount of information. The results reported below are based on these composite scores.

NEGATIVE INDUCEMENT EFFECTS

In terms of non-institutionalized bargaining, the critical dimension of an anti-recruiting demonstration is the extent to which it represented a negative inducement to administrators. Negative inducements are efforts to win concessions from authorities by making the maintenance of the status quo appear to be more costly than granting the concession. For example, holding a sit-in could be a negative inducement if it communicated to the university authorities the likelihood of continuing disorders with respect to the particular grievance, or the likelihood of increasing support among students on the particular grievance. These prospects might be undesirable to authorities for several reasons, but especially if the apparent inability to control a student disorder would result in loss of support from major financial or political backers.

The main goal of authorities in response to negative inducements would be one of avoidance—to prevent or stop, whichever may be the case, the undesirable state of affairs. In the context of anti-recruiting demonstrations, one preventive response open to administrators was to place new restrictions on on-campus recruiting, as the activists sought. Another possibility was to place new regulations on demonstration conduct. The common sense expectation is that administrators would have made one response or the other, but certainly not both, depending on how "permissive" or how "tough" were their attitudes toward student activists. Surprisingly then, at least from this viewpoint, the stronger the protest activity,

TABLE 1—POLICY CHANGES DURING 1967–68 FOR SCHOOLS WITH DIFFERENT
LEVELS OF ANTI-RECRUITMENT PROTEST ACTIVITY

POLICY CHANGE	PROTEST LEVEL		
	NO PROTESTS	ORDERLY PROTESTS	CIVIL DISOBEDIENCE PROTESTS
New restrictions on on-campus recruiting	19% (26)[a]	33% (70)	61% (33)
New regulations on demonstrations	23% (26)	37% (70)	42% (33)

[a] Number of schools on which percentage is based. Not included in this table are three schools with missing data.

the more likely administrators were to make both forms of preventive response (Table 1). Administrators at schools which had protests involving organized civil disobedience subsequently put new restrictions on recruiting twice as often as at schools with orderly demonstrations, and three times as often as at schools with no demonstrations. Organized civil disobedience was operationally defined as the refusal to obey directives from police or administrators by more than 10 demonstrators. Usually this involved some form of sit-in or human blockade at the recruiting site. Strongly associated with the occurrence of organized civil disobedience were the total number of demonstrators and the extent to which campus activities were interrupted by the protest activity.

The implementing of demonstration rules appears less strongly related to the intensity of protest activity than does the changing of recruiting policy, based on Table 1. New rules were announced in the aftermath of orderly demonstrations almost as often as after the demonstrations involving civil disobedience. Further analysis, however, revealed that this was mainly because the orderly protests were more likely than the civil disobedience protests to have occurred at schools with no prior history of demonstrations. These schools consequently were less likely to have in existence any demonstration rules, and thus were more likely locations for the implementation of new regulations as a preventive response.

An examination of the content of the changes enacted reveals more clearly the overall preventive nature of the administrative response. With respect to recruiting policy, administrators implemented restrictions at 44 (42 percent) of the 106 schools with protests. At 34 of the schools the restrictions involved withdrawal of special location privileges from military recruiters. Military recruiters would no longer be able to set up tables in areas of high student density—the student union, the cafeteria, the halls of class buildings, and so on—but would instead have to share with all other recruiters the placement center or other more remote locations. Although these restrictions predominantly affected military recruiters, they took place nearly equally often at schools where the reason for the initial demonstrations was a recruiting visit from Dow Chemical Company. At 9 schools either some or all recruiters were temporarily banned until a new recruiting policy, usually the above, could be agreed upon. Finally, at one school all recruiting and placement services were dropped permanently. To some extent, these changes met the protestors' concerns about reducing complicity with the war effort, but in all cases the changes meant that disruptive recruiting protests could less easily take place.

An interesting off-campus effect was that in Washington, D.C., where isolated events are more likely to be viewed as an aggregate whole, there is some evidence that these changes may have been of more serious concern. This was particularly so for those worried about the growing antiwar sentiments at the time, and more specifically, about the increasing difficulties of attracting military recruits. In May the Pentagon released a list of 22 schools which had placed bans on military recruiters (only 4 of these schools were included in the present study). Following this, the Senate amended in June to its National Aeronautics and Space Administration appropriation bill a provision denying grants (NASA had given $100 million in grants to universities the previous year) to schools which bar military recruiters.[11]

Tighter regulations on demonstrations were put into effect at 50 (47 percent) of the 106 protest schools. The primarily preventive, versus punitive, nature of these changes is apparent from the fact that at most of the schools, 31 in all, the change involved a formalization of previously ad hoc or even non-existent procedures, with guidelines being set for permissible actions and penalties stipulated for their violation. At other schools, in 13 the tighter regulations took the form of warnings that the recurrence of a similar demonstration would result in severe disciplinary action, and in 6 schools, existing regulations became more strictly enforced. Thus at only this last minority of schools did the tighter regulations appear in any way to be punitive in nature.

The principal alternative explanation for this primarily conciliatory response to student activists is that any student-oriented policy change comes about to the extent that administrators hold permissive and liberal attitudes toward students. According to this argument, the more liberal the administrators at a particular institution, the more likely that changes sought by students will take place there, regardless of the nature of the protest activity and felt need for preventive measures. The matched sample analysis, however, indicated that there was a substantial protest effect independent of any possible response predisposition of administrators (Table 2). The protest institutions had nearly three times the rate of change in recruiting policy, and over twice the rate of change in demonstration regulations, as did the non-protest institutions matched on administration liberalism.

11. *Science* (June 21, 1968), p. 1320. Also reported in *College and University Business* (August 1968), p. 39.

TABLE 2—POLICY CHANGES OF TWO MATCHED GROUPS OF SCHOOLS
VARYING IN INCIDENCE OF PROTEST ACTIVITY[a]

DEGREE OF CHANGE	NON-PROTEST SCHOOLS	PROTEST SCHOOLS
	ON-CAMPUS RECRUITING	
No change	21	11
Restrictions	5	9
Ban, all recruiting	0	1
Ban, some recruiting	0	4
Total	26	26
	DEMONSTRATION REGULATIONS	
More liberal	1	0
No change	19	12
More restricted	6	14
Total	26	26

[a] Using a one-tailed, Wilcoxen two-sample rank test, the group differences on recruiting policy change are significant at the .001 level, and on demonstration regulations are significant at the .01 level. See: K. A. Brownlee, *Statistical Theory and Methodology in Science and Engineering* (New York: John Wiley & Sons, Inc., 1965), pp. 251–255.

A somewhat more refined argument for the importance of administration attitudes grants that the protests may have served to make administrators aware of the recruiting issue. The more disruptive the protest, the more administrators became aware of the issue, and hence the more likely they were to change. This argument, however, assumes administrators were previously unaware of the issue, an assumption which is contradicted by the evidence. According to the informants, prior to demonstrating, students had expressed their objections to recruiting through an average of 4 out of 7 communication channels asked about in the questionnaire—campus newspaper editorials, meetings reported in the campus newspaper, student government resolutions, petitions, leaflets, conversations with administrators, and conversations with faculty.

When administrators did respond to these student objections, they confined themselves to affirming existing recruiting policy and warning against interference during the impending recruiting visits. They were aware of student plans to hold a demonstration at 83 percent of the protest schools studied. The following statement released to students at a state university in the East, is representative of this approach.

College Placement activity is a service provided to students on our campus. . . . The agency personnel who come to visit us represent education, service to underdeveloped areas, and government, as well as business and industry. The place most convenient for students to have these contacts with these agency representatives is on the college campus. The opportunity for placement interviews should be equally available to all students.

Therefore, in keeping with the University's commitment to orderly procedures and the rights and freedoms of all, the following policies are set down regarding protest activity related to recruitment practices. . . .

The contrast between this statement and the following student position, a student government resolution passed prior to the demonstration at a private Eastern university, illustrates how far apart many students and administrators were on this issue:

Whereas we affirm the right of free speech by all parties on the campus, in that the expression of all views is a basic function of the university, and

Whereas we regard active recruitment as distinct from the basic principles of free expression in that it embodies an attempt to enlist individuals to engage in actions and accept principles which we, the student body, may regard as antithetical to the operations of a free society, and,

Whereas we regard the university's providing facilities for recruiting organizations as enabling the implementation of the principles of those groups, therefore, we . . . respectfully request that the University take the following actions:

First, that the University rescind permission of the above-mentioned organizations to recruit on campus, and

Second, that the University encourage representatives of the said organizations to engage in an open discussion with concerned members of the University community as an activity substituted for recruitment.

The net effect of this predemonstration communication seems to have been to polarize the positions of the two sides. The more students tried to communicate, probably the more convinced they became that allowing on-campus recruiting for an illegal war was wrong, and the more occasions there were for the administration to appear intransigent. In fact, the amount of communication on the issue correlated positively with the occurrence later of organized civil disobedience at the demonstrations (Table 3). When communication was low (0-2 channels used), civil disobedience occurred in 12 percent of the demonstrations, whereas when there was a medium (3-4) or high (5-7) amount of communication, the incidence of civil disobedience was 36 percent and 43 percent respectively.

TABLE 3—OCCURRENCE OF CIVIL DISOBEDIENCE BY AMOUNT OF PRIOR ISSUE DISCUSSION

Civil Disobedience	PRIOR DISCUSSION		
	Low	Medium	High
Yes	12%	36%	43%
No	88%	64%	57%
Total	100%	100%	100%
	(25)	(39)	(37)

In summary, the most meaningful communication, from the student position of bringing about a favorable response, was engagement in a disruptive protest. Even though administrators were well aware of the student position on the issue, it took this direct action to convince them that the students really "meant it," that they were willing to risk disobedience for the sake of their convictions, and might well do so again. It is in this sense that many of the protests represented effective negative inducements, a non-institutionalized form of student bargaining with administrators.

FORMALIZED INFLUENCE TRENDS

As suggested earlier, the movement toward formalized influence relations extends over a period of time considerably longer than any one protest and its aftermath events. The particular impact of each of these anti-recruiting protests in generating more formalized relations thus depended upon the degree of movement that had already occurred. At schools with a history of protest activity, protest effects were quite different from those at schools with no previous demonstrations. One might, for example, expect the immediate impact to be smaller at the previously active schools, but at the same time, some of their resultant institutional changes may represent more meaningful approaches to formalized influence. Much of this variation became apparent in the final comments from the informants regarding what they felt was the overall impact of the demonstration.

At schools with little or no previous protest activity, the demonstrations, most of which were non-disruptive, had a general arousal effect. This represents the first stage of formative influence. Students, faculty, and administrators became newly aware of and involved in protest issues. As one faculty informant put it, the demonstration and aftermath "generally shook up this sleepy hollow university." A somewhat more dramatic statement was the following:

It had a profound effect. Activism gained a high degree of respectability. An ad hoc meeting held at noon of the same day was attended by over 25,000 [sic], a phenomenon hitherto unknown at _____.

At many of these institutions, however, such new involvement was only temporary, subsiding with the decline of the particular protest issue nationally, or as the new, relatively uncommitted protestors weighed the potential costs of further protest activity. One temporary faculty activist expressed his disillusionment as follows:

It [the demonstration and aftermath] gave the "liberals" an opportunity to say that the issues raised were freely and openly discussed in the legitimate representative bodies on campus, and that all demands were rejected. As a result, many persons who were beginning to get involved recognized the costs that would be involved if they further participated, and so they went back to tending their gardens. In a sense the school simply went through a rite of passage, and by Spring was engaged in activities similar—although weaker—than those in other schools.

A more predictably enduring effect occurred at schools where a general issue awareness and concern already existed, but where involvement had never reached the extent of active opposition to an existing administration

policy. Demonstrations at schools in this second stage of formative influence often produced a new sense of campus polarization. In part, this polarization arose from the emergence in the protest aftermath of recognized student and faculty conflict groups, as stated by the following two faculty informants:

It was one of the first acts of open defiance by both students and faculty against a university policy. I think it led to a greater sense of potency, and I believe that the level and form of protest will definitely increase and change as a result of it.

While the proximate cause of the demonstrations was the presence of military recruiters, the basic causes relating to university goals and facilities were unaffected. The demonstrations established both faculty and student conflict groups and provided some successes. They represent only the start of more serious conflict, and only a handful of faculty are aware of this.

Greatly magnifying the polarization at several schools were physical confrontations that resulted from the use of police to control the demonstration. Police were used at 27 percent of the demonstrations. A faculty informant at one of these schools expressed this effect as follows:

Although the demonstration began as an objection to Navy recruiting, it was quickly transformed into an anti-administration, anti-cops on campus demonstration. I think it radicalized many students and faculty, and infused the college with a political fervor which had been there, but sporadic at best. Student government has collapsed (its president resigned and joined SDS) and the students have a greater sense o⁰ mission and of their power. Faculty has polarized. In short, the place is a powder keg.

It is in this second stage, where the initial enthusiasm was joined by an awareness of polarization, that protest activity was likely to be the most intense, and have its broadest student, as well as faculty, support. An activist-supporting student government president, not directly involved in the protest at his school, expressed the following judgment:

The massive sit-in radicalized much of the student body. It gave birth to a student/faculty alliance of sorts (when the Academic Council voted in favor of the demonstrators' demands), it alienated some alumni, elicited ominous warnings from the administration and trustees, and probably cost the University a bit of money. But students now realize that in cases of clear injustice they can act effectively. One unfortunate result was that it gave a sizable, normally inert reactionary segment of the students a focal point for organization. But it seems to have dissolved.

The anti-recruiting demonstrations probably had their strongest negative inducement effects at schools in this stage, and consequently administrators at these schools began to actively seek means to diminish and rechannel this protest activity.

Several schools appeared to be in a third stage of formative influence. At the time of the anti-recruiting demonstrations, conflict groups at these schools had already been established, this particular protest representing only a new, expanded foray on the part of activists. As a result, assessment of the demonstration impact was a little more sober in tone. Activists in particular began to weigh the gains of the protests with the costs to themselves, in the form of penalties for rule violations. The possibility of the protest generating an alternative, less risky form of influence, namely a coalition with faculty, was often an important consideration in their assessment of the outcome. The following statement by an SDS activist suggests much of this:

Even the "fink liberals" eventually came out and admitted that we were probably

the only campus organization that was doing anything—and this all started with the October demonstration. Not only did it raise the question of recruitment, but also the questions of student power, civil disobedience, relation of administration to the educational process, and faculty powerlessness. The base of support has been broadened, both among students and faculty. However, those students suspended were completely screwed, and though our demonstration showed all students and faculty that these questions did indeed exist, we feel that in relation to educating the administration, it induced only paranoia and harsh and capricious controls.

Administrators at these schools often represented themselves as effective counter-demonstration strategists, or at least as astute analysts of protest. These new signs of confidence contrasted with the defensive posture of many administrators at the second stage schools. In many instances a paternalistic concern for activists seemed to be replaced by a recognition, almost an admiration, for activists as skillful opponents in a game of confrontation. One implication of this new stance toward activists, however, was a diminished concern about penalizing them. Administrators' evaluation of the protests, along with that by the demonstrators, now rested importantly on the extent that each demonstration generated new support from the faculty and non-demonstrating students. The following assessment from a dean of students is illustrative of the type of thinking at this stage:

The subsequent faculty vote recommending that the President . . . must also be considered a student victory. The immediate upshot of the sit-in seems to be a new distaste of the majority of students for the use of coercion to gain reform, and a new awareness on the part of faculty of the responsibilities they must assume in their community. Both of these things are good, but it is obvious that, unless inflammatory issues are handled with extraordinary delicacy in the future, student power of a coercive nature will be seen again.

A dean of students at another school expressed confidence on the basis of external support from alumni and the public, even though admitting activists currently appeared to have the bulk of internal support.

The demonstration moved SDS into an important position of influence in the campus community. Faculty and student hostility gained momentum and provided the impetus for revision of our disciplinary structure as recommended by the Faculty Senate Committee on Student Affairs. Because of the shift in concern from a national issue (recruiting) to a local issue (University discipline), it provided a new vehicle for the gradual buildup of student support and involvement around the concept of "student power." This culminated in the spring semester with mass rallies, demands, negotiations, and concessions to students. In addition, the demonstration helped to solidify support (because of disciplinary action) for the institution from alums and the general public.

Faculty at these schools were less inclined to consider their new involvement in terms simply of coalition support for one side or the other. Instead, they saw themselves as relatively independent agents, examining the sources of conflict and seeking solutions that would serve the best interests of their school.[12] The following faculty statement is illustrative:

I would say that this is the major result: much more faculty involvement and interest among faculty members not connected

12. A more detailed examination of the role of faculty in campus disorders and their aftermath is given in William R. Morgan, "Faculty Mediation of Student War Protests," presented at the 1969 meeting of the American Sociological Association, San Francisco, and reprinted in part in Julian Foster and Durward Long, eds., *Protest: Student Activism in America* (Clifton, N.J.: Morrow, 1970).

with "activist" movements. The faculty council was moved to appoint a number of committees to make special investigations and to develop policies on such things as recruiting. The faculty is also much more aware of the actions and reactions of the administration (particularly the Dean of Students office) and now "oversees" this office much more regularly.

This third stage of formative influence, although an important movement in itself, probably provides the greatest barriers to further development of effective formalized influence patterns. Faculty involvement was likely to be temporary only, gradually dissolving as the immediate crisis passed and efforts were made to catch up with delayed research and teaching duties. Initiatives taken by administrators to increase student participation in the committee machinery of the campus were likely to be met with cynicism and distrust, by faculty as well as students, especially those most polarized. They were likely to be seen as control techniques, which of course they were, but as control techniques only, without any mutual gains of formalized influence. Instead of facilitating the effective exercise of student influence, this administration-defined participation was often seen as an effort to permanently subordinate student influence. According to a suspended demonstrator, "the nature of the liberal techniques of co-optation were revealed to several hundred poltically oriented students."

Unlike the original activists, the newly involved students were much less critical of this reformist response by administrators, and may even have been enthused by it. Yet even among them there appeared to be serious doubts about the adequacy of these new influence channels, and an uncertainty as to how permanently they would be willing to work within them. The following came from a student newspaper editor:

The aftermath of the protest definitely increased the amount and ease of student/faculty and student/administration communication. The punishment and veiled threats which followed the Dow demonstration may have helped direct protest into other channels. This is not necessarily to say there could be another obstructive demonstration here. As the memory recedes and the threat becomes more obscure, appropriate issues might mobilize another demonstration.

Finally, at a few schools, the anti-recruiting protests had the effect, not of generating new modes of student influence as previously, but of legitimizing certain ones recently put into existence. From the students' point of view, legitimacy was granted these formalized influence procedures to the extent of their ability to present the student position against recruiting. Faculty and administrators were likely to be favorably impressed to the extent that the influence group was able to formulate a meaningful solution to the recruiting issue, the formulation being in a manner and style that met their own standards of rationality and wisdom. The two-fold test of gaining student trust while also winning faculty and administration respect was a difficult one for persons holding these new positions. The following faculty statement suggests that at his school there was a good measure of success on at least the second count:

The issue of recruiting did more than any other single issue to help establish the relatively new (two-year-old) College Council, of faculty, students, and administrators, as a responsible and respected agency of college government. The College Council took the responsibility for framing a major report on the issue, hearing and responding to all interested views, recommending temporary suspension of recruiting, . . . The faculty voted strongly to support the Council's recommendations, and the administration followed them.

In summary, this last section has offered impressionistic evidence on the ways these anti-recruiting demonstrations generated moves toward the inclusion of students in more formalized influence relations. This effect of the protests depended not only on their intensity, but also on the current stage of development of influence patterns at each school. At some schools the protest simply led to the first stage of expanded issue awareness and discontent. At others the demonstration produced increasingly polarized forms of protest activity and response. At a smaller number of schools, the increased costs of this particular protest episode, compared to previous ones, generated an increased interest, among students, faculty and administrators alike, in finding more co-operative forms of influence. Finally, in a few schools, the anti-recruiting protest activity provided the opportunity for legitimizing a recently organized co-operative influence mechanism.

Indirectly, this evidence suggests the possibility of any one school eventually moving through all four stages of formative influence, although this cannot be demonstrated within the one-year time span of the data presented here. One would expect the speed and course of this movement to vary across universities, depending on the size and selectivity of the student body and the existing governance arrangements among faculty, administrators, and trustees. In addition, the modes of formalized student participation most feasible at any one school may depend in large part on these institutional characteristics.

22

Local Political Leadership and Popular Discontent in the Ghetto

By Peter H. Rossi and Richard A. Berk

Peter H. Rossi is a professor of Sociology in the Department of Social Relations at Johns Hopkins University. He has served as director of the National Opinion Research Center and has taught at the University of Chicago and Harvard University. He is the author of several books, including Why Families Move *and* The Education of Catholic Americans, *and of articles on political sociology, community studies, and the sociology of education.*

Richard A. Berk, Ph.D., is a research associate in the Department of Social Relations at Johns Hopkins University and a lecturer in Sociology at Goucher College. He has an appointment as an assistant professor in the Sociology Department at Northwestern starting in the fall of 1970. He is interested in political sociology, social change, and methodology, and has authored several articles in these areas. He is co-author of a book on class and racial conflict in American cities, to appear early in 1971.

The research reported here has been supported by grants from the Ford Foundation and the National Institute of Mental Health (MH 16549). This assistance is gratefully acknowledged.

NATIONAL problems have a way of coming home to local roosts, as many urban mayors have discovered. The national unemployment rate is an abstraction, the concrete manifestations of which are persons without jobs and factory layoffs in specific places. The state of the national economy determines largely, if not entirely, the size and the nature of the welfare problems which an urban community has to face. The Kerner Commission pointed to centuries of national neglect and white racism as being among the more important causes of the urban disorders of the sixties, but the riots were local events manifesting themselves in the destruction of local property and the defiance of local police forces.

The extent and the quality of local social problems may be viewed as being made up of two parts: a national component, determined by society-wide trends, and a local component, determined by the special characteristics of the locality in question. Thus, a local unemployment rate is determined by the health of the national economy (the national component) and local factors: the special mix of industries and businesses of which the local economy is composed, the special characteristics of the labor force, and the like. For some social problems, the local components may not be very large; whereas for others, the local components may be the most significant parts. The relative sizes of the local and national components in a particular problem largely condition the extent to which local communities can materially ameliorate a given social problem through changes in local policy. For example, there may be very little that a local community can do directly about inflationary trends in the prices of retail goods. In contrast, there may be a great deal that it can do to reduce the amount of consumer fraud prevalent.

The amelioration of social problems which have very large national components has to proceed on different bases than do problems which are more local than national. Thus, an appropriate strategy combatting inflation on a local level is one which seeks to lessen the impact of higher prices on purchasing power—perhaps through an educational campaign instructing citizens on how to substitute lower priced goods for high priced ones. Local communities could not attempt to regulate prices through local legislation (even if such legislation would be considered constitutionally proper) because by so doing they would merely penalize local retail establishments, possibly crippling the local retail distribution system. In contrast, there are problems which are almost entirely local in origin. For example, the cleanliness of streets and sidewalks can only be attacked through local efforts, by changes in local legislation and services. Attempts to affect the cleanliness of streets through changes in national policy can only succeed if local practices and services are thereby modified substantially.

One of the major strategic policy problems faced by the urban leaders today is how to determine, at least crudely, the extent to which urban social problems are local or national in origin. Indeed, this question lies at the base of the current conflict among several ideological positions concerning local social problems. On the one hand, the philosophy underlying such federal programs as Model Cities and the Office of Economic Opportunity's Community Action Program (CAP) is that many of the problems of slum neighborhoods have very large local components, and that significant improvements in the level of life in urban slums can be accomplished by providing organizational frameworks and funds for the delivery of missing services to slum neighborhoods and the better "coördination" of existing services. Similarly, those in favor of decentralization of schools and other public services operate on the assumption that the local components are at least large enough so that enhancing the efficacy of local communities will make for significant improvements.

The contrasting social philosophy emphasizes the importance of national and regional policy shifts for the amelioration of social problems. Thus, an alternative to Model Cities and CAP programs would be some policy of income maintenance administered directly by the federal government and raising the level of life in slum neighborhoods by providing more adequate household incomes. Similarly, policies which call for the federal government to provide employment directly are also based on the assumption that there is little that local communities can do to raise the employment level high enough to affect local rates.

At least until very recent years, political philosophies of the "right" emphasized that social problems had very large local components and those of the "left" argued the opposite position.[1] The apparent failure of national programs to affect substantially very local problems, particularly those of the urban black ghettos, has now led some on the left to argue for more local autonomy, on the grounds that only local residents who know their own problems can effectively produce the policies which will lead to their amelioration.

1. Note that the classical traditional position of relying on local efforts to ameliorate social problems may be viewed as the social structural analogue to social philosophies which view changes in individuals as the sources of social change. Thus, the level of life in a community is a function of the community's efforts on its own behalf, just as an individual's social status is a function of the efforts on his own behalf.

Thus, the drive for decentralized control of schools is bolstered by the argument that changes in local school policies can materially affect educational outcomes and that the local community is better equipped to judge which policies are achieving that end.

LOCAL DETERMINISM IN CIVIL DISORDERS

The study reported here grew out of attempts to discern how large are the local components in one of the more serious social problems of recent times, the urban disorders of the sixties. Its origins were in the Kerner Commission's preliminary ideas about the causes of the civil disorders. In the fall of 1967, one of the more significant features of the distribution of ghetto riots was that the riots had touched some cities and not others and that some cities had had riots early in the sixties and others some years later. At first glance it seemed to the commission staff and consultants quite appropriate to entertain a theory of local determinism in the causation of the civil disorders. The model developed, and later discarded, by the Kerner Commission's research staff envisaged civil disorders in a city as dependent on two major factors: the level of grievances held by the black population and the responsiveness of local city administrations. The timing of a disorder depended on being triggered by an event which could be interpreted by the black community as a particularly grievous and unwarranted assault on the rights of its members. The "facts" appeared to support the triggering concept, since each of the civil disorders appeared to have had its triggering event. In Newark the event was the arrest of a black taxi driver and his alleged mistreatment by the police; in Detroit it was a police raid on a "blind pig," and in Watts it was the arrest of and maltreatment of a black couple by the police.

It was also clear that there were grievances suffered and articulated by the black communities in the cities which had riots, and variations among cities in both the vigor and the styles of city administrations. This theory of local determinism seemingly had much to commend it. First of all, it seemed to fit the "facts"; secondly, it was politically attractive to a "national" commis-

Hopkins University sociologists,[2] who undertook qualitative surveys of leaders within each of the same cities together with structured interviews with educators, police, social workers, ghetto merchants, major employers, and political workers in the same cities.[3]

Fifteen cities were chosen by the researchers and the research staff of the Kerner Commission to represent a full range in the experience of civil disorders in Northern urban places, as follows:

CIVIL DISORDERS IN 15 NORTHERN CITIES

Cities which had major civil disorders in 1967	Newark, Detroit, Cincinnati, Milwaukee, and Boston
Cities with minor disturbances in 1967, or disturbances in previous years but not in 1967	Philadelphia, Cleveland, San Francisco, Chicago, and Brooklyn, N.Y. (Bedford-Stuyvesant)
Cities with no civil disorders	Washington, D.C., Baltimore, Pittsburgh, Gary, Ind., and St. Louis

sion because it placed the "blame" on local institutions, personalities, and events and shifted attention away from the national scene and the federal administration.

The research design appropriate to testing this model was fairly obvious. It called for a comparative study of cities, looking for the relationships among levels of grievances, activities and attitudes of public officials and other leaders, and the activities of the delivery systems of local institutional complexes. The Kerner Commission sought and successfully obtained funds from the Ford Foundation to undertake such a study, with the specific research activities involved being divided between the Survey Research Center at the University of Michigan, which undertook sample surveys of blacks and whites within each of fifteen cities, and Johns

It should be noted that this sample of cities contains all the fifteen largest Northern metropolitan areas (with the exception of Los Angeles and San Diego), the two largest areas being represented each by two subcenters (Gary[4] and Chicago from the Chicago

2. The Johns Hopkins group consisted of Peter H. Rossi and James S. Coleman. Mainly responsible for the Survey Research Center activities were Angus Campbell and Howard Schuman.

3. Preliminary results from the sample surveys and the delivery system studies were published in The National Advisory Commission on Civil Disorders, *Supplemental Studies* (Washington, D.C.: Government Printing Office, July, 1968).

4. To be entirely candid, Gary was included in the sample not to provide extra weight to the large metropolitan areas but because it had just elected a black mayor (Richard Hatcher). Nor were Los Angeles and San Diego omitted for good sampling reasons; Watts had already been investigated (the McCone Commission

metropolitan area, and Brooklyn and Newark from the New York metropolitan area). The sample was confined to Northern and border state cities because it was felt that with very few exceptions, race relations in Southern urban centers were still being governed by peculiarly regional customary rules which all but ruled out the possibility of civil disorders without an almost immediate and harsh repression.

By the time data were collected in the early part of 1968, the Kerner Commission had already abandoned the local determinism model as an explanation for civil disorders. In addition, the early analysis of data from the Johns Hopkins part of the study indicated that there were really no systematic differences among the three groups of cities. The final blow to the local determinism model was dealt by the riots which broke out after the assassination of Martin Luther King, Jr.: three out of the five cities in the non-riot category had very serious disorders in April, 1968 and one city in the medium riot category (Chicago) had its most serious disorder.

Clearly, the occurrence of civil disorders had nothing to do with whatever differences existed among cities. Sooner or later, each of the major Northern metropolitan areas had its riot, with some, like Chicago and Cleveland, experiencing more than one. The civil disorders, as the Kerner Commission pointed out in its report, were local manifestations of national problems to which national remedies had to be directed. This is obvious when we consider that the assassination of Martin Luther King, Jr.—a national event— was the spark for the last major round of civil disorders. Less obvious was the

discovery that levels of grievances, practices of delivery system personnel, and the characteristics of local leadership groups were not related to either the timing of civil disorders or whether or not a disorder occurred. This is not to say that there were no significant differences among cities in these respects. There just were no differences that were correlated with disorders.

LOCAL DETERMINANTS OF LEVELS OF GRIEVANCES

It is clear from both the data that were gathered by the Johns Hopkins group and the Survey Research Center that the fifteen cities studied varied considerably in the styles of public leadership cadres, in the ways in which the delivery systems of major institutional areas operated, and in the ways in which black and white residents of the cities expressed satisfaction with those services.

The problem to which the remainder of this paper is addressed concerns the sources of variation from city to city in the level of grievance held by the black populations of the fifteen cities we studied. In one sense, the analysis is an exercise in understanding the formation of public opinion, because we will be seeking for those circumstances which materially affect public opinion assessments of community institutions. In another sense, it is a study of political leadership, for we will be concerned with how the leaders of a community, black and white, affect the level of grievance in those communities.

It should be noted that we will concentrate particularly on aspects of community life which are likely to have larger local than national components— the business practices of ghetto merchants and the behavior of the police.

For heuristic purposes, it is useful to

Report), and San Diego was not even considered.

consider two alternative models as representing processes in the formation of grievances. Both models rest on the assumption that the grievances ultimately reflect some objective basis: that is, that people do not become dissatisfied with some aspect of the community in which they live unless there is something objectively wrong with the aspect in question.

The Elitist Model postulates that before an objective situation can affect the level of grievance, the objective situation has to be identified by an elite, then transformed into an issue to which the mass responds with a heightened level of grievance. Thus, no matter how bad (or good) the schools may objectively be, it is only when elites make education into an issue that the objectively bad condition of the schools becomes formulated as a grievance held widely by the masses.

The alternative model, the Populist Model, postulates a causal process in which the objective conditions directly affect the level of grievance, which in turn determines whether or not elites raise the matter to the level of a public issue. Thus, according to the Populist Model, the direct negative experience of the public (for example, with public transportation) leads to a high level of dissatisfaction which, when communicated to the political and civic leaders, leads to their raising public transportation to the level of an issue.

Of course, no set of empirical data ever fits very closely simple models of the sort described above. Errors of measurement as well as the fact that "real life" is usually more complicated than the models we can construct usually make a set of empirical data depart to some appreciable degree from almost any model with which the data can be compared. This looseness of fit will also be the case with respect to the data to be presented in the pages which follow.

Nevertheless, we believe that one set of data tends to conform to the general outline of one model and the other set conforms more closely to the other model.

The data to be used in this analysis come from four sources, each collected independently.[5] The four sources also correspond to different levels in the social structures of the cities studied. They are as follows:

Demographic and Documentary Data: Data drawn from the decennial Census and special censuses, labor force statistics, documentary sources, e.g., *National Municipal Yearbook.*

Elite Interviews: Qualitative interviews with approximately forty community leaders in each city. Interviews were conducted by a team trained at Johns Hopkins, and covered a standard set of topics, including salient local issues, the sympathy of local leaders to black grievances, and the like.

Delivery System Personnel:[5] Structured interviews were undertaken among police, social workers, educators, and political party workers whose work brought them into the ghettos, as well as merchants and the major employers in the city. In this article we will be concerned only with the forty ghetto merchants and fifty policemen who were interviewed in each city. Interviews covered perceptions of local problems, activities engaged in as professionals, and the like.

5. Interviews were collected by Audits and Surveys, Inc. of New York City. See National Advisory Commission on Civil Disorders *Supplemental Studies*, where the schedules used are reproduced.

Sample Survey
Interviews:[6]   Structured interviews conducted by the Survey Re-
search Center using probability samples of the white
and non-white residential
areas of each city. Ap-
proximately 200 respon-
dents were interviewed in
each city, half from
among white and half
from among black resi-
dents.

The analysis presented below is based
upon correlations across the fifteen cities
using data aggregated within each of
four data sources described above. Because we deal with aggregated data,
there are only fifteen cases (the cities
studied), posing severe limitations on
the number of variables we can study
simultaneously without using up too
many degrees of freedom.[7]

GRIEVANCES AGAINST GHETTO
MERCHANTS: THE ELITIST
MODEL

A frequently voiced complaint of
black leaders is that the retail merchants who are located in the ghetto and
cater to residents offer goods of a lower
quality and/or at higher prices. Indeed, the alleged exploitation of the
ghetto resident by merchants has been

6. We are grateful to Howard Schuman and
Angus Campbell of the Survey Research Center for graciously making these data available
to us in the form of marginals for each of the
fifteen cities.

7. In evaluating the statistical significance of
the results, the small number of observations
(15) is a decided handicap, especially if the
observations are looked upon as a sample.
However, there is some justification for looking
upon the fifteen cases as almost a total enu-
meration of the universe of large metropolitan
areas and hence for regarding the statistics as
descriptive of a universe rather than as samples
drawn from a universe. Since there are good
arguments for either viewpoint, we prefer the
argument which presents a more sympathetic
view of our data and hence present the statistics as universe-descriptive rather than as
samples.

pointed out as one of the reasons why
commercial establishments are likely to
be vandalized and looted during civil
disorders.

There are many problems in trying to
come to an assessment of whether, in
fact, ghetto retail mechants do exploit
their customers. Several studies comparing prices in ghetto stores with
prices in white neighborhoods have
shown that prices tend to be higher
in the ghetto.[8]   However, it may also
be the case that the costs of doing business in the ghetto are higher and that
the price differentials reflect these costs.
For example, the higher interest rates
charged on consumer loans available to
the poor are alleged to be functions of
the higher default rates among the poor.

There are enough obvious differences
between the retail establishments located
in the ghetto and those located in non-
ghetto neighborhoods to give rise to the
possibility that the services rendered to
ghetto residents would be perceived by
them as inferior and give rise to grievances against this sector of the economy
of local communities. The question we
want to raise here concerns the conditions under which these differences became translated into grievances and into
public issues.

Table 1 presents the zero-order correlations among data taken from the
three levels described above, plus the
proportion of blacks in the cities in
question. Note that although the correlations are not very high,[9] they generally support the underlying postulate

8. David Caplovitz, *The Poor Pay More*
(Glencoe, Ill.: Free Press, 1962).

9. When we consider that the measurement
error in these variables is undoubtedly high,
these correlations have to be considered as
probably reflective of even higher correlations
between better measures of the variables.
Thus, merchants were asked to indicate their
agreement to statements about retail practices
in a context in which they must have known
that they were being asked to reveal whether
or not they exploited their customers.

TABLE 1—ZERO ORDER CORRELATIONS: GHETTO MERCHANT MEASURES

	PROPORTION BLACK IN CITY 1	MERCHANT SHARP PRAC- TICES INDEX 2	MERCHANT EXPLOITATION AS ISSUE 3	BLACK DISSAT- ISFACTION WITH MERCHANTS 4	MERCHANT BARGAINING 5
Prop. Black 1	—	− 07	22	− 01	25
Sharp Pract. 2		—	44	30	22
Exploitation 3			—	47	− 05
Black Dissat. 4				—	35

EXPLANATION OF VARIABLES

Proportion Black =	Proportion of Negroes in city population
Merchant "Sharp Practices" Index	Composed of two items from Merchant Questionnaires: Merchants were asked to express agreement or disagreement to ". . . merchants feel that in business the main thing in a neighborhood like this is to learn how to price their merchandise to cover the extra costs of poor credit risks, petty thievery, and the like" and ". . . merchants say the main thing to do is buy bargain merchandise so that they can keep their retail prices low enough for people to afford."
Merchant Exploitation as an Issue	Protocols of qualitative interviews with public and civic leaders were pooled for each community and read by four raters, who made judgments on a 10–point scale as to how salient merchant exploitation was as an issue in the black community of that city. Ratings were done independently and achieved a high degree of consensus.
Black Dissatisfaction with Retail Merchants	Composed of responses to three items in SRC questionnaire covering whether respondents felt they were overcharged in local stores, sold inferior goods, or treated disrespectfully by merchants.
Merchant Bargaining	Composed of an item asking the extent of merchant agreement with the statement ". . . [merchants] feel that the best way to stay in business in a neighborhood like this is to bargain with each customer and take whatever breaks you can get."

of both models: that it is in the objective situations facing people that the basic cause of popular dissatisfaction lies. Thus, two out of the three highest correlations (r_{34} and r_{45}) in the matrix are between measures of merchant practices and black dissatisfaction with merchants. The highest correlation in the matrix, however, is between mass dissatisfaction with merchant practices and the importance of merchant exploitation as an issue among elites. This pattern of relationships suggests that the Elite Model described earlier is likely to be a closer fit than the Populist Model.

Indeed, when we arrange the relationships into a causal model, as in Figure A, the Elite Model appears to be fairly plausible. Following Blalock's formulation of causal models in nonexperimental data, in which the correlations between any pair of variables in a causal chain would be a product of the correlations between adjacent members of intervening pairs,[10] the model shown in Figure A is a better fit than an alternative arrangement in which the salience of the issue of merchant exploitation is seen as the outcome of black dissatisfaction.[11] Note, however, that one of the measures of merchant sharp practices

10. Hubert N. Blalock, *Causal Inferences in Non-Experimental Data* (Chapel Hill, N.C.: University of North Carolina Press, 1961).

11. The essential comparisons are as follows: The Elitist Model postulates as causal chain BED or $r_{BD} = r_{BE} r_{ED}$ or $(.44)$ $(.47) = .21$ which is not too different from the actual $r_{BD} = .30$

The Populist Model postulates BDE as a causal chain or $r_{BE} = r_{BD} r_{DE}$ or $(.30)$ $(.47) = .13$ which compares very poorly with the actual $r_{BE} = .47$

FIGURE A

CAUSAL MODEL FOR GHETTO MERCHANT ANALYSIS

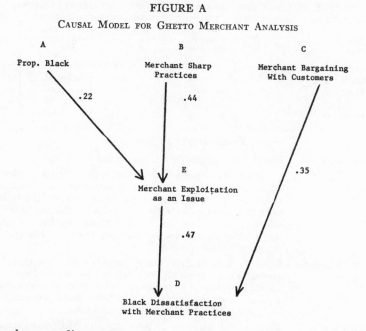

is seen to have a direct effect upon black dissatisfaction: The more merchants in a city say that they bargain with customers and take advantage of whatever breaks they can get in the process, the more likely are blacks to be dissatisfied with merchant exploitation. One can interpret this finding as representing a measure of merchant practice which individual blacks can experience in a direct fashion, while the other measures of merchant sharp practices (pricing high to cover overhead and buying bargain goods) are less visible because they are practices which are not performed in direct interaction with customers and require a comparative perspective to detect.

The proportion of blacks in a city is seen in the model of Figure A as having a direct effect on the appearance of merchant exploitation as an issue in the city. At this point, the interpretation becomes speculative. It may be that the proportion of blacks is an index of the potential political power of the black community. Hence, the larger the pro-

portion of blacks, the more likely are black leaders to be able to transform a grievance into an issue. It may also be that the proportion of blacks is a measure of the extensiveness of the problem of merchant exploitation: the more blacks in the city, the more extensive is merchant exploitation and the more likely it is to be detected.

Although the Elitist Model is a better fit to the data than the Populist Model, there is still considerable looseness. By and large, it appears that it takes the identification of merchant sharp practice by elites and their raising such practices to the status of a public issue for mass dissatisfaction to arise concerning such exploitation. Thus, the experience of blacks in their day-to-day dealings with retail merchants is not sufficient for them to be able to develop dissatisfaction. Their experience has to be interpreted to them as arising from exploitation for a sense of dissatisfaction with retail merchants' treatment of them to arise among the masses of black residents. This applies with particular force to retail merchant pricing policies and quality of goods offered. It is less true of merchant behavior which is expressed in direct dealing with customers, as in the case of bargaining with customers over prices.

This interpretation is at least consistent with, if not bolstered by, an analysis of the kinds of merchants who are vandalized during ordinary times, or looted and vandalized during a period of civil disorders.[12] The analysis found that merchants who admitted to sharp practices were no more likely to be hit than merchants who did not admit to engaging in such practices. The best predictors of whether a business was hit during a disorder was the attractiveness of the goods sold in the store and the frequency with which consumers used stores of that type. If a store contained valuable merchandise and experienced frequent customer patronage, it was most likely to suffer some damage during a civil disorder. This finding is consistent with the interpretation that merchant sharp practices are not easily detectable by their customers.

A QUASI-POPULIST MODEL: THE POLICE AND THE GHETTO

In many cities, ghetto/police relations are close to the head of any list of complaints that black leaders might draw up. In many cities, blacks have complained that the police act in the ghetto as if they were troops stationed as occupation forces among a hostile and conquered enemy. In other cities, the complaints have been milder, amounting to charges of occasional discriminatory behavior. But in all cities there are some complaints, with levels varying from city to city.

12. For a detailed exposition of this analysis, see Richard A. Berk, "The Role of the Ghetto Retail Merchant in Civil Disorders," Ph.D. diss. (Johns Hopkins University, 1970).

The complaints are not one-sided, for the police have their grievances too, usually concerning the frustrations encountered in attempting to pursue their tasks in a hostile environment.[13] The high level of tension between police and black residents can be seen in the fact that police have been involved in the triggering events that have set off almost every one of the civil disorders in the sixties (outside of those which were reactions to the assassination of Martin Luther King, Jr.).

The structure of public opinion concerning police abuse is quite different in the black as compared to the white populations of the fifteen cases studied, as Table 2 illustrates. The correlations shown are across cities and express the extent of relationships in levels of general belief concerning police abuse, personal experience with police abuse, and observations of abuse directed against others. Separate sets of correlations are shown for white and black residents. Note that whites and blacks tend, as it were, to be living in separate worlds. There are high coefficients among the indices for blacks (as shown at upper left) and high coefficients among the corresponding indices for whites (as shown at lower right), but the correlations among the two sets of indices (as shown at upper right) tend to be low and as often negative as positive.

Whites and blacks have some common experiences. The correlation between personal experience indices for the two races is .51, the highest correlation in the upper right corner. In other words,

13. For an analysis of police perceptions of the ghetto populations in the fifteen cities, see W. Eugene Groves and Peter H. Rossi, "Police Perceptions of a Hostile Ghetto: Realism or Projection," *The American Behavioral Scientist* (forthcoming). A detailed description of ghetto resident and police complaints for the fifteen cities can also be found in *Supplemental Studies*, op. cit.

TABLE 2—CORRELATIONS AMONG INDICES OF PERSONAL EXPERIENCES WITH AND
PERCEPTIONS OF POLICE ABUSE: BLACKS AND WHITES

		AMONG BLACKS			AMONG WHITES		
		GENERAL BELIEF (1)	PERSONAL EXPERIENCE (2)	OBSERVATION (3)	GENERAL BELIEF (4)	PERSONAL EXPERIENCE (5)	OBSERVATION (6)
Among Blacks	General Belief (1)		68	91	− 13	32	− 37
	Personal Experience (2)			69	21	51	− 11
	Observation (3)				− 18	28	− 38
Among Whites	General Belief (4)					82	55
	Personal Experience (5)						17

Correlations are computed across cities using averages of indices derived from Survey Research Center interviews with black and white residents in each city. The items involved are as follows:

"Some people say that the police don't show respect for people or they use insulting language. Do you think this happens to people in this neighborhood? Has it ever happened to you? Has it happened to anyone you know?"

"Some people say the police frisk or search people without good reasons. Do you think this happens to people in this neighborhood? Has it ever happened to you? Has it happened to anyone you know?"

"Some people say the police rough up people unnecessarily when they are arresting them or afterwards. Do you think this happens to people in this neighborhood? Has it ever happened to you? Has it happened to anyone you know?"

The index entitled "general belief" sums answers across the three items to the subquestion concerning whether the respondent believes that the abuse in question is prevalent in the neighborhood. The other two indices have been formed in a similar fashion using respectively the subquestions concerning personal experience and knowing about abuses experienced by other persons.

in cities where there are high levels of personally experienced police abuse among whites, there tend also to be high levels of personally experienced abuse among blacks. The commonality of personal experience does not spill over into common definitions of the beliefs concerning police abuse, however.[14] The

14. It should be noted that the items are phrased in terms of abusive practices "happening to people in this neighborhood" and this locality frame of reference may be affecting the relationships across cities in a way that restricts the correlation. For example, if the incidence of police abuse in white areas is very low, it may not be obvious to those who have had direct experience with such abuse that the abuse is part of a general pattern rather than an isolated incident that just "happened" to an "unlucky" individual.

correlation between the two groups' assessments of the general abusive behavior of the police is slightly negative (−.13).

If we examine the relationships among the three indices within each of the racial groups, it is obvious that there are quite different patterns. For blacks, the correlations tend to be considerably higher: personal experience, observations about the experience of others, and general beliefs about police abuse tend to go hand in hand. There is a particularly strong relationship (.91) between observations of others experiencing police abuse and general beliefs about the prevalence of such abuse, indicating the reliance of general beliefs on

TABLE 3—CORRELATIONS AMONG MEASURES RELATING TO POLICE ABUSE OF BLACKS

		GENERAL BELIEF (1)	PERSONAL EXPERI- ENCE (2)	OBSERVA- TION (3)	POLICE COMM. KNOWL- EDGE (4)	POLICE ABUSIVE PRACTICES (5)	POLICE CHIEF RESPONSE (6)	POLICE ABUSE ISSUE (7)	PROP. BLACK (8)
General Belief	(1)		68	91	− 62	40	− 53	49	− 49
Personal Exper.	(2)			69	− 64	58	− 59	55	− 25
Observation	(3)				− 49	53	− 74	69	− 35
Police Comm. Knowledge	(4)					− 34	− 08	− 29	36
Police Abusive Practices	(5)						− 54	48	− 11
Police Chief Response	(6)							− 57	21
Abuse Issue	(7)								17

Police Abusive Practices Index based on items in police interviews asking about frequency with which police stop and frisk suspicious people, search on suspicion without a warrant, break up loitering groups, and interrogate suspected drug users.

Police Community Knowledge Index based on how many people policemen knew from the following categories: important adult leaders, residents in general, youth leaders, and "continual" trouble-makers.

Police Chief Responsiveness Index based on composite ratings of police chief as accessible to black leaders, sympathetic to black grievances, and responsive to such grievances.

observations of the incidence of abuses in the ghetto neighborhoods.

In contrast, white beliefs about police abuse appear to be more dependent on personal experience (.82) than upon observations of others' experience, and indeed, there is very low relationship (.17) between levels of personal experience and levels of observations of the experiences of others.

This patterning of relationships suggests that blacks integrate their personal experience and especially their observations of police treatment of their neighbors into generalizations about usual police practices. In contrast, whites believe that the police are abusive in general, primarily through their own personal experience with police abuse. This patterning may have more to do with the density of police activities in white and black areas than with anything else. Although the

incidence of police abuse among whites tends to be high in cities where blacks also experience high levels of abuse, the racial differentials in the levels of abuse in each city may be such that blacks experience and observe abuse much more frequently than the whites.[15] There may be a point when the incidence of police abuse becomes so frequent that the experience is all-pervasive, when the observation of others' experience can hardly be avoided, and where such experience becomes translated into generalized belief.

The argument developed so far is one which supports a Populist Model, in which personal experience becomes gen-

15. Indeed, such is the case: The mean on the indices for personal experience for whites is .109 and for blacks is .263, indicating that on the average there is more than twice as much personal experience with police abuse among blacks.

eralized into generalized belief and then develops into an issue. To develop this argument further, we need to consider data from elite interviews on the salience of police abuse as a public issue, and data from interviews with policemen on their police practices. The correlations across cities for these variables and the indices considered earlier are shown in Table 3, with two other relevant variables: the proportion of blacks in the cities, and ratings of the responsiveness of the police superintendent (from the elite interviews).

Unfortunately, we can present data only for blacks. The policemen interviewed were those whose duties were in black neighborhoods, and the issues focused on in elite issues were those concerning black residents of the cities studied. Because the structure of beliefs in the white populations is so different from that of blacks, as shown in Table 2, we can speculate that the processes involved in the formation of issues concerning police brutality directed toward whites would be quite different, although in ways that are difficult to discern in advance.

The first three variables in Table 3 have been repeated from Table 2, and consist of indices of black residents' beliefs about, personal experience with, and observations of police abuse in their neighborhoods. The next two variables are taken from interviews with the police in each of the cities.[16] Variable 4 is an index of police knowledge and acquaintance with residents of the ghettos which they patrol. Note that there are strong negative relationships between this index and the three measures of residents' grievances against the police: in cities where the police know relatively more residents, there are fewer complaints of police abuse.

Variable 5 is an index of the extent to which policemen admit engaging in practices which could be viewed by ghetto residents as abrasive. Note that the correlations between this index and complaints are positive and fairly large, indicating that in cities in which the police admit engaging in such practices, the level of ghetto residents' grievances tends to be high.

It is important to stress that the relationships discussed in the above are between data collected from two different sources; on the one hand, interviews with ghetto residents, and, on the other hand, interviews with the police. The signs and sizes of the correlations indicate that we are dealing in the case of ghetto residents' grievances with reflections of reality. In other words, there appears to be some substantial basis for the complaints that ghetto residents make about the police.

The next two variables (6 and 7) are obtained from qualitative interviews with elites in each of the fifteen cities. Ratings were made using interviews with elite persons on how sympathetic and responsive the chief police officers in each of the cities were to black leaders and black complaints and grievances. The more responsive the police chief was rated, the lower the level of grievances.

16. Interviews were held with policemen in thirteen of the fifteen cities, permission not being granted to conduct interviews in either Milwaukee or Boston. Forty policemen were interviewed in the cities from among police who served in precincts largely or exclusively populated by blacks. Policemen to be interviewed were selected by quotas for rank and race and were interviewed on the job. Since the specific policemen interviewed were selected by Police Department officials and our interviewers, they probably represent a biased sample, with the direction of the bias toward overselection of the kinds of policemen who supervisors thought would put their police departments in the best light. In other words, this sample contains policemen who are probably more liberal in race issues than the police in general.

Again, it should be stressed that these are correlations between data collected independently and hence add further weight to the bases of reality for ghetto resident complaints.

It should also be noted that the police chief's responsiveness is negatively related to the index of police abusive practices: The more responsive the police chief, the less likely are police to engage in abusive practices in the ghetto.

The next to last column of correlations indicates that the greater the level of grievances, the more abusive are police practices, and the less responsive the police chief, the more likely are police practices in the ghetto to be a public issue.

The final column contains correlations involving the relative size of the black population of the cities. The pattern of these correlations indicates that as the proportion of blacks increase, police abusive practices tend to decline, the police chief tends to be more responsive, and the level of grievances held concerning the police declines. Apparently in cities with relatively large ghettos, the police are more sensitive to black complaints.

The data that are contained in Table 3 allow the posing of two questions: First, what are the causal links among the variables which lead to differences among cities, in the extent to which police departments engage in abusive practices? Here we would be concerned very specifically with the impact of the police chief's responsiveness upon police practices. Second, are black levels of grievance a factor in the appearance of police practice as an issue, or does the causal direction go the other way around?

The most likely configuration of factors is shown in Figure B. Here we postulate a model in which the proportion of blacks in the community affects the responsiveness of the police chief, who in turn affects police practice (but not the police rank and file knowledge of the residents of the ghettos). The experiencing of police abuse is dependent on the responsiveness of the police chief and police practices. Finally, the existence of police brutality as a salient local issue is dependent on the experiences of blacks with police abuse.

How well do the data fit the model? A good place to begin is to look at the effects of percentage of blacks at the top left of Figure B. The proportion of blacks correlates .21 with the responsiveness of the police chief, and the more responsive the police chief, the less frequently police engage in abrasive practices (−.54) concerning members of the black community. In any event, the causal chain is a good fit: The predicted correlation is −.11. Perhaps the process involved is that when the black ghetto is relatively small, police precincts include both black and white residents— with the blacks regarded as the minor constituency to which the police need attend. In contrast, in cities where the proportion of blacks is high, the precincts covering the ghetto are exclusively concerned with a black constituency and hence develop networks of acquaintance among black residents. A high proportion of blacks may also indicate that the ghetto settlement has been in existence longer and hence is more likely to have developed visible leaders whom police can identify and relate to.

The other link in the causal chain which relates police knowledge of black residents to the experience of abuse is more obvious. Where the police know the residents in their patrol areas, they are less likely to make arbitrary and seemingly capricious errors and more likely to discriminate among residents according to some reasonable estimate of the likelihood that the residents in

FIGURE B

PROPOSED CAUSAL MODEL FOR BLACK EXPERIENCES WITH POLICE ABUSE
AND THE APPEARANCE OF POLICE ABUSE AS LOCAL PUBLIC ISSUE

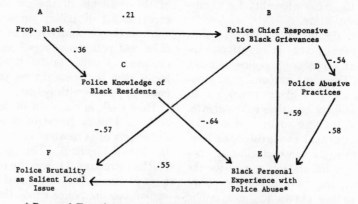

* Personal Experience with police abuse was chosen as the index to represent black levels of grievance although it would have been possible to use either general belief or observations of police abuse as the end variable. Table 3 indicates that the patterning of correlations for the three variables is essentially alike indicating that the causal model would not change much if one of the other two indices of levels of grievances had been chosen.

question are law violators. This may not mean that the police actually engage in different actions when they know the community better, but that the actions are more appropriately directed and that residents are less likely to interpret any actions as abuses. In short, the residents may be better able to understand and accept the rationality of a given police action, and have greater trust in the intentions of the police, when they are more familiar with the police in their neighborhoods.

Beyond these two causal chains the model becomes less one-dimensional. In Figure B we see that there are three elements which make independent contributions to black experience of police abuse: the police chief's responsiveness, the level of community knowledge of the police, and abusive police practices. In short, the level of grievance concerning personal experience of police abuse is lowest in cities where the police know their black communities, where they en-

gage in less abrasive practices, and where the police chief has a reputation for being sympathetic and responsive to black grievances.[18] In fact, if we compute the multiple regression using these three factors to predict the level of experienced police abuse, we find that the multiple correlation is .85, explaining approximately 72 percent of the variance in city levels of experiencing police abuse.

Finally, when we attempt to account for the appearance of police brutality as a salient local issue, the picture that emerges is far from one of a clear-cut causal chain. Black personal experience with police abuse and the reputation of

18. This can be seen, for example, in the following way: If there were a causal chain BDE, the correlation between B and E would be −.31. In fact, the correlation is −.59, indicating that the police chief's reputation makes a direct contribution to the level of black grievances over and above the contribution it makes through changing police abusive practices.

the police chief both contribute independently (and with about the same strength) to the salience of police brutality as a local issue. Indeed, the best way to represent the relationships is again to use the linear regression model. The multiple correlation, using police-brutality-issue salience as a dependent variable and police knowledge of black residents, black experience of police abuse, abusive police practices, and police chief's responsiveness, is .64, explaining 41 percent of the total variance in police brutality issue salience. Although, because of the small number of cases, not too much reliance can be placed upon partial correlations, it does appear that the police chief's responsiveness independently determines more of the variation from city to city in the existence of police brutality as an issue than any other variable in the multiple regression.

In other words, the general line of interpretation that has emerged from the analysis of these data supports an interpretation which relies on both the Populist and the Elitist Models. Police brutality appears as an issue in local community affairs both as a function of the reputation of the chief police officer and the level of black residents' grievances. It does appear as if community leaders—black and white—are attending both to their estimation of the police chief's handling of the police and the level of grievance expressed by residents.

It also appears that the office of the chief of police is a critical one for understanding the conditions under which police brutality is actually experienced and the conditions under which police brutality becomes a public issue. The police chief has an influence on police practices, and his reputation affects both black residents' interpretation of police actions and the raising of police actions as a public issue.

CONCLUSIONS

Using a unique set of data which enables the analyst to relate several levels of community social organization, we have attempted to study the conditions under which objective situations are translated into levels of grievance and into public issues. The analysis was concerned with two areas of community life over which issues have arisen in local communities throughout the country. Retail merchant exploitation of black communities has been pointed out as one of the conditions underlying the civil disorders of the sixties, and alleged police brutality has most uniformly been involved directly, except in the civil disorders following the assassination of Martin Luther King, Jr.

Analysis of the data concerning retail merchant practices indicates that the appearance of such practices as an issue is heavily dependent on the elite's raising of such practices as an issue. Where merchants engage in questionable practices, elites are more likely to raise merchant exploitation as an issue, and when they do so, the rank and file members of the ghetto community perceive the practices as a focus for complaint.

A more complicated process seems to be at work with respect to police abuse, however. Although police practices and knowledge of black communities are directly and strongly related to the levels of grievance held by black communities concerning the police, the reputation of the local chief police officer has an independent effect, both on levels of grievance and on whether or not police brutality is a salient issue. Where the police chief is sympathetic and responsive to black leaders, the rank and file of policemen are less likely to be abusive and police brutality is less likely to be a salient issue. Of course, black experience with police abuse tends to be related to its appearance as a public issue, but such experience is by no means the sole determinant.

Two major conclusions emerge from these analyses: First, the complaints of black residents concerning local services have a basis in reality. Complaint levels vary from city to city and are sensitive to the objective conditions to be found in those cities. Second, the development of grievances and their translation into public issues is a complicated process involving objective conditions, public leadership, and the actions of elites.

23

The Emergence of Muted Violence in Crowd Behavior: A Case Study of An Almost Race Riot

By RICHARD A. BERK

I want to thank Jane Taylor, Lee Bradford, Alice Hartmann, and Joe Blake for their help; and especially thank Howard Becker, who carefully read earlier drafts of the paper.

THE history of the United States has been characterized by a tragic amount of inter-racial violence which has taken a variety of forms and produced a variety of outcomes. Among the most dramatic kinds of inter-racial violence has been the Black/White race riot made highly visible by the large number of impassioned participants. Although such confrontations can be analyzed along many dimensions, a starting point, for this chapter, is the heuristic dichotomy proposed by Allen D. Grimshaw of "Southern style" and "Northern style" race riots.

The Atlanta riot of 1906 and the Springfield, Illinois riot of 1908 are examples of Southern style riots. . . . In every such riot violence is largely one-sided and consists of attacks, of varying degrees of organization, by Whites on Negroes and on the Negro community. In all such riots, whatever may have been the actual background of the riot, there are charges of Negro assaults upon White women.

The Chicago riot of 1919 may be taken as the type-case of the Northern style urban race riot. Here the causation, both in background and in actual precipitating incident, is secular in nature and there is no focusing on the alleged violation of the sanctity of White womanhood. Rather, there was a long period of constantly increasing tension in other areas, and a series of assaults upon the accommodative pattern by Negroes, indeed, a challenge to the very continued existence of that pattern. The assault was felt particularly in the areas of housing, labor competition, and the use of public facilities, especially transportation. The actual precipitating incident was the death, perhaps accidental, of a Negro youth during a dispute over segregated swimming. The riot found organized and unorganized groups of both races engaged in occasional pitched battles and widespread occurrence of attacks upon isolated individuals of one race by roaming gangs of the other race. While there were claims of police partiality and governmental inefficiency, the role of government was far more neutral than was the case in disturbances in the South, urban or rural.[1]

Grimshaw believes that the Southern style race riot is unlikely to occur again in the United States primarily because the Black population will no longer adopt a passive stance to White assaults. While much of the civil rights movement has epitomized Gandhian non-resistance, many Blacks are now willing to employ more aggressive tactics.

And just as there are prayerful young Negroes courting arrest in "sit-ins" there are Negroes of many ages who sit in darkened homes with shotguns on their knees, prepared to defend themselves if the necessity arises. And particularly in Northern cities, there are some young Negroes who do not wait for violence to come to them but are prepared to carry it into the enemy camp.[2]

Thus, the style from now on will be largely Northern.

Although Grimshaw's analysis of changes in the Black community and resulting alteration in the patterns of race riots may be useful as far as it goes (newer types of racial violence of a more calculated and overtly political style have recently added a new dimension or category of racial confronta-

1. Allen D. Grimshaw, *Racial Violence in the United States* (Chicago: Aldine Publishing Co., 1969), pp. 25–26. For purposes of this paper the important point is not the geographical dimension—Southern style riots often took place in border states—but the relative aggressiveness and passivity of the racial groups involved over time. Note that in the Southern style, the Whites are aggressive and Blacks passive, while in the Northern style both are aggressive and that the Southern style riot may have ceased to occur. Also Grimshaw is talking about *race* riots, i.e., confrontations between Whites and Black citizens, and the typology is not intended to cover other kinds of riots such as civil disorders of the late 1960's.

2. *Ibid.* p. 114.

tion), his presentation focuses primarily on changes in patterns of Black violence. After correctly noting that Whites are motivated somewhat differently in the Northern style riot than the Southern style, he stresses only new types of militant patterns emerging from the Black community. Potential changes in the tactics and techniques of Whites during race riots in response to these patterns are not discussed.

In the past five years the militant side of the Black movement has received wide publicity. What Morris Janowitz has labeled "commodity riots" have been covered intensively by the media.[3] News broadcasts have presented blow-by-blow accounts of ongoing civil disorders, and magazines have published many accounts of the violence with large color pictures of the destruction, personal injury, and fatalities. The federal government has underscored these accounts through the Kerner Commission. With the emergence of Black Nationalists groups, self-avowed revolutionaries, and guerrilla-type confrontations, the militant reputation of the Black community has been further enhanced. Books such as *Shoot-Out in Cleveland*,[4] media stories on Black revolutionary groups, and the visibility in urban centers of organizations such as the Panthers have made it well-known through all levels of the white society that to some extent Whites are to be "dealt with." Even popular

television series such as "The Name of the Game" have presented shows exploiting such issues. Is it not reasonable to expect that Whites have had their views about Blacks greatly altered?

In the analysis by Grimshaw and in accounts of race riots for which we have detailed information, it seems that large numbers of Whites, especially young white males, have been relatively eager in many situations to attack Blacks. If there was fear of counterviolence from Blacks, it appears not to have been a salient consideration once the riot began.[5] (It may also be that reporters of race riots simply failed to observe such ambivalence.)

This chapter will present an analysis of data on what may be a new elaboration of the Northern race riot in the face of wide public belief that many Blacks have organized for violence and are prepared to use whatever means necessary to attain their ends. We will attempt to show that new respect for the capacity of the Black community to engage in mass and/or organized violence alters the form that the Northern race riot can take.

The analytical context in which the data will be presented is based on a social psychological approach to mass violence taken by Roger Brown.[6] He suggests that a useful way to analyze the behavior of crowds is to examine the kinds of evaluations and decisions made by individual members of the collectivity. The heuristic device proposed is a pay-off matrix intended to represent the thought processes occurring within each member of the crowd.

3. Morris Janowitz, *Social Control of Escalated Riots* (Chicago: University of Chicago Press, 1968). Important from the point of view of the general public is that analyses such as Janowitz's seem to have vastly overestimated the amount of violence directed against white persons by Blacks (e.g., sniping), giving the impression that the civil disorders of the 1960's were more consciously hostile towards white citizens than they probably were.

4. Louis H. Masotti and Jerome R. Corsi, *Shoot-Out in Cleveland* (New York: Bantam Books, 1969).

5. For example, see case studies in R. H. Turner and L. M. Killian, *Collective Behavior* (Englewood Cliffs, N.J.: Prentice-Hall, 1957).

6. Roger Brown, *Social Psychology* (New York: The Free Press, 1965), chap. 14. In building his analysis Brown draws substantially from Turner and Killian, ibid., especially their first chapter.

The matrix is seen as a two-person or one-person group game in which the individual is trying to maximize his pay-off based on what actions he can implement and what action he can expect from others. Whether or not a group takes action is seen as a result of each individual trying to arrive at the highest pay-off cell in the matrix.

In the discussion to follow, the use of pay-off matrices will be extended to characterize not only the processes that trigger mob action, but also the *form* of action taken by the mob. Further, crowd participants will be viewed as holding different sets of pay-offs, consequently different pay-off matrices will be employed depending on the type of participant and the situation. It is first necessary to describe in general terms the events to be detailed at a later point so that the current discussion will be less abstract.[7]

The setting is an urban White working class community which feels threatened by a spreading "commodity" riot. Blacks in adjacent neighborhoods are looting and burning stores, with police officials apparently helpless to check the violence. The white citizens know of the civil disorder (through rumor, actual observation, and mass media) and as the riot spreads sense an immediate danger of Blacks invading their community. Further, they feel outrage that Blacks are challenging in a very direct way the current distribution of power and consumer goods. Small groups of Whites gather to talk over the events and, while attempting to get the facts of the situation, begin to exchange ideas of what they might do either to throw back an invasion or to put the Blacks "back in their place." With discussions proceeding, clusters

7. The data for this paper was part of the material gathered during four years of participant observation by the author in an Appalachian White neighborhood in Baltimore.

of people start drifting toward the streets that mark the boundary between the two neighborhoods, and soon large numbers are massed on the boundaries. This sets the stage for crowd behavior, and is a point at which to apply the Brown model.

People arrive on the scene with a variety of motivations behind their presence, ranging from passionate commitment to fighting Blacks to simple curiosity. As there are many motivations for people's congregating on the boundary, there are many reasons for staying away. Some have moral objections to violence, some do not want to take the law into their own hands, some fear police actions against perpetrators of assaults, and some are afraid of getting severely injured (or worse) at the hands of Blacks. Although, a large number of those present can clearly articulate such concerns, for many, motivations and fears are dimly focused, barely intruding on consciousness. The aggregate result is a large group of ambivalent people and a collective lack of direction.

In spite of the overall lack of direction, the people gathered on the boundaries can be visualized as belonging to one of two factions in the crowd. For purposes of analysis it will be useful to think of these two groups as agitators and followers. The agitators can be characterized as having a confident analysis of the situation and as very anxious to take aggressive action against the expected assault. The followers are more confused and hesitant, with some interest in vigilante techniques but less belief in their ultimate utility.

The highly motivated agitator is not without ambivalences, but for him the potential gains in a violent confrontation with Blacks far outweigh the costs. And although different agitators bring varying insight and somewhat different components to bear on such a conclusion, one can reasonably speculate what the balance of rewards and punishments might appear to be for a typical agitator. He would believe strongly that action was needed for defense of the white community and to put Blacks back in their place. He would be the type of person who enjoys the excitement surrounding crowds and aggressive behavior. He would also be likely to gain a variety of psychological satisfactions (such as shoring up a type of self-image) of which he would be only dimly aware. On the cost side of the balance sheet would be the high risk of personal injury at the hands of Blacks, the danger of arrest and/or a beating from police, moral reservations about the use of violence, and some psychological inhibitions towards the intended tactics. Clearly this is just an example and in reality the perception of specific rewards and costs would vary somewhat between individuals. Nevertheless, an ideal type cognitive "tally sheet" favoring action can be postulated for all agitators.

Along with the content and conclusions of the tally sheet, a central point not to be overlooked is that the agitators do not reach the scene and immediately act on the first impulse they feel, nor are they passively swept along by the actions and emotions of others in the crowd. Rather, they appraise the situation, weighing the facts with potential gains and losses before deciding what to do. Through such concepts the behavior cannot be well characterized as contagion.

The conclusions from the balance sheet of the follower differs considerably from that of the agitator. He can be seen as weighing somewhat different considerations, or evaluating the same variables, but giving them different values. In the latter case, for example, he may think it not especially important to try to put Blacks in their place,

and he may feel that the only real reason to engage in violence is in response to an actual invasion. Whatever the variables and/or the values given to each consideration, the result is that benefits closely approximate costs. The follower is ambivalent and consequently immobilized in vacillation.[8] Note that people in the crowd are not simply reacting to impulses; they are consciously evaluating the situations and possibilities for action as best they can.[9]

Up to this point, the specific components of the balance sheets have been relatively unimportant; the totals and cognitive processes have been the focus. This will remain the case with the exception of one of the potential costs. The risk of injury at the hands of Blacks is an important issue for this analysis because, as Grimshaw notes, this is a new development. White rioters of the not-too-distant past did not have to contend with a black population that appeared to be armed and prepared to "deal with" Whites. White balance sheets did not include a high risk element based on Black-perpetrated vio-

8. This is the classic approach-avoidance conflict described by Dollard and Miller in their book, *Personality and Psychotherapy* (New York: McGraw-Hill, 1950). For our purposes it is not necessary to use as sophisticated an analysis as employed by Dollard and Miller. We do not need, for example, to examine if the vacillation with both rewards and costs at higher values is more intense than vacillation at lower values, even though in principle such extension would be possible. For present purposes it does not especially matter what the actual considerations are (with one exception to be examined later) or what values they are given; we require only that for the agitator the benefits of action far outweigh costs; and for the follower costs and benefits are about equal.

9. It is important to stress that their evaluations may be "wrong" either because they are weighing the wrong components or have given them unrealistic values. This might be especially likely to happen in the case of psychological considerations.

lence. Thus, with such a component missing it would have been more likely (other things being about equal) that they would feel it in their interest to engage in an assault on Blacks. One might think then, that a potential white rioter in earlier years could have a balance sheet like either of the two we have discussed, with the primary difference a smaller total on the cost side of the tally.[10]

Agitators and followers, having different totals for their balance sheets, join the crowd with different pay-off matrices (Figure 1). Each matrix is meant to represent the evaluations by either agitators or followers for one of two actions by himself and the crowd. The issue is whether to launch an assault or not, and each person has some estimation of the cost and benefits for him and the other group members based on the actions taken. For example, in the eyes of the agitator the best result for both him and the crowd (+3) is for everyone to riot. A poor result in his eyes is for neither him nor the crowd to attack. The worst result would be for the crowd to remain inactive and for the agitator to charge into the Black community by himself. Such an action would do little to inhibit a Black assault and would likely result in severe injury. It is clear from the agitator's matrix that the only two cells with positive pay-offs are those in which the crowd takes collective actions, and of those two choices, the best pay-off for the agitator is when he is part of that action. Thus, the evaluations by the agitator lead him to the conclusion that he must get the crowd to act.

10. It is also probable that the self-defense component on the benefit side would not be as large as in this case where there is a threat of invasion, but in terms of the total evaluation this is probably less important than the change in the costs side of the sheet where the element of fear of Blacks would have been almost entirely missing.

FIGURE 1. PAY-OFF MATRICES: FOR CROWD MEMBERS* IN THE MIND OF THE AGITATOR

| | | GROUP | |
		RIOT	NO RIOT
Person	Riot	+3 for P / +3 for G	—2 for G / —3 for P
	No Riot	+2 (+3?) for G / +1 (+2?) for P	—2 for G / —2 for P

IN THE MIND OF THE FOLLOWER

| | | GROUP | |
		RIOT	NO RIOT
Person	Riot	0 for G / 0 for P	0 for G / —3 for P
	No Riot	0 for G / 0 for P	0 for G / 0 for P

*(3 = high, 2 = medium, 1 = low, 0 = vacillation)

The pay-off matrix for the follower reflects the indecision of his balance sheet. About all that he is sure of is that for him to launch an individual assault on the Black neighborhood would involve a high personal risk. All of the other possibilities find him vacillating.

Given the pay-off matrices in Figure 1, the roles of agitators and followers become clear. An agitator must try to move the crowd to join him in a vigilante action. If this cannot be done, the group violence against Blacks will not occur. The agitator's goal must be to change the balance sheet of the followers so they will conclude that collective action will produce substantial gains. Such an alteration might be accomplished by introducing, highlighting, or minimizing certain "facts" about the situation along with appropriate evaluations so that followers become convinced that the benefits are very high, or that the costs are not too severe, or both. In some cases a clever agitator may help to mold the facts by acting in ways that bring useful responses for important actors on the scene. For example, he might attempt to provoke an imminent confrontation with Blacks.

In the crowd processes to be described later, the communication techniques employed by agitators to alter the balance sheets and pay-off matrices for the followers take a variety of forms. The most overt tactic of rousing public speeches is not the only approach. Agitators discuss the issues from their point of view while in small groups, or on a one-to-one basis. Nor is verbal communication the only way information is exchanged. Symbolic gestures, displays of emotion, and tentative actions are employed to transmit the notions of the agitators to the followers. It is crucial to realize that the agitators are not engaged solely in transmitting information. Like the followers, they must absorb the words, emotions, and actions of crowd members because their pay-off matrices also depend on the responses of other people. They must discover points of resistance among followers and determine whether followers are being moved. Thus, there is an extensive dialogue occurring with agitators trying to motivate followers, and everyone trying to gain information about what is going on. These communications processes are crucial because it is through such mechanism that new facts, evaluations, and collective definitions emerge.[11]

In the events to be documented in this chapter, we will find the agitators unable substantially to alter the pay-off matrices of followers. The followers are too frightened of the potential outcome of a violent confrontation with Blacks to launch an assault. Thus, full-scale violence ceases to be a viable choice, and crowd members begin to seek an-

other kind of action that will provide a more favorable pay-off matrix. The immediate goal is the same—to thwart a Black invasion—but people begin casting about for tactics that involve less risk. The dialogue begun in an attempt to move the crowd toward vigilante action now broadens to include alternative strategies.

Some of the suggestions for action evolve from the logic of a certain perspective on the situation, others seem more a result of nearly random trial-and-error. In this case study, the white crowd eventually arrives at a consensus that with full-scale violence ruled out, confrontation employing limited violence, supplemented by posturing and ritual conflict, is an approach that might bring to crowd members a reasonable balance of benefits. Such a conclusion is not arrived at by all people, or even by a large number of people all at once. Further, the pay-off matrices produced by this new strategy do not necessarily emerge in verbal terms. Agitators frequently begin to act out and/or explain some sort of ritual conflict, and followers respond with gestures and actions as well as words. For example, when a leader rips up a black flag (a symbol of Black Power) and the crowd cheers and begins to engage in similar actions, it is clear to all that there is a consensus in support of that action (people agree that rewards outweigh costs). In similar ways a number of actions are proposed, tested, and evaluated until eventually a "program" appears, embodying tactics that satisfy large numbers of people in the crowd. (The testing of tactics that are symbolic may become an end in itself because symbolic gestures can be inherently satisfying—or may be the first in a series of more extensive symbolic acts.) Finally, along with the programmatic consensus a number of emergent norms appear that indicate a range of appropriate actions.

11. Ralph H. Turner, "Collective Behavior" in Robert E. L. Faris, ed., *Handbook of Modern Sociology* (Chicago: Rand McNally Co., 1964). See especially the material on emergent norms.

It is important to keep in mind that most of the possible actions desired by the agitators require support and co-operation from the rest of the crowd. In a very real sense there exists for a relatively short time a group of people who need each other and can only function effectively if the majority, or a large number, agree on the proposed actions. And thus, in the exchange of information between crowd members, important dialogue exists, and the final outcome represents a form of democratic decision to be implemented through norms indicating acceptable actions.

We can turn now to the case study of a Northern race riot that forms the empirical base for this paper. In this case study, one will be able to see White perceptions of "Black Power," group processes that shape the final actions of the crowd, and a confrontation—a mixture of physical and symbolic conflict. The events will illustrate ways in which broad changes in White perceptions of ghetto Blacks may influence the behavior of crowds during race riots and how individuals involved in the mob processes act in a manner that appears consistent with the theoretical concepts of cost and benefits, pay-off matrices, group decisions, and emergent norms.

BACKGROUND FOR THE RIOT

The city of Baltimore is blighted by two large and impoverished ghettos, one located on the west side of town and the other on the east side. The events to be described occur in 36 square blocks directly south of a main avenue separating the White and Black slums of East Baltimore—an area populated by Appalachian Whites and Lumbie Indians. As one moves farther south and east, the community quickly becomes a solid working-class neighborhood of Polish and Italian ethnic stock. These people, though crucial to the political and social functioning of Baltimore, do not have a central role in the confrontation documented here. We will largely be concerned with the recent migrant Appalachians and Lumbie Indians that live along the northern and western ghetto boundaries.

The migrant Appalachians who reside near the boundaries that separate the Whites from the Blacks in East Baltimore live in conditions as impoverished as any in the Black sections of the city. Housing consists of over-crowded and run-down tenements that are hazardous to health and safety. Crime is rampant. Families often show matriarchal structure similar to that associated with Black ghettos. Very few youths finish high school, and unemployment, especially among the young, is very high. About the only advantage Whites have over the Blacks living several blocks north is slightly greater success in finding jobs. This advantage is counter-balanced, however, by the fact that the White community has no spokesman, and thus cannot get government services and action even as well as the Black community. The lack of political influence is at least partly the result of divisions among Whites along ethnic and class lines. The Appalachians who have been the most recent to arrive in the city and are the poorest and least well-educated, are looked down upon by the Italians and Poles living to the south.

Also living in the immediate area, south and east of the Black/White dividing line are a group of about 4,000 Lumbie Indians. These recent migrants are descendants of Indians many of whom, in their native North Carolina, had probably intermarried with Blacks. As a result, large numbers of the current residents show facial and skin characteristics of both Blacks and Indians. One will find, for example, men with bronze skin, high cheekbones, and extremely curly hair.

There is remarkable group solidarity within the Lumbie community, strong identification with the tribe, and great attachment to their ethnic background. It appears that, at least in Baltimore, intermarriage with Blacks is infrequent, and even to be seen associating with Blacks is frowned upon. Yet in spite of strong group identity and basically sound family life, there is great poverty among the Lumbies. The standard of living is not as low as among the Appalachian Whites, but it is not nearly as high as among the blue-collar Whites several blocks south. Many in the community exist on welfare. The crime rate, especially crimes against persons, is very high.

Race relations along the Black/White boundaries since 1966 had been characterized by increased tension, and both the Indians and the Whites felt growing fear and dislike of Blacks. Many had individual Black friends, but the generic term Negro could elicit intensely hostile responses. The Indians and Whites related to each other in a distant sort of way, with both accepting the right to be different but neither wanting to exchange places. Their interactions were rarely social but, because of the proximity of their living quarters and similarity of occupations, Whites and Indians became acquainted. (There was some intermarriage, although it usually brought disapproval from both groups.) As lukewarm as the Indian/White relations were, there was a strong alliance against the Blacks. The Indians especially underscored this point, and the quickest way to get "cut" on Baltimore Street (a main street in the ghetto) was to call an Indian a "nigger."

Although the mounting hostility along the northern racial border was manifested in a number of violent White/Black episodes, several stood out as especially visible indicators of the increasing tension. One hot, muggy night late in the summer of 1967, four White youths, members of a group called the Blue Royales, attacked ("banked") a Black youth at a neighborhood sandwich shop. The Black teenager, apparently minding his own business as he came out of the store, was grabbed, thrown to the ground, and "stomped" senseless. The sandwich shop had been considered neutral territory, although technically located about a block south of the northern boundary. Blacks had been using the sandwich shop for a long time, and while getting to it often meant being subjected to a barrage of insults when passing through the White area, there had rarely been any violence. This attack was a clear escalation of the previous, largely verbal, hostilities.

Violence among teenagers was common in this neighborhood, but in the past had been primarily intra-racial. White gangs aligned along ethnic ties, and "warring" with each other periodically, supplemented a high rate of individual assaults. During the summer of 1967, however, the teenage hostilities became increasingly inter-racial. What at one time had been merely an exchange of racial insults had now become open violence.

The transition to more dangerous kinds of confrontation seems to have been caused largely by changes taking place within the Black community. Formerly, most Blacks living several blocks north had been afraid to venture into the Appalachian community. Those who did, acted in timid and unassuming ways that were calculated not to antagonize Whites. By the summer of 1967 this subservient demeanor was no longer in evidence, especially among teenagers. Young Blacks were starting to strut, wearing symbols of their new pride. Black became beautiful in East Baltimore, and as the display of racial pride increased, so did violence between youths of the two communities.

The response to the sandwich shop incident was swift and vicious. The next night a group of young Blacks caught one of the White gang members alone and carved his back with knives and razors. He required more than a hundred stitches. In the months that followed, the swapping of atrocities between races became a typical week-end event.

Teenagers were not the only ones involved in racial conflict. The summer of 1966 had brought with it a race riot to an all-White city park when a States Rights party rally was counter-picketed by C.O.R.E. The inflamed Whites, urged on by the most vicious and absurd racist propaganda, turned on the peaceful pickets from C.O.R.E., and only quick police action prevented serious and possibly fatal beatings of the Blacks.

After the rally, States Rights party workers and KKK organizers continued to agitate in the White community. The common response to their efforts was apathetic sympathy. Most members of the Appalachian community harbored great prejudice and fear of Blacks and so, although few would encourage or approve of violence, they did nothing to stop it. Somewhat in contrast was a small vocal group which preached conflict and encouraged the escalation in racial warfare. From this group the teenagers got a great deal of verbal support.

The result of the overall increase in hostilities was that both the White and Black communities in East Baltimore entered the month of April 1968 with great and increasing feelings of anger and fear. The Black community had been growing more verbal and more militant about the rights of black men. The White community had shown a bit of sympathy for equality for all, but the majority seemed to be getting progressively more hostile. Cries of "Black Power" from the Negro community elicited cries of "White Power" (literally) from the whites. More and more of the social ills faced by the poor Whites were blamed on the "pushy niggers" and the "nigger-lovers downtown." If a White could not get a job, he blamed it on Blacks getting special treatment. If a White could not get what he or she wanted from welfare, the White accused the welfare department of giving Blacks preferred status. Further, many Whites honestly believed that one night the black "savages" would rise up and attack the Whites, raping and looting as they went. Black Power was interpreted as physical, military power.

The Indians seemed to take a neutral position of isolationism. They wanted to leave everyone else alone and expected similar treatment in return. However, if forced to ally, they would choose the Whites.

Thus, the assassination of Martin Luther King, Jr., came at a time when tempers were already short. Everyone was anticipating a long hot summer, especially in escalation of racial conflicts. The assassination not only brought summer in April; it introduced a new form of White/Black confrontation. The bulk of the remainder of this chapter will be a detailed description of that confrontation.

CHRONOLOGY OF EVENTS

Saturday, April 6, was the first day of a civil disorder triggered by the death of Martin Luther King, Jr. By sunset, Blacks in the poor sections of the city were engaged in looting and burning that was to last four days. (The riot began the day after the assassination.) Although violence diminished in the early morning hours of

April 7, by noon the riot was once again at full intensity, with groups of Blacks ranging farther and farther in an effort to exploit new neighborhoods. It appeared that the spread of violence would soon involve the invasion of White neighborhoods by Blacks.

About 12:30 p.m., I arrived in the White neighborhood just south of the boundary separating Whites from Blacks in East Baltimore. Driving north on a major avenue to get to the street where I anticipated a potential racial confrontation, I noticed an unusually large number of Whites gathered on the east side of the street five blocks south of my intended destination. The largest number were gathered on the southeast corner of a small side-street running east and west, and many of the faces were recognizable as teenagers who had been prime actors in the "guerrilla" race war of the past ten months. These White youths had not only been involved in many attacks on Blacks, but had been agitators for "teaching the niggers a lesson."[12]

After pulling over and parking my car, I walked to the corner where the crowd was gathered. The north-south street on which I had been driving was a main, four-lane avenue, the central shopping district for those living in the area. Besides retail stores, there were large numbers of service industries and places of entertainment. In addition to being an important commercial area, the avenue was the eastern boundary separating Blacks from Whites in the east-side slum of the city. Blacks lived west of the avenue, Whites to the east. On any day, especially a day when

12. I had been in the area approximately 2 years when these events occurred and knew the community and its people well. For details of how this was accomplished, see Richard A. Berk and Joseph M. Adams, "Establishing Rapport with Deviant Groups," *Social Problems* 18 (No. 1, 1970), pp. 102–117.

there was no school, the corner was crowded (a sandwich shop and drugstore on the corner made it a "hangout"), but even considering that it was Sunday, the crowd seemed too large and too active to be accounted for in terms of the usual activities. Also strange was the almost complete lack of Black faces in the crowd. Although the avenue was considered White territory, especially on the east side of the street, Blacks did use the stores and movie houses. On this Sunday, however, only a few Blacks could be seen.

The drugstore and sandwich shop were crowded with about 40 white teenagers, mostly boys. Very few adults could be seen, and those present were in their 20's and early 30's. There were two Blacks in the gathering, and they seemed, on the surface, to be on very friendly terms with the Whites. They moved in and out of the crowd chatting casually, but were "hanging loose" and it seemed calculated. The speed with which they moved from group to group and their overly friendly manner (they greeted people they hardly knew as old friends) suggested that they were really quite anxious about the situation. (One Black youth whom I knew very well and who associated with a White group exclusively often told me of the special anxiety he felt when racial confrontations took place. His friends happened to be White, but he also felt some racial loyalty. As a result, neither side completely trusted him. His solution in times of trouble was to hide from *both* sides.)

Most of the white youths were well-dressed in slacks or stay-press cotton pants and button-down shirts. Very few were dressed in the more "hoody" style of blue jeans and black leather jackets. Well-combed hair, of either an Ivy-league or longish Beatle cut, was prevalent. Few had the long side-burned ducktail style often associated with juvenile delinquency (at least until the mid-1960's). Especially noticeable was the presence of several rival groups who seemed, at least for the time being, to be getting along very well. The situation appeared to generate active, if uneasy, friendships between former enemies. The usual "sounding" was cut to a minimum, and ethnic slurs were virtually eliminated.

As I got to the corner, I went immediately to one of the youths I knew and tried to find out the reason for the gathering. I spoke with him for about ten minutes, during which time several others came over to add their opinions. It soon became clear from what they said and from what I observed that the crowd was forming out of concern for an attack that was expected from the Black community. New people kept arriving and the primary topics of conversation were the "facts" of the situation and what could be done about them. Some youths who were particularly outspoken seemed to be trying to agitate the crowd.

Knowing one of the agitators well, I walked over to him and we began to talk about what was occurring. The ideas he was passing on to the crowd seem to have been as follows. He believed that the Blacks were massing several blocks west to attack the southern section of the avenue. After all, he argued, they had already looted the northern section (i.e., in the Black ghetto), and the southern part seemed a sure target. There were plenty of ripe places to loot, and it was very close to the Black neighborhoods. Further, he felt that the police could not protect the area; either they were simply outmanned by extensive rioting or they were coddling the Blacks. In any case, the only thing that stood between the Blacks and the avenue was the might and will of the White community. In addition, the attack on the avenue was

viewed as an intermediate step. He also predicted an assault that would take the Blacks into White residential neighborhoods, burning, looting, and raping. The black flags (in mourning for King) seen on cars were interpreted as coats of arms, signifying Black Power. In short, there was a firm belief that vigilante action was needed, and he was trying to arouse the crowd for that purpose. His agitating style toward this end was not to stand on soap boxes making political speeches, but rather to move among the people, speaking to groups of three or four at a time.

It was now nearly 1:00 p.m. The size of the crowd was growing so that on the east side of the avenue there were about 100 Whites. At about this time, two white girls, approximately 16 years of age, crossed over from the west side (the Black side) and joined the crowd. They moved into the white gathering, saying that they had just been a couple of blocks into the Black area and that the Blacks were threatening to burn the avenue. The two girls had promiscuous reputations, and it became clear from the reaction of those in the crowd who knew them that they were "equal opportunity employers." Their relegation to the level of "funky bitches" probably explained the fact that no one seemed offended that these girls had "friends" in the Black ghetto.

The message they brought reinforced the rumors that were already spreading, but after they had told their story several times, the crowd lost interest in them and the two girls disappeared up the street. No other girls appear to have had any salient role, and only a few were present.

During the forty minutes or so that I had been on the corner, police cars had cruised slowly by on several occassions. One of the youths I knew informed me that the day before, two police officers had kept a close surveillance on this corner and had cleared off the streets in the immediate vicinity on three occasions. Curfew had been very strictly enforced, and it seemed to him that the police were operating with unusual seriousness.

With the crowd now at over 100 on the White side and a small group of 15 or so Black youths gathering on the west side of the avenue, two police cars pulled over near the median strip. Two policemen from one car walked toward the Blacks and two toward the Whites; all four carried riot clubs. The Blacks ran, but the Whites at first stood their ground. The policemen calmly but firmly told the people to "break it up," and the crowd pulled back about 50 yards. The policemen did not pursue the crowd past the corner, but stood resolutely on the corner swinging their clubs. After about five minutes they returned to their cars, and both crowds moved back to the corners.

People now seemed to take the situation more seriously. Police presence verified the rumor that trouble was expected, and the tough manner of the officers suggested that they expected some difficulties in keeping order. Two agitators moved swiftly through the crowd, verbally attacking the police as "nigger-lovers" and urging the people to drive the Blacks out of Baltimore. Their style was aggressive yet quite sophisticated. Exuding confidence and poise, they could drop their rhetoric when necessary and give a reasonable rationale as to why the Whites needed to protect themselves. In contrast were the attempts of several others to arouse the crowd. One youth in particular, although known as a tough fighter, was far less successful in agitating. He was not verbally skilled enough to persuade people that violence was required in their own self-interest. Consequently, teenagers in the crowd respected him for his toughness and liked the idea of

his being on their side, but they were not particularly inspired by his style.

About 1:15 p.m., two cars driven by Blacks and flying black flags on the aerials drove west down the side street toward the avenue. They approached the White crowd from the ethnic territory to the rear. As soon as people noticed the cars approaching the intersections, they poured into the street, shouting insults. A barrage of stones and spit followed. The drivers of the automobiles understandably panicked and ran the red light at the intersection.

Shortly after, four cars driven by white youths and flying white flags on their aerials arrived. They were greeted with cries of "White Power," and people in the crowd became increasingly animated in speech and movement. More cars with white flags arrived and lined up along the side street. What was at first defined as a defensive confrontation now took on "search and destroy" overtones.

Meanwhile, across the avenue, a crowd of about 30 Blacks had gathered apparently in response to the massing of the Whites. The two mobs, Black and White, began to exchange provocative gestures and hostile words. The police, sensing the rising tension, had little success in once again attempting to clear the corners. Although the crowds would retreat as the police advanced, retreat was merely token. The crowds never withdrew more than 25 yards from the corners.

With police stationed in the middle of the street between Blacks and Whites, an uneasy balance of power emerged. Closer scrutiny of the white crowd suggested that the majority really did not want a confrontation with the Blacks. Most were content to stand back, fading into the large mass of milling people. Many were genuinely frightened by the potential violence, and spoke about their fears in hushed tones to close friends. Only about twenty appeared eager to mix with the Blacks, and they did not show the ambivalence about racial violence that the others evidenced. These twenty kept the mob agitated. They spoke of the "inevitable race war," of the necessity to "show those niggers once and for all," and described the situation in such a way that Whites appeared to have no choice but to prepare for certain attack. Since they were verbal in the language of racism, one had only to grant one or two assumptions for the rest of their propaganda to follow logically.

The more passive majority of the White crowd were not nearly so able to verbalize why they were there or what was happening. They seemed to be drawn to the corner largely by curiosity and a search for excitement. Firm in stating that if the Blacks attacked their homes they would fight back viciously, they were most ambivalent about defending the stores on the avenue and very cool to the idea of attacking Blacks in the ghetto. As a result most stood back from the corner or gathered in the nearby poolroom about 50 yards from the corner. (The pool room normally had about 10 people inside; on this afternoon the number was close to 50.)

About this time many parents of teenagers in the crowd reached the scene. Several mothers of younger boys present tried to get them to come home with promises of rewards and threats of punishment. The mothers told their children that rioting was dangerous and that they should not participate. The issue was not articulated as an ethical question of the use of violence or of participation in racial confrontation, but rather as a high-risk situation. The children refused to comply with requests to return home. Several older men also appeared, apparently fathers of some of the youths. Unlike the mothers, they did little to get their boys home. Some, in fact, encouraged the crowd, although none seemed actually to join in. Thus the crowd of approximately 300 remained largely a group of teenagers led by teenagers.

The uneasy stalemate between the crowds lasted about 15 minutes. During this time, those wanting to attack the Blacks who were standing on the opposite corner continued to agitate the crowd. Still avoiding speeches to large numbers of people, they continued to employ a more intimate technique: talking to groups of three or four at a time in a conversational manner. The technique seemed to be having an effect, and the Whites in the cars appeared particularly ready to mix. Several drove their cars recklessly out onto the avenue and made screeching left turns which brought them within several yards of the Black crowd, now numbering about 50. As they passed, they yelled insults at the Blacks and urged them to come across to the White side and fight it out. Whites witnessing these challenges cheered.

Meanwhile, on the White side of the street, several of the leaders had bought rolls of white adhesive tape which many in the crowd used to make white arm bands. The tape was also employed to fashion white crosses and KKK initials to be put on the clothing of anyone who felt it necessary to make clear where he stood on racial questions. Most of the agitators were among the first to dramatize their position, and the white KKK stood out impressively on their clothing.

Partly in response to the actions of the people in cars and partly in response to the insignias, new shouts of "White Power" were heard, and the intensity of activity in the white mob continued to grow. For the first time now, large numbers of people became outspoken, and inhibitions which originally minimized the expression of racial hatred and advocacy of violence seemed to slip away. Opinions originally discussed in quiet tones were being shouted. Police were included as a prime target for insults, accused of protecting Blacks, even of being on their side. Apparently unrattled by this new development, the police remained outwardly calm.

Despite the increased level of hostility within the crowd overall, there was still a clear distinction between the agitators and the rest. Twenty or so of the most aggressive youths (all appearing to be about 18 years old) actually stood in the street (about 5 yards from the curb), inching slowly toward the Black side of the avenue. The rest of the crowd hung back, watching carefully and not participating as extensively in the exchange of challenges and insults.

Around 2 p.m., five Blacks in their early teens feigned a break across the avenue toward the Whites. They acted as if they were going to pick up the white gauntlet, but stopped several yards short of going half-way across the street. In response to this, the group of 20 Whites in the front of the crowd charged toward the Blacks. Although the rest of the crowd moved out partially into the street, they did not follow.

Seeing the Whites approaching, the Blacks turned and ran. Several were not fast enough, and a brief fight involving about 15 Whites and 5 Blacks took place on the Black side of the avenue. The police, who at that moment were not standing in a position to intercept the White attackers, hurried over, and the conflict immediately ceased. Several of the Blacks, but no Whites, who participated in the brief skirmish were arrested.

Within a few minutes three more police cars pulled up; the policemen jumped out and pursued the entire Black mob (50 or so) for about a block back into the ghetto along the side street. At that point they were met with a barrage of bricks and bottles, and the chase ended. Nevertheless, about ten more Blacks were caught and arrested. The police largely ignored the White side of the street, and the crowd stood watching, cheering them on.

Those who had participated in the attack returned and were taken in as heroes. They told anyone who would listen how "we showed those niggers who's boss," and they bragged at length about the way the Blacks ran. It was as if they had won a final victory against the hated enemy.

Everyone stood watching as the police mopped up, and about five minutes later, national guard troops arrived. Even before the troops came down the avenue, however, the spirit of the crowd seemed to change from anxious hostility to victorious festivity. Those who had charged across the street were especially enthusiastic, although no blood was spilled and no booty taken. A crowd that a few minutes earlier had claimed it was ready to fight to the death was now preparing to throw a party. During the positioning of troops along the avenue the victory euphoria remained; in addition, the crowd seemed relieved as the threat of dangerous racial violence disappeared.

The conflict on the avenue ended with a minimum of actual combat. As the crowd continued to watch the deployment of police and troops, the passions of the crowd died away and many people began to drift home. Then a new rumor began to spread through the crowd, and with it the holiday spirit abruptly vanished. The word circulating was, "the niggers have looted the Volcano Bar."

The Volcano was a symbolic center for the Indian section of the eastern ghetto. Located on an east/west street about two blocks west of the avenue, it lay on the northern border that separated the Blacks from the Whites and Indians. It was clear to everyone who knew the Indian neighborhood that the bar was a hang-out for the Indians, and white Appalachians referred to the bar as "Indian hunting grounds."

Looting bars and liquor stores had been a salient aspect of the Baltimore riot, but the Volcano was not just any bar. To attack it meant an attack on the Indians themselves. Knowing this and anticipating some excitement, the mob, then breaking up, began to move quickly toward the northern boundary. The crowd was almost completely white (with some 10 or so Indians). Motivations appeared to involve a search for action rather than a deep-felt sympathy for the violation of Indian territory.

I arrived at a corner about three blocks west of the Volcano at 2:15 and tried to evaluate the situation. On the street that passes by the Volcano, Indians and Whites, allied, were fighting Blacks. There were at least 300 men and boys involved, fighting with bricks, bottles, and anything else that could be easily picked up from the street. The confrontation extended over about three blocks along the northern boundary, and two police cars drove up and down the street trying to break the mobs apart. As the cars approached a knot of people, they would separate, only to join in battle once again as the police car moved to another group.

Large numbers of "artillery" operatives, probably about three-fourths of the people involved, were throwing stones, cans, bottles, and bricks from the sidewalk toward the opposition on the other side of the street. (Blacks were deployed on the north side and the Indians and Whites on the south.) Meanwhile, more daring groups of five or six, making up about one-quarter of

the crowd, were engaging the enemy in hand-to-hand combat in the middle of the street. Most of these incidents were of short duration—30 seconds or so—with people darting briefly into skirmishes from sidewalk sanctuaries. (However, several groups of Indians chased Blacks across the street and into their homes.) It appeared that it was primarily Blacks and Indians who were engaging in the close combat and that Whites were largely on the sidewalks throwing rocks.

Two things were particularly surprising. First, although most of the participants, especially the Indians, owned knives and/or guns, no weapons (other than improvised ones) were to be seen. I had noticed several Indians carrying pistols earlier in the day, and knew that many Blacks also had access to guns. One particular home near the boundary was used as an armory by a group of Black teenagers. Yet, with virtually everyone having access to guns, not a shot was fired. People on either side could have stationed themselves in tenement buildings overlooking the battle and sniped at whomever they chose, or, in the milling and noisy crowd, fired at the enemy at point-blank range. There was no evidence of either taking place. Further, from what I could see, and later confirm, knives were not employed either. People seemed content to throw stones at each other and to exchange blows. On this very street on many a Friday night, knifings and occasional shootings occurred, but on this day of rioting violence was limited to less dangerous actions.

The second surprising feature was that although the police cars were driving up and down the street trying to break up the crowds, not a bottle or brick was directed toward the police. With hundreds of objects being thrown, the patrol cars were never struck. If there was any intent toward the police, it was to *avoid* hitting the cars. In this neighborhood, as in any slum, there had always been a great amount of distrust and dislike for the police, but this hostility was not in evidence. Considering the limited presence of only four policemen in two patrol cars, the crowd could have chosen to force them to retreat rather than try to stay out of their way (as has frequently happened during civil disorders). Yet, this did not happen. The atmosphere of the "riot" was like a big football game in a neighborhood park, where the police appeared to be needed to keep the game within the rules.[13] The "rioters" seemed to be having a great time; many participants could be seen cheering and laughing! In a community where groups of pre-teens often engage in playful rock-throwing fights, this large-scale confrontation appeared to be taken as sport. In a culture where fist fights among friends are common, the small group conflicts in the middle of the street seemed almost "business as usual." Most of the people were enjoying the excitement.[14]

13. In fact, if the crowds really wanted to engage in an armed escalation against one another, it is unlikely that the 4 policemen in the 2 cars could have prevented it. There were simply too many people spread over too wide an area. In the eyes of the participants, however, it is not clear to what extent the police acted as a deterrent. I suspect the deterrence was minimal, based on the demonstrated ability of crowds during riots to rout city police when they choose.

14. It is difficult to account more specifically for the sporting atmosphere—probably similar to the carnival atmosphere described in civil disorders—without a detailed discussion of a variety of psychological variables that could have been operating. I do not see this case study as being rich enough in data probing the emotions of individuals during actual confrontation to warrant such an analysis. My speculations are that the enjoyment evidenced by the participants was at least in part a result of aggressive activity often

Though a sporting event to most of the participants, many observers of the scene took a more serious view. One middle-aged Appalachian migrant had a shotgun draped over his arm and was very frank about his intentions should the Blacks try to burn his block. He stated the case for many of the older adult White residents very simply: "If they leave me alone, I'll leave them alone. But if they want trouble, they'll get more than they bargained for. I know how to use this thing." (He referred to his shotgun.) He went on to say that the Whites had had just about enough of this looting and burning and that the police should shoot a few Blacks just to show them they couldn't push people around.

Younger observers reflected more closely the attitude of the participants (who were generally under 30). Most supported the sporting event atmosphere. Although many had now adopted the white arm band as a symbol of White Power, they seemed preoccupied with the excitement of the confrontation and did not take seriously the political implications or the danger of the events. They just stood on the corner rooting for their side. The older adults, by comparison, seemed much more concerned about the possibility of racial war and the use of guns.

About 3 p.m., the national guard troops arrived and things immediately quieted down. Few arrests were made, and apparently there were few critical injuries. Those teenagers who had participated in the rock-throwing came back with stories of their prowess, but their tone was not that of participants in a political or racial war. There was

being fun for its own sake, of the fact that the muted tactics were working, and of the relief that the confrontation was staying within acceptable limits (almost like hysterical laughter following a crisis).

not even the seriousness or anxiety that had been so often present after an inter-gang skirmish.

By 3:15, the troops had restored order. The streets were reasonably quiet; the main concern had become where to get beer and whiskey (no alcohol was allowed to be served or sold) and what to do for fun now that everyone had to be off the streets. By 4 p.m., curfew time, the only people outside were soldiers.

In the week that followed, normality gradually returned. Although there were two serious arson attacks directed against White businesses (one of particular interest against a lumber yard that had refused to close for the national day of mourning), the boundary areas of previous trouble were quiet. Things seemed to have returned to *status quo*, with possibly even a reduction in the general level of anxiety and hostility. The riot seemed to have been taken in stride as nothing too out of the ordinary, and no special new problems appeared to arise. Most of the people in the affected White area returned to their habitual way of life and left it to the politicians and social scientists to figure out what had happened. Many appeared to look back on the riot with favor, as something that had added a bit of excitement to their lives.

For a variety of reasons, I maintained close contact with the Appalachian community for two more years. During that time I expected to see continued racial fighting and an escalation in the violent aspects of such confrontations. However, there were no more large-scale conflicts, and the guerrilla warfare between White and Black gangs completely disappeared. Blacks continued to push for what they saw as their rights, and Whites continued to express anger at what they felt to be reverse discrimination. But neither group chose to express their grievances

by physically assaulting one another. Both groups stayed within the boundaries of their neighborhoods, and such inter-racial contact as occurred took place rather civilly.

Summary of Events

From the details of the events in the confrontations, several occurrences should be highlighted.

(1) Prior to the outbreak of the "commodity" riots in the Black community, respect for Black militancy had been growing among the members of the White community. This was in part a result of real experiences with Blacks and in part a result of mass media presentations.

(2) The immediate reason for Whites to gather on the boundaries of their community was the spreading civil disorder. An invasion was a real possibility.

(3) The White groups that formed were clearly made up of leaders and followers, with leaders playing the role of agitators. The agitators moved among the crowd, giving and receiving information. Their job was made especially difficult by fears held by followers that a violent confrontation with Blacks would be extremely dangerous.

(4) Instead of just plotting alternative strategies where the only goal was effectively thwarting a Black invasion and controlling more general Black advances, the leaders spent great amounts of energy making and displaying symbols of "White Power" and exchanging verbal insults with Blacks. Part of this behavior can be attributed to their role as agitators (an instrumental action); part seems more appropriately labeled as symbolic posturing (a consummatory action).

(5) In spite of all attempts to move the crowd, the physical violence in the first confrontation was very minor (especially considering past police rec-

ords of many of the leaders), involving at most 25 Whites out of a crowd of several hundred.

(6) The victorious merriment after the first confrontation was far out of proportion to the actual "victory" achieved. There was a symbolic victory when the Blacks were forced to retreat, but an honest strategic interpretation was at best a stand-off.[15] A serious attempt at an invasion was not thwarted, and there was little reason to believe that the token resistance put up by Whites would act as a future deterrent. Thus, the joyousness of the White crowd may have been largely due to the symbolic victory and the fact that troops arrived, preventing (for the moment) further violence. However, if the primary emotion following the small confrontation and arrival of the troops was relief (that is, thank God there will be no more trouble), then there would be little reason to celebrate as if there were a victory. Returning leaders who had engaged in the violence would not have been welcomed as heroes.

(7) The second confrontation demonstrated the form that the first confrontation might have taken if it had been allowed to continue. The violence was muted, and police were not attacked. People acted as if they were participating in or watching a sporting event, not a race war. Most of the participants were satisfied simply to throw rocks and to cheer for their side. A minority engaged in actual hand-to-hand combat, and even this was limited by the absence of knives and guns. In short, few people really wanted a

15. Blacks may have not viewed the results as a total defeat because they withdrew only when outnumbered by Whites and police. Also the fact that the White community was obviously concerned about Black intentions and that police had to be employed clearly indicated that they had successfully flexed their muscles.

full-scale race war, and a solution to each person's pay-off matrix emerged that muted the confrontation and encouraged symbolic expression. To cries of "Black Power" and black flags, the Whites responded, not with guns but with cries of "White Power," white arm bands, and a few rocks.

(8) Instead of the race riot encouraging further violence, it appeared to be the last salient White/Black confrontation in the area, at least as of 1970. The grievances of both sides did not change appreciably, only the techniques used in expressing those grievances. There were no more riots, and inter-racial gang warfare among teenagers all but ceased. In effect, the race riot of April 1968 brought about a "cease fire."

Conclusions

In Chapter 6 of this volume, H. L. Nieburg discusses the role of ritual in collective conflict:

Ritual action is the redressive, reconciling means of reaffirming loyalties, testing and changing them at times or offering new ones to replace the old, but expressed in a kind of muted symbolic display with a symbolic response which changes attitudes and values without major and unlimited conflict, and without the necessity of total and simultaneous involvement in the new value systems by all members of the society. The potential for disruptive revolutionary change by escalated violence and internal warfare is always present, unpredictable in its outcome, costly in its logistics, dangerous in the secondary conflicts which may be engendered; ritual controls and moderates these undesirable tendencies.

It seems reasonable to interpret the form of the confrontation described in the present chapter in the context of ritual conflict. Violence was muted and there were a wide range of symbolic actions. A potential race war was transformed into a sporting event. Equally important, however, was the manner in which the agreement on alternative behavior evolved. Besides the obvious role of verbal exchange of information, two other complementary processes appear to have been operating.

First, a consensus may have emerged at least in part from large numbers of people independently constructing similar pay-off matrices. Given similar inputs and similar evaluation procedures, it is not unreasonable to expect that many people might independently arrive at similar conclusions. In this process, the role of information exchange between participants in the crowd would be minimal.

Second, a wide variety of information was exchanged by non-verbal communication. The tone and style of crowd members conveyed important cues, and tentative actions by various individuals acted as "trial balloons" to which the crowd could respond.

Given these processes which provided the foundation for widespread agreement, it may not be useful to characterize all mobs as something especially different from other groups of people. In the case study presented, one can reasonably interpret the data to suggest extensive exchange of information, the weighing of benefits and costs, the evolution of a group decision in a way that approximates democratic procedure, and the emergence of norms. What is different is not the mental process of participants, but the means of conveying information, the short life of the group, and its informality. And the actual confrontation that emerged, although probably appearing on the surface to be wild, expressive behavior, in fact reflected a great deal of group discipline and self-control. Thus, mobs may be only different in degree from other kinds of human groups.

Finally, it is important again to address the historical pattern of race riots described by Grimshaw. His characterization of Northern race riots emphasized aggressive violence by both Whites and Blacks. Here we have seen evidence suggesting that when Whites (and probably Blacks as well) believe that a racial confrontation will involve high risks, they will try to find less costly ways to accomplish their goals, making symbolic conflict salient in a confrontation. However, even this involves some risk, and there is always a chance that serious violence may occur anyway, once the confrontation begins. Thus, one could reasonably expect that with both sides believing that both groups are capable of armed racial war, they may simply choose not to fight. The sudden decline of inter-racial fighting following the "race riot" is quite possibly an example of this kind of "cease fire." However, one must remember that the choice to engage in high risk actions depends in part on the potential for rewards, and continuing injustice and oppression could again make it in the interest of either or both groups to employ violence.

24

Police Violence and Its Public Support

By WILLIAM A. GAMSON AND JAMES McEVOY

William A. Gamson is professor of Sociology and a staff member of the Center for Research on Conflict Resolution at the University of Michigan. He is the author of Power and Discontent *for which he received the 1969 Sorokin Award of the American Sociological Association. He is also the author of a teaching game,* SIMSOC: Simulated Society *and a forthcoming book with André Modigliani,* Untangling the Cold War. *He has written on community conflict and coalition formation; for work in the latter area, he received the 1962 Socio-Psychological Prize of the American Association for the Advancement of Science (AAAS). His current work involves a study of the careers of relatively powerless groups that have challenged the American political system since 1800.*

James McEvoy is assistant professor of Sociology at the University of California, Davis. He is the author of a forthcoming book, Radicals or Conservatives? The Contemporary American Right *and an editor, with A. Miller, of* Black Power and Student Rebellion. *He served as a special consultant to the National Commission on the Causes and Prevention of Violence.*

We are indebted to John P. Evans, David Segal, Edward Laumann, and Leon Mayhew for their criticisms of an earlier draft of this paper, and to Richard Juster for his suggestions and assistance in getting our data in and out of the computer.

DURING the winter of 1970, a United Press International correspondent was taken into custody by police and held for twenty hours. He had been covering a student riot in Santa Barbara. During the period he was detained he was neither formally charged nor allowed to make a phone call. "War correspondents," California Governor Ronald Reagan explained with a grin, "have to realize that sometime they are going to get it. . . . He should be happy he was captured by the good guys." [1]

For many Americans, there is apparently a thin blue line between order and chaos. Breach it and untold furies lie beyond. The police require unconditional support when they are in combat; sins are understandable and forgivable when they occur in the stress of battle.

For others, of course, it is a quite different story. The police are a crude instrument of power, often failing to differentiate between criminals and bystanders and full of barely controlled aggressive impulses. Norman Mailer expresses this view eloquently in his description at the time of the 1968 Democratic Convention.

Every public figure with power, every city official, high politician, or prominent government worker knows in his unspoken sentiments that the police are an essentially criminal force restrained by their guilt, their covert awareness that they are imposters, and by a sprinkling of career men whose education, rectitude, athletic ability, and religious dedication make them work for a balance between justice and authority.[2]

This paper explores the sources of public support and opposition to police violence. The most highly publicized police violence of the last decade has

1. Reported in the *San Francisco Chronicle*, Wednesday, March 4, 1970.
2. Norman Mailer, *Miami and the Siege of Chicago* (Cleveland: World Publishing Co., 1968), p. 175.

taken place in a political context with the police confronting organized groups rather than isolated individuals. Since police frequently appear in such conflicts as protagonists, attitudes toward them are likely to be closely bound to support and opposition to the social movements that have occurred within American society during this period. Hence, we start with the more general issue of the nature of social movements before turning to the more specific phenomenon of attitudes toward the police.

SUPPORT FOR POLITICAL MOVEMENTS

Two broad orientations run through efforts to understand the sources of support for such movements as the radical right, student activism, black power, and the like. One orientation has roots in the theory of mass society and views the recruitment to such movements as primarily *reactive*. Potential supporters presumably become available to a movement because they are supposed victims of social strains or personal anxieties. In addition, certain social controls are thought to be absent for these individuals, making them especially promising targets for mobilization by the leaders of mass movements.

The second orientation has roots in class or conflict group analyses and views the recruitment to these movements as more *proactive*. Rather than being acted upon, the participants are seen as goal-directed actors pursuing social change through collective action. At the risk of overdrawing the differences, we will attempt to sketch these two orientations as competing models.

Reactive Model

The reactive model is characterized by weak social attachments and personal vulnerability.

In this model, there are two steps leading to participation in mass movements.

The first of these is the formation of an aggregate of individuals who are psychologically ready for participation. Readiness to participate comes from the *absence* of those conditions that constrain others from involvement in essentially irrational forms of political action. In this model, the mass movement participant presumably lacks the series of institutional affiliations and group loyalties that bind people into the political system and create loyalty to it. Those who are heavily embedded in such intermediate associations are less available for new loyalties. Those who are weakly attached and are peripheral to existing social networks are "loose" in the system. Being loose, there are few constraints preventing the development of support for proffered social movements.

Being unconstrained, however, is only part of the story. Mass movements must also promise to meet some important need to energize the unattached, potential recruit. Several different motivational bases have been suggested but, for our purposes, it is unnecessary to distinguish among them. We will use them here as examples of the same basic argument.

One might, for example, emphasize the personal anxiety that results from lack of strong social attachments. Participation in a mass movement provides the emotional satisfaction of being part of a group with strong solidarity—a satisfaction that the participant lacks prior to his participation. In this argument, participation in a movement fills an important psychological need of belongingness; Fromm and Hoffer write in this spirit.[3]

A structural example might empha-

size status insecurity. Individuals occupying marginal social positions may experience common strains as social change occurs. Among these groups losing status in society, it will be especially those individuals with weak and conflicting group loyalties who will manifest these strains to the greatest degree. Those with inconsistent statuses, for example, may find that their claims based on their higher status characteristic are no longer socially validated; at the same time, they reject the lower status group into which they are moving and the psychological support that it might provide. Hence, their social marginality gives them a special kind of psychological vulnerability. There are other potential sources of status insecurity besides that of objectively inconsistent statuses but the argument is, in general, similar: By the symbolism and the meaning they give his social condition, by their myth of a better future, by the camaraderie and group support they provide, mass movements supply some important satisfactions for the unattached and vulnerable individual. Kornhauser and many of the authors in *The Radical Right* argue along these lines.[4]

Note that the participants in mass movements are primarily *reactive* in this model. A major part of the dynamic of mobilization is supposed to be provided by elites and, in some cases, demagogues who skillfully exploit the vulnerabilities of the masses for their own political ends. The primary empirical implication of this argument is that degree of social attachment will be negatively associated with support for social movements. In addition, degree of insecurity about one's social identity and degree of

---

3. Erich Fromm, *Escape from Freedom* (New York: Rinehart and Co., 1941); Eric Hoffer, *The True Believer: Thoughts on the Nature of Mass Movements* (New York: Harper & Bros., 1951).

4. See especially Daniel Bell, Seymour Martin Lipset, and Richard Hofstadter in Daniel Bell, ed., *The Radical Right* (Garden City, N.Y.: Doubleday, 1964); and William Kornhauser, *The Politics of Mass Society* (New York: Free Press, 1959).

social marginality should be positively associated with movement support.

Proactive Model

The proactive model is characterized by conflict groups and group identification.

The mechanisms invoked in this second model are much more conventional. Participation in a social movement is assumed to involve much the same process as group participation in general. Those most available for participation will be those who are not handicapped by constraints such as cross-pressures or social isolation. Thus, the more socially imbedded one is in a group, the more likely he is to become involved in a social movement that involves the group's interest.

Note the underlying assumptions here about social movements. They are seen to embody challenges by relatively powerless groups. These challenging groups are the activist portion of some underlying solidary group. They represent a constituency on behalf of whom they are attempting to change the society. Much of their effort centers on the mobilization of this constituency and its conversion into an active political force. This political struggle takes the form of a mass movement because the groups involved initially lack the scale of organization, access, and appropriate response to operate effectively *inside* the existing political arena. If they ultimately acquire such access and resources, their organizational strategy will shift from that of a mass movement to the tactics of conventional politics.

This model assumes, then, that if groups were equal in their access to resources and were all well integrated into the political system, there would be little occasion for collective action outside of institutional channels. To a greater or lesser degree in different societies, however, political integration is not uniform among social groups. Groups with less access forge their own instruments of change and, in American society, this often takes the form of a mass movement. Tilly, Gamson, and Rogin write in this spirit.[5]

The activists in this political struggle are those members of the challenging group that most strongly identify with and are most strongly embedded in the group. Those with the weakest group attachments will be less likely to be drawn into participation. In contrast with the previous model, this one is proactive; and the mass movement is viewed essentially as an instrumental form of organization by a group that lacks institutional power. The leaders are not "outsiders" who are using the movement for their own, separate purposes but "insiders" who embody the group's norms and values.

Thus, the empirical implications concerning group attachment contrast sharply with the first model. If a movement embodies a challenging group's interest, then the participants will tend to be those who are most strongly attached to the group. Those who are peripheral, who are socially isolated, cross-pressured, or otherwise marginal will be the least likely to participate in movement activities.

McCarthyism, Goldwater Support, and Student Activism

Both models may be helpful in explaining a given social movement, up to a point. Movements may change their

5. Charles Tilly, "From Mobilization to Political Conflict," multilith (Ann Arbor, Mich.: University of Michigan, 1970); William A. Gamson, *Power and Discontent* (Homewood, Ill.: Dorsey, 1968) and "Stable Unrepresentation in American Society," *American Behavioral Scientist* 12 (Nov.–Dec., 1968) 15–21; Michael Paul Rogin, *The Intellectuals and McCarthy: The Radical Specter* (Cambridge, Mass.: M.I.T. Press, 1967).

character, appealing at one time to relative social isolates and at another to those with strong loyalties to a challenging group. Or, one wing of a complex movement may be best understood by one model while another part of it is handled by the other. Having conceded this, however, it is difficult for both to be generally correct, because they differ in their assumptions about the basic nature of the phenomenon being explained.

Take the case of McCarthyism in the early 1950's. Labeling McCarthy supporters as members of the "radical right" rather than as "conservative" invokes the first model. Bell, Hofstader, Lipset, and other students of Joe McCarthy's support emphasized status anxiety as the underlying cause of participation in the movement.[6] "Communists in government" provided a psychologically rewarding (i.e., simplistic) conspiratorial explanation and scapegoat for the alleged insecurities and anxieties that the McCarthy followers were supposed to be experiencing.

Recently, however, Rogin has taken a fresh look at the McCarthy phenomenon and his analysis suggests that the proactive model is more appropriate. A close look at county voting records and at other evidence leads him to conclude that "McCarthy capitalized on popular concern over foreign policy, communism, and the Korean War, but the animus of McCarthyism had little to do with any less political or more developed *popular* anxieties. . . . McCarthy did not split apart an elite, the parts of which had been equally conservative before him. He rather capitalized on an existing liberal/conservative split within the existing Republican elite."[7] Polsby's analysis of poll data points in the same general direction. Party

affiliation is the single best predictor of support for McCarthy—Democrats opposed him and Republicans supported him.[8] Rogin concludes from his own review, "In these polls, as in the data reported by Polsby, no other single division of the population (by religion, class, education, and so forth) even approached the party split."[9]

Rogin rejects the notion that McCarthy was sustained primarily by the vague discontents of frustrated groups. "McCarthy had powerful group and elite support. He did not mobilize the masses at the polls or break through existing group cleavages. . . . Communism and the Korean War played crucial roles."[10] Strange as it may seem, the issues on which McCarthy mobilized support were apparently real ones for his followers, not merely symbolic of private anxieties.

The first model is also a popular apparatus for explaining the support for Senator Goldwater in 1964. It was frequently assumed that the early supporters of Goldwater were anomic, institutionally detached "cranks," neofascists, or "infiltrators" into the Republican Party. "Little old ladies in tennis shoes" became the popular phrase to capture the lunatic fringe imagery.

McEvoy has demonstrated that the evidence sharply contradicts this image of the Goldwater phenomenon.[11] Preconvention supporters of Goldwater were compared on a number of variables with those who ultimately voted for him even though they had preferred another nominee prior to the convention. The early Goldwater supporters were very

6. See Bell, op. cit.

7. Rogin, op. cit., pp. 216, 220.

8. Nelson W. Polsby, "Toward an Explanation of McCarthyism," *Political Studies* 8 (October, 1960), 250–271.

9. Rogin, op. cit., p. 234.

10. Ibid., p. 268.

11. James C. McEvoy, *Radicals or Conservatives? The Contemporary American Right* (Chicago: Rand McNally, 1970).

significantly higher on such variables as church attendance, income level, and education. They were more likely to be married. Furthermore, they were much higher in past participation in Republican Party politics. Finally, they exhibited average to low levels of objective status discrepancy. None of this evidence suggests lack of attachment; on the contrary, early Goldwater supporters seem to be strong conservatives with social support and respect from their friends and neighbors.[12]

The persistence of social science support for the reactive model in the absence of much data that support it suggests something about its ideological biases. It typically has a pejorative ring, suggesting that supporters of a political movement are irrationally seeking simple, illusory solutions for complex problems. Since social scientists who study right-wing movements are typically hostile to them, this model readily suggests itself and receives far less critical examination than it deserves.

When attention turns to movements of the left, there is much less tendency to invoke the reactive model. Although the McCone Commission Report on the Watts riot suggested that rioters were recent migrants with weak attachment to the community, social scientists were quick to test and demolish this hypothesis.[13] Similarly, this model has failed to gain a foothold as an explanation of student activists. While popular articles about student "rebels" may have postulated their personal maladjustment, serious studies put this myth to rest. Student activists, it turns out, are not the most marginal members of the student body but those most embedded in many aspects of life at the university. They are not academic failures, psychological wrecks, or social isolates, but those with better than average academic performance, with more liberal parents, with higher self-esteem, and with friends who have similar political views. They are, in short, well socialized and personally well-adjusted members of politically militant sub-groups in the university.[14] We do not mean to imply here that activists are "typical" students, but merely that they are actively and centrally involved in life at the university—in fact, more so than the typical student.

In all the above studies, the evidence seems more nearly to support the proactive model. We would not argue that this is necessarily true for all recruits to social movements. But at this point, we would be skeptical any time the reactive model is invoked to explain a movement when the person who invokes it is far removed from or unsympathetic to the movement or the issue in question.

MEASURING SUPPORT FOR POLICE VIOLENCE

The models discussed above apply rather generally to social movements. The issue of police violence, we argue, must be viewed in this more general context. Police may play two different roles in group conflict situations. They may take a relatively neutral posture, remaining on the sidelines as much as possible and operating to make sure that the means of carrying on conflict remain

12. The weak attachment model might conceivably account for some "deviant" Goldwater supporters—that is, supporters from areas where few people were sympathetic.

13. See, for example, Nathan Caplan and Jeffery M. Paige, "A Study of Ghetto Rioters," *Scientific American* (August, 1968), 15–21, and Jeffery M. Paige, *Collective Violence and the Culture of Subordination* (Ph.D. diss., University of Michigan, 1968).

14. See the various articles in Edward E. Sampson, ed., *Stirrings Out of Apathy: Student Activism and the Decade of Protest*, special issue of the *Journal of Social Issues* 23 (July, 1967), for documentation of this point.

within certain limits. Or, they may be used as a partisan instrument or ally of one group in the conflict. The latter role is especially likely when the conflict is between the authorities and those challenging them.

Our underlying concern in this paper is with the presence or absence of constraint on the use of police as a partisan instrument against challenging groups. One aspect of this constraint is the climate of opinion that is reflected in public attitudes toward police violence. By understanding where the sources of public support and opposition to police violence are located, we can understand something about the nature and strength of this possible source of constraint on police behavior. The two models discussed above, as we will argue shortly, have direct implications for this issue. Before considering this, we turn to a description of our data and our measure of support and opposition for police violence.

The data we report were obtained from a national cross-section probability sample of adult Americans conducted for the National Commission on the Causes and Prevention of Violence, by Louis Harris Associates of New York in October, 1968.[15] The sample consists of 1176 completed interviews and is more fully described in Kirkham, Levy, and Crotty, and McEvoy.[16]

The interview schedule contained a section of 25 statements about violence in various contexts—personal, political, international, and so forth. Respondents were asked to express varying de-grees of agreement or disagreement with each statement. A factor analysis of the entire set identified several distinct clusters, including one that we have labeled "police violence." This factor showed high loadings on three items:

1. The police are wrong to beat up unarmed protestors, even when these people are rude and call them names. (Factor loading: .79)

2. The police frequently use more force than they need to when carrying out their duties. (Factor loading: .62)

3. Any man who insults a policeman has no complaint if he gets roughed-up in return. (reversed item, Factor loading: .61).

The overall distribution on these three items is included in Table 1. A score on support for police violence was computed for each individual by reversing the direction of the third item and summing it with scores on the other two items. These total scores were then reduced to a seven-point scale, with high scores representing greater favorableness toward police violence. The distribution of the sample on this index is reported in Table 2.

RESULTS

Our attempts to explain the variation in the index of support for police violence will be guided by two models derived from the more general models described in the first section of this paper.

Reactive Model

In this argument, we suggest that police violence raises a fundamental question for our respondents: Do they see police as embodying the law, or as subject to its constraints like other citizens? To appreciate this second view, one must embrace a complex normative principle. Those who have allegiance to it resemble those who are usually

15. McEvoy served as special consultant to the Commission Task Force on Political Assassination.

16. James Kirkhan, Sheldon Levy, and William J. Crotty, *Assassination and Political Violence*, A Report to the National Commission on the Causes and Prevention of Violence (Washington, D.C.: U.S.G.P.O., 1969), and McEvoy, *Radicals or Conservatives?* op. cit.

TABLE 1—DISTRIBUTION OF RESPONSES TO ITEMS IN POLICE VIOLENCE INDEX

	PERCENTAGES				
	STRONGLY AGREE	AGREE	DISAGREE	STRONGLY DISAGREE	DON'T KNOW
The police are wrong to beat up unarmed protestors, even when these people are rude and call them names.	12	37	36	9	6
		49			
The police frequently use more force than they need to when carrying out their duties.	9	19	46	18	7
		28			
Any man who insults a policeman has no complaint if he gets roughed-up in return.	13	44	32	7	4
		57			

$N = 1171$.

found to support principles of civil liberties. This means, especially, those who are well educated and have other characteristics associated with high normative integration into the political system.

More specifically, this model implies the following hypotheses:[17]

1) The higher the educational level, the more opposition to police violence.

2) Assuming that whites are higher in normative integration than blacks, whites will be more opposed to police violence than blacks.

3) Registered voters will be more opposed to police violence than those who are not registered.

4) People who identify with a major political party will be more opposed to police violence than those who lack such identification.

Proactive Model

In this argument, the police violence index primarily taps trust in the police.

During periods of sharp challenge to the distribution of power and privilege in a society, the police tend to be used as a partisan instrument in defense of privilege. When this happens, they usually become agents of established groups and opponents of challenging groups. Gamson defines trust in these terms: "Confidence in authorities means that they are perceived as the group's agents, that the group members identify with them. . . . Alienation from authorities means that . . . they are . . . the agents of groups with conflicting goals."[18]

The past decade has been a period of high conflict between challenging groups and authorities. Consequently, individuals will differ sharply in trust of the police, depending on whether they are part of groups attacking the established order or of groups defending it. Not only will group memberships determine attitudes toward the police, but the strength of group identifications and attachments will determine the degree of such support.[19]

17. It implies many others beyond those stated here. However, we confine ourselves to those hypotheses that our data enable us to test.

18. Gamson, op. cit., pp. 54, 56.
19. Unfortunately, we lack the data to test this part of the argument here.

More specifically, this model implies the following hypotheses:

1) Blacks will be more opposed to police violence than whites.
2) Young people will be more opposed to police violence than older people.
3) Poor people will be more opposed to police violence than rich people.
4) Financially dissatisfied people will be more opposed to police violence than financially satisfied people.

Table 3 presents a series of bivariate relationships between the police violence index and the variables suggested by the hypotheses listed above. It should come as no great surprise to most readers that race sharply differentiates toward police violence: blacks are much more likely to be against police violence than are whites. Furthermore, there is some additional evidence that this difference is not merely a reflection of general distrust of authority, but is more specifically directed at the police. The interview schedule contained a rather extreme item expressing political distrust: "The government in Washington is the enemy, not the friend, of people like me." Only 8 percent of the whites in the sample agree with this statement; and the percentage for blacks is identical. Thus, the great difference between blacks and whites on the police violence index seems to reflect attitudes toward this specific object of trust or distrust.

Education shows a moderate effect. As education increases, so does opposition to police violence, from 31 percent

for those with less than a high school diploma to 45 percent for college graduates. Family income shows no simple relationship to police violence, but age does: the younger group shows more opposition. However, those who are financially most dissatisfied are higher in their opposition to police violence (42 percent) than are those who are happiest with their financial position (29 percent).

As for our measures of political involvement, Republican Party identifiers show the least opposition to police violence (25 percent); Democrats and those without a major party identification are more opposed (38 percent). Finally, those who are registered to vote show slightly less opposition to police violence (34 percent) than those who are not participants in the electoral process (40 percent).

A multivariate analysis adds some additional information. Chart 1 presents the interaction between education and race. The figures in this chart represent the percentage of respondents in each category who fall at the antiviolence end of the index (categories 0–2). Education has no additional effect for blacks; those at all educational levels are opposed to police violence. For whites, education has some explanatory power; the percentage of whites opposed to police violence increases from 19 in the lowest group to 43 in the highest but remains considerably short of the overall black figure of 70.

Given the importance of race and of

TABLE 2—DEGREE OF SUPPORT OF POLICE VIOLENCE

VIOLENCE INDEX	Oppose			Support				TOTAL
	0	1	2	3	4	5	6	
Number Interviewed	54	103	246	298	287	146	23	1157
Percentage	5	9	21	26	25	13	2	100
			35		26		40	

education for whites, Table 4 controls for these variables in exploring the relationship between the police violence index and several other relevant variables. Family income still shows no consistent relationship; at best, there is a slight suggestion that whites in the lowest income group are more opposed to police violence than their wealthier counterparts at each educational level. For blacks, the direction is reversed, and only 51 percent of those with income under $5,000 fall at the oppose-police-

violence end of the index. Financial satisfaction shows a similar but more pronounced relationship for whites—the least satisfied are most opposed to police violence at each educational level; there is no clear direction on this variable for blacks. Age differences emerge more sharply, particularly for the college group. Of white college graduates under 30 years of age, 58 percent oppose police violence compared to one-third of those over age 50 with similar education.

TABLE 3—RELATIONSHIP OF SELECTED VARIABLES TO ATTITUDES
TOWARD POLICE VIOLENCE

RESPONDENTS	OPPOSING POLICE VIOLENCE* Percentage	MIDDLE Percentage	SUPPORTING POLICE VIOLENCE* Percentage	NUMBER INTERVIEWED
Race				
White	27%	27%	46%	(929)
Black	69%	18%	13%	(215)
Education				
Not high school graduate	31%	28%	41%	(488)
High school graduate but not college graduate	36%	24%	40%	(542)
College graduate	45%	24%	30%	(125)
Age				
Under 30	45%	25%	30%	(276)
30–49	40%	23%	37%	(417)
50 or over	24%	28%	48%	(447)
Family Income				
Under $5000	36%	29%	36%	(222)
$5000–$9,999	36%	24%	40%	(361)
$10,000 and above	34%	26%	40%	(572)
Financial Satisfaction				
"Not satisfied at all"	42%	22%	37%	(257)
"More or less satisfied"	36%	27%	37%	(473)
"Pretty well satisfied"	29%	27%	44%	(425)
Party Identification				
Republican	25%	29%	46%	(288)
Democratic	38%	25%	38%	(576)
Independent, other, or none	39%	27%	35%	(238)
Voting Registration				
Registered	34%	26%	41%	(919)
Not registered	40%	26%	35%	(235)

* This column includes those in categories 0–2 in Table 2, the middle column contains category 3, and the third column combines categories 4–6.

CHART 1

RACE AND EDUCATION BY POLICE
VIOLENCE INDEX

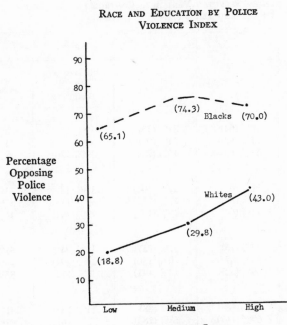

EDUCATIONAL LEVEL

The earlier results on party identification and voting registration emerge more clearly with race and education controlled. Those without a major party identification have the greatest opposition to police violence, while Republican identifiers show the lowest opposition.[20] Furthermore, whites who are registered to vote are less likely to oppose police violence than those of the same educational level who are not registered voters. For blacks, this relationship is reversed.

INTERPRETATION

How well do our two models handle these results? The first model fares rather badly. It successfully predicts the positive relationship between education and opposition to police violence. However, it is not clear from this model why blacks, who most would argue are less normatively integrated, are so much

20. There are no differences on this variable, however, for low education whites.

higher on opposition to police violence. It seems reasonable to assume that registering to vote is a mark of integration into the political system. If so, it is not clear from this model why those who are not registered to vote should be more opposed to police violence. The argument for the effects of major party identification is similar; but those who lack such identification are, if anything, more opposed to police violence.

The second model does considerably better. As predicted, blacks are more opposed to police violence than whites. Young college-educated whites are more opposed than other whites. The hypothesis concerning poor people receives equivocal support at best, with subjective satisfaction proving a better predictor than actual income. Perhaps the have/have-not dimension of conflict is less relevant at this time than the racial dimension.

By and large, then, the proactive

TABLE 4—PERCENTAGE OF PEOPLE INTERVIEWED OPPOSING POLICE
VIOLENCE BY SELECTED VARIABLES CONTROLLED FOR
RACE AND EDUCATION FOR WHITES

	BLACKS	WHITES		
		NOT HS GRADUATE	HS GRADUATE BUT NOT COLLEGE GRADUATE	COLLEGE GRADUATE
Age				
Under 30	70%(64)	31%(35)	34%(141)	58%(36)
30–49	77%(82)	24%(93)	32%(193)	41%(49)
50 or over	56%(68)	15%(224)	22%(126)	28%(29)
Family Income				
Under $5000	51%(63)	22%(104)	35%(48)	71%(7)
$5000–$9999	75%(88)	17%(132)	30%(115)	35%(23)
$10,000 and above	71%(68)	19%(122)	29%(293)	46%(79)
Financial Satisfaction				
"Not at all"	63%(75)	27%(73)	32%(94)	57%(14)
"More or less"	74%(87)	20%(136)	29%(194)	46%(46)
"Pretty well"	69%(52)	13%(141)	30%(172)	35%(52)
Party Identification				
Republican	56%(18)	18%(88)	24%(135)	31%(42)
Democrat	69%(169)	18%(183)	28%(187)	47%(32)
Independent, other, none	88%(17)	18%(62)	38%(117)	51%(39)
Voting Registration				
Registered	72%(153)	17%(273)	27%(375)	42%(105)
Not registered	60%(60)	24%(79)	38%(81)	56%(9)

Percentages include those who fall at the anti-police-violence end of the index (categories 0–2);
the number next to the percentage refers to the total number of respondents with the specified
characteristic.

model makes good sense of our data. There is one exception to this success, and an important one: it fails to account for the effect of education. To the extent that education is solely a measure of privilege, increasing it should make one more supportive of police violence rather than less so. This hypothesis not only fails to be supported but, as Table 4 indicates, education has an effect on white attitudes even when income is controlled. This suggests that, as we might expect, there is something about education other than the privilege it brings that may be contributing to attitudes toward police violence. How,

then, can this model be enlarged to account for this additional result?

Each model treats education as an indicator of something else—of social integration (in the reactive model), or of privilege (in the proactive model). But perhaps it has an effect in its own right, through influencing the conceptual sophistication of the respondent. The more highly educated the respondent, the greater his cognitive differentiation between the police and the law. A highly educated respondent who is generally opposed to contemporary challenging groups may give his fealty to a more abstract conception of the law.

Transgressors should be treated harshly but with due process; the legal system, not the police, is the proper bulwark against extra-legal dissidence.

This conception leads to recognition that not only the control of dissidents but also the control of the police can become a problem. Mailer describes the reactions to police behavior in the streets of Chicago at the time of the 1968 Democratic convention:

What staggered the delegates who witnessed the [police] attack . . . on Michigan avenue was that it opened the specter of what it might mean for the police to take over society. They might comport themselves in such a case not as a force of law and order, not even as a force of repression upon civil disorder, but as a true criminal force, chaotic, improvisational, undisciplined, and finally—sufficiently aroused—uncontrollable.[21]

Education, we suggest, gives enough of a glimpse of this specter to sober the sympathetic attitudes toward the police that the sophisticated "law and order" supporter may have. We argued earlier that the police violence index taps trust in the police, and this trust is primarily a function of privilege. For respondents with low trust in the police—blacks, for example—the education factor is largely irrelevant, because differentiating between police and the law does not make them any more trusting toward the police. Respondents with high trust in the police but low education do not have their support for police violence inhibited by awareness of the police control issue. But as education increases for high trust respondents, this additional factor becomes more salient; their inclination to support police violence is retarded by their greater awareness of the problem of controlling the police.

21. Mailer, op. cit., p. 175.

CONCLUSION

Police comportment has an important effect on the degree of violence with which political conflicts are waged by challenging groups. As Stinchcombe argues,

Military control and liberty function together to stabilize political conflict. If the violent means of conflict are made much more expensive by effective enforcement by the police and army, while nonviolent means are made cheaper by the condition of liberty, then a rational organizational leader . . . will prefer less violent means. If the police and army are either ineffective, or enter into the conflict as full-fledged participants themselves by denying not only the right to riot but also the right to speak, then the comparative effectiveness of violent means in the competitive struggle increases, while the effectiveness of nonviolent means declines. Under these conditions, a rational organizational leader will choose a higher proportion of violent means.[22]

It is important to ask what constraints exist on the use of police as a partisan instrument or ally of one group in a conflict situation. Some of these constraints may be structural, including both aspects of internal police organization and linkages between the police and political, economic, and other organizations. This paper does not address these possible structural constraints but it does raise the question of normative constraints on police behavior. If police violence violates widely held norms in American society, then a public outcry against such behavior might serve to constrain it and to mobilize institutional pressure against it.

We find scant cause for optimism

22. Arthur L. Stinchcombe, "Social Structure and Organizations," in James G. March, ed., *Handbook of Organizations* (Chicago: Rand McNally, 1965), p. 176.

about any constraint from public opinion. Robinson describes what a sample of 1,005 respondents thought about police action at the Chicago convention in 1968.[23] Only 19 percent believed that the police had used too much force; 25 percent felt that they had not been forceful enough, and the rest were either satisfied with the amount of force used or had no opinion.

Our own data have the same thrust. With the possible exception of the effect of education, we have not found any

23. John P. Robinson, "Public Reaction to Political Protest: Chicago 1968," *Public Opinion Quarterly* 34 (Spring 1970), 1–9.

support for the proposition that police violence seriously violates American political norms. Extra-legal police actions directed against unpopular targets are unlikely to draw censure or even disapproval from those substantial segments of the American public for whom the police are the "good guys." And for those who, like ourselves, see police participation in conflicts in a partisan role as an invitation to counter-violence on the part of challenging groups, we offer this warning: Nurture whatever organizational and structural constraints exist, for you will find few normative constraints in the present American political culture.

25

The Police and Collective Violence in Contemporary America

By GORDON E. MISNER

Gordon E. Misner is professor and director of the Administration of Justice program, University of Missouri—St. Louis. He has taught at San Jose State College and at the University of California, Berkeley, where he was acting associate professor of criminology and associate research criminologist for the Center for Planning and Research Development. He is co-author, with Joseph D. Lohman, of The Police and the Community, *published by the President's Commission on Law Enforcement and Administration of Justice.*

ANY analysis of the police and their relationship to collective violence must begin with the realization of the policeman's unique position in American society today. The policeman does not operate within a cultural vacuum; nor can the policeman deny his cultural heritage, or the value system of the social class position from which he arose. Individually and collectively, the policeman is a product of his society and of the pressures, strains, and demands which he feels the larger society places upon him. Prior to entering the police service, his previous socialization had provided him with a shorthand system for accepting or rejecting personal and social values. Socialization within the police service generally assures that the individual policeman's personal value system can be accommodated to that of the organization which he now serves.

Socialization within the police organization is accomplished in a variety of ways: by the selection process, itself; in the training academy; in the informal associations with peers and with "outsiders"; and in the actual performance of his daily routine and duties.[1] Time spent in a training academy makes the recruit aware of the definition of his role which the organization has made; it also provides him with a set of basic skills which the organization has decided he will need, while at the same time making him aware of the performance standards which have been established. Whether programmed or not, the training experience also stimu-

lates a sense of solidarity or *camaraderie,* not only with associates in his own department, but also with "policemen everywhere."[2]

Technology and the increased access to rapid information has obviously contributed to a feeling of police solidarity.[3] This development assures that policemen throughout the nation—whether they work in Chicago or Fargo, North Dakota—are made almost instantaneously aware of incidents occurring thousands of miles away. Through radio and television newscasts, individual policemen throughout the nation were made aware of the confrontations between the police and demonstrators at the Democratic National Convention in Chicago. Recently, within hours policemen throughout the nation were informed of the killing of four California highway patrol officers in one incident. The point to be made is that anger, frustration, horror, fear, and revulsion among policemen has now become a national collective phenomenon through the media of radio and television. In previous times, the bounds of these feelings may very well have been limited to the area immediately surrounding the location of a particular

1. Jerome H. Skolnick, *Justice Without Trial* (New York: John Wiley & Sons, Inc., 1966); Arthur Niederhoffer, *Behind the Shield* (New York: Doubleday & Co., 1967); John H. McNamara, "Uncertainties in Police Work: the Relevance of Police Recruits' Backgrounds and Training," in David J. Bordua, ed., *The Police* (John Wiley & Sons, Inc., 1967), pp. 163–252.

2. The attitude that "co-operation is the backbone of effective law enforcement" has been carefully nurtured for generations by the F.B.I. and other police agencies. Repetition of the phrase and the concepts which flow logically from it cannot fail to have an impact upon in-group, occupational solidarity. Stress placed upon such virtues as reliability, dependability, etc., take on a special occupational flavor in policing.

3. See, for example, Jerome H. Skolnick, *The Politics of Protest*, A Staff Report to the National Commission on the Causes and Prevention of Violence (Washington, D.C.: U.S. Government Printing Office, 1969), chap. 7; Daniel L. Walker, *Rights in Conflict*, A Staff Report to the National Commission on the Causes and Prevention of Violence (Washington, D.C.: U.S. Government Printing Office, 1969).

dramatic incident. Today, however, the policeman in Bloomington, Illinois may feel just as angry, just as frustrated, and just as alienated as does his counterpart in San Francisco or Philadelphia. This development cannot be ignored when attempting to make an analysis of police response to collective violence.

Nor can the impact of the electronic media be ignored when attempting to analyze the general public's attitudes toward the threat of crime, violence, disorder, and other threats to their feelings of personal security. In this writer's opinion, the political risks have changed as a result of the public's access to "fast-breaking news." Inevitably, we are confronted with a "chicken and egg" question when attempting to delineate between which comes first, the threat of collective violence or a political leader's vulnerability to the threat. Relatively few areas of the nation are immune to the political shockwaves of even an isolated incident of collective violence. Demonology pervades the political arena, and political leaders can ignore supposed and alleged threats of collective violence only at very real peril to their own careers. The old, geographically-bound insularity is gone. The effects of its passing upon the political process and upon the police organizational response to threats or actual instances of collective violence should not be overlooked.

PROBLEMS IDENTIFIED

In responding to threats or actual instances of collective violence, the police apparatus has enjoyed little success. Effective police performance in these difficult situations has been a rarity, an exception rather than the rule. Partly, this poor "track record" has been a result of the fact that collective violence

is a relatively new phenomenon[4] and the police have been relatively unprepared. More important, however, have been structural defects within the police apparatus itself, and within the political structure of which the police are supposedly a part. Threats or actual instances of collective violence pose a network of problems consisting essentially of five sub-sets, each inter-related and interdependent. This problem-set consists of the following elements:

1. Political
2. Organizational
3. Informational
4. Ideological
5. Tactical

The Political Problem

In theory, police agencies are responsible to elected political officials or, in city manager forms of municipal government, to their appointed, professional administrators. Often, the amount of actual leadership and control of police agencies by political superiors is more illusory than real. What leadership and control that has existed previously has rested primarily in the area of budgetary management and control. In fact, police agencies have largely been self-directing and

4. It is quite true, as Skolnick points out in *The Politics of Protest* (ibid., pp. 6–14), that violence as a form of protest is ingrained in American history. Despite this historical fact, it was a new phenomenon to the personnel who staffed police agencies in the 1950's and 1960's. The most relevant experience was that which marked many violent confrontations between the police and organized labor. For the most part, these confrontations had taken place 20 or 30 years previously, and were not part of contemporary police experience. More recent confrontations took place spasmodically in widely separated parts of the nation. Furthermore, electronic mass media were not saturated with stories of these particular episodes. Consequently, it seems accurate to regard collective violence as a new phenomenon for the police.

self-regulating. There seem to be interesting parallels between political control of the police and civilian control of the military. Today, probably more than ever before, there is need for the assertion of civilian, political leadership over the police; in this regard, there seems to be no compelling reason to treat the police any differently than any other executive arm of the government. Such leadership and control necessarily means that the political leadership must take an active role in the selection of local governmental goals. Unfortunately, in the realm of police operations, most goals are stated in such general terms as to create ambiguity (for example, the protection of life and property, the prevention of crime, etc.). Similarly, the selection of appropriate means for the attainment of goals must also be made. Obviously, this task involves the clear and decisive rejection of *inappropriate* means (such as the use of excessive force, or the unnecessary use of deadly force).

Obviously, it is easier to write about the selection of goals than it is to participate in the selection process; and it is easier to talk in terms of generalities than to talk in terms of specifics. Recent history should amply demonstrate the desirability, however, of thinking through many of the dilemmas which spring from a consideration of how best to deal with the threats of collective violence. In the last five years, there has been sufficient experience to demonstrate the utility of certain public postures, and the utility of certain strategies and techniques. A study of these experiences would seem to suggest that the operating style or "administrative style" of principal public officials is an important ingredient in the way in which police agencies react to situations. For example, a political leader's public pronouncements of the importance of freedom of assembly and

of his commitment to guarantee the right of assembly for all persons has often contributed to a de-escalation of planned violence. Unfortunately, political leadership and control over police agencies can take a variety of forms. In the case of the Democratic Convention in Chicago, there seemed to be rather general agreement that what took place was *because* of Mayor Daley's domination and control of the police, not *in spite* of it. In another city, or in Chicago in another period of time, the mayor's dominance over the police department might have a radically different result.

The municipal reform movement and "police professionalization" have shared the goals of eliminating the political spoils system, political favoritism, and of insulating civil servants from the vagaries of political domination and control. Today, the suggestion that city hall has a proper role to play in the determination of police policies and in the investigation of complaints against policemen is likely to bring shouts of outrage. Few have seriously suggested that city hall should concern itself with day-to-day police operations, or that it should intervene in routine personnel matters, or that it should interfere with arrest dispositions. Political and administrative superiors do have an important role to play, however, in attempting to maintain the fragile balance of domestic peace. Ideally, political and administrative superiors are expected to have a more global view of the world and of its interdependencies; ideally, they are unencumbered by the occupational myopia of individual municipal departments. Theoretically, they are more sensitive to the competing demands of a pluralistic society.

Difficulties often arise when mayors or other political leaders attempt to gain control—or regain control—over police departments which had hitherto operated without too much external executive control. When to exercise control, how to exercise control, and the strategies for maintaining control are key questions. Long-range planning and analysis of alternative strategies for dealing with collective violence are subject matter areas over which political leadership can be exercised. Both activities also provide an opportunity to assess the abilities and perceptions of second- and third-level staff personnel in police agencies.

The Organizational Problem

There is nothing about the traditional closed police personnel system which guarantees the emergence of capable executive leadership.[5] Some would suggest that instead, police personnel practices actually stifle the development of creative leadership and contribute to rigid "no think" behavior patterns. Consequently, goals remain traditional goals; operational practices become institutionalized; each new social development is often unanticipated and has to be dealt with on a crisis basis. Everything about the closed personnel system works inexorably toward the development of police personnel who have limited social perspective, hence little genuine understanding about what is actually taking place in society. It is only the unusual police officer who recognizes the perils of the system and takes steps to broaden his own perspective. It is only the unusual department which recognizes its present and future manpower dilemmas and takes steps to correct the situation through

special training or educational endeavors, or through innovative, selective assignments and career patterns.

Another organizational problem which has only recently been identified is the presence of a *patrolman sub-culture,* operative within the police department itself.[6] To generalize about a police sub-culture is one thing. Understanding that a patrolman sub-culture may exist and may actually be at odds with the administration of the department and with other organizational units within the department gives quite a different perspective to the matter of organizational response. In mass disturbances, rank-and-file policemen may engage in assorted types of conduct which are in direct violation of departmental rules. There may be many explanations for these occurrences: a breakdown of discipline, excitement, hysteria, fear, improper leadership, inadequate training, etc. One explanation which is as plausible as the others is that the patrolman sub-culture was operative and dictated the field tactics to be used, in open defiance of department plans and directives.[7]

Discipline and coordination are key attributes to the effective handling of mass disturbances by the police. Not every mass disturbance results in instances of collective violence. Once deployed, it is essential that police resources be disciplined and that their efforts be coordinated. In reviewing

5. Previously, I have emphasized the point that police leadership is actually much better than the citizens have any right to expect. Despite its shortcomings as a career field, for some reason policing has seemed to attract an unusually high caliber of person. Gordon E. Misner, "Enforcement: Illusion of Security," *Nation* (April 21, 1969), pp. 488–491.

6. Thomas A. Johnson, *A Study of Police Resistance to Police Community in a Municipal Department*, unpublished doctoral dissertation (Berkeley: School of Criminology, University of California, 1970), pp. 58–68.
7. On more than one occasion, chiefs of large cities have privately told the writer that their most difficult task is to maintain control over the men in their departments. Some have felt, although they dare not openly admit it, that rank-and-file personnel are close to "open rebellion" against "the administration."

procedures used by the Metropolitan Police Department in Washington, D.C., a ranking police official made the following comment:

Rigid training impresses upon each officer the necessity for maintaining discipline. Officers who resort to individual action are dropped from membership in the Civil Disturbance Unit.[8]

Coordination and discipline become more complicated as the number of different agencies involved in a police action increases. Proper planning with specific attention being paid to the matters of discipline, control, and co-ordination can reduce the likelihood of failures in these organizational matters.

Finally, the matter of intelligence gathering must be addressed. An anathema to liberal democratic traditions, intelligence gathering is viewed by many not only as "dirty business" but also as directly contrary to the best interests of the body politic itself. The writer shares many of these concerns; he is aware of some of the grosser abuses. Pragmatically, however, he realizes that intelligence gathering will continue as an activity and that the best to be hoped is that it will be adequately controlled and that the information gained will be safeguarded from abuse. If one accepts the fact that intelligence gathering will continue as a clandestine activity, one should wish that the information gained is worth the expenditure and that it is accurately interpreted.

In reviewing some domestic intelligence gathering endeavors, one may wonder if this activity doesn't often suffer from certain structural defects

within the apparatus itself.[9] How well, for example, is the typical police intelligence officer able to interpret what he sees, what he hears, and what he reads? Without a rather extensive background in social movements and political protest, he may be ill prepared to differentiate between the substance and the rhetoric of protest. Accurate and timely intelligence gathering is a highly specialized skill; in the writer's opinion only a limited number of agencies possess the skilled resources to perform the function competently. Performed competently or incompetently, however, the information gathered frequently makes its way into the information base passed on to rank-and-file policemen and their supervisors.

The Informational Problem

Experienced police officials who are known for their expert handling of mass disturbances have emphasized to the writer that there is a direct relationship between the quality of intelligence gathered and their ability to avoid violence in dealing with explosive situations. They reiterate their experiences in using intelligence information in order to make decisions about the tactics which they were to employ. Uniformly, they have been convinced that "there is no substitute for carefully gathered and correctly interpreted intelligence." They make the point that proper intelligence can be used as a safeguard against over-reaction by the police. Some of these same officers have condemned crudeness of many of the intelligence gathering efforts by some police agencies, making the point that few police officers possess the degree of

8. Earl L. Drescher, "Diary of a Peace March," *The Police Chief* 37 (March 1970), p. 22.

9. One federal intelligence officer complained to the writer about the tactical handicaps under which he labored. His supervisor insisted that all personnel wear white shirts, ties, and business suits. Even sideburns were forbidden in his agency!

sophistication necessary for the task. One explanation for this lack of skill is the educational level of many of the policemen; another explanation relates to the inadequacy of training about social change, change agents, and the broad range of constitutionally protected political activities. Without this background and knowledge, the occupational life style and peer group relationships of policemen almost guarantee that simplistic notions about *agent provocateurs* will prevail as the *dominant* explanation for collective behavior and collective violence.

During the course of one of the field studies conducted in 1966 for the Commission on Law Enforcement and Administration of Justice, the writer had an opportunity to interview one of the nation's most prominent police chiefs. During the course of the interview, this respected police official decried the status of police training, the fact that much of it was antithetical to democratic values. He startled the writer by advocating that primary responsibility for police training be taken out of the hands of the police, and that the police be given an advisory capacity and the responsibility for conducting only a small portion of the actual training. In his opinion, little was being done to assure that police recruits identified themselves with the preservation of democratic institutions, or with the positive values of constitutionally guaranteed rights of political dissent. Without this input to recruit training, he was pessimistic about the young policeman's ability to withstand the rigors and strains of street policing.

The Ideological Problem

The information base which should be provided to policemen in order to perform even their routine daily duties comprises a continuing set of theoretical and operational problems. The sit-uation is severely aggravated when policemen are injected into situations where there is a reasonable likelihood of large-scale disorder and violence. In these situations adequate information, coupled with skillful organization and command and control, are absolutely essential. Without these ingredients, policemen are likely to become groups of individual actors, motivated and directed by their own ideological predispositions. Skolnick, Walker, Marx, and others have outlined the social consequences of these situations, and the instances in which police partiality to certain causes has been demonstrated.[10] Adherents of "popular" causes have often been protected, while agitators for "unpopular" causes have been penalized.

The small number of instances in which the police have fulfilled truly impartial roles in mass demonstrations is so significant as to deserve special comment in the press. In these instances, care has been exercised by police leaders to identify the ideological biases of rank-and-file policemen and to take steps to neutralize these biases.[11] Special recognition has been made by police leaders themselves, of the typical policeman's tendency to reject non-conformist behavior. Recognition has also been made of the fact that policemen

10. Skolnick, op. cit.; Walker, op. cit.; Gary T. Marx, "Civil Disorder and the Agents of Social Control," unpublished paper presented to meeting of the American Sociological Association, (1968).

11. Joseph R. Sahid, *Rights In Concord: the Response to the Counter Inaugural Activities in Washington, D.C.*, A Special Staff Study submitted to the National Commission on the Causes and Prevention of Violence (Washington, D.C.: U.S. Government Printing Office, 1969); Gordon E. Misner, *Police-Minority Group Relations at the Cow Palace: the 1964 Republican National Convention*, unpublished doctoral dissertation (Berkeley: School of Criminology, University of California, 1967).

are beset not only with "commonplace" anxieties, but also that their peculiar occupational setting is likely to give rise to a unique set of psychological strains. Unless these conditions are realized and addressed, policemen are inadequately prepared to cope with certain types of emergency situations.

The Tactical Problem

For the most part, the police were tactically unprepared to deal with the mass demonstrations, large-scale civil disobedience, and urban rebellions of the late 1950's and the 1960's. For the most part, in emergencies reliance had to be placed upon outdated, pre-World War II army field manuals. Except in Philadelphia, Washington, D.C., and New York, the police seldom had had experience in using small unit tactics. Most of their routine duties involved working individually or with only one other fellow officer. Preparedness plans were often either non-existent or could not be located when needed. The use of chemical agents had normally been reserved only to remove a barricaded person from a building. In brief, the truly reactive character of the police was demonstrated time and time again as they were called upon to deal with new situations.

From an intelligence point of view, the police were often no better prepared. Without adequate knowledge about the phenomenon they were dealing with, no adequate strategy or tactic could be devised. Nor was there a systematic literature on alternative strategies, or a cataloging of the variety of tactics which had been used in dealing with various situations. The building of such an information base on strategy and tactics has been undertaken only in recent years. In some cases, opportunities have been missed to capture experiences police depart-

ments themselves have had. In Chicago, for example, there was no systematic effort at de-briefing policemen involved in the turmoil surrounding the Democratic Convention.[12] This was either an oversight, decided against as a result of the perceived exigencies of the next day's activities, or considered to be too highly "sensitive" to be undertaken. In any case, "evaluation" of police performance in Chicago was done essentially by outsiders. Such evaluation can certainly serve essential public purposes, but police agencies could also benefit from an "in-house" administrative evaluation of performance.

Conclusion

Tragically, it is difficult to be optimistic about the likelihood of a general de-escalation of violence in urban America. Several different factions seem to be inexorably headed on collision courses. Unquestionably large-scale, massive, collective violence can be suppressed, if that is the option which is selected—either consciously or unconsciously. This can be done, of course, only at great peril to our existing political and social institutions—and at great personal risk to both citizens and civil servants! Other options exist, and one can hope that these will present more attractive alternatives to political and administrative decision-makers. The futility of placing virtually total reliance upon the police apparatus of the nation should be patently obvious. Civil policing agencies are not designed to devote a major share of their resources and energies to these types of duties.

Certainly, in many instances police response has been a contributing factor in the escalation of violence. To

12. Personal observations by the writer and interviews with officials of the Chicago Police Department.

say otherwise would be to ignore historical fact, and to overlook one of the great dilemmas of the time. On the other hand, it is foolish and grossly unfair to scapegoat the police and to make them the culprits for all the social and political ills which beset the nation.

As is true of so many "police problems," resolution of the underlying problems lies outside the police system boundary. And as is true in so many cases, the police can have only a marginal impact on the problem, for better or for worse.

Part V

In Search of Alternatives

26

The Nonviolent Alternative: Research
Strategy and Preliminary Findings

by A. Paul Hare

A. Paul Hare is professor of sociology, department of sociology and anthropology, Haverford College. He is the principal investigator of a grant from the National Institute of Mental Health to study nonviolent direct action. He served as deputy representative for the Peace Corps in the Philippines; and has lectured at universities in Africa, and as a visiting professor at the Institute for Advanced Studies, Vienna. He is co-editor of Small Groups *(with E. F. Borgatta and R. F. Bales),* Nonviolent Direct Action *(with H. H. Blumberg), and* Studies in Regional Development *(with S. Wells). He is author of* Handbook of Small Group Research; *and currently is deputy editor of* Sociological Inquiry.

This research was supported by NIMH Grant 5 RO1 MH 17421-02 SP.

THE nonviolent alternative to collective violence as a factor in the process of social change has developed in depth and in scope over the past two years. In 1968 when we applied to the National Institute of Mental Health for a three-year grant for a "social-psychological analysis of nonviolent direct actions," the focus of the proposed research was on the direct confrontation between the nonviolent protestor and some counter-player such as a counter-demonstrator or a member of a policing force. By Fall 1970 we had broadened our project to include the analysis of nonviolent life styles, the response of universities to campus violence, and nonviolent revolutions, thus to keep track of the change in face and pace of the "movement."

In this chapter I will first outline some of the recent developments in the movement and then give some examples of our research in each of the four areas. It will be apparent that the "findings" are in a very preliminary stage since much of the first year of the grant was spent in reviewing the literature, developing psychological tests, developing category systems, and testing our field observation methods. Even with a team of 12 persons, full- or part-time, drawn from the movement or from academic halls, we find it difficult to keep up with the pace at which nonviolence is breaking out in the United States. Even though the research product is uncertain at this point, the process is an exciting one, one that we hope makes some contribution to the movement and to the institutions we study.

Research Strategy

With the radical critique of research still in full swing, it may be best to start by describing our research strategy with regard to the people we study, the ways in which we "use" them, and the purpose for which our research

findings will be used. We have to tell this story over and over again in the "field" since people in the movement can be quite concerned about having someone with a United States government grant sitting in on their meetings. No explanation we can give will satisfy some groups. For example, the Puerto Rican Independence Party does not want us to observe their training workshops for nonviolent action. So we agree. If we cannot be present openly, we will not try. Secrecy and subterfuge have no place in the ideal nonviolent action and should have no place in scientific research.

Too often in the past, in the typical research survey of some minority people or social movement, someone from the "establishment" decided on the research questions without consulting persons from the social movement, procured his own funds and staff from outside the movement, and conducted the research using the people in the movement only as subjects. The data were taken home to be analyzed and published, some years later, in a journal or monograph which probably never reached the hands of the subjects who supplied the data. Although in many cases the research process still takes this form, in others the process has evolved through the stage of participant observation, on to a stage of mutual cooperation between researchers and researched, and finally to a stage in which the research becomes a part of the process of social change rather than a preliminary step toward beginning the process of change.

In our own case, we work out an agreement with any group we are going to observe before we begin our observations. We tell them about the kinds of observations we wish to carry out and ask if they can suggest further observations which would help them. Since most nonviolent groups would like to have more observation and evaluation than their own staff can provide, they welcome the opportunity to have outside observers. We come fully equipped with notebooks, tape recorders, and still and movie cameras. Where appropriate we summarize our observations on the spot and later send copies of field reports to both the group observed and the National Institute of Mental Health. We plan to publish as much of our material as the journals will accept. There are no secret reports to anyone. The NIMH does not ask for one and none is given. As in all basic social scientific research, the goal is a greater understanding of the social process. Anyone may use the results for any purpose; however, the people in the movement will be among the first to know.

Fortunately for us, there is no conflict between this research strategy and the Gandhian emphasis on search for truth. We want to know not only what is true of men today in their interpersonal relations but also what may be true of them in the future when they have broadened and deepened their sense of common humanity.

Research Objectives

Our original research objective was to observe the inter-action between the nonviolent demonstrator and some counter-player in the "field" (which might be the steps of the Capitol, the gates of an army base, or a public street). In a review of previously published research on social-psychological aspects of non-violence, we had collected 11 case studies representing some of the major confrontations in the United States in recent years.[1] Only two of these were free from direct violence. Both of these were attempts to sail boats into restricted areas. Since the "theory" of nonviolence calls for treating an opponent with love so that he will respond with love, there would seem to be no occasion for violence to occur at a "nonviolent" demonstration. Where did the violence come from?

Our plan of research called for selecting a sample of groups or individuals who represented some degree of nonviolent philosophy, along a continuum from, for example, a dedicated Gandhian who is completely immersed in a nonviolent "life style," to an individual who is consciously nonviolent for tactical reasons. We had no mandate to study persons committed to violence since they were already studied by many research teams and institutes. Some of the groups in our sample include the Friends Peace Committee (Philadelphia Quakers), AQAG (A Quaker Action Group), the Southern Christian Leadership Conference, Resistance, and the Life Center at Kent State University.

For each case in our sample, we would like first to conduct a content analysis of the literature of the group as one indicator of its commitment to nonviolence. We may also interview key members or attend evaluative and planning sessions conducted by the group. After assessing the commitment to nonviolence, we would like to give a short personality test and background questionnaire to the members to identify their salient personality and background characteristics, and then observe the group in a training workshop or planning session where the role to be played in a demonstration is rehearsed. Finally, we would follow the group to the field to observe how the personalities of the members combine with the role of demonstrator or marshal in an actual confrontation.

For our observations at the training

1. A. Paul Hare and Herbert Blumberg, *Nonviolent Direct Action: American Cases: Social-Psychological Analyses* (Washington, D.C. and Cleveland: Corpus Books, 1969).

sessions and in the field we ideally have a team of five persons present. Each team member has a different task to perform:

1. A narrative account of the action, illustrated by still photos, motion pictures, and tape recordings, plus other documentation.

2. An inter-action process analysis using a four-dimensional category system based on the work of Bales and Couch.[2] The four dimensions are: dominant vs. submissive, positive vs. negative, serious vs. expressive, and conforming vs. nonconforming.

3. A functional analysis based on the work of Parsons and Effrat.[3] The four major functional categories are: (A) Adaptation, (G) Goal-attainment, (I) Integration, and (L) Latent pattern maintenance and tension management.

4. An exchange theory analysis based on the work of Homans and Blau, where we ask what values the actors seem to be willing to give and what they seek in return.[4]

5. A dramaturgical approach based on the work of Goffman and Burke, which asks how the action is being staged.[5] Since many

demonstrations include "guerrilla theater" and many of the demonstrators are permanently in "costume," there is a continuing interplay between a theatrical performance and "real life."

Although we still plan to collect as many cases as we can, using this team approach, it became apparent by the end of our first year of research that for all the thousands of persons who take part in some of the mass demonstrations, only a few of these have been specifically trained in nonviolent techniques, and only a few of these in turn ever directly confront a violent counter-player. Thus we are unlikely to have a very large sample of observations of actual field situations.

Noting this, we designed a questionnaire to give to the participants at the first National Workshop for Trainers in Nonviolent Direct Action held in September 1970. A dozen of the 130 persons there had more than 20 years' experience in the movement. Almost all of the experienced trainers in the country were present. Yet only a half of those who returned the questionnaire had had a direct confrontation with a violent counter-player during their entire lifetimes, and some of these cases had occurred in a school corridor or in their neighborhood when they were growing up. Nevertheless, we plan to continue to collect case material using the questionnaire approach, and plan to send quesionnaires to some of the hundreds of persons who have taken part in workshops on nonviolence over the past several years.

2. R. Freed Bales, *Personality and Interpersonal Behavior* (New York: Holt, Rinehart and Winston, 1970); A. S. Couch, *Psychological Determinants of Interpersonal Behavior*, doctoral dissertation (Cambridge: Harvard University, 1960).

3. Andrew Effrat, "Editor's Introduction: Applications of Parsonian Theory," *Sociological Inquiry* 38 (Spring 1968), pp. 97–103.

4. P. Blau, *Exchange and Power in Social Life* (New York: John Wiley & Sons, Inc., 1964); G. C. Homans, *Social Behavior: Its Elementary Forms* (New York: Harcourt, Brace and World, 1961).

5. Erving Goffman, *The Presentation of Self in Everyday Life* (New York: Doubleday Anchor, 1959); Erving Goffman, *Behavior in Public Places* (Glencoe, Ill.: Free Press, 1963); Kenneth Burke, *The Philosophy of Literary Form: Studies in Symbolic Action* (New York: Vintage Books, 1957); Kenneth Burke, *A Grammar of Motives and a Rhetoric of Motives* (Cleveland: World Publishing Company, 1962).

A further result of our experience at the National Workshop for Trainers in Nonviolence was to be told, rather abruptly, by some of the participants, especially by women, that direct confrontations were not where nonviolence "was at." This was just more evidence of "male chauvinism." The women said that the men were going around showing their participation in demonstrations as if they had earned "battle stars." The main point about nonviolence, the women said, was in the way you lived it day by day. It was in *life style*. This life style was more likely to be found in *communes* than it was in demonstrations on the street.

So we are now studying communes. The preferred method is participant observation. We hope to compare a sample of six "regular" communes with six devoted to a nonviolent life style. In both sets of cases, the major dimensions to consider are whether the communes are rural or urban, activist or retreatist, religious or secular, and largely self-sufficient or dependent on the outside community. We have already completed a review of the literature to find that the systematic study of communes has just begun in the past two years.

In addition to communes, we now find ourselves involved with students, faculty, and administrators at Kent State University who are attempting to find nonviolent solutions to the problems leading up to the events of May 4, 1970, when four students were killed on campus by members of the National Guard. This might be called an institutional response to institutional violence. Already one group, primarily of students, has established a "Life Center" devoted to a nonviolent life style and to forms of creative protest. A University Commission, appointed to propose a "living memorial" to the four students who died, has brought forward a plan for an "Institute for Peaceful Change" which would include teaching, research, and action inspired by a nonviolent philosophy. Other universities are following suit either in direct response to the events of May 4 or in response to the general wave of violent protest on college campuses since 1970. Several faculty members and students at Kent will join us in recording the Kent State story. This major case study will in turn serve to highlight the nonviolent response on other campuses.

A final research objective, not anticipated at the time the research was proposed, is to follow the growing discussion and action on the theme of "nonviolent revolution." Discussions of nonviolent revolution are just beginning to spread throughout the movement in the United States. The use of the word "revolution" seems to reflect two concerns. The first is to overcome the feeling that the movement in the past had been characterized more by "passive resistance" rather than by "active intervention." The second is to emphasize the fact that it is no longer enough to demonstrate dissatisfaction at the feet of the powerful, hoping that some unspecified change will result. The nonviolent actor must also have some clear idea of the dimensions of the new society he wishes to bring about. This calls for a degree of economic and social planning which goes far beyond the content of the typical workshop on nonviolence as it exists today.

Since our NIMH grant limits our research to the United States, we are unlikely to be able to observe any bona fide nonviolent revolutionary attempts. However, the activities of the Puerto Rican Independence Party probably can be viewed within this framework. In any event, we would like to develop a profile of a "nonviolent revolution" as an "ideal type" against which to compare current forms of nonviolent activity.

Although it is too soon to be able to present any findings from our observations of communes or of nonviolent revolution, we can present some preliminary findings on the personality dimensions of nonviolent actors, some observations at a workshop for nonviolence and at demonstrations, and a report from Kent State University.

Personality Dimensions of Nonviolent Actors

We have developed a short form of personality test based on tests developed by Couch and Borgatta and Corsini for use in the field and at workshops and training sessions for nonviolent action.[6] The test scales measure the four personality dimensions of anxiety, aggression, conformity, and extroversion, and also verbal intelligence.

The personality test has been given to over 700 persons representing samples of college students, persons attending summer music festivals, and participants in workshops for trainers in nonviolent direct action. After comparing the mean scores for the different samples using appropriate statistical tests, we find no significant differences between the samples on the anxiety measure. Apparently they are all about equally anxious. However, persons in the movement are less aggressive, less conforming, and more extroverted. Since we expected to find that persons actively engaged in training for nonviolent action would have these characteristics, we can use these results as

6. A. S. Couch, *Psychological Determinants of Interpersonal Behavior*, doctoral diss. (Cambridge: Harvard University, 1960); E. F. Borgatta and R. J. Corsini, "The Quick Word Test (QWT) and the WATS," *Psychological Report* 6 (1960), p. 201.

evidence that the personality test measures what it purports to measure. Later we hope to be able to compare personality scores with behavior in field situations. Probably the best predictor of actual behavior in a confrontation between a nonviolent actor and some counter-player will be a combination of the role the nonviolent actor has been trained to play and his general tendencies to act as measured by the personality test.

The measure of verbal intelligence also seems to be working as one would expect. The sample with the lowest level of education had the lowest mean score, and the sample with the most college graduates had the highest mean score.

A Functional Analysis of Group Development

As an example of the analysis of a workshop on nonviolence we can follow the events in a workshop held by the Friends Peace Committee of Philadelphia on a weekend in February 1970. The workshop was held at a Quaker meetinghouse in the suburbs. Thirty-five persons were present, about equally divided by sex, with an average age of 26 (range 14 to 60 years). The majority had a college education. Although all participants were given personality tests and rated by several judges on the four interaction process dimensions, the major findings result from the functional analysis using the four functional categories (AGIL).

As the workshop progressed from Friday night through Saturday afternoon, it was possible to identify typical stages in group development. The workshop turned out to be successful because the trainers and members were able to deal with the basic functional problems faced by any group in the order that is most effective for learning groups.[7]

The functional theory of groups was developed primarily by Parsons.[8] This approach begins with an analysis of the four basic problems which every social system must solve in order to survive. These problems are Latent pattern maintenance and tension management (L), Adaptation (A), Integration (I), and Goal-attainment (G). (See summary of theory by Effrat.)[9] For a whole society, the solution to these problems is usually centered in four types of institutions: L, the church, family, and educational institutions (which give the basic meaning to the society and bring new members into the system) ; A, the economic institutions (which create materials to be used by the society) ; I, the law (which defines the norms for the activities of the society) ; and G, the political institutions (which coordinate the activities in the interest of goal-attainment).

A category system based on the AGIL scheme has been developed by Effrat and Hare, which makes it possible to analyze the content of the activity of a social system, to determine the functional nature of each unit of activity, and to test an hypothesis about the "typical" sequence of development of the system.[10] This developmental sequence of L/A/I/G with a terminal stage of L is similar in many respects to the previous analyses of group development based on data from therapy groups, self-analytic groups, classroom groups, and work groups.[11]

When the AGIL categories are applied to the description of a learning group such as a classroom group, the forces at work seem to be as follows: the work of the group requires that the purpose of the group be defined (L), that new skills be acquired (A), that the group be reorganized so that the members can try out the new skills without being too dependent on the leader (I), and that the group members work at the task (G). Finally there is a terminal phase in which the group returns to L to redefine the relationships between the members and the group as the group is disbanded. The amount of time the group spends in each phase is determined by the activity of the leader (his direction or non-direction) and by the skill and emotional strengths of the members. Presumably the leader is "ready" for each stage at the outset since he has been through the stages before. However, members come to the group with different degrees of problem-solving skills

---

7. A. Paul Hare, *Theories of Group Development and Categories for Interaction Analysis*, Report No. 4, NVA Project (Haverford, Pa.: Haverford College, 1970).

8. T. Parsons, R. Freed Bales, and E. A. Shils, *Working Papers in the Theory of Action* (Glencoe, Ill.: Free Press, 1953) ; T. Parsons, "An Outline of the Social System," in Parsons, T. et al., eds., *Theories of Society* (New York: Free Press of Glencoe, 1961), pp. 30–79.

9. Effrat, *op. cit.*

10. A. Paul Hare, "Phases in the Development of the Bicol Development Planning Board," S. Wells and A. P. Hare, eds., *Studies in Regional Development* (Bicol Development Planning Board, 1968) ; A. Paul Hare and A. Effrat, *Content and Process of Inter-action in "Lord of the Flies,"* Report No. 8, NVA Project (Haverford, Pa.: Haverford College, 1969).

11. W. G. Bennis and H. A. Shepard, "A Theory of Group Development," *Human Relations* 9 (1956), pp. 415–437 ; R. D. Mann, *Interpersonal Styles and Group Development* (New York: John Wiley & Sons, Inc., 1967) ; T. M. Mills, *Group Transformation: An Analysis of a Learning Group* (Englewood Cliffs, N.J.: Prentice Hall, 1961) ; W. C. Schutz, *FIRO: A Three-dimensional Theory of Interpersonal Behavior* (New York: Holt, Rinehart, and Winston, 1958) ; B. W. Tuckman, "Developmental Sequence in Small Groups," *Psychological Bulletin* 63 (June 1965), pp. 384–399.

or preferences for different emotional modalities (for example: a preference for fight-flight or pairing or dependency.[12] Subgroups tend to form on the basis of these skills or emotional modalities. If the subgroup with the appropriate skills and emotional state for each stage is large enough, it can carry the whole group through that phase.[13] If not enough members of the group are ready for a particular stage, more intervention by the leader may be necessary. Some groups may never progress beyond the early stages.

Group Development During the Workshop

Before the analysis of group development begins, the life of the group is divided into natural time periods. The duration of these time periods depends upon the length of time the group is in existence. In the Friends Peace Committee Workshop, the days provide the major breaks in activity and within each day the morning, afternoon, and evening sessions. If more detailed records of each session had been kept, the units might have been based on each change of activity, since each session included several different activities. However, in this case, the major trends of development are evident when the session is used as a unit. The sessions were: (1) Friday night, (2) Saturday morning, (3) Saturday afternoon, (4) Saturday evening, (5) Sunday morning, and (6) Sunday noon.

On Friday night some of the L or pattern-maintenance functions were performed as group members were registered, names and brief backgrounds given, and the trainers made an opening statement about the purpose of the workshop. Some orientation had been

12. W. R. Bion, *Experiences in Groups, And Other Papers* (New York: Basic Books, 1961).

13. Bennis and Shepard, *op. cit.*; Mann, *op. cit.*

provided by the registration and announcement forms sent out prior to the workshop. Much of the definition of the basic goal of the workshop was given through actual participation in role-playing or other skill groups. The basic message was that the workshop would concentrate on skills rather than on philosophy or tactics of nonviolence. This definition was challenged by some group members who thought that there should be more emphasis on philosophy or a greater self-awareness in dealing with skills.

Actually it is possible to identify subphases within each of the major phases. In the L phase, for example, the subphases are L_1, L_a, L_i, and L_g. That is, in order to establish the general meaning of the workshop, the "big idea" is introduced by one or two individuals (L_1 or L sub 1); next, information is given or resources collected which will help to implement the idea (L_a); next, the group is organized to endorse the idea (L_i); and finally the idea is agreed upon (L_g).

On Friday night the main idea of the workshop was presented by the trainers (L_1). The idea was tested through actual role plays so that information could be gathered about the feasibility of the approach (L_a). The trainers indicated that they were "loose" and would entertain suggestions for sessions other than the ones originally proposed, thus bringing all the group members into the L process (L_i). Finally a definition of the workshop was fashioned which included new as well as old ideas (L_g).

We can guess that there must have been a similar set of pre-group subphases in the L sector when the Friends Peace Committee members met to outline their ideas about the workshop before they issued a call for participants. Here we see that many levels of analysis are possible. When we begin the workshop in the L phase, we are taking the point of view of the participants. From the trainers' viewpoint, this is the *work* which they planned to do sometime before, and therefore represents the G phase for them.

Friday night's session was effective as an L stage because it allowed for a modification of the overall plan to meet the needs and skills of the particular set of participants who attended. This tended to give a higher degree of commitment to the program than any formulation which is simply laid on by someone in authority.

Saturday morning was primarily in the A sector as participants learned a variety of new skills. Saturday afternoon continued in A with two groups working on street speaking and guerrilla theater. When the group left the site of the workshop and drove into town to speak and perform in front of a supermarket, the group might seem to have moved into the G sector since they were actually doing the *work* they had come for. However, this was still in A since the group was not yet reorganized for the new task. The trainers were still in control. They had made all the arrangements and were directing the sessions. This is the point where classroom education usually stops. The teacher gives the students skills and perhaps tries them out on practice problems, but the students never act independently.

The move toward independence from the trainers began Saturday night, a traditional time for integrative (I) activity. The following morning one of the participants remarked that the singing the night before had given the group "soul." Group members now felt "together" enough to do something on their own.

The opportunity for independent action was provided Sunday morning when the trainer asked for volunteers to prepare a presentation for the Forum of the Friends Meeting whose facilities were being used. A group of participants took over this activity, planned it according to prinicples learned in the workshop, incorporated techniques and skills already learned, and produced an outstanding performance. Thus the group moved into the G sector, using their own resources.

We note that the participants who took the lead in this activity had shown their strength early in the workshop by volunteering to lead special sessions. A group composed of persons with less experience than the trainers who were the participants in this workshop might not have been able to "take over" as readily. Most teachers never give their students a chance. The student is put firmly in his place as "student" throughout the learning experience and never given an opportunity to use the new skills with his former teacher as resource person, co-participant, or subordinate.

The group passed again into the L stage during the evaluation at noon on Sunday. Here members summed up their experiences, prepared to sever their relationships with the workshop, and began to shift their commitment to the groups and tasks they had left behind.

In sum, the group passed through the expected stages of group development from L to A to I to G and back to L again. However, the trainers seemed to have placed their main emphasis on the L and A stages. The singing and integrative events which highlighted the I stage seem to have occurred because of the day of the week (Saturday night) and were more casually organized.

A Demonstration Against War Taxes

On April 15, 1970, members of our research team were on hand at the internal revenue headquarters in Philadelphia to observe a demonstration conducted by the Philadelphia War Tax Resisters group. During the early hours of the morning there were as many observers on the street as demonstrators. We sought to test the reliability of our four-dimensional category system for rating inter-action process. Several observers would watch the demonstrator for about five minutes and then make a summary rating on each of the four dimensions. In this case, we had previously observed the demonstrators in the course of weekend workshops and had obtained personality and background information from them. Two short sequences of inter-action will illustrate the use of the category system.

The first demonstrator, a man of about 60 years whom we will call Bill, had been walking back and forth in front of the main entrance of the internal revenue headquarters. He carried a sign which read "Don't pay war taxes." In general he seemed serious and intent on his work but would smile when a pedestrian stopped to talk to him. It was a cold, windy day. After a few hours of picketing, Bill decided to go inside the building to visit the toilet. He was stopped at the door by two men, and the conversation went something like this:

Man: Where are you going?
Bill: I don't have to tell you where I'm going.
Man (showing his U. S. marshal badge): Why do you want to come in here?
Bill: Just because you have a badge doesn't mean I have to tell you anything.
Man: You still can't come in here.
At this point Bill left the entrance and solved his problem elsewhere.

Although Bill had been dominant and positive with passing pedestrians, he was clearly negative with the U.S. marshals. In both cases he was serious, but with the marshals he was definitely non-conforming since he refused to go along with their definition of the situation. Here we see a marked difference in Bill's behavior toward the pedestrian whom he would like to influence and the marshal whom he makes no attempt to reach. This may provide a partial answer to the initial research question concerning the origins of the violence in nonviolent demonstrations. It is possible that demonstrators are not uniformly loving and concerned about all persons present at a demonstration. It is also possible that when authority figures "come on strong" as they did in this instance, it is difficult for a demonstrator not to respond defensively without very specific training in his role.

A second incident occurred at the same demonstration. The demonstrator, of college age whom we will call Fred, entered the foyer of the internal revenue headquarters with his income tax form. He had hoped to make some verbal protest while handing in his form at the office inside. The following conversation was recorded on a tape recorder he was carrying.

Agent: Can I help you, buddy?
Fred: I have a tax form. I want to give it to someone inside.
Agent (asking to see the form): Are you going to file it? Do you want to mail it?
Fred: No. I want to give it to them.
Agent: Do you want to file it?
1st Agent: Put it in the basket over there.
2nd Agent: I'll take it. I suggest you sign it. (The agent has noticed that Fred has not yet signed his form.)
Fred: Oh, yeah.
Agent: W-2 form attached?
Fred: I can't go into the office?
Agent: No!

Fred: Why is that?

Agent: We are using the place over here to collect returns. There is a mailbox over here. Right here.

Fred: I want to go into the office to give it to them.

Agent: Drop it here, this is it. This is the mail drop right here. This takes care of it. Have you got a pen? (To sign the form.)

Fred: Why is it that I can't go into the office to give it to them?

Agent: There is no purpose.

Fred: I want to talk to them about it.

Agent: Well, there is nobody you can talk to about it. We're just employees here. Talk to your congressman if you have a problem. The forms are right here. It's a bureaucracy, you'll have to recognize that. (His tone was consoling.)

Fred: I understand that it's bureaucracy. I just don't see why I shouldn't be able to talk to, say, you, to people who work for the public.

Agent: Who's that?

Fred: Whoever it is who's working for the public, collecting the taxes.

Agent: What taxes?

Fred: They go to fight wars.

Agent: Why don't you write your congressman?

Fred: I've tried to do a number of things to contact my congressman. It seems to be pretty ineffective. I just wanted to talk to. . . .

Agent: It does you no good. . . .

Fred: Okay, thank you for your time. (This last is rather sarcastic.)

In contrast to the first incident, Fred did seem to want to engage the agent in conversation, and possibly win him over, or at least talk his way past. Fred was not too dominant, fairly positive, serious, and conforming (to the suggestions of the agent). If anything, the agent was even more outgoing and helpful. He noticed the form had not been signed, offered a pen, and was consoling about the nature of bureaucracy. Had he also had training in a nonviolent role?

In fact, the police have been issued quite detailed instructions on arrest procedures for civil disobedience demonstrators. They are cautioned that time is not important in making arrests of demonstrators and there should be no haste. Civil disobedience teams are told that the policy of the police department is to recognize and respect the right to protest or demonstrate against a social custom or condition. Agents are cautioned to avoid picayune arrests because an arrest can be seen by the demonstrators as the successful climax of a demonstration and can be interpreted as a denial of the right to demonstrate. Thus an agent who has read the rules need not assume a position which is too dominant, negative, serious, or conforming in the first instance, although eventually he will have to assert his dominance in the interest of the conformity he has been trained to enforce, if the demonstrator persists in nonconforming behavior. In this case, Fred did not insist on going through the police line and the encounter seems to have ended in favor of the agent.

SOME OBSERVATIONS AT KENT STATE
UNIVERSITY: OR, WHO NEEDS A
REVOLUTION TO BE A
HUMAN BEING?

It was Thursday night, October 1, 1970, at Kent State University. "Think Week" was going well so far. For the past several years, the first week of classes had been designated by the student government as "Think Week." During this period outside speakers were brought on campus for a series of lectures and discussions on current topics. This year Kent had plenty to think about following the events of the previous May when four students were killed and others wounded by members of the national guard. This year the subject of discussion was nonviolence and its application to Kent State in the form of life style, avoiding further violence, and creative dissent. The theme was "Power to the Peaceful."

The week before, many of the students, faculty, and administration were fearful that the University would not be able to last through the first week. Someone might place a bomb in a building, the president of the university might be attacked while giving his opening speech to students, dissident students who were rumored to have transferred to the campus in large numbers might start a riot. Between 30 and 40 rumors were actively circulating about the campus, and all of them boded no good.

However, from Monday to Thursday there had been no major problems. The president had spoken at the opening convocation without incident. The memorial service Monday night—with songs by Phil Ochs, and stirring speeches by Ralph Abernathy, recalling the power of nonviolence in the days of Martin Luther King, and Ira Sandperl, representing the California "life style" approach—roused the audience of about 7,000 to the possibilities of nonviolent action. The candlelight march from the gym to the common where the students had been shot closed an emotional evening.

On Tuesday, Wednesday, and Thursday there was an almost continuous stream of nonviolent activity flowing across the campus. Representatives from "Nader's Raiders," the Berkeley Peace Brigade, and the "Harvard Peace Action" conducted workshops on nonviolent life styles and forms of protest. James Michener, Mark Lane, and Congressman Robert Eckhart gave major addresses in the evening, and journalists, legislators, and attorneys spoke about problems of civil liberties and the democratic system. Friday was to bring more workshops, speeches by Allard Lowenstein, Democratic congressman from New York, and Sargent Shriver, former Peace Corps director. The final event was to be an informal celebration of Gandhi's 101st birthday featuring a film of Gandhi's life and discussions of new directions for those who had been moved to join some form of nonviolent activity.

Since the number of students attending the various speeches and workshops had ranged from about 30 to about 300, the number of students who would participate in the final event was not expected to be high. By my count, about 40 were actually present the next night, not including the outside resource people and the 20 or so students who were committed to nonviolence before Think Week began. This is a very small percentage of a student body of 20,000. However, it would increase the number of activists about three-fold, giving more than enough problems to the "old timers" as they sought to *integrate* the activities of all these new *individuals* into the "movement."

The emphasis was clearly on the word "integrate" since the word "organize" was ruled out as a "no-no." The problem that the "old timers" had set for themselves was to help the newcomers find their places in the nonviolent life without "organizing" them and without clear directions from any appointed or self-appointed leaders. The problem was to bring about change in old forms of social institutions, including Kent State University, using a seemingly new form of group process which allowed much more freedom to the individual but at the same time called on the individual for more commitment and responsibility in his actions and more concern for his fellows. The goal was to become more "human" and to treat others in more humanizing ways rather than to dehumanize them in large formal institutions or, in the extreme case, to treat them as objects for target practice in a shooting gallery. For some, old and young, who felt comfortable with clearly designated leaders, agenda, and formal controls, this new life style seemed strange, ineffective, even revolutionary. Why should it seem so revolutionary? Who needs a revolution to be a human being? To discover something of the nature of this "revolution" let us return to the events of Thursday night at Kent State to watch the process unfold.

Problem Solving

The first students arrived at the apartment about 10:30 p.m., after the evening speaker. Over the next hour about eight students assembled, some first passing by the kitchen for snacks, others lying on a large mattress in the corner of the room where they rested, attempting to recover from the fatigue of the many preceding nights of planning and "organizing" with little sleep. The apartment was one of several rented by members of an informal "commune" of students who shared each others' food and facilities and were always open to any visitors from the movement who might want to stay overnight.

As students joined the group they would volunteer information about their activities during the day, or they might be drawn out by another group member. There was no appointed leader for the group and no agenda. The center of the discussion would shift from one person to another as the topic changed. In general, the person with the most information on a particular subject became the "leader" of the discussion while that subject held the floor. Early in the evening one member reported his conversation with some students who planned to burn their draft cards. He had suggested they say that they were inspired by the president of the university, who had made a public statement endorsing nonviolence. Other group members challenged this stand, arguing that one should not single out an individual for attack in a nonviolent campaign. Variations on the theme were suggested as the group sought to assess the proposed action in the light of Gandhi's search for truth.

Later in the evening the phone rang. A member of the nonviolent action group was calling in from another part of the campus to report yelling in front of one of the dorms. One member of the group took the initiative to go off to check out the report. On his return he reported that it was only a "panty raid" conducted by some male undergraduates at one of the women's dorms. The campus police were on hand and there seemed to be no need for student marshals. Since all members of the group had been trained to act as "third party" marshals in the event of any campus disorder, there was some anxious discussion while the report of the yelling was being checked. The previous events leading to the shooting had taken place over a weekend from May 1 to 4. This was now October 1 and a weekend was approaching. Would this be some sort of "anniversary" of the first event? Would this be the long-feared riot which would provide an occasion for outside authorities to close the university? If so, what could be done to keep it open? Fortunately the group never had to give a final answer to these questions that night, but they realized that plans had to be made for each contingency and that they had no clear plans at present.

As the evening wore on into the early hours of the morning, the group moved back and forth between a number of topics. Plans were developed for a proposed Life Center, schedules were considered for further training of marshals, co-ordination with other colleges was discussed, and a list was drawn up of current issues which might be the focus of student protest. One woman spoke of her plans for a new course on nonviolence to be given as part of the "free university." Group members considered their own need for more organizing experience. To meet this need and to provide some respite from the stress of opening week, group members planned a weekend workshop with a local resource person at a site some distance from the campus.

Content and Form of Interaction

By the time the evening was over, the group had dealt with three social system levels: their own group, their group as part of a Life Center, and the Life Center as part of Kent State University. At each level they had discussed aspects of the four basic problems of all social systems: pattern maintenance, adaptation, integration, and goal-attainment. For example, for their own group they discussed their basic values of nonviolence and also the ways in which they would introduce new members to these values (Pattern Maintenance); they considered new sources of information and skills for problem solving (Adaptation); they shared in the fellowship of food and drink—potato chips and soft drinks— (Integration); and they actually carried out their responsibility as third

party marshals by checking out the potential riot (Goal-attainment).

In planning for the Life Center they considered its basic purposes (L); the amount of money, floor space, and office supplies that would be needed (A); the type of committee structure and leadership necessary (I); and the type of programs it would sponsor (G). Similarly, they considered the ways that the Center would fit into the activities of the university.

Thus this form of "leaderless group discussion" was handling a complicated set of problems which the group faced. It was able to do it without the heavy authoritarian structure which the nonviolent movement seeks to replace. The means were consistent with the ends. However, this probably represented the group working at its best. Would the group always be able to perform this way? Would other groups composed in different ways be as successful? Some of these same students were reported on another occasion to have taken 15 or 20 minutes to decide which restaurant to choose for dinner. Why was there a difference?

The literature on role differentiation in groups suggests that when there is a clear basis for role differentiation, group members can more easily recognize informal leaders and spend more time on the task and less time on interpersonal relationships.[14] Perhaps on the evening of October 1 there was a fairly clear differentiation of skills and information for the different topics of discussion. Thus different members would be able to "take over" the "leadership" as the group moved from topic to topic. This would maintain an overall equality of participation and yet reward mem-

14. A. Paul Hare, "Groups: Role Structure," D. L. Sills, ed., *International Encyclopedia of the Social Sciences* 6 (New York: Macmillan and Free Press, 1968), pp. 283–288.

bers for visible abilities. In contrast, the task of choosing a restaurant was probably more one of personal opinion. If no one had any obvious basis for taking the lead, then one person's suggestion could only be followed at the expense of having another's "put down." This would seem an assertion of undue authority to people who are very sensitive about the subject. In any event, this is only one aspect of the situation. After more data have been collected we would hope to be able to describe the process in more detail.

Summary

By the end of the first year of a three-year grant to study nonviolent direct action, members of the research team had developed four category systems for social-psychological analysis of interpersonal behavior and a short form of a personality test. The four category systems, all adapted for field use from previous theoretical statements, include: (1) Four functional categories (AGIL) for content analysis, (2) Four interpersonal dimensions (dominate, positive, serious, conforming) for process analysis, (3) a set of exchange categories, also for content analysis, and (4) a set of dramaturgical dimensions for structural analysis. The personality test includes measures for: anxiety, aggression, conformity, extroversion, and verbal intelligence.

Although we still plan to observe actual encounters between nonviolent demonstrators and their counter-players in field situations, we find that the probability of obtaining a very large sample is rather small. We are now turning to interviews and questionnaires to recover accounts of past encounters from persons who have been active in the movement.

Further, we discover that the field of nonviolent action has broadened and deepened since we first proposed our study. To keep pace with the new developments, we have now begun observing at institutions (such as Kent State University) which are trying to respond nonviolently to recent violent events. We also plan to study nonviolent communes as examples of nonviolent "life style" and to follow the discussions of those in the movement who are beginning to talk of nonviolent revolution.

As we go about our work in the field we try to make some contribution to the people we study as well as to social science. We feel that the process of peaceful change is served by bringing the best theories and methods available to bear on the analysis of the social system and its components.

As a sample of our preliminary findings, we present personality test data which indicate that nonviolent activists do not differ from samples of college students or persons who attend summer music festivals, on the dimension of anxiety, but that they do have significantly lower scores on aggression and conformity and higher scores on extroversion. Next we describe a weekend workshop for trainers in nonviolent action which passes successfully through the expected phases in group development from L to A to I to G and back to L again. Two short transcripts of the inter-action between nonviolent demonstrators and government agents at an income tax demonstration illustrate the use of the four inter-action process dimensions. Finally, an account of the inter-action at a gathering of students involved in planning a Life Center at Kent State University is used to compare the problem-solving process within the movement with that of more traditional organizations.

27

The Usefulness of Commission Studies of Collective Violence

By James S. Campbell

James S. Campbell is a practicing attorney in Washington, D.C. In 1968–1969 he was general counsel for the National Commission on the Causes and Prevention of Violence, and a co-director of the Task Force which produced Law and Order Reconsidered *(1969; rev. edition forthcoming). Formerly he was special assistant to the Assistant Attorney General in charge of antitrust cases, and has written articles for legal periodicals in antitrust and other fields.*

TODAY it has become a common-place to assert that national commissions are useless. Despite our political leaders' penchant for creating such bodies, none of them, it is said, ever seems to "do any good." The assertion is made about all kinds of commissions, but it is the commissions which strongly emphasize recommended solutions for the problems they have studied that are the chief target of popular pessimism. The Kerner Commission is probably the best example of an apparently program-oriented commission that, according to this view, "didn't really accomplish anything." Indeed, that commission seemingly provided the text for its own epitaph when it featured in its concluding section Dr. Kenneth B. Clark's comment about the reports of earlier riot commissions:

I must again in candor say to you members of this commission, it is a kind of *Alice in Wonderland*, with the same moving picture reshown over and over again—the same analysis, the same recommendations, and the same inaction.[1]

When such sentiments are voiced about the Kerner Commission, the Eisenhower Commission, and other similar groups, the premise is that a national commission is a failure if it does not prompt swift executive and legislative action on its program of reforms. The correctness of this premise depends in turn upon the further assumption that the chief function of a commission is to make specific recommendations for immediate governmental implementation. No doubt this is the announced purpose of most commissions, but I would submit that the "recommendations function" is usually only a

1. *Report of the National Advisory Commission on Civil Disorders* (New York: Bantam Books, 1968) [hereinafter, the Kerner Report], pp. 29, 483.

secondary and accidental part of the commission process. If some useful, concrete recommendations emerge and are quickly acted upon, that is a bonus; it is not normally the real measure of a commission's usefulness.

TWO REASONS

My reasons for thus contradicting the received opinion are of two kinds and can be briefly stated. First of all, the kind of commission which I am talking about—the ad hoc national advisory commission—is wholly without either legislative power or executive authority: it can neither make laws nor assume any day-to-day operating responsibility in the areas of its concern. Indeed, it tends naturally to shun any direct involvement in the political process, intentionally closing off what little access it may have to the power centers of government, for fear that such involvement may expose it to pressures that will destroy its objectivity and integrity. The national advisory commission typically asserts its total independence of politics and leads a brief life of its own, often measuring its success almost solely by the degree to which it is able in its final report to "tell it like it is." We should not be surprised, I suggest, that the frequently utopian recommendations of a body so deliberately isolated from political decision-making are rarely translated into governmental action on any simple, one-to-one basis.

My second set of reasons for minimizing the recommendations function of most national commissions reflects what I believe to be the true measure of the usefulness of commissions. Both in terms of the way most commissions actually operate and in terms of the tangible results they produce, it is not the recommendations that are paramount, but the findings. The real usefulness of commissions lies simply and primarily in their ability to present significant facts about national problems to those who possess political power and make political decisions.[2] Judged by this standard, many of our national commissions have indeed been highly useful and successful, and, as I hope to suggest in this paper, the work of future commissions studying episodes of collective violence can be even more valuable for public policy purposes if the social science community can give these commissions some additional help in several perplexing problem areas.

I am not principally concerned here with trying to demonstrate the correctness of my view that it is the fact-finding function of commissions which is the most valuable to society. Instead, my purpose is chiefly to offer some observations on what is necessary to improve commission fact-finding about episodes of collective violence, whatever the ultimate value of such fact-finding may be. But I do not think it takes me too far afield to cite three items of evidence in support of my views about the true usefulness of commissions, especially if I confine my examples to the field of collective violence.

THREE EXAMPLES

Item: The Walker Report on the Democratic Convention disorders of 1968, produced by a "subcommission" of the Eisenhower Commission, contained really only one explicit recommendation for governmental action—namely, that the policemen who used unlawful force against demonstrators and bystanders be held accountable for their conduct.[3] Yet this exhaustive, de-

finitive account of what happened in Chicago made credible to millions of Americans, for the first time, the long-standing complaints of Black ghetto residents and political dissidents about "police brutality." To be sure, surveys after the event showed that a majority of our citizens felt the demonstrators got what they deserved [4]—but at least it could no longer be denied that they and others like them had in fact gotten it.

Item: At the present time, more than two years after the Kerner Commission filed its Report, relatively few people hold to the notion that "agitators" or "conspirators" were principally responsible for the ghetto riots of the 1960's. Yet how many white citizens—and their legislators [5]—believed in the summer of 1967 that Stokely Carmichael, H. Rap Brown, and other less-publicized operators of the same ilk were, simply, the cause of the riots? An important part of the reason for this advance in understanding lies with the Kerner Report's careful accounts of the major riots, its massive documentation of the oppressive conditions of life in the racial ghetto, and its convincing finding that there was no evidence of any of the disorders

---

2. I refer here to the people and their elected leaders. Others, believing this to be naïve, may take the reference to be to the "establishment," or whatever, without detracting from the basic point.

3. *Rights in Conflict,* A Report to the National Commission on the Causes and Preven-

tion of Violence (New York: Bantam Books, 1968), p. 11.

4. Fifty-six percent of the nation's adults (59 percent of the whites, only 18 percent of the Negroes) approved of "the way the Chicago police dealt with the young people who were registering their protest against the Vietnam war" (Gallup Poll, Sept. 18, 1968). Compare the finding of the recent CBS News survey that three out of four adult Americans believe extremist groups should not be allowed to organize protests against the government, even when there appears to be no clear danger of violence. See 116 *Congressional Record* (daily ed., April 27, 1970) at S6261.

5. Cf. the debate surrounding the federal anti-riot statute, 18 U.S.C. §§ 2101–2102, as it passed the House of Representatives on July 19, 1967.

having been "planned or directed by any organization or group, international, national or local." [6] The Kerner Report's recommendations for governmental action may not have evoked an adequate response from the larger society, but these findings on the conspiracy issue have undoubtedly helped to hold in check the forces of backlash and repression.

Item: Finally, we can see the usefulness of commission findings concerning episodes of collective violence by looking at a situation where we have no such findings. After the shoot-out between police and Black Panthers in Chicago on December 4, 1969, a group of Congressmen called on the Eisenhower Commission to conduct an investigation of this episode and of other similar clashes. The Commission was, however, in the process of going out of business at the time the request was made, and no investigation could be undertaken. Efforts to have a private citizens' group make the investigation have proved fruitless, and today, for want of a commission, the average American citizen is almost entirely uninformed about the true state of relations between the Panthers and the authorities.[7] The result, of course, is that official actions which may have the most serious sorts of long-term political consequences are effectively freed from the restraints normally imposed by

6. Kerner Report, pp. 2, 202.
7. After the Chicago shoot-out, the seven surviving Panthers were indicted for attempted murder and other alleged offenses; subsequently, however, the prosecution dismissed the indictment, stating that it lacked sufficient evidence to proceed with the case (*The New York Times,* May 9, 1970, p. 1, col. 1). Shortly thereafter a federal Grand Jury reported that the Chicago police had vastly exaggerated the degree of resistance offered by the Panthers to the police raid (*The New York Times,* May 16, 1970, p. 1, col. 8).

the democratic process on significant governmental activity.

THE IMPORTANT FACT-FINDING ROLE

What these examples all suggest is that in the area of collective violence, national advisory commissions have a distinctive fact-finding role to play that is related to—in a sense, lies midway between—the respective roles of both the news media and the social sciences. Commissions, media, and science all have the responsibility, among others, of presenting the facts to the citizenry about episodes of collective violence so that an appropriate response by the social order to such episodes becomes at least a possibility. Commission reports differ from news reports in that they appear months after the event (rather than hours, days, or weeks) and are usually far more informative. On the other hand, commission reports usually precede more thorough scientific or historical studies by months or even years, and they achieve a level of public visibility which such studies rarely attain.

At least part (and, I would urge, the major part) of the true usefulness of commissions lies, then, in their special ability to transmit to the public, with reasonable speed and thoroughness, significant information about the causes and consequences of episodes of collective violence. Now, to return to my main topic, how can this fact-finding function of commissions be improved? I suggest that the most promising avenue of improvement lies in the direction of having the social sciences provide commissions with sharper analytical tools for coping with a number of intensely practical problems in the field of collective violence.

When commissions study and report on episodes in this field, they inevitably make heavy use of such concepts as "political action," "cause," "intent," "leader," "demand," "grievance." These are notions which appear frequently in ordinary discourse, and commissions are understandably inclined to the view that such concepts present no special problems when they are used as analytical tools in the study of collective violence. In fact, however, each of these simple-seeming words is a hornet's nest of difficulties. Do we really know how to identify, for example, the "leader" of a group whose members have engaged in violence? Is it significant for a given purpose that he seems to have some control over whether the group will resort to violence—or is it more important that he can formulate "demands" which reflect the real "grievances" of the group? Perhaps our "leader" can do neither—should he still be regarded as a "leader" because of a symbolic position he holds?

Two Tools in Need of Sharpening

In the remainder of this paper I want to discuss, with examples from current commission literature dealing with ghetto riots, two of these frequently used concepts: "political action" and "cause." These are fundamental elements in any commission analysis of contemporary collective violence. There are others, of course, but these two will serve nicely as illustrations of my point that our basic analytical tools could use some sharpening.

"Political action"

In his provocative report to the Eisenhower Commission, Skolnick urges that the recent urban riots must be understood as "political acts," "spontaneous" or even "primitive" in nature, but nonetheless showing "a considerable degree of structure, purposiveness, and rational-

ity." [8] He objects to "the substitution of a psychological analysis for a political one," because an approach that "underestimates the political significance of riots" may rely too heavily on forceful control techniques and thus "channel expressive protest into more organized forms of political violence." [9] Similar ideas, implicitly relied on rather than explicitly developed, are found in many portions of the Kerner Report's analysis of the riots, especially in conclusions such as the following: "What the rioters appeared to be seeking was fuller participation in the social order and the material benefits enjoyed by the majority of American citizens." [10]

These findings have a substantial degree of plausibility for anyone who has reflected upon the nature of the urban riots; yet one withholds judgment until a closer examination is made of the central analytical concept of "political action." What are the criteria by which we are to judge whether and to what extent an episode of collective violence is a "political" act? The closest we get in Skolnick's report to an explicit answer to this question is the evident equation of the concept of "political action" with (rearranging the order of words for the sake of clarity) "activity aimed at altering the existing arrangements of power and authority in contemporary society." [11] Manifestly, however, this standard of what constitutes "political action" is inadequate.

That a collective activity such as a riot is "aimed at" a redistribution of power is, no doubt, one factor bearing on the extent to which it is political in character, but there are certainly others,

8. *The Politics of Protest*, A Report to the National Commission on the Causes and Prevention of Violence (New York: Ballantine Books, 1969), pp. xxvii, 335, 342.
9. Ibid., pp. 338 (italics omitted), 345–346.
10. Kerner Report, p. 7.
11. *The Politics of Protest*, p. 7.

some of which may be more important. For example, the acts of the Presidential assassins in United States history would have to be regarded as thoroughly political by this standard, since all of the assassins "tended to link themselves to a cause or a movement and to relate their crime to some political issue or philosophy." [12] Yet, as the Eisenhower Commission and its Task Force on Assassination have demonstrated, Presidential assassinations in this country, in contrast with those in other parts of the world, have not been political in character, if by political assassination we mean "assassinations that are part of a *rational* scheme to transfer power from one group to another or to achieve specific policy objectives." [13] To treat U.S. assassinations as political, as Skolnick's standard would require us to do, runs us into difficulties which are the exact opposite of those against which he has aptly warned us: we substitute the political analysis for the psychological one—and gravely misunderstand the nature of assassination in this country.

Do we not risk the same kind of misunderstanding if the Skolnick test of "political action" is applied, for example, to collective violence on the campuses? Probably all of these episodes are "aimed at" altering existing arrangements of power and authority; yet despite this fact, surely some, at least, of the clandestine fire-setting and bomb-planting is best understood primarily in psychological terms, as the result of individual personality factors that are, at bottom, unrelated to politics. Similarly, qualifying the assertedly political nature of ghetto riots with the term "primitive" may not adequately reflect the degree to which the riots are (or were) "expressive," undirected acts, arising out of a non-specific anger and frustration and quite innocent of any genuinely instrumental, "political" content. [14]

My point, however, is not to quarrel with the apparent breadth of Skolnick's concept of "political action," but to argue that social science should assist commissions in becoming rather clearer than they now are about the standards by which one determines whether and to what extent episodes of collective violence are in fact "political." Not all crimes are pre-revolutionary acts, and it seems to me that we urgently require a more refined and incisive test of the "political" element in collective violence.

We need a test that will make us consider, for example, the degree to which the collective violence is buttressed by, and rationally expressive of, a developed ideology, a *Weltanschauung* which condemns the existing order and rationalizes unlawful acts to achieve the new order. We probably also need to consider whether, and under what conditions, this ideology has the capability of attracting adherents and paralyzing opponents in sufficient numbers to make an alteration of existing arrangements of power and authority a reasonably likely outcome. We may further need to attend to the leadership resources and other assets of the violent group to determine whether it can impact significantly on the status quo. Doubtless many other factors are also relevant.

12. *To Establish Justice, To Insure Domestic Tranquility,* Final Report of the National Commission on the Causes and Prevention of Violence (New York: Bantam Books, 1970), p. 106. See also *Assassination and Political Violence,* A Report to the National Commission on the Causes and Prevention of Violence (Washington, D.C.: Government Printing Office, 1969), pp. xvii–xviii, 64–65.

13. *Assassination and Political Violence,* p. xvii (emphasis added); cf., *To Establish Justice, To Insure Domestic Tranquility,* p. 104.

14. Cf., J. Q. Wilson, "Why We Are Having a Wave of Violence," *The New York Times Magazine,* May 19, 1968.

The issue of when collective violence constitutes "political action" is not merely a question of definition, nor is it simply of theoretical interest: as I have indicated, this question goes to the heart of intensely practical problems. In the absence of a more sensitive, multidimensional test for the "political" element in episodes of collective violence, I fear that we may be uncritically describing some of these episodes in a manner that mis-states, or at least overstates, their meaning for public policy. If, for example, the ghetto riots of the 1960's must be explained exclusively in political terms, then we should probably have to agree with the Kerner Report's basic conclusion that "our nation is moving toward two societies, one black, one white—separate and unequal."[15] On the other hand, if we are permitted to see in the riots important non-political elements, such as psychic breaking of the Negro/white "dependency bond" and the freeing of Blacks to express the full measure of their anger,[16] then our conclusion may well be that this nation is, for the first time, really moving toward one society, albeit not nearly fast enough. These two conclusions have, of course, radically different implications for public policy.

"Cause"

The Kerner Commission found that "the causes of recent racial disorders are imbedded in a massive tangle of issues and circumstances," but that the "most fundamental" strand in that tangle is "the racial attitude and behavior of white Americans toward black

15. Kerner Report, p. 1.
16. See Comer, "The Dynamics of Black and White Violence," in *Violence in America*, A Report to the National Commission on the Causes and Prevention of Violence (New York: Praeger, 1969), p. 460.

Americans."[17]   In the now famous words of the commission, "white racism is essentially responsible for the explosive mixture which has been accumulating in our cities since the end of World War II."[18]   By thus identifying "white racism" as the basic cause of the ghetto riots, the Kerner Commission touched a nerve since rubbed raw by the tremendous currency which this phrase has achieved.

The objection has often been raised that the Kerner Commission's concept of "white racism" is an imprecise one, but the nature of the imprecision never seems to be adequately spelled out. From the context in which it is used, "white racism" obviously means "race prejudice" of whites against Blacks,[19] and that is tolerably clear: we know the sort of facts that are relevant to the question of whether, for example, a nominee to the Supreme Court is or is not prejudiced against Negroes. I do think there is imprecision in the Kerner Report's use of "white racism" but I suggest that it lies not so much in the "white racism" concept itself as in the report's lack of an adequate analytical approach to the problem of causation.

It would appear to have been worthwhile, for example, for the commission to have attempted a more explicit and systematic distinction between the immediate and the underlying causes of the riots. The report, after all, treats the phenomenon of white racism only as a basic, underlying, non-proximate cause. White racism is said to have had certain "bitter fruits," i.e., discrimination in education, employment, and housing; formation of black ghettos; conditions of poverty, crime, and

17. Kerner Report, p. 203.
18. Ibid; also, p. 10.
19. Ibid.

social disorganization in the ghettos.[20] The "mixture" created by these fruits of white racism was in turn "catalyzed" by three more recent ingredients (frustrated hopes, legitimation of violence, and powerlessness);[21] and finally, the riots came when a "spark" (incitement by extremists, police action) was applied to the total mixture.[22] This is manifestly a long and complicated causal chain, with "white racism" somewhere near the beginning.

With even this crude distinction between immediate and underlying causes made explicit, two further issues relating to causation are at once exposed, forcing us to deal with them. First, we want to know whether there may not be other underlying causes that are either more basic than the cause we propose to designate as the underlying cause (here, white racism), or, at least, equally basic. Second, we become concerned as to whether or not we have correctly and convincingly traced the causal sequence that extends from our proposed underlying cause to the effect we are analyzing (here, ghetto riots). Grappling with these two additional issues is sure to improve the quality of our analysis.

A DEEPER CAUSE

Thus, if we ask whether the riots may not have a deeper cause that underlies even white racism, we will not overlook the possibility of a further historical and sociological analysis of the sources of prejudice against Negroes in this country. We can meaningfully ask what caused, and what continues to sustain, these attitudes which we have denominated "white racism." We can consider, for example, what the institu-

20. Ibid., pp. 203–04.
21. Ibid., pp. 204–05.
22. Ibid., pp. 205–06.

tion of slavery and the failure of Reconstruction did to Blacks and whites, and hence to their attitudes toward themselves and toward each other. We can further try to identify those features of contemporary life (e.g., high Negro crime rates and low media visibility of Negro accomplishments) which tend to reinforce the attitudinal legacy of centuries of white supremacy and Negro subordination. By inquiring, therefore, whether white racism really deserves to be treated in our analysis as the first cause—the unmoved mover, as it were—we are led to abandon, largely, the position that the basic cause of the riots is to be found in a distorted set of individual attitudes essentially unrelated to external conditions. Instead, without minimizing the attitudinal factor, we find these attitudes themselves to be the effects of yet more basic causes of an institutional kind. In short, we avoid substituting a psychological analysis for a socio-historical one.

Similarly, our analysis will be sharper if we realize that we must identify, and connect with one another, the several intermediate causes that lie between our supposed underlying cause and its ultimate effect. Many readers of the Kerner Report were not persuaded by the metaphorical melange of fruits, mixtures, catalysts, and sparks by which the commission sought to explain how white racism had caused the riots. The convincing part of the report was the exhaustive factual description of the conditions of life in the racial ghetto: it was more understandable how those conditions could cause people to riot. But that white racial attitudes (*my* attitudes!) caused the riots—that was hard to swallow.

Of course, the demonstration can be made, and the Kerner Report would have been the stronger for focusing more attention on it. For example, let us assume that our white reader is a member of a social club which does not admit Negroes to membership. He is, *pro tanto,* a white racist, and the Kerner Report ought to be able to show him how he caused the riots. The showing would have to explore concepts of class and status, and in outline might go something like this.

The riots were caused by the rage and frustration of a lower-class ghetto population. Part of this rage and frustration is due to the fact that the traditional "up and out" road traveled by other ghetto-ized minorities leads, for Negroes, to a different destination: educated, middle-income Blacks are denied the opportunity to cash in their achievements for a true middle-class status, signifying the recognition of those accomplishments by the rest of the community. Even when the Negro has made it by all the standards of the dominant white society, he still doesn't have it made. He is still black. Thus it is by no means fanciful to assert that support for an exclusive social club (or whatever else in our society denies that a complete escape from the bondage of the ghetto is possible) contributed to the sense of hopelessness and alienation out of which the riots arose.[23]

ONE MORE EXAMPLE

There are other examples which could be adduced in support of my thesis that a clearer, more analytical approach to questions of "cause" would be of major benefit to commissions studying collective violence. To mention in passing

23. Cf. Wade, "Violence in the Cities: A Historical View," and Pfautz, "The American Dilemma: Perspectives and Proposals," in *Urban Violence* (Chicago: University of Chicago Center for Policy Study, 1969), pp. 26, 59–61.

just one more example: A careful application of the hoary distinction between necessary and sufficient causes might have prodded the Kerner Commission into a more detailed discussion of why the riots occurred in the latter half of the decade of the 1960's. Discrimination, poverty, and powerlessness are indeed causes of the riots but, having been part of the Negro's lot in America for so long, they do not suffice to explain why the riots erupted when they did. Further analysis is required to give us a really sufficient causal explanation—and the Kerner Report probably didn't go so far in this direction as it should have.

I can offer no model of an adequate analytical approach to the "causes" of episodes of collective violence—any more than I could propose a standard for determining the extent to which an episode of collective violence is "political" in character. What I have tried to suggest is that we need to make some progress in clarifying basic concepts like these. National advisory commissions, and others, are going to go on making findings about the "intent" of the demonstrators, the "causes" of the violence, the "political" character of the disorders, and so on, even in the absence of adequate scientific criteria for the use of these terms. Their findings will continue to influence public policy to a significant degree; for, as I have said, commission reports are more accessible than scholarly studies—which, in addition, sometimes avoid the tough issues which commissions can't avoid—and are more sophisticated than the instant analysis of the media accounts.

Commission studies of collective violence are useful. Social science can make them even more useful by improving the blunt and clumsy tools with which commissions have to do their job.

Name Index

Subject Index

Accommodation, 42
"Action System," 187
Activity orientation, 239–40, 248; and conflict resolution, 248; of personality, and student protest, 239; of personality, U.S.A., 239; of personality, and the university, 240
Acts of violence, 108
Administration attitudes toward student activists, 285–86
Advocacy of violence, 107
Aggression, 187, 188, 194, 196; cultural, 189, 190; defensive, 194; intra-group, 187, 190; sadistic, 194; sanctioned, 189, 190; the social structure and, 197; violence as, 13
Aggressive action, 312, 313
Aggressive behavior, 172
Aggressive factors, 196
Aggressive minds, egoistic, 194
Aggressive style, 194
Aggressive violence, 328
Aggressiveness, predisposition toward, 194
Agonistics, 82–99; among animals, 82, 84, 85; defined, 82; functions of, 89; as political behavior, 82, 84; as ritual behavior, 82, 83
Alcohol and violence, 151, 152, 164
Algiers Motel Incident, The, 40
Alice's Restaurant, 89
Allen controversy, 256–59
American violence, 37, 201–9
Assimilation, 42

Berkeley Solidarity protest, 255, 256
Black militancy, 326
Blank Panthers, 95; Chicago shoot-out, 373, 373n

Black Power, 19, 24, 316, 318, 320, 327; attitudes toward, 259
Black Student Union, and protest, 255
Blacks in U.S.: constituency, 97; revolution and, 97
Brawling, 164

Campus unrest and value conflict, 17
Campus violence, 19
Cannibalism, 183
Canticle for Liebowitz, A, 39n
Carnegie Commission, 27n
Ceremonial violence, 165, 166–68, 174–75
Ceremony vs. ritual, 87
Chicago Convention, 1968. *See* Democratic Convention, Chicago, 1968
Civil disobedience, 284
Civil disorder, a general theory of, 133; in Northern cities, 295
Civil rights: age categories questioned, 230; attitudes about, 229; discussions of, 229
Clan violence, 166
"Collective behavior" theory, 6, 60, 61
Collective violence: and police, 345; political implications of, 7; scholarly concern with, 6; social contexts of, 10; in U.S., 201–3
Commissions, national, 4n, 29–31
"Commodity riots," 311, 326
Communes, 359
Communication techniques, of agitators, 315
Community Action Program (CAP) of OEO, 293, 294
Conflict: bases for, 150; political, 102, 154; resolution of, 245–48, 280; as ritual, 327; rituals of, 7, 24; value, 104; and violence,

383